THE SIX YEARS WAR

A Concise History of Australia in the 1939-45 War

The Six Years War

A Concise History of Australia in the 1939-45 War

GAVIN LONG

THE AUSTRALIAN WAR MEMORIAL AND THE
AUSTRALIAN GOVERNMENT PUBLISHING SERVICE
CANBERRA 1973

Published jointly by
The Australian War Memorial and the
Australian Government Publishing Service

Registered at the General Post Office, Sydney,
for transmission through the post as a book

ISBN 0 642 99375 0

PRINTED IN AUSTRALIA BY JOHN SANDS PTY. LTD. HALSTEAD PRESS

Foreword

Gavin Long, O.B.E., the author of this distinguished work, was General Editor of the 22-volume official history, *Australia in the War of 1939-1945*, and wrote three volumes in the Army series of that history. In *The Six Years War* he marshals between single covers for the first time the events described in the multi-volume series of the history.

Long died in October 1968 after the drafting of the volume was complete except for some checking and the selection of illustrations. Publication was deferred, however, pending the completion of two major works in the larger series—*Royal Australian Navy, 1942-1945* by G. Hermon Gill and *The Government and the People, 1942-1945* by Sir Paul Hasluck. The present volume seems bound to become the standard text-book on Australia during the Second World War.

E. F. HERRING

Chairman, Board of Trustees,
Australian War Memorial

Canberra
30 August 1972

Contents

Illustrations

Maps

SKETCH MAPS

Preface

The plan for a government sponsored history of Australia in the war of 1939-45, agreed to in its final form by the War Cabinet in 1946, provided for the writing of a single book covering the ground explored in detail in the multi-volume history. This was intended as a companion book to C. E. W. Bean's *Anzac to Amiens* (then unwritten) in which he distilled the essence of the twelve-volume history of Australia in World War I which he had edited and largely written.

The several short studies of Australian history during the six years war concentrate on politics and on wartime measures that were to produce radical changes in national policies and administration after the war ended, but describe only sketchily the work of the War Cabinet and the men and women in uniform and in the factories. This work attempts to complement these discussions by telling the story of the nation's leaders and men engaged in the immediate business of war.

Inevitably this work is derived almost entirely from that of the thirteen authors of the longer history, whose readers will soon recognise the extent to which that rich source has been plundered. Indeed substantial parts of this book were drafted by some of those authors. At the same time any bias, reflected in assessments, selection and proportion, is mine.

The sources on which the longer history are based are referred to in its various volumes. Even a select bibliography would be an inappropriate and bulky burden for this volume to carry. The 'official' histories of allied and enemy countries referred to by writers in the longer series number more than 100, Australian unit histories more than forty, memoirs and the like referred to in single volumes of the longer history sometimes add up to more than fifty. And in any event published works contributed only in a small degree to the longer histories, which were written for the most part from unprinted papers and personal knowledge.

This book owes much to all who served on the research and editing staff of the War History Section and in particular to three of them: Joyce Fisher, who from her encyclopaedic knowledge of the political and economic story drafted several sections; A. J. ('Bill') Sweeting, who with his comprehensive grasp of the military story contributed much advice and editing; Mary Gilchrist, who detected some errors and inconsistencies in the drafts, chose the illustrations and wrote the index. One of the first to join the Official History Staff in 1946 and last to leave, this volume and the history as a whole owe much to her continued devotion to the task.

GAVIN LONG

Canberra
April 1968

List of events

1939	1 Sep	Germany invades Poland
	3 Sep	Britain and France declare war on Germany; Australia and New Zealand declare war on Germany
	29 Sep	Soviet-German treaty partitioning Poland
	30 Nov	Soviet Union invades Finland
1940	10 Jan	First convoy of Second A.I.F. (6th Division) sails for the Middle East
	9 Apr	Germany invades Denmark and Norway
	10 May	Germany invades Holland, Belgium and Luxembourg; Mr Churchill becomes Prime Minister of Great Britain
	26 May	Evacuation of British and Allied forces from Dunkirk begins
	10 Jun	Italy declares war
	22 Jun	France signs armistice with Germany
	10 Jul	Battle of Britain begins
	19 Jul	H.M.A.S. *Sydney* sinks Italian cruiser *Bartolomeo Colleoni* in Mediterranean
	13 Sep	Italian army invades Egypt
	22-23 Sep	Japanese occupy bases in Indo-China
	27 Sep	Tripartite Pact between Germany, Italy and Japan
	11 Nov	Fleet Air Arm attacks Italian naval base at Taranto
	9 Dec	Battle of Sidi Barrani begins
1941	3-5 Jan	Battle of Bardia
	21-22 Jan	Tobruk captured
	6 Feb	Australian troops enter Benghazi
	18 Feb	8th Australian Division arrives Singapore
	11 Mar	President Roosevelt signs Lend-Lease Bill
	28-29 Mar	Battle of Cape Matapan
	Mar-Apr	6th Australian Division arrives Greece
	31 Mar	Axis forces counter-attack in North Africa
	6 Apr	German army invades Greece and Yugoslavia
	11 Apr	Siege of Tobruk begins
	22 Apr	Embarkation of troops from Greece begins
	20 May	German troops descend on Crete
	27 May	German battleship *Bismarck* sunk by British ships
	8 Jun	Allied invasion of Syria begins
	15 Jun	British offensive opens in Western Desert
	22 Jun	Germany invades Soviet Union
	12 Jul	Armistice in Syria
	14 Aug	The Atlantic Charter—Mr Attlee broadcasts news of Churchill-Roosevelt meeting
	7 Oct	John Curtin becomes Prime Minister of Australia
	18 Nov	Second British offensive in Western Desert begins
	19 Nov	H.M.A.S. *Sydney* sunk in action with German raider
	7-8 Dec	Japanese land in Thailand and Malaya and attack Pearl Harbour

	10 Dec	H.M. Ships *Prince of Wales* and *Repulse* sunk
	11 Dec	Germany and Italy declare war on the United States
	26 Dec	Hong Kong falls
1942	23 Jan	Japanese capture Rabaul, New Britain
	19 Feb	First Japanese air raids on Darwin
	20 Feb	Japanese invade Timor
	27 Feb	Battle of Java Sea
	28 Feb-1 Mar	Japanese forces land in Java
	8 Mar	Japanese troops enter Rangoon and occupy Lae and Salamaua
	17 Mar	General Douglas MacArthur arrives Australia
	26 Mar	General Blamey becomes Commander-in-Chief, Australian Military Forces
	6 Apr	41st United States Division arrives Australia
	9 Apr	United States forces on Bataan surrender
	18 Apr	General Headquarters South-West Pacific Area established at Melbourne
	5-8 May	Battle of the Coral Sea
	20 May	Allied forces withdraw from Burma
	26 May	German offensive in Western Desert begins
	31 May-1 Jun	Japanese midget submarines raid Sydney Harbour
	4-6 Jun	Battle of Midway Island
	21 Jun	Axis forces capture Tobruk
	25 Jun	General Auchinleck assumes command of the Eighth Army; 9th Australian Division ordered to move to Egypt
	21 Jul	Japanese land in Gona area, Papua, and begin advance towards Kokoda
	7 Aug	Americans land in the Solomons
	8-9 Aug	Naval Battle of Savo Island
	13 Aug	General Montgomery takes command of the Eighth Army
	19 Aug	Dieppe raid
	25-26 Aug	Japanese forces land at Milne Bay
	30-31 Aug	Battle of Alam el Halfa
	25 Sep	Australians begin counter-offensive in the Owen Stanleys
	23-24 Oct	Battle of El Alamein begins
	2 Nov	Kokoda recaptured
	7-8 Nov	Allied landings in French North Africa
	12-15 Nov	Naval Battle of Guadalcanal
	19 Nov	Russians launch counter-offensive at Stalingrad
	9 Dec	Australians capture Gona
	21 Dec	British and Indian troops cross Burma frontier and advance in direction of Akyab
1943	18 Jan	Siege of Leningrad ends
	23 Jan	Organised Japanese resistance in Papua ends
	29 Jan	British Eighth Army enters Tripoli
	2 Feb	German forces at Stalingrad capitulate
	18 Feb	9th Australian Division arrives at Fremantle
	2-4 Mar	Battle of the Bismarck Sea
	13 May	Campaign in North Africa ends
	14 May	Japanese sink hospital ship *Centaur*
	30 Jun	Americans land on New Georgia in the central Solomons
	10 Jul	Allies invade Sicily
	21 Aug	Australian Labour Party wins Federal Election

	26 Aug	Headquarters 5th Australian Division takes over direction of Salamaua campaign
	3 Sep	Allies invade Italy
	11 Sep	Australian troops enter Salamaua
	16 Sep	7th and 9th Divisions enter Lae
	2 Oct	Australians capture Finschhafen
	1 Nov	American troops land on Bougainville, northern Solomons
	28-30 Nov	Churchill, Roosevelt and Stalin attend conference at Teheran
	15 Dec	Americans land on New Britain
1944	31 Jan	American forces invade Marshall Islands
	22 Apr	Americans land at Hollandia and Aitape, New Guinea
	24 Apr	Australians enter Madang, New Guinea
	6 Jun	Allied forces invade Normandy
	19-20 Jun	Naval Battle of Philippine Sea
	21 Jul	United States Marines invade Guam in the Marianas
	15 Aug	Allies invade southern France
	17 Sep	First Allied Airborne Army lands in Holland
	20 Oct	United States Sixth Army invades Leyte in the Philippines
	23-26 Oct	Naval Battle of Leyte Gulf
	24 Nov	Superfortresses attack Japan from bases in the Marianas
	16 Dec	Germans open counter-offensive in the Ardennes
1945	3 Jan	Allies occupy Akyab, Burma
	9 Jan	American forces land on Luzon in the Philippines
	11 Jan	Burma Road reopened
	4 Feb	Churchill, Roosevelt and Stalin meet at Yalta Conference
	19 Feb-1 Apr	American forces land on Iwo Jima, Mindanao and Okinawa
	12 Apr	Death of President Roosevelt. Harry S. Truman becomes President of the United States
	28 Apr	Mussolini shot by Italian partisans
	30 Apr	Hitler commits suicide in Berlin
	1 May	Australian troops land on Tarakan Island, Borneo
	3 May	British troops capture Rangoon
	7 May	Germany surrenders unconditionally
	11 May	6th Australian Division captures Wewak, New Guinea
	10 Jun	9th Australian Division lands Brunei Bay, North Borneo
	26 Jun	United Nations Charter signed at San Francisco
	1 Jul	7th Australian Division lands at Balikpapan, Borneo
	5 Jul	Death of Australian Prime Minister, John Curtin
	13 Jul	J. B. Chifley becomes Australian Prime Minister
	16 Jul	Potsdam Conference—representatives of United States, Britain and Soviet Union meet to draw up terms for Japanese surrender
	26 Jul	Clement Attlee becomes Prime Minister of Britain
	6 Aug	First atomic bomb dropped on Hiroshima
	8 Aug	Soviet Union declares war on Japan, effective from 9th
	9 Aug	Atomic bomb dropped on Nagasaki
	15 Aug	VJ-Day—all offensive action against Japan comes to an end
	2 Sep	Japanese envoys sign Allied instrument of surrender aboard U.S.S. *Missouri* in Tokyo Bay

Chapter 1 **Between the wars**

Australia emerged from the war of 1914-18 and the period of settlement which followed it with her status as an adult member of the family of nations more clearly defined than hitherto. The independence of the self-governing Dominions had been affirmed; Australia was a full member of the League of Nations and her voice had been heard at the Peace Conference; she controlled colonial territories far more extensive than in 1914, and had acquired a military tradition in which she took much pride.

Thereupon she resumed the interrupted task of national development, one which generations of Australians had been convinced they must hasten forward with the greatest possible speed. By national development was meant increasing the population, then just above 5,000,000, putting more land under the plough, building more factories, and bigger cities and towns—'men, money and markets' was the slogan. Australia's attitudes towards the outside world were largely controlled by her concentration on this task and by the shape of the national economy which she had built. She was bound closely to Great Britain by sentiment, trade and common interests in defence. Britain was her principal customer, and the main supplier of immigrants and imported capital. On her oversea public debt Australia was paying interest amounting to some £20,000,000 a year, nearly all in London. Three-quarters of her oversea trade was carried in British ships; she possessed few ships of her own—a serious obstacle to economic or military independence for an island nation. The Government looked to Britain for leadership in foreign and defence policy.

In common with the other Allies victorious in 1918 Australia looked forward hopefully to continued peace and stability, with the League of Nations ensuring the maintenance of the post-war settlement: the Austrian Empire broken up into its member nations, Germany disarmed, frontiers redrawn. Yet in the Far East the settlement emphasised Australia's isolation in the eastern hemisphere. As an outcome of the Four-Power conference at Washington in 1921-1922 the twenty-years-old Anglo-Japanese Alliance ended and a naval treaty was signed limiting the tonnage of cruising warships and establishing a capital ship ratio of 5:5:3 as between Britain (including the Dominions), the United States and Japan—a subordination to which Japan agreed with reluctance.

In the next year leaders of the British nations—a league within the League of Nations—met at an Imperial Conference in London and set out principles that should govern their common policy towards the world outside. The conference affirmed the primary responsibility of each independent member of the Empire for its own local defence and the need for adequate safeguarding of the Empire's maritime communications, naval equality with any foreign power, and the development in Empire countries of air forces similarly trained and equipped and able to co-operate efficiently and without delay. The conference 'took note of' the deep interest of Australia, New Zealand and India in the provision of a naval base at Singapore (recognition of the growing power of Japan), the necessity for maintaining 'safe passage along the great route to the East through the Mediterranean and the Red Sea', and the need for Great Britain to maintain 'a home defence air force of sufficient strength to give adequate protection against air attack by the strongest air force within striking distance of her shores'.

The next Imperial Conference, in 1926, defined procedures by which the British Dominions might independently conduct foreign affairs, while recognising that 'in this sphere, as in the sphere of defence, the major share of responsibility rests now, and must for some time continue to rest with His Majesty's Government in Great Britain'. The Australian Government's attitude towards its responsibilities in these fields was expressed by the Prime Minister, S. M. Bruce, when reporting to Parliament on this conference:

> Our first obligation is to play a part, by consultation, in the foreign policy of the British Empire. Our second obligation is to co-operate in the defence of the Empire as a whole. Regarding the first, we have demanded for ourselves the status of full equality with Great Britain and the right of consultation respecting her foreign policy. We found ourselves involved in the Great War because of a foreign policy about which we had never been consulted and I think we are all determined that we shall never again be so involved by a policy of which we have no information. For our own protection and in the interests of our people we must recognise that we are part of the Empire, and if Britain were confronted with a great disaster we should be involved . . . When nations like Canada, Australia, South Africa and New Zealand all look in one direction and are animated with a desire to promote world's peace, their right of consultation in the foreign policy of Great Britain must exercise a tremendous influence upon the world.[1]

Bruce's Ministry represented a coalition of the Nationalist Party (the liberal-conservative group) and a newly-formed Country Party. The Labour Party would have agreed with Bruce's affirmation of the right to consultation but perhaps not with his statement that Australia was obliged to co-operate in Imperial defence and must be involved if Britain was at war. The close links with Great Britain were welcomed by the leaders of the right-wing parties and their supporters, who regarded the British Empire not only as offering security to Australia but as something worth preserving for its own sake. The Labour leaders, who included a strong contingent of Irish origin, were critical of aspects of British policy and anxious that Australia should not be drawn into European or Asian quarrels which they believed were not the affair of the citizens of the young Commonwealth. Consequently they argued that Australia's defence forces should be designed not so much to co-operate in a common plan as to defend Australia's shores against an invader. Specifically they advocated reliance on aircraft and submarines —new weapons whose powers had been demonstrated in the four years war. Concentration on such forces had attractions to Labour minds also from a political point of view because, they believed, aircraft and submarines would be not only cheaper but less likely to be sent on oversea expeditions and might make a large conscript army unnecessary.

[1] *Commonwealth Debates*, Vol. 115, p. 71.

Military writers in Australia, with some support from writers in England, during the 1920s and 1930s argued that, if Japan attacked, it would be when Britain was engaged in a European war, and, if this was so, a long time might elapse before substantial British (or American) naval power came to the defence of British (or American) interests in the Far East. In the meantime the Japanese were likely to have captured Singapore from the landward side, to have overrun the European colonies and perhaps invaded Australia. These writers advocated reorientation of British Far Eastern defence policy in the light of such possibilities and heavier expenditure on Australian military and air defences with the object of ensuring that the vital south-eastern crescent of Australia, containing virtually all the industries of military value and a great part of the population, could hold out until naval help arrived. However, for all but two of the years between the wars, the right-wing parties held power in the Commonwealth (though Labour was sometimes in power in a majority of the States) and the defence policy formulated in 1923 was followed consistently up to and beyond the time when it was to undergo the test of war.

The adoption by Allied nations of a co-operative plan of defence brings forward the question of the share to be carried by each partner. To those Australians who were eager to speed national development, expenditure on defence seemed a deduction from the money to be spent on the main objective. Yet it was evidence of Australia's awareness of her vulnerability that, in this period, her per capita expenditure on defence was greater than that of the other Dominions put together, and somewhat more than half that of the United Kingdom.[2]

Even so, in the four years which followed the end of the war of 1914-18 the Australian Army and Navy had been greatly reduced; the strength of the compulsorily-enlisted militia, in training for only a few weeks of each year, from some 90,000 to fewer than 40,000, of the Navy from 4,800 men to 4,000. In consequence of the naval reduction agreed to at the Washington Conference the battle cruiser *Australia* was sent to the bottom outside Sydney Heads and the number of naval ships in commission reduced from twenty-three to thirteen.

Few voices were raised against these reductions. Nevertheless, as the war receded, the Bruce-Page Government (Nationalist Party-Country Party) prudently fed the forces with at least enough new men and material to preserve an efficient nucleus. In keeping with the policy formulated at the 1923 conference it allotted the largest share of the funds to re-equipment of the navy, to which, in the five years to 1929, were added two heavy cruisers, a seaplane tender and two submarines. A diminutive air force, sustained with a vote of some £500,000 a year, had been established in 1921, its leaders being drawn mainly from the Australian Flying Corps which had formed part of the wartime army overseas. The strength of the militia was slightly increased, and the government-owned factories for producing small arms, explosives and ammunition were maintained.

[2] In 1925-26 per capita expenditure on defence was: UK 51s 1d; Australia 27s 2d; New Zealand 12s 11d; Canada 5s 10d; South Africa 2s 6d. The forces of Great Britain had the double task of defending the homeland and the oversea empire; normally half of the army, for example, was at home and half distributed among the oversea garrisons.

At a Federal election in 1929 the Labour Party obtained a majority and in October took office with J. H. Scullin as Prime Minister. In the election campaign the Labour candidates had promised the abolition of compulsory military training, and before Parliament met it fulfilled this promise. The result was that a militia of 47,000, about 40,000 of whom had been compulsorily enlisted, was replaced by a purely volunteer force which in 1930 dwindled to a strength of 27,000. The new Government at first made only inconsiderable reductions in the defence Estimates, but in the next few months a world-wide trade depression provided a compelling reason for reducing Commonwealth expenditure. The axe fell particularly heavily on the fighting Services, whose Estimates were cut by about 13 per cent. Five naval ships were paid off into reserve and the seagoing personnel reduced by 700, some regular military officers and men were retired, and the naval and military colleges reduced to microscopic size and removed from their pleasant quarters at Jervis Bay and Duntroon, the one to the Flinders Naval Depot and the other to Victoria Barracks in Sydney.

In January 1932, after another election, the Scullin Government was replaced by one supported by the United Australia Party, a combination of the former Nationalist Party with some dissenting members of the Labour Party, one of whom, J. A. Lyons, became Prime Minister. Lyons's Government, like Scullin's, was convinced that expenditure must be cut to the bone. When its Estimates were presented in November 1932 they allotted slightly less to defence than had the previous Government.

By 1932 nearly all nations were reducing their forces, and a disarmament conference of the League of Nations was about to meet. One great Power —Japan—was an exception to this rule. Coming increasingly under the control of a military junta she had in September 1931 begun to occupy Manchuria. Her economy was rapidly expanding. Already in 1932 she was spending 37.6 per cent of her revenue on the fighting Services. (Australia was spending 4.4 per cent.) In March 1933, ruffled by disapproval of her attack on China, she withdrew from the League of Nations. In October of that year Germany, since January under the leadership of Adolf Hitler, who was preaching defiance of the peace treaties, also withdrew from the League. In Australia, now slowly emerging from the poverty and anxieties of the trade depression, the response to these rumblings was a modest, though prompt, addition to the defence vote, which was increased in 1933 by £1,000,000 to a total of over £4,000,000. The purchase of a cruiser, the building of smaller vessels in Australian yards and the rearming of coastal batteries were authorised.

Thus the 6,600,000 Australians of 1933 were armed less strongly than the 4,600,000 of 1914. But in the intervening twenty years the industrial capacity of the nation had greatly increased. Steelworks, established in 1915, were producing somewhat more than 1,000,000 tons a year. Other large-scale metal-working industries, capable of conversion to the making of weapons of war, had been established. In the 1920s some light aircraft, but not their engines, had been made in both government and private workshops. Essington Lewis, managing director of the Broken Hill Pty Ltd, after a world tour in 1934 was convinced that steps should be taken to prepare the Australian steel industry to meet the demands of war. Plans were put in hand to extend plant, improve efficiency and make new kinds of steel.

The war of 1914-18 had shown that in another war Australia was likely to be handicapped by lack of shipping. In 1916 the Prime Minister, W. M. Hughes, had partly repaired this deficiency by establishing a government shipping line which eventually possessed fifty-four steamers including five liners each of 13,850 tons. Twenty-one cargo ships were built in Australian yards between 1919 and 1924. The line lost money, the Nationalist-Country Party Government was averse to state ownership of industries, and in 1928 the ships had been sold to British firms. Thereafter Australian shipowners possessed only the coastwise merchant fleet and a few vessels trading overseas, and the shipyards were dependent almost solely on refitting work and occasional naval orders.

In 1935 the League Powers, now rapidly losing faith in the ability of the League to preserve peace, began rearming in earnest, urged on by eloquent advocates, such as W. S. Churchill in England—and Hughes in Australia—who considered that too little was being done too late. In June 1935 Britain and Germany reached an agreement by which Germany, restricted by the Treaty of Versailles to only the nucleus of a navy, might build ships aggregating 35 per cent of the British tonnage—in other words a navy equal to the French or Italian in weight, and, since it would be new, superior to them in quality. This agreement, entered into without consulting France, altered the whole balance of naval power; the British battle fleet, said Churchill, would in the near future be 'largely anchored to the North Sea . . . that means to say the whole position in the Far East has been very gravely altered'.

It was now evident that if peace among the Powers was disturbed it would be by one or more of three ambitious States—Germany, Japan or Italy. Later in 1935 it became likely that Italy would invade Abyssinia, and for a time a Mediterranean war seemed imminent between Italy and the League Powers (who since 1934 included Russia). The Mediterranean Fleet was reinforced by British ships from every ocean. Here was a test of Bruce's statement that if Britain were confronted with 'a great disaster' Australia should be involved, and of the character of Australia's membership of the League. The cruiser *Australia* was then serving on exchange in the Mediterranean and during this crisis remained there. The British cruiser on exchange in Australia was released and hurried to the Mediterranean, and the Australian cruiser *Sydney*, just taken over in England, joined them.

These distant alarms led to relatively rapid increases in defence expenditure in Australia—to £5,400,000 in 1934-35, £7,500,000 in 1935-36, £8,800,000 (about 9 per cent of Federal revenue) in 1936-37. In books, pamphlets, speeches and newspaper articles, the hitherto neglected problems of Australia's responsibilities in world affairs and defence were being discussed. Archdale Parkhill, the Minister for Defence, in 1935 gave the Government's answer to some of these questions when, in a long speech on defence, he said that Australia's 'interests to be safeguarded' were *(a)* seaborne trade 'for the maintenance of economic strength, for the payment of external obligations and preservation of overseas credit', and *(b)* maintenance of the integrity of Australian territory and continuity of Australia's national life. The order in which these interests were placed was significant of the Government's view of Australia's role and her place in the world; the Opposition party would probably have reversed the order.

An opportunity for intimate discussion of what constituted the foreign policy of the British nations and what were the military measures by which they should help to carry it out was provided by an Imperial Conference in London in May 1937—the first for seven years. Six months earlier the British Foreign Secretary, Eden, had defined the circumstances under which Great Britain might go to war: in defence of British territory or of France and Belgium, in defence of Germany against unprovoked aggression, and in bringing help to any victim of aggression in a case where it would be proper in Britain's opinion so to do. Was this also Australia's policy? Were there other possible occasions of war not mentioned by the British Foreign Secretary? He had said nothing specific about what might impel Britain to resort to war in the Far East.

The Australian delegates, led by Lyons, went to the Imperial Conference armed with searching questions, particularly concerning policy in the Far East. What was Britain's attitude towards Japan? Would Britain go to war in defence of Hong Kong or the Netherlands Indies? The conference, like its predecessors, could establish no new commitments and decide no definite courses of action, but it provided an opportunity for Ministers and their advisers to state opinions, and seek clarification of the views of others; and, in committee, officers of the Services and the civil administration were able to discuss their problems. It was the last such meeting before the outbreak of war.

During the conference the British nations announced to the world that their aim was the maintenance of peace by conciliation, but that at the same time they would continue to rearm. In private discussions the Admiralty made reassuring statements that a British fleet would be sent to Singapore if war broke out against Japan; the British Chiefs of Staff declared that, in a world war, the opening phase would be the most dangerous and therefore help given early would be more valuable than help in six months—advice that would have been merely platitudinous were it not that the only armies the 20,000,000 Britons overseas maintained were part-time militias which would need months of training before they were fit for battle.

A particularly important outcome of the conference was the British experts' assertion of the inability of British factories to rearm their own Services in a few years, much less those of the Dominions. The Dominions would need to expand greatly their own ammunition and aircraft factories and shipyards. The Imperial Conference of 1930 had recommended that Dominion Governments should establish Principal Supply Officers' Committees to help their industries to meet the demands of war, and such a committee had been formed in Australia in 1933. So far, however, Australian rearmament from home sources had entailed little more than giving orders to the main shipyard at Cockatoo Island, hitherto half-idle, and to the small though well-equipped Commonwealth munition factories. For some years these factories had been devoted largely to making civilian goods—not rifles but moving picture projectors, cutters and combs for shearing machines, golf irons, lipstick holders and so on. It was now evident that it would be wise for the Dominions to organise civilian industry for conversion to weapon production. Already, in 1935, Essington Lewis had come forward with a plan for forming a company with Commonwealth support to produce military aircraft on a fairly large scale, and in October 1936 the Commonwealth

Aircraft Corporation had been formed to make, as a beginning, a fighter aircraft of American design and its engine. In 1937 a plan for giving educational orders for weapons to private firms and for installing twenty-one government annexes in selected factories had been developed. Although more than 500,000 people were now employed in Australian factories—about the same number as in agriculture—relatively little high-precision engineering work was being done, and the consequent shortage of machine tools and skilled workers would have to be overcome before weapons, military vehicles, fighting ships and the like could be produced on a large scale. By 1939 the government munitions factories were employing some 5,000 workers and about 4,000 more were in the aircraft factories.

A plan to produce engines and chassis for motor vehicles (the body-building industry was already well established) was examined but abandoned; so was a proposal to make tin-plate. Attempts to find worth-while quantities of oil in Australia or New Guinea having proved fruitless, a beginning was made with the large-scale extraction of petroleum from shale.

An important step was the establishment by Imperial Chemical Industries of Australia and New Zealand of plant for the local production of alkalis, synthetic ammonia and nitric acid, thus freeing many factories from dependence on imported chemicals. The growing awareness of the need for extending the scope of Australian industry was also indicated by the decision in 1936 that the Council for Scientific and Industrial Research, founded in 1926, should interest itself in the problems of secondary as well as primary industries. One result was the establishment of a National Standards Laboratory to extend the limited work in this field hitherto done by the government munitions organisation. Without exact standards of measurement it would be impossible for the factories to co-operate in the production of precision weapons and other equipment.

The growing threat of war, and in particular the lessons given at the 1937 Imperial Conference, led to acceleration of other plans to organise the nation for war. In the Department of Defence the secretary, F. G. Shedden, and his staff kept themselves well informed about the principles of wartime planning that had been evolved in Britain since the war of 1914-18. In this department the War Book, a detailed statement of the steps to be taken by government departments on the outbreak of war, was compiled, air raid precautions were co-ordinated, and plans to control manpower prepared. In war this department would act as the executive of a small War Cabinet which, advised by the Chiefs of Staff Committee, would make decisions on major matters affecting the fighting Services and their supply. Parallel with the War Cabinet would be an equally small Economic Cabinet to deal with wartime economic and financial policy. In November 1938 a Manpower Committee was established by the department under the chairmanship of Major-General Sir Thomas Blamey, a former regular soldier. Its task was 'to prepare allocations of personnel in emergency to the armed forces, munitions factories, key industries and essential services', basing its estimates on information obtained through a National Register or census of youths and men, eventually compiled in July 1939. By June of that year a list of reserved occupations had been drafted, based on a British schedule, which in its turn was a revision of a similar schedule used in the First World War.

In Australia, as in Britain, there was a fairly clear conception in the minds of the leaders in the Defence Department and the army of the approximate share of the nation's manpower that could be allotted to the Services. The army's working assumption was that it would be able to maintain at full strength in a long war not more than one division over and above the seven which existed in nucleus in the militia—an allocation proportionately a little higher than that on which the British War Office founded its own estimates at the outset. Senior army leaders had long based their plans broadly on the rule of thumb that an industrialised state—and Australia was one—could spare one in ten of its population to the fighting Services, a rule the soundness of which was later confirmed. Thus the Service leaders and Defence officials had estimated the number of men who should be available to them and knew how they would organise them; but plans for the allocation of manpower within industry itself did not exist.

A main task of the planners in the Department of Defence was to arrange for co-ordination of Commonwealth and State activities in war. A conference of Commonwealth and State authorities in 1936 had discussed air raid precautions, and from September 1938 onwards a series of conferences agreed on broad principles of collaboration and exchanged views on details such as transport, use of State police, and the allotment of priorities to public works of value for defence. The larger States prepared War Books modelled on the Commonwealth's; but, in general, progress was slow and difficult, as is usual at conferences of Federal and State authorities, and there was failure (before war began) to make co-ordinated plans for price-fixing, public works and wartime transport, to choose some examples. Although Commonwealth officers had urged the employment of State technical colleges in the urgent task of training munition workers, and the two larger States had offered to co-operate, Lyons, in February 1939, declined to agree to 'the diversion of funds from defence projects of much greater importance and urgency for the purpose of increasing the facilities for technical education in the several States'.

As planning proceeded it was recognised that some of the tasks hitherto undertaken by the Defence Department would have to be distributed. Thus in 1939 a Ministry of Supply and Development was established, to be 'an essentially industrial Defence Department'. It took over the munitions factories and annexes, and had a general responsibility for supplying the Services and co-ordinating secondary industry for emergency tasks. Other planning was being carried out unobtrusively within the administration. For example, since 1936 wartime control of food exports had been discussed with the British Board of Trade, and Australia had been warned that shortage of shipping might cause Britain, the principal customer, to seek supplies from places nearer home. One of the first tasks of a Financial and Economic Advisory Committee, consisting of three economists and appointed early in 1939, was to assess the effect of this possible interruption of seaborne trade. It made proposals for stock-piling, control of imports, and readjustment of domestic industry. To help co-ordination with the private manufacturers on whom the Government would largely depend for supplies in war an Advisory Panel of Industrial Organisations was created, with Essington Lewis as chairman and four other leaders of industry as members.

Meanwhile the replenishment of the Services had continued. In August 1937 a new three-year program was undertaken; in the first year £11,500,000 would be available. In April 1938 Lyons announced that £43,000,000 would be spent in three years, distributed thus: navy £15,000,000; army, £11,500,000; air force, £12,500,000; munitions supply, £3,000,000; plans for organisation of industry, £1,000,000.

Lyons added that a senior officer of the British Army would be obtained to report on the state of the Australian Army, and a senior officer of the Royal Air Force to report on the Australian Air Force. These proposed appointments, like the allocation of the funds among the Services, were in keeping with that deference to British strategical advice which the Government had shown throughout the period between the wars and earlier. Australian defence, Lyons said, was 'related to a wider pattern of Empire defence and its fundamental basis is Empire sea-power and the Singapore naval base'. It was logical, therefore, that the largest share of the new money should go to the navy, the next to the air force. The basic strategic policies having been formulated by the leaders of the British Services and accepted by Australia it was consistent now to seek the advice of such leaders. These decisions demonstrated not that the Government's Australian advisers were not reliable—they included men of greater experience and capacity than those now being imported—but rather that the Ministers were conscious of their own inexperience in the field of strategy. In the event Lieut-General E. K. Squires came from England to report on the Australian Army and Marshal of the Royal Air Force Sir Edward Ellington to report on the air force.

For the navy, from the new funds, two more cruisers were to be bought in Britain and smaller ships built in Australia, including destroyers of 2,000 tons—but even so naval shipbuilding at home would not have regained the scale of 1916.

Since 1928 the air force had been developing in accordance with a plan designed by an officer of the British force, Air Marshal Salmond—a predecessor of Ellington—who had been invited to inspect it and make recommendations about its future. In 1937 its striking force comprised only two squadrons, but now it was to be expanded until in 1939 it would contain twelve, with seven more soon to be formed. Its chief problem was to obtain modern aircraft, and by 1939 the delay in deliveries from Britain and the United States had become so disturbing that it was decided to establish a second group of aircraft factories to make bombers—Beauforts, of English design. The Government gave an initial order for 180.

These measures were a response to an alarming march of events in Europe, where Germany's policy was becoming more theatening, and in East Asia where the Japanese had driven the Chinese forces back into the interior. Since early in 1938 the British Prime Minister, Neville Chamberlain, had been seeking 'a general appeasement throughout Europe which will give us peace', but without success. In March 1938 the German Army marched into Austria; in September it was threatening Czechoslovakia. Chamberlain thrice flew to Germany to placate Hitler, and on the third occasion at Munich in September took part in the agreement ceding the Sudetenland of Czechoslovakia to Germany.

Had the Australian Government shared in the making of British policy in this critical year? It had been kept informed, and had expressed agreement. On 28th September Lyons had gone somewhat farther and had cabled to

Chamberlain a suggestion that he should make a personal appeal to Mussolini. After the event the Ministers announced their approval of the Munich settlement, an opinion that seems to have been shared by a majority of Australians. The Ministers appear to have taken the view that neither they nor their administration—which since 1935 had included a separate but still embryo Department of External Affairs—were equipped to create an Australian foreign policy. Their best contribution would be to help maintain a united front among the British nations. In October 1938, when explaining Munich, R. G. Menzies, the Australian Attorney-General, declared that it would be folly for Australia to produce a separate foreign policy; 'rather Australians should have minds sufficiently informed and sufficiently strong, positive and constructive to be able to say useful things at the right time to the Government of the United Kingdom'. He added: 'My doctrine is that so long as the British Empire is constituted as it is today, it is not possible for Australia to be neutral in a British war.' The Leader of the Opposition, John Curtin, declared that Australia should not be embroiled in the disputes of Europe, and specifically that no men should be sent out of Australia to participate in another war overseas. A few weeks after Munich, on 16th November, Australia followed Britain's example in granting *de jure* recognition of the incorporation of Abyssinia in the Italian Empire.

The Munich crisis, which involved a definite threat of war, had produced a rehearsal of the defence measures which Australia had decided to take when war seemed imminent; the naval squadron was concentrated, reserve ships were manned and the forts were put in a state of readiness. In December 1938 £19,500,000 was added to the £43,000,000 already to be spent on defence during the three-year program. A recruiting campaign was opened with the aim of increasing the militia from 35,000 to 70,000. This was achieved by April and a few months later 80,000 was reached. It was a remarkable result, perhaps unparalleled (per capita) in any country in peace, and demonstrated that a large proportion of young Australians were ready to spring to arms in a crisis threatening Britain. (The total number of men aged 18 to 26 was estimated at 482,000.)

At this stage General Squires recommended the formation of a small regular army of 7,500 organised in two brigades—a similar proposal had been advocated by Curtin, a few months earlier. Earle Page, who had succeeded Lyons as a stop-gap Prime Minister on Lyons's death in April, approved this plan and decided that three units should be raised within the coming year. However, in August, Menzies, who succeeded Page after a few weeks, cancelled this decision in terms which made plain that the Government still hoped that war could be avoided and did not wish to be committed to 'measures which possess a permanent character'.[3]

Meanwhile the British Government had abandoned its search for appeasement which began in June 1935 with the Anglo-German naval treaty and ended on 31st March when Britain guaranteed the independence of Poland. There is no indication that the Australian Government was consulted before this last step, but again it knew what was happening and after the event assured the British Government of its support.

We have seen how for years the Services and their attendant factories

[3] *Sydney Morning Herald*, 3rd August 1939.

were starved for money. Now they had more than they had dreamed of, but were having difficulty in spending it. In the first year of the 1937-40 program £1,736,000 remained unspent, in the second year more than £3,000,000. One reason was that all the Powers were hurriedly arming and orders for aircraft and weapons placed by small nations were not being delivered. Also the habit of cautious budgeting, reinforced by the experiences during the depression, persisted. Ministers, hoping that at the eleventh hour war might be avoided, sought to escape lasting defence commitments. From this point of view it might prove more economical to order equipment abroad rather than establish factories to make it at home, to increase the militia than recruit long-service regular units. The allotted funds and far more could have been spent had the Ministers recognised what the evidence in front of them had clearly shown: that for a nation in Australia's situation one of the foundations of military strength—second in importance only to morale—is an ability to produce a full range of weapons, ships, and vehicles of war from its own resources; and had taken heed of the suggestion made at the Imperial Conference in 1937 that, if war broke out, forces ready for immediate action would be needed urgently.

Chapter 2 **Raising oversea forces**

Only two nations outside Europe—Australia and New Zealand—were immediately involved in war as a result of the German invasion of Poland. Great Britain declared war at 11 o'clock in the morning of 3rd September 1939. While it was still the 3rd in the Antipodes official proclamations had been signed in Australia and New Zealand that a 'state of war' existed, war having broken out between Great Britain and Germany. The terms of the Australian proclamation implied what the Prime Minister had declared long before: that if the Crown was at war so was Australia. More important than consitutional theory was the fact that an overwhelming majority of Australians wished their declaration to be prompt and unequivocal, principally because of sentimental ties, partly because of their consciousness that Australia was a member of the closely-welded British group of nations and her membership carried responsibilities. When the Commonwealth Parliament met three days later the Leader of the Opposition, Curtin, declared on behalf of his followers that Australia was part of the British Commonwealth and his party would do its utmost to maintain the integrity of that Commonwealth.

South Africa declared war on 6th September and Canada on the 10th. By then Poland had been overrun and there were ranged against Germany and her subject states Great Britain and her Empire, France, and four young British nations.

The most sweeping of the Australian Parliament's early measures was a *National Security Act* giving the Ministers wide powers to govern by regulation. According to Maurice Blackburn, one of the few Labour members who had opposed the legislation, it authorised the Government 'to pass any laws it liked and disregard existing laws'. With this weapon in its hand the Government set about establishing control over trade. Already, on 28th August, regulations had been made under the power given to the Government by the *Defence Act* to prevent Australians from sending capital overseas; on 22nd September all proceeds from exports were directed into the banking system and thus made subject to government control; Australians were later prevented from selling securities held abroad so as to obtain foreign currency; and in December the control of exchange was completed by the introduction of regulations requiring importers to obtain permission before bringing in imports from non-sterling areas. These problems had arisen and been grappled with in 1914; now the Government mainly followed precedent or improved on it.

During 1939 export prices had fallen sharply and Australian funds in London in September totalled only some £45,000,000. Before the war contracts were being negotiated with Britain to supply her with wool, dairy products, eggs, meat, dried fruits and sugar; now it seemed likely that it would be difficult to obtain enough shipping space to carry away the usual cargoes of wheat, fresh fruit and wine. Soon after war broke out the Commonwealth bought the entire wheat crop, and from 1st March 1940 similarly bought the apple and pear crops and took control of their distribution. The political influence of the exporting groups was considerable and the Government's anxiety about markets was partly a result of that influence. The export cargoes at this stage fell into three groups: products such as wool, all future production of which had been bought by the United Kingdom, and for which she would find ships; products such as hides for which war created a strong demand both at home and abroad; and products such as wheat and raw fruit for which shipping was likely to be difficult or impossible to find because Britain would supply her needs from less distant sources. In the event, whereas in November 1938 13,400,000 bushels of wheat remained in the country, in November 1939 there were 21,000,000 bushels; in November 1940 there would be 77,500,000. On 9th September 1939, as part of the traditional system of economic warfare, an Act was passed to prevent any trading with the enemy.

It was desirable to ensure that speculators did not profit from the upsets caused by the declaration of war. After conferring with the States the Commonwealth Government on 28th September introduced control of prices: an announcement could be made that the price of an item might not be increased until an investigation had been carried out, and it became an offence to sell or buy above a prescribed price. In November, in a revised budget, it was estimated that £62,000,000 would be spent on defence in the year. Despite the advice of its Financial and Economic Committee that it should increase taxation and take firm measures to control private investment, the Government announced that for the present its policy was to avoid action likely to disturb private industry, then recovering from a slight recession, and it would raise the new money required almost entirely by borrowing. Chiefly with the object of reducing the competition for capital between the Government and private companies, regulations were made whereby permission had to be obtained to raise any amount of capital over £2,500. (Mortgages were exempt up to £5,000.)

The shortage of skilled labour soon became acute. There were fewer than 20,000 engineering and other skilled tradesmen and it was estimated that by June 1942 industry and the Services would need 56,000. In an effort to limit the number of skilled workers enlisting in the Services men in various age-groups whose trades were listed in the Schedule of Reserved Occupations were not allowed to join up unless they were to be employed in their trade in one of the Services. Skilled men were offered wages above the ruling rates if they would work in munition factories, and training was accelerated. Yet, although there was a shortage of skilled workers in the metal and engineering industries, it was estimated that about 10 per cent of all members of trade unions were unemployed—a point to which Labour leaders frequently directed attention in Parliament—and in November the Government made an effort to use some of these by allotting £2,000,000 for public works of value for defence, to be undertaken by men hitherto unemployed. Another consequence of unemployment was that the Government was anxious to avoid such measures as the restriction of building or rationing of petrol which, although they would divert labour to defence works, or conserve strategic supplies, might also increase unemployment in some trades.

Argus (Melbourne)

Inaugural meeting of the Australian War Cabinet held at Victoria Barracks, Melbourne on 27th September 1939. *Left to right:* The Minister for Commerce, Senator George McLeay; the Minister for External Affairs and for Information, Sir Henry Gullett; the Minister for Supply and Development, Mr R. G. Casey; the Prime Minister and Treasurer, Mr R. G. Menzies; the Minister for Defence, Mr. G. A. Street; and the Secretary of the Department of Defence and to the War Cabinet, Mr F. G. Shedden. (The Attorney-General, Mr W. M. Hughes, was absent.)

The program of increased aircraft production, naval shipbuilding and weapon production was sufficient to underline the shortage of skilled tradesmen, but was on so modest a scale as to make no notable inroads into the nation's total manpower. In December 1939 7,600 were employed in munition factories; it was estimated that 2,200 more would be added by June 1940—a small increment considering that there were in Australia 1,750,000 wage and salary earners and many thousands of unemployed. The munition factories were then making chiefly small-arms, heavy anti-aircraft guns, and ammunition. Except for the relatively simple 2-pounder anti-tank gun no new weapons had been undertaken. On 29th September 1939, when the Minister for Supply and Development presented to the War Cabinet a proposal for capital expenditure totalling an additional £2,755,000 for the production of munitions, the War Cabinet agreed to items totalling £1,900,000, mostly for making increased quantities of ammunition, but rejected a proposal that £855,000 be spent on factory extensions to enable the new 25-pounder field guns and their ammunition to be made. This proposal was partly in anticipation of continued orders for ammunition from the United Kingdom, and officials of the munitions organisation used these orders to justify increased capacity, which they rightly foresaw would be needed even to cope with local demands. Opposition to this expenditure came from sections such as the Treasury Finance Committee, whose chairman, Sir Walter Massy-Greene, declared concerning the first batch of orders that 'it is difficult to escape the conclusion that a piece of commendable salesmanship has opened up a market for any potential surplus production . . .' Undaunted, munitions officials succeeded in manoeuvring the 25-pounder project through the War Cabinet on 18th January.

When war broke out, one destroyer, a sloop and two boom-defence vessels were being built for the navy; in November 1939 the building of four 650-ton corvettes was authorised, and these orders were distributed among four shipyards whereas hitherto naval shipbuilding had been concentrated at one. Soon the building of a second destroyer was approved. One aircraft factory was producing Wirraway single-engined aircraft and another was hoping by 1941 to produce Beaufort bombers; in October the War Cabinet authorised an order for 350 Tiger Moth aircraft, an elementary training machine, from a third factory—the Australian works of De Havilland's—and approved the manufacture of twin-row Wasp engines and Gipsy Moth engines in addition to the single-row Wasp engines already being made.[1] One hundred Hudson bombers were on order from the American makers and other aircraft from Britain.

The Government had promptly found its answer to the question whether or not Australia should enter the war, but was finding that the decision as to what size and shape her contribution to Allied strength should take was a more difficult one. The Ministers approached it cautiously. The problem was complicated by two main factors; one external and the other internal. There was the uncertainty about the policy of Japan, and there was the fact that the strongest individual party in the House of Representatives had declared itself opposed both to sending forces overseas and to raising home defence forces by conscription. Obedient to tradition the Australian Government asked the British Government what it should do. The British views were received on 8th September 1939 in a telegram which stated that if Japan 'adopted an attitude of reserve towards the democratic countries' Australia might be unwise to send an expeditionary force overseas though she could assist by having formations ready to reinforce Singapore, New Zealand or British and French islands in the western Pacific. On the other hand, if Japan was friendly the British Government hoped that Australia would prepare an expeditionary force and would consider whether it would prefer to relieve United Kingdom units and formations in, say, Singapore, Burma, or India as brigades became available, or would prefer to wait until complete divisions could be sent to the main theatre. A somewhat similar telegram was sent to New Zealand, one difference being that the New Zealand message referred to 'a complete division' not 'complete divisions'.

The day after the arrival of the British telegram the New Zealand Government—a Labour government—announced that it would raise a special military force for service within or beyond the Dominion; as a first step 6,600 officers and men to form one infantry brigade and some divisional units would be enlisted. Six days later Menzies announced that Australia would raise a 'special force' of one division and auxiliary units—20,000

[1] By June 1940 75 Wirraways, 8 Moths and 76 single-row Wasp engines had been produced; in the following year 225 Wirraways, 453 Moths, 195 single-row Wasp engines and 319 Gipsy Majors.

men in all—for service at home or abroad 'as circumstances permit'. At the same time the militia, some units of which were already on full-time duty, would be called up for a month's training in two drafts each of 40,000. By this time Japan had stated that she would remain 'independent' in the crisis, which appeared to mean that she would not be dragged into the war at Germany's heels but would wait and see. At the same time she advised European powers and the United States to withdraw their ships and troops from the Japanese-controlled areas of China. The opinion of the Australian military Intelligence staff was that Japan was too deeply involved in China to embark on an attack on European colonies in the Far East in the coming winter, but that she might do so if the Allies had a set-back in Europe. In fact, the Russo-German alliance had caused consternation in Japan, the Government lost face and at the end of August was replaced.

Uncertainty about Japan was not the only reason for the cautious tone of Britain's suggestions to the Dominions. Another factor was the general shortage of arms and the knowledge that many months must elapse before even the forces in the United Kingdom could be adequately armed. Until the Munich crisis Britain had been planning for 'a war of limited liability' in which the army would not be allowed to expand as it had in 1914-18. After Munich Britain had agreed with France that she would enlarge her army to thirty-two divisions (six regular and twenty-six Territorial) which would be ready before the end of the first twelve months of the war. This entailed doubling the Territorial Army, then equipped only on a training scale. After war broke out the British War Cabinet decided to take steps to provide arms for fifty-five divisions—the thirty-two mentioned above plus twenty-three from the Dominions, India and 'prospective Allies'. The assumption evidently was that the Dominions' contribution would be on the scale of 1916-18 when, from smaller populations, twelve Dominion divisions were serving in France and Palestine. At this time not even the regular British divisions were fully armed for a European war, and the equipment of the Territorials was similar to that of the Australian militia.

Because the conscription controversy in Australia had been solely concerned with military service the interest of politicians and the public was concentrated on the question whether or not an expeditionary army should be formed, but in the meanwhile Australian naval and air forces were already serving overseas. Naval mobilisation had been swiftly completed and the navy's total strength brought to 10,250 by the calling up of some 4,800 reserves including 450 former regular officers. The navy possessed two heavy cruisers (*Australia* and *Canberra*) and four light cruisers (*Perth, Hobart, Sydney* and *Adelaide*), five old destroyers (*Stuart, Waterhen, Vampire, Vendetta* and *Voyager*) and two sloops. (In 1914 one battle cruiser, four light cruisers, three destroyers and two submarines had been in commission; the total tonnage of the 1939 squadron was somewhat greater than that of the 1914 squadron.) During September 1939 eight small vessels were requisitioned and armed as minesweepers, and merchant ships were armed with a gun at the stern. Three liners, *Moreton Bay, Arawa* and *Kanimbla,* were converted into armed merchant cruisers and manned by Australians, though as units of the Royal Navy. Two other liners, *Manoora* and *Westralia,* were armed and commissioned in December and January as merchant cruisers in the R.A.N.

On 24th August the Admiralty had asked the Commonwealth Government to be allowed to retain on the West Indies station the cruiser *Perth*, then in the Caribbean on her way to Australia from England, where she had been commissioned as an Australian ship in June. The Commonwealth Government agreed, with a proviso that the decision be reconsidered if war broke out in the Far East. On 29th August the Admiralty had cabled a request that the ships of the Australian Navy should begin moving towards their war stations. The Naval Board informed the Government that this entailed sending a cruiser to the Mediterranean, its prearranged station in time of war. An Order-in-Council transferring *Perth* to the King's Naval Forces had been issued, but the Government did not wish to send a second cruiser away. The acting Chief of the Naval Staff urged compliance, pointing out that New Zealand and India had placed their naval forces at the Admiralty's disposal, but the Government still would not agree, and on the 30th cabled the United Kingdom Government that, although it wished to place the ships of the R.A.N. at the Admiralty's disposal, it was necessary to stipulate that no ships other than *Perth* be taken from Australian waters without its concurrence. On 8th September the British Government asked that both the second cruiser and five destroyers be lent for service elsewhere than on the Australia Station. On the 6th October the War Cabinet agreed to send the destroyers to Singapore and place a second cruiser at the disposal of the United Kingdom Government with the proviso that she should not proceed west of Suez. *Hobart* left Sydney on 13th October, three destroyers on the 14th, and two destroyers left Fremantle on the 14th. The destroyers were still on passage when a further United Kingdom request sought permission for them to proceed to the Mediterranean. This request was agreed to by the War Cabinet on 17th October though, as the Chief of the Naval Staff informed the First Sea Lord, 'with some misgiving'. The result was the offer by the Admiralty of a *quid pro quo*, the transfer of the light cruisers *Colombo* and *Ceres* to the Australia Station. Full Cabinet approved this proposal on 31st October. (*Ceres* and *Colombo* were in fact transferred to other duties and did not arrive on the Australia Station, and the War Cabinet formally relinquished any claim to them in May 1940.)

It was taken for granted that, although there would be some controversy about sending Australian soldiers overseas, Australian seamen went there as a matter of course. However, while the Australian destroyer flotilla was on passage from Australia to Singapore, Commander H. M. L. Waller signalled the Naval Board that many reserve ratings in his flotilla claimed that they had joined for service only in Australian waters, and he asked for a ruling. In fact, the *Naval Defence Act* provided that members of the naval forces might be required to serve anywhere. By joining the naval reserve, or, in the case of a conscript, by expressing a preference for service in the navy, a man in effect volunteered for service anywhere in the world, but this had not always been made clear to youths joining the reserve. It was not long before the young reservists, their protests answered, were giving fine service under daunting conditions.

Finally, on 7th November, an Order-in-Council placing all Australian naval ships then in commission at the disposal of the Admiralty was signed. The transfer of Australian ships to Admiralty control had taken place in slower motion than in 1914, when it had been made on 10th August, six days after the declaration of war, but not before the Admiralty had been persuaded to agree that the strongest ship—the battle cruiser *Australia*—should not join the China Squadron, as the Admiralty wished it to do, until it had searched New Guinea waters for powerful German cruisers whose whereabouts were then uncertain.

In December 1939 the Admiralty agreed that *Perth* should return to Australian waters and *Sydney* join the East Indies Station. To the same station in March went the armed merchant cruiser *Manoora*, to augment a force of eight British naval vessels which were patrolling the Netherlands Indies in case some of the nineteen German merchantmen sheltering in ports there should try to break out.

When the war began the nucleus of an Australian flying-boat squadron (No. 10) was in England preparing to take delivery of its Sunderland aircraft from an English factory. At the request of the British Government the Australian Cabinet decided in October to bring this squadron to full strength in England and place it under the control of the British Air Ministry. Meanwhile on 20th September the War Cabinet had offered the British Government an air expeditionary force of four bomber and two fighter squadrons with a strength of 3,200 officers and men. There were then fourteen squadrons in the air force, including No. 10 and a squadron being formed to go to Port Moresby though equipped only with two converted passenger-carrying flying boats; the total strength when war began comprised about 3,000 regulars, 500 in the Citizen Air Force, and about 150 officers in the reserve; there were some 1,400 civilian pilots. Thus the expeditionary force, if promptly formed and sent away, would take many of the available trained men, particularly of the ground staff.

However, two days after this offer, the Australian High Commissioner in London, Bruce, had recommended to the British Under-Secretary for Air that the Dominions be approached with a proposal that the Empire's training resources be pooled, that elementary aircrew training be carried out in each Dominion, that post-elementary training be largely concentrated in Canada, and that Dominion graduates of these schools should join Dominion squadrons to be formed in Great Britain. (The possibility of co-ordinated Empire air training in war had been discussed since 1936 but hitherto without result.) On 26th September a proposal along these lines was sent to the Dominions. The objective would be to train 50,000 aircrew a year, of whom five-ninths would come from Canada, Australia and New Zealand (South Africa had not yet decided to participate) and the remainder from the United Kingdom. If they were in general agreement with the plan the Dominions were invited to send a delegation to a conference in Canada to discuss details. They did so and at a conference at Ottawa an agreement was hammered out. The Australian delegate—J. V. Fairbairn, the Minister for Air—insisted that about half the Australians should be fully trained at home—a sage precaution from the point of view of local defence because it would entail stationing in Australia large numbers of advanced training machines possessing some military value. Finally it was agreed that the intake of the Canadian schools should be some 2,800 every four weeks, about half from Canada, somewhat over a third from Australia and the remainder from New Zealand and Great Britain. In Australia were to be established 4 initial training schools, 9 elementary flying training schools, 7 service flying training schools and 13 other schools.

In October the Government decided to cancel the decision to send away the six-squadron air expeditionary force partly on the ground that the crews would be needed to staff these schools. This decision was made on advice from London, where there was an evident desire to build up a unified Empire air force commanded at senior levels by United Kingdom officers rather than one containing substantial Dominion formations. From the point of view of the R.A.A.F. one result was that its senior officers would be unlikely to obtain commands in the main theatre of war; their role would be to organise the air force at home and the training of individuals who would be sent to join the British-led Empire air force overseas. In the event no squadrons were broken up to staff the training schools and the net result was simply that well-officered Australian squadrons that might have gone overseas remained at home. By January 1940 there were some 280 pilots in the fourteen squadrons; about forty regular and 180 Citizen Air Force pilot officers had graduated since the war began and about 100 regular air cadets were in training; about fifty C.A.F. officers were under instruction as flying instructors. The sending away of the personnel of six squadrons would not have affected the development of the training schools, yet would have established overseas a nucleus of a self-contained Australian air force along the lines of the proud Australian Flying Corps of 1916-18.

In the last quarter of 1939 there were already about 450 Australians in the Royal Air Force, nearly all of them pilots. That is to say, there was a somewhat larger number of Australian aircrew in the R.A.F. than in the regular R.A.A.F. at the outbreak of war. This contingent ranged from marshals like Sir William Mitchell, Air Officer Commanding in the Middle East, and Longmore, soon to be his successor—Australians by birth who had joined British Services as youths before the earlier war—through a quota of Australians who had joined the R.A.F. just after that war, such as Air Commodore R. M. Drummond and the McCloughry brothers—Group Captains W. A. McCloughry and E. J. Kingston-McCloughry—down to relative juniors trained by the R.A.A.F. for the R.A.F. in the last five years or so. Most squadrons of the R.A.F. contained an Australian or two, and consequently some Australians took part in practically all the main exploits of the R.A.F. in the following eight months.

Meanwhile crews of No. 10 Squadron had been taking part in operations since September. When war began the nucleus of this squadron consisted of seven pilots and fourteen others. In the last quarter of 1939 and in January 1940 more pilots and airmen arrived from Australia and the squadron, now complete and based at Pembroke Dock, made its first normal sortie on 6th February. In March it moved to Mount Batten in Plymouth Sound whence it made anti-submarine patrols over the south-western approaches. It was one of only three long-range flying-boat squadrons in the United Kingdom and was highly skilled, being manned by picked regular officers and airmen.

While still undecided about the destination of the 'special force', now entitled the 6th Division—there being four infantry divisions, the 1st, 2nd, 3rd and 4th, and the components of a fifth in the militia—the Australian Cabinet on 19th October took the important step of reintroducing compulsion for home service in the army: unmarried men who became 21 in the year ending on 30th June 1940 would be called up for three months training. In the debate which followed Menzies undertook that he would not introduce conscription for oversea service.

On 5th November the Australian Ministers had in front of them for the first time a comprehensive picture of the strategical situation in Europe, as seen in London, and definite proposals for the employment of military forces which might go overseas. These came from R. G. Casey, a Cabinet Minister who had been sent to London as Australian member of a group of Dominion Ministers who were to confer on war plans. Casey's experience in the infantry and as an officer on the staff of the Australian Corps in the previous war, and as Australian political liaison officer at the Foreign Office from 1924 to 1931, qualified him to make good use of this opportunity. He reported that the Chiefs of Staff in London hoped that until April there would be no attack on the Western Front, where, they said, the German army now outnumbered the combined French and British armies.[2] It was thought that the probability of attack by Japan was remote. The Chiefs of Staff tentatively suggested that the Australian division be sent to Egypt or Palestine for training as soon as possible, thus relieving British troops there, and that a second Australian division should be sent to the Middle East, making an Australian corps. On 13th November the Australian Defence Committee recommended that these suggestions be adopted. The question was considered by the War Cabinet on the 15th and again on the 16th when, no decision having been made, it was decided that it should be discussed by the Full Cabinet.

Meanwhile on the 20th the New Zealand Government informed Britain that it wished the first contingent of its force to be shipped to Egypt as soon as ships were available. Menzies immediately cabled to the New Zealand Prime Minister, M. J. Savage, that 'the closest co-ordination' between Australian and New Zealand policies was essential, and added a statement of the reasons why his Government had decided to watch developments for three or four weeks before committing itself to sending the division away: the Government was uncertain about Japan's policy; Australian public opinion would warmly support sending troops abroad if land warfare in Europe assumed a critical character, but there was a feeling that with only five British divisions in France, and as yet no casualties, the dispatch of Dominion troops could not be very urgent. He added: 'Another consideration which has puzzled us is that whereas we are finding the greatest possible difficulties in obtaining even a fraction of the shipping needed for some of our export commodities, it seems to be assumed that there would be no difficulty in securing ships and naval convoy for a military force.'

However the Australian Government did not wait for two or three weeks, but on 28th November decided that the division should go abroad early in 1940. It then decided that it was opposed to sending away artillery weapons with this contingent, but on 22nd December modified this decision to the extent of allowing the shipment of enough guns to arm one of the three field

[2] It was discovered later that this was an over-estimate of German strength. In September 1939 Germany had 102 divisions, France 110, Poland about 45; Britain sent five divisions to France up to October 1939. During the campaign in Poland Germany had only thirty-three divisions on her western frontiers. Late in October, however, she was planning to attack in the west with 102 divisions.

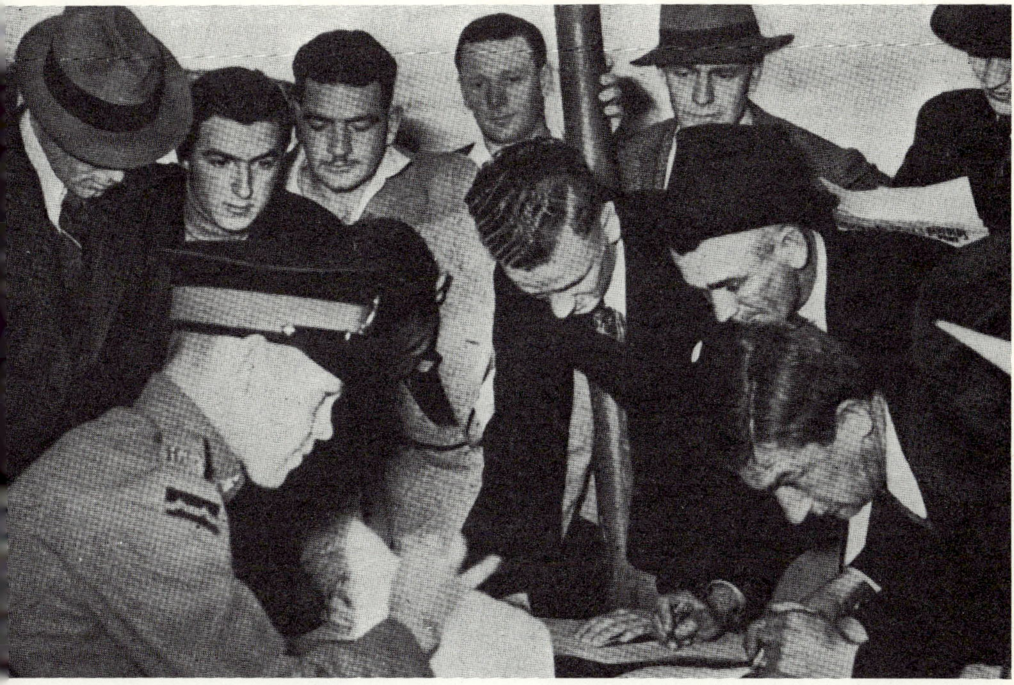

Sun (Sydney)

Victoria Barracks, Sydney, 16th September 1939. Volunteers for service at home or overseas in the 'special infantry division of 20,000 men'—the 6th Division of the future.

regiments. This was typical of the hesitancy that marked this period. There were then in Australia guns and howitzers enough to equip the field artillery of five infantry and two cavalry divisions—a larger force than the British Expeditionary Force in France at that time; and three months earlier the Australian War Cabinet had rejected a recommendation that steps be taken to manufacture field guns in Australia. The recommendation of the British and Australian Chiefs of Staff that a second oversea division be formed, making a corps, was not adopted. Earlier in December the War Cabinet had deferred a decision about a request from Britain for Australian forestry companies until details of the sharing of the cost of Australian forces abroad had been decided. The Ministers were, indeed, contemplating 'a war of limited liability'.

Meanwhile during October and early November the 6th Division had been formed. Indecision as to the need for the new force and what its role would be was so evident that only the most eager—the most adventurous and those most keenly conscious of their obligation to the State—came forward to enlist. From the 80,000 militiamen, most of whom had enrolled during the recruiting campaign which followed the Munich crisis, fewer than 5,000 volunteered—less than half the quota the Government had sought from this source. The divisional commander's official diary gave as the reasons for this failure: the absence of an inspiring lead by the Commonwealth Government, a reluctance on the part of members of the militia to relinquish well-paid positions to join a force which might not go overseas, and opposition by commanders of militia formations and units. About half the recruits had had no military experience. For the reasons given above, and because more than twenty years separated 1918 and 1939 whereas only twelve years separated the South African War from the outbreak of war in 1914, the 6th Division of 1939 contained fewer men who had seen active service than the 1st Division of 1914. The 1st Division had contained 1,300 former British regulars and about 7,300 present or former members of the militia and the British Territorial Army. It had 104 officers who had seen active service whereas the 6th Division had only about sixty; two of its infantry battalions had none at all.

The age limits for private soldiers were 20 to 35 and men who had fought in the previous war were therefore barred, but, in the same way that many who were eager to enlist mis-stated their occupations to avoid the manpower restrictions, many mis-stated their ages and joined up. Medical examination was conducted in crowded noisy halls by busy doctors; men anxious to enlist concealed defects, and a noticeable number of unfit men were enlisted. The poor accommodation at hastily-built camps and the fact that the camps were generally in colder climates than most Australians were accustomed to helped to weed out the unsuitable men.

As commander of the division the Government had chosen Major-General Sir Thomas Blamey who in 1918, as a brigadier-general aged 34, had been chief of staff of the Australian Corps in France. In 1926 he had retired from the regular army to become Commissioner of Police in Victoria. He left this appointment in 1936, and, as mentioned, in 1938 he was made chairman of the Manpower Committee. Probably most of the senior leaders of the old A.I.F. would have recommended his appointment. He had a mind which comprehended the largest military and politico-military problems with singular clarity, and by experience and temperament was well-equipped to cope with the special difficulties which face the commander of a national contingent which is part of a coalition army in a foreign theatre of war. As his senior staff officers he chose two regulars, Colonel S. F. Rowell as G.S.O.1, and Colonel G. A. Vasey as senior administrative officer; as brigadiers he chose four militia officers who had served with distinction as young regimental officers in the earlier war—A. S. Allen (16th Brigade), S. G. Savige (17th Brigade), L. J. Morshead (18th Brigade) and E. F. Herring (artillery). Both Allen and Morshead had commanded battalions in battle; Savige had varied experience as an infantry officer and on the staff, and Herring had risen to the rank of major in the British artillery in the war of 1914-18.

It will be recalled that in 1938 Major-General Squires had been brought to Australia to inspect and report on the army. On the day on which the Cabinet appointed Blamey, a former regular, to command the new A.I.F., it made Squires Chief of the General Staff in place of Major-General J. D. Lavarack, who had held that post since 1935 and when war broke out had been on an overseas tour of duty. Lavarack was transferred to the Southern Command. This action, combined with an announcement by Menzies that all commands in the 6th Division were being given to militia officers, created considerable resentment in the regular officer corps, to which the Prime Minister's announcement was taken not merely as a statement of present fact but as an indication of future policy.

The Chief of the Naval Staff, Admiral Sir Ragnar Colvin, appointed in

1937, and the commander of the naval squadron, Rear-Admiral J. G. Crace, were officers of the British Service—although Crace was an Australian who had joined the Royal Navy as a youth. So far no Australian-trained officers of the R.A.N. had reached flag rank; the senior of these was H. B. Farncomb who had become a captain in 1937.

When war broke out the senior officers of the air force were Air Vice-Marshal Richard Williams who was serving on exchange in the Royal Air Force in England, and Air Vice-Marshal S. J. Goble who was acting as Chief of the Air Staff in the place of Williams, who had occupied that post for most of the time since the foundation of the force eighteen years before. Both had seen exacting service in the war of 1914-18, in which Williams had finally commanded a wing; both were still in their late forties and had varied their between-wars service in the small Australian Air Force with courses in British schools and tours of exchange duty in the R.A.F. But the Cabinet decided to seek a British officer as its senior air adviser, and in February Air Chief Marshal Sir Charles Burnett, aged 57, who had been Inspector-General of the R.A.F., became Chief of the Air Staff; and thus the heads of all three Australian Services were British Officers.

In his discussion with the New Zealand Prime Minister Menzies had indicated that already, in the early months of the war, his Government was beginning to foresee a difficulty which Hughes, his predecessor in the earlier war, and now a junior colleague, had not found acute until 1916—Australia's lack of shipping. In 1916, finding that Australia could not ship her wheat except at exorbitant freight charges, Hughes, as mentioned, had bought tramp steamers and embarked on local shipbuilding on a fairly large scale (though no ships were completed until the war was over). Menzies now faced a similar problem, springing from similar causes. Britain had somewhat less merchant tonnage than in 1914; she had omitted to build up substantial emergency stocks of grain, and in the early months of the war ships were delayed in port while being armed or while waiting for convoys. All this reduced the volume of Britain's imports by about one-third and she began to seek cargoes from the nearer sources—grain, for example, from North America rather than Australia.

In 1939 virtually the only ships registered in Australia were those engaged in the coastwise trade—154 in all. The passenger ships could be useful as armed merchant cruisers or troop transports and, as we have seen, several were now thus employed. At length, on 8th December, the Government obtained the passing of a *Ship Bounty Act*, under consideration since before the war, which provided for payment of a bounty ranging from £10 to £12 10s a ton on ships built in Australia, total payments to be limited to £50,000 a year; thus the encouragement would cease when some 5,000 tons of shipping had been built! The Government next (in January) considered the possibility of chartering neutral shipping. Soon afterwards the British Government, which from 1st February had requisitioned all British shipping, hitherto under somewhat easy-going control and wished to obtain the use of as much neutral shipping as possible, informed the Australian Government that it was anxious lest competitive chartering should send up the rates. In the event the Australian Government by 21st March had succeeded in chartering only one ship.

When Menzies had said that he was puzzled because ships could be found for troops but not for cargoes, he evidently overlooked the fact that Australian wheat, in common with other bulky cargoes, was carried chiefly in tramp steamers; troops were carried in passenger ships, a large proportion of which had to be converted into transports as soon as war began. Troop transports were normally accompanied by some freighters carrying heavy equipment and stores, but these would not need to accompany a movement of Australian troops because the Government had decided to provide only a little of the heavy equipment needed by its expeditionary force. In the event the convoy which was assembled to carry the first Australian and the first New Zealand contingents consisted of ten passenger liners and one British trooper.

On 28th November the Admiralty had informed the Australian Naval Board that if the convoy could sail from Sydney early in January it could be escorted by the battleship *Ramillies*, then part of a raider-hunting group in the Aden area; it proposed that an Australian 6-inch gun cruiser be sent as additional escort from south-west Australia to Colombo. Some days later Churchill, the First Lord of the Admiralty, suggested to the First Sea Lord that a second cruiser be added leaving *Ramillies* freer to engage an enemy if the convoy was attacked. He added: 'The transportation of the Australian divisions is an historic episode in Imperial history. An accident would be a disaster.' The Australian naval staff proposed that the cruisers *Australia*, *Canberra* and *Sydney* should accompany the *Ramillies* on the

Australian War Memorial

Men of the 6th Australian Division boarding transports at Sydney, 9th January 1940.

convoy from Fremantle to Cocos Island, and the *Sydney* thence to Colombo. This would leave only *Adelaide* and, if they were then ready, two armed merchant cruisers in Australian waters. However, the War Cabinet, though it wished the escort to be strengthened, would not agree so to weaken the local forces and asked the Admiralty to provide two other 8-inch cruisers from Fremantle onwards. The Admiralty agreed and allotted H.M.S. *Kent* and the French cruiser *Suffren*. On 15th December, immediately after the successful action against the adventurous German battleship *Admiral Graf Spee* off Montevideo, Colvin urged that his original proposal be agreed to, the Australian cruisers escorting the convoy to the limits of the Australia Station, but the War Cabinet decided to adopt the Admiralty's proposal. Outside Sydney Heads on 10th January four liners containing the 16th Australian Brigade and attached divisional and base troops joined six ships carrying the 4th New Zealand Brigade. On the 12th the eleventh ship, containing other divisional and base troops, joined the convoy outside Port Phillip Bay; on the 20th the convoy and its 13,000 troops—the largest the war had yet seen—sailed for Fremantle.

A few days before the embarkation of this first contingent General Squires had again recommended to the War Cabinet that a second division be formed, making a corps for service overseas. Eight weeks later, on 28th February 1940, the Cabinet adopted this recommendation and also decided, in response to an appeal from Britain, to raise forestry companies (first asked for early in December) and railway companies for service in France. It decided also that an air force squadron should be attached to the new army corps.

As soon as the ranks of the 6th Division had been filled the recruiting rate had declined sharply. Only 811 enlisted in January and 217 in February, but in March and April, after the formation of the new division was announced, 6,757 enlisted. The administrative machine moved slowly and commanders for the corps and the new division were not appointed until five weeks after the Cabinet's decision. Blamey was promoted to command the corps, and took Rowell up with him as his chief of staff. Major-General Iven Mackay, a schoolmaster by profession, who had been an outstanding company commander on Gallipoli and battalion and brigade commander in France, and was then leading a militia division, was appointed to command the 6th, and Lavarack the 7th. Mackay was a modest, austere officer who would not be satisfied with less than the highest standards of military efficiency and would be practical, cool and resolute in action; Lavarack, temperamental and ambitious, whose status had for five years been higher than that of a divisional commander, dropped a step in rank for the sake of taking a division into the field. In consequence of a decision to adopt the new British divisional organisation, with three instead of four battalions to a brigade, one of the new brigades could be formed from the surplus battalions of the 6th Division. Command of this brigade, the 19th was given to a regular soldier, H. C. H. Robertson; of the 20th and 21st to citizen soldiers, J. J. Murray and J. E. S. Stevens.

In the first six months far more men applied for enlistment in the air force than in the A.I.F.: service in the air force appealed to many adventurous and mechanically-minded young men, and the Government had proclaimed that Australia's contribution of aircrew would be of greater importance than her contribution of troops. By the end of March 11,550 had applied for enlistment as aircrew, 56,770 as ground staff. Of the aircrew applicants the recruiting staffs had by that time managed to interview only 4,610 of whom 1,970 had been accepted. Of the ground staff applicants fewer than one-tenth had so far been enlisted. Progress with training of crews under the Empire scheme was necessarily gradual: the regular force in peace had trained only about 100 pilots a year. As an early and wise measure more than fifty experienced civil pilots had been given an 8-weeks course for instructors in October and November, and other similar courses followed; at a flying school the ratio was one instructor to five or six pupils. In April the last batch of pilot trainees who had been enlisted before the outbreak of war graduated. The air force was then about 6,000 strong, having more than doubled since September, and had on its waiting list all the men it could cope with for six months.

In February the first of the new air training schools had opened, and by the end of March 184 potential aircrew had been entered. This was the beginning of the flow which was planned to increase until by early in 1943 it had reached a total of 57,000 in aircrew alone. In peace pilots had been given a comprehensive training and emerged ready, after some experience in a unit, to fly any aircraft, to navigate, or to take a junior administrative post. Under the Empire plan time would be saved by specialisation. Each pupil first spent three months at an initial training school, learning mathematics, the elements of navigation, Morse and other subjects. Those survivors of this course who were chosen to become pilots went on to an elementary flying training school where, in two months, they were taught to fly a light aircraft. Those who succeeded entered service flying training schools, and spent four months learning to fly an advanced trainer. Those considered suited by temperament to become pilots of single-engined machines, such as fighters, went to service schools equipped with Harvards or Wirraways (by March fifty-one Wirraways had been delivered). Those considered suited to become pilots of multi-engined machines, such as bombers, went to schools equipped with Ansons, a small bomber or reconnaissance machine now being discarded by R.A.F. squadrons. After the initial training school the potential air gunners or potential navigators were diverted to their special schools, whence six months later they rejoined their contemporaries trained as pilots. The upper age limit for pilots was 31, for air gunners and navigators 32. Youths could enlist at 18 but since, in 1940, the great majority would spend six months, perhaps more, awaiting a place at an initial training school and their training would take nine months, relatively few of those enlisting in the early months of 1940 were likely to go into action before they were 20. About one in five pupils failed to graduate; of the unsuccessful about half 'remustered' as ground staff.

Thus there grew up side by side a big training organisation, producing contingents of aircrew for service over Europe in R.A.F. squadrons, and a small but expert air force which had one squadron on service in England and another soon to go to the Middle East, but otherwise was occupied with the local defence of Australia. In November Goble had eased the pressure on the staff at Air Force Headquarters by creating two group headquarters, one at Sydney and one at Melbourne. In February Burnett amended this arrangement: there would be four 'areas'—Southern, Central,

Northern and Western (though the Northern and Western Areas were not actually established until the next year). Burnett also reorganised the headquarters staff on lines that would enable it to cope with the coming expansion both in the schools and the areas. Williams, the father of the force, was given the new post of Air Member for Organisation and Equipment; Group Captain W. D. Bostock, who had become Deputy Chief of the Air Staff in 1939, remained in that appointment under Burnett; the increasingly important post of Director of Training was given in April to Group Captain George Jones. In April the air force medical service was removed from the control of the director-general of the army's medical services and the last link between the army and its offspring was severed.

By the end of March about 100,000 Australians had volunteered for service overseas in the war against Germany. Some 22,000 were in the A.I.F., 68,000 had signed applications to join the air force, about 7,000 were in the navy. The army figure does not include 12,000 regulars and garrison troops. The air force figure includes all who signed applications; there were so many that there was a long delay in calling them up and when their time came about 25 per cent did not respond. Some of these may have enlisted in another Service; others may have changed their minds. Nevertheless it was a remarkable response by men of a distant Dominion in view of the lack of fighting in Western Europe in those months, the Government's delay in deciding what form the Australian contribution should take (the citizen could only guess at the causes of the delays), and the knowledge that the air force had vastly more volunteers than it could handle. In the Australian population there were about 600,000 men aged 20 to 29. A number equal to one in six of those had volunteered. Relatively few had been outside that age group. It was as though in the United States, with nearly twenty times Australia's population, 2,000,000 had volunteered so soon for service against an inactive enemy in another hemisphere. The number who had come forward equalled about half the number likely to be required up to June 1942, provided that the scale of the Australian effort was not increased. In February this requirement was estimated at 151,000 for the army, 54,000 for the air force, and 25,000 for the navy.

This response seemed to indicate that the nation's 'morale' was sound, and did not need to be pepped up with propaganda. Faith in the power of propaganda to rapidly mould people's opinions and elate or depress their spirits was a fundamental political doctrine in the two great totalitarian Powers, Germany and the Soviet Union, and as a result of this and of the recent elaboration of means of mass communication, this faith gained many adherents in countries where liberal or socialist doctrines were dominant; enough to ensure that, in a new war, organisations would be built up on both sides to bombard the enemy with dispiriting ideas and their own people with encouraging ones, and to cajole possible allies. The doctrines on which totalitarian propaganda methods were based left little room for the conception that the character of a community is a product of centuries of slow growth and not to be fundamentally changed overnight, or in a year or two.

Soon after the outbreak of war in Australia as in England, a Department of Information was established, but Australia's first steps in this direction were modest and cautious. The portfolio was allotted to Sir Henry Gullett, a former journalist, who also held another portfolio. As administrative head of the department he chose, not a publicity expert, but a museum director, Major J. L. Treloar, an able and retiring public servant who was in charge of the Australian War Memorial at Canberra. Unlike the corresponding British department, which at this time plastered the cities with posters appealing to the people to be resolute, proclaiming the invincibility of the British Navy and so on, the Australian department as yet distributed no exhortations, but confined itself chiefly to forming consultative councils including representatives of the newspapers, to supplying information to the newspapers and news films to the cinema, and to giving short-wave news broadcasts in several languages. The department was also given control of censorship of news, with the aid of liaison officers from the Services.

We have seen that about one-sixth of the men of military age, as then understood, volunteered in the first uneventful seven months of the war. It is difficult to assess the sentiments of the remainder at this time, but there is evidence that the Government considered them to be unwilling to accept measures which would disturb normal business or pleasure. For example, no decisive step to reduce consumption of petrol was taken for eight months: on 6th May the Government imposed a small tax of 3d a gallon —about one-eighth of the retail price. And doubts whether all the people had their hearts in war may have seemed to receive confirmation when from March to May occurred a 67-day strike on the New South Wales coalfields.

The Ministers themselves were handicapped by doubt about what Japan would do. They and the people were perplexed by the fact that since the fall of Poland there had been little actual fighting in and around Europe; it seemed a 'phoney' war. There was, indeed, a conviction in the minds of many influential people concerned with finance that a settlement would be reached with Hitler's Germany without further serious conflict. The Australian Ministers had shown that they were keeping a weather eye on possible post-war difficulties; one reason given for the financial policy was that it would ease the economic crisis which some experts regarded as inevitable after the war.

In these first few months of the war the Labour Party's opposition to the dispatch of expeditionary forces had dwindled. In the course of a by-election, consequent on the resignation of Casey to become the first Australian Minister to Washington, Curtin had affirmed that if Labour was in power it would continue to reinforce the A.I.F. Thus a major cause of political controversy seemed to have been removed. On the other hand the Government had only a slender majority and was supported by a coalition of two parties whose interests and policies were not identical. Thus handicapped, it had postponed decisions, both military and economic, in a manner perilous in warfare. One course of military action open to the Government was full mobilisation of the Services and an open cheque for the manufacture of arms—a course the neutral United States would adopt in a few months. Another course was to encourage without stint the formation of a volunteer army and to plan to arm it fully from Australian factories. A third course was adopted: to enlist a small military force, then for three months to allow enlistment almost to cease; to begin to send the force overseas but with few heavy weapons; to embark upon a cautious increase in arms production in Australia; to leave the home army unmobilised.

Chapter 3 **After Dunkirk**

Since 9th October 1939 Hitler and his staffs had been planning an invasion of Holland and Belgium and since early in December had been plotting a *coup d'état* in Norway in which the local National-Socialist party would seize power and a German occupation would follow. In March the German leaders had decided that Norway would have to be conquered by military not political means, and on 2nd April Hitler set the hour—4.15 a.m. on 9th April. That day Denmark and southern Norway were overrun, but resistance continued in northern Norway, where British troops landed from 14th April onwards.

Between the wars soldiers had been striving to develop tactics and weapons which would enable them to overcome the kind of deadlock that had occurred on the Western Front and elsewhere in 1915-18. This was to be achieved, they believed, by the use of large armoured forces, close support by aircraft and improved infantry tactics and transport. The new German Army in particular was imbued with the doctrine of the *blitzkrieg*, the swift-moving offensive that would break through the opposing defences, bewilder the enemy and be pressed without any interval for reorganisation until victory was complete. The German Army and Air Force had won rapid success with these tactics in Poland and now set out to repeat that success in western Europe. At dawn on 10th May German troops invaded Belgium, Holland and Luxembourg and soon were sweeping on into northern France. They rapidly thrust back the defending armies. Fighting ceased in Holland on 15th May; the King of the Belgians surrendered on the 28th; on the 26th the British Expeditionary Force and those French troops who were isolated round Dunkirk by the rapid German advance across their lines of communication had begun to embark for England; air force men and base troops had been embarking at other Channel ports for several days. Italy declared war at midnight on 10th June. The German advance southward through France continued, and on the 17th France asked for an armistice. Britain and the Dominions then stood alone against Germany and Italy.

Meanwhile, in Britain, on the day the German attack opened Winston Churchill had become Prime Minister. He was a worthy spokesman for the sturdy resolution of the common people of Britain as they prepared to meet the apparently inevitable German onslaught upon their own land—'Let us . . . so bear ourselves that, if the British Empire and its Commonwealth last for a thousand years, men will still say: "This was their finest hour".'

In Australia the news of the disasters in Europe transformed the mood of the government and the people. The Prime Minister expressed the convictions of the majority when, on 21st May, he told the War Cabinet that the whole situation had changed and henceforth Australia must conduct herself in a totally different way. There must be an all-in war effort. No longer could they depend on obtaining munitions from Britain; indeed, they might have to be ready to send them to her.

Menzies added that he proposed to appoint Essington Lewis as Director-General of Munitions with extensive powers; the Service Ministers were to consult their advisers and return with demands for all they needed on the assumption that the war would last three years. He proposed also to appoint Sir Keith Murdoch, a leading newspaper manager and a former journalist, as Director-General of Information; when this appointment was made the Prime Minister himself replaced Sir Henry Gullett as Minister for Information.

In the House next day Menzies announced these decisions, and added that Essington Lewis would be given the utmost authority to get things done by means of existing government machinery and by pressing private factories into service. A third A.I.F. division (the 8th) would be raised. Australia would man ten corvettes being built in Australia for the Admiralty and new destroyers being built in Britain. The building of a graving dock at Sydney capable of taking capital ships would be begun—it had been under discussion since 1938.

In the course of May and June the Government decided to send further naval and air forces overseas to reinforce British stations: it was then that it agreed that the small British cruisers *Ceres* and *Colombo*, which were at Singapore and destined for the Australia Station, should not come to Australia but be used elsewhere; the armed merchant cruiser *Westralia* and two sloops were made available for service on the East Indies Station, and the heavy cruiser *Australia* placed under direct Admiralty control. Later the heavy cruiser *Canberra* was allotted to convoy duty in the Indian Ocean. It was decided to send three air force squadrons—Nos. 1, 8 and 21—to Malaya to relieve British squadrons there for service elsewhere. Thus, although in October the Government had decided that it could not afford to send away an expeditionary force of six squadrons, it would soon have five squadrons overseas—three in Malaya, one in England and one in the Middle East. Thirteen squadrons remained at home.

On 16th June Menzies, in a broadcast appealing for 'all-round sacrifice, unremitting toil and unflinching devotion', announced that Parliament would be called together to consider a Bill to enable the Government to requisition property, to direct employers and employees, and to call up and train the manpower of the nation.

In June it was decided that 250,000 men would be raised, trained and equipped for the home defence army—the number needed in the event of general mobilisation. However this was not to entail a true mobilisation of the seven militia divisions. It was estimated that there would always be 30,000 to 40,000 A.I.F. volunteers in Australia; the aim would now be to increase the militia to about 22,000 but to train units for three months, then disband them for three months, and so on.

As the crisis became graver men crowded the recruiting offices in unprecedented numbers. The air force soon had enough volunteers to fill the training schools for a year. In March and April recruits for the 7th Division had been enlisting at so slow a rate that it seemed that two more months might pass before it was filled, but in May 8,000 were accepted and in June 48,500; already enough men were available to fill not only the 7th and 8th

Divisions but two more. On 11th July the War Cabinet decided to suspend recruiting for the army on the grounds of lack of equipment, the depletion of the militia and the loss of men by industry. It decided that the strength of the A.I.F. in Australia should be stabilised at 80,000. However, far more than 80,000 had either already enlisted or were in the process of enlisting, or had been accepted but had obtained permission to defer actual enrolment. In July 21,000 enlistments were recorded, in August 32,500, making the total for three months 102,000. The Government had authorised the formation of a corps of three divisions, with an establishment of 65,000; it now had about twice that number of volunteers. The people, not the Government, were deciding policy in this field.

The German invasion of Norway, the defeat of France and the entry of Italy into the war had promptly produced new naval tasks and dispositions in which Australian ships were concerned. There were twenty-four Norwegian and Danish merchantmen in the waters of the Australia Station on 9th April; all complied with signals to go to the nearest Australian port except one which was intercepted and escorted to Fremantle.

When Italy declared war two Italian liners, *Remo* and *Romolo* (each 9,780 tons), were in Australian waters. The *Remo* was seized in Fremantle harbour; the *Romolo*, after being chased northwards from Queensland waters by *Manoora*, was scuttled by its crew on 12th June, 220 miles south-west of Nauru, the *Manoora* rescuing the passengers and crew. A week later the liner *Niagara* (13,415 tons) was mined four hours out of Auckland. This led to a vigorous naval and aerial search for possible minefields in the Australian shipping lanes but none were then found.

It was learnt long afterwards that the mines off the New Zealand coast were laid by the German armed merchant cruiser *Orion* (7,800 tons). She had entered the Pacific round Cape Horn and laid these mines on 13th and 14th June, had then cruised along central Pacific routes, and at length turned south through the Coral Sea and into the Tasman. On 16th August she sank the French steamer *Notou* (2,489 tons) near Noumea and on 20th August met the large freighter *Turakina* (8,706 tons) on passage from Sydney to Wellington. *Turakina* refused to stop and replied to *Orion's* fire from six 5.9-inch guns with her single 4.7-inch gun, thus opening the first naval action ever fought in the Tasman Sea. Inevitably *Turakina* was sunk: her captain and thirty-five others were killed and twenty-one survivors became prisoners. The New Zealand cruiser *Achilles*, the Australian cruiser *Perth* (one of only two cruisers now remaining on the Australia Station) and Australian aircraft searched for the raider but she made off to the south. In September she steamed back through the Tasman Sea and into the Pacific to meet a supply ship off the Marshall Islands. Next month she joined a second raider, the *Komet* (3,287 tons), which had reached the Pacific by way of the Arctic Ocean and the Bering Sea. They steamed southward in company to intercept shipping off the east coast of New Zealand. There in November they captured a small ship and sank the liner *Rangitane* (16,712 tons). Thence the raiders went north towards Nauru. Round Nauru on 6th, 7th and 8th December they sank five phosphate-carrying vessels totalling 25,900 tons which had congregated there because bad weather had delayed loading. Later in December they landed 343 European and 171 Chinese and native prisoners at Emirau Island in the Bismarck Archipelago. On

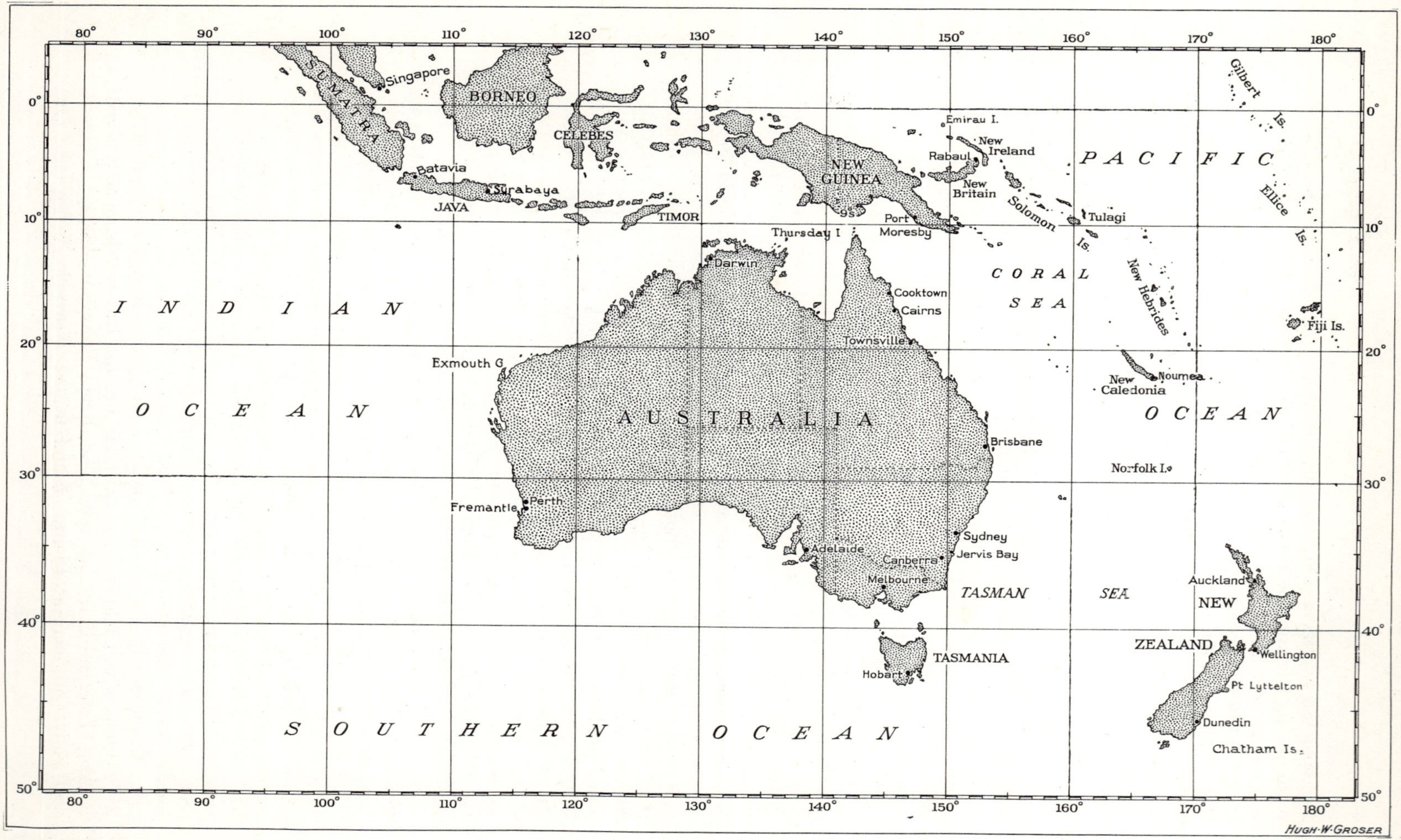

Australia Station

27th December *Komet* again appeared off Nauru where she fired 200 shells into the phosphate plant and wrecked it, with the result that loading was interrupted for ten weeks.

In October and November a third raider, the *Pinguin* (7,766 tons) coming by way of the Indian Ocean, laid mines off the south and east coasts of Australia; these sank three merchantmen. The *Pinguin* then returned to the Indian Ocean where in November she sank three big cargo ships. She will reappear in this chronicle later. The success of these raiders demonstrated that the protection of trade in the long Australian and Pacific sea lanes was a task far beyond the reach of a few relatively short-range aircraft and the four cruising ships then remaining on the Australia and New Zealand Stations—*Hobart, Achilles, Adelaide* and *Manoora.* But this was a risk that could be avoided only at the cost of gravely depleting the combined British naval forces in the Indian Ocean, the Mediterranean and the Atlantic, where, as will be seen later, the Australian cruisers absent from their home waters were doing vital tasks.

The fall of France and Holland radically altered the situation in the Far East; and in their decisions concerning the deployment of their forces the Australian Ministers had to take into account the possibility of Japan seizing the opportunity to attack the European colonies in East Asia.

In May and June Japan sought to extract a promise from the Government of the Netherlands Indies that the export to Japan of specified quantities of certain raw materials would not be hampered and at length the Dutch agreed. In June Japan demanded that Britain should withdraw her troops from Shanghai and close the Hong Kong frontier and the Burma Road against supplies of war materials to China; Japan demanded that the French Government should allow Japanese observers to enter Indo-China to supervise the execution of an agreement that no military equipment be transported thence to China and France agreed.

In what proportions should Australia distribute her forces among what seemed the three main tasks—the reinforcement of Britain in western Europe and the Mediterranean, the reinforcement of British garrisons in the Far East, and the local defence of Australia? On 13th June Britain announced to the Dominions her probable inability to send adequate naval reinforcements to the Far East in the changed circumstances. In a review of the new situation presented to the Australian War Cabinet by its military advisers on 18th June they had emphasised that Britain, without the aid of the French Fleet, could not contain both the German and Italian Fleets and at the same time send a fleet to the Far East. Yet Singapore must be held. The question was raised how much Australia could do to help defend it. On 28th June the British Government asked whether Australia could at once move to Malaya a division equipped from the militia's pool of weapons. The Australian Chiefs of Staff reported that to send away the 7th Division equipped on even a modest scale would seriously hamper the training of the remainder of the A.I.F. and the equipment of the 6th Division and the militia (in other words would hamper local defence and the Australian contribution to the defence of the Middle East). As a result of this advice the War Cabinet decided not to send a division to Malaya.

Already the Government had resisted a British proposal for distributing its oversea force rather than concentrating it in the Middle East. When Germany had attacked in the west, one brigade group of the 6th Division was in Palestine and two convoys containing the remainder of the division and some corps troops were on the way thither. The British Government wished both these contingents to be diverted round the Cape to England because of possible dangers on the Red Sea route and the possible difficulty of shipping equipment to the Middle East. After some discussion the second convoy completed its voyage to Egypt, but the third, which contained about 8,000 Australians and 6,800 New Zealanders, was diverted to Britain, where it arrived late in June and was sent to Salisbury Plain. It included the 18th Australian Brigade, plus artillery and other units, and a high proportion of technical troops and reinforcements. Largely from the technical troops a second brigade was improvised and the whole force placed under the command of Major-General H. D. Wynter. Thus, by July, an Australian division—the 6th—lacking certain units was in Palestine, a force of about half a division was in England, the 7th Division was training in Australia, and the 8th was being formed there.

When the Japanese demanded that the Burma Road and the Hong Kong frontier be closed, the Australian Government urged Britain to agree, arguing that 'the concessions that we can give together are very likely to be considerably less than Japan will be able to take by war'. After consulting the United States, Britain closed these doorways to China from 17th July. That day Prince Konoye, an eminent nobleman, replaced Admiral Yonai as Prime Minister, and General Tojo, representing the army leaders who were gaining control of the Government and were eager to seize the European and American colonies in east Asia, became War Minister. The new Government's immediate policy was rapidly to bring about the defeat of China and to begin southward expansion by measures short of war.

Between Japan and the United States a keen diplomatic conflict was now in full swing. Also in July conscription was enacted in the United States, with the object of bringing the army up to full strength and having it continuously under arms. The effect of this would be to mobilise and train an army including thirty-three divisions, four of them armoured, with a total strength of 1,400,000; the ultimate aim was to establish forty-five divisions, ten of them armoured. At the same time President Roosevelt authorised an unprecedented naval building program which when completed would provide a fleet more than twice as large as Japan's. The United States placed limitations on the export of aviation fuel and certain scrap metal to Japan.

Australia's special interest in the diplomatic struggle in the Far East led to the appointment on 18th August of Sir John Latham as Minister to Tokyo. He had been a Federal Minister, and as such had led an Australian mission to the East in 1934; since 1935 he had been Chief Justice of the High Court.

In Australia shortage of equipment seemed to the Ministers to be the main obstacle to the adoption of more weighty military measures. It had been a factor in the decision not to send a division to Singapore and to suspend recruiting; the air force schools were short of training machines and one of the nineteen squadrons authorised nearly a year ago for the home air force had, for lack of aircraft, not yet been formed. It was to help solve this problem that Essington Lewis had been appointed Director-General of Munitions, with autocratic powers; in July Menzies announced that Lewis had been told that 'the sky was the limit'. Plans were soon being made to more than quadruple the number of men and the amount of money allotted to making weapons of war. For example, it was decided to increase the number of munition workers and workers in aircraft factories, then estimated at 15,200, to 80,000 within the coming year.

When Lewis took command the undertakings begun either before the war or in the first nine months of the war were beginning to produce results. The first 3.7-inch anti-aircraft guns, by far the most elaborate weapons yet made in Australia, had been finished and others were being produced at the rate of one a week. (Thirty of the less-complicated 3-inch anti-aircraft guns had been completed and production had ceased.) Twenty Bren-gun carriers were being delivered each month. Production of rifles and medium machine-guns had been increased, rifles to 170 a week, machine-guns to twenty. The factory to produce 25-pounder field guns and one to produce 2-pounder anti-tank guns had been partly built, two explosives factories in addition to the one existing when war broke out were being built, as was a second gun-ammunition factory. The output of small-arms ammunition would be doubled between January and December 1940. Since before 1914 the policy had been followed of siting munitions factories outside the Sydney-Newcastle area, which might be expected to be the main objective of an invader, and hitherto all but a few such factories had been placed in Victoria. The factories now planned were dispersed more widely, partly for security and partly to tap new supplies of labour. For example, a small-arms ammunition factory and a gun-ammunition factory were to be established in South Australia, a cartridge-case factory in Queensland, a branch of the small-arms factory at Bathurst (New South Wales), inland from Lithgow where the main factory was situated.

By October orders for munitions exceeded £100,000,000—more than five times the sum allotted to all defence services in the last pre-war year. On 26th June, when news was arriving of the success of the German armour in France, the War Cabinet had authorised the building of 859 cruiser tanks. The order for machine-gun carriers was increased to more than 2,000. These projects, like the manufacture of aircraft engines, were extremely ambitious ones for an engineering industry which had only just produced its first modern artillery weapon, and in 1939 had, for example, not been equipped to make complete motor vehicles. The size and complexity of these programs underlined the engineering factories' main handicaps, namely their long-foreseen shortage of skilled workers and machine tools. These were now being gradually overcome. For instance, in September 1939 there were only five firms in Australia making machine tools, gauges and jigs, but by August 1940 there were twenty-eight.

It will be recalled that between September and April a modest naval shipbuilding program had been approved: one destroyer and four corvettes being built at four yards. Substantial additions were made from April to July: one boom defence vessel and twenty more corvettes, ten being for the Admiralty. It was these ten Admiralty corvettes which it was later decided to man with Australian crews. Three more yards were now recruited to build corvettes. In the second half of the year a third Tribal-class destroyer was ordered, and twenty-four more corvettes making a total of forty-eight—twenty-four for the Australian Navy, twenty for the British Navy, and four for the Indian. Naval shipbuilding was now at last on a larger scale than in 1914-19, when two 5,400-ton cruisers, three 700-ton destroyers, and a naval oiler were launched in Australia. However, plans for merchant shipbuilding had not progressed beyond a Cabinet decision of 23rd May to obtain drawings from a Scottish shipbuilder of a 9,000-10,000 ton freighter with the object of building ten such vessels.

The number of aircraft ordered from Australian factories was increased early in June when 200 Wackett trainers, 100 more Moths, making a total of 450, and more Wirraways, making a total of 476, were ordered. The slow rate at which aircraft had been delivered from abroad during the first eight months of the war had indicated that Australia would be wise to increase the output of her own factories. In that time seventy-nine Hudson bombers and twenty-five Tiger Moth trainers had been landed—only a fraction of the machines needed to equip the schools and a home air force of nineteen squadrons. However, from May to December, over 240 trainers (Ansons, Battles and Moths) arrived from England, and from America twenty-one additional Hudsons and eight flying boats.

The need to reinforce Malaya had again been considered by the Australian War Cabinet on 9th July, when it had before it an appreciation by the British Chiefs of Staff in which they emphasised the danger in which the United Kingdom itself stood, its inability for the present to reinforce the Middle East, yet the necessity to hold that area so as to protect the oil supply from Persia, maintain a blockade of occupied Europe, and defend the Red Sea route. In response the Australian Chiefs of Staff now recommended that the 7th Division might be moved to India, one brigade group at a time, possibly releasing a fully-equipped Indian division for Malaya.

The War Cabinet deferred a decision until it had received from London an appreciation of the situation in the Far East asked for some time before. This arrived early in August, and was accompanied by an assurance by Churchill that, if Japan 'set about invading Australia and New Zealand on a large scale', Britain would cut her losses in the Mediterranean and go to their aid, sacrificing every interest except the defence of Great Britain. In their comment on this appreciation the Australian Chiefs of Staff now went a step farther. In June they had been opposed to sending an Australian division to Singapore; in July they had recommended sending one, a brigade group at a time, to India. In August, arguing that Singapore was of primary importance in that it provided a base for the operations of a British or American fleet, and this in turn governed the strength of the forces which Japan would have to dispatch successfully to invade Australia, they recommended that the 7th Division less a brigade group but plus certain ancillary units should be sent to Malaya about October, the remainder following as soon after December 1940 as possible.

However, the War Cabinet decided to inform the British Government that, although it was agreeable to the division going to Malaya, it would (as before) prefer it to go to India to relieve Indian troops for service in Malaya. It considered that in India it would have wider scope for training and a role more suited to the Australian soldier's temperament than garrison duty in Malaya, and was influenced also by the desire that their forces should be in an active theatre and concentrated in one army corps. The British

Government replied that, after considering these Australian opinions, it would prefer the 7th Division to go direct to the Middle East. The War Cabinet approved this course on 23rd September. After four months of proposals and counter-proposals the question of the deployment of the Australian oversea force was back where it had begun. Also on 23rd September the Cabinet decided to form a 9th Division using the two brigades then in England as its nucleus. Later transfers of brigades from one division to another, generally in consequence of a wish to send the better-trained troops into action earliest, produced by early 1941 the following final groupings:

6th Division (16th, 17th, 19th Brigades)
7th Division (18th, 21st, 25th Brigades)
8th Division (22nd, 23rd, 27th Brigades)
9th Division (20th, 24th, 26th Brigades)

In August command of the 8th Division was given to Major-General H. Gordon Bennett, a militia officer who had distinguished himself in 1915-18 as a forceful young battalion and brigade commander—he had led a brigade at the age of 29. Wynter was appointed to command the 9th Division.

The Cabinet's decision of July to discontinue recruiting became effective from September onwards and in the last four months of the year only 5,500 enlistments were recorded, most of them evidently of men who had reasons for deferring their arrival in camp.

When the Government approved, in July 1940, the manufacture of 859 tanks, the implication was that an A.I.F. armoured division would be formed; on 1st January 1941 the Government formally authorised such a division, thus increasing the oversea volunteer force to a strength of five divisions, with their supporting corps and depot troops. At the same time the establishment of the militia remained unchanged — five divisions or their equivalent of infantry and two of cavalry. Thus the Government's desire to maintain a force in a main theatre of war and yet retain a home army for defence against Japan, combined with the objection to conscription for oversea service and the fact that such a large number of volunteers had enlisted, had led to the establishment of an army of twelve divisions, five fully-maintained and seven for the present partly-maintained. Before the war the army staff had contended that Australia could not support more than seven or eight divisions at full strength in active operations, and events were to prove them right. At this time the United Kingdom (46,000,000 people) was planning to maintain thirty-four divisions, of which seven were to form the permanent garrison of the British Isles; Canada (11,000,000) had two divisions in Britain and two at home; New Zealand (1,500,000) had one division overseas; South Africa (2,000,000 Europeans) had two serving in the Middle East. Two divisions of the Indian Army were then serving outside India.

Meanwhile Japan continued her peaceful penetration of South-East Asia. On 22nd September the French Government agreed to admit Japanese troops to Tonkin and allow them to establish airfields there. On the 27th Japan, Germany and Italy signed a Tripartite Pact recognising Japan's leadership in East Asia and agreeing to assist one another if attacked by Powers not yet engaged in war, but with a provision that the pact would not affect any party's relations with Russia. On 30th September the United States Government, its attitude to Japan steadily hardening, placed a virtual embargo on the export of iron and steel scrap. In October, with the agreement of the United States, Britain reopened the Burma Road to China; at the same time Britain, Australia and Holland pressed the United States to take even more positive action to deter Japan.

The collapse of France had left the French islands in the Pacific virtually unprotected against possible Japanese attack. On 26th June the local council in New Caledonia had resolved to carry on the war against Germany, and to encourage continued resistance both in New Caledonia, with its valuable chrome and nickel, and the New Hebrides (governed by a joint British-French administration). The Australian Government, late in June, offered to open trade discussions with the object of arranging to buy New Caledonian metals and supply goods hitherto imported from France; in August B. C. Ballard, an Australian solicitor who since 1934 had been acting for Australian interests in the New Hebrides was appointed Australian official representative at Noumea.

Although most of the people of New Caledonia supported the decision to continue the war and defy the Vichy Government there was a group among the officials and wealthier merchants which supported Marshal Pétain. Early in August the British High Commissioner for the Western Pacific warned his government that recent incidents in New Caledonia indicated that it would be wise to send a French warship with French officials to Noumea to take control of the administration and remove the supporters of Pétain. The Australian Government, however, asked that no steps be taken before the arrival of Ballard at the end of August. Meanwhile the Vichy Government had ordered the sloop *Dumont d'Urville* to Noumea. The outcome was the replacement of a governor who had been trying to hold the balance between the two parties by a Vichyite governor, and on 30th August the British Government asked the Australian Government that a British ship should convey M. Sautot, the French Resident Commissioner in the New Hebrides, to Noumea to rally New Caledonia to the Free French cause. Later the Free French leader General de Gaulle appointed Sautot to be Governor of New Caledonia. After some hesitation on the part of the Australian Government it was decided that Sautot should travel to Noumea in a Norwegian steamer, escorted by the cruiser *Adelaide*. His arrival was to coincide with a *coup de force* by the followers of de Gaulle. Sautot was landed on 19th September and marched at the head of a crowd of supporters to the Governor's office and at length placed him under arrest. The *Dumont d'Urville* sailed for Indo-China whither she was followed later by a steamer carrying 132 French who wished to leave New Caledonia. It had been an unusual experience for an Australian Government to be faced by a delicate diplomatic problem demanding prompt and unequivocal decisions.

East of New Caledonia lie the Fiji Islands in the path of an advance from the north towards New Zealand. In pre-war planning New Zealand had accepted responsibility for the defence of this remote British colony, and in June had begun to form a brigade group to garrison it. In addition she assisted the Fiji administration to raise a local territorial force about 1,000 strong. In November 1940 the 8th New Zealand Brigade arrived in Fiji. Apart from the R.A.A.F. squadrons sent to Malaya in July this was the first

Dominion force to help garrison a Crown colony outside the war theatres.

Meanwhile in an effort to co-ordinate military preparations against attack by Japan the British Government in August had suggested a Far Eastern defence conference attended by staff officers from the United Kingdom, Australia and New Zealand, to be followed possibly by staff talks with Netherlands and American representatives. Co-operation between allies is achieved slowly and not before time-consuming correspondence, and it was October before the conference opened at Singapore. It agreed that the forces garrisoning Malaya were gravely inadequate, and should be promptly reinforced. For example, whereas there were eighty-eight first-line aircraft in Malaya and Burma, half of them of obsolescent types, the conference recommended that 582 were needed. It was estimated that, if these aircraft were available, the military garrison should include twenty-six infantry battalions (including three for Borneo) and the necessary supporting artillery.

A further step towards co-ordination was taken in November when Air Chief Marshal Sir Robert Brooke-Popham arrived at Singapore to become Commander-in-Chief in the Far East with authority over four of the commanders in the area—the general officers commanding Malaya, Burma and Hong Kong and the air officer commanding in the Far East, but not the naval commanders of the China and East Indies Stations.

The Australian Government found the conclusions reached by the conference alarming and approved a proposal that the Prime Minister should go to London to discuss this problem and others with Churchill. The conference had the effect of causing the Government to adopt a proposal that it had three times rejected: that an Australian contingent should, directly or indirectly, be used to reinforce Singapore. It offered a brigade group (of the 8th Division) for service in Malaya as a temporary measure until it could be relieved by Indian troops and transferred to the Middle East. No further air force reinforcement of Malaya from Australia was proposed. Australia still lacked enough modern aircraft to bring the home air force to a strength of thirty-two squadrons, which had been the target since August; indeed, it was January before the former objective of nineteen squadrons was reached.

While the Singapore conference was sitting an 'Eastern Group Supply Conference' was held at New Delhi to organise the distribution of equipment produced in the factories of Australia, New Zealand, South Africa, India and the African and Asian colonies to the forces in the area. Australian policy in this field was defined by Menzies as 'production up to the maximum capacity of the things that we can produce, and, having provided for our needs first, we would be prepared to be importers of the balance'. Australia was not willing to import things she could produce herself; 'there was no intention of entering into commitments which might cramp the development and expansion of our secondary industries'. The conference led to the establishment at New Delhi of an Eastern Group Supply Council on which the countries concerned were represented.

During the critical middle months of 1940 local political problems pressed heavily upon the Australian Ministers. The plan for enlarging the scope and intensifying the effort of the Department of Information suffered an early setback. On 19th June, Murdoch proposed and the War Cabinet agreed that a regulation be made insisting on a journal publishing 'the truth' in an appropriate form if required by the Government. The Ministers had been under fire from some newspapers, particularly the Sydney *Daily Telegraph*, and the prospect of being able to correct mis-statement in the same newspapers was attractive. A month later, when regulations to this effect were gazetted, there was an outcry by the newspapers. The regulation was watered down and a new version announced on 31st August, but the outcome was that the reorganised department made a bad beginning and the criticism aimed at it by newspapers increased. In December Murdoch resigned. The department carried on its necessary duties of supplying material to the Press, giving background information to editors, taking and distributing official photographs and films, broadcasting, and performing other tasks.

In July Menzies had offered Curtin and his followers five or six seats in the Cabinet, but a majority of the Labour Party leaders were rigidly opposed to the establishment of an all-party government, and determined that the general elections due in September should not be postponed. Menzies' offer was rejected. Meanwhile, at a conference in June the Labour Party had adopted a resolution on defence in which it declared its determination that the whole resources of the country, including 'all productive and financial organisations', should be devoted to winning the war; declared its support for the Empire Air Training Scheme and the reinforcement of the A.I.F.; and affirmed the need for an excess war profits tax of 100 per cent, and other measures. These would be the main planks on its election platform.

The House of Representatives rose on 22nd August and the elections were fixed for 21st September. Nine days before the House rose the nation and the Ministry had suffered a severe loss: an aircraft crashed near Canberra and the Minister for the Army (G. A. Street), the Vice-President of the Executive Council (Gullett), the Minister for Air (Fairbairn) and the Chief of the General Staff (General Sir Brudenell White, who had succeeded Squires when Squires died in March) were killed. The loss was particularly telling in that, Casey having gone to Washington, the Ministry was robbed of nearly all its members who had been officers in the previous war. Major-General V. A. H. Sturdee was appointed Chief of the General Staff.

The Government parties lost some seats at the elections with the result that they had a majority of only one and, after providing a Speaker, would have to rely on the support of two Independents. These were A. W. Coles, a Melbourne businessman who had stood as an Independent supporting the United Australia Party, and A. Wilson, an Independent Country Party member, who was a vigorous advocate of the wheat farmers' interests. The swing against the Government had been limited to New South Wales, a phenomenon probably explained partly by the vehemence with which Sydney newspapers had criticised Menzies and his Cabinet and partly by more astute Labour campaigning in that State. The election in New South Wales brought into the House two influential Labour leaders—J. B. Chifley, who had been a member from 1928 to 1931, and H. V. Evatt, at one time a member of the State Parliament and, until his nomination for this election, a justice of the High Court.

Immediately after the elections Menzies again asked the party leaders whether they were willing to join an all-party Government, but a majority of the Labour members were still opposed to it. The compromise was adopted of establishing, in October, an Advisory War Council consisting initially of four Ministers and four members of the Opposition. Partly as a result of the loss of the three Ministers in the air crash of August, fifteen out of twenty of the members of the new Cabinet were new to their portfolios.

In the last quarter of 1940 the need for more rigid and comprehensive control of materials and labour became increasingly evident. In the early months of the war the Government's chief concern had been to direct money into the war effort; now it was to direct resources and men into it. A difficulty was that the State Governments had their own works programs and were sensitive to Commonwealth interference. With a view to reducing these programs a Loan Council[1] meeting in May had approved the appointment of a Co-ordinator of Works. On 15th November, to restrict civilian building, a regulation was introduced that buildings costing more than £5,000 might not be erected without a permit; thenceforward the establishment of such controls would follow one another in fairly rapid succession. In October a Commonwealth Department of Labour and National Service was created to co-ordinate the diverse authorities and policies on employment-finding, industrial relations and industrial welfare, but State Governments regarded industrial matters as being their field, and the new department made headway very slowly.

The Budget introduced by the new Government in November illustrated the extent to which the nation's resources were now being concentrated on war. In 1939-40 actual war expenditure had been £55,000,000; in May it had been estimated that in 1940-41 it would be £79,000,000; in November the estimate was £186,000,000.

An immediate and alarming problem was a shortage of coal as a result of an increasing demand, the strike on the New South Wales fields earlier in the year, and inadequate transport. In 1940, 1,810,000 fewer tons of coal had been won than in 1939. In November the Cabinet was informed that coal was 'desperately short in most States'. In addition, for lack of ships iron ore was being used at Newcastle more rapidly than it could be carried from the source in South Australia, and timber was accumulating on the wharves in Queensland. At length, on 5th December, shipping was placed under the control of the Minister for Commerce; control of coal distribution was discussed but no decision was made, nor would be until February when a Commonwealth Coal Board was formed and given the task of allocating supplies.

During these months small contingents of Australians had taken part in the operations which followed the German onslaught in the west. Some had served in the British air squadrons which fought in France in May and June, and about 100 Australian pilots fought in the 'Battle of Britain'—the long and crucial struggle with the German Air Force in the northern summer of 1940. The intended invasion of England was tentatively fixed for 21st September, but the German fighter force failed to gain an ascendancy

[1] The Australian Loan Council, a permanent body modelled upon an earlier voluntary arrangement in the middle 1920s, operated under the financial agreement of 1928. Representatives of Commonwealth and States met, usually after a Premiers' Conference, to reach agreement on raising and management of public debt especially with a view to minimising competition.

over the R.A.F., German Intelligence overestimated the strength of the defending army, and on 13th September the British bombers successfully attacked the invasion ports and naval ships bombarded them. On 17th September Hitler postponed the invasion indefinitely. The losses suffered by the relatively few who defeated the German air offensive were severe. For example, of the thirty Australians in fighter squadrons who survived the costly conflict in France ten were killed and one became a prisoner. Of seventy-three Australians in coastal and bomber squadrons which took part in attacks on German territory thirteen were killed and six shot down and captured.

The possession of the western coast of Europe from northern Norway to southern France enabled Germany to intensify her submarine offensive against shipping, although her losses were heavy—up to the end of August, twenty-eight submarines. As one of the three long-range flying-boat squadrons in Coastal Command, No. 10 Squadron R.A.A.F. had a relatively large role. A detachment of the squadron was transferred to Oban, on the west coast of Scotland, to patrol against submarines there. On 1st July a Sunderland of the squadron with the corvette *Gladiolus* sank the *U26*, the second definite sinking of a submarine in which Coastal Command aircraft shared. A Sunderland, on 13th July, beat off the first attack made by a German

Australian War Memorial

Four of the original Sunderland flying boat captains of No. 10 Squadron, R.A.A.F., conferring at Pembroke Dock R.A.F. Station in Wales in December 1939. *Left to right:* Flying Officer I. S. Podger and Flight Lieutenants W. H. Garing, C. W. Pearce and W. N. Gibson.

fighter on a flying boat of this squadron. Henceforth such attacks were not infrequent, but the heavily-armed though slow flying boats, boldly handled, were generally a match for fighters or bombers encountered out at sea.

During these months when Britain was threatened with invasion General Wynter's Australian force formed part of the garrison. Even so small a group, armed at first with little more than the rifles and machine-guns it had brought from Australia, was a useful reinforcement to the army defending England, which, immediately after Dunkirk, contained only one division —the 1st Canadian—that was at full strength, well trained and fully armed. The Australian forestry companies and railway construction companies had also arrived in England in mid-1940 and begun work there. The task of the foresters, with others from Canada and New Zealand, was to increase British local production of timber so as to reduce demands on shipping. The intended task of railway companies had been to build lines behind the western front. Between November and January the main body of the Australian force embarked to join the remainder of the Australian Corps in the Middle East.

In the summer of 1940 the Middle East had been transformed into a main theatre of war. As a result of losses round Norway the German surface fleet had temporarily been reduced to three cruisers and four destroyers. Thus, even before France was defeated and before Italy entered the war, the Admiralty could afford to strongly reinforce the Mediterranean Fleet, which at the beginning of the year had consisted only of three small and aged cruisers and the five old Australian destroyers. The destroyers had reached the Mediterranean in December 1939 and had seen exacting and strenuous service often in heavy weather and bitter cold throughout a particularly hard winter. In April and May ships were hurried to the Mediterranean and the Red Sea from east and west and south, among them being H.M.A.S. *Hobart* which with H.M.S. *Liverpool* formed a Red Sea Force in April, and H.M.A.S. *Sydney* (Captain J. A. Collins) which reached Alexandria on 26th May and joined the 7th Cruiser Squadron (Vice-Admiral J. C. Tovey). On 27th May the Australian destroyers in the Mediterranean joined four British destroyers to form the 10th Destroyer Flotilla, with Waller in command.

The proposal, mentioned earlier, that the crews of the Australian destroyers should be used to man new British destroyers had originated with Tovey, who considered that these crews were being wasted in such old ships. Admiral Sir Andrew Cunningham, commanding the Mediterranean Fleet, passed the suggestion on to the Admiralty in April with the comment: 'They certainly are the most lively and undefeated fellows I have ever had to do with.'

Opposing the Allies in the Mediterranean in June 1940, the Italians had 6 battleships, 19 cruisers, some 50 destroyers and at least 115 submarines. These were mainly concentrated in Italy, with light forces in the eastern Mediterranean at the Dodecanese Islands, and some destroyers and submarines based on Massawa in the Red Sea. Italy hoped that her air force, in conjunction with her submarines, would exercise a powerful influence on the conduct of the naval war. Midnight of the 10th June—the moment when war with Italy began—found most of the Mediterranean Fleet in Alexandria harbour but within an hour it was putting to sea on the first of

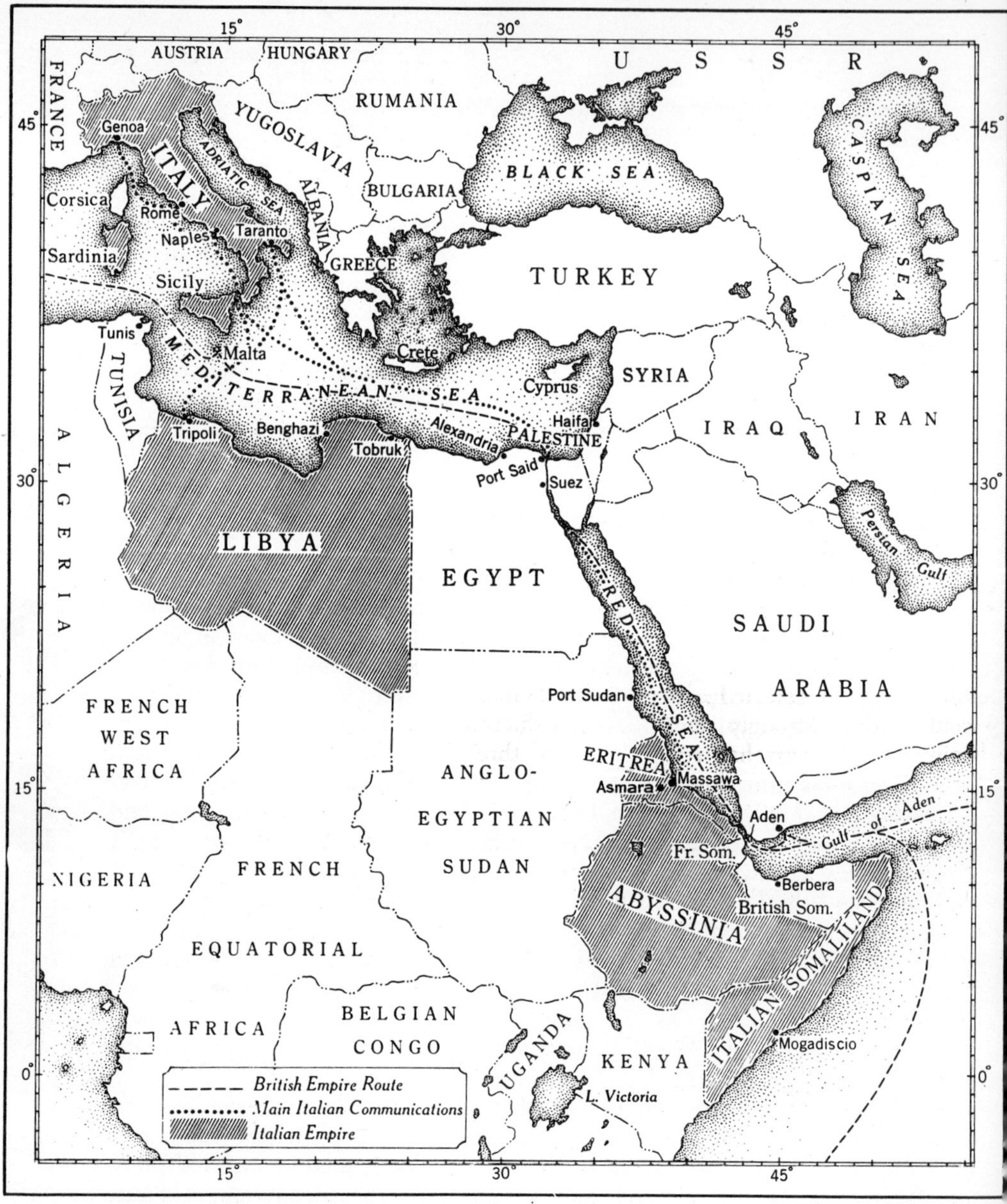

Middle East

the aggressive sweeps with which Cunningham seized and held the initiative. For four days he cruised the central Mediterranean as far as the south coast of Italy without encountering any opposition.

Italy opened naval hostilities with a submarine campaign and an attempt to confine the fleet in Alexandria by mining the approaches. Ships of the 10th Destroyer Flotilla found and marked the minefields and hunted submarines. H.M.A.S. *Voyager* and H.M.S. *Decoy* made a promising attack on 13th June off Alexandria and damaged a submarine which later escaped. By the end of the month—within nineteen days of the start of hostilities—

the Italians had lost ten submarines: six in the Mediterranean, two in the Red Sea, one in the Gulf of Aden, and one at the entrance to the Persian Gulf.

On 21st June the first of a series of bombardments of the Libyan coast in support of the army's harrying operations was carried out, the object being 'to destroy military objectives at Bardia'. The French battleship *Lorraine* took part in the first Bardia bombardment, the last operation against the Italians in which Admiral R. E. Godfroy's ships in the eastern Mediterranean were to share. When the French ceased fighting the naval situation in the Mediterranean was radically changed. In the western Mediterranean no Allied naval bases now existed between Gibraltar and Malta. In the eastern Mediterranean shore resources available to the fleet were limited to those of Egypt, Palestine and Cyprus, with Malta in the central Mediterranean under heavy and constant air attacks. To pass ships through the central Mediterranean now entailed a major fleet operation, and replenishment of stores and ammunition for forces in Egypt and east of Suez had to be carried out by way of the Cape and Red Sea. It now became impossible to divert naval forces from the Mediterranean to the Far East, as had been intended. For a few days the French ships in Alexandria constituted a problem, but the sage and resolute Cunningham solved it peacefully. On 27th June, Godfroy, who had requested permission to sail, appeared relieved when this was refused, and on 4th July an arrangement was reached whereby his ships would be demilitarised and remain at Alexandria.

In the western Mediterranean the first action of a force of three capital ships, an aircraft carrier, a cruiser and seven destroyers hurriedly sent from the Atlantic was against the Vichy French fleet at Oran on the 3rd and 6th July. On 8th July and again in September British ships including the *Australia* made partly successful efforts to disable the French battleship *Richelieu* at Dakar. These attacks greatly intensified French bitterness towards Britain.

The first Italian surface vessel to be sunk in the Mediterranean was a victim of *Sydney's* guns when the 7th Cruiser Squadron, at sea to provide cover for an east-bound convoy, intercepted three enemy destroyers taking troops and supplies from Italy to Libya. The encounter took place some 120 miles north of Benghazi on the evening of 28th June, and was a chase in failing light, *Sydney* engaging the destroyer *Espero* while the other cruisers pursued her consorts. *Espero* put up a gallant fight before being overwhelmed by *Sydney's* heavier gunfire and went down with her colours flying, forty-seven survivors being rescued.

On 7th July the fleet left Alexandria, again to cover a convoy; and the result of this operation was the Battle of Calabria on 9th July, the first clash between the opposing battle fleets, and the first fleet action in which Australian ships had ever taken part. The British force commanded by Cunningham consisted of the flagship *Warspite* with five destroyers; the 7th Cruiser Squadron of four ships including *Sydney*, with *Stuart*, and the 1st Battle Squadron—*Royal Sovereign* and *Malaya*—the aircraft carrier *Eagle*, and eleven destroyers including *Vampire* and *Voyager*. The enemy had two battleships, some sixteen cruisers, and three flotillas of destroyers. The action, fought westward of the toe of Italy on sparkling blue seas in perfect weather, took the Mediterranean Fleet to within twenty-five miles of the Calabrian coast. Because of the superior speed of the Italians, *Warspite* was the only British capital ship to get within range of their battleships; she made a lucky hit on one of them at 26,000 yards. The enemy turned away and retired at high speed behind an effective smoke-screen.

The material results of the brief meeting were disappointing, but the strategical effects were far-reaching. A degree of moral ascendancy was established by the British fleet, while the action showed those without previous war experience how difficult it was to hit at long range, and therefore the necessity of closing in. It showed, also, that the same applied to bombing: high-level bombing yielded few hits. On the Italian side, the battle did nothing to induce self-confidence in a navy in which there was little love for the Fascist regime and correspondingly little real fighting spirit and enthusiasm. Italian training was sketchy, and control, not only of strategy but tactics, was vested in the Ministry of Marine ashore, where the policy was to avoid committing the fleet to a battle in which heavy losses might be suffered.

The Calabrian experience was of value ten days later when *Sydney* (6,830 tons, eight 6-inch guns), in company with five British destroyers, fought an action with two Italian cruisers (each 5,069 tons, eight 6-inch guns) off the coast of Crete. At dawn on 19th July a division of British destroyers was on anti-submarine patrol off the western end of Crete when the enemy was sighted. Outranged by the heavier weight of gunfire of the Italian cruisers which also held the margin of speed, the destroyers retired to the northward under fire towards *Sydney* who, with the destroyer *Havock*, was some forty miles distant, hastening south as she worked up to full speed in the sparkling light of the early Aegean morning. She sighted the Italians at 8.26, and the welcome orange flashes of her opening 6-inch salvos were seen by the destroyers three minutes later. At 8.35 her fire appeared to be effective on the leading enemy ship, and at 8.41 Vice-Admiral Ferdinando Casardi, in *Giovanni delle Bande Nere*, under the impression that the newcomers were two 8-inch gun cruisers instead of one 6-inch gun cruiser and a destroyer, turned away to the south-west, and the action developed into a chase, the British force steaming roughly in line abreast, and the Italians making heavy smoke which intermittently obscured the target. Soon the rearmost Italian, *Bartolomeo Colleoni*, came under effective fire from *Sydney*, her punishment increasing as her reduced speed closed the range. At 9.25 she was stopped, and apparently out of action. Leaving three destroyers to complete her destruction, *Sydney*, who had received only one hit with superficial damage on the forward funnel, continued the pursuit of *Giovanni delle Bande Nere* with the other two destroyers. But the quarry had too much speed and at 10.37 *Sydney*, whose ammunition was low, and who was dropping astern, abandoned the chase, the Italian making Benghazi safely.

The *Bartolomeo Colleoni* was torpedoed by the destroyers, who rescued 545 of her complement. Rescue operations were hampered by Italian bombing attacks, one of the destroyers receiving a direct hit. The ships arrived at Alexandria on the morning of the 20th, and *Sydney* received an ovation from the fleet. *Sydney* had repeated the exploit of her namesake of the 1914-18 war.

Admiralty

The Italian cruiser *Bartolomeo Colleoni* shattered and sinking on 19th July 1940 after her engagement with H.M.A.S. *Sydney* in the Mediterranean, off the island of Crete.

The naval war in the Mediterranean had now taken shape. On the British side, an energetic and aggressive strategy—in which the scope of Cunningham's earlier intentions was considerably expanded—aimed at securing and maintaining east-west communications and keeping Malta supplied and defended, harrying the Italians wherever possible, at sea, on the Libyan coast, and in the Dodecanese, and losing no opportunity to force a fleet action. On the Italian side maintenance of African and Albanian communications was the main occupation; aggressive action would be left to submarines and aircraft and a fleet action avoided.

In the air Italian numerical superiority was equally marked, for, not counting obsolescent types, the Italian Air Force had about 2,000 front-line aircraft of which there were at least 200 bombers and 200 fighters in Libya with a further 110 bombers and sixty fighters in East Africa. To oppose this considerable force, Air Marshal Sir Arthur Longmore, in command of the British Air Force in the Middle East, controlled some forty fighters and about 130 other aircraft in Egypt and Palestine. A few Gladiator fighters and eighty-five bombers were available for the defence of Kenya, the Sudan and Aden. Longmore gained an initial advantage by attacking Italian airfields from the first day onwards. Italian air reinforcement of Libya was simple; but now that France was virtually overrun, British aircraft destined for the Middle East could no longer use the planned route from the United Kingdom, a particularly serious situation in view of the lack

Air Ministry

Gladiators of No. 3 Squadron R.A.A.F. returning to a landing ground near Salum from a patrol over Bardia in January 1941. The squadron's mobile operations room is in the left foreground.

of modern fighters. Despite Longmore's pressure only six Hurricanes arrived via Malta before France capitulated. Until the opening in September 1940 of a reinforcement route through West Africa, Middle East Command was obliged to live on its own resources. In the Middle East as elsewhere there was a contingent of Australians in the R.A.F. squadrons. For example, in the third quarter of 1940 four Australians were commanding squadrons there. In consequence of the Australian Government's decision to send a complete army co-operation squadron to the Middle East, No. 3 (Squadron Leader I. D. McLachlan) arrived in August.

The Italians had some 250,000 troops in Libya and 200,000 in Abyssinia. Thus the British Commander-in-Chief, General Sir Archibald Wavell, had to conduct operations in two widely-separated areas in both of which his forces were outnumbered, since he had only 85,000 troops of whom about one-third were in training or on garrison duty in Palestine. At the outset his fighting formations included only four divisions—the 7th Armoured, 1st Cavalry, 4th Indian and 6th Australian, all of them incomplete. Wavell decided that in the Sudan, on the northern frontier of Abyssinia, and in Kenya, on the southern, he would hold the frontier posts with light forces and harass the Italians if they advanced; it seemed unlikely that they would have time to mount an effective offensive before the rainy season began in July.

In North Africa 500 miles of either desert or highlands separated the Nile Delta from the farmlands round Benghazi in western Cyrenaica. Along the intervening coast the Italians had established fortress areas at Tobruk and Bardia and the British had established one at Mersa Matruh. Wavell decided to garrison Matruh, which was also his railhead, as strongly as he could and send mobile forces to the frontier to observe and harry the Italians, an occupation highly congenial to the expert, desert-trained troops of the 7th Armoured Division to whom this role was allotted.

From Abyssinia the Italians acted fairly promptly. In July they cut the Port Sudan-Khartoum railway and advanced a little distance into Kenya. Early in August they moved into British Somaliland in considerable force and, after a hard fight, the British garrison of about a brigade retired on Berbera and began to embark. H.M.A.S. *Hobart* (Captain H. L. Howden) took part in this operation as headquarters ship. The troops ashore possessed no weapon to deal with medium tanks so Howden landed a 3-pounder with a gun's crew of one petty officer and two able seamen. During the night of 18th August *Hobart* embarked the demolition parties, and she sailed next day after bombarding the town.

In the Western Desert during July and August small columns of the 7th Armoured Division made a series of successful raids across the frontier where a formidable Italian force—the *Tenth Army*—was slowly assembling. On 10th September this army began to advance, and seven days later, after being severely harried on the way by the Support Group (infantry and artillery) of the armoured division, reached Sidi Barrani, seventy miles within the Egyptian frontier. There four Italian divisions and two of Libyan troops, all under General Bergonzoli, established themselves in an arc of fortified camps stretching from the sea to an escarpment fifty miles to the south.

Meanwhile Wavell had received useful reinforcements and been promised more. Among them was another Indian division—the 5th—which he proposed to use against the Italian force in northern Abyssinia. He was promised two tank regiments to bring his armoured division to full strength. In Kenya were now assembled a South African division and two small and lightly-armed divisions of British-led African colonial troops. The Australian force in the Midldle East had been growing in strength and would soon form the largest individual contingent of fighting troops in a force which included formations from the United Kingdom, India, New Zealand, South Africa, the African colonies and Poland. General Blamey had reached the Middle East on 20th June. His force then comprised the nucleus of a corps headquarters, some corps troops and the incomplete 6th Division, with barely enough equipment to train with. Blamey persuaded the Australian Government to send to Palestine the remaining units of the 6th Division as soon as possible and to ship some more equipment to it, including twenty-four additional field guns and half the machine-gun carriers then coming from Australian factories. In November the greater part of the 7th Division arrived from Australia. The 6th Division, which had been training hard and had greatly benefited by sending young leaders to British Army schools in Palestine and Egypt, was now concentrated round Amiriya on the eastern edge of the Western Desert. It was in fine fettle.

In October Mussolini had taken a step which would profoundly affect the shape of the war in the Middle East. He was envious of Hitler's military and diplomatic successes, which had given the Germans mastery of most of Europe west of the Russian frontier. Hitler was then planning to march through Spain to North Africa, hoping thus to drive Britain from the shores of the Mediterranean and to outflank Russia. Germany and Italy had signed their pact with Japan hoping to increase Russia's fears and those of the United States, whose support of Britain was causing Hitler increasing anxiety. The plan for conquering North Africa was delayed by the hard bargaining of the Spanish leader, General Franco, and the hesitations of the French, on whom American diplomats were exerting heavy pressure. It was at that stage that Mussolini, on 28th October, having given Hitler only a few days' warning of his intention, invaded Greece from Albania.

On his own initiative Longmore immediately dispatched a fighter squadron to Athens. A further three squadrons moved to Greece during the third week of November and another flight of fighters early in December. The resultant deficiencies in strength in Egypt were met by withdrawing flights from squadrons in the remoter areas, and by calling into the line No. 3 Squadron R.A.A.F.

British troops landed in Crete to support the Greeks on 1st November, and later in that month a force of some 4,000 British soldiers and air force men landed at the port of Athens. Britain had gained an ally in the fight against Italy, but Wavell and Longmore had now, from their meagre resources, to support operations in a third area.

In November aircraft from *Illustrious* attacked the Italian fleet at Taranto, delivering a crippling blow. *Sydney* was part of a cruiser and destroyer force under Vice-Admiral H. D. Pridham-Wippell which made a night penetration of the Strait of Otranto into the Adriatic during the Taranto operation and severely cut up a convoy crossing from Albania.

The Italian offensive against Greece was a failure. The Greeks, though ill-equipped, were formidable fighting men in their own mountains. They defeated the Italian columns and drove them back into Albania, demonstrating (as the Finns had done when the Russians had earlier invaded their country) that in difficult terrain high-spirited infantry on familiar ground can hold a more numerous and heavily-armed invader. It was a notable and encouraging victory—the first the Allies had achieved on land.

Before the invasion of Greece General Wavell, with Lieut-General H. Maitland Wilson (commanding the British Troops in Egypt) and Lieut-General R. N. O'Connor (commanding the Western Desert Force), had planned an attack that would cripple General Bergonzoli's army and drive it back to the frontier. As planning proceeded the scope of the attack was widened. On 28th November Wavell wrote to Wilson that it was 'possible that an opportunity may offer for converting the enemy's defeat into an outstanding victory . . . I do wish to make certain that if a big opportunity occurs we are prepared . . . to use it to the fullest.' At length it was decided that the initial attack should be delivered early in December by the 7th Armoured and 4th Indian Divisions, and that as soon as it was over the 6th Australian Division should relieve the 4th Indian, which would join the 5th Indian for an offensive against Abyssinia.

Chapter 4 The campaigns of 1941

Hitler's plans had been seriously upset by the Italian attack on Greece and his own failure to reach an agreement with the calculating Franco. His ambition to defeat Britain by invasion had not been realised, and now the Spanish leader was frustrating his projects in the Mediterranean. The immediate effect of the Italian attack on Greece had been to strengthen Britain in the Mediterranean: she now occupied a naval base in Crete and airfields on the Greek mainland. November 1940 was a month of indecision and exploration for the German leaders. Negotiations with Spain were strenuously continued. Molotov, the Russian Foreign Minister, visited Berlin in the second week of November but refused to commit himself about a German proposal that Russia should combine forces against Britain and share the spoils. Hitler gave instructions that these political discussions should not interrupt plans for a campaign which he had been considering for some time—an invasion of Russia; and on the day when the Molotov talks began he ordered preparations for the occupation of Greece.

The negotiations with Spain broke down decisively on 7th December when Franco said that he would not take part in an attack on Gibraltar planned for 10th January, on the grounds that he feared the loss of his colonies to Britain and that his forces were unready and he lacked supplies; in short British sea power, silently exerted, had robbed Hitler of this ally. On 9th December Hitler, whose staff had been urging him to recognise the threat offered by the British reinforcements which were arriving in the Middle East and the danger of a front in the Balkans, decided to advise Italy not to renew her offensive in North Africa as she was planning to do. At dawn that day the carefully-rehearsed British Western Desert offensive opened—an event that was to end Hitler's indecision and swiftly shape the coming year.

On 7th December seventy miles of open desert had separated the main opposing armies. That night the attacking force moved forward some forty miles. Next day the four fighter squadrons of the supporting air force kept enemy aircraft away and the British advance remained undiscovered. The approach march was resumed on the night of the 8th. The first warning received by the Italians was the hum of tank engines to the west of their fortified camps before dawn on the 9th. These camps were in four main groups: from the north, El Maktila, Tummar, Nibeiwa and Sofafi, with a wide gap separating the last two. In the darkness, the 4th Indian Division had driven its trucks through that gap. Led by a battalion of formidable infantry tanks not hitherto used against the Italians and supported by 25-pounder field guns, one Indian brigade took the Nibeiwa camps from the rear, another attacked the Tummar camps. An armoured brigade followed the Indian and British infantry through the gap and advanced north-west towards Buq Buq and the main coast road. By dusk that day Nibeiwa and all

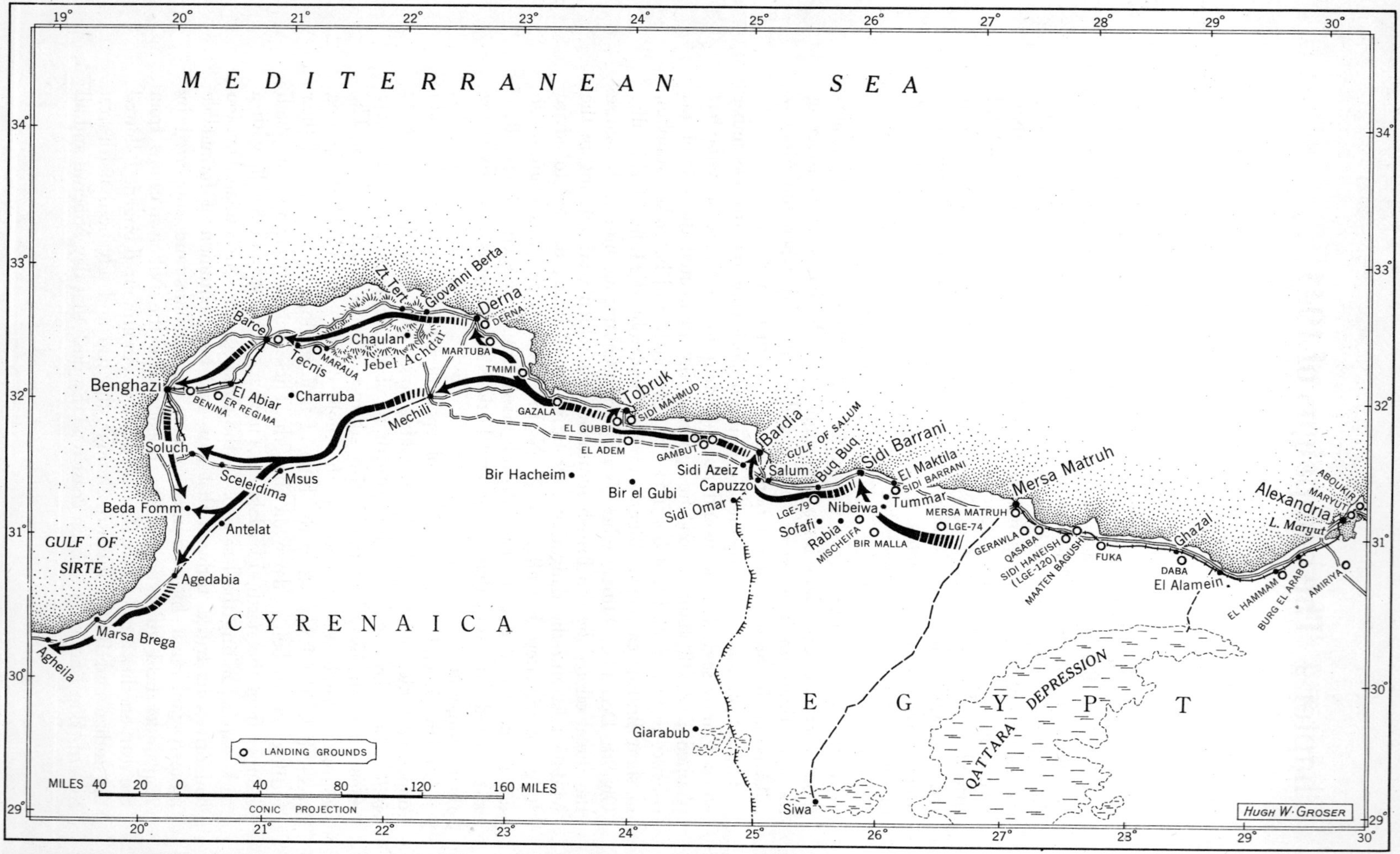
MEDITERRANEAN SEA
CYRENAICA
EGYPT
GULF OF SIRTE
QATTARA DEPRESSION
Benghazi
Barce
Tecnis
MARAUA
Chaulan
Jebel Achdar
Zt Tert
Giovanni Berta
Derna
DERNA
MARTUBA
TMIMI
El Abiar
BENINA
ER REGIMA
Charruba
Mechili
GAZALA
Tobruk
SIDI MAHMUD
EL GUBBI
EL ADEM
GAMBUT
Bardia
GULF OF SALUM
Sidi Azeiz
Salum
Capuzzo
Sidi Omar
Buq Buq
Sidi Barrani
El Maktila
SIDI BARRANI
Tummar
Nibeiwa
LGE-79
Sofafi
Rabia
MISCHEIFA
BIR MALLA
MERSA MATRUH
LGE-74
Mersa Matruh
GERAWLA
QASABA
SIDI HANEISH
(LGE-120)
MAATEN BAGUSH
FUKA
Ghazal
DABA
El Alamein
EL HAMMAM
BURG EL ARAB
AMIRIYA
L. Maryut
Alexandria
MARYUT
ABOUKIR
Soluch
Sceleidima
Msus
Beda Fomm
Antelat
Agedabia
Marsa Brega
Agheila
Bir Hacheim
Bir el Gubi
Giarabub
Siwa
LANDING GROUNDS
MILES 40 20 0 40 80 120 160 MILES
CONIC PROJECTION
HUGH W·GROSER

but one of the Tummar camps had been captured, the armoured brigade had cut the road behind Sidi Barrani, and the Matruh Force was engaging the Italian left flank at El Maktila.

On 10th December after hard fighting, particularly in the coastal zone, Sidi Barrani was captured and most of the Italian force was in confusion. There remained, east of a line Buq Buq-Sofafi, one Italian division south-east of Buq Buq (where the British Intelligence staffs had not suspected its presence) and another in the Sofafii area forty miles to the south. That day an opportunity was presented for a deep advance by the armoured brigades, leaving the infantry to deal with the remaining enemy camps. The opportunity was missed, and on the 11th it was found that the enemy had withdrawn from the camps near Buq Buq and Sofafi. His northern division was pursued by tanks and most of its men captured; but two divisions withdrew eventually to Bardia. However, two Italian and two Libyan divisions had been virtually destroyed, and 38,000 prisoners including four generals taken, with 237 guns and 73 tanks. At the time the British staffs believed that they had achieved even greater success and that only some 20,000 troops had been able to reach the fortified zone at Bardia; in fact four divisions and remnants of others were there. On the 14th a column of the armoured division was astride the road leading west from Bardia, and by 16th December the Italians had abandoned all positions outside the Bardia fortress, where they then lay isolated, awaiting the next blow.

This British victory was followed within nine days by a series of crucial decisions at Hitler's headquarters. Having now given up hope of obtaining Spanish co-operation, he cancelled the plan for attacking Gibraltar, but ordered (Directive No. 19) that plans be made to occupy Vichy France; he ordered that German air formations should be sent to south Italy to attack British communications; he ordered (Directive No. 20) that the German attack on Greece should open in March and allotted more divisions to it than before; on 18th December he issued Directive No. 21, 'Barbarossa', which required that preparations 'to overthrow Soviet Russia in a rapid campaign' should be completed by 15th May. The planned invasions of Greece, Russia and unoccupied France were still far in the future; in the next three months a main preoccupation of the German leaders would be to prevent an Italian collapse. The German naval staff, which had persistently urged that an Axis offensive in the Mediterranean was essential, was now despondent, both because of the Allied successes and the decision to attack Russia before Britain has been defeated. Admiral Raeder reported to Hitler on 27th December:

> The enemy has assumed the initiative at all points and is everywhere conducting successful offensive actions—in Greece, Albania, Libya and East Africa . . . The decisive action in the Mediterranean for which we had hoped is . . . no longer possible.

On the British side the victory was regarded as an immensely heartening success but a local one. Churchill concluded a congratulatory message to Wavell on the 13th by saying: 'As soon as you come to a full-stop along the African coast we can take a new view of our prospects, and several attractive choices will be open.'

The British force was small—much smaller than the German and Italian staffs realised—but it had the great advantage of an ascendancy in the air and command of the sea, so that its ships could bombard the enemy's flank and carry supplies forward to the harbours the army captured. Thus by the end of December Salum had become the main supply port for the force investing Bardia; the Desert Air Force was bettering the Italians though they were still fighting back. For example, the Gladiator flights of No. 3 Squadron R.A.A.F. (now the most forward squadron) operated regularly over the army units as they approached the frontier. On 10th December four and on 12th December three enemy aircraft were claimed to have been destroyed without loss, but 13th December brought disaster when six Gladiators encountered five Savoia-79 bombers attacking near Salum. One bomber was destroyed and the rest dispersed, but in the ensuing fight with attendant Italian fighters one Australian was killed, two had to bale out and two more had to make forced landings. With four Gladiators destroyed and two damaged the squadron virtually ceased to operate, only two sorties being possible the next day.

It will be recalled that before the battle of Sidi Barrani began Wavell had decided to send the 4th Indian Division to reinforce the 5th Indian for the proposed advance into Abyssinia from the Sudan and to replace it in the Western Desert with the 6th Australian Division. Therefore, as soon as the Indians had completed their initial role in the Western Desert, Wavell halted them, left the armoured division and the 16th British Brigade to continue the pursuit, and ordered General Mackay's 6th Division forward.

The division, although still short of equipment, was now in fine form. Its officers had been well chosen from the regular officer corps and the militia. The units had been in training for a year, and in Palestine had exercised against expert British regulars. As was to be expected of men who had volunteered in the first few weeks of the war they were keen to learn and eager to test themselves in battle. Most of their senior officers had been outstanding young leaders in the Australian Corps in France in 1918, when that corps became probably the most audacious and successful formation on either side of the Western Front, and they had inculcated the same standards into the new force. Since October the division had been in the desert immediately west of the Delta, where it was responsible for a defensive position covering Lake Maryut and the Rosetta Nile in case the Italians overcame or bypassed the Matruh position. Thence on 12th December, by rail and road, its leading brigades had set off westward.

From the railhead at Mersa Matruh a bitumen road travelled through the desert to Sidi Barrani and thence an earth road to Salum, where the 600-foot escarpment which to the east lay about twenty or thirty miles from the coast touched the sea. Two principal tracks climbed the escarpment near Salum, one to the Italian frontier and beyond. A good road ran from the frontier by way of the ports of Bardia, Tobruk and Derna and over the Jebel Achdar to Benghazi.

When Mackay arrived at O'Connor's desert headquarters on 14th December he found its staff convinced that the Italian army in Libya had been reduced to impotence and would probably abandon Bardia without a fight. Indeed Wavell had ordered that one of Mackay's brigades be held temporarily at Alexandria in case it could move to Bardia by sea and land unopposed. Meanwhile the remainder of the division was carried forward

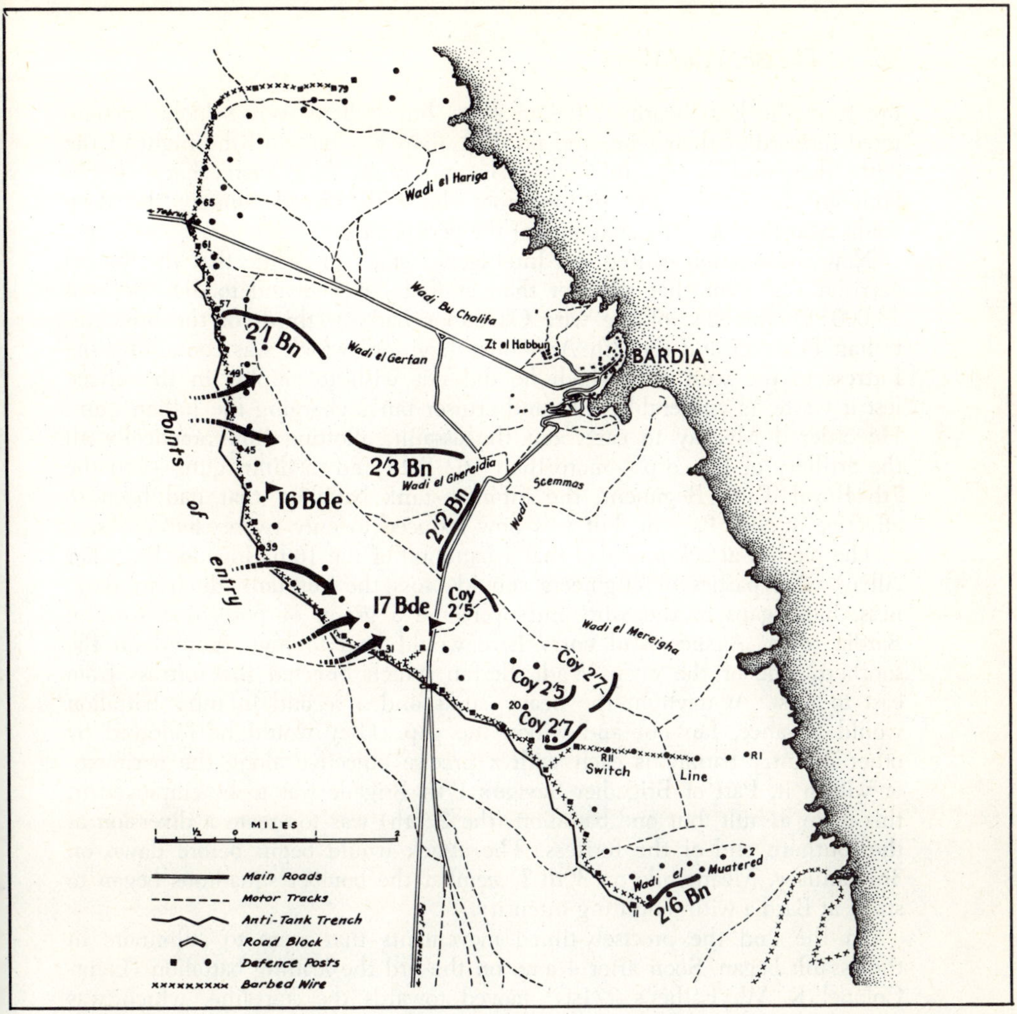

Bardia

over a battlefield littered with tanks, trucks and weapons discarded by the retreating army. On the 19th it began to relieve the British infantry astride the road south of Bardia.

The little port of Bardia was defended along an 18-mile arc consisting of a double line of concreted underground posts fronted by an anti-tank ditch and barbed-wire barriers. The posts in the forward line were about 800 yards apart and each was armed with one or two light guns and from two to four machine-guns (captured maps supplemented by aerial photography had given the attackers a fairly clear picture of the line). The rearward posts lay some 400 yards behind. Farther back were many artillery positions, then calculated to include about 110 field and medium guns.

As soon as they arrived the Australian battalions began making stealthy night patrols across the featureless no-man's land to measure the width and depth of the anti-tank ditch, test the wire, and observe the habits of the enemy. Often these parties of scouts, stalking forward with muffled boots, and warmly clad against the intense cold of the desert nights, drew deafening fire from the heavily-armed Italian posts, but Italians were seldom encountered forward of their wire, and no Australian was hit until the night of the 28th; then and on the following day and night there were sharp clashes between the enemy and patrols from the 17th Brigade among the deep wadis near the southern extremity of the perimeter.

New information caused the Intelligence staffs to decide that the Italian garrison was somewhat stronger than at first believed and totalled perhaps 23,000. On his side of the wire O'Connor had two-thirds of the 6th Australian Division and the 7th Armoured Division, which was containing the fortress to the west and which he did not wish to employ in the attack lest it waste its vulnerable light and cruiser tanks charging the Italian guns. He ordered Mackay to carry out the assault, allotting him practically all the artillery of his corps—more than 162 field and medium guns—and the 7th Royal Tank Regiment, the infantry tank battalion that had been so effective at Sidi Barrani, but was now reduced to only twenty-five tanks.

The plan of attack provided that a battalion of the 16th Brigade (Brigadier Allen) with parties of engineers should cross the anti-tank ditch in darkness, blow gaps in the wire and overcome a group of posts due west of Bardia town. A successful entry here would lead to high ground on the southern side of the deep Wadi Gerfan which bisected the fortress from east to west. At daylight the heavy tanks and a second infantry battalion would advance, fan out and widen the gap. They would be followed by other infantry battalions each with a precise objective along the perimeter or within it. Part of Brigadier Savige's 17th Brigade was to be employed in this main assault, but one battalion (the 2/6th) was to create a diversion at the southern end of the fortress. The attack would begin before dawn on 3rd January. Meanwhile on 30th December the bomber squadrons began to strike at Bardia with mounting intensity.

On the 2nd the precisely-timed movements that were to culminate in the assault began. Soon after 4 a.m. on the 3rd the leading battalion (Lieut-Colonel K. W. Eather's 2/1st)[1] moved towards the start-line, which was taped with lengths of rifle-cleaning flannel knotted together. The men were heavily clad with greatcoats and leather jerkins over their uniforms, and laden with weapons, tools, ammunition, grenades and three days' rations. At 5.30 a.m. the guns opened fire and the two leading companies, extended 300 yards from flank to flank, advanced, the men singing and shouting, the hammer of guns drowning their voices. Under the fire of the Italian artillery, engineers and pioneers carried forward long bangalore torpedoes, blew gaps in the Italian wire, and began breaking down the sides of the ditch to make crossings for the tanks. In less than half an hour the infantry had moved through ditch and broken wire and taken the four posts immediately opposite them, and the Italian line was breached. At 7 a.m. the 2/2nd Battalion (Lieut-Colonel F. O. Chilton) with the 7th Royal Tanks moved through the gap and swung south as far as the main road, overcoming the posts and the batteries behind them. Eather's battalion fought its way north along the perimeter; Lieut-Colonel V. T. England's 2/3rd, which next passed through the gap, advanced east, capturing Italian sangar

[1] Units of the Second AIF were so numbered to distinguish them from corresponding units of the first AIF.

positions and fanning out along the top of the escarpment opposite the point of entry. At some posts and in their battery positions the Italians fought with determination and Australian casualties, particularly among junior leaders, were severe. Elsewhere the Italians surrendered with little resistance, and during the morning long columns of Italians began pouring back towards the Australian rear. By midday some 6,000 had been assembled.

Meanwhile, between 8 and 9 a.m., the Mediterranean Fleet had heavily bombarded a sector north of the Bardia-Tobruk road (in which large concentrations of enemy trucks and tanks had been reported) to prevent the formation of a counter-attacking force. The bombardment succeeded in its principal objective—the moral effect of the fire sent the enemy to the ground, and he hardly moved in the northern sector all day.

The Italians made one effort to counter-attack. Soon after the 2/3rd Battalion reached its objective it was attacked by six tanks which moved along the face of the battalion, at one point winning the temporary release of some hundreds of prisoners. As the tanks were advancing on England's headquarters they were met by three anti-tank guns mounted on trucks. After a rapid and deadly duel one gun-truck was on fire, but the hulls of all six of the Italian tanks had been perforated and their crews killed.

On the right of the 16th Brigade one battalion (the 2/5th) of the 17th Brigade with companies of the 2/7th was to advance in the early afternoon and swing south towards a switch-line which ran from the perimeter to the sea near the southern end of the perimeter. In the morning Lieut-Colonel H. Wrigley, commanding the 2/5th, was wounded. The tanks which were to support the attack did not arrive in time. When the battalion advanced it moved under direct fire at short range from Italian batteries and was halted with heavy loss. However, the attack was carried forward on either flank; on the left by a small party which advanced along the Wadi Ghereidia deep into the enemy artillery and headquarters areas, and on the right by a company of the 2/7th which advanced along the perimeter southward taking post after post until, at dusk, this company, now with two others on its left, was facing the switch-line and had breached it at its western end. Meanwhile, on the extreme right, Lieut-Colonel A. H. L. Godfrey's 2/6th Battalion had launched a diversionary attack against the Italian posts facing it across the deep Wadi Muatered. The left company climbed through the wadi and reached the wire round Post 11 without losing a man, but when it charged towards the circular post forty yards within the wire the Italians met it with the fire of machine-guns and rifles and with grenades, and after a bitter fight only two Australians remained alive and unwounded. Farther right two posts were taken and Italian counter-attacks repulsed; at dusk the battalion clung to some 600 yards of the north bank of the wadi.

At the end of the day the Australians held about two-thirds of the perimeter and had penetrated more than a mile within it. Brigadier Allen was ordered to encircle the town of Bardia next day. In the morning he sent one battalion with a troop of tanks to clear the wadis south of the town and another, with a squadron of the divisional cavalry (mounted in carriers) and two tanks to advance through the deep Wadi Gerfan into upper Bardia (part of the town was at the top of cliffs, part at the beach below). This advance was carried out with great dash, and in the afternoon the 2/2nd Battalion took a fort on the southern headland and entered the lower town, and tanks, followed by the cavalry and the 2/3rd Battalion, entered upper Bardia, having captured some thousands of prisoners on the way.

Thus by the end of the second day the fortress had been cut in two. In both the north and the south the enemy occupied an area only about one mile deep by two wide. Over 30,000 Italians had been captured—more than the estimate of the entire garrison. After its hard fight and its losses on the day and night of the 3rd the 17th Brigade was able to make little progress on the 4th and at midday Brigadier Savige had been ordered to halt: the reserve brigade, Robertson's 19th, would attack southward through the 17th next morning. Accordingly on the 5th, while the 16th Brigade advanced north and occupied the remaining Italian posts, the 19th, with tanks and behind supporting artillery fire, marched south taking the surrender of the Italians who remained there. There was not much resistance except by the stout-hearted defenders of Post 11—the most strongly manned and best armed post of all. There the 2/6th Battalion pressed forward, and when Robertson's tanks and infantry appeared and the Italian commander hoisted a white flag, Godfrey went forward with his leading men, sought out the Italian commander and shook his hand.

The number of prisoners probably exceeded 40,000. The captured guns included 26 coast defence guns, 7 medium guns, 216 field guns and 213 anti-aircraft and anti-tank. There were 12 medium and 115 light tanks, 708 motor vehicles. Some hundreds of Italians, including General Bergonzoli, escaped from the perimeter and began walking towards Tobruk. The Australian losses totalled 130 killed and 326 wounded.

To many Australian soldiers, as diaries and letters revealed, this battle had been a test of their equality with the men of the old A.I.F., and they felt they had passed that test. The plan was bold yet practical: an intrepid one in those days when the strength of fortified lines was over-estimated and when tanks, of which the attackers had few to employ in the assault, were considered essential to success. The troops had carried out a difficult enterprise—a night attack on a narrow front followed by a precisely-arranged time-table of advances through narrow gaps in the defences—and done it with dash and accuracy. In the few places where they were called upon to do so they had pressed on regardless of casualties that might have deterred less resolute and well-trained troops in a first battle.

During the assault the air force's effort was applied at points farther west to reduce any likelihood that the Italian Air Force, constantly reinforced from Tripolitania and Italy but still surprisingly ineffective, would intervene. Every landing ground east of Derna was bombed. Fighters ranged the Tobruk-Bardia road strafing vehicles and providing cover for the 7th Armoured Division already moving against Tobruk.

By 15th January Bardia was in use as a supply base, the navy having swept a channel and cleared the harbour of wrecks. Owing to off-loading difficulties, it was capable of handling only 100 tons daily, but it eased the strain on the roads up the Salum escarpment. The Italian prisoners created a sea transport problem, some 35,000 being carried from Salum, where a large cage was built, to Alexandria or Mersa Matruh at the rate of about 3,000 a day.

This new Italian defeat further alarmed Hitler and he expressed a fear that the whole of North Africa would be lost. He decided that steps must

Australian War Memorial

Imperial War Museum

Libya. Heavily-laden Australian infantrymen advancing on Bardia, 3rd January 1941. *Inset:* Looking down on the harbour and lower town of Bardia. Upper Bardia is on the top of the cliffs in the background.

be taken to prevent an Italian collapse, and on the 11th directed that an improvised German force including anti-tank and anti-aircraft batteries and an armoured unit be sent to Africa. It was estimated that it could begin embarking on 15th February.

O'Connor's 30,000 men did not dream that their two-day fight had caused Hitler to picture them pressing on as far as Tripoli. Moreover, Churchill in London saw the campaign in Cyrenaica only as a defensive operation. On 6th January Churchill proposed to the Chiefs of Staff that the objective should be to capture Benghazi 'any time during March': this would secure the western flank of Egypt and enable priority to be given to supporting Greece. On that day the Foreign Secretary, Eden, warned Churchill that the Germans seemed likely to descend on Greece through Bulgaria, now evidently willing to comply with any German demands, in March or perhaps earlier. Thereupon Churchill and his Chiefs of Staff agreed to do 'everything possible, by hook or by crook, to send at once to Greece the fullest support within our power'; and on 10th January Wavell was instructed that, after taking Tobruk, not Benghazi, all operations in the Middle East were to be subordinated to the sending of help to the Greeks. Wavell protested and was sharply instructed by Churchill to give 'prompt and active compliance'; he and Longmore were to go to Athens and offer the Greeks five air squadrons, one squadron of infantry tanks, a regiment of cruiser tanks, and ten regiments of artillery—a force similar to that which Hitler offered the Italians next day. However, the Greek leaders declined the offer on the grounds that it would not be an effective reinforcement yet might provoke German attack. Consequently, on 21st January Wavell was instructed again to concentrate on advancing to Benghazi.

Before the Australians had finished collecting prisoners at Bardia and counting the booty the 7th Armoured Division had surrounded Tobruk. By 8th January two brigades of the 6th Division were in position outside the eastern half of the Tobruk perimeter while the armoured division lay across the roads leading west and south-west. Tobruk, like Bardia, was protected by a semi-circle of concreted underground posts which lay behind an anti-tank ditch and belts of barbed wire. At each end the line included a deep wadi, but for most of its length it had been dug into the flat floor of the desert. With Tobruk isolated, the Italians abandoned all airfields east of the Derna-Martuba area and Italian air opposition was greatly reduced.

For fifteen nights the Australian infantrymen and engineers sent patrols forward across the flat no-man's land stealthily to measure the anti-tank ditch round the Tobruk defences, explore for mines, disarm booby traps and place landmarks to guide the coming attack. The forward troops lived in shallow trenches which they dug for protection against intermittent artillery fire and occasional aerial bombing raids, and these served to give shelter from dust-storms sometimes so dense that they reduced visibility to a few yards.

Before dawn on 21st January the attack opened. Again the infantry tanks (now reduced to only twelve) and the whole of the 16th Brigade moved in the darkness close to a sector of the Italian line; an artillery barrage was put down by eighty-eight guns, the naval ships bombarded Italian concentrations, and before it was light the leading battalion—the 2/3rd—attacked on a front of 600 yards. In a series of sharp fights it took five Italian posts

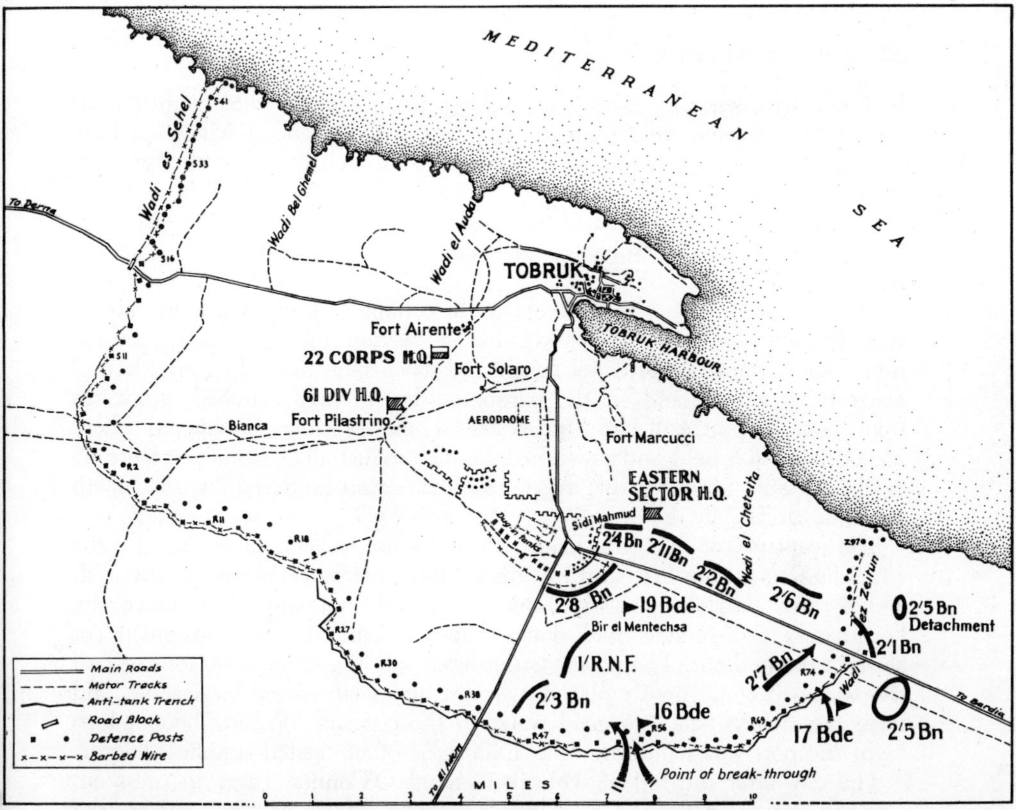

Tobruk

thus opening a door for tanks and infantry to pass through. Parties of engineers had disarmed mines and blown gaps in the barbed wire ahead of the leading infantry and while the first posts were being taken, had broken down the sides of the anti-tank trench so that the tanks could cross. While the 2/3rd Battalion, sometimes with the help of tanks, sometimes without, fought its way west along the line of posts, often against unusually determined opposition, tanks and the 2/1st Battalion rapidly widened the gap on the eastern side until, by 9 a.m., they had crossed the Bardia road and the way into the fortress was wide open. After them the 2/2nd Battalion, with tanks, advanced deep into the Italian area to capture the guns that were in close support. Then two battalions of the 17th Brigade went in.

At 7.55 the 19th Brigade entered and, behind a moving barrage, marched north, the men dispersed across a wide front, to the edge of the escarpment overlooking Tobruk harbour. This phase, like that which preceded it, went like clockwork until the left of the 2/8th Battalion, itself on the left flank of its brigade, ran into an arc of posts round the junction of the Bardia and El Adem roads, shielding the Italian *XXII Corps* headquarters outside the town, and the town itself. Here the battalion wheeled, and from 11 o'clock until dusk fought its way west along the escarpment against the fire of stationary tanks dug into the ground and machine-gun posts and artillery. One company lost all but one of its officers and sergeants and nearly half its men before the fight was over. Meanwhile the 2/4th Battalion on its right had also wheeled and, advancing against weaker opposition, captured the Italian headquarters and, with it, the commander, General Manella. Thus by nightfall the eastern half of the fortress had been taken except for some pockets of Italians in the wadis at the eastern end, and the line of weary Australians, some of whom had marched and fought nearly twenty miles in the day, ran from Fort Solaro in the north to a point on the perimeter just west of the El Adem road.

Next morning (the 22nd) all resistance collapsed. Cavalrymen in carriers who entered the town, with Brigadier Robertson following close behind, found some thousands of depot troops and naval men (including an admiral) ready to surrender, and on the perimeter the infantry marched westwards from post to post collecting prisoners. These prisoners numbered about 25,000 with 208 field and medium guns. The Australian casualties were 49 dead and 306 wounded; of these losses 104 were suffered by the 2/8th Battalion, and 57 by the 2/3rd.

The capture of Tobruk made a capacious harbour available to the advancing corps; the first ship to unload stores reached Tobruk on the 27th and by the 29th the port was able to unload four ships simultaneously. Fortunately the Italians had done little to demolish port equipment or obstruct the harbour. The power station was working, some 4,000 tons of coal had been left conveniently placed, two distilling plants were serviceable, and there was a large stock of good water in the cisterns. Within about a fortnight the port was handling some 1,400 tons of off-loaded supplies daily.

The day after the fall of Tobruk General O'Connor, eager to press on, sent the armoured division to Mechili, a track centre at the south-eastern corner of the Jebel Achdar, where the Italians were believed to have concentrated an armoured brigade; and he ordered an advance-guard of the Australian division to move next day along the coast road towards Derna, a pleasant town at the mouth of the wadi of the same name, an immense cleft, in some places a mile wide from lip to lip and 700 feet in depth, extending about 12 miles south and south-west from Derna and then turning west into the uplands. The road zigzagged down to the coast at Derna and then wound up the coastal escarpment again to the timbered Jebel Achdar.

When the leading infantry—the 2/11th Battalion—arrived on 25th January, they advanced towards the airfield which lay next to the road near the top of the escarpment. During the afternoon the West Australians attacked with determination across the flat, fire-swept plain, where at length after dusk some occupied the hangars and others had reached the edge of the escarpment. That night and next day the 2/4th Battalion on the left sent about a company across the great wadi at a point where it was about 500 yards in width. Meanwhile O'Connor ordered Major-General M. O'M. Creagh of the armoured division to surround the enemy tank force at Mechili.

On the northern flank the Italians resisted stubbornly, sending over intense artillery fire; west of the wadi they sharply counter-attacked the small force precariously assembled there. On the 27th, greatly to the chagrin of O'Connor, it was found that the enemy force at Mechili had vanished in the night. O'Connor would have liked to pursue the Italians directly across the desert south of the Jebel, cut the road south of Benghazi, and thus encircle what remained of the enemy in Cyrenaica, but wear and tear and lack of enough vehicles to carry petrol forward immobilised his armoured force. His staff decided that it would be a fortnight before it could advance.

Mackay ordered Savige's brigade, which had now come forward, to extend the left flank and swing round into the hills south of Giovanni Berta on the road west of Derna—an imposing task in country cut by a tangle of steep-sided wadis. Again Bergonzoli, who was commanding the rearguard, anticipated his enemy's move. On the night of the 29th the Italians slipped out of Derna, but continued to fight for the wedge of highland pinched between the 19th Brigade, now west of Derna, and the 17th, now toiling towards Giovanni Berta. On the night of the 31st the 2/8th Battalion stealthily climbed the cratered road leading up the Jebel beyond Derna. Meanwhile Savige, with armoured cars and carriers scouting ahead, had been pressing on from the south and on the afternoon of the 2nd his carriers entered Giovanni Berta. The Italian rearguard had now made a long withdrawal. That day and the next reports from the pilots of aircraft searching the roads over the tableland convinced O'Connor that what remained of the Italian army was scurrying out of Cyrenaica as fast as it could.

O'Connor decided that if he struck with his armoured force on the 12th, as he had planned, he would be too late to catch the retreating Italian army, and therefore he ordered Creagh immediately to advance to Msus, and Mackay to continue to pursue the enemy along the roads over the Jebel, ferrying forward a unit at a time if need be. The largest force Mackay could fully motorise was one brigade. On the afternoon of the 4th the 19th Brigade began rolling along the smooth Barce road, meeting no opposition until, a little beyond Tecnis, the armoured cars leading the force were ambushed and the long column halted while the foremost infantry battalion deployed.

At dawn that day the armoured division, its tanks now reduced to fewer than half the normal number, set off across the stony foothills of the Jebel. At 3 p.m. the advance-guard reached Msus and drove out the little outpost there. Creagh decided to send one force westward towards Soluch, and another south-west through Antelat to block the Italian retreat on the road west of that place, in case the retreat had already moved so far. At midday on the 5th the latter established itself astride the road south-west of Antelat just in time to block the head of a densely-packed enemy column retreating from the north. Into the flank of this column and others that followed drove the regiments of the armoured division. That evening and all next day a series of bitter fights took place, chiefly round Beda Fomm, between the depleted British armoured forces and the Italians, trapped in a pocket about forty miles long with the sea behind them. A few enemy vehicles broke through; the Italians that remained surrendered early in the morning of the 7th. The prisoners exceeded 20,000, with 216 guns, 112 medium tanks and 1,500 wheeled vehicles. General Tellera, the army commander, was killed and Bergonzoli captured. In two months an Italian army of ten divisions with some 1,300 guns and 400 tanks had been virtually destroyed.

Meanwhile the advance-guard of the Australian division had reached Benina airfield outside Benghazi on the evening of the 6th, and a small party had entered that city. Next morning a column set off southward to take part in the Beda Fomm battle, but that battle was already over.

The Italian Air Force in Africa had now been practically eliminated as a factor in the land fighting. Despite its losses it was still numerically stronger than the R.A.F., but, incessantly harried, it now had neither will nor organisation to fight, and at Beda Fomm, despite the inability of the R.A.F. to be present, Italian aircraft made no attempt to influence the course of the battle.

There remained in Tripolitania four Italian infantry divisions of which three lacked their artillery regiments and all four lacked their machine gun battalions, these having been sent forward into Cyrenaica. There was also a recently-arrived Italian armoured division, but it possessed only light tanks. The first shiploads of German reinforcements were expected in the third week of February. Before Derna fell the Italian High Command had informed the Germans that the best it could do with existing resources would be to defend a fortified camp round Tripoli. On 5th February Hitler wrote angrily to Mussolini that he was disappointed with the Italian conduct of the campaign; provided the Italian army held on and did not retreat to Tripoli, which could not be defended, he would contribute a full armoured division in addition to the German force, now named the *5th Light Division*, already on the way. Mussolini replaced General Graziani, the commander in Libya, with General Gariboldi and ordered that the defence of Tripoli be conducted in the Sirte area. Thereupon Hitler, on 26th February, gave orders that the *15th Armoured Division* be sent to North Africa. It would begin to move to Tripoli about 20th March when the transport of the *5th Light Division* should have been completed. Two days later Hitler wrote to Mussolini:

> If we could have fifteen days more time in North Africa I am certain that a new British attempt to advance towards Tripoli would fail.

General O'Connor was convinced that, given generous naval and air support, he could have taken Tripoli. His casualties had been low and his troops were not tired. Two fresh regiments of the 2nd Armoured Division were on their way forward. He was able to equip one of his veteran regiments with the remaining serviceable tanks of the 7th Armoured Division, another with brand-new Italian medium tanks captured at Beda Fomm. He planned to send his Support Group to Sirte immediately and considered that he could begin to move from Sirte towards Tripoli on 20th February. We now know that the Italian and German officers who were in Tripolitania when Benghazi fell were equally convinced that O'Connor could have taken Tripoli. However Churchill's eyes were firmly fixed on the 'several attractive choices' he had mentioned to Wavell after Sidi Barrani, and especially on one of them—a front in the Balkans. In his congratulatory message to Wavell on 12th February after Beda Fomm he said:

> We are delighted that you have got this prize (Benghazi) three weeks ahead of expectations[2], but this does not alter, indeed it rather confirms, our previous directive, namely that your major effort must now be to aid Greece and/or Turkey. This rules out any serious effort against Tripoli.

[2] The 'expectations' were those contained in Churchill's directives, not estimates by Wavell or O'Connor.

Churchill halted the advance before it was known whether the Greeks could be persuaded to accept a British force. In his message to Wavell he added that he was sending Eden and the Chief of the General Staff, General Sir John Dill, to Cairo whence with Wavell they would go to Athens to offer the Greeks at least four divisions and additional air forces. If agreement could not be reached the advance on Tripoli could then be re-considered.

Thus in the last half of February, while the Axis army in Tripolitania was being reinforced, the British army in Cyrenaica was being whittled away. General Wilson took command of Cyrenaica as Military Governor until 27th February when General Philip Neame replaced him. O'Connor was given command of the troops in Egypt and his fine Corps staff was dispersed. General Blamey, with the staff of I Australian Corps, assumed command of the fighting troops in Cyrenaica. The 7th Armoured Division set off for Cairo, being replaced on the Tripolitanian frontier by the 17th Australian Brigade and units of the newly-arrived 3rd Armoured Brigade; after 24th February, when the 19th Brigade was withdrawn to east of Derna to ease the supply problem, Savige's three battalions were the only infantry left in western Cyrenaica. Four days earlier armoured cars of the King's Dragoon Guards exchanged fire with German armoured cars—the first seen in Africa. Since 13th February German aircraft had been bombing Benghazi and the surrounding area, and the forward troops. By the third week of February there was only one defending squadron forward—No. 3 R.A.A.F. at Benina—and on the 18th the naval convoy supplying the force through the port of Benghazi was withdrawn because it was inadequately defended against air attack.

While O'Connor's corps was advancing through northern Cyrenaica an isolated Italian garrison of some 2,000 Italian and Libyan troops had remained at Giarabub, an oasis 145 miles south of Bardia on the edge of the Great Sand Sea of the Sahara. In September Wavell had sent a company of British infantry to Siwa, the larger oasis across the Egyptian frontier from Giarabub, to counter this enemy outpost. In December he replaced it with the headquarters and two squadrons of the 6th Australian Cavalry under Lieut-Colonel M. A. Fergusson. These cavalrymen were mounted in trucks, which could travel faster over the desert than tanks or carriers and would not wear so rapidly. In December they drove in the enemy outposts and, although the Italian force outnumbered them about ten to one, confined it to the defences round the oasis itself, which, after the fall of Bardia, was supplied by air. As the long siege continued the Libyan troops lost heart and by the middle of February practically all had deserted. Nevertheless, in the middle of March, a month after the fall of Benghazi, some 1,500 Italians remained in a tactically strong position, entrenched and well supplied with artillery. On 10th March Brigadier G. F. Wootten of the 18th Brigade was ordered to take an augmented battalion to Giarabub (there were not vehicles enough to support a larger force so deep in the desert) and capture the fortress. Wootten decided to achieve surprise by sending his attacking force over difficult tracks through the marshy depression south of the oasis and assault from that direction. On the 19th and 20th the 2/9th Battalion moved along this route and patrolled among the enemy's forward posts; on the 21st in a dense dust-storm the battalion attacked while the cavalry advanced from the north. After bitter fighting in which the attackers lost ninety-four men the Italians surrendered. Perhaps 250 Italians were killed; 1,300 were captured, with 36 guns and more than 100 machine-guns.

When he received orders to send the greatest possible aid to Greece Wavell decided that the most that could be spared were the 6th and 7th Australian Divisions, the New Zealand Division, a brigade of the 2nd British Armoured Division, and the Polish infantry brigade, consisting of soldiers who had made their way to the Middle East after the defeat of Poland. This subtraction would leave two Indian divisions, one South African division and the two small African colonial divisions to carry on the campaign in Abyssinia. Cyrenaica would be garrisoned by the 9th Australian Division and the remainder of 2nd Armoured Division; the only other divisions would be the 1st Cavalry Division in Palestine and the 7th Armoured, refitting in Egypt. Wavell was apprehensive about the outcome. 'Personally I can never see much prospect of the Balkans being an offensive military front from our point of view . . .' he wrote on 17th February. 'Our forces available are very limited and it is very doubtful whether they can arrive in time.'

At a conference in Athens in the third week of February the Greek leaders met Eden, Dill, Wavell and others of the delegation and accepted the offer of the military force and an addition of five Royal Air Force squadrons to the seven then fighting in Greece. The Greeks now had fifteen divisions facing about twenty-one Italian divisions on the Albanian front and six in reserve or on the Bulgarian frontier. However these six possessed only thirty-two battalions between them and were lightly armed and thus were the equivalent of only three British or German divisions. From Athens the British envoys went to Ankara where they failed to persuade the Turks to join an alliance against Germany. On 1st March the German army entered Bulgaria. Until Yugoslavia's policy had been defined, and since possession of Salonika was vital to the support of that country, three Greek divisions were left on the Bulgarian frontier and three began to deploy on the Olympus Line where the British force was to join them, the whole line coming under the command of General Maitland Wilson.

The Australian Prime Minister, Menzies, had visited the Australian troops in the Middle East and was now in London. Early in March, when news reached London of the failure of a British attack on an island of the Italian Dodecanese, the German entry into Bulgaria, the persistent mining of the Suez Canal by German aircraft, and the possible arrival of German troops in Tripolitania, he asked that the Greek expedition be re-examined. The vacillating Churchill cabled to Cairo that he could not now see any reason for expecting success, could not forecast Dominion assent to the venture, and was reconsidering resuming the advance on Tripoli. However, it was now too late to draw back: a convoy of troops was already arriving in Athens and the Greeks were taking up their position in the Olympus Line. From Cairo Eden cabled that the commanders there considered there was a 'reasonable fighting chance' of success, and the British War Cabinet authorised Wavell to carry on with the expedition. The Australian War Cabinet was greatly disturbed when three days later it received a cable from General Blamey that he considered the enterprise hazardous and unwise.

On 24th March the Yugoslav Government, from whom Britain had been expecting co-operation against Germany, decided to follow an opposite

Australian War Memorial

H.M.A.S. *Perth*, later to be sunk off Java, thrusts her way through rough seas while on patrol off Crete at the end of January 1941.

YUGOSLAVIA
ALBANIA
LAKE OCHRID
LAKE PRESPA
Monastir
Serrai
Axios R.
Florina
Vevi
Yiannitsa
Edessa
Koritza
Salonika
Stavros
Klisoura
Veria
Veria Pass
Kozani
Katerini
Aliakmon River
Servia
Dolikhe
Grevena
Gerania
Platamon
Mt. Olympus
Elasson
Tempe Gorge
GULF OF SALONIKA
Tirnavos
Kalabaka
Yannina
Larisa
PINDUS MTS.
Trikkala
Koila
Pinios River
Volos
Agria
Mileai
Karditsa
Demerli
Pharsala
Arta
Domokos
Akheloos
Preveza
Lamia
GREECE
Brallos
Agrinion
Gravia
Brallos Pass
EUBOEA
River
THERMOPYLAE
Khalkis
Levadia
Moulki
Thebes
Patras
GULF OF CORINTH
Kephissia
Eleusis
Megara
Rafina
ATHENS
Corinth
Piraeus
Porto Rafti
PELOPONNESE
Lavrion
Pirgos
Argos
Miloi
Navplion
Tripolis
IONIAN SEA
Sparti
Kalamata
Monemvasia
SCALE
MILES 10 5 0 10 20 30 40 50 60 70 MILES
HUGH W. GROSER

Greece

policy and joined the German-Italian-Japanese alliance. Next day, however, a group of Yugoslav officers and others expelled this Government and established another which rejected the alliance with Germany. Churchill, again filled with hope, now pictured a Balkan front manned by seventy divisions—Greek, Turkish, Yugoslav and British.

In spite of frequent air attack the transport of some 58,000 troops to Greece was achieved without the loss of a man. On 27th and 28th March the Italian fleet attempted to attack the convoy route. Admiral Cunningham had good warning and his cruisers (*Orion*, *Ajax*, *Perth* and *Gloucester*) intercepted the leading Italian cruisers on the morning of the 28th. After an exchange of fire the Italians made off westward, shadowed by the British cruisers and with Cunningham with three slow battleships and an aircraft carrier trying to catch up. The speed of the Italian battleship, *Vittorio Veneto*, was reduced by air attacks, but the best speed the British battle squadron could achieve was only 22 knots. At 10.25 p.m. the British battle fleet sighted two Italian cruisers (*Zara* and *Fiume*) barely two miles away and disabled them with a few accurate salvoes. A few minutes later three Italian destroyers attacked out of the darkness. They were engaged by the battleships and Captain Waller's division of four destroyers—*Stuart*, *Greyhound*, *Havock* and *Griffin*—and driven off. In a confused night action the destroyers sank two enemy destroyers and finished off the heavy cruiser *Pola*, which had been crippled by air attack the previous day, and also the *Zara* and *Fiume*. At dawn no Italian ships could be found by *Formidable's* aircraft. Under heavy air attack the fleet returned to Alexandria. The encounter was named the Battle of Matapan, having been fought off Cape Matapan in southern Greece.

By 3rd April the 1st Armoured Brigade, the New Zealand Division and about two-thirds of the 6th Australian Division had arrived in Greece. The Germans had assembled two armies for the conquest of Greece and Yugoslavia: the *Twelfth*, hurriedly reinforced from France and Germany until it consisted of thirteen divisions, four of them armoured, was given the task of taking northern Yugoslavia; the *Second* (Field Marshal von Weichs) with fifteen divisions including four armoured (one of these was to watch the Turkish frontier) would invade southern Yugoslavia and Greece. In three days much of Yugoslavia was overrun and such formations of the defending army as had been in action were in confusion; on the 17th Yugoslavia capitulated. After severe fighting German troops broke through the line of Greek forts opposite the Bulgarian frontier; an armoured division thrust down the Axios valley towards Salonika, which fell on the 9th. It now remained for the invading army to deal with the British-Greek force which was on the Olympus Line guarding the gateways into central Greece. The Germans proposed to attack it both from the front and, by advancing from Yugoslavia into the Florina valley, from the rear. Before a shot had been exchanged with the British force the German Air Force had dealt it a severe blow. On the night of the 6th-7th aircraft bombed Piraeus, an ammunition ship blew up, many transports were sunk and the harbour wrecked.

The likelihood of the Germans marching down the Florina valley and taking the Olympus Line in the rear had been foreseen, and a force under General Mackay including the 1st Armoured Brigade and the 19th Australian Brigade had been hurriedly formed to stop such a *blitzkrieg*.

Shots were exchanged by German and British guns in the Florina valley on the morning of the 10th; on the same day German troops engaged the New Zealand cavalry on the right flank. General Papagos, Commander-in-Chief of the Greek forces, had agreed that the Olympus Line was now untenable and that the Greek forces holding the passes east of the Florina valley should be switched to the passes west of it. Wilson's plan for this new 'Aliakmon Line' was that the New Zealanders would hold three main passes round Olympus, one between the mountain and the sea, one leading west from Katerini, and one about Servia through which the road from Florina travelled south. The 16th Australian Brigade, which had been hurried forward to the Veria Pass, was now to march back through the snow-covered mountains to fill a gap in the New Zealand front west of Servia; the 19th Australian Brigade would be on the far side of the Aliakmon River linking with the Greeks, who would hold the three passes through which roads climbed into the range flanking the headwaters of the Aliakmon.

To cover the Greek withdrawal across the wide valley Wilson ordered Mackay to hold until the night of the 12th-13th—three days, two nights and part of a third after the first contact with them. The Germans were finding heavy going on the bad roads and their attack developed slowly. On the afternoon of the 10th their infantry deployed, and patrols reached the Australian line on the right that night. Brigadier Vasey, commanding Mackay's infantry, had three weary battalions spread across ten miles of front, much of it covered with snow—the 2/8th Australian Battalion on the right, the 1/Rangers (a raw English battalion belonging to the 1st Armoured Brigade) astride the road in the centre, and the 2/4th on the hills to the left. A German infantry attack on the afternoon of the 11th was beaten off, but it was resumed next day and soon the rearguard's situation was precarious. The Rangers were thrust back but the supporting regiment of the Royal Horse Artillery and Australian anti-tank gunners, firing their guns until they were under machine-gun fire from a few hundred yards away, held back German infantry and tanks. By dusk German tanks were among the forward posts of the 2/8th Battalion and it was out of touch with brigade headquarters. It withdrew in some confusion but most of the men managed to reach the vehicles farther south. On the left the 2/4th withdrew successfully except for a company which unknowingly walked into the German lines and was captured. On the 13th after two sharp and successful rearguard actions by the armoured brigade the force was extricated and the infantry reached the Aliakmon Line.

Wilson now knew that he might expect no substantial reinforcement from Egypt. Early in April the German-Italian force in Tripolitania had attacked, and Wavell had informed him that the 7th Australian Division must be retained in Africa to help cope with this new threat. On 13th April Wilson decided that the Greek divisions on his left could no longer be relied on and next day he ordered that the 17th Australian Brigade should move to Kalabaka to cover the western flank and informed Blamey (but not yet Papagos) that he had decided to withdraw about 100 miles to a shorter line from Thermopylae to the Gulf of Corinth. Blamey, who on the 12th had renamed his corps the Anzac Corps, would conduct the withdrawal. On the 15th General Wavell, Admiral Cunningham and Air Chief

Australian War Memorial

Troops of the 6th Division crossing the Aliakmon River during the brief campaign in Greece in April 1941.

Marshal Longmore had decided that evacuation of the force was unavoidable; outline plans for an embarkation were ready in Cairo.

Blamey's orders for the withdrawal provided that the 6th New Zealand Brigade would occupy a rearguard position astride the roads near Elasson, through which the two forward New Zealand brigades would withdraw; the 16th Brigade would occupy a position west of Larisa through which the 17th would withdraw, and the 19th would form a final rearguard at Domokos to cover the final move to the new line.

At this stage the German divisions were hastening south and west over muddy, cratered roads; one infantry division was thrusting west against the Greeks in the passes, an armoured division was moving down the Florina-Larisa road, and an armoured division and two mountain divisions were approaching the more easterly Olympus passes. After a lull on the 14th Austrian infantry of the *9th Armoured Division* attacked the New Zealanders in the Servia Pass on the 15th and were beaten off, losing 180 prisoners and probably as many killed and wounded. That day German aircraft destroyed thirty British fighters and bombers on the Larisa airfield, a crippling blow to the small supporting air force.

Whereas Wilson expected the main force of the German attack on his left and particularly against the Greeks, the Germans, as shown above, were in fact concentrating against his right. On the 16th they drove back a New Zealand battalion defending the narrow pass at Platamon on the Aegean

Australian War Memorial

coast and pressed hard on the New Zealand brigade in the Olympus Pass. Blamey ordered Brigadier Allen and the two available battalions of his 16th Brigade to the Pinios Gorge, where the German thrust threatened to reach the main road where it bottle-necked through Larisa and to cut off practically the entire British force. On the 17th there was again a comparative lull while the German force struggled forward over cratered roads, and a providential mist prevented heavy air attacks on the defenders' vehicles. That night the four forward brigades left their positions, embussed and drove south, leaving (from the right) the 16th, 6th and 17th Brigades astride the three main roads.[3]

All next day the Germans attacked the 16th Brigade (2/2nd, 2/3rd and 21st Battalions) in the Pinios Gorge and the 6th Brigade about Elasson. The 16th held the road until late that night but not before German tanks and infantry had forced the 2/2nd and the 21st into the hills above the road. In the Elasson position accurate artillery fire held the German armour off all day. The 17th Brigade at Kalabaka was not in contact with the enemy. Again there was a night withdrawal, and by dawn on the 19th every unit except parts of those disorganised in the Pinios Gorge were south of Larisa. It had been an anxious and arduous day on the road leading south. In clear weather German aircraft attacked the vehicles all day as they moved slowly along a crowded road or stood halted because of craters in the road or damaged trucks ahead. However, losses of men and vehicles were light and by the end of the day it was evident to the leaders that aircraft in the

[3] Henceforward the Australian and New Zealand brigades and battalions will be referred to by their numbers alone. The prefix 2/ distinguishes an Australian battalion. The New Zealand brigades were the 4th, 5th, and 6th, the Australian the 16th, 17th and 19th.

Greece and Crete

Opposite page: Brallos Pass viewed from the arch bridge during the withdrawal from Greece in April 1941.

numbers available to the Germans could not seriously impede the force's movements.

On the 19th there were some fifty miles of cratered roads between the Anzac Corps, now deploying in the Thermopylae position, and the German army. It took the Germans five full days to cover that distance and prepare for the next attack. Meanwhile it became evident that Greek resistance was collapsing. Koryzis, the Prime Minister, committed suicide on the 18th; the commander of the Greek army in Epirus wished to surrender—but to the victorious and respected Germans not the despised Italians; and on the 20th when German troops arrived at Yannina he did so, without authority from Athens. On 19th April Wavell arrived in Athens and, after conferences with the Greek leaders and with their agreement, gave Wilson orders to embark the British force.

The plan of withdrawal and embarkation provided for the establishment of a covering force astride the Athens road near Thebes and embarkation from various beaches in the Athens area or in the Peloponnese. Each brigade would withdraw to its embarkation place by night, lie concealed next day, and embark the following night. To lift the troops there were 6 cruisers, some 24 destroyers and escort vessels, 2 'Landing Ships, Infantry' (L.S.I's)—*Glenearn* and *Glengyle*—14 troopships and a number of landing craft.

The withdrawal from the Thermopylae Line and also the first large-scale embarkation was to take place on the night of the 24th-25th. On the 24th the Germans, who now had two armoured and two mountain divisions crowding the road from Larisa to Lamia, attacked the Thermopylae Line, now held by the 6th Brigade on the right and the 19th on the left. Tanks tried to break through along the coastal road held by the New Zealanders while mountain troops attacked the high pass held by the Australians. The

New Zealanders knocked out at least twelve tanks and damaged others, and both they and the Australians held their ground and broke away after nightfall. That night the 5th Brigade and some 6,000 corps and base troops embarked at beaches farther south. At dawn on the 25th the 4th Brigade was in its rearguard position astride the road to Athens and the remainder of the force was either lying concealed at its place of embarkation or on the way thither. Both Blamey and Mackay had now been flown out of Greece, and Wilson and the New Zealand General, B. C. Freyberg, commanded the remaining troops.

On the 25th the orders were amended to provide for the embarkation of a greater part of the force from beaches in the Peloponnese. That night the 19th Brigade embarked. Early on the 26th German paratroops descended round the Corinth Canal, overwhelmed the troops defending it and thus cut the only road linking the two parts of the British force. However, that night troops, mainly of the armoured brigade, were embarked from the Athens beaches and 8,000, including the 16th and 17th Brigades, from Kalamata far to the south. Wilson handed over to Freyberg who now, on the 27th, had one brigade at the Athens beaches, one in the Peloponnese, some 2,000 ill-organised men about Navplion and more than 8,000 at Kalamata. The 4th Brigade in the Athens area fought off the Germans that day and was smoothly embarked at night; the next night the last New Zealand brigade embarked; but except for a few hundred taken off at Kalamata, the groups there and at Navplion were captured, in each case after a fight with German forces.

According to Admiral Pridham-Wippell (who was in charge of the operation afloat) the total number embarked in the whole series of embarkations was about 50,662, which was apparently accepted as the official figure by the Admiralty and the British Government. About 14,000, largely base troops and Cypriot and Palestinian labourers, were left behind. Many who were embarked were landed temporarily in Crete. In the campaign the German army suffered some 5,200 casualties. Only four British transports and two destroyers were sunk by aircraft, about 500 troops being lost in these sinkings. The commanders concerned had entered upon this expedition with justified misgivings, and embarkation was being planned before the battles opened. Wilson began a withdrawal as soon as he decently could, and Blamey and his staff planned the retirement expertly. Mackay and Freyberg, cool and sage infantry veterans, maintained firm and inspiring control of the fighting formations. The skill and resolution of the navy ensured that almost every fighting unit was embarked practically intact. From a severely military point of view the gravest loss was that of the vehicles and heavy weapons which the force had to destroy and abandon.[4]

[4] The description of the campaign in A. J. P. Taylor's *English History 1914-1945* (1965), p. 525, the final volume of the *Oxford History of England*, is less than accurate: 'Early in April the Germans overran Yugoslavia and arrived in Greece before the British had begun to move. The inferior British forces never came to grips with the enemy. They were retreating and being withdrawn almost as soon as they landed.'

During the invasion of Greece another Axis army was making an equally rapid advance in North Africa. When the 6th Australian Division was replaced in Cyrenaica by Major-General Morshead's 9th Australian Division, the 20th Brigade (Brigadier Murray) had relieved the 17th Brigade in its position astride the main road between Marsa Brega and El Agheila, where the road ran close to the sea and on the left a marsh stretched some ten miles southward. The 3rd Armoured Brigade continued to patrol south and south-west of the marsh. In the first half of March the German *5th Light Division* was still arriving in Libya, but embarkation of the *15th Armoured Division* had not begun. However Morshead, like Mackay and Savige before him, was convinced that the enterprising German patrols operating across the frontier were heralding an offensive. He recommended that the slow-moving infantry brigade should be withdrawn from Marsa Brega leaving only the mobile 3rd Armoured Brigade forward. By the 23rd the 20th Brigade had been withdrawn 160 miles and the infantry division occupied the line of the escarpment overlooking the Benghazi farmlands and facing north-west, while the gateway into Cyrenaica was guarded by Major-General M. D. Gambier-Parry's small 2nd Armoured Division. In the last week of March General Rommel, commander of the new German *Africa Corps*, though he still possessed only slender armoured forces, ventured to advance. At Marsa Brega on 31st March and Agedabia on 2nd April he gave the 2nd Armoured Division a rough handling and destroyed most of its tanks. The route across the desert to Mechili was now open to Rommel and he took it. Wavell now sent O'Connor forward; at his own suggestion O'Connor did not replace Neame but acted as an adviser.

The German advance-guard entered Benghazi early on 4th April, whereupon Neame ordered the 9th Division to withdraw to the second and higher escarpment east of Benghazi, the 2/13th Battalion (Lieut-Colonel F. A. Burrows) in the pass at Er Regima being the last unit to move. At 4 p.m. it was attacked but it held the German tanks and lorried infantry until after dark, when it embussed and withdrew to Barce. That day the 3rd Indian Motor Brigade moved to Mechili where it was intended that the remainder of the British armoured units should join it.

By the 6th it was evident that the Germans were moving along the route to Mechili in force and O'Connor ordered the 9th Division and the infantry of the armoured division to withdraw along the northern routes towards Tobruk while the armour went to Mechili. In a confused withdrawal Generals Neame and O'Connor and part of the 2/15th Australian Battalion were taken prisoner, and the 3rd Armoured Brigade retired not to Mechili but Derna.

The Mechili garrison, now surrounded, was ordered to break out eastward. Part did so, but most of the garrison including Major-General Gambier-Parry, and part of the 2/3rd Australian Anti-Tank Regiment, were captured. Protected by this rearguard at Mechili and by the Support Group east of Derna, the 9th Division had continued its withdrawal through Derna.

On 8th April Wavell and Major-General Lavarack of the 7th Australian Division landed on the Tobruk airfield. Two days earlier the three commanders-in-chief, with Dill and Eden, had met in Cairo and decided that Tobruk should be held even if isolated. It was then that Wavell decided that the 7th Division (less the 18th Brigade which Wavell had moved forward to Tobruk where it arrived on the 7th) must go to Mersa Matruh not Greece. Lavarack would succeed Neame in command in Cyrenaica. In Tobruk Wavell gave Lavarack written orders and instructed him that 'to gain time for the assembly of the required reinforcements it may be necessary to hold Tobruk for about two months'.

Within the thirty-mile perimeter Lavarack and Morshead now had some 31,000 troops of whom 24,000 were fighting troops. There were the three brigades of the 9th Division, the 18th Brigade, the 3rd Armoured Brigade (two regiments), four regiments of British field artillery, and two of anti-tank and two of anti-aircraft artillery.[5]

Morshead decided to place seven of his thirteen infantry battalions on the perimeter each with a reserve company half a mile behind it.[6] Thus each forward company usually held a front of more than a mile. About two miles within the perimeter an inner line—the Blue Line—was gradually dug and wired; each forward brigade had one battalion in this line. Farther back Morshead held in reserve one brigade and his tanks, armoured cars and carriers.

By 11th April (Good Friday) the Germans were astride the road leading

[5] Of the twenty-seven infantry, artillery and armoured units fifteen were Australian, eleven British and one Indian.

[6] The thirteenth 'battalion' was the 18th Indian Cavalry Regiment. Later the 2/1st Pioneer Battalion was used in the line.

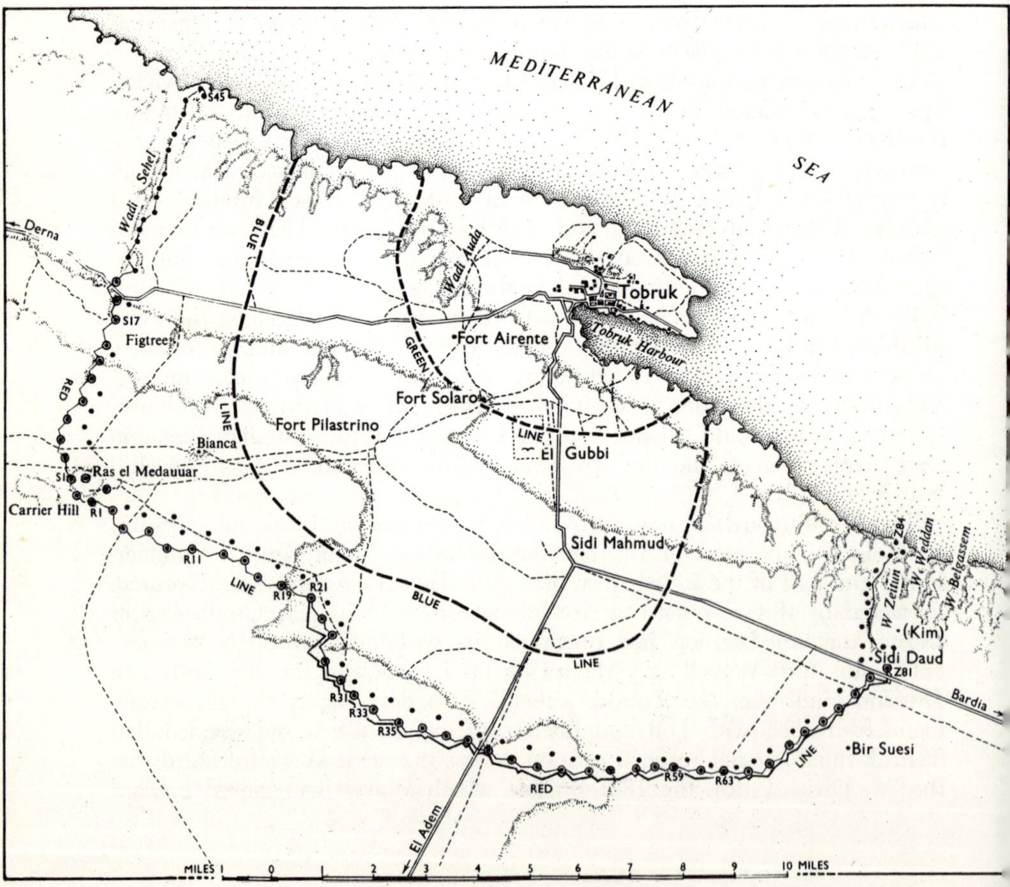

Siege of Tobruk

east from Tobruk. The siege had begun. On the 13th Rommel had most of the *5th Light* and part of the Italian *Ariete Armoured Division* outside Tobruk. He attacked that night using a tank regiment and a machine-gun battalion, just west of the El Adem road in the 2/17th Battalion's sector. A group of Germans who established themselves inside the wire with two guns, a mortar and eight machine-guns were dislodged with grenades and bayonets by Lieutenant F. A. Mackell, Corporal J. H. Edmondson and five men. Edmondson fought on after being severely wounded and died next day. He was awarded the Victoria Cross, the first won by an Australian in that war. At dawn some fifty tanks thrust on towards the escarpment overlooking the port. The forward infantry waited in their posts for the German infantry to follow up. When the tanks came under fire from the guns of the 1st Royal Horse Artillery and anti-tank guns of the 3rd R.H.A. and 2/3rd Anti-Tank Regiment, eight were soon knocked out. The infantry in the perimeter shot down the German infantry and gunners as they advanced to join the tanks, which by 7 a.m. were being attacked on all sides by artillery and the defending tanks. They fled, leaving seventeen wrecked tanks, 150 dead and 250 prisoners within the perimeter. As the tanks were fleeing forty German aircraft attacked, and ten were shot down. The garrison suffered only eighty casualties.

While this fight was in progress the Germans had reached Bardia and Capuzzo and an improvised force round Salum under Brigadier W. H. E. Gott was also under attack. On 13th April the enemy captured Salum but Gott's force, supported by fire from naval vessels, halted them. On the 15th Gott, reinforced by the 22nd Guards Brigade, forced the enemy back to Capuzzo; on the 20th British commandos landed from destroyers, including the five Australian destroyers, raided Bardia and caused damage and alarm there.

On the 14th Lavarack's Cyrenaica Command ceased to exist and Morshead took complete control at Tobruk, where the garrison consisted mainly of his division. The Western Desert Force was now commanded by Lieut-General N. M. Beresford-Peirse who had commanded the 4th Indian Division at Sidi Barrani. On the frontier he had what was left of Gott's Support Group; round Mersa Matruh were the 7th Australian Division and 6th British, each with only two brigades. Wavell had not even one complete division in Egypt or Palestine. However, decisive successes in Abyssinia in late March and early April had enabled him to order the 4th Indian Division to return to Egypt. In Abyssinia on 27th March Keren had fallen after a long, hard battle; by 8th April Asmara, Addis Ababa and Massawa had been captured, and only remnants of the Italian army remained at large.

This success was soon offset by disturbing events in remote Iraq. There, late in March, a group of anti-British officers under Rashid Ali had deposed the pro-British Regent. By treaty Iraq was required to assist Britain in war and allow passage of troops, and Britain had control of air force stations at Habbaniya, forty miles from Baghdad, and Shaiba near Basra. Both had been denuded of all operational aircraft, but at Habbaniya was a training school protected by Kurdish troops under British officers. The British Government decided to send troops to Basra and a brigade group from India was landed there on 18th April. When Rashid Ali learnt that further brigades were to arrive he refused to agree, on the ground that this would infringe the treaty, and so in late April there was a prospect of a new conflict.

Thus, in March and April, there had been a calamitous decline in British fortunes in the eastern Mediterranean. By February the Italian Navy and Air Force had been severely mauled, the Italian army in Cyrenaica had been destroyed, the army in Tripolitania was in confusion, Wavell had an army of two armoured and four infantry divisions in Palestine and North Africa. Now, in April, Cyrenaica had been lost except for the Tobruk fortress and Egypt was in danger, Greece had been lost and it was known that the Germans were planning to attack Crete, in Iraq trouble was developing which might spread to other Arab countries, and of the six divisions mentioned above only two (the 7th and 9th Australian) were still effectively equipped. Churchill then called on the navy: on the 14th April (the day of the defeat of the German attack on Tobruk and the day before the decision that the evacuation of Greece was inevitable) he ordered that the fleet must render the port of Tripoli unusable. Cunningham was instructed to carry out a combined blocking and bombardment; the battleship *Barham* was to be sunk across the entrance. As a result of Cunningham's outspoken protests the blocking proposal was dropped but the fleet did bombard Tripoli for an hour on 21st April and—'incredibly fortunate' in Cunningham's opinion—emerged unscathed. Only one enemy ship was sunk in the harbour. Far greater damage was done on the 16th by four destroyers which Cunningham had stationed at Malta to raid the Axis route to Tripoli. These sank five ships for a loss of one destroyer.

The next effort to restore the balance in North Africa was also originated by Churchill. On 22nd April he decided that tanks, now coming from the factories in substantial numbers, must be shipped to Egypt through the Mediterranean and a convoy of six ships carrying 295 tanks was loaded. This reinforcement got through early in May in providentially thick weather with the loss of one transport.

During the second half of April Rommel prepared for a second attempt to take Tobruk. Meanwhile Italian infantry was given the task of maintaining pressure. The Italian probing cost them dearly, the 2/48th Battalion, for example, on 16th April capturing almost an entire Italian battalion, colonel and all, at a cost of one man killed and one wounded.

In the last three weeks of April 677 sorties against the anti-aircraft batteries and the harbour were made by German aircraft. The fighters brought down about thirty aircraft and the guns probably about forty.

Late in April a map taken from a German aircraft shot down in Tobruk warned the defenders that the awaited German attack would fall along the Acroma road and through Hill 209. This was in the centre of a front of four miles and a half held by the 2/24th Battalion (Lieut-Colonel A. Spowers). In the afternoon of 30th April the posts round Hill 209 were shelled and bombed. At dusk German pioneers and machine-gunners advanced in the dust and smoke, disarmed the mines and blew gaps in the wire at several points and moved through the gaps between the posts. There was confused fighting all night. Mist covered the area in the morning until 8 a.m. When it lifted it was evident that the Germans had taken seven perimeter posts; there were forty tanks round Hill 209. These advanced eastward and ran into a minefield where seven were damaged. In an hour

Australian War Memorial

A section of Tobruk during the siege. The town and port through which supplies were fed to the garrison were about nine miles from the dusty perimeter where much of the fighting took place. Dispersed vehicles, some of them derelict, can be seen in the foreground.

Tobruk, August 1941. Australians in action in a shallow front-line trench on the perimeter. The enemy is only about 400 yards away.

Australian War Memorial

this attack had halted, probably half the tanks having been damaged. Meanwhile some forty tanks with infantry were thrusting along the perimeter south from Hill 209. By 9.30 a.m. they had advanced three miles under artillery fire. At that stage they encountered fourteen British cruisers of the 1st Royal Tank Regiment, which Morshead had sent forward, and after intermittent fighting for more than an hour the Germans made off. In the afternoon there was severe fighting round the posts just south of Hill 209 where the garrisons were holding out sturdily. By dark the Germans held fifteen posts on a 5,000-yard front, but had been checked with severe losses.

At 7.15 p.m. the 2/48th Battalion, in the Blue Line, was sent out to counter-attack and recapture Hill 209. The attacking companies lost heavily and by 9.30 had begun to withdraw, but the attack forced the enemy on to the defensive. Next day a dust-storm covered Tobruk and the enemy made no serious attack, yet were under intense fire all day. It was expected that the attack would be resumed on the 3rd, but it did not come; more than half the tanks of the attacking regiment had been knocked out and Rommel decided not to press on. The enemy now held a large salient about three miles wide and three deep. The 18th Brigade counter-attacked early in the night of 3rd-4th May but came under heavy fire and made no gains except on the left where the 2/9th Battalion recaptured one perimeter post. In the three days the Germans and Italians lost some 950 men, and the garrison about 800. But 'the achievement was not to be measured in casualties. The real achievement was the fact that the aggressive conduct of the defence compelled Rommel to hold his salient in strength with some of his best troops, which augmented the inhibiting effect of the Tobruk fortress on his power to strike at the frontier of Egypt'.[7] For the defenders the attack marked the end of a phase. Henceforth, for some time, the emphasis was on strengthening the line round the salient and general reorganisation.

Meanwhile on 2nd May fighting had begun in Iraq and there too a decisive success had been achieved. The Iraqi Army concentrated a force of more than a division overlooking Habbaniya. On 2nd May improvised squadrons from the flying school and some bombers from Shaiba attacked the Iraqis. After four days of fighting the boldly-handled aircraft, part of a British battalion, and the five companies of Kurdish troops had defeated the Iraqi force. To confirm this local success a brigade of the 1st Cavalry Division was sent 500 miles across the desert from Palestine. It reached Habbaniya on the 18th and the outskirts of Baghdad on the 30th. Next day Rashid Ali fled and the Regent was restored.

To enable them to help Rashid Ali the Germans had obtained an agreement with Vichy France that their aircraft might refuel on Syrian fields and also that war material under Axis control in Syria might be sent to Iraq. From 9th May onwards small numbers of Axis aircraft staged in Syria and gave support—too little and too late—to the Iraqi nationalists. Promptly Churchill instructed Wavell that there was no alternative to allowing General Catroux, leader of the Free French in the Middle East, to march into Syria. Wavell was most unwilling to accept this new commitment. The Free French forces then consisted of only five battalions (mostly of Africans) and some artillery.

[7] B. Maughan, *Tobruk and El Alamein* (1966), p. 235.

Wavell was hard-pressed in the Western Desert; the only part of the cavalry division which he could equip with vehicles was on its way to Iraq; the onslaught on Crete was soon expected; air support for an invasion of Syria could be only sketchy.

The R.A.F. attacked German aircraft on Syrian airfields from 14th May onwards, but Wavell told the Chiefs of Staff that nothing less than a corps including an armoured division would be sufficient for the effective occupation of Syria. They replied that he must advance into Syria as soon as possible. On the 20th Wavell ordered the 7th Australian Division to move from Mersa Matruh to Palestine and on the 21st instructed General Maitland Wilson to prepare plans for the invasion. On the 20th the long-awaited German airborne attack on Crete had opened.

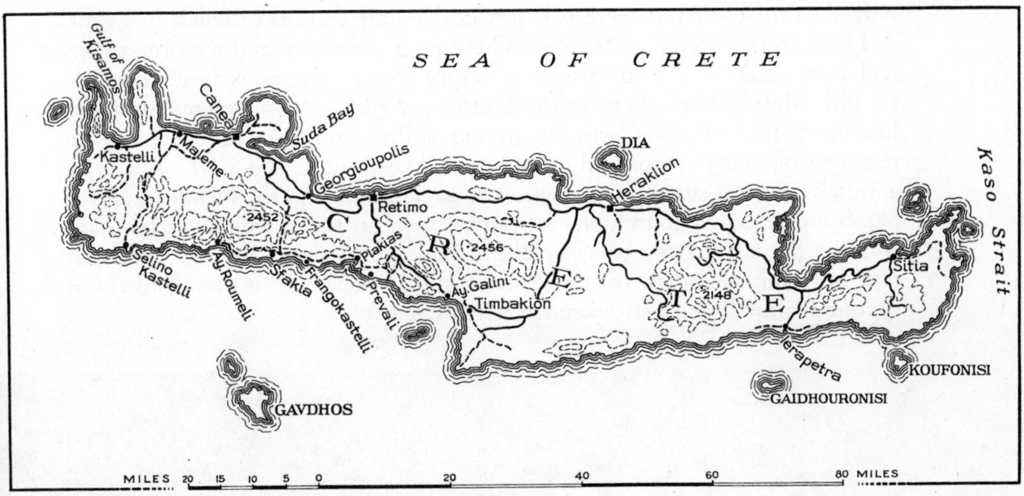

Crete

When the embarkation from Greece began the garrison of Crete consisted of the 14th British Brigade, some anti-aircraft and other units, and a few thousand Greeks who had not even enough rifles to go round. Part of the British Mobile Naval Base Defence Organisation was due to arrive soon. From 23rd April onwards some 30,000 troops from Greece, with no heavy weapons, were landed in Crete and on the 30th General Freyberg, who had arrived the previous day imagining that he was on his way to rejoin his division in Egypt, learnt that most of it was in Crete and that he was required to take command of all forces on the island and defend it against probable attack by German airborne troops. In the next fortnight the force on the island was hurriedly reorganised. Some 7,000 men were shipped to Egypt, leaving a force including 15,000 British, 7,700 New Zealanders, 6,500 Australians and about 11,000 Greeks; the Greeks, organised in eleven rifle battalions, were practically untrained and were poorly armed.

There were four likely landing places to be defended on the narrow coastal plain lying between the mountainous spine of Crete and the sea: the area round Maleme airfield west of Suda Bay, Suda Bay itself, Retimo some twenty miles to the east, and Heraklion forty miles farther east. Of the seventeen British and Anzac battalions (excluding battalions improvised from incomplete units and technical troops from Greece), five (of the 5th and 10th New Zealand Brigades) were allotted to the Maleme area and one to Suda, three (4th New Zealand Brigade) being in force reserve in this area; four (19th Australian Brigade) were allotted to Georgioupolis-Retimo, and four (14th British Brigade) to Heraklion. Brigadier E. Puttick who succeeded Freyberg in command of the New Zealand Division commanded in the Maleme sector, Major-General E. C. Weston commanded at Suda Bay, Brigadier Vasey at Georgioupolis-Retimo, and Brigadier B. H. Chappel at Heraklion. The force was gravely short of equipment, particularly of efficient artillery weapons. There were 50 obsolete field guns, mostly captured Italian weapons, 36 heavy and 32 light anti-aircraft guns, 9 heavy tanks. On 13th May systematic large-scale bombing of Crete began. By the 19th only six British aircraft were still serviceable and they were flown to Egypt.

The German decision to capture Crete with parachute and airborne troops had been made in the third week of April and preparations were complete by 14th May. General Lohr of the *Fourth Air Fleet* was in command; under him were the *XI Air Corps* (including a division of parachute troops, a regiment of glider troops and a mountain division) and the *VIII Air Corps*, a purely air formation. The plan was to land the glider regiment and a parachute regiment round Maleme and Canea on the morning of the 20th, and, in the afternoon, two parachute battalions round Retimo and four round Heraklion. Part of the mountain division was to be landed on captured airfields and part taken to Crete by sea.

Australian War Memorial

Suda Bay, Crete, during a bombing attack preceding the German invasion in May 1941.

The garrison of Crete had been under heavy air attack daily during the third week of May. On the morning of the 20th a larger force of bombers and fighters than ever before attacked round Maleme and Canea. Then the defenders saw a fleet of slow transport planes approaching over the sea, some towing gliders. Most of the gliders landed just west of Maleme, where the transports spilled out their paratroops over a wide area. Many paratroops were shot before they reached the ground and in every area but two only small disorganised groups remained by midday. The exceptions were the area of the westernmost New Zealand battalion, where the Germans captured ground round the vital Maleme airfield, and the hills south of the centre of the New Zealand position.

The force round Retimo—the 2/1st and 2/11th Battalions and four Greek battalions, commanded by Lieut-Colonel I. R. Campbell—was some miles from the remainder of the 19th Brigade and Vasey's headquarters at Georgioupolis. In the afternoon the planned landing round Retimo took place. Most of the paratroops were soon overcome but at the end of the day one group held strongly on a ridge south-east of the airfield and others were astride the road leading west. At Heraklion all who dropped within the defended area were killed or captured except small parties, but some Germans gained a foothold in the town itself.

During 21st May the western flank of the New Zealand Division held its ground under heavy attack, but control of the airfield at Maleme had been lost and that afternoon German aircraft began landing on it in a steady stream, bringing in a battalion of the mountain division. The enemy had

Australian War Memorial

H.M.A.S. *Voyager* off Suda Bay during the evacuation of Crete in May 1941.

gained his first main objective. Late in the afternoon it was decided that a two-battalion attack would be made towards Maleme that night, after one of Vasey's battalions from Georgioupolis had replaced one of the attacking New Zealand battalions in the New Zealand area. At Retimo that day the 2/1st Battalion dislodged the Germans from the heights south-east of the airfield, but a group remained astride the roads both west to Canea and east to Heraklion. At Heraklion the Germans had gained no vital ground round the airfield but again were astride the coast road both east and west. That night a British naval force patrolling north of Crete met a convoy consisting chiefly of caiques crowded with about 1,000 German mountain troops and sank several of them, drowning some 400 men.

The night attack by the New Zealanders temporarily gained some ground but failed to achieve the main objective—command of the airfield. The German plan was now to send the mountain troops on a wide outflanking move over the hills south of the New Zealanders. That evening the Germans in the hills attacked north towards the centre of the elongated New Zealand position, but after heavy fighting they were driven back. It was decided that night to withdraw the western flank to a creek some two miles to the east —in effect to accept German possession of the airfield. At Retimo on the 22nd Campbell's force attacked both east and west but failed to open the roads. Early in the morning of the 22nd a force of three cruisers and destroyers engaged enemy vessels off the eastern coast of Crete. *Perth* sank a caique and others were seen in the distance, but the squadron was under heavy air attack and withdrew. Intense air attack on the ships round Crete continued and on this day and the next the cruisers *Fiji* and *Gloucester* and the destroyers *Greyhound*, *Kelly* and *Kashmir* were sunk; the destroyer *Juno* had been sunk on the 21st; two battleships and three cruisers had been damaged. Naval protection of the force in Crete was becoming dangerously costly.

On 23rd May the New Zealanders carried out their withdrawal, the Germans following closely. That night there was a further withdrawal. The line covering Canea and Suda Bay was now held by the 4th Brigade on the right and the 19th (2/7th and 2/8th Battalions) on the left. Crete had received some reinforcements during the battle. One infantry battalion reached Timbakion on the south coast on the 20th and the fast minelayer *Abdiel* and destroyers landed two commando units at Suda Bay on the 24th and 26th. On the 24th the Germans probed forward and at length began an attack on the New Zealanders which seemed likely to grow in intensity the next day.

There were now two airborne regiments and a mountain regiment concentrated against the weary New Zealand Division and a second mountain regiment was moving towards Suda Bay through the hills where a Greek regiment was offering sturdy resistance. There was hard fighting all through 25th May on the New Zealand front, but in the evening a resolute counter-attack decisively halted the Germans. Puttick doubted, however, whether his line would hold another day, and that night a further withdrawal was made.

On the morning of the 26th Freyberg informed Wavell that his position was hopeless. The Germans pressed hard all day and the mountain regiment in the hills was encircling the inland flank. At night a withdrawal was made past Canea to a new line at the head of Suda Bay, the Australians on the right and the New Zealanders on the left. The Germans followed fast and by 11 a.m. on the 27th were nearing the new line, where the 2/7th Battalion (Lieut-Colonel T. G. Walker), which had not yet been heavily engaged, made a spirited charge in which the Maori Battalion and others joined. Perhaps 200 Germans were killed and the rest fled; the enemy made no further attack that day.

Freyberg was manoeuvring his force for a withdrawal over the mountain road from Suda Bay to the village of Sfakia on the south coast where embarkation might be possible. Already the road was crowded with troops. The rearguard battalions withdrew to the road on the night of the 27th. That afternoon Freyberg had received orders to abandon Crete. Communication with the force at Retimo was now non-existent and all efforts to inform it of the decision to embark failed. Early on the 28th yet another effort was made by the 2/11th Battalion to thrust the Germans off the road leading west, but in vain. On the morning of the 30th German tanks and artillery appeared from the west, making it evident that western Crete had been abandoned. That day the Australians surrendered except for some groups who escaped into the mountains.

At the western end of Crete plans were now made to hold a series of rearguard positions on the Sfakia road while on three consecutive nights—29th-30th, 30th-31st and 31st-1st—the force was embarked at Sfakia. Intensely weary and often short of food and water, the defenders retreated along the narrow road winding over the backbone of Crete. On the night of the 28th four destroyers embarked about 1,000 men including 230 wounded at Sfakia, and the same night three cruisers and six destroyers embarked practically the entire British-Australian force from Heraklion. On the way to Egypt the Heraklion convoy was attacked by aircraft. A destroyer was damaged and had to be sunk, a second destroyer was sunk, the cruiser *Orion* was hit and about 800 seamen and soldiers were killed or wounded.

Next night, the 29th-30th, four cruisers including *Perth*, a landing ship, and six destroyers, including *Stuart*, embarked 6,000 men from Sfakia. Aircraft attacked the convoy on the return journey and *Perth* was hit and damaged. The beach at Sfakia was now protected by the 2/7th and 2/8th Battalions, British marines and commandos. The German advance-guards pushed boldly forward on the 30th but were roughly handled and lost heavily.

The naval force allotted to Sfakia for the night of the 30th-31st consisted of four destroyers, but two were damaged by air attack and ordered back. However, two Australian destroyers, *Napier* and *Nizam*, embarked 1,500, the full quota allotted to the four. There now remained some 1,500 British, 1,250 Australian and 1,200 New Zealand infantry and 5,000 depot troops and detachments.

After their losses on the 30th the Germans made no attempt to advance against the rearguard on the 31st. At the same time they were systematically encircling the Sfakia position.

On the 31st a cruiser, the minelayer *Abdiel* and three destroyers set out to make the final embarkation. It was evident that they would not be able to lift all the 9,000 troops who remained, but Cunningham, who now had

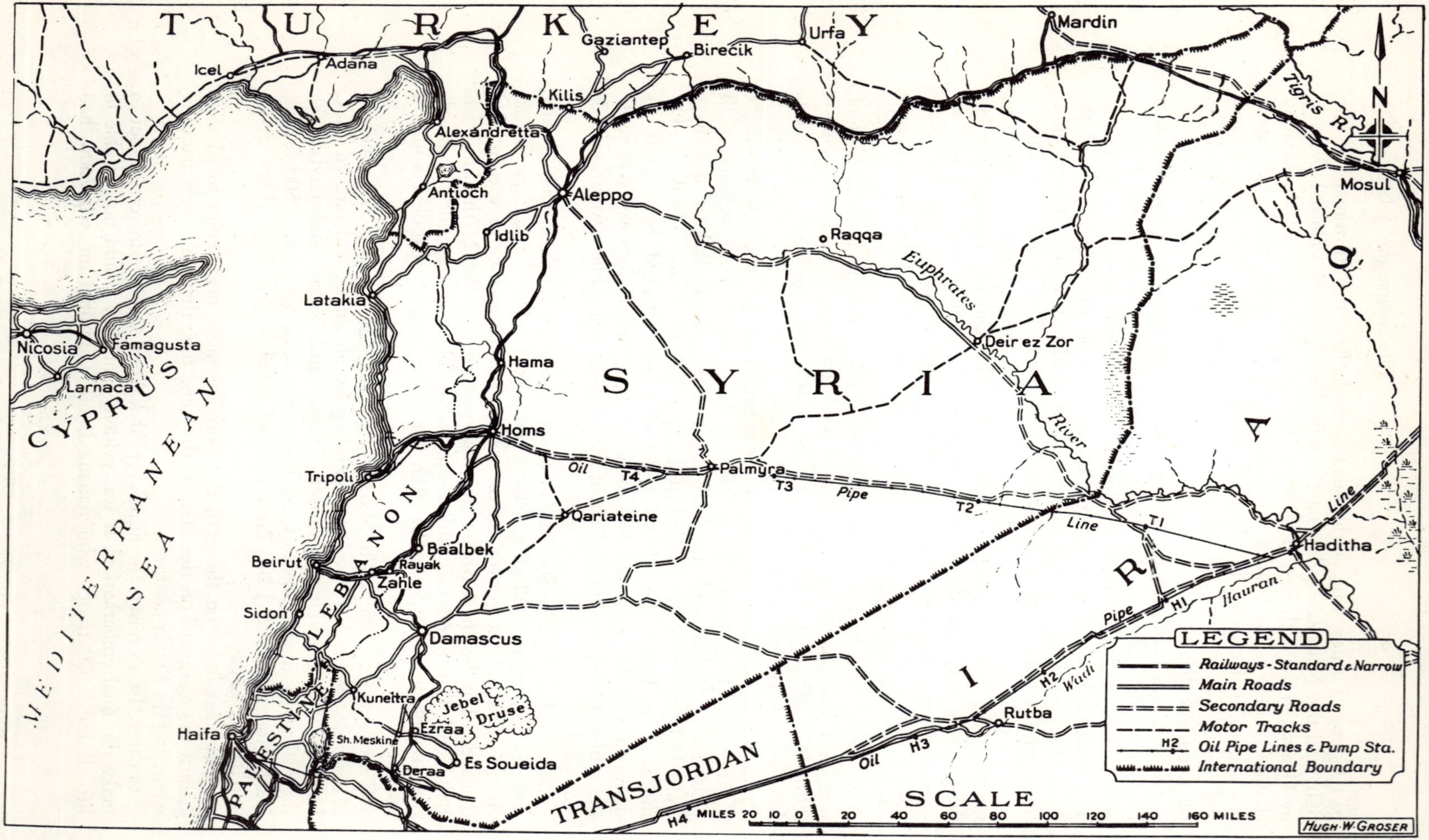

Syria and Iraq

only two battleships, three cruisers, a minelayer and nine destroyers fit for action, was resolved that his diminishing fleet should be risked no longer.

The naval force embarked about 4,000 men but, when the ships sailed, practically all of the 2/7th Battalion, the marines and the commandos, and some 3,000 others, were left behind. About 15,000 men in all had been embarked at Sfakia and Heraklion; about 12,000 were taken prisoner in Crete, including over 3,000 Australians. In fighting units the Australian force lost heavily—three full battalions captured. In the operations round Crete the fleet lost 3 cruisers and 6 destroyers; and 2 battleships, an aircraft carrier, 2 cruisers and 2 destroyers were damaged so severely that they would be out of action for some months. 'A disastrous period in our naval history', Cunningham called it.

Thus, by the beginning of June, British fortunes in the Middle East had sunk very low. The fleet had been reduced to a few ships yet still had the urgent tasks of attacking the Axis supply line to North Africa and maintaining Tobruk and Malta. The air force, now possessing only some 200 serviceable aircraft, was greatly outnumbered yet had to cope with German aircraft based in Crete as well as the Dodecanese. Two of Wavell's most experienced infantry divisions—the 6th Australian and the New Zealand—would need months to re-equip and re-form after the losses in Greece and Crete, yet he was scheduled to attack in the Western Desert and make an unheralded invasion of Syria. He decided that he could not attack in the desert before 15th June when he would have the 7th Armoured Division and the 4th Indian—the same force which had won the victory at Sidi Barrani six months before—to face perhaps twice that number of German and Italian divisions.

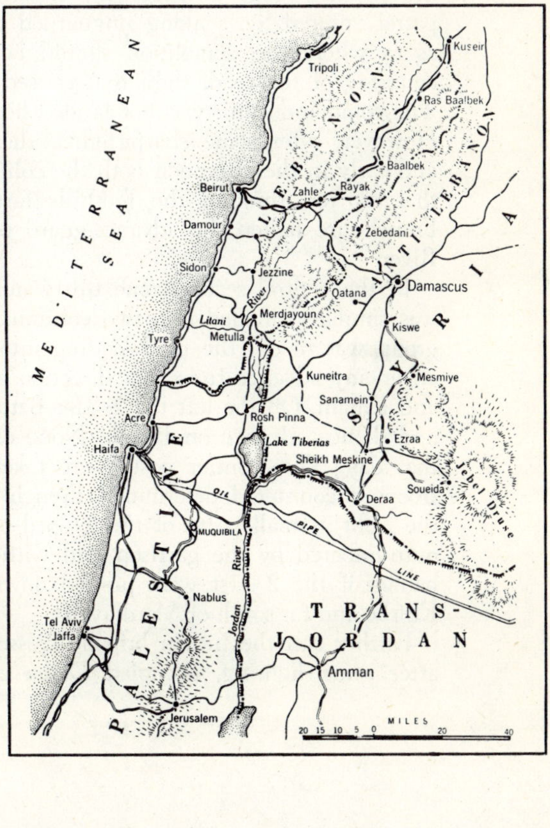

In Syria the French Commander, General Dentz, had 28,000 French and African troops, including six regiments of regulars, and about 10,000 Lebanese and Syrians, and he had ninety tanks. It was believed that some 300 German technicians were in Syria (actually there were never more than fifty). To carry out an invasion Wavell could spare no armoured troops and only three British infantry brigades—the 21st and 25th Australian and 5th Indian—and two Free French brigades, weak in numbers and ill-equipped.

Three main routes led into Syria from Palestine: one over desert roads to Damascus, another along mountain roads between Mount Hermon and the Lebanons to the Damascus-Beirut road near Rayak and Zahle, a third along the narrow coastal plain to Beirut and beyond. The plan was to advance with one brigade along each of these. On the left the 21st Australian Brigade (Brigadier Stevens) would thrust along the coast to Beirut; in the centre the 25th Australian (Brigadier A. R. Baxter-Cox) over the mountain roads to Rayak airfield; on the left the 5th Indian Brigade (Brigadier W. L. Lloyd) would overcome the first opposition and form a bridgehead through which General Paul Legentilhomme's Free French would advance through the desert to Damascus. When the line Damascus-Rayak-Beirut had been taken Lieut-General Lavarack and the headquarters of I Australian Corps were to control the whole operation, Major-General Allen, formerly of the 16th Brigade, succeeding him in command of the 7th Division. Wilson's staff at Jerusalem were confident that the French would offer only weak resistance and that a swift advance would be made to Beirut and Damascus, but the commanders of the troops waiting on the frontier did not share these opinions.

The coast road ran along a narrow shelf between the mountains and the sea. Two early obstacles were foreseen: that the French would demolish the road north of the frontier where it was a mere ledge cut into the mountain side, and that they would blow up the bridge over the Litani River farther north. Stevens decided therefore to send in a small patrol early on the night of the advance to prevent the demolition of the road; in addition a plan had been made, but not properly co-ordinated, to land a commando unit to seize the bridge over the Litani. In case the road was blocked Stevens ordered one battalion and some cavalry to move along mountain paths to bypass the coast road, where it travelled round the steep headland, and descend on Tyre from the east.

Thus on 7th June, while the main body of the brigade lay concealed on the frontier ready to begin the invasion before dawn next morning, the patrol entered Syria along unguarded mountain tracks. Wrongly informed as to where the demolition should be expected, it failed to prevent the cratering of the road, though it caused confusion behind the French lines. The commando unit was not landed because a dangerous surf was running. However, after some sharp fights, the French frontier posts were taken, and early in the afternoon both the column advancing on the coast road and that moving through the foothills farther east were about Tyre. Heavy French fire halted the advance-guard on the slopes overlooking the Litani River.

In the central sector, some thirty miles to the east, Baxter-Cox's brigade was similarly divided into two columns. On the right the 2/33rd Battalion group was to cut the road leading into the area from Kuneitra to prevent an enemy advance from that direction and advance north through Hasbaya and Khiam. On the left the 2/31st Battalion group was to take Merdjayoun and thence advance on Rayak. None of the main objectives were achieved that day. The frontier posts were taken, but farther north the advancing troops encountered determined French troops in well-chosen positions. On the right a small party of the 2/33rd entered Fort Khiam, but was greatly outnumbered by the garrison and withdrew. At daylight the leading companies of the 2/31st were pinned down by fire in open country south of Khirbe and far south of Merdjayoun.

Farther east the Indian brigade crossed the frontier in four columns and, after some fighting, occupied Deraa and were soon on the outskirts of

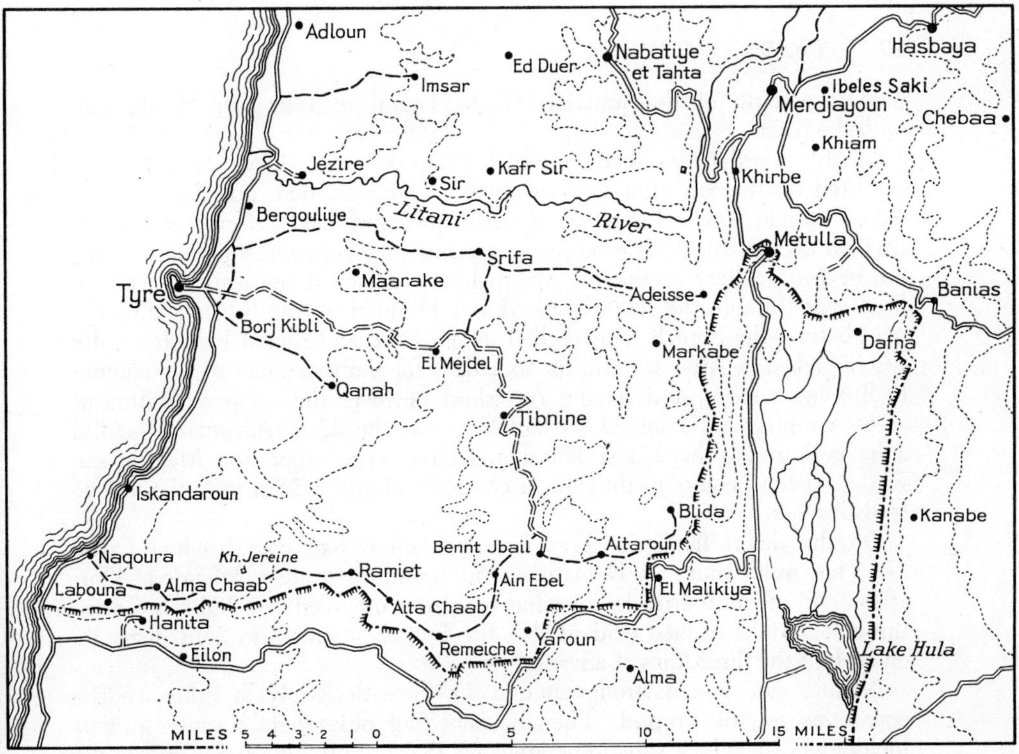

Palestine-Syria frontier

Sheikh Meskine and Kuneitra. Early next morning those towns and Ezraa were occupied and the Free French contingent passed through towards Damascus.

It was arranged that the commandos should again attempt to land before dawn on the 9th and that the 21st Brigade should launch an attack across the Litani River at 7.30 a.m. and link with them. One group was landed north of the river mouth as intended, but another south of it and in rear of the Australian infantry. Their object—to seize the bridge—was not achieved. When the 2/16th Battalion advanced towards the river the bridge was blown up ahead of them. An assault boat was carried forward and a man swam the river carrying a tow-line made of painters from the boats knotted to a length of telephone wire. Section by section a platoon reached the far bank and thrust forward. Others followed and by afternoon they were firmly established. West of the bridge the commando party advancing with others of the 2/16th suffered severe losses crossing the river under fire but in the afternoon they too had captured the French positions beyond. Of the commandos who landed north of the river some, including the commanding officer, were killed, others captured, but others succeeded in joining the Australians who had crossed the Litani. By 1.30 a.m. next morning the engineers had built a pontoon bridge across the river.

That night the 2/27th Battalion crossed and overcame the remaining enemy defences. Early next morning the cavalry carriers thrust north to find the next French positions—near Adloun some five miles beyond the river. These were overcome next day, but that afternoon the advance was again held just south of the junction of the lateral road linking Merdjayoun with the coast.

In the Merdjayoun sector, Fort Khiam and the village beyond were captured on the 9th after a sharp artillery concentration, but the infantrymen who had attacked towards Merdjayoun could make no progress. It was decided that on the 11th a set-piece attack would be made supported by the fire of two artillery regiments. Meanwhile a detached company which had been sent through the foothills of Mount Hermon on the 8th to harass the road behind the French had reached its objective and routed French cavalry who attacked it. After waiting for four days for the remainder of the column to link with them, and having run short of food, the company withdrew across country and rejoined its battalion—on the 13th. Advancing behind a heavy barrage, the 2/31st Battalion on the 11th swept into Merdjayoun while, on the heights to the east, a company of the 2/25th took the village of Ibeles Saki.

On the desert flank the Free French column had now reached Kiswe some ten miles south of Damascus, and found it strongly defended. Thus at the end of the fourth day of what had been intended as a lightning drive through Syria it seemed evident that the French intended to fight doggedly on each of the three lines of advance.

Neither side had a strong enough air force decisively to influence the operations on the ground. The attackers had only some seventy aircraft including two fighter squadrons (No. 80 R.A.F. and No. 3 R.A.A.F.); the French had about 100 at the outset. At sea French destroyers made some

Australian War Memorial

An artillery troop command post at Merdjayoun during the Syrian campaign against the Vichy French in June and July 1941.

forays and briefly bombarded positions ashore, but were driven off by artillery fire or by an inshore squadron, including H.M.A.S. *Perth* and the Australian destroyers, which lent increasing strength to the Australian western flank as the campaign continued.

On 12th June Stevens' column pressed on. After a prolonged attack the leading troops approached Sidon, which was occupied on the 15th after an advance on a wide front by two battalions—the 2/16th and 2/27th. Meanwhile Lavarack had decided that, because the Merdjayoun area offered such advantages to the defender and the coastal column was outpacing the advance in the centre, he would switch the 25th Brigade to the left along a mountain road over the eastern slopes of the Lebanons to Jezzine, due east of Sidon, to support Stevens' advance. One battalion and most of the cavalry were left at Merdjayoun while Baxter-Cox with the 2/31st (Lieut-Colonel S. H. W. C. Porter) and strong detachments of cavalry and artillery, on the 13th-14th made an arduous night journey in trucks along the winding road towards Jezzine which was taken next evening in a dashing attack. Thus, on the 15th, after eight days of hard fighting, Baxter-Cox at Jezzine and Stevens at Sidon were at opposite ends of a lateral road some forty miles north of the frontier, but Beirut was still twenty-five miles ahead.

At Kiswe it was evident that the French positions were so strong that only a carefully-organised attack with artillery support would take them. Bit by bit the Indian brigade was moved forward, except its English battalion the 1/Royal Fusiliers which remained at Kuneitra. On the morning of the 15th Lloyd's Indians made a brilliant night attack and took Kiswe, breaking the deadlock there that had lasted five days.

The advance seemed to be gaining impetus, but that day the French seized the initiative. Lloyd received news that an enemy column was advancing southward toward Kuneitra and another column had driven the little Transjordan Frontier Force out of Ezraa—in fact that the enemy had cut one of the roads in his rear and was closely threatening the other. He promptly dispatched a company of French native troops and some British guns to hold the road at Sheikh Meskine. In the afternoon the French attacked also the depleted force at Merdjayoun. There had remained in that area the 2/33rd Battalion, the 2/2nd Pioneers (on engineering work), the Scots Greys and part of the 6th Australian Cavalry. All but one company of the infantry battalion were out among the foothills of Hermon making a wide flanking advance towards Hasbaya to cut the road behind the enemy, and the cavalry were astride the two roads leading north from Merdjayoun both of which were commanded by French artillery. The French attacked towards Merdjayoun and Ibeles Saki with an infantry regiment and tanks, strongly supported by artillery, and forced the defenders out of their positions. The guns of a battery of the 2/5th Field Regiment were extricated with difficulty, some of them being hauled over steep terraced hillsides. Alarm spread behind the lines where rumours flew that tanks had broken through and a general withdrawal was in progress. However, the gunners knocked out a number of French tanks and the attack lost impetus. Late in the afternoon the one company of the 2/33rd was holding the fort at Khiam on the right, and on the left a company of the veteran 2/5th Battalion, which had recently arrived in the area for garrison duties, was astride the road north of Merdjayoun with a detachment of the Greys

Australian War Memorial

Syria, July 1941. The road known as the 'Mad Mile', near Jezzine. All the supplies for units had to be taken along this road which was under continuous enemy observation and shell fire.

and two anti-tank guns. In accordance with orders this company withdrew through Merdjayoun next morning before dawn, having first sent a patrol forward 500 yards and found no sign of the enemy. The French attack was not resumed next day. On the afternoon of the 15th the French had attacked also at Jezzine but were soon stopped by rapid and accurate artillery fire.

The general French counter-attack transformed the situation. General Wilson and General Lavarack threw in their few reserves to meet it. The leading battalion of the 16th British Brigade, which Wavell had recently ordered from Egypt to Syria, was dispatched towards Deraa. Lavarack sent Lieut-Colonel A. S. Blackburn with two companies of his 2/3rd Machine Gun Battalion to hold the crossings over the Jordan lest the enemy, already astride or threatening the roads behind the Indian-Free French column, should swing into northern Palestine and cut the roads behind the 7th Division also. He ordered the 2/25th Battalion, then on its way to Jezzine, to return to Merdjayoun and placed his artillery commander, Brigadier F. H. Berryman, in command of all troops in the Merdjayoun area. On the 17th he ordered Stevens to halt the advance along the coast and send a battalion inland to reinforce Baxter-Cox at Jezzine.

Before dawn on the 16th the French column—some 1,500 troops, with tanks—attacked Kuneitra, which was defended by the depleted 1/Royal Fusiliers supported by one small Italian gun. After fighting all day the surviving Fusiliers surrendered that evening. Lloyd however, undeterred by the French successes along his lines of communication, turned the tables on them by sending an Indian battalion from Kiswe to the Kuneitra road, thus cutting the road behind the French, and continued his thrust towards Damascus.

The French counter-attack had now spent itself. On the 17th the situation was restored in every threatened sector. That morning Free French Senegalese attacked Ezraa but were repulsed, whereupon a force of fewer than 100 men from Sheikh Meskine made a determined attack and retook Ezraa capturing 160 prisoners. That afternoon the 2/Queens (the battalion that had been ordered to Deraa) arrived and drove the French out of Kuneitra with little difficulty.

In the Merdjayoun sector next day Berryman launched a counter-attack on Merdjayoun by part of the 2/2nd Pioneer Battalion along the main road and the 2/25th Battalion from the west through the ravine in which the Litani flows. It failed, the Pioneers, fighting as infantry for the first time, losing heavily. At Jezzine on the 16th and 17th the enemy continued to attack but were again repulsed. The Australians took some seventy prisoners, mostly Senegalese, who were weary, hungry and dejected.

On the 18th Lavarack took command of I Australian Corps and assumed control of all operations in western Syria. He took over a problematical situation. Practically all his reserves had been committed; in the Damascus sector dangerous enemy attacks had been defeated; at Merdjayoun a counter-attack had failed; at Jezzine the enemy was still attacking; on the coast, where, with the support of the navy, the best progress had been made, the advance had been discontinued and the force reduced to strengthen another area. Wilson instructed Lavarack to concentrate the main effort on the drive along the coast against Beirut. It was decided on the 19th to place Major-General J. F. Evetts of the 6th British Division in command at Merdjayoun and concentrate the 7th Division west of the range for the thrust to Beirut.

Meanwhile the forces at Damascus and Merdjayoun, which together comprised three-quarters of the whole corps, engaged in a series of attacks in those sectors. On the night of the 18th Lloyd launched his Indians on a twelve-miles advance through Mezze to cut the Damascus-Beirut road. Moving in darkness they took Mezze and one company reached the Beirut road but was forced back. Next morning the French attacked the Indians in Mezze with tanks and surrounded them; the fight went on all day and the following night. On the morning of the 20th the survivors of the brigade surrendered, their food and ammunition exhausted. A complementary attack by the Free French along the Deraa road failed completely, and the French commander decided that his men had lost heart and would not move again unless British troops were there to encourage them. In consequence, Evetts, whose incomplete 6th British Division had been intended to relieve the Australians at Merdjayoun so that they could reinforce the coastal drive, was placed instead in command of all troops east of Mount Hermon and his 16th Brigade—the only one then available—and two battalions of the 6th Australian Division were to be used in that sector. Evetts was ordered to take Damascus.

He promptly sent forward Blackburn with one machine-gun company and some anti-tank guns to inspire the Free French to advance. On the afternoon of the 20th the machine-gunners, normally supporting troops, led a steady thrust towards Damascus. That evening the 2/3rd Battalion, newly arrived from Palestine, opened a renewed attack towards Mezze and the Beirut road on a much wider front than the Indians had used, their left flank companies advancing against a group of forts on the hills overlooking

Damascus from the south-west. The Australians scaled the heights and took the forts; a night attack by the French captured the colonel and headquarters of the Australian battalion but they were retaken next morning. A detached company of the 2/3rd cut the Beirut road and then climbed up the face of the gorge and helped to capture a fort. The defenders of Damascus had surrendered to the Free French-Australian column before midday on the 21st. Thus after fourteen days the first of the three main objectives had been taken.

Evetts then decided to advance west along the Beirut road, which travels through the deep Barada gorge. The 16th British Brigade (to which the 2/3rd Australian Battalion was now attached) advanced to the foot of Jebel Mazar, a dominating mountain on the south side of the road. The Australians twice attacked this eminence, and it was taken by a company on the 27th in a daring night attack. If an artillery observer with signalling gear had reached the summit of the hill it would probably have been possible to drive the French from the lower ground beyond, but none arrived and the following night, after withstanding attacks by strong French forces all day, the isolated company, then almost surrounded, withdrew.

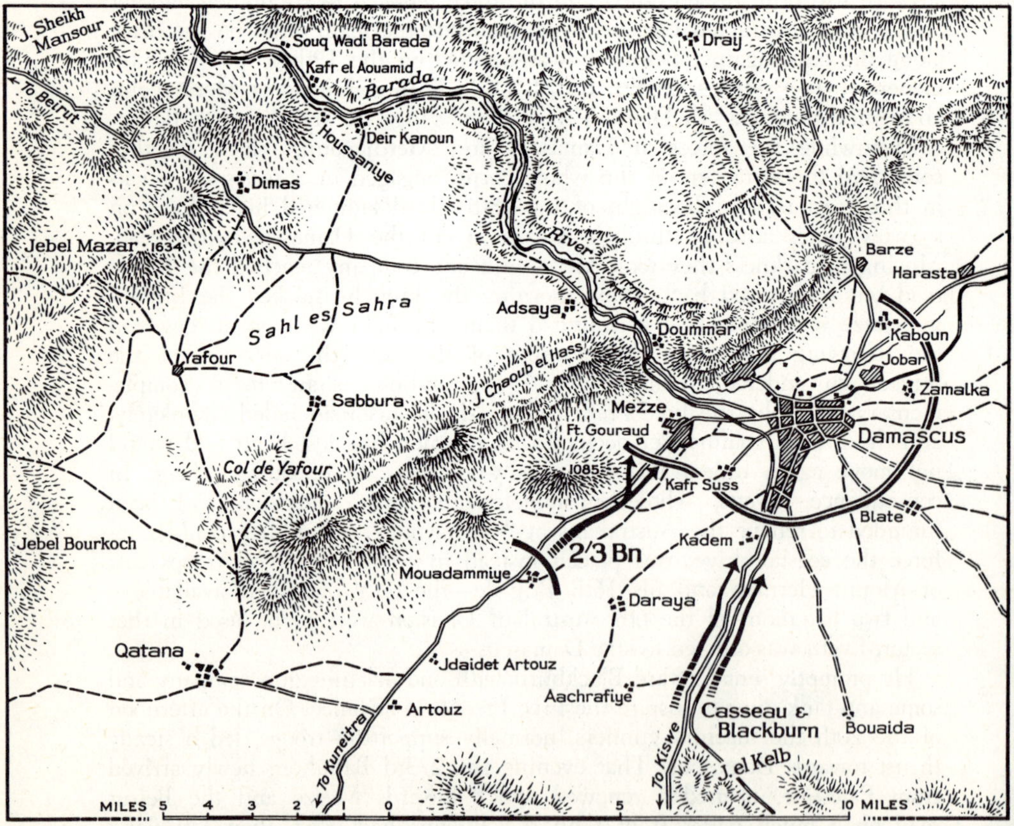

Damascus area

Merdjayoun had been the scene of a similar series of attacks. One, made on the 19th, resembled in plan the attack of the 17th, and again failed, although for a time the Queenslanders of the 2/25th were fighting within the town. Thereupon Berryman ordered an attack towards Ibeles Saki on his right flank by the 2/33rd and the 2/King's Own. On the 23rd, advancing close behind a strong artillery barrage, the Australians stormed their objective and held it against counter-attacks, but the English infantry failed to reach theirs. In the meantime, however, a patrol of the Pioneers had found that the enemy had abandoned Merdjayoun, probably because of the galling artillery fire to which it had been subjected. Next day the force was more or less back in the positions it had lost when the French counter-attack opened on the 15th, but the execution of the decision of five days before to concentrate on an advance towards Beirut was still delayed. Berryman attacked again on the 27th, this time employing one company of the Pioneers against the lofty ridge dominating the junction of the two roads leading north from Merdjayoun. The Pioneers reached the summit, but the ridge was held by two French battalions, who withdrew to avoid the barrage and then counter-attacked and drove back the handful of Australians. More than half the attackers were killed, wounded or taken prisoner.

Meanwhile a fruitless attack had also been made on equally strong French positions north of Jezzine. On the 24th two companies of the 2/14th, recently transferred from the coast, attacked towards the flank of the lofty hills dominating the road leading north from Jezzine. After suffering heavy losses the two companies were withdrawn. The troops, both French Africans and Australians, who were fighting in this tangled mountain country were now beginning to suffer from severe fatigue. On the 25th Baxter-Cox himself was taken out, tired and ill, and Brigadier E. C. P. Plant, a cool and widely-experienced soldier, replaced him. Next day Allen, at Plant's suggestion, decided to make no more infantry attacks there but to blast the French off the hill tops with artillery fire, and at the same time to relieve the pressure by sending a small mobile force into the tangled Lebanons between the coast and Jezzine. The policy of pounding the French hill-top positions produced prompt success. On the 28th and 29th patrols found the main French positions empty, and the rocky crests scarred in a close pattern and scattered with dead whom the defenders had not waited to cover or carry away.

On the 21st, the day Damascus fell, the 4th Cavalry Brigade—the same which had crossed the desert from Palestine to help suppress the rebellion at Baghdad—advanced from Iraq towards the remote town of Palmyra, which was held by only three companies, two of them of the Foreign Legion. As the column approached Palmyra, and on the following days, it was attacked persistently by French aircraft. As a result of these attacks and the stubborn resistance of the little garrison, the French held Palmyra until 3rd July, when the survivors, 165 men including eighty-seven Germans and Russians of the Foreign Legion, surrendered, having withstood for twelve days the attacks of four cavalry regiments (counting the Arab Legion as one) and an infantry battalion. On the 1st the leading brigade of the 10th Indian Division (Major-General W. J. Slim) had entered eastern Syria from Iraq, and on the 3rd it took Deir ez Zor from a small outpost garrison there.

On 26th June General Lavarack decided that he could now promptly carry

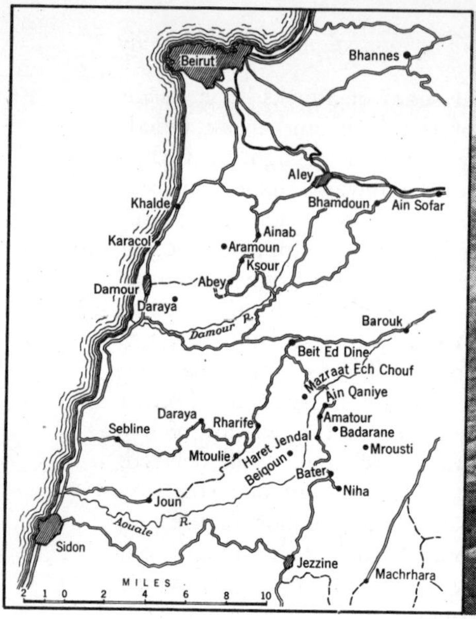

Australian War Memorial

Left: Damour-Beit ed Dine. *Right:* Tomahawks of No. 3 Squadron R.A.A.F. on patrol over Syria in July 1941.

out the plan outlined seven days before: namely, to concentrate the 7th Division on the coast and round Jezzine, the 23rd British Brigade (which had now arrived) replacing the units of the 7th Division at Merdjayoun. Allen's division was to be brought up to strength by adding the 17th Brigade (Brigadier Savige) which would be pieced together from the 2/3rd and 2/5th Infantry and 2/2nd Pioneer Battalions. This plan necessitated transferring six of the nine Australian infantry battalions westward to new sectors.

Since mid-June, when he had been ordered to halt, Stevens had in fact been steadily gaining ground by vigorous patrolling and had been planning an attack on the main obstacle that lay between him and Beirut, the great ravine through which the Damour River flowed. By 30th June the whole of the ridge overlooking the river was in Australian hands, and on the following nights the southern wall of the ravine and suitable river crossings were stealthily explored. As a preliminary to a full-scale assault on the Damour positions the 2/25th Battalion (Lieut-Colonel C. B. Withy) reinforced by part of the 2/2nd Pioneers was instructed to clear the enemy from the southern part of a road winding into the rear of the Australian positions from Beit ed Dine. This they achieved in the next three days, having fought a series of sharp actions on the heights of the Lebanon.

In the meantime the assault on Damour had been planned. One of Stevens' battalions was to attack heights just east of the main road, which led into Damour through banana plantations. His other battalions were to secure the right against possible enemy counter-attack from Beit ed Dine, and, crossing the Damour by a goat track, to make a wide flanking move into the mountains sloping down to the town from the east. Through the corridor formed by these battalions two battalions of Savige's brigade were to advance still farther and fan out until their left flank was astride the road leading out of Damour on the north. Thus, if all went well, the main enemy force would be surrounded.

This led to a set-piece battle lasting four hard days. In a frontal attack on the left the 2/16th Battalion suffered sharp losses but gained important ground. The large-scale flanking movement through the mountains to the east, carried out by the 2/14th and 2/27th, succeeded in spite of some strong counter-attacks, and the road leading north from Damour was cut by the 17th Brigade. Meanwhile the 25th Brigade pressed on from Jezzine towards Beit ed Dine; and the 6th British Division, which still included several Australian units, attacked toward Jebel Mazar. Threatened from south and east and with his forces weary and depleted, Dentz sought an armistice, and fire ceased on 12th July. It had been a hard-fought campaign which cost the Australians some 1,600 casualties including 416 killed.

While the Syrian campaign was being fought news arrived of the German invasion of Russia. This meant that there was no immediate likelihood of a concentrated Axis offensive against the eastern flank in the Middle East, and thus that the main reason for a hasty invasion of Syria had been illusory. But a rapid German victory in Russia was expected by most British leaders and consequently steps were taken to garrison Syria as strongly as possible.

On 15th June (the day of the French counter-attack in Syria) the British Western Desert offensive (BATTLEAXE) had opened: the force in Egypt was to deal with the German armour on the frontier and relieve Tobruk. There was some success on the first day, but on the second and third Rommel, bringing up tanks from Tobruk, counter-attacked and the British-Indian force was forced to withdraw having lost more than half of its tanks. Thus Tobruk was still besieged.

Early in May Air Chief Marshal Longmore had been recalled to England —an action 'most deeply regretted' by Cunningham—and was later replaced by Air Marshal A. W. Tedder. On 21st June, soon after the failure in the Western Desert and on the day Damascus fell, General Wavell learnt from Churchill that he was to change places with General Sir Claude Auchinleck, Commander-in-Chief in India. Afterwards Churchill wrote that he held Wavell responsible, in part or wholly, for the loss of Benghazi 'which had undermined and overthrown all the Greek projects on which we had embarked', and for failure in Crete and the Western Desert, and that he was displeased by Wavell's opposition to the reinforcement of Iraq from the Middle East and to the plan to invade Syria. But it was Churchill and his advisers in London who were responsible for the decision to denude North Africa to send an expedition to Greece, and it was the failure of that adventure that had led to the subsequent set-backs. Cunningham was 'desperately sorry' about the departure of Wavell whom he considered 'one of the great generals thrown up by the war, if not the greatest'. Soon the axe would fall also on General Dill, the Chief of the Imperial General Staff.

Among the three main military contingents in the Middle East—British, Australian and Indian—the Australians had carried a large share in the first six months of 1941. Now two of their three divisions were in need of rest and replenishment. Soon the 6th, the battalions lost in Crete now re-formed, joined the 7th in Syria, where a British Ninth Army was being formed.

In Tobruk the 9th Division continued to fight on what was now the most active front in the Middle East. Throughout May the positions in the Salient had been improved and the vigorous program of night patrolling continued. Morshead insisted that every forward unit must strive to gain and retain mastery of no-man's land. It was in this phase that the 'bush artillery' came into its own. Before the siege opened infantry units in Tobruk had begun to equip themselves with captured Italian guns, often in imperfect condition but with an inexhaustible supply of ammunition. In May one battalion, for example, possessed eleven guns, another nine, ranging up to 149-mm calibre.

In mid-May the garrison began to press forward more strenuously all along the line and particularly in the Salient; and, as a brigade instruction said, 'incessantly to exert pressure upon the enemy and relentlessly drive him back bit by bit on battalion fronts, under arrangements made within battalions'.

The Germans too were active and on 16th May attacked the northern corner of the Salient but without success. A counter-attack by three companies gained several posts in that area but they could not be held. In June the 20th Brigade pressed systematically and steadily forward and succeeded in shortening the line in the Salient by about 600 yards and this arduous process was continued until by early July the line round the Salient had been advanced by about 2,000 yards, leaving the Salient about 3,000 yards deep at its middle.

The ships supplying Tobruk in the face of enemy air attack had brought in only bare essentials in the weeks before BATTLEAXE, but the failure of that offensive made it necessary to greatly increase the monthly tonnage, at length to 170 tons a day on an average. To ease the supply problem the base personnel were drastically reduced in June and July until of a total garrison of 22,076 only 1,400 were in base units.

On 2nd August, in the belief that the enemy was thinning out along the Salient, an attack was launched by a company of the 2/43rd Battalion along the perimeter from the north and a company of the 2/28th Battalion from the south. In fact there were three German battalions in the Salient, facing two Australian battalions and the left flank of a third. The attack was carefully planned. It was supported by more than sixty guns but the enemy artillery swiftly replied, and his infantry were ready. The attack was gallantly pressed but failed with very heavy losses in the assaulting companies. This was the last effort to straighten the line. Thenceforward it was chiefly a task of holding the dented perimeter and making increasingly aggressive patrols into no-man's land and, for the navy, of keeping the supply line open. All the Australian destroyers (including the new *Napier*, *Nizam* and *Nestor*) took part in running supplies to Tobruk. The old Australian destroyers were now 'literally dropping to bits', yet one of them, *Vendetta*, made thirty-nine trips—the record. The following ships were sunk on the Tobruk run: the fast minelayer *Latona*, destroyers *Defender*, *Waterhen* (Australian), sloops *Auckland*, *Parramatta* (Australian), *Grimsby*, and twenty-one smaller vessels. Thus the only Australian ships sunk so far in the Mediterranean were lost on this service.

From July onwards Blamey, since 24th April occupying the dual appointment of Deputy Commander-in-Chief in the Middle East and Commander of the A.I.F., urged that the 9th Division should be withdrawn from Tobruk and the Australian divisions concentrated in the Australian Corps. It had been part of Blamey's instructions from his Government to avoid the dispersal of the A.I.F. Events had forced dispersal. At one stage in June part of the A.I.F. was in Tobruk, part in Palestine, part in Syria where some Australian formations and units were included in the 7th Australian and some in the 6th British Division, part in Cyprus. In addition Blamey strongly held the opinion that, in general, the Middle East forces had been dispersed in too many improvised forces and what was needed was a compact and powerful fighting force of full-strength divisions. He also wished to form in effect an Anzac Army of two strong corps of Anzac infantry and British armour. The Australian War Cabinet, fearing that its manpower would not stand the strain, would not agree to the raising of the new units needed to produce an Anzac Corps, but it consistently backed Blamey's request that the 9th Division be relieved. The request was supported first by the Menzies Government, then by one led by A. W. Fadden, then one led by Curtin. It brought Blamey into conflict with Auchinleck, who considered that the relief would unnecessarily endanger naval ships and impede preparations for a desert offensive. The discussion was transferred to Cabinet level with Churchill supporting Auchinleck's views and Curtin Blamey's. At this stage the main argument employed on the Australian side was that the troops were becoming physically weak and run-down. At length in August the 18th Brigade Group, including a British and an Indian unit, was withdrawn to rejoin its own division—the 7th—in Syria, and was replaced by the fresh Polish Brigade. In September and October the 9th Division was replaced by the 70th British Division (a new name for the 6th British Division which had last fought in Syria). On the last night of the relief the convoy proceeding to Tobruk was attacked from the air and turned back with the result that the 2/13th Battalion remained at Tobruk until the siege ended.

The necessity for securing the Persian oilfields and the supply route through Persia to Russia and of expelling German agents who were assembling in Persia led in August to a rapid and economical occupation of that country by Indian and British troops from the south and Russian from the north. The Australian manned H.M.S. *Kanimbla* and H.M.A.S. *Yarra* were part of a motley naval force which covered the landings, immobilised the small Persian Navy and captured Axis merchantmen interned in Persian waters.

In the summer of 1941 Auchinleck's forces in North Africa and the Levant were greatly strengthened as a result of transfer of formations from Abyssinia; the re-equipment and reinforcement of divisions which had suffered heavy losses in Greece, Crete and the desert; and arrivals from India, the United Kingdom and South Africa. There were now three Indian divisions in Persia and Iraq, two Australian divisions in Syria and one in Palestine, the 5th Indian Division in Cyprus; the Eighth Army, of six divisions—7th Armoured, 70th British, 4th Indian, 2nd New Zealand, 1st and 2nd South African—and several independent brigades had now been formed in the Western Desert. The Eighth Army possessed considerably more tanks than Rommel; the Desert Air Force was about equal in numbers to the enemy force. Incidentally, there were now in the Middle East, in addition to No. 3 Squadron R.A.A.F., two Australian squadrons—Nos. 450

and 451—formed under the Empire Air Training Scheme. However, at this stage they were Australians in little more than name, the Australian Air Board's unwillingness to transfer pilots from regular R.A.A.F. squadrons such as No. 3 to Empire scheme squadrons having delayed their manning by Australians.

Learning that Rommel was planning an attack on Tobruk late in November Lieut-General Sir Alan Cunningham, commanding the Eighth Army, advanced the date of an offensive intended to roll up the Axis army and drive on to Tripoli. On 18th November the XXX Corps thrust across the frontier near Sidi Omar with Tobruk as an objective; on the right the New Zealanders attacked towards Bardia and Gambut. After nine days of heavy and costly fighting the attacking force linked with a group, including the 2/13th Battalion, which had attacked eastward from Tobruk. Rommel counter-attacked, and cut Tobruk off again, but a British flanking move at length persuaded the enemy to abandon the whole battle area. By 10th December the Germans and Italians were in retreat. They stood west of Tobruk, but were forced back again, this time to the El Agheila position from which Rommel had begun his advance nine months before.[8]

Auchinleck announced that the siege of Tobruk had ended on 7th December, though in fact it had been ineffective for some days before. It had lasted eight months. Writing of his period of command Auchinleck said that 'freedom of embarrassment in the frontier area for four and a half months is to be ascribed largely to the defenders of Tobruk. Behaving not as a hardly pressed garrison but as a spirited force ready at any moment to launch an attack, they contained an enemy force twice their strength . . . they held back four Italian divisions and three German battalions from the frontier area from April until November.' The Australian historian of the siege wrote:

> If the greatest single factor in repelling the German assaults and holding the besiegers off was the steadfast, efficient and brave work of the field artillery which for some of the time was solely and for the whole time preponderantly from the British Army; if the greatest call on deep resources of courage was laid most often upon the anti-aircraft gunners who stood to their guns day and night even when they themselves were the direct target of the strike; if the most dreadful burden borne by the defenders was the constant manning of shallow and sun-scorched diggings and weapon-pits in the regularly bombed, bullet-raked Salient, in which to stand in daylight was to stand for the last time; these judgments only illustrate that each man had his own job in the conduct of the defence. The spontaneous respect of all arms and services for the performance of the others and the loyalty with which they combined were the things that made Tobruk strong in defence and dangerous to its besiegers . . .
>
> That such success was achieved was due most of all to Morshead's own insistence on an aggressive conduct of the defence; his determination that the enemy should be attacked wherever he came within reach; his single-minded rigid resolve, to which he adhered in the face of counsels for a more flexible defence, that his forces should never yield ground nor give quarter, that if any place was wrested from them, they should not relent until they recaptured

[8] In Cyrenaica the 9th Division suffered 3,349 casualties including 788 killed; in Cyrenaica, Greece and Crete the 6th Division had lost 750 killed; in Syria the 7th Division and attached units lost 416 killed.

it. There were some misjudgments. Sometimes the tasks prescribed could not be done with the means given. Nonetheless Morshead's policy left his opponent no other choice than to let the garrison forces keep their ground, at least until he felt able to mount a massive attack.[9]

By October practically all the A.I.F. was away from the battle fronts and the Australian naval force in the Mediterranean had diminished. Between August and October the old destroyers were sent home for refit, leaving only *Hobart* (which had replaced *Perth* in August) and the Australian-manned 'N'-class destroyers in the Mediterranean. One of these, *Nestor*, spent October and November undergoing engine repairs in England. On 15th December, when off Cape St Vincent on her way to the Mediterranean, she saw a submarine on the surface and sank it; it was *U 127*, the first submarine to be destroyed during the war by a ship of the Royal Australian Navy.

During 1941 Australians took an increasing part in the air war over western Europe and the Atlantic. In January it was decided to form 25 Canadian, 18 Australian and 6 New Zealand squadrons within the R.A.F., as crews trained under the Empire scheme became available. From April to December nearly 3,000 Australian aircrew and 1,500 ground staff passed through the reception centre in England, and in the same period three fighter squadrons (Nos. 452, 456 and 457) and three bomber (455, 458, 460) were formed in England; as mentioned two fighter squadrons were formed in the Middle East; and one (453) in Malaya. It was difficult to co-ordinate the formation of such squadrons and the intake of suitably-trained crews and sometimes, in the early stages, there were few Australians in the nominally Australian squadrons, nor were the men themselves greatly interested in the aspirations of their seniors at home who wished Australians to be grouped together in their own units.

The most urgent task of the Air Force in Britain in 1941 was to assist the Navy to protect the Atlantic convoys on which Britain's life depended. Sinkings by an expanding U-boat fleet rose to a perilous level during the first half of 1941. In April, when, for example, 249,375 tons of shipping were

[9] Maughan, pp. 400-1.

Pilots of No. 452 Squadron in the dispersal hut at Kenley R.A.F. Station in England, late in 1941.

sunk in the North Atlantic alone, a new policy was adopted of making systematic air sweeps aimed at intercepting the submarines far from the shipping lanes and preventing them from congregating. As a result the number of submarines sighted trebled in the later months of 1941 and, partly as a result of these tactics, sinkings were reduced spectacularly. No. 10 Squadron R.A.A.F. continued to play an arduous part in these operations, and, at the same time, in common with No. 3 in the Middle East, acted in effect as an operational training unit in which a steady stream of young regular officers gained active service experience and then returned to Australia.

Early in 1941 the fighter force in Great Britain went over to the offensive. When the Battle of Britain ended, twenty-four out of the total of sixty-two fighter squadrons were fit for service only in quiet areas, but by mid-1941 there were eighty-four expert fighter squadrons. Patrols over occupied territory became stronger and more aggressive; in May, when the Germans delivered their last big bombing raids on English cities before concentrating for the invasion of Russia, sixteen squadrons took part in a single offensive patrol; and after the German attack on Russia opened these forays were intensified. The first Australian fighter squadron to be formed under the Empire scheme, No. 452, rapidly gained fame, in August destroying more German aircraft than any other squadron in Fighter Command.

Britain's bomber force was still far too small to do important damage to German industry or transport. The year 1941 was a period of experiment and training, often bought at high cost. As a rule raids were made by fewer than fifty aircraft. The British factories had concentrated on making fighters so that, in June, whereas there were eighty-four fighter squadrons there were only forty-nine bomber squadrons. A vastly larger force would be needed if Germany was to be effectively attacked from the air, or if Europe was to be invaded.

At the beginning of December the Allies were in a far stronger position than six months before. The Russians had not only withstood the German onslaught but were themselves attacking. In North Africa a successful offensive had been carried through. The campaign against the German submarines seemed to have been won. Britain had gained a modest air superiority in Western Europe.

At this stage, on 8th December, Singapore time, Japan attacked British and American colonies in the Pacific and Far East.

It had been vital to deny the Middle East to the enemy, and Australian forces had played a large part in carrying out that task—relatively a far larger one than they or their leaders at home had foreseen. The navy had provided a substantial and highly-efficient reinforcement to the Mediterranean Fleet. The A.I.F. had contributed about a third of the infantry divisions in Wavell's army during the critical first half of 1941 and one or other of these had played a leading part in nearly all his campaigns. Incidentally the Australian forces in the Middle East had built up an asset of immense value for the defence of Australia against the Japanese. The existence of these veterans, who had fought Germans, Italians and French in Africa, Europe and Asia, at sea and in the air, meant that Australia now possessed leaders and men who were vastly more confident and expert than they would have been had they not gone overseas to fight against the more distant enemies.

Chapter 5 **Japan coming nearer**

During 1941, while the greater part of the A.I.F. and the Australian Navy were engaged in the Middle East, the southward advance of Japan had been causing increasing anxiety at home. The Japanese Army had marched into northern Indo-China in September 1940. It was because the situation in the Far East seemed so threatening that the Australian Government had decided to contribute a brigade of infantry to the garrison of Malaya, where it already had three air force squadrons, and decided that the Prime Minister should go to London to confer with Churchill.

Australian interest in defence against Japan had always largely concentrated on Singapore. Successive Australian Governments had been assured that in time of need a British battle fleet would be sent there, whence it should defeat any Japanese attempt to advance into the Indian Ocean or the South-West Pacific—a strange notion since more than 2,000 miles separated Singapore from the nearest Japanese island bases in the Pacific. The problem remained of providing Malaya with an air force and army strong enough to hold out until such a fleet arrived. At the time of the October conference at Singapore, mentioned earlier, there were eighty-eight aircraft in Malaya and Burma, and most of them were outdated; the conference decided that 582 were needed for successful defence. At that time the military force in Malaya included the few battalions which had formed the peace-time garrison, plus an Indian brigade sent there at the outbreak of war and two battalions withdrawn from Shanghai in August 1940 as a result of Japanese pressure; but the conference estimated that twenty-six battalions and the necessary supporting units would be needed to provide a sufficient garrison—if the 582 aircraft had been supplied.

The garrison of Malaya was substantially increased in the seven months after the October conference. The 11th Indian Division arrived before the end of the year, the headquarters of Major-General Gordon Bennett's 8th Australian Division and the 22nd Brigade Group of that division in February, the 9th Indian Division in March and April. In May arrived the III Indian Corps headquarters under Lieut-General Sir Lewis Heath, who had recently commanded the 5th Indian Division in the successful operations against the Italians in Abyssinia. There were now twenty-four battalions—almost the number required—but air reinforcements had been few: two fighter squadrons armed with American Buffaloes and manned chiefly by pilots from the bomber squadrons already in Malaya had been formed and two more were being formed. In addition there were only four regiments of field artillery to support the eight infantry brigades whereas a normal allocation would have been at least eight. In 1939 there had been enough artillery in all India to complete only from three to four divisions.

INDIA
Calcutta
BURMA
Akyab
Toungoo
Rangoon
Mingaladon
Moulmein
THAILAND
Tavoy
Tenasserim Pen.
Mergui
Andaman I.
Victoria Point
Kra Isthmus
Bangkok
Gulf of Siam
Hanoi
CHINA
INDO CHINA
Saigon
Camranh B.
Hainan
Hong Kong
Formosa
Singora
Patani
Kota Bharu
Sabang I.
Alor Star
MALAYA
Kuala Lumpur
Singapore
SUMATRA
Banka I.
Palembang
Sunda Str.
Oosthaven
Batavia
JAVA
Surabaya
INDIAN
OCEAN
Singkawang
Kuching
Sarawak
Miri
Labuan
Brunei
BORNEO
Samarinda
Balikpapan
Tarakan
Vigan
Lingayen G.
Luzon
Aparri
Manila
PHILIPPINE
ISLANDS
Legaspi
Leyte
Mindanao
Davao
Menado
Ternate
Morotai
Halmahera
CELEBES
Kendari
Macassar
Ambon
Banda Sea
Flores
Koepang
Portuguese
TIMOR
Dutch
Timor Sea
Tanimbar Is.
Manokwari
Babo
NEW GUINEA
Wewak
Merauke
Lae
Pt. Moresby
Thursday I.
Horn I.
Rabaul
New Ireland
New Britain
Millingimbi
Darwin
Cooktown
Broome
AUSTRALIA
PACIFIC
OCEAN
Marianas
Saipan
Tinian
Guam
Yap
Palau
Caroline
Islands
Truk
ELAINE OATES

Anglo-American staff conversations about plans for co-operation in a war in which Britain and the United States should be engaged against Germany and Japan simultaneously had been held at intervals since 1937. At one of these, in May 1939, the American naval staff was informed that if Britain was fighting Germany and Italy it would be impossible to send a battle fleet to Singapore, and thenceforward plans were based on that assumption. On 16th January 1941 President Roosevelt, after consultation with his Secretaries of State, War, and Navy, and his Chiefs of Staff, had issued a general strategical directive which stated that, in the event of war against Germany and Japan, America would stand on the defensive in the Pacific with the Fleet based on Hawaii, there would be no naval reinforcement of the Philippines, and 'the Commander of the Asiatic Fleet would have discretionary authority as to how long he could remain based in the Philippines and as to his direction of withdrawal—to the East or to Singapore'.[1] At staff talks in London in September 1940 and at Washington in January-March 1941 a difference of opinion between the American and British naval leaders became manifest. The British delegates wished America to send some warships to Singapore, where Britain could now not afford to send a naval force strong enough to counter the Japanese fleet, but the Americans did not wish to divide their main fleet. 'It was agreed that for Great Britain it was fundamental that Singapore be held; for the United States it was fundamental that the Pacific Fleet be held intact.'[2] At the same talks a basic strategical decision, already implied in the President's directive, was reached: that the Atlantic and European area should be considered the decisive one, and if Japan entered the war the strategy in the Far East would be defensive, though the Pacific Fleet would be employed 'in the manner best calculated to weaken Japanese economic power, and to support the defence of the Malay barrier by diverting Japanese strength away from Malaysia'.[3]

In February the Australian Chiefs of Staff had advised the War Cabinet that Australia's area of responsibility should include Timor and Ambon and that the whole of the 8th Division should be retained for service in Australia and the Far East and arrangements for its transfer to the Middle East cancelled. The War Cabinet agreed. At this time the War Cabinet was told that President Roosevelt had informed the British Ambassador, Lord Halifax, that if the United States were at war with Japan the main theatre would be the Atlantic and Europe and she would have to fight a 'holding war' in the Pacific; in this way the Australian Ministers learnt of this basic strategic decision, but it seems doubtful whether they and their advisers realised its full implications at the time. Later in February at another defence conference at Singapore, this one attended by Dutch representatives also, the Australian proposal to prepare to reinforce Timor and Ambon was accepted.

As an outcome of this conference and of the German raid on Nauru the

[1] Quoted in M. S. Watson, *Chief of Staff: Pre-War Plans and Preparations* (1950), p. 124, a volume in the official series *United States Army in World War II*.

[2] Quoted in S. E. Morison, *The Rising Sun in the Pacific* (1948), p. 50, a volume in the series *History of United States Naval Operations in World War II*.

[3] Quoted in Morison, p. 51.

Australian War Cabinet, also in February, decided to send an A.I.F. battalion to garrison Rabaul, capital of the mandated territory of New Guinea. Hitherto the only military force in the territory had been a detachment of about eighty men of a small part-time force, the New Guinea Volunteer Rifles, led by officers of the old A.I.F. who had settled in New Guinea after the war. (The Rifles also had detachments on the New Guinea mainland.) Thus the 2/22nd Battalion arrived at Rabaul in March and April. Later two 6-inch coast defence guns, two 3-inch anti-aircraft guns and their crews were added to Rabaul's defences. In July the remote and thinly-manned Australian outpost line was extended right and left by posting sections of the 1st Independent Company at Vila in the New Hebrides, at Tulagi and Buka in the Solomons, in New Ireland and at Manus in the Admiralties; and later the 3rd Independent Company (333 strong) was sent to Noumea. Early in December an air force squadron armed with four Hudson bombers and ten Wirraways was sent to Rabaul.

Along the outpost line was another small but very valuable force. In the 1920s the Naval Intelligence Division had organised and instructed a network of 'coastwatchers' chosen from suitable people living in Papua and New Guinea and in remote places round the Australian coast. In the islands they were recruited from patrol officers, planters, missionaries and others. When war broke out this secret service was about 800 strong, most of them on the Australian mainland. A retired naval lieut-commander, E. A. Feldt, who had had long experience in New Guinea, was posted to Port Moresby to enlarge the organisation and equip the coastwatchers with portable teleradios. At length there was a line of watchers with teleradios spread out at intervals of 50 to 150 miles all along the chain of islands from the Ninigo group in the north-west, through the Admiralties and New Ireland to the southern Solomons, and similar inner lines along the north coast of the New Guinea mainland and along New Britain—about sixty posts in all.

In London in March Menzies had sought and obtained from the United Kingdom Chiefs of Staff a detailed statement about the prospects of reinforcing Malaya; particularly he asked when warships and fighter squadrons equipped with Hurricanes might go there, and whether agreement could not be reached with the United States to inform Japan that if she advanced beyond a certain line it would entail war. Menzies was informed by the Chiefs of Staff that there were then 118 aircraft in Malaya, whereas, in their view, 336 were needed. They added: 'The majority of the 450 shore-based aircraft which the Japanese can marshal against us are of obsolete types, and . . . we have no reason to believe that Japanese standards are even comparable with those of the Italians.' Hurricanes could be sent to the Far East only at the expense of the Middle East, they said, but the American Buffalo fighter 'would probably prove more than a match for any Japanese aircraft'. (Better circulation of Intelligence then available would have prevented this error which, however, was typical of the European tendency at the time to underestimate the technical achievements and military ability of the Japanese, and indeed of all Oriental people. As for naval reinforcements: at the opening of a war with Japan a battle-cruiser and a carrier would be sent to the Indian Ocean. Ability to do more would have to be judged on the situation at the time.

The responsibility of the recently-appointed Commander-in-Chief in the Far East, Air Chief Marshal Sir Robert Brooke-Popham embraced not only Malaya, but Burma, British Borneo and Hong Kong. In Burma he had one weak division and it was estimated that two more were needed; there was only a very small air force. The garrison of Borneo in May comprised one Indian battalion, of Hong Kong two British and two Indian battalions. It was considered that reinforcement of Borneo and Hong Kong would be unwise from a purely military point of view unless America was likely to be allied with Britain in a war against Japan and ready to strongly defend the Philippines, and at this stage the American general staff was convinced that the Philippines could not be held.

Of the surviving colonial Powers in the Far East Holland controlled some 53,000,000 Asian people, Great Britain about 26,000,000 and the United States 17,000,000. The Philippines, the main part of the American empire, had reached somewhat the same degree of progressive realisation of responsible government as had India, except in one important field—defence. Whereas there was a veteran Indian Army which had now sent five divisions abroad and had more in training at home, only a beginning had been made with the establishment of a Philippine Army. In 1935 General Douglas MacArthur, formerly Chief of Staff of the United States Army, had been appointed Military Adviser in the Philippines. Conscription was introduced, an officers' school established, and it was hoped by ten years after 1st January 1937 (when the first conscripts began training) to have an army of 200,000 Filipinos. By 1941 about 160,000 men had been through the training camps. There were also in the Philippines, in May 1941, an American garrison which included some locally-enlisted 'Philippine Scouts', two American army regiments, a regiment of marines, and a small air force. The American Asiatic Fleet, based on Manila, included three cruisers, a flotilla of destroyers and one of submarines. Farther east lay the American Pacific Fleet, based on Pearl Harbour in Hawaii. In May, after the transfer of three battleships to the Atlantic, it included 9 battleships and 3 aircraft carriers. Japan possessed 11 battleships and 10 carriers.

In February 1941 the German Foreign Minister, Ribbentrop, had urged upon the Japanese Ambassador in Berlin that Japan should attack Singapore at once and secure her position by the time of the peace treaty—he pictured an early peace treaty dictated by Germany, with Japan like Italy receiving the crumbs from the Fuehrer's table. Germany's object in trying to push Japan into the war was to ensure the defeat of Britain, compel the Soviet Union to disperse her forces, and deter the United States. The German leaders recognised that a Japanese offensive against Britain might have the opposite effect on the United States to the one intended but considered that the risk had to be taken. On 4th April Hitler himself met Matsuoka, the Japanese Foreign Minister, who was visiting Berlin, and urged upon him also that Japan should attack Singapore and accept the risk of the United States entering the war. Matsuoka said that 'Japan would do her utmost to avoid a war with the United States'. Although he was encouraging Japan to strike, Hitler instructed his subordinates that Japan must not be told about his coming attack on the Soviet Union.

Matsuoka was probably sincere when he said that Japan wished to avoid war with America: he appears to have been convinced that the isolationist

Americans would not go to war if they could possibly avoid it, and he considered that Japan could attain her objectives without fighting the United States. The Japanese military leaders, however, did not trust their diplomats and did not confide in them, nor did they confide in their German and Italian allies. In January Admiral Yamamoto, commander of the Japanese Combined Fleet, had ordered his staff to study the possibility of a surprise attack on Pearl Harbour by carrier-borne aircraft. That month news reached London and Washington from Tokyo that Japan seemed likely soon to enter the war, the American Ambassador, Joseph C. Grew, specifically mentioning that he had heard talk of an attack on Pearl Harbour. On 13th April Japan signed a pact of non-aggression with Russia, thus (if she could trust Russia) securing her northern flank in preparation for a southward advance. Early in May Allied Intelligence staffs learnt that a Japanese force of three divisions was being concentrated on the island of Hainan evidently as the spearhead of some thrust to the south.

In Australia during the first six months of 1941 the Government was called upon to make few decisions of great moment. It was a period in which policies established in the last half of 1940 were carried through. The oversea forces had been designed on as large a scale as reliance on volunteers would permit. In January 1941 the navy was 16,000 strong. Of its six cruisers three were in the Mediterranean or the Atlantic, three in the Pacific or Indian Oceans; the five destroyers were in the Mediterranean. The A.I.F. contained four infantry divisions and corps troops equivalent to a fifth, and an armoured division was being formed. It had 62,000 men overseas and 53,000 at home. As had happened in 1915, news that Australians were in action produced a rush of volunteers, and in the six months from March to August 40,500 were enlisted. In January 25,000 of the militia were on full-time duty, and the regular forces and garrison battalions were 13,000 strong. The air force numbered 33,000, and, in addition, 7,900 men had been selected as aircrew and were waiting to be called up when there was room in the training schools. In January the nineteen-squadron plan was achieved.

The objectives of the arms production program then included the manufacture, each year, of 840 25-pounders, 300 anti-aircraft guns, 1,500 2-pounder anti-tank guns, 3,000 Vickers machine-guns, 6,000 Brens, 100,000 rifles, 1,000 tanks, 2,000 carriers—projects that would have seemed incredible in 1939. The labour force directly employed making aircraft, munitions and warships in June 1941 numbered about 53,000. By that month all these weapons and fighting vehicles except tanks, 25-pounders and Brens were being delivered. By August new projects were being undertaken: the manufacture of the 6-pounder anti-tank gun, of the locally-designed Owen sub-machine-gun, and the Bofors light anti-aircraft gun. By June the aircraft factories had delivered 313 Wirraways or Wackett trainers and 461 Tiger Moths, but had then not yet completed a bomber—the first Beaufort bomber would be delivered in August and the first twin-row Wasp engine in November. The air force squadrons were still poorly equipped. Their only fighter type was the Wirraway which was actually only a training machine. Virtually the only front-line machines received from overseas from the outbreak of war up to June 1941 had been 100 Hudson bombers and four Catalina flying boats, though there were in the training schools some hundreds of obsolete light bombers which might be used in a crisis.

By September 1941 the navy had sixty-eight ships in commission ranging from cruisers to a tug, and 19,740 men were serving. Of these, 8,640 were in ships on the Australia Station, 3,500 in Australian ships overseas, 300 in the armed merchant cruiser *Kanimbla*, 900 on service in the Royal Navy or in armed merchant ships, and 6,400 in Australian shore establishments. In July Australia had agreed to man eight new British destroyers. Eventually seven were manned: *Napier*, *Nizam*, *Norman*, *Nepal*, *Nestor*, *Quiberon* and *Quickmatch*.

The naval building program at home was now making rapid progress: by March 1941 3 destroyers, 2 sloops, 26 corvettes and 3 boom vessels had been or were being built; in eight days of October, for example, four corvettes were launched—*Gawler* on the 4th, *Broome* on the 6th, *Cairns* on the 7th and H.M.I.S. *Punjab* on the 11th. By July a total of sixty corvettes had been ordered plus some frigates of 1,420 tons. Seven yards were now building naval vessels. Four-inch naval guns to arm some of the corvettes were being produced, though at a slow rate. At last, in March 1941, a decisive step was taken towards establishing merchant shipbuilding on a scale comparable with that attained in the First World War. Four yards—Mort's, Cockatoo, Evans Deakin and the Melbourne Harbour Trust's—were each given orders for two 9,000-ton vessels and the first keels were laid in July.

What were Australian leaders and people thinking and feeling at this time? The newspaper files give an impression of impatience and irritation, and there are many apparent contradictions. Newspapers were upbraiding Ministers for not taking sterner measures to intensify the war effort. Ministers were bombarding the people with vague exhortations to realise that 'the position' was 'very grave' and an 'all-in effort' essential. The Acting Prime Minister and the Leader of the Opposition combined in a particularly ominous-sounding appeal of this kind in February 1941—at a time when the people were reading news of one victory after another. A few days earlier the Chief of the General Staff, General Sturdee, had arrived from Cairo and announced in an interview that the Italians did not want to fight and that the biggest fight in North Africa was against the terrain not the Italians. This seemingly-authoritative statement, with its promise of sweeping and bloodless victories, was confusing to people who were reading long casualty lists in each day's paper. The defeats in Greece and Crete produced much newspaper criticism of the higher management of the war, though the extracts cabled from London newspapers contained sharper criticism than was voiced in the Australian Press or in the Commonwealth Parliament. Political leaders responded by charging the people generally with 'complacency'. Evidently in search of a cure for this alleged malady the Department of Information in June published a series of maudlin advertisements. One showed a large-eyed child caressing a dog; and carried, in big letters, the following ambiguous legend:

> From a little girl in England whose father fought at Dunkirk. Later he visited Sydney. He left on a boat and has not been heard of since.
> Please Tell Daddy the Bombs Killed My Doggie.
> All in Australians. This Can Happen Here.

From another such advertisement a woman's anxious face stared out and beneath it appeared:

> I believe that I should no longer excuse myself as a woman from facing up to and thinking about the full horror that threatens my home, my family and my children.

The impression existed also in America that the Australians were in need of reassurance. In May 1941 four American cruisers and some destroyers visited Australian and New Zealand ports and were given the enthusiastic reception usually given to visiting naval squadrons. In 1948 the American naval historian wrote, concerning this cruise: 'At the request of the [State] Department, the Navy sent four cruisers and a destroyer squadron to visit New Zealand, Australia, Fiji, and Tahiti, in order to demonstrate to Japan our solidarity with the British Commonwealth and hearten our Antipodean friends, who felt forgotten and virtually abandoned by Mother England.'[4] On the other hand, at that time volunteers were streaming into the recruiting offices and there were many indications of pride in the achievements of Australian forces overseas. It is notoriously difficult for diplomats, moving in a limited circle, to gauge the mood of a foreign people, and it was specially difficult for Americans, anxious to extend their own influence, to discern the nature of the sentiments then felt by most Australians towards England.

It seems that in Australia during 1941, as in England in 1940, the exhortation of the people by the political leaders and their interest in the people's 'morale' were indicative mainly of the weight of the politicians' own perturbations and anxieties, and that the people were well able to endure the shocks of war. For example, on 8th May the Leader of the Opposition, Curtin, suggested at a meeting of the Advisory War Council that the Allies should evacuate the Mediterranean before the British Fleet was hemmed in, and instead should strengthen the forces in the Far East. Certainly the troops and probably most of the people would have indignantly repudiated such a proposal, had they known of it.

The attack on the Soviet Union had the effect, in Australia as elsewhere, of bringing the Communists and their followers enthusiastically behind the war effort. Hitherto this small but active and regimented group had done what it could to impede the Government. Now its pronouncements echoed those of the right-wing leaders—to the embarrassment of the conservative wing of the Labour Party which was resolved that even the accidents of war should not produce an unholy alliance with the Communists. Because of his insistence on joining a Communist-led 'Australian-Soviet Friendship League' Maurice Blackburn, an otherwise-revered Labour member of the House of Representatives, was expelled from his party.

Probably a sufficient reminder that a war was in progress was provided by the daily casualty lists in which in June the names totalled up to 700 a day—the killed and missing in Crete, the killed and wounded in the May fighting in Tobruk, and, late in the month, the casualties in Syria. By the end of June the total Australian losses in six months in the Middle East exceeded 12,000.

The continued depredations of German raiders in the Pacific and Indian

[4] Morison, *The Rising Sun in the Pacific*, p. 56.

Australian War Memorial

Workmen erecting a brick screen to protect a Brisbane city building in December 1941 soon after the outbreak of war with Japan.

Oceans also brought the war home to Australians, and references to them were employed by Ministers in their battle against 'complacency'. In January 1941 two German raiders—*Orion* and *Komet*—were operating in the Pacific and two—*Pinguin* and *Atlantis*—in the Indian Ocean. A fifth raider had left Germany on 3rd December and was on her way to the Indian Ocean. In an earlier chapter the story of the *Pinguin* was carried to November 1940 when she sank three large freighters in the Indian Ocean. She then steamed far to the south-west, and captured a Norwegian whaling fleet consisting of a factory ship, a supply ship and eleven whale catchers. Prize crews took the whaling fleet to France, except for one catcher (350 tons) which was renamed *Adjutant* and remained with *Pinguin*. On 8th May the *Pinguin* was found and sunk by the cruiser H.M.S. *Cornwall* in the north-west Indian Ocean. In eleven months she had sunk or captured thirty-one ships totalling 156,000 tons.[5] On 4th March the cruiser *Canberra* had encountered two German supply ships in the Indian Ocean, *Coburg* and *Ketty Brovig*. When she opened fire on them they were promptly scuttled. The *Komet*—the raider which had shelled Nauru—steamed thence far to the south-east seeking ships on the New Zealand-Panama route, but found none. She then went south to within sight of the Antarctic Continent and on to Kerguelen where she met the *Pinguin*, the *Adjutant* and the supply ship *Alstertor* and took on stores. She cruised fruitlessly in the Indian Ocean until May when the *Adjutant* joined her. Together they headed for the Pacific. From a rendezvous at the Chatham Islands *Adjutant* boldly steamed to the entrance of Port Lyttelton (New Zealand) by night and there laid ten magnetic mines. She then went to Wellington and laid ten more there. The *Komet* sailed north-east, and on 14th August sank the *Australind* (5,020 tons)—her first victim for eight months. In the next five days she captured the Dutch *Kota Nopan* (7,322 tons) and sank the *Devon* (9,036 tons). She then turned about to evade pursuit, and, on 20th September, met the raider *Atlantis* which had recently entered the Pacific after a successful career in the Indian and Atlantic Oceans and had captured the Norwegian *Silvaplana* (4,793 tons). The *Komet* set off homewards via Cape Horn and at length arrived at Hamburg on 30th November. The *Atlantis*, however, was sunk by the cruiser *Devonshire* near Ascension Island on the 22nd of that month.

In February the *Orion* had set out from the Marianas for the Indian Ocean. Off the Solomons she was seen by a flying boat of the R.A.A.F. but changed course and evaded further discovery. She gained no victims in the Indian Ocean and was at length recalled. On the way home she sank one ship—her only success in nine months.

At the end of May the Australian Prime Minister, Mr Menzies, arrived home after four months spent visiting the troops and the battlefields and consulting Churchill and other British leaders. He returned full of newly-acquired knowledge and new plans. Within a few days after his return he appealed again, as he had done from London in April, for an all-party government, but Labour again would not agree. Next he set about shaping the administration on lines suggested by the observations he and his lieutenants had made in England. Five new departments were created: Aircraft Production, Transport, War Organisation of Industry, Home Security and External Territories. This entailed increasing the number of Ministers from twelve, with four Assistant Ministers, to nineteen.

The task of the Department of War Organisation of Industry was to discover what industries could be reduced or diverted without impairing 'the real strength of the nation', to devise ways of doing so, and to relate

[5] In 1940 disguised German surface raiders sank fifty-four ships totalling 366,644 tons; in 1941, forty-four ships totalling 226,527 tons. In 1941 submarines sank 2,172,000 tons of Allied and neutral shipping, aircraft 1,017,400 tons, mines 231,000 tons, surface craft other than disguised raiders 202,000 tons; ships totalling 421,000 tons were sunk by other or unknown agents.

the consequent limitation of civilian production to the needs of military production. Menzies gave this portfolio to E. S. Spooner, an accountant and company director who was a newcomer to the Federal Parliament but had been a Minister in New South Wales for a number of years. As a further step towards the organisation of industry W. C. Wurth, since 1939 chairman of the New South Wales Public Service Board, was, in July, appointed Director of Manpower Priorities.

For the past six months it had been realised that shortage of manpower would soon become acute. At the end of 1940 70,000 unemployed workers were registered but nearly all of these were unskilled. A parliamentary committee which examined the problem in February 1941 decided that by the end of the year 112,000 more men would be needed—31,000 by the Services and 81,000 by munitions factories. The Government might decide what the Services needed, but it was left to the individual citizen to decide what the Services got, and from March until the end of the year not 31,000 but 64,000 men enlisted in the A.I.F. alone.

In September the War Cabinet received a new statement of the manpower requirements of the Services and their attendant factories. It was forecast that by 30th June 1943 the Services, Aircraft Production and Munitions would need 794,000 men and 52,000 women, and that industries providing supplies for the munitions factories would need 60,000. The population contained only 1,140,000 men aged 18 to 60 who were not already engaged in the Services or war industry. To maintain the Services at their present level would require a total of 280,000 volunteers by September 1942.

Meanwhile plans were being made to divert or recruit large numbers of women to the Services or to essential industries. By July 1941 666,000 women were in employment, 100,000 more than in 1939, and in addition 24,000 were estimated to have left domestic service and found other work. It was planned to increase the number of women in the Services and the munitions factories from 13,000 to 52,000 in two years.

The wage-earners were now experiencing some of the benefits which war can confer. As a result of controls prices had risen only slightly. Real wages were higher than in 1939 and unemployment was almost non-existent. At the same time there had been little curtailment of the production of consumer goods or of services, and, despite the restriction of dollar imports, shortages were negligible.

Side by side with efforts to divert manpower to essential tasks went efforts similarly to divert capital, to economise in shipping, and to use less petrol and produce more coal. So sensitive was the Government, with its small majority in the House, to pressure from one direction or another that, up to June 1941, only timid measures had been taken to reduce consumption of petrol and these had produced negligible results. A 12-horsepower car was allowed 11 gallons a month, compared with 6 in England and 7½ in New Zealand. By April failure to restrict the use of private cars had produced a crisis: stocks of petrol had fallen to 63,000,000 gallons—about two months supply. In June it was decided to ration petrol in such a way as to allow each private car to travel only 1,000 miles a year.

Ever since the strike of March-May 1940 shortage of coal had been a recurring problem. At the end of 1940 there was only about six weeks supply throughout Australia. Such a shortage of reserves was the more dangerous because the New South Wales coal on which industry in other States largely depended had to be carried to them by sea, just as the iron ore from South Australia had to be carried to New South Wales by sea, and it was most desirable that stocks should be maintained to provide against possible interruption of coastal shipping. In February 1941 a Coal Board was established with, as chairman, Mr Justice Davidson, who before the war had been chairman of two Royal Commissions on the coal industry. It had power to issue directions concerning the production and distribution of coal. In August this board was replaced by a commission with enlarged powers, and presided over by N. R. Mighell, formerly chairman of the Repatriation Commission. Meanwhile on 30th January a Shipping Control Board, also with a judge (Sir Owen Dixon) as chairman, was given control of all Australian shipping, of any other ships in Australian waters, and of coastal freights.

The problems created by the breaks in the Australian railway gauges at State borders now faced the industrial planners as threateningly as they had always faced the military planners. The possibility of having to move coal and iron ore by rail had already, in November 1940, persuaded the Commonwealth to provide some money to assist in building a new bridge over the Hawkesbury River on the main Sydney-Brisbane line and duplicating the remaining single-line sections of the Melbourne-Sydney railway. In July the new Department of Transport took over the transport organisation established by the Defence Department and at length brought into being a War Railway Committee modelled on the War Railway Council which had long existed as a purely military agency. Thus in yet another field an organisation well-thought-out by the Army or by the Defence Department in peace, under the pressure of wartime expansion hived off as a civil department.

The German invasion of the Soviet Union was soon followed by far-reaching decisions in the Pacific area. On 2nd July the Japanese Emperor and Cabinet met and decided that a southward advance would be made. The United States Government, whose Naval Intelligence had broken the Japanese diplomatic code, knew of this decision within a few days but not whether Japan was resolved directly to provoke either America or Britain. On 21st July Japan obtained the French Government's agreement to a joint protectorate over Indo-China and to the entry of Japanese troops into south Indo-China. On the 26th President Roosevelt who, through intercepted radio messages, had known in advance of the terms being extracted from

Opposite: A Melbourne housewife doing her weekend shopping. One section of the community on whom the burden of war pressed most heavily, particularly after the outbreak of war with Japan, was the housewife. Absence of menfolk, shortages of transport and rationing of goods frequently forced her into the role of the tired packhorse, often combined with the dual responsibility of mother and father to a growing family.

Australian War Memorial

Indo-China, issued orders that Japanese assets in America be frozen—in effect that trade between the two countries would cease; and the British Commonwealth countries and, in some degree, the Netherlands Indies did likewise. Also on the 26th Roosevelt ordered that the Philippine Army should become part of the United States Army, General MacArthur taking command of all American army forces in the Far East. Since 80 per cent of Japan's oil came from the United States, either she must abandon her ambitions, including her hope of subduing China, or she must attack and, incidentally, conquer oil before her stocks—then only enough for about one year of war—were exhausted. On 6th August Japan presented her terms to the United States: the United States should resume trade with Japan, cease reinforcing her possessions in the eastern Pacific, discontinue helping the British and Dutch in the Far East, put pressure on China to negotiate, and recognise Japan's special status in Indo-China. These terms were not acceptable by the United States.

Later in August Roosevelt and Churchill met at Argentia Bay, Newfoundland, and signed the Atlantic Charter. On the other side of the world the Japanese Emperor and Cabinet met on 6th September and decided that if, by early October, there was no hope of Japan's terms being accepted Japan should get ready for war, but that diplomatic negotiations with the United States were to continue.

Throughout this period the Australian Government had been pressing for definite declarations by the United States and Britain which might halt Japan; it did not seem to realise the force of Roosevelt's challenge of 26th July. At the same time it urged the reinforcement of the Far Eastern garrisons, and had itself sent a further contribution to the forces in Malaya. A few weeks after Menzies' return the War Cabinet decided that the 27th Brigade should go to Malaya when ships were available, which would not be until August. When this had been done the only A.I.F. formation remaining in Australia apart from the embryo 1st Armoured Division would be the 23rd Brigade (the third brigade of the 8th Division) which was scheduled to send battalion groups to Ambon and Timor if Japan attacked.

In search of means of improving the home forces, the War Cabinet in August brought General Mackay back to Australia to command them. It was decided that the new commander would be equal in status to the Chief of the General Staff, General Sturdee, and would have direct access to the Minister, but that his authority would not extend over New Guinea or the Northern Territory. This was an inefficient arrangement. One satisfactory alternative would have been to appoint a commander-in-chief who would become the Government's principal military adviser with the Chief of the General Staff as his immediate subordinate; another to appoint an army commander, with two or three corps commanders, to train and deploy the main army formations. In any reorganisation aimed at making use of the recent battle experience gained by Australians in the Middle East it would not be enough to bring back one lonely general; a substantial cadre of commanders, staff officers and junior leaders would be needed. On the other hand, so long as the militia remained unmobilised, the keenest A.I.F. officers would not be enthusiastic about returning from an active theatre to serve with it, yet the longer the A.I.F. remained overseas the wider would become the separation between it and the militia. Mackay took up his appointment on 1st September, and set about improving the training of the militia and planning the defence of the vital area of eastern Australia.

It was mentioned in the last chapter that in May 1941 General Blamey had recommended that both an Australian Corps and an Anzac Corps should be formed in the Middle East, this necessitating the creation of additional corps and base units. The War Cabinet had postponed a decision on this proposal first until Menzies' return from London and then until the comprehensive review of manpower had been presented to it. It decided, on 2nd July, that Australia could not maintain a larger overseas force. In August General Sturdee, who based his calculations on an assumption that 7,400 reinforcements a month would be needed to maintain the A.I.F. in the Middle East and Malaya, informed the War Cabinet that the intake of volunteers was not enough to maintain the existing force (5,910 had been enlisted in July, but there would be 7,622 enlistments in August). On 13th August the War Cabinet decided that it might become necessary to abolish one of the infantry divisions in the Middle East, and on 17th September—Fadden had now become Prime Minister in circumstances described below—it specifically decided to convert the force in the Middle East into a corps of three divisions less a brigade group but including a tank brigade; and to maintain only the armoured units of the Armoured Division. If the 1st Armoured Division went to the Middle East its artillery, infantry and other units were to be provided by breaking up one of the infantry divisions there. The Curtin Ministry confirmed this decision, but, fortunately, it also summoned General Blamey home for conferences. At a meeting on 26th November, Blamey convinced the War Cabinet that the reduction of the A.I.F. would damage the force's morale and in any event was not necessary; there were enough reinforcements in the Middle East to maintain the corps during operations in the spring of 1942. The Ministers reversed their decision.

When he returned from London, Menzies had found that at home he had to cope not only with criticism from the Opposition but with a progressive disintegration within his own party. A small group of members on the Government side, with the support of some newspapers, notably the *Sydney Morning Herald*, circulated the criticism that, in general, the Government was not achieving enough, and, in particular, that Menzies lacked the qualities required in a wartime leader. The reconstruction of the Cabinet in June probably sharpened the discontent of certain members who were not allotted portfolios. On 17th July one junior member publicly demanded that Menzies should resign in favour of Fadden, the Country Party Leader.

On 9th August the Australian Cabinet learnt of the coming meeting between Churchill and Roosevelt in North America. Thereupon the Full Cabinet decided that Menzies should again go to London to discuss the Far Eastern problem. The deputy Leader of the Opposition, F. M. Forde, declared that the Advisory War Council should have been consulted before this decision was made. Under sharp fire from both sides Menzies on 22nd August again invited Curtin to join an all-party government and offered to serve under him if necessary. The offer was rejected, the Labour Party maintaining, as before, that a strong Opposition was a necessity. On the 28th after a meeting of the United Australia and Country Parties which Coles, one of the two Independent members on whom the Government depended for existence, afterwards described as 'nothing but a public lynching', it was announced that Menzies had resigned in favour of Fadden. Except for this exchange of chairs the Cabinet remained as it was; Fadden retained the Treasury, Menzies continued as Minister for Defence Co-ordination.

Fadden was commissioned on 29th August and on 17th September Parliament met. The Opposition vigorously attacked the Budget proposals. (No very important principle was involved.) At length Coles announced that he had come to the conclusion that the House of Representatives was unworkable and that he would vote against the Government; it was defeated on the Budget by 36 to 33, Wilson the other Independent also voting against it. On 3rd October Curtin became Prime Minister.

Ten years had passed since a Labour Government had been in power, and fifteen out of the nineteen new Ministers, including Curtin himself, had not held office before. Forde, the second-in-command, became Minister for the Army; Chifley became Treasurer, a portfolio for which he was well qualified by temperament and experience; Evatt became Attorney-General. The other members of the War Cabinet were J. A. Beasley (Supply and Development), N. J. O. Makin (Navy and Munitions) and A. S. Drakeford (Air).

In September Fadden's War Cabinet had decided to send Earle Page, a former Prime Minister and an eminent member of the Country Party, to London to represent Australia at the British War Cabinet, and, specifically, to seek the reinforcement of Singapore. The Curtin Government confirmed this decision. On his way to London Page visited Singapore and General MacArthur at Manila. Early in November he was in London pressing for more naval and air reinforcement of Malaya, and keeping his colleagues at home closely informed about British Cabinet discussions and decisions. When he arrived, however, the nature of that reinforcement of the Far East in which Australia was most deeply interested — the battle fleet — had already been decided.

Soon after the German attack on the Soviet Union the British Admiralty had decided that the time had come to send such a fleet to the Far East. By December Britain would have sixteen capital ships — five of the *Queen Elizabeth*-class and four of the 'R'-class all built in World War I; *Nelson* and *Rodney*, built in the 1920s; two battle cruisers, *Renown* and *Repulse;* and three new battleships, *King George V*, *Prince of Wales* and *Duke of York*. All but one of the *Queen Elizabeth's* had long formed the backbone of the Mediterranean Fleet. There were strong reasons for retaining at least two new battleships and a battle cruiser always ready in home waters to counter the powerful and modern *Tirpitz*, and other fast German ships. The Admiralty planned, therefore, to send to the Far East *Nelson, Rodney, Renown* and the four older 'R'-class battleships, with two or three aircraft carriers. Churchill stepped in, however, and proposed that 'a small but very powerful and fast force' should be sent: one of the new battleships, one battle cruiser, and one aircraft carrier. He overruled the Admiralty. Instead of seven capital ships and two or three aircraft carriers, two capital ships (*Prince of Wales* and *Repulse*) and one aircraft carrier (*Indomitable*) were chosen. The *Indomitable* was damaged while on a training cruise and could not join the squadron. On 2nd December the two capital ships arrived at Singapore, attended by only four destroyers, two of which were in such poor repair that they were immediately docked. Already at Singapore were two antiquated destroyers — the Australian *Vampire* and the British *Tenedos*.

While this attenuated and ill-balanced battle squadron was on the final stages of its voyage to Singapore the naval forces in the Mediterranean suffered losses which greatly reduced the possibility of reinforcing the Far East from that quarter. On 13th November the aircraft carrier *Ark Royal* and on the 25th November the battleship *Barham* were torpedoed and sunk.

Also on 25th November the loss was confirmed of the Australian cruiser *Sydney* (Captain J. Burnett), which had been silent for several days. From February 1941 *Sydney* had been employed mainly on patrols and escort duty in Australian waters. The knowledge that German raiders were still operating made it more necessary to retain some cruisers on the Australia Station. On 11th November *Sydney*, then in the Indian Ocean, had signalled her expected date of arrival at Fremantle as the 20th. No more was heard of her, but on the 24th a tanker picked up a raft carrying twenty-six German naval men from the raider *Kormoran*, and by 30th November six boats and two rafts had been found, carrying 315 German officers and ratings. By then it was known that about 4 p.m. on the 19th the *Kormoran* was 150 miles south-west of Carnarvon, Western Australia. When *Sydney* approached her *Kormoran* tried to pass herself off as a Dutch ship. At 5.30 *Sydney*, then less than a mile from *Kormoran*, made the signal: 'Show your secret sign.' To this Captain Anton Detmers of the German ship could not reply, and he immediately opened fire. Salvoes were exchanged and by about 5.45 both *Sydney* and *Kormoran* were crippled and on fire. At 6.25 Detmers ordered abandon ship. The glare from the burning *Sydney* was last seen about 10 p.m. and it must be assumed that she blew up. All that was found was a float recovered about 160 miles north-west of Carnarvon. Why Captain Burnett did not keep his distance from an unidentified ship remains a mystery.

Meanwhile the trickle of military reinforcements into Malaya had continued. Another Indian brigade landed a few weeks after the 27th Australian Brigade, and in November and early December much-needed field artillery reinforcements arrived—four regiments making a total of seven. The army commander in Malaya, Lieut-General A. E. Percival, now re-deployed his force. General Heath's III Indian Corps (9th and 11th Divisions) was concentrated in northern Malaya and the 8th Australian Division in Johore; two brigades were allotted to the defence of Singapore Island and one held in reserve. Not only was the main strength of General Percival's force concentrated far away in northern Malaya but a plan was made to advance into southern Thailand and anticipate the Japanese by occupying likely landing beaches and two airfields there. It was decided that this operation would be practicable if the British force had twenty-four hours start. British officers in plain clothes who went into Thailand to reconnoitre found that the Japanese 'were obviously doing the same thing. The two parties frequently met and even stayed together in the same rest houses.'[6] Until 5th December Brooke-Popham's instructions were that he should not invade Thailand without reference to London, but on that day the Chiefs of Staff authorised him to

[6] A. E. Percival, *The War in Malaya* (1949), p. 55.

undertake the invasion if a Japanese expedition violated any part of Thailand or was approaching with the apparent intention of landing in southern Thailand.

The arrival of Buffalo fighter aircraft had now made it possible to complete four fighter squadrons in Malaya, including No. 453, a squadron manned by Australian Empire Air Training Scheme men, and No. 488 a similar New Zealand squadron; also No. 21 R.A.A.F. was rearmed with Buffaloes in place of Wirraways. The Buffalo was no match for the Japanese Zero fighter — a fact now well known to Intelligence staffs in Singapore and Melbourne, but not widely enough circulated.

The appointment of General MacArthur to command all American Army forces in the Far East gave a new aspect to American planning in that area. Whereas the long accepted plan was that if the Japanese attacked in strength the defenders would attempt to hold only Manila Bay, MacArthur since February had been urging a more ambitious policy: defence of all Luzon and the Visayan Archipelago and the expansive waters they contained. In August the American Chief of Staff, General George C. Marshall, influenced by MacArthur's optimism and by the increasing output of long-range bombers (Flying Fortresses), decided to send considerable reinforcements to the Philippines. By the end of November MacArthur had 29,000 American Army troops (including the Philippine Scouts), 2,700 more were on the way, and 19,000 due to sail in December. These were in addition to about 80,000 men of the Philippine Army. The Americans and the Philippine Scouts formed one division and there was also the regiment of American marines. The Philippine Army, still poorly trained and equipped, was organised in eight under-strength divisions. The air force possessed 30 long-range bombers — Flying Fortresses — and 90 efficient fighters, and more were on the way; in Hawaii were 72 bombers and 149 fighters.

In September nine of the Flying Fortresses had been flown into the Philippines from Hawaii by way of Midway Island, Wake Island, Port Moresby and Darwin. Next month the Australian War Cabinet eagerly agreed to an American plan, which was kept secret, that an air route from Hawaii to Manila be established including bases suitable for heavy bombers at Rabaul, Port Moresby, Townsville and Darwin. Bombers used this route in November. On 1st December General H. H. Arnold, the Chief of the American Army Air Forces, decided to send every available B-17 (Flying Fortress) to the Philippines as soon as possible, and two squadrons of them left San Francisco on 6th December.

While America was planning to reinforce her advanced base in the Philippines, Britain was seeking Canadian reinforcements for her advanced base at Hong Kong. On 29th September the Canadian Government agreed to send two battalions to reinforce the four battalions (two British and two Indian) which were already there. This brought the garrison to about 14,000.

As mentioned, it had been decided in Tokyo on 6th September that Japan should get ready for war if agreement with America had not been reached by early October. The Premier, Prince Konoye, was inclined to give way to the United States but General Tojo and his army colleagues were resolved to go to war. The navy was lukewarm. Admiral Yamamoto, com-

Japan's initial assaults, 7th-8th December 1941

manding the Combined Fleet, foresaw early successes but eventual defeat if the war lasted long. On 16th October the Konoye Cabinet resigned and next day Tojo, a would-be Hitler, became Premier. He continued as Minister of War and took over the Home Ministry, thus controlling the police. An Imperial Conference on 5th November decided that if the negotiations with the United States had not produced a satisfactory result by 25th November Japan would make war on the United States and Britain. Despite the efforts of leading Japanese diplomats to avoid war, Tojo had his way. An Imperial Conference on 1st December confirmed the decision to go to war, and next day the Japanese forces were ordered to attack in accordance with plans already distributed.

In the coming offensive Japan could deploy a fleet somewhat more powerful in ships of all main types than the American Pacific Fleet. Her air forces (both navy and army possessed their own air arms) were numerically stronger and better equipped than those of the combined American, British and Dutch forces in the Far East. Her army, of some fifty divisions plus many smaller formations, was heavily committed in China, but it was decided that about ten divisions should be used for a southward offensive.

Japanese strategy was determined by Imperial General Headquarters, but it consisted of separate army and navy branches and those branches issued their own separate directives. There was no Japanese equivalent of the British Chiefs of Staff Committee or the American Joint Chiefs of Staff, and thus, if a difference of opinion developed between the two Japanese Services, there was no higher authority to resolve it. Tojo was Prime Minister, Minister for the Army, and, during 1942, also Chief of the Army General Staff, but he was not Minister for Defence in the British sense. He and his vice-chief met the Navy Minister (an admiral) and the two senior officers of the naval staff twice or thrice a week. After obtaining such agreement as proved possible on this level, the army staff's directives concerning the operations, of for example, the newly-formed *Southern Army*, which was to include all expeditionary forces outside China and Manchuria, went directly to the commander of that army, General Count Terauchi. The corresponding directives of the naval staff went to Yamamoto.

The Japanese staffs had been intensively planning the southward advance during 1941. Because they were running short of oil they considered that they must capture the oil-producing centres of Borneo, Sumatra and Java as soon as possible. After discussing various alternatives the staffs decided to attack the Philippines and Malaya more or less simultaneously and then advance into the Netherlands Indies. The intention was to occupy all territories within the arc stretching from the Kurile Islands through Wake Island, the Marshalls and New Guinea, and round the southern and western limits of the Indies to the western border of Burma.

Four main combined forces were to be employed: the *XXV Army*[7] supported by the *Second Fleet* was to take Malaya, including Singapore; the *XV Army* was to conquer Burma; the *XIV Army* supported by the *Third Fleet* was to take the Philippines; and finally the *XVI Army,* supported by combined naval forces, was to occupy the Netherlands Indies.

[7] A Japanese 'army' was the equivalent of a British or American 'corps'—from two to four divisions augmented by corps units.

The surprise attack on the American Pacific Fleet at Pearl Harbour was included in the proposed campaign and plans for it were ready by the end of October, as had been ordered. On 7th November the date of the attack was fixed at Sunday, 7th December at Pearl Harbour, because it was the practice of the American ships to spend the week-end in harbour. On 22nd November the Japanese *Carrier Fleet*, including six aircraft carriers, made a rendezvous in the Kurile Islands. Thence it steamed east until 3rd December when it turned south-east towards Hawaii.

In the opening stages there would be two subordinate operations: the *38th Division* advancing from the Chinese mainland was to take Hong Kong; the *Fourth Fleet*, with an amphibious force of marines and infantry, was to take Guam, Makin and Wake Islands. Late in January the *Fourth Fleet*, reinforced by a carrier division, then replenished after the Pearl Harbour raid, would cover a force which would take Rabaul and exploit south through the Solomons and west into New Guinea proper. The *Carrier Fleet* would then support the final operations in the Indies — against Ambon, Timor and Java. Having occupied their objectives the Japanese staffs proposed that their forces should go on the defensive. They counted on defeating any attempts to break through their perimeter and at length destroying their enemies' will to fight.

Chapter 6 **Defeat in the East**

During 7th December the Japanese convoy which was to fire the first shots in the Pacific War was steaming north-westward across the Gulf of Siam. Influenced by a report that the few slow ships some distance ahead of the main flotilla were steering north-west, Air Chief Marshal Sir Robert Brooke-Popham after conferring with Vice-Admiral Sir Geoffrey Layton decided that the convoy was on its way not to the Malayan coast but to the west coast of Indo-China in preparation for a later move against this area, and he decided that he would not yet be justified in ordering his troops to march into southern Thailand. About 8 p.m., however, news arrived at headquarters at Singapore that a Hudson aircraft (of No. 1 Squadron R.A.A.F.) had seen Japanese vessels off Singora steaming south and that another Hudson had been fired on by a Japanese cruiser. It was now too late to put into operation the plan to occupy Singora and the south Thailand airfields.

The *XXV Japanese Army*, allotted to the conquest of Malaya and Singapore, included the *Guards, 5th, 18th* and *56th Divisions*. The convoy now advancing across the Gulf of Siam contained six battalions and attached troops to land at Singora, three to land at Patani and three at Kota Bharu. In support were navy and air units with some 530 machines. There were 161 first-line aircraft in the British air force in Malaya.[1]

Soon after midnight on the 7th-8th, Malayan time, Japanese battalions began landing at Kota Bharu, where one Indian battalion—the 3/Dogras—was covering the beaches with the three other battalions of Brigadier B. W. Key's 8th Indian Brigade disposed southwards. The second brigade of the 9th Indian Division was about Kuantan some 200 miles farther south. The 11th Indian Division was in north-western Malaya. It was easy for the Japanese to achieve local superiority over forces so widely dispersed.

[1] Soon after the Japanese attack opened the air force squadrons were distributed thus:

Mainland of Malaya:		
Kota Bharu	No. 1 R.A.A.F. (General Reconnaissance)	12 Hudsons
Kuantan	No. 8 R.A.A.F. (General Reconnaissance)	12 Hudsons
	No. 60 (Bomber)	8 Blenheims
Alor Star	No. 62 (Bomber)	11 Blenheims
Sungei Patani	No. 21 (Fighter)	12 Buffaloes
	No. 27 (Night Fighter)	12 Blenheims
Singapore Island:		
Seletar	No. 36 (Torpedo Bomber)	12 Vildebeestes
	No. 100 (Torpedo Bomber)	12 Vildebeestes
	No. 205 (General Reconnaissance)	3 Catalinas
Sembawang	No. 453 R.A.A.F. (Fighter)	16 Buffaloes
Tengah	No. 34 (Bomber)	16 Blenheims
Kallang	No. 243 (Fighter), No. 488 R.N.Z.A.F. (Fighter)	32 Buffaloes

There were also three Catalinas manned by Dutch crews on Singapore Island.

THAILAND
MALAYA
KELANTAN
JOHORE
Singora
Haad Yai
Patani
Khlaung Ngae
Ban Sadao
Jitra
Alor Star
Muda R.
Gurun
Sungei Patani
Kroh
Kota Bharu
Gong Kedah
Machang
Kuala Krai
Georgetown
Penang
Butterworth
Krian R.
Grik
Lubok Kiap
Perak R.
K. Trengganu
Taiping
Kuala Kangsar
Ipoh
Sitiawan
Kampar
Kuala Lipis
Telok Anson
Jerantut
Kuantan
Slim River
Raub
Fraser's Hill
K. Kubu
Selangor
Kuala Lumpur
Port Swettenham
Gemas
Batu Anam
Endau
Segamat
Labis
Mersing
Port Dickson
Malacca
Kahang
Jemaluang
Bakri
Yong Peng
Muar
Kluang
Parit Sulong
Ayer Hitam
Batu Pahat
Senggarang
Rengit
Tebrau
Johore Bahru
Singapore
Occupied Airfield
Unoccupied "
Landing Ground
MILES 20 10 0 20 40 60 80 100 MILES
HUGH W. GROSER
Johore Bahru
Strait
Johore
SEMBAWANG
SELETAR
TENGAH
SINGAPORE I.
Changi
Tanglin Bks
KALLANG
Singapore
Alexandra Bks
Keppel Hbr.
0 5 MILES 10 15

Malaya

The Dogras and the supporting artillery brought down damaging fire on the Japanese ships and on the landing craft as they struggled ashore through heavy seas. Hudsons of No. 1 Squadron R.A.A.F. from the Kota Bharu field, little over a mile from the beach, and torpedo bombers from other airfields, joined in the defence. The Hudsons sank one Japanese transport (the *Awagisan Maru);* two others were damaged. Soon, however, the Japanese had got ashore and were extending their foothold, fanning out along and behind the beaches. Key sent forward a second battalion—the 2/12th Frontier Force Regiment—and then his third—the 1/13th Frontier Force Rifles. These counter-attacked but at dusk the Japanese still held their bridgehead. They had lost 320 killed and 538 wounded—probably about one in three of the men who landed on that day.

Meanwhile, about 3 a.m.—later than they intended—the Japanese had landed at Singora and Patani in Thailand. When a squadron of Blenheims arrived their attack was unsuccessful as defending fighters caused hurried bombing. This unit was caught on the ground at Alor Star soon after its return. On near-by Sungei Patani airfield No. 21 Squadron R.A.A.F. also was caught on the ground, and at the end of the day had only four serviceable aircraft; withdrawal to Butterworth was ordered.

General Percival, at his headquarters in Singapore, obtained permission to send columns from the 11th Indian Division into Thailand to intercept the Japanese forces which, he was certain, would land at these beaches, and that day (the 8th) one column set off north along the Singora road and another along the Patani road. The Singora column occupied a position some ten miles north of the frontier where about 9.30 p.m. a Japanese column led by tanks ran into it; two tanks were knocked out. The Japanese deployed and began an enveloping movement and in the night the Indian column withdrew. The Patani column was delayed by skirmishes with Thai troops on and beyond the frontier and at nightfall had not reached the good defensive position which was its objective. Thus on the night of the 8th the Indians were in action against the invaders on the eastern and on the western highways leading south on each side of the jungle-covered mountain spine of northern Malaya, and were awaiting them on the central road from Patani. The Japanese were ashore in three places on the Thailand-Malayan coast and other landings farther south were likely. Their *Guards Division* was marching into Thailand from Indo-China. At 4 a.m. on the 8th about seventeen Japanese naval aircraft operating from Indo-China had bombed Singapore, moonlit and ablaze with lights, doing little military damage but causing about 200 civilian casualties; to the civilians this was the first news that war had broken out.

At Pearl Harbour the Japanese attack went in at 7.55 a.m., 7th December, local time.[2] Radar had picked up unexpected aircraft an hour and ten minutes earlier, but this warning was not taken seriously. For three hours about 360 Japanese aircraft attacked the American ships in Pearl Harbour and the airfields on Oahu. Of the eight battleships in Pearl Harbour four were sunk

[2] At 6.45 a.m. an American destroyer had sunk a Japanese midget submarine off Pearl Harbour, but this was not known at headquarters ashore until more than an hour later. In terms of Greenwich time the landing at Kota Bharu took place at 4.55 p.m., 7th December, and the attack on Pearl Harbour at 6.25 p.m.

and one run ashore; 120 aircraft were destroyed; 2,403 men were killed. The Japanese lost twenty-seven aircraft. Fortunately for their enemies the Japanese had decided not to follow their crippling raid with invasion, although this had been considered by their planners. Such an enterprise could hardly have failed. After the raid only eighty-seven aircraft of the Army Air Force were usable and most of those were unarmed. Not only was Hawaii unready, but alarm prevailed along the west coast of America, where during the following week an attack in force was daily expected. It was fortunate too that the three aircraft carriers of the Pacific Fleet—*Lexington, Enterprise* and *Saratoga*—were at sea that day, and that part of the battle fleet was in the Atlantic.

The colony of Hong Kong consisted of Hong Kong Island, about twenty-nine square miles in area, and an area on the mainland about twelve times as large. Major-General C. M. Maltby deployed one brigade (two Indian battalions and one British) on the mainland and one (two Canadian battalions and one British) on the island. At 8 a.m. on the 8th (local time) about fifty Japanese aircraft bombed the only airfield and destroyed or disabled the few R.A.F. machines there. Troops of the *38th Japanese Division* crossed the frontier that morning and by the afternoon had reached the defence line on the mainland which formed an arc some eight miles long.

When Pearl Harbour was being bombed it was still before dawn at Manila. General MacArthur learnt of the attack while it was still dark. Major-General Lewis H. Brereton, commanding the United States air force in the Philippines, wished to send his bombers against the Japanese bases in Formosa. There is controversy about exactly what orders were given in the next few hours, but at 11.20 a.m. the heavy bombers were belatedly ordered to attack Formosa. They were still loading with bombs soon after midday when fifty-four Japanese aircraft appeared over the main airfield and destroyed or damaged seventeen of the thirty-five Flying Fortresses and fifty-six fighters—about half of Brereton's heavy bombers and a third of his fighters. The Japanese attack had been delayed by fog, but vacillation at Manila had enabled them to achieve as satisfactory a result as if they had made an unexpected raid.

Thus by the end of the first day the Japanese achievements had been spectacular. They had disabled the United States main fleet and the U.S. air forces in Hawaii and the Philippines, and had established bridgeheads in Malaya and Thailand.

Churchill heard the calamitous news that evening at Chequers. He immediately telephoned Roosevelt. 'We are all in the same boat now,' said Roosevelt. Churchill remembered saying: 'This certainly simplifies things. God be with you,' or words to that effect. He was now confident that Britain must emerge from the war 'however mauled or mutilated, safe and victorious'. Next day he sought and obtained the King's approval of a visit to Washington.

The news of the attack on Pearl Harbour was heard in Australia at 5.45 a.m. on the 8th—about an hour and a quarter after the event, Australian time being 20½ hours fast on Hawaiian. The War Cabinet was called together, and later in the day Mr Curtin announced that the 'partial mobilisation' of the army would be 'extended'. Parliament would meet next day. 'This is the gravest hour of our history,' he said in a broadcast speech. 'We have a heavy responsibility. I ask every Australian, man and woman, to go about their allotted task with full vigour and courage.'[3]

The event which Australians had long feared had now happened: attack by Japan at a time when the navies of the two great colonial powers could not effectively intervene. The British Navy was engaged in a European war, the main American Fleet, except for its carrier force, was disabled at Hawaii. When the Australian Chiefs of Staff were asked to advise the War Cabinet about Australia's situation they said that they saw two main possibilities: that Japan would move southward step by step or that she would make a direct advance against Australia, on the lines of the Pearl Harbour attack. If she advanced step by step, capture of Singapore and the Netherlands Indies would enable her to invade Australia. It was possible that she would seek to take Rabaul, Port Moresby and Noumea as advanced bases, and an attempt to take Darwin with its 100,000 tons of oil would be a strong possibility.

What forces could Australia deploy? In Australian or Far Eastern waters she had four cruisers, New Zealand had one; the War Cabinet decided to ask for the return of the fifth Australian cruiser, *Hobart*, from the Mediterranean. On 11th December she had at home fifteen first line air force squadrons, about half of them armed only with Wirraways (to serve as fighters), fifty-three Hudson bombers, twelve Catalina flying boats and some hundreds of training aircraft. There were 168,800 troops in training in Australia, of whom 32,000 were volunteers of the A.I.F. and 4,500 were regulars; about 120,000 men of the A.I.F. were in the four divisions overseas.

The War Cabinet decided to call up 114,000 men to bring the five infantry and two motorised cavalry divisions of the home army to full strength—246,000—and ordered that militiamen should not be allowed to enlist in the A.I.F. By the 12th all formations were in camp. There were not yet enough weapons fully to arm them: the field artillery regiments, for example, each had sixteen guns not twenty-four, the infantry battalions thirty-eight light machine-guns not fifty-eight, the 1st Armoured Division only eighteen tanks and needed more than 500. However, weapons were now being delivered by the factories at a steadily-increasing rate.

Meanwhile Australia had to carry out her long-standing agreement with the Netherlands Indies Government that, when war broke out, Australia would reinforce the garrisons of Ambon and Timor. The 2/40th Battalion group was landed at Koepang in Timor on 12th December and the 2/21st Battalion group in Ambon on the 17th. Also on the 17th the 2/2nd Independent Company and some Netherlands troops were landed at Dili in Portuguese Timor.

At Rabaul was a third battalion group of the A.I.F. (the 2/22nd) and a few local troops; at Port Moresby the 49th Battalion and other units and

[3] In 1939 the Commonwealth Government had announced that it was at war by means of an announcement in the *Commonwealth Gazette* that war had broken out between Great Britain and Germany and a request to the United Kingdom to inform Germany that Australia was associated with her in war; this time Mr Curtin's Government employed a different method with the aim of making it clear that, on such an occasion, the King acted exclusively on the advice of his Australian Ministers. The advice of the King's Ministers in Australia that Australia should declare war on Japan was placed before the King by telegram on the 8th. On the 9th, Assent having been received, the Australian Government declared war as from the 8th.

detachments, 1,200 men in all. On 3rd January 1942 General Sturdee increased the Port Moresby garrison to a brigade group by the addition of the 39th and 53rd Battalions, the 13th Field Regiment and other units. Farther out Ocean and Nauru Islands were each defended by a troop of Australian field artillery placed there to resist German commerce raiders. By the third week of December No. 2 (Hudson) Squadron R.A.A.F. was being established at Koepang, No. 13 (Hudson) at Laha in Ambon, Nos. 11 and 20 (both Catalina flying boats) were at Port Moresby, No. 24 (Hudsons and Wirraway fighters) was at Rabaul.

In these circumstances—the American Pacific Fleet severely damaged and the British battleships based on Singapore sunk—the Australian Chiefs of Staff considered three courses of action at Rabaul: to reinforce the garrison to a brigade group, to withdraw the garrison, or to leave it by itself. They recommended the third course and the War Cabinet on 12th December made the hard decision to accept this advice.

The importance of the Darwin base had been steadily increasing. Work on an all-weather road from Alice Springs had begun in September 1940; by December of that year it was ready, and soon 100 vehicles were engaged moving men and supplies overland to Darwin, hitherto maintained almost entirely by sea. In 1941 an all-weather road from Mount Isa to Tennant Creek was begun. Late in that year Darwin was being used as a staging point from which American aircraft were being flown to the Philippines. When two A.I.F. battalions were sent from Darwin to Ambon and Timor two militia battalions (the 27th and 43rd) were sent north from South Australia to replace them, and the garrison was maintained at a strength of about 6,600. One air force squadron—No. 12 (Wirraway)—was based there.

There remained elsewhere in Australia eight squadrons armed with Wirraways or Hudsons. On 11th December the War Cabinet had decided to increase the establishment of the air force from thirty-two to sixty squadrons—an objective which could not be attained for many months. It decided also that for the present no more Empire Air Training Scheme men were to leave Australia for Europe.

In New Zealand, when the Japanese war began, there were 13,000 troops in training not counting the brigade in Fiji; the air force possessed sixty-five operational aircraft (but no fighters) and 251 training aircraft. The Territorials were called up and by January 1942 40,000 were in camp; the force in Fiji was increased to two brigades later to be named the 3rd Division.

Each of the two main combatants in the Pacific was strong where the other was weak. The Japanese had much recent experience of war; for over seventy years the Americans had had relatively little. On the other hand the population of the United States was half as large again as that of Japan and her industrial capacity immensely greater. The United States produced about 70,000,000 tons of steel a year, Japan and Manchuria only about 7,500,000. Japan's engineering industries had been developed largely in the service of her fighting forces and she had a relatively small reserve of civil industry to fall back upon in war. A great asset was her big mercantile fleet of 5,600,000 tons, the third largest in the world. In 1939 the British Empire had 21,000,000 tons, the United States 9,000,000, excluding lake shipping.

The Japanese citizen—and therefore the Japanese soldier—was schooled in devotion to his country and respect for his superiors to a degree that aroused wonder among Europeans. Japanese drama and literature made war appear glorious; American films and literature pictured it as futile and tragic. The American was impatient and volatile; the Japanese patient and obedient.

> Japan's one chance of success in the event of hostilities (wrote a British soldier in 1935) would lie in her ability to strike hard and strike rapidly, so as to ensure a war of short duration and to ensure, too, that the enemy was kept out of bombing distance of her own shores . . . rapidity of attack is a marked feature of all her training on land and sea as well as in the air . . . Where . . . rapid thinking is required in order to improvise against the unexpected the Japanese probably leave something to be desired; but provided nothing intervenes to upset their carefully thought-out plans . . . they have few equals and no superiors.[4]

Japan was an island nation whose military and industrial leaders were possessed by an ambition to conquer a great part of the mainland of Asia and the islands of the Indies. This could be achieved only by landing forces on hostile shores. In 1937 foreign observers in China were surprised by the appearance off the coast of 400 efficient landing craft and a 10,000-ton landing craft carrier. At that time Britain possessed three motor landing craft of unsatisfactory design and was building six more. The United States Navy had one converted destroyer-transport able to carry 120 marines. In 1938 the United States marines experimented with a self-propelled tank lighter for the first time; otherwise their landing exercises were carried out in ships' boats. In 1938, spurred by Japanese success, Britain had established an Inter-Service Training and Development Centre to develop and test doctrines and equipment for combined operations, and by September 1939 had designed and built a variety of landing craft, and, soon after war began, three transports were fitted out each to carry 850 troops and thirteen landing craft. Early in 1940 more than eighty landing craft were being built in England. The Norwegian campaign tested the craft in action and it and the fall of France led to production of landing craft on a far larger scale. The transports mentioned above were fitted out as L.S.I. (Landing Ship, Infantry) and new types including the L.S.T. (Landing Ship, Tank) were developed. By April 1941, 235 L.C.T. (Landing Craft, Tank) of an improved model were being built. Early in 1942 an L.C.I. (Landing Craft, Infantry) would be designed and the design sent to America.

Thus when the Japanese war began, British staffs and designers had produced most of the types of landing craft that would be employed in later operations and most had been tested in action. Experiment had proceeded also in America in 1940 and 1941, where an 'alligator'—a tracked amphibian, forerunner of the L.V.T. (Landing Vehicle, Tracked)—had been tested, and a conventional landing craft had been approved and ordered in large numbers by the British Government. For the present, however, the British and American forces were merely experimenting in a department in which the Japanese were far advanced.

[4] Capt M. D. Kennedy, *The Problem of Japan* (1935), pp. 235-6.

Throughout December the carefully thought out Japanese plan was in highly-successful operation. Each day their perimeter was extended.

Between the Philippines and Hawaii lay two American stepping-stones, Wake Island and Guam, the intervening stretches of ocean being from 1,500 to 2,000 miles. A strong Japanese force landed at Guam on 10th December and after a brief clash, in which seventeen of the defenders were killed, the Governor surrendered.

At Wake Island, a lonely atoll about seven miles in length, there was a longer fight. The island was severely bombed on the 8th (7th December at Pearl Harbour), and before dawn on the 11th an invasion force of three cruisers and two destroyers carrying 450 troops appeared. The defenders' gunfire sank one destroyer and drove away the remaining ships. They made off pursued by four American aircraft which sank another destroyer. The Japanese returned, greatly strengthened, on the 20th. The island had now been systematically bombed. Before dawn on the 23rd about 1,500 Japanese marines landed in barges, and about 8 a.m. the garrison surrendered.

At Hong Kong on the night of the 9th-10th the Japanese penetrated the British line on the mainland and by the 13th all British troops had been withdrawn to the island. On the 18th the Japanese crossed Victoria Harbour in small boats and landed on a two-mile front, fanned out, and by 25th December had thrust the main body of the defenders to a line defending the city on the west and a smaller body into a small peninsula in the south. General Maltby capitulated on the 26th.

Meanwhile the Japanese had taken possession of one of their main strategic prizes—the oilfields of British Sarawak. On 8th December a British military detachment laid the fields waste. Japanese troops landed at Seria, the main field, on 15th December; on the 24th they landed near Kuching where the garrison—the 2/15th Punjab Battalion—was concentrated. The Indian unit made a fighting withdrawal southward into Dutch Borneo, where the survivors were captured by the Japanese.

The Japanese plan provided that, after having knocked out the American Pacific Fleet and the air force in the Philippines on the opening day, they would not land troops on Luzon until 10th December and then only in small force. They came ashore that day at Aparri and Vigan near the northern end of the island, and at Legaspi at the southern end on the 12th. In northern Luzon were four Philippine divisions but General MacArthur held them well south of the north coast being convinced, rightly as it turned out, that the main Japanese landing would be farther south. It was not until 16th December that the first real clash occurred in Luzon when a Philippine outpost ambushed two truck-loads of Japanese.

On the 20th a Japanese force landed at Davao on Mindanao in the southern Philippines; next day the Japanese in northern Luzon reached a main American outpost, which they outflanked and dispersed. On the 19th the fourteen surviving Flying Fortresses had been flown out to Darwin; there was now little air support for the defenders. On 22nd December the *48th Japanese Division* came ashore where the American commanders had long expected a landing—along the shores of Lingayen Gulf—and on the 23rd and 24th December part of the *16th Division* landed in Lamon Bay on the east coast, south-east of Manila. This was the *Southern Army's* second big amphibious operation. At Lingayen Gulf 37,000 troops were put ashore, at Lamon Bay 7,000. Altogether 200 landing craft of from three to eight tons were used. Soon the defenders were hard-pressed and MacArthur ordered his subordinates in the north to put into operation the long-standing plan to withdraw into the Bataan Peninsula, which forms the western shore of Manila Bay, thus abandoning the city of Manila. The Philippine-American force succeeded in extricating itself but not before some costly rearguard actions. By 2nd January it was within the peninsula; Major-General Jonathan M. Wainwright's corps which had borne the brunt of the fighting so far had been reduced from 28,000 to 16,000. Across the 20-mile neck of the peninsula or in reserve farther south now stood nine small Philippine divisions and the one regular division of Philippine Scouts and Americans—about 80,000 in all—but there had been delay in building up supplies in Bataan and it was inevitable that the defenders must eventually be starved into submission.

Up to this stage, although heavy Japanese landings had not begun until 22nd December, events had moved somewhat more swiftly in Luzon than in Malaya. There on the morning of 10th December the column ('Krohcol') moving into Thailand along the Patani road was carried forward to a point four miles short of the strong Ledge position which it intended to occupy, and thence marched forward. Less than a mile ahead they encountered a strong Japanese advance-guard, with light tanks.

Meanwhile, round Kota Bharu, the fight continued. On the afternoon of the 8th the Kota Bharu airfield had been abandoned by the air force in haste and before stocks of bombs and petrol had been demolished or the runways cratered. Throughout the 8th the Japanese bombed the forward airfields, often catching the defending aircraft on the ground, and at the end of the day only fifty of the 110 machines based on these fields were serviceable. The Japanese used some 330 aircraft and had few losses.

On the evening of the 8th Brigadier Key decided to withdraw his troops to positions covering Kota Bharu, and next morning, when the Japanese were infiltrating through and round his positions, to withdraw farther south. By the 11th he had broken contact and was south of Machang.

Early in the afternoon of the 8th the Commander-in-Chief of the Eastern Fleet, Admiral Sir Tom Phillips, had decided that his two capital ships should raid the Japanese convoys unloading at Singora and Kota Bharu. Thereupon soon after 5 p.m. the *Prince of Wales* and *Repulse* with four destroyers (including the Australian *Vampire*) sailed from Singapore. As they were leaving the naval base Phillips learnt that fighter cover could not be provided as far north as Singora; the losses of the day had been too great. On the evening of the 9th Japanese aircraft appeared and shadowed the ships until nightfall. Thereupon Phillips, sure that surprise had been lost, altered course for Singapore. In the night, however, a signal reached the squadron that Japanese were landing at Kuantan and Phillips altered course south-west towards that place. At 8 a.m. on the 10th Kuantan was in sight, but there were no Japanese ships there. Soon after 11 a.m. Japanese high-level bombers attacked, then a formation of torpedo bombers, then more high-level bombers and finally more torpedo bombers. The *Repulse* and the *Prince of Wales* were both sunk. Admiral Phillips and more than 800 others were lost. No Allied capital ships now remained to dispute Japanese domination of the Far Eastern seas.

From 9th December onwards the R.A.F. and R.A.A.F. squadrons were not able to do much to influence the battles below and their effective strength dwindled daily. Road transport was attacked and some good results observed, but after 9th December, when a number of Blenheims were shot down and others destroyed on the ground at Butterworth, Air Headquarters ruled that there was to be no more bombing of land targets without fighter escort. That day Butterworth, after an attack by twenty-seven Japanese bombers, was evacuated by all squadrons which had serviceable aircraft, but reinforcements arrived at Singapore: the four promised Dutch squadrons armed with twenty-two Glenn Martin bombers and nine Buffaloes. However, the bomber crews had not been trained for night flying, and their aircraft were slower than the Blenheims. One squadron was sent back to the Indies. By the 10th no British aircraft were based in north-eastern Malaya. The defending force had lost about a quarter of its aircraft in two days. It was estimated that the Japanese already had 100 aircraft based in the Singora-Patani area and at least 280 in Indo-China.

On 10th December Mr Duff Cooper, a member of the British Cabinet who had been examining the situation in the Far East since August, was appointed Resident Minister for Far Eastern Affairs, to relieve the Commanders-in-Chief of 'extraneous responsibilities', give them broad political guidance, and settle urgent matters on the spot. It was arranged that he should preside over a War Council on which sat the Governor, the Commanders-in-Chief, General Percival, Air Vice-Marshal C. W. H. Pulford, V. G. Bowden representing the Australian Government, and later Sir George Sansom, who was responsible for propaganda and press control. Major-General Gordon Bennett could also attend if he wished.

On the Kedah front the 11th Indian Division was now in position astride the road junction at Jitra, covering the main road leading south and the airfield at Alor Star. The Japanese were in touch with the outposts near the frontier by the morning of the 10th and that day and the next attacked, enveloped and virtually destroyed two Indian battalions which had been sent forward to delay the enemy—a heavy loss. On the night of the 11th the Japanese began a concerted attack on the main Jitra position.

Meanwhile 'Krohcol' was attacked by strong Japanese forces. An enemy advance along this road would threaten the 11th Indian Division round Jitra, but when the divisional commander, Major-General D. M. Murray-Lyon, sought permission to withdraw thirty miles General Percival decided that such an early and long withdrawal would have a demoralising effect on the troops and civilians and the battle must be fought at Jitra. There on the evening of the 12th the Japanese advance-guard attacked east of the main road and drove a wedge into the defenders' position. Soon the 15th Brigade was in some confusion and Murray-Lyon was given permission to withdraw. That night the division came out. Though not closely followed by the enemy, its spirit had been shaken; traffic jammed the roads and much equipment was lost. Some units withdrew to Alor Star along the railway, others to the sea. The Japanese advance-guard, with tank support—the main strength of their *5th Division* had not been employed—had routed a whole Indian division, taken 3,000 prisoners, and delivered a blow to the British forces in Malaya from which it would be difficult to recover.

The operation thus far had been ill-managed. There had been indecision about implementing the plan to advance into Thailand, a sudden change from an offensive to a defensive plan, delay in occupying the Jitra position, the early loss of two battalions far forward of the main position, the costly night withdrawal on a crowded road. In addition the battle had revealed weakness at the brigade and unit level. Reserves had been expended prematurely. In some units control was lost. It was being demonstrated that the Indian Army units had lost much of their value as a result of the rapid expansion of that army and the consequent dilution of the units with raw troops and equally raw junior leaders. The old Indian Army had been a force of long-service professional soldiers bound together less by national feeling than by personal loyalty to their officers. The principle was accepted that an Indian ranker was not fitted for command of a platoon until he had had perhaps fifteen years of service. The army was not geared for the rapid wartime expansion accepted as a matter of course in Western armies.

On 12th December one more attempt had been made to hit the enemy's aircraft on the ground at Singora. Eight Blenheims set out from Tengah but few reached Singora because of bad weather. Air Vice-Marshal Pulford decided to move No. 453 Squadron to Ipoh to join the depleted No. 21 Squadron and give support to the ground forces. On the 13th, the day this movement was made, three Buffaloes of No. 453 claimed five bombers over Penang. Later in the day the squadron engaged more than forty enemy fighters of which four were shot down. On this and the next few days the squadrons attacked Japanese columns moving south, but by 15th December the two squadrons had only three aircraft fit for combat until twelve replacement aircraft were flown in from the base. After having lost seven more aircraft on the ground the squadrons were withdrawn, No. 21, with no serviceable aircraft, to Sembawang and No. 453, with five, to Kuala Lumpur, where it fought hard for a week, probably shooting down ten enemy aircraft. It too was then withdrawn to Sembawang where Group Captain J. P. J. McCauley now commanded these two, the two R.A.A.F. Hudson squadrons and two Dutch bomber squadrons.

On the 12th, the day of the disasters at Jitra, the Kroh column was severely attacked and withdrew with heavy loss. On the 14th General Heath, commanding III Indian Corps, placed what was left of the column under the command of Brigadier A. C. M. Paris, whose 12th Indian Brigade —Percival's sole reserve—had been hurried north by rail and road to take over the central sector. On the 15th Percival withdrew the 8th Indian Brigade from Kelantan, it now being evident that the main thrust was down the west coast.

On the night of the 13th-14th the 11th Division completed a withdrawal to Gurun astride the main road and railway with mountains on the west and jungle to the east. The enemy arrived on the 14th and soon penetrated the Indian lines. That night they broke through and Murray-Lyon ordered a further withdrawal; many vehicles were abandoned. By the morning of the 16th December the division was south of the Muda River. The city of Penang had been severely bombed from the air and would soon be exposed; the Europeans and nearly all the troops were evacuated, but without destroying a large flotilla of coastal craft lying in the harbour.

Before there had been any substantial attack along the Muda the 11th Division and also the 12th Brigade were withdrawn to the Krian River, which offered a position of greater natural strength. The whole force was south of this line by the 18th. Meanwhile a Japanese column thrusting unexpectedly along the inland road through Grik threatened the communications of the division, and a withdrawal to the Perak River was authorised by Percival. His plan was that the 11th Division should hold the enemy here while the 9th continued to deny the Kuantan airfields.

On the 19th and 20th a sharp engagement was fought by the 12th Brigade on the Grik road. On 23rd December the 11th Division completed its withdrawal behind the Perak River. Next day Brigadier Paris replaced Major-General Murray-Lyon in command of the 11th Division and new commanders were appointed to each of the brigades; and, as a result of a decision made before war broke out, Lieut-General Sir Henry Pownall arrived in Singapore to replace Air Chief Marshal Sir Robert Brooke-Popham as Commander-in-Chief of a force which was principally military.

The wide Perak River delayed the Japanese but on 26th December there was a heavy engagement between the advancing Japanese and the 12th Brigade north of Ipoh; on the 27th-28th the whole force was south of Ipoh and in semi-circular position some four miles in extent about Kampar. The Japanese followed fast and on 1st January attacked the Kampar position after an intensive bombardment but were held that day and the next. Meanwhile Japanese had been detected landing from small craft at points on the west coast including Telok Anson. The 12th Brigade, though in need of rest, was put in on this flank with the 2/Argyll and Sutherland Highlanders forward. It was thrust slowly back, and soon there was no alternative to withdrawal from the Kampar position; the next stand was to be made on the Slim River.

Meanwhile the Allied Governments had been planning the reinforcement of the Far East, a task made difficult by distance, Britain's commitments in other theatres, the crippling of the American battle fleet, and America's unreadiness. Japan had the initiative and was working along interior lines of communication. She commanded the sea and air and was able to carry out her conquests with land forces which in total were numerically smaller than those opposed to her. Altogether ten divisions had been allotted to the southward advance.[5]

The question of unified command of the Allied forces soon arose. On 11th December the Australian Government urged the necessity of this upon the British Government. The matter had to await settlement at a conference between the British and American leaders to be held at Washington in the last week of December. A more immediate problem was to set reinforcements in motion. On the 12th Mr Churchill informed General Wavell, now Commander-in-Chief in India, that the 18th British Division and four fighter squadrons then rounding the Cape on their way to Egypt would be diverted to India and that he should retain in India the 17th Indian Division, intended for Iraq. On the 15th Churchill suggested to his staff

[5] Initially the *XXV Army* (Malaya) included the *Guards, 5th* and *18th Divisions*, the *XV Army* (Burma) the *33rd* and *55th*, the *XIV Army* (Philippines and Borneo) the *16th* and *48th*, the *XVI Army* (Java) the *2nd*. The *38th* attacked Hong Kong and later was to undertake other tasks. The *21st* was in reserve. Later the *4th* and *56th* would be added to the *Southern Army*.

that an Australian division should be transferred from the Middle East to Singapore. On the 13th a convoy containing 4,600 American troops and seventy crated aircraft intended for the Philippines was diverted to Australia where it arrived on 22nd December.

On 14th December Brigadier-General Dwight D. Eisenhower, a trusted officer just appointed to General Marshall's staff, who had been General MacArthur's chief staff officer in the Philippines in the 1930s, recommended that America 'must instantly move to save Hawaii, Fiji, New Zealand and New Caledonia' so as to secure a line of communications leading to Australia, and must 'make certain of the safety of Australia itself'. 'Our base must be Australia', he said. Marshall accepted this policy.

The possibility of sending effective British naval reinforcements was reduced when, on the 19th, Italian 'human torpedoes' disabled the battleships *Queen Elizabeth* and *Valiant* in Alexandria harbour. Within a few weeks more than one-third of Britain's capital ships had been sunk or put out of action; all that remained of the Mediterranean Fleet were three cruisers and a few destroyers.

As one setback followed another, more reinforcements were diverted to Malaya. By early January two brigades from the 17th Indian Division, all the 18th British Division, and four Hurricane squadrons from the Middle East and the United Kingdom had been allotted to that area; Australia was sending a machine-gun battalion (one of the two A.I.F. battalions remaining in Australia) and some 1,800 reinforcements. On 16th December General Bennett had asked for at least one Australian division from the Middle East. On the 25th the Australian Government sent a strong request to Churchill and Roosevelt (who were conferring in Washington) that Singapore should be reinforced. Churchill replied, also on the 25th, recording what was being done to reinforce Malaya, stating that he did not share the view that Singapore would soon fall, and that Roosevelt was 'quite willing to send substantial United States forces to Australia'.

On the 25th the Australian Government sent a further appeal through its Minister in Washington, Casey. It said: 'Please understand that the stage of gentle suggestion has now passed. Continuous over-statements by British Far East Commands as to the degree of preparedness have produced a very serious effect upon public opinion . . . This is the gravest type of emergency and everything will depend upon a Churchill-Roosevelt decision to meet it in the broadest way.'

At this time the Australian Ministers had been receiving disturbing messages from V. G. Bowden, its representative on the Singapore War Council. On the 25th Bowden declared that only the dispatch from the Middle East by air of powerful reinforcements might save Singapore. 'Anything that is not powerful, modern and immediate is futile', he said.

On the 27th Curtin published a newspaper article in the course of which he said:

> . . . the war with Japan is not a phase of the struggle with the Axis Powers, but is a new war . . . we take the view that, while the determination of military policy is the Soviet's business, we should be able to look forward with reason to aid from Russia against Japan. We look for a solid and impregnable barrier of democracies against the three Axis Powers and we refuse to accept the dictum that the Pacific struggle must be treated as a subordinate segment

> of the general conflict . . . The Australian Government, therefore, regards the Pacific struggle as primarily one in which the United States and Australia must have the fullest say in the direction of the democracies' fighting plan. Without any inhibitions of any kind, I make it quite clear that Australia looks to America, free of any pangs as to our traditional links or kinship with the United Kingdom. We know the problems that the United Kingdom faces . . . But we know, too, that Australia can go and Britain can still hold on. We are, therefore, determined that Australia shall not go, and shall exert all our energies towards the shaping of a plan, with the United States as its keystone, which will give to our country some confidence of being able to hold out until the tide of battle swings against the enemy.

This, according to Churchill, 'produced the worst impression both in high American circles and in Canada'. Maie Casey, the wife of R. G. Casey, Australian Ambassador to the United States, wrote afterwards that 'it was a cause of embarrassment to Australians in Washington. President Roosevelt sent for Dick and told him that if it was thought that this statement would ingratiate Australia with the United States he assured him that it would have the opposite effect. It tasted of panic and disloyalty. The President insisted that his remarks were to be regarded as personal and were not to be reported officially.'[6]

Australian dissatisfaction continued to express itself. The Australian Chiefs of Staff advised the Ministers on 30th December that the situation was 'most unsatisfactory'. The American Pacific Fleet was 'unable or unwilling to assist'; the British plan to establish a separate fleet in the Indian Ocean was unsound and the assembly of one main fleet should be the objective. These views were sent to Churchill.

At their conference at Washington the British and American leaders promptly established a combined staff for the strategical planning of the war—the Combined Chiefs of Staff. This group was to sit in Washington, and would include the American Chiefs of Staff and a senior British officer of each Service. It was in General Marshall's words 'the most complete unification of military effort ever achieved by two Allied nations'. At the same time the basic strategic concept—to beat Hitler first—was confirmed. Thirdly, an Allied Supreme Commander was appointed to the 'South-West Pacific Area'. Roosevelt asked that Wavell be given the appointment. The British Chiefs of Staff opposed the appointment of a Briton to a command which seemed doomed to defeat, but wished 'an American commander [to] be given the post (and the blame)'; the American leaders were insistent, and Wavell was appointed.[7] He would control the commanders in Burma, Malaya, Netherlands Indies and Philippines, but not India, China or Australia.

The appointment of Wavell was announced without having obtained the approval of the Netherlands Government whose territory comprised the greater part of his command, and this wounded the feelings of the Dutch. The Australian Government was not consulted about the appointment, nor had it yet been clearly informed about the important decision to concentrate first on the defeat of Germany and stand on the defensive in the East.

[6] Maie Casey, *Tides and Eddies* (1966), p. 83.

[7] R. E. Sherwood, *The White House Papers of Harry L. Hopkins*, Vol. I (1948), p. 470.

On 1st January and later the representatives of the Allied Nations—henceforth the United Nations—signed a joint declaration subscribing to the Atlantic Charter, pledging themselves to employ their full resources against the enemy Powers and inviting other nations to join them in the struggle.

It happened that the largest well-trained and experienced formation not engaged in operations in the Middle East was the I Australian Corps. India having been almost denuded of trained troops the logical course would be to send the Australian corps to the East. On 19th December Earle Page in London had informed Curtin that the sending of one Australian division to Malaya was contemplated.

At length on 3rd January the British Government suggested that two Australian divisions should be sent to the Netherlands Indies, and on the 5th the Australian War Cabinet approved the sending of those two divisions plus the Australian corps staff and corps units. Wavell's plan at first was to use the corps to counter-attack in Malaya but he soon decided that it would not arrive in time and that one division should be landed in south Sumatra and one, with a British armoured brigade, also from the Middle East, in Java. On 4th January the first Japanese bombs fell on Australian territory when Japanese aircraft attacked the Rabaul airfields.[8]

The first substantial military reinforcements to reach Malaya after the outbreak of war arrived on 3rd January: the 45th Indian Brigade from the 17th Division, mentioned above. General Percival instructed General Heath that III Corps should deny the Kuala Lumpur and Port Swettenham airfields to the enemy until the 14th so that their aircraft could protect the disembarkation of fifty Hurricanes and the 53rd Brigade (the leading brigade of the 18th Division). After withdrawal from Kuala Lumpur the III Corps would be responsible for the eastern area and the A.I.F. for the western; the main line of resistance would be through Mersing, Batu Anam, Muar.

On the east coast the 9th Indian Division's main defensive position was now on the line of the Kuantan River, where the 22nd Indian Brigade was deployed. The Japanese advancing along the coast reached the Kuantan

[8] Reputable English historians have circulated the notion that, soon after Japan entered the war, the Australian Government began to demand the return of her divisions from the Middle East. Thus, in *The Turn of the Tide* (1957), p. 288, Arthur Bryant wrote concerning the last days of December and the first days of January: 'For as, with the turn of the year, the Japanese fanned rapidly outwards in the islands of the South-West Pacific and the Eighth Army followed up Rommel's retreating forces to Agheila . . . an alarmed Australian Government began to clamour for the withdrawal of its divisions from the Middle East to defend Singapore, New Guinea and its own threatened shores.' In fact, as we have seen, the tranfer of a corps of two Australian divisions from the Middle East to the Far East (not Australia) was proposed by the British Government and promptly agreed to by the Australian Government. In mid-February, when one of the divisions was at sea and it was proposed by the British Government that it be landed not in the Netherlands Indies, as had been planned, but in Burma, where the defence was then collapsing, the Australian Government insisted that it be diverted to Australia. Soon afterwards, at the suggestion of the Australian Government, two brigades of the second division were landed in Ceylon to strengthen the small garrison there. The return of the 9th Division was sought by Curtin, on the advice of his Chief of the General Staff, in mid-February, but, as we shall see, the division did not embark from Egypt until early 1943.

River area on 30th December and there was fierce fighting. The Japanese advance along the western roads was now threatening the communications of the brigade and on 3rd January it broke contact and withdrew to the Raub area.

Meanwhile, in the central area, the 11th Indian Division was deployed north and south of the Slim River. One brigade was in depth astride the road and railway for some miles north of the river, another in support. Japanese attacks were repulsed on 5th January, but before dawn on the 7th they attacked again, a force of fifteen tanks with infantry driving straight down the road while other infantry moved round the flanks. There were few anti-tank weapons in the forward areas. The tanks thrust along the road and before 8 a.m. the thirteen tanks which survived had advanced nineteen miles and were well south of the Slim River, which they crossed on the still-intact bridge. There they ran into an artillery regiment which was moving forward along the road believing it was still far from the front. A howitzer was hurriedly put into action and knocked out the leading tank at thirty yards. The Japanese pulled back but few men of the two Indian infantry brigades managed to withdraw past the Japanese column, which had succeeded in dispersing and virtually destroying the greater part of the 11th Indian Division.

During the advance down the peninsula a main problem for the Japanese was to get their men across the many rivers whose bridges had been blown. It was then that their bicycles came into their own. When heavy vehicles were halted at a broken bridge the troops waded across carrying their bicycles, or crossed on log bridges supported on the shoulders of engineers standing in the stream. When the troops went into action they left their bicycles in the rear with a few men on guard, like the horse-holders of old-fashioned mounted infantry.

Next day General Wavell arrived at Singapore on his way to the headquarters of his new South-West Pacific Command in Java. He visited the shattered 11th Indian Division and saw its condition. Next day he laid down a plan for the defence of Johore which generally followed the lines of one Percival had prepared: the III Indian Corps, after delaying the enemy north of Kuala Lumpur as long as possible, was to be withdrawn into Johore; the 8th Australian Division with only one brigade was to be deployed on a line from Segamat to the mouth of the Muar River, where the 22nd Brigade would join it as soon as it could be relieved at Mersing; the 9th Indian Division, made up from the freshest troops of the III Indian Corps and the newly-arrived 45th Brigade, was to be placed under General Bennett on the Muar line; when it was withdrawn the III Indian Corps was to take over responsibility for the east and west coasts of Johore south of the Mersing-Kluang-Batu Pahat road.

While the main body of the 11th Indian Division was being thrust back from the Slim River the amalgamated 6th/15th Brigade was deployed round Selangor to prevent Japanese landings. By the 9th, however, the Japanese were ashore in strength and pressing eastward. Withdrawal from Kuala Lumpur was ordered. The survivors of the 11th Division were clear of Kuala Lumpur by the night of the 10th-11th and made a long withdrawal back to the new main line of resistance, just forward of which, at Gemas, an Australian battalion was now deployed. The 11th Division was withdrawn to the south. The depleted 9th Division came under command of Bennett whose force was designated Westforce and comprised the 27th Australian Brigade (Brigadier D. S. Maxwell), the 8th and 22nd Brigades of the 9th Indian Division and the newly-arrived 45th Indian Brigade.

After his visit to the Malayan front Wavell had flown to Java, met the principal members of his staff and worked out the organisation of his command. His headquarters were to be established near Bandung but signal communications were not yet available and he decided not to take over his command until the 15th. On the 13th he flew back to Malaya and again conferred with the commanders there.

Bennett's plan was to hold the crossings over the Muar and Segamat Rivers strongly, while, to the west, localities were to be held with striking forces which could prevent the enemy from moving round this flank. Forward on the main road near Gemas the 2/30th was to place an ambush. The commander of the 2/30th, Lieut-Colonel F. G. Galleghan, had a battery of field artillery and a battery of anti-tank artillery under command. Farther east the 2/26th Battalion was north of the main road with the 2/29th behind it. In the coastal area the 45th Indian Brigade was given the task of guarding the coastal area behind the Muar River.

The place chosen for the ambush was a stretch of road travelling from the north-west through the dense bush to a long cutting and beyond it to a bridge over the Gemencheh River. The 2/30th Battalion was deployed with one company in the ambush position three miles ahead of the main body of the battalion. At 4 p.m. on the 14th 200 to 300 Japanese cyclists rode through the ambush position; after an interval 700 to 800 more followed. When these were within the ambush the Australians blew the bridge. The infantry did great slaughter among the Japanese crowded on the road, killing some hundreds, but at this moment it was found that the signal line had gone dead and artillery fire could not be directed against the Japanese who were following up. The forward company then withdrew through the jungle and through an area now occupied by the Japanese who had been let through the ambush, followed fast by the main body of the Japanese force. This company had not come in when, at 9 a.m. on the 15th, Japanese tanks appeared at the road-block covered by the supporting company. One tank was destroyed and another disabled by anti-tank guns; then four more were hit. The Japanese pulled back and did not push on again that morning, though their aircraft concentrated on the Australian area. A company of the 2/30th made a counter-attack and drove the enemy back. In the afternoon the Japanese tanks thrust forward again but were driven off. In mid-afternoon the 2/30th, under heavy pressure, withdrew in good shape. In the two days it had lost five officers and seventy-six men killed, wounded or missing, but it estimated the enemy's casualties at 1,000. That evening the battalion was behind the main line. It was now deployed with the 8th Indian Brigade astride the main road and railway, the 2/26th Battalion in a mobile offensive role near by and the 2/29th Battalion in reserve. To the left was the 22nd Indian Brigade.

Meanwhile on the east coast the Japanese were pressing forward from Kuantan towards Mersing. In this area on 7th January Brigadier H. B. Taylor, commanding the 22nd Australian Brigade, had sent two companies northward to the Endau River, where patrol clashes occurred on the 14th and 15th. By the 17th the Japanese were in strength about Endau. That day Taylor was instructed to send his 2/19th Battalion to join the 45th Indian Brigade and the 2/29th Battalion in the Muar sector for reasons given below. Thereupon he ordered the demolition of bridges and cratering of roads between Endau and Mersing and withdrew the Endau force.

The 45th Brigade, guarding the west-coast flank, had been deployed on the Muar River with four companies on its northern bank. The Japanese arrived on the Muar on the 15th and next day attacked and scattered the untried Indians; the commanding officer of each of the two battalions engaged and many other officers were killed, and the supporting Australian battery lost a gun in an ambush during the withdrawal. Alarmed by this threat Percival decided to make III Corps responsible for the roads leading from the coast to the main road to Singapore and sent the newly-arrived 53rd British Brigade forward. It placed a battalion at Batu Pahat and another at Bukit Pelandok, on the road to Yong Peng. On the 17th Bennett decided also to send his 2/29th Battalion from the 27th Brigade and the 2/19th Battalion from the 22nd Brigade to the Muar area to strengthen the 45th Brigade. The 2/29th reached Bakri on the afternoon of the 17th and patrols soon found that there was nothing between it and the enemy two miles away. That night the Indians on the 2/29th's left were driven back to within a mile of Bakri but re-established their position in the early hours of the 18th. Japanese light tanks attacked at Bakri early that morning. Australian anti-tank gunners whose weapons were sited at both ends of a cutting destroyed eight tanks.

Australian War Memorial

The rear 2-pounder gun of an Australian anti-tank regiment in action on 18th January 1942, ahead of Bakri, during the Malayan campaign. From this position the forward and rear guns accounted for eight Japanese tanks.

Meanwhile the 2/19th was arriving at Parit Sulong, where it learned that the 45th Brigade had lost heavily, was out of contact with one of its battalions—the Jats—and the 2/29th was heavily engaged. Brigadier H. C. Duncan of the 45th Brigade now received an Intelligence report that he was being attacked by the Japanese *Guards Division*, not yet encountered in Malaya, augmented by strong armoured units. He decided to deploy the 2/19th Battalion to give depth to the 2/29th's position, and, when the Jats were found, to counter-attack. The 2/19th cleared a way through the Japanese who had blocked the road to the 2/29th. In the course of the night it became evident that the 45th Brigade was a spent force. General Percival, now learning that the *Guards Division* was attacking at Bakri and the *5th Division* advancing down the main road, placed General Heath in command of the Muar sector. General Bennett, anxious about the threat from the west, obtained Percival's agreement to a withdrawal behind the Segamat River preparatory to a consolidation round Kluang. In short the Mersing-Segamat-Muar 'main line of resistance' had been lost. The Japanese had pressed the 2/30th and 2/26th, stationed forward of Segamat, on the 17th and 18th; on the 19th the 27th Brigade broke off and withdrew to the Segamat area.

On the west coast the 2/19th attacked along the road to Muar on the 19th to gain touch with the Jats, who were cut off there. Using outflanking tactics they routed the Japanese on their front, but a strong group of Japanese cut the road behind them, and Japanese aircraft made a direct hit on 45th Brigade headquarters, stunning Brigadier Duncan and killing or wounding nearly all his staff. Lieut-Colonel C. G. W. Anderson of the 2/19th took command and wisely decided that the 2/29th must be withdrawn behind the Bakri road junction and that he must concentrate on holding the road east to Yong Peng. At a conference at Yong Peng about that time Percival instructed Bennett to pull his main force back to Labis.

Anderson delayed the withdrawal of the 2/29th, awaiting the arrival of the Jats, and meanwhile both Australian battalions became heavily engaged. At length the Jats came in and on the morning of 20th January a fighting withdrawal to Parit Sulong began. The leading company broke through a Japanese force, Anderson himself leading the final attack. Farther on they encountered another road-block and the Japanese following close behind the Australian-Indian column pressed the rearguard until a counter-attack was launched in which Brigadier Duncan was killed. Meanwhile Anderson with the advance-guard organised a three-company attack which put the enemy to flight. That night Anderson learnt that the enemy was already in Parit Sulong. Japanese had landed in the Batu Pahat area and forced the 53rd Brigade and the Indian troops back towards Yong Peng. Not only was Anderson's force cut off but Bennett's main force was threatened. Percival now ordered Bennett to withdraw the 27th Brigade on the central road to Yong Peng instead of halting it at Labis.

On the 21st Anderson's force encountered the Japanese strongly established round Parit Sulong and attacked but had gained only a few hundred yards by nightfall. It now had many wounded and its artillery and mortar ammunition was almost exhausted. The Loyals, a battalion of the 53rd Brigade, were to have attacked from Yong Peng towards Parit Sulong but the attack was delayed, delayed again, and finally abandoned on the 22nd. Early that morning Japanese tanks broke into the perimeter of Anderson's force from its rear but were stopped by gunfire. The isolated force was bombed from the air and shelled by artillery, as it had been throughout its withdrawal. At 9 a.m. Anderson ordered that his vehicles and guns be destroyed and the men withdraw eastward in small parties. Of the 2/19th only 271 reached Yong Peng, of the 2/29th only 130.

At conferences at Yong Peng on the 21st and Rengam on the 23rd Percival had issued orders that Heath should take command of all troops in Johore except those in the extreme south. Under Heath, Brigadier Taylor was given the task of holding Jemaluang and Kluang with detachments forward at Mersing; General Bennett, with the remainder of his division and the depleted 9th Indian Division, was to defend Kluang and Ayer Hitam; Brigadier Key with what was left of the 11th Indian Division was to hold the Batu Pahat area and the coast road generally. The 53rd Brigade was to join Key's force as soon as Bennett could spare it. The intention was now to hold a line along the road Jemaluang-Kluang-Ayer Hitam-Batu Pahat; one aim was to deny to the enemy the airfields of southern Johore until the transports carrying the remainder of the 18th Division had arrived. On the 22nd and 23rd, however, the enemy reached the Batu Pahat-Ayer Hitam road and on the evening of the 23rd the commander of the force round Batu Pahat began withdrawal to Senggarang. He was ordered, however, to hold at Batu Pahat and did so, while efforts were made to send relieving columns forward. These failed and the force withdrew to Senggarang on the 25th-26th but found the road blocked there. Units were ordered to make their way out as best they could.

A convoy bringing, among other reinforcements, fifty-one crated Hurricanes, had arrived at Singapore on 13th January. These were assembled and on 20th and 21st January Hurricane crews shot down fourteen Japanese aircraft for a loss of five, but by the end of the month only a third of the Hurricanes remained. Already Far East Command had ordered the bombers and other long-range aircraft to Palembang in Sumatra.

On 22nd January the 44th Indian Brigade arrived in Singapore. It was no better trained than the 45th, which had suffered so severely at Muar, and Percival decided to keep it on the island for further training. With it came 7,000 'extremely raw' Indian reinforcements. From Australia on the 24th arrived the 2/4th Machine Gun Battalion (942 all ranks) and 1,900 ill-trained reinforcements. The remaining brigades of the 18th British Division were expected on the 29th.

Meanwhile, in the forward area, the 5/11th Sikhs had delivered a successful counter-attack at Kluang which temporarily halted the Japanese advance, but on the 25th Percival decided that, because of the threat from his western flank he must withdraw from Kluang and Ayer Hitam forthwith. A new danger now appeared in the east. On the 25th an aircraft sighted an enemy convoy approaching Endau. Next day a concerted air attack was made on these ships by nine Hudsons of Nos. 1 and 8 Squadrons R.A.A.F. with twenty-one Vildebeestes and three Albacores of Nos. 36 and 100 Squadrons R.A.F., covered by Buffaloes and Hurricanes. In the course of this attack eighteen aircraft were lost; five ships were hit but none was sunk. It was the last heavy attack which the defending air force was able to deliver in Malaya. On the night of the 26th-27th the destroyers *Vampire* and *Thanet*, practically the only naval force still available at Singapore, attacked the convoy but fell in with Japanese cruisers and destroyers which sank the *Thanet*.

Four Australian corvettes—*Bendigo*, *Burnie*, *Goulburn* and *Maryborough*—had been based on Singapore when war broke out. In January the cruiser *Hobart*, the sloop *Yarra*, and the corvettes *Wollongong*, *Toowoomba* and *Ballarat* arrived. All these were constantly employed on patrol, minesweeping and escort work, often under air attack.

Since the 18th, in the eastern sector in Malaya, clashes had been occurring between Australians and Japanese north of the Mersing River. On the 26th the enemy crossed the river west of Mersing. On the Nithsdale Estate, ten miles north of Jemaluang, Brigadier Taylor placed the 2/18th Battalion in an ambush position with one company each side of the road and two astride it to the rear. After dark on the 26th a Japanese column estimated at a battalion in strength advanced into the ambush. At length the Australians opened fire and a long and bitter fight followed in which the Australians lost ninety-eight killed or missing and the Japanese suffered heavy casualties. After that encounter the 22nd Brigade withdrew to Jemaluang unmolested.

In the central sector the withdrawal was also being carried out without mishap. On the 27th, however, Percival decided that the danger of an enemy advance down the main west coast road was so great that he must withdraw right out of Johore and back to Singapore Island. This movement was to take four days. The day after the decision was made Japanese troops advancing along the railway penetrated between the 22nd Indian Brigade and the 8th which was supporting it. Major-General A. E. Barstow commanding the 9th Indian Division was killed, and all but about 100 of the 22nd Brigade were lost. Elsewhere the withdrawal was successful, and at 8 a.m. on 31st January the rearguard crossed onto Singapore Island and a gap was blown in the causeway.

About 35,000 Japanese had fought on the Malayan mainland; they had lost 1,793 killed and 2,772 wounded. In a little more than seven weeks they had driven some 60,000 Indian, Australian and British troops from Malaya, capturing much of their equipment and many thousands of prisoners. Three out of the seven Indian brigades had ceased to exist, and only one or two of the remainder were fit for a major task in the coming battle.

The Japanese army comprised picked and, for the most part, battle-wise troops, eager, well-trained and aggressively led. They had been taught to press on regardless of loss, to improvise; they had tanks and boats and bicycles. Most of the Indian units were poorly-trained, contained a dangerous proportion of recent recruits and too few experienced officers. The British deployment at the outset and the tactics during the campaign contributed to the ease with which the Japanese overcame the defence. About half of Percival's army was arrayed in the northern third of the peninsula to protect airfields and perhaps to advance into Thailand in anticipation of a Japanese landing. After the initial defeat at Jitra and the success of the Japanese landing at Kota Bharu the Indian Corps attempted to hold a series of positions along the 600-mile road to Singapore. Each time the defenders were defeated with heavy loss of men and material and the Japanese gained more and more vehicles and stores. It would have been a wiser course, once the air force had been withdrawn from the northern fields and the lesson of Jitra had been learnt, to have swiftly withdrawn the Indian Corps to Johore, blown the bridges and prepared to meet the Japanese there in prepared positions with a fresh and more or less intact force of three divisions, with two Indian brigades and another division arriving. Once Johore was lost the capitulation of the island could not be long delayed, if only because of lack of food and water for the civilians crowding Singapore, normally about 550,000 but now increased by refugees to twice that number.

At the end of December the advance of the Japanese *Second* and *Third Fleets* and *XVI Army* in the Indies had reached Davao in the southern Philippines and the Miri oilfields in Sarawak. The January program provided for a series of strides that would bring the front line to Rabaul, Ambon, Kendari (in Celebes), and Balikpapan. Then there would be a lull of about a fortnight before a third series of advances began late in February. On 11th January Tarakan in Dutch Borneo and the Menado peninsula in Celebes were occupied. Wavell, in command of what was now named ABDA (American-British-Dutch-Australian) Area, decided that he could not send support to MacArthur, and that the enemy was likely to cut the air route to Australia by taking Ambon and Timor. On the 23rd and 24th the Japanese took Balikpapan. There, in the early morning of the 24th, four American destroyers in a night attack sank four Japanese transports and a patrol vessel: it was the first surface action by American ships in the war and caused the heaviest loss yet suffered by a Japanese convoy. Also on the 24th the Japanese occupied Kendari. Rabaul was attacked on the 23rd. Here there was a stronger garrison.

Rabaul lies near the north-eastern extremity of New Britain round the northern shore of a deeply-indented harbour. The main airfield, Vunakanau, lay some ten miles south of Rabaul, a second one, Lakunai, was adjacent to the town. The fertile and well-developed Rabaul area was well served by local roads but no motor-road led through the mountains to the south to link it with the remainder of the island. The harbour of Rabaul was overlooked on the north, east and south by volcanic craters, one of which, Matupi, had been in eruption from July to October and had covered the surrounding country with black ash.

At this isolated outpost the 2/22nd Battalion was supported by two coast guns and two anti-aircraft guns and other detachments including about eighty men of the New Guinea Volunteer Rifles, the whole force being commanded by Colonel J. J. Scanlan, an officer of 51 who had served in the infantry throughout the First World War. The only air unit was No. 24 Squadron (Wing Commander J. M. Lerew) with four Hudsons and eight Wirraways.

From 4th January onwards Japanese aircraft in relatively small numbers had bombed the Rabaul airfields. On the 9th a single Hudson bomber made

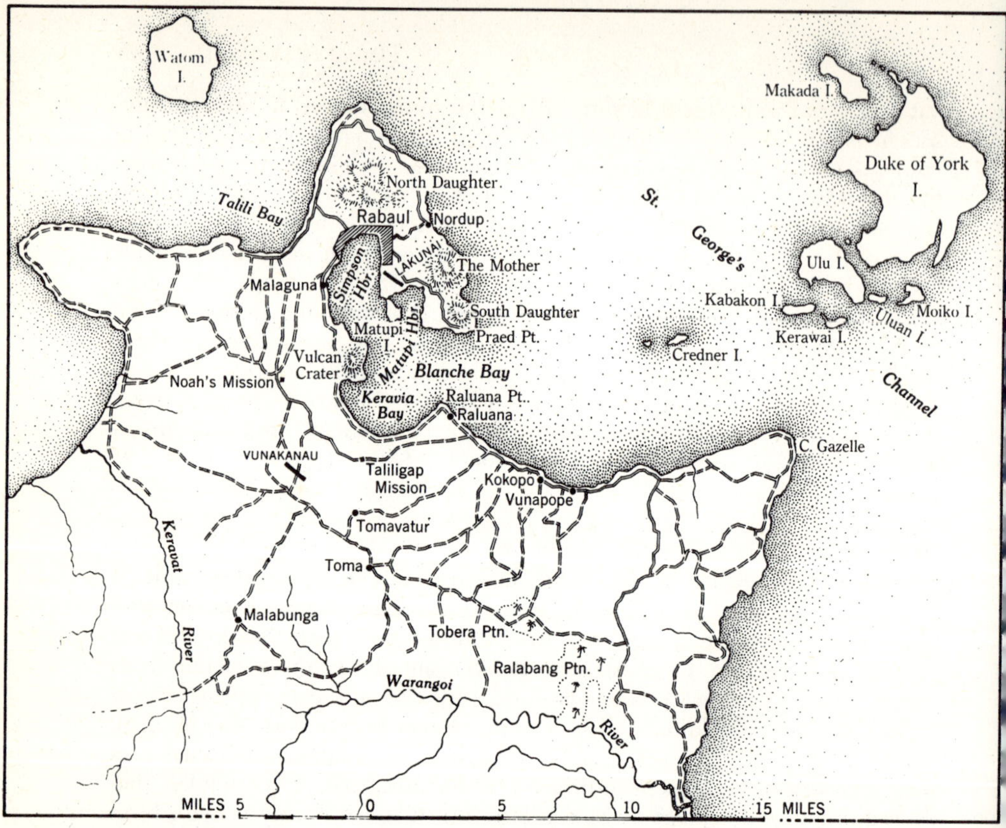

Rabaul area

a reconnaissance over Truk, a main Japanese base about 700 miles from Rabaul. On the afternoon of 20th January over 100 Japanese aircraft attacked Rabaul. The eight Wirraways went up against this force; three were shot down and only one remained undamaged; six of the sixteen men in their crews were killed and five wounded. The Japanese aircraft leisurely bombed and strafed airfields and the harbour. Next day Lerew was ordered to withdraw the remaining aircraft to the mainland of New Guinea and two Wirraways and one Hudson were flown out.

Reconnaissance aircraft now reported that a large convoy was heading towards Rabaul. (It contained General Tomitaro Horii's *South Seas Force,* including the *144th Regiment* and battalions of marines.) Air attacks continued, and on the 22nd the coast guns were put out of action. Later that day a big dump of bombs was demolished. The explosion broke the valves in all wireless sets and the force's link with the outside world was severed.

Hitherto Scanlan's force had been sited in defence of the harbour and the main airfields. He now withdrew those companies which were in the Rabaul peninsula and deployed his force south of Blanche Bay, of which the harbour is a northern arm, and along the road leading south to Vunakanau airfield.

About 1 a.m. on the 23rd Japanese landing craft could be seen in the bay, and soon after 2 a.m. troops were coming ashore north and south of Vulcan. The two reinforced companies of Australians widely-separated on the southern shores of Blanche Bay fired with mortars and small arms. Before

3 a.m. the commander of the eastern company was captured and the survivors were withdrawing. At dawn the western company, round Vulcan, was still firmly in position but enemy patrols were working round its flanks and threatening the road behind it, and it was being heavily attacked from the air. At 7 a.m. it withdrew in good order to a road junction—Four Ways—in the Vunakanau area where the four reserve companies were deployed, and south of which Colonel Scanlan and Lieut-Colonel H. H. Carr, the commander of the 2/22nd, had their headquarters. Two companies were deployed to cover the withdrawal of the men retiring from Blanche Bay. They were soon being pressed by the Japanese.

By 9 o'clock trucks were moving back through the headquarters area. Both Scanlan and Carr were out of touch with the forward companies, signals having broken down. Scanlan decided that it would be useless to prolong the action and ordered a withdrawal. At length the northern companies were ordered to withdraw west to Keravat, the southern companies south towards the Warangoi River, all moving in small parties. The forward companies retired in good shape during the late morning and early afternoon. The fighting had ended, but for the Australians there began a period of great suffering and privation. Many, overcome by their circumstances, elected to surrender, among them Colonel Scanlan. About 200 who did so in good faith became involved on 4th March in a brutal massacre at Tol and Waitavalo plantations on the south coast, in which the Japanese killed about 150 Australians. Mass rescues on the north and south coasts, in which officers of the administration played a large part, saved over 400 survivors in late March and early April, and as late as May small parties were still arriving from New Britain.

In the meantime, about 7 a.m. on 21st January, about sixty Japanese aircraft had attacked Kavieng, which was defended by the headquarters and part of the 1st Independent Company. Probably four aircraft were shot down. The Independent Company's vessel, *Induna Star* (81 tons), was attacked while seeking a more sheltered anchorage and ran on to a reef. The company commander, Major J. E. Wilson, sent all his men except a rearguard inland to positions overlooking the harbour or to a camp where stores had been assembled in case withdrawal became necessary. Before dawn on the 23rd Japanese landed at Kavieng. In the darkness Wilson and the rearguard blew up the remaining dumps and cratered the airfield. A few days later Wilson decided that his little force, in which most of the men were now suffering from malaria or diarrhoea, could serve no useful purpose by remaining on New Ireland and on the 30th it embarked in the *Induna Star*, which had now been made seaworthy. The vessel was about ninety miles south of Rabaul on 2nd February when Japanese aircraft hit it with a bomb and shepherded it into port.

The little garrisons on Ocean Island and Nauru were now left far within the Japanese perimeter and they remained there until late in February when they and most of the European civilians were embarked by the French destroyer *Le Triomphant* and the steamer *Trienza.* Seven Europeans including the Administrator, Lieut-Colonel F. R. Chalmers, remained on Nauru, and six, including Mr C. G. F. Cartwright, who was in charge at the time, on Ocean Island. Nauru was not occupied by the Japanese until August 1942.

Curtin's newspaper article of 27th December had led to an interchange of long telegrams between him and Churchill, and at length to one sent on 23rd January in which Curtin stated that Earle Page had reported that the Defence Committee in London was considering the evacuation of Singapore (they had done so on the 21st but without reaching a conclusion). 'After all the assurances we have been given,' Curtin added, 'the evacuation of Singapore would be regarded here and elsewhere as an inexcusable betrayal.'

> It is not true to say that Mr Curtin's message decided the issue (wrote Churchill later).[9] If we had all been agreed upon the policy we should . . . have put the case 'bluntly' to Wavell. I was conscious however of a hardening of opinion against the abandonment of this renowned key point in the Far East. The effect that would be produced all over the world, especially in the United States, of a British 'scuttle' while the Americans fought on so stubbornly at Corregidor was terrible to imagine.[1] There is no doubt what a purely military decision should have been. By general agreement or acquiescence however all efforts were made to reinforce Singapore and to sustain its defence. The 18th Division, part of which had already landed, went forward on its way.

The remainder of the 18th Division, less several units, arrived at Singapore, as previously arranged, on 29th January.

Ambon, in the path of the Japanese flotilla of men-of-war and transports advancing south through the Moluccas, and possessing the strongest garrison yet encountered by the Japanese in the Indies or New Guinea, was next on their program. When the 2/21st Battalion (Lieut-Colonel L. N. Roach), supplemented by ancillary detachments, disembarked at Ambon on 17th December there were already some 2,600 Netherlands Indies troops there. In the next ten days Roach complained strongly to Army Headquarters in Melbourne that his force was inadequate and particularly that it lacked heavy weapons. He asked for field and anti-tank guns, anti-aircraft guns, mortars and medium machine-guns. He was informed from Melbourne that his role was 'to put up the best defence possible'. The first Japanese air attack came on the night of 6th January when forty-two aircraft bombed the Ambon area. On the 13th Roach signalled Melbourne that his force could not hold out for more than a day against the strong Japanese force then operating in Celebes. (It included a substantial fleet and some sixteen transports carrying an infantry regiment plus two battalions of marines.) Roach recommended evacuation. Next day he was informed that Major W. J. R. Scott would be flown from Melbourne to replace him.

On 24th January, after the Japanese landing at Kendari, Admiral Thomas C. Hart of the United States Navy, Wavell's naval commander, also recommended that Ambon be evacuated but his advice was rejected. Indeed on the 27th Wavell decided to meet the threat offered by the Japanese advance from Celebes by reinforcing Koepang in Timor, likely to be the next Japanese objective after Ambon. The main role of the Netherlands

[9] Churchill, *The Second World War*, Vol. IV (1951), pp. 51-2.

[1] In fact from mid-February until early April there was practically no fighting in the Philippines.

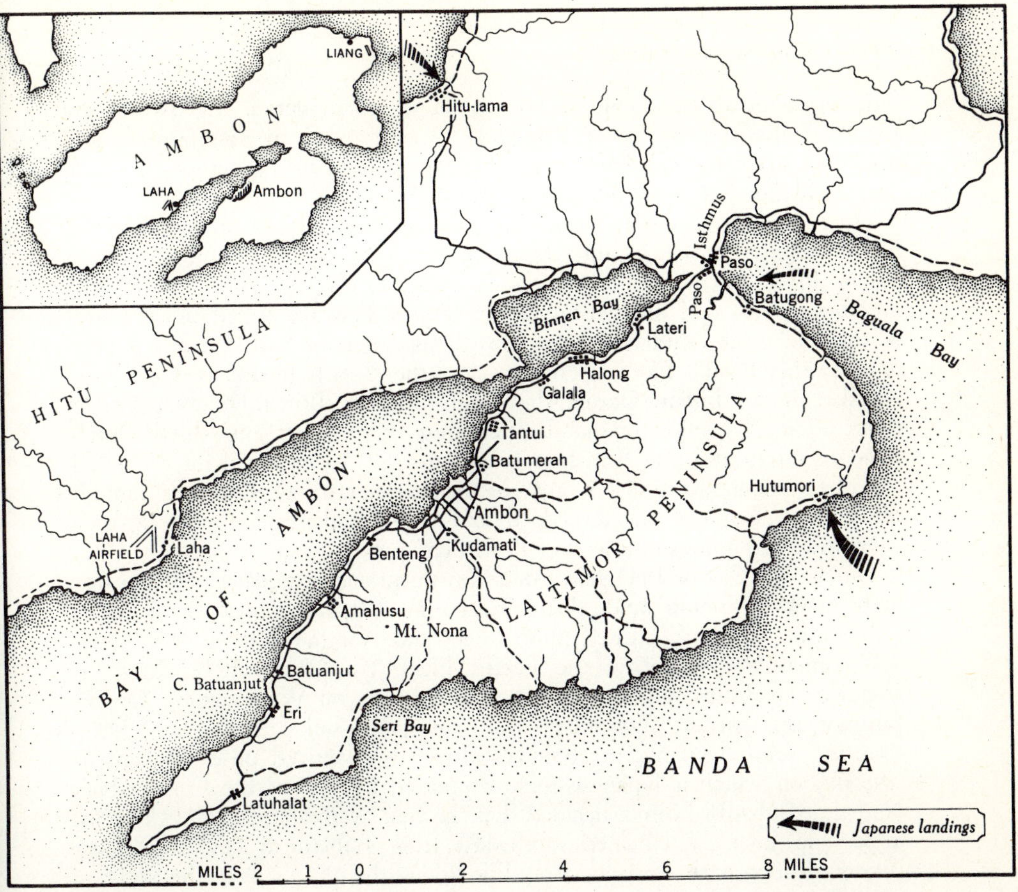

Ambon

Indies troops on Ambon and of 'Gull Force', as the 2/21st Battalion group was named, was to defend the bay of Ambon and two airfields, where some Netherlands and Australian aircraft were based. The Australians accepted from Lieut-Colonel J. R. L. Kapitz, the Netherlands officer commanding the combined force, the task of defending Laha and also the area south of Ambon on the eastern side of the bay. The main body of Netherlands troops was deployed about Paso to defeat any attempt to land in the Bay of Baguala, which Kapitz considered the most likely place.

In the second half of January attacks by Japanese aircraft increased in number and intensity, the aircraft from two carriers, *Soryu* and *Hiryu*, being used. By the 30th the last of the defending aircraft were withdrawn. On the previous day they had reported the approach of a convoy estimated at five warships and seventeen transports. On the night of the 30th-31st Japanese troops landed at the southern end of the Laitimor Peninsula where a landing was least expected, about Hitu-lama, and near Paso. Once ashore they thrust north to Paso and west towards the town of Ambon. They soon overran the Paso defences, and on the afternoon of the 31st some Netherlands troops surrendered. The advancing Japanese pushed the Australians back and by nightfall on the 31st they were concentrated in a confined area about Eri. On 3rd February Scott decided that further resistance by his weary and depleted force would serve no useful purpose. He sent an envoy to the Japanese and at length surrendered. Meanwhile the two Australian companies at Laha had been attacked on 31st January and overcome after a long hard fight. Several parties of Australians escaped and made their way back to Australia in small craft.

Up to mid-January, apart from an abortive effort ending on 23rd December to relieve Wake Island, the aircraft carrier forces of the American Pacific Fleet, including the carriers *Saratoga, Lexington, Yorktown, Hornet* and *Enterprise*, had not ventured far west of Hawaii. Allied naval power in the Pacific and Indian Oceans was divided among four widely-separated groups: this Pacific Fleet far to the east, the British force based on Trincomalee in the Indian Ocean, the small American-British-Dutch-Australian force under Wavell's command (including three American, three Dutch, one Australian and one British cruiser), and the Anzac naval force (including three Australian cruisers and one American cruiser). On 11th January the carrier *Saratoga* was torpedoed and severely damaged by a Japanese submarine 500 miles south-west of Pearl Harbour.

On the last day of 1941 new American naval commanders had taken over both at Washington and Pearl Harbour—Admiral Ernest J. King as Commander-in-Chief, United States Fleet and Admiral Chester W. Nimitz as Commander-in-Chief of the Pacific Fleet. (In March 1942 King also assumed the duties of Chief of Naval Operations, at Washington.) On 6th January the carriers *Yorktown* and *Enterprise* sailed from San Diego escorting reinforcements for Samoa, where they arrived on 23rd January (the day on which a Japanese force supported by part of the *Carrier Fleet* landed at Rabaul). Nimitz decided that the best available means of deterring a possible Japanese advance southward from Rabaul to cut his line of communication with Australia would be to raid the Marshalls in the Japanese rear. Consequently *Yorktown* and *Enterprise* with attendant ships joined forces near Samoa and steamed north. On 1st February they carried out air attacks and bombardments against islands in the Marshalls. Little damage was done, but useful experience was gained. Meanwhile on 27th January the Australian Government had warned Nimitz that Japanese troops at their present rate of progress might take New Caledonia before an American division then on the way reached it. This was a faulty appreciation of Japanese tactics as revealed during the past two months, because each stage of their advance through the archipelago had not exceeded the range of a fighter aircraft, but Nimitz sent the carrier *Lexington* into the Anzac Area and by 12th February she was near Fiji.

In the first week of February it had become evident that hope of holding Singapore or Sumatra, or perhaps even Java, was meagre. The balance of the 18th British Division had landed at Singapore but other reinforcements were still far away: the 7th Armoured Brigade could not arrive in Java until late in February, the 7th Australian Division could not be ready for action in Sumatra until about 21st March, the 6th not until the middle of April. On the eastern flank the Japanese were in Rabaul whence they might move across the route from America to Australia, and in Ambon whence they might soon cut communications between Australia and Java. On the western flank they were moving steadily into Burma.

There, at the outbreak of war, the British garrison had comprised chiefly the 1st Burma Division (which then consisted of one Indian and two

Burma Brigades). The 17th Indian Division (reconstituted after the subtraction of the 44th and 45th Brigades, which were sent to Malaya, until it included two Indian brigades later augmented by a Burma brigade from the 1st Burma Division) was assembled there in December and January. In December the Japanese landed their *55th* and *33rd Divisions* in southern Burma, to be followed some months later by two more. Their aircraft bombed Rangoon on 23rd and 25th December, causing great panic. Meanwhile the *55th Japanese Division* had advanced north along the narrow southern arm of Burma, taking Tavoy on 19th January and Moulmein on the 31st. The 17th Indian Division was now deployed about Martaban and the Salween River.

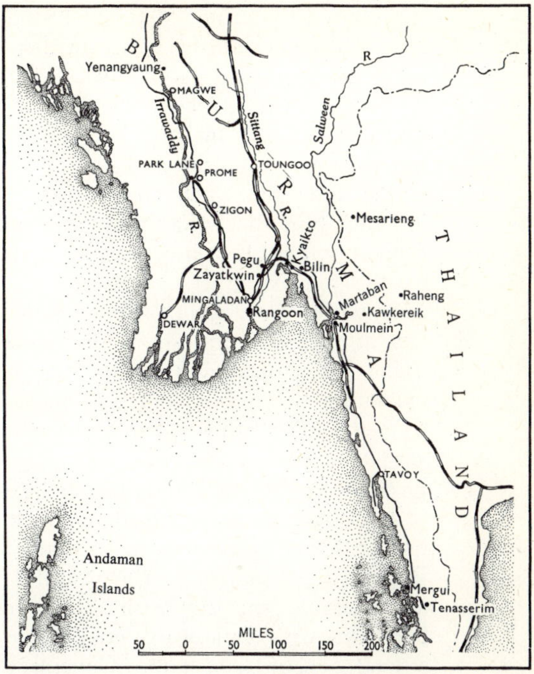

Southern Burma

On 6th February Wavell flew from Java to the headquarters of Lieut-General T. J. Hutton, the commander in Burma, and visited the 17th Division. He decided to divert the 7th Armoured Brigade, then on its way to Java, to Rangoon; on the 9th a brigade of Gurkhas from the north-west frontier of India joined the 17th Division, making a total of six brigades in Burma.

Meanwhile there had been a naval setback to the combined naval force of ABDA Command. Rear-Admiral K. W. F. M. Doorman (of the Netherlands Navy) led a force of two Dutch and two American cruisers with seven destroyers towards Macassar Strait to attack an enemy convoy bound probably for Macassar. On the 4th February they were attacked by thirty-six Japanese bombers; two American cruisers were damaged, one severely. On 9th February the Japanese landed at Macassar. The Allied naval striking force now included five cruisers (three Dutch, one British and one Australian) and ten destroyers.

Farther east in the Philippines, late in January, the Japanese had forced the defending line back to the waist of the Bataan Peninsula. On 8th February Manuel Quezon, President of the embryo Commonwealth of the Philippines (over which the United States reserved control of finance, foreign trade and foreign relations, immigration and defence) with MacArthur's approval sent a message to President Roosevelt proposing that the Philippines be given independence and forthwith neutralised by agreement between Japan and the United States. The American High Commissioner, Francis B. Sayre, added a message that if American help could not arrive he supported the proposal. General MacArthur also added a message in which he said that the Filipinos felt 'almost violent resentment' against the United States and that the President 'must determine whether the mission of delay would be better furthered by the temporising plan of Quezon or by my continued battle effort'. MacArthur predicted 'a disastrous debacle'. These messages shocked Roosevelt and his colleagues. Roosevelt replied to Quezon rejecting his proposal and assuring him that eventually American forces would drive the invaders out; and to MacArthur authorising him to choose the time when the Filipinos serving under him might capitulate, ordering him that American forces must resist as long as they could, and proposing that Quezon be evacuated via Australia.

Meanwhile the assault on Singapore had begun. Crowded into Singapore city at the southern tip of the island were about 1,000,000 people. The island has a maximum length from east to west of twenty-six miles and a maximum width from north to south of fourteen. The straits separating it from the mainland vary in width west of the Causeway from 600 to 2,000 yards and east of it from 1,000 to 5,000. Thus a modern medium artillery piece sited in Johore could drop shells into the city.

The force now assembled on Singapore Island numbered about 85,000, but 15,000 of those were base troops. There were 17 Indian battalions, 14 British, 7 Australian, 2 Malay and 2 of local volunteers—enough infantry and machine-gun units to fill about four divisions, but about eight of these battalions were greatly depleted. In support were artillery units armed with a total of 266 field guns. General Percival estimated, correctly, that the Japanese commander had three divisions: the *Guards, 5th* and another (later known to be the *18th*); he considered that other Japanese divisions might be brought in from farther north.

Percival decided that, because of the lack of room to manoeuvre, the thick vegetation, and the adverse moral effect of a successful landing, he would have to fight the enemy on the beaches rather than hold the coast thinly, reserve his main force for a counter-attack and fight the decisive battle after the enemy had landed and thus revealed the direction of his attack. He divided the island into three areas: Western, extending from the Sungei Jurong to the Causeway; Northern, from the Causeway to Changi; Southern from Changi to the Jurong. At first Percival considered that the main attack would be launched against the Northern Area, and there he placed the III Indian Corps, including the 11th Indian Division (into which the 9th had now been absorbed) and the 18th British Division, it being his freshest formation. Six field artillery regiments were allotted to this sector. Later Percival decided that the main attack was likely to fall west of the Causeway, where the Australians were, but he considered it too late to change the dispositions, and not even artillery regiments were transferred to the west. This area was commanded by General Bennett who had the 22nd and 27th Australian Brigades and the 44th Indian with three field artillery regiments—only half the number allotted to the Northern Area. Major-General F. Keith Simmons, commanding the Southern Area, which was unlikely to be heavily attacked, had the 1st and 2nd Malaya Brigades and the Straits Settlements Volunteer Force, and one field artillery regiment. The 12th Indian Brigade, only 900 strong, and the 6th/15th Indian Brigade were in general reserve.

Bennett placed the 27th Brigade in the sector from the Causeway to the

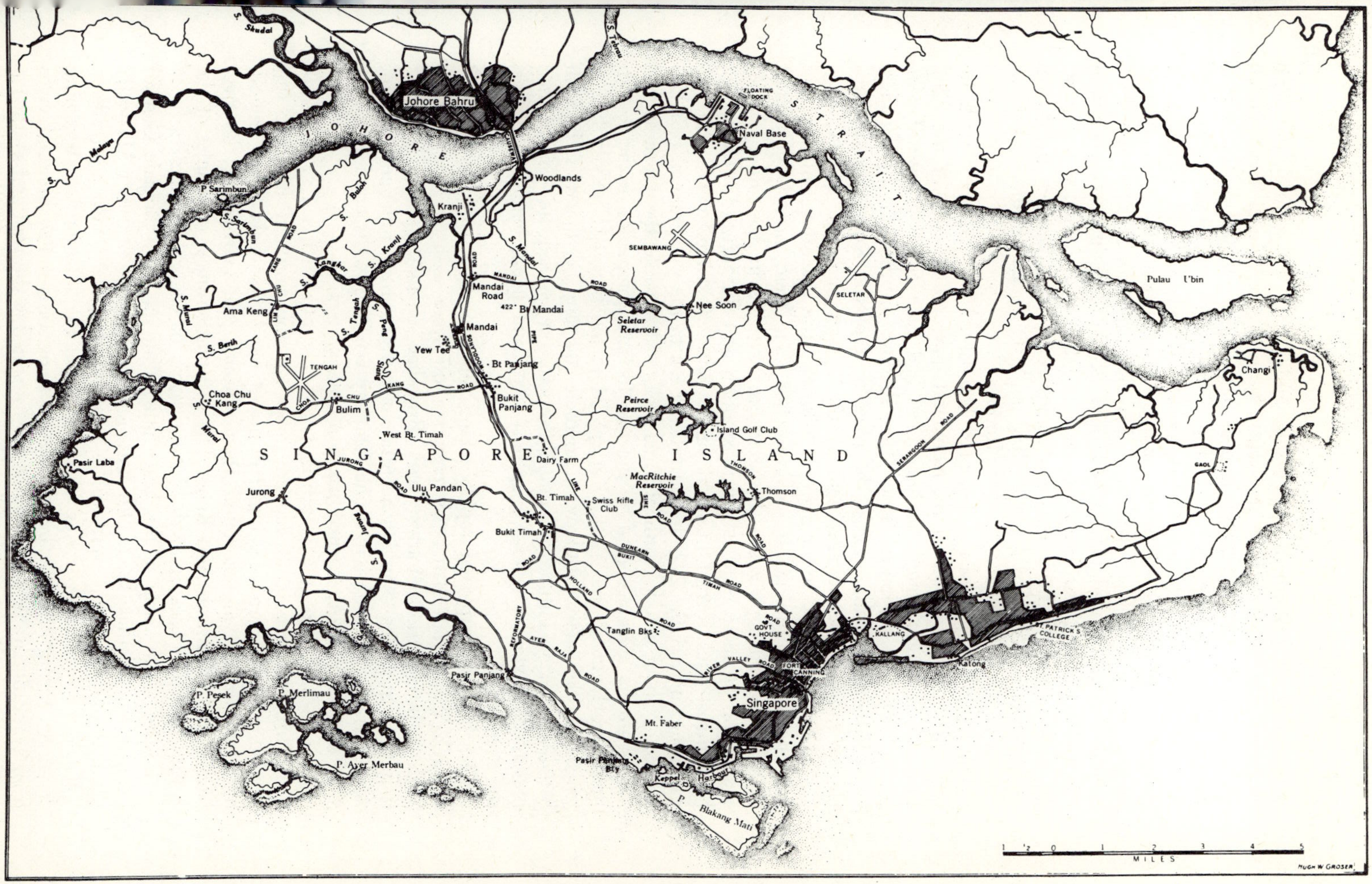

Singapore Island

wide Sungei Kranji (more than a mile and a half of coastline), the 22nd Brigade from the Kranji to the south bank of the Sungei Berih (about eight miles of coast), and the 44th Indian Brigade thence to the Sungei Jurong (about ten miles of coast). Brigadier Taylor's front was so long that he decided that he must place all three battalions of the 22nd Brigade on or near the coast, with local reserves, and gave instructions that if the forward troops were overwhelmed those who remained were to fight their way back to their company headquarters and form defensive perimeters, whence, if again overwhelmed, the companies were to fall back to battalion perimeters on a line across the neck of land through Ama Keng, between the Kranji and the Berih. A second defensive line might be formed farther east across the neck between the Kranji and the Jurong.

During 8th February the Japanese bombarded the defenders with increasing intensity, concentrating more and more on the area of the 22nd Brigade. At length many telephone lines had been cut and forward companies were out of touch. Soon after 10 p.m. on the 8th the Japanese launched their assault, against the coast west of the Kranji. In the area on the right of the brigade, held by the 2/20th Battalion (Lieut-Colonel C. F. Assheton) and a company of Chinese, the defending infantry and machine-gunners inflicted heavy losses but there were more landing craft than they could cope with—the attackers used 260 in all—and by about 1 a.m. the Japanese were ashore in strength and the forward infantry had been thrust back several hundred yards. Between 2 a.m. and 7 a.m. the rifle companies of the 2/20th had fallen back to the pre-arranged battalion perimeter about a mile north of Ama Keng. Meanwhile the Japanese had landed in the areas occupied by the two forward companies of the 2/18th Battalion (Lieut-Colonel A. L. Varley). Here too they lost heavily but at length the defenders withdrew on to their company headquarters. In each battalion's sector failure of communications, or inadequate liaison, had prevented maximum defensive artillery fire from being employed against the attackers.

The Japanese exploited rapidly along the two roads running eastward through the 2/18th Battalion's position and were soon pressing towards Varley's headquarters; Varley, with Brigadier Taylor's approval, ordered that the companies should concentrate about the road junction north of Ama Keng. In the withdrawal one company was greatly dispersed, and only 45 of another company reached battalion headquarters.

Next to the left was the 2/19th Battalion (Lieut-Colonel A. E. Robertson). Some fifty Japanese craft landed troops on the northern flank of this battalion. The Australians inflicted heavy losses and held their ground, but the Japanese moved round them through the marshes at the river mouth and on towards Ama Keng. The two northernmost companies of the 2/19th then fell back from the coast towards battalion headquarters.

As soon as he learnt of the heavy attacks on the 22nd Brigade General Bennett ordered that the 2/29th Battalion deployed on Brigadier Maxwell's left rear should be sent westward to reinforce Brigadier Taylor's brigade.

Taylor considered by 6 a.m. on the 9th that the situation was becoming desperate. Firing could be heard in Ama Keng, only a few hundred yards from his headquarters, and Japanese were reported to the west and south. He ordered that his headquarters be moved to a position near Bulim, and that the 2/29th, when it arrived, should line the road just south of Ama Keng; the plan was to form a line in depth along the neck from Ama Keng to the Berih, north of the Tengah airfield. The 2/29th arrived and then the 'Reserve Battalion', formed of Army Service Corps men and others, and both were placed in the new position. Forward of the Tengah position the 2/20th and 2/18th were hard pressed, as was the 2/19th farther south. By the time they reached the 2/29th's line all had lost heavily.

Satisfied that the Japanese were committed to an attack on the western area General Percival placed his command reserve—the depleted 12th Indian Brigade (Brigadier Paris)—under Bennett's command. Bennett at 9.30 a.m. had ordered Taylor to counter-attack and occupy the Kangkar-Berih neck, through Ama Keng. Taylor went forward to the 2/29th and found that this battalion and the Reserve Battalion were being heavily assailed. He cancelled the counter-attack and reported this by liaison officer to Bennett's headquarters. It seemed to Taylor that his main task was, in co-operation with the 44th Indian Brigade on his left, to rally on the Kranji-Jurong line, which as yet was unprepared and unmanned. His own brigade had been reduced to about 500 men; he had in addition the 2/29th Battalion, the Reserve Battalion, both chiefly raw reinforcements, and the Jind Battalion, an inexperienced Indian State unit guarding the Tengah airfield. He estimated (fairly accurately) that the Japanese could by midday bring twelve battalions against him. He decided to form a line east of the Tengah airfield through Bulim.

Meanwhile, round the airfield, the hurriedly-assembled force had halted the Japanese, and fragments of the 22nd Brigade's battalions came in. Paris reported to Bennett with his 12th Brigade and Bennett ordered him forward to join Taylor, which he did at midday. Brigadier G. C. Ballentine of the 44th Brigade now telephoned Bennett's headquarters that unless the Japanese were held his brigade would soon be cut off. Colonel J. H. Thyer, Bennett's Chief Staff Officer, told Ballentine that he should make plans on the assumption that Taylor would have to withdraw to the Kranji-Jurong line. Early in the afternoon the two brigades prepared a plan to occupy that line but Bennett refused to sanction this. It was then about 2 p.m. Soon afterwards Percival arrived forward at Bennett's headquarters. While he was there news arrived that the 22nd Brigade was being thrust back to the Kranji-Jurong line. At this stage Percival ordered his only remaining reserve—the 6th/15th Indian Brigade—to the Bukit Timah area to cover the vital road junction there.

Later that afternoon Percival and his staff began preparing plans for a general withdrawal to a line round the city itself, enclosing the Kallang airfield, the MacRitchie and Peirce reservoirs and Bukit Timah, and swinging thence to Pasir Panjang. A provisional order for a withdrawal to this area was circulated.

Meanwhile Taylor's brigade and Paris's were occupying the Kranji position. About 4 p.m. Bennett ordered Ballentine to withdraw to this line and late that night ordered Taylor to withdraw to it too, after denying Bulim to the enemy until 6 a.m. on the 10th. The Japanese did not attack Bulim that night.

The withdrawal of the 2/29th Battalion to reinforce Taylor had uncovered the left flank of the 27th Brigade along the Kranji and groups of the 2/20th crossing the Kranji into its area had indicated that that battalion had been thrust back. Brigadier Maxwell was anxious about this flank and obtained permission to place two companies along the east banks of the Kranji and the Peng Siang. Artillery and air attack was intensified during the morning of the 9th and Maxwell made a further request to Bennett's headquarters about midday that he be permitted to occupy a north south line from the junction of the Kranji-Woodlands road to the 12-mile post on the Woodlands road. This appears to have been granted subject to the oil storage depots near the Causeway first being destroyed. Lieut-Colonel R. F. Oakes of the 2/26th was to co-ordinate the move of his own and the 2/30th Battalion.

About 9 p.m. on the 9th Japanese barges crowded with troops began crossing the straits to the eastern side of the Kranji mouth and the Mandai River. The Japanese were kept under heavy fire for some hours. About 4.30 a.m. a party of Australian engineers, working close to the enemy, set fire to the petrol storage, starting immense fires in which 2,000,000 gallons were consumed. Blazing petrol flowed along the creeks and on to the waters of the strait and the fires filled the air with fumes; throughout the night black oil was mixed with the heavy rain which was falling. The petrol having been set on fire the pre-arranged withdrawal of the 27th Brigade might begin. Oakes decided that the situation of the two battalions was so perilous that he must make a longer withdrawal than the one planned. After concentrating heavy mortar and machine-gun fire on the enemy the battalions began to fall back before dawn on the 10th to an arc north and west of Bukit Mandai. This uncovered the left flank of the 11th Indian Division.

It was learnt later that the main assault, on the 22nd Brigade's front, had been made by the *5th* and *18th Japanese Divisions* whose first objective was the Tengah airfield and whose second was a line from Bukit Mandai to the Jurong. They would then wheel southward against the Bukit Timah area. Meanwhile on the night of the 9th the *Guards Division* was to cross the strait just west of the Causeway. The enemy was supported by the concentrated fire of 168 field and medium guns, not counting infantry guns—about one gun to every forty yards of the front on which the main assault was made.

At daylight on the 10th the 27th Brigade was moving into position between Mandai and Bukit Panjang with the *Guards Division* following up; between the right of the 27th Australian Brigade and the left of the 28th Indian Brigade, not yet under attack, was a gap of about three miles. To the south-west four brigades—the battered 22nd Australian and the 12th, 6th/15th and 44th Indian—were going into position on the Kranji-Jurong neck. In anticipation of further set-backs General Percival had issued a provisional order for abandonment of the greater part of the island and the defence of an arc embracing Singapore and its immediate surroundings.

In the Jurong position the 12th Brigade was astride the Bulim road

Australian War Memorial

Singapore, February 1942. Smoke from the naval base overshadows the city.

with the Australian Reserve Battalion on its left and the 6th/15th and 44th covering the Jurong road. Of the Australian units falling back to this position the 2/18th was reorganising just in rear of the 12th Brigade and the 2/29th went in between the 12th Brigade and the Reserve Battalion.

At this stage Taylor, having received the order about the retirement to 'a final perimeter' in 'certain circumstances', took the order to mean that the retirement should begin immediately, and ordered his units to take up their allotted positions along the Reformatory Road. The troops remaining with him were: the remnants of the 2/18th, one company of the 2/19th and about one company of the 2/20th, about 500 infantry all told, with some supporting detachments. Taylor then reported to Bennett, who told him that the order had not required immediate withdrawal and that Taylor's units should still be on the Jurong line.

General Wavell, always insistent on going forward and seeing for himself, arrived on the island on the morning of the 10th, and visited Percival, Heath and Bennett. Percival now allotted more reinforcements to Bennett: three battalions from the 18th Division, the group being named 'Tomforce' after Lieut-Colonel L. C. Thomas their commander. Percival also decided to place the 22nd Brigade under the command of General Key of the 11th Indian Division and ordered the 27th Brigade to secure Key's left by regaining the Mandai road junction.

In the meantime the Japanese had pressed on from Bulim on the morning of the 10th and, in danger of encirclement, the Argylls (of the 12th Brigade) and the 2/29th had been withdrawn to ground near Keat Hong, about one and a half miles to the east. Paris, learning that the Causeway road was undefended, placed the 2/29th astride it facing north with the Argylls in depth behind them and the Hyderabads—facing west astride the Bulim road. Thus the northern sector of the Kranji-Jurong road was abandoned. The Reserve Battalion on the right, still with nobody in touch with it, fell back towards the 6th/15th Brigade on the Jurong road.

Here, early in the afternoon, the *18th Japanese Division* had thrust between the 6th/15th and 44th Indian Brigades; the inexperienced battalions of the 44th had taken alarm and fallen back right out of the area to Pasir Panjang on the south coast. After this collapse on its left the 6th/15th Brigade (including the Reserve Battalion) withdrew to a position west of Bukit Timah village. Thus, in the afternoon, the line was along the Causeway-Pasir Panjang road, except that, in the south, the 1st Malaya Brigade, not yet attacked, was forward on the Jurong. Also that afternoon General Key, anxious to secure his left, gave Brigadier W. A. Trott's 8th Brigade the task of occupying the high ground overlooking the road and the Causeway and it fought its way forward to this position. Later, on Key's orders, the 2/30th Battalion occupied a position running south from the Mandai junction.

That afternoon Percival, learning something of the set-backs on the Kranji line and having been exhorted by Wavell, ordered Bennett to regain it, and at 4.5 p.m. Bennett issued instructions for a large-scale counter-attack in three phases, the first to be completed by 9 p.m., the second by 9 a.m. on the 11th and the third by 6 p.m. The 12th Brigade was to attack on the right, the 6th/15th in the centre and the 22nd on the left; the 44th and Tomforce (the only fresh troops) were to be in reserve positions. When the orders were given the three brigades, one weaker than a battalion and the others little stronger, were on a five-miles front along the main road some three or four miles from the final objective which was occupied by two Japanese divisions. The attack could not hope to succeed.

Before preparations for this ambitious project were complete, Japanese of the *5th Division* had advanced along the Bulim road through the Hyderabads and into the 2/29th, which that evening was pushed west and south and at length with Paris's agreement withdrew on to the 22nd Brigade. The Japanese, who had a strong force of tanks, then encountered the Argylls and during the night thrust through them to Bukit Timah village.

An 'X' Battalion consisting of raw reinforcements was now sent forward to a position about two miles along the Jurong road where it established itself, unaware, as was the 6th/15th Brigade behind it, that the Japanese were entering Bukit Timah behind them. 'Merrett Force' (200 survivors of the 2/19th and 2/20th) went into position on the 'X' Battalion's left.

About 3 a.m. on the 11th Japanese of the *18th Division* advancing along this road attacked the 'X' Battalion, which was overwhelmed, its commander and many others being killed and others captured. Hearing firing behind him Major R. O. Merrett withdrew his force to Reformatory road. After heavy fighting only remnants of the force reached the road. By 6 a.m. the leading Japanese were nearing the outskirts of Singapore. Later in the morning Japanese aircraft dropped several copies of a message demanding surrender and one of these was delivered at Percival's headquarters.

Bennett now ordered Tomforce to retake Bukit Timah village. Early on the morning of the 11th Tomforce, joined by the 2/29th Battalion, attacked but could not reach the objective. While Tomforce was pressing towards Bukit Timah from the east, part of the 6th/15th Brigade, isolated west of the village, was obediently carrying on with the counter-attack ordered the previous day. An order cancelling the attack did not reach the Jats, who went forward and were soon isolated. Meanwhile the Japanese attacked the remainder of the brigade. During a cross-country withdrawal to Reformatory road the columns ran into an enemy force and were dispersed, only 500 men reaching the railway east of the road.

In the northern sector the proposed attack on Mandai village was abandoned and instead Maxwell was ordered to assist in the recapture of Bukit Panjang. Orders arrived late, the attack was cancelled and at length, in the confusion, the 2/26th Battalion began withdrawing towards the perimeter not along the road but along a pipeline about a mile east of it while the 2/30th and the 8th Indian Brigade became heavily engaged with the Japanese *Guards Division*, which was thrusting east towards Nee Soon. The 8th Indian Brigade withdrew to Nee Soon. The 2/30th Battalion withdrew south of Nee Soon and by nightfall was astride the road leading south towards Peirce reservoir. The 2/26th, withdrawing south along the pipeline, clashed with Japanese moving east from the main road and lost heavily before some detachments reached the 2/30th and some reached the perimeter area in the south, east of Bukit Timah.

The Japanese were now—about 5 a.m.—pressing hard against the 22nd Brigade round Reformatory road. Taylor's headquarters were attacked and several of his staff killed or wounded in close fighting. The line was held but Taylor obtained Bennett's permission to shorten the line, to conform with the withdrawal of Tomforce, until it formed an arc forward of Holland road linking with Tomforce near the racecourse. On the morning of the 12th the defending force was deployed along a north-south line from the Causeway, where the 28th Indian Brigade was still in its original position, to Sembawang airfield (53rd British Brigade), Nee Soon (8th Indian Brigade and 2/30th Battalion), Peirce and MacRitchie reservoirs (Massy Force—an improvised brigade group drawn from the 18th Division), the racecourse (Tomforce), and thence to Pasir Panjang (as described above).

Japanese tanks thrust along the Bukit Timah road towards the city at 8.30 a.m. on the 12th but were turned back. After this Percival and Heath agreed to put into effect the plan to form a close perimeter about twenty-five miles long round Singapore. Meanwhile, as a result of a suggestion by his senior administrative officers, Bennett had decided to bring all Australian base troops, except those in the hospitals, out of the city proper, and from this proposal developed a plan to create an Australian perimeter round the Tanglin Barracks area.

Along its narrowing front the defending force was now obtaining strong artillery support and the Japanese attack was not pressed so effectively during the 13th. Brigadier Taylor, utterly worn out, collapsed and was taken to hospital, Bennett replacing him with Colonel Varley.

It was now evident that either a capitulation or slaughter of the defenders could not be delayed much longer. The nursing sisters from the hospitals had been embarked on the 10th, 11th and 12th. On the night of the 13th some 3,000 men, including 1,800 soldiers, were placed on some of the small vessels which remained in Singapore Harbour. These men included groups of staff officers and other specialists, no longer needed, whose knowledge and experience might be useful elsewhere.

At 2 p.m. on the 13th Percival held a conference of senior commanders. All agreed that a counter-attack could not succeed. Early on the 14th the shortage of water became critical. Percival reported the position to Wavell, who told him that resistance 'must be continued to limit of endurance'. There was heavy fighting on the perimeter all day, and chiefly on the left and round the MacRitchie reservoir. Early on the 15th (a Sunday) Percival was told that the water would not last another day; the Japanese were infiltrating deeply on the left and on the front of the Indian Corps. A signal arrived from Wavell (who had consulted Churchill) giving Percival discretion to cease resistance. That evening Percival met General Yamashita and capitulated. Fighting ceased at 8.30 p.m.

General Bennett had decided some days earlier that he would try to escape. Leaving Brigadier C. A. Callaghan, his senior artillery officer, in command of the division, Bennett, with two staff officers, embarked in a sampan and at length reached Java, whence Bennett was flown to Australia. He was convinced that it was his duty to escape and 'return to Australia to tell our people the story of our conflict with the Japanese, to warn them of the danger to Australia and advise them of the best means of defeating the Japanese tactics'.[2]

On Singapore Island the Japanese lost 1,714 killed and 3,378 wounded. During the whole campaign they took about 130,000 prisoners. The defenders losses were: Indian, 67,340; United Kingdom, 38,490; Australian, 18,490 (including 1,789 killed and 1,306 wounded); local volunteers, 14,380.

Disaster now followed disaster. The air force concentrated in Sumatra was now based at 'P1' airfield eight miles north of Palembang and 'P2' forty miles to the south-south-west, where McCauley was in command. At P2 were eight bomber squadrons, some having only three or four aircraft, and at P1 two fighter squadrons equipped with Hurricanes most of which had been flown off the British carrier *Indomitable*. The bombers attacked enemy airfields in Malaya with success, but on 13th February a convoy was sighted approaching Sumatra.

Allied aircraft attacked the convoy on the 14th when it approached the mouth of the Musi River and scored hits on transports. Japanese paratroops floated down on Palembang and forced the small improvised force defending P1 to withdraw. Next day the aircraft at P2, where all squadrons were now based, spent their bombs and ammunition against ships and barges approaching Palembang. All air force units were then ordered to Java.

Two transports carrying the first reinforcements from the Middle East had arrived at Oosthaven in Sumatra on the 14th and 15th. These included a squadron of British light tanks, two Australian battalions—2/3rd Machine Gun and 2/2nd Pioneer—and other small units and detachments, fore-

[2] H. G. Bennett, *Why Singapore Fell* (1944), p. 198.

runners of I Australian Corps. Since 27th January General Lavarack and part of his staff had been in Java and on the 13th General Allen of the 7th Division and five of his staff arrived. That day the first main convoy of Australian troops, containing the 21st Brigade, had left Bombay.

On the 13th February Lavarack had prepared an appreciation for Curtin in which he said that if Singapore fell large Japanese forces would be freed and south Sumatra could be lost before the 7th Australian Division arrived there. (It would not be ready for action until 21st March.) Even with the addition of the 6th Division, which would not be ready for operations before the middle of April, the prolonged land defence of Java was not possible. Lavarack said that I Australian Corps was the only striking force within reasonable distance of the Far East and emphasised the value of 'two highly trained, equipped and experienced divisions'. After seeing Lavarack's signal Wavell's staff prepared a somewhat similar one and sent it to London and Washington.

Wavell diverted the two transports from Oosthaven to Tanjong Priok, port of Batavia. Lavarack urged Wavell that the Australian troops (in *Orcades*) be not disembarked, but Wavell said that he wished to avoid compromising British relations with the Dutch and lowering British prestige; he wanted these troops to protect airfields. They disembarked at Batavia on the 18th.

Meanwhile on 14th February there had been a change in American policy towards the reinforcement of the base in Australia, hitherto used principally as a staging point for the air force. In Washington Brigadier-General Eisenhower proposed and General Marshall approved the dispatch of the 41st Division and 8,000 service troops to Australia.

On 15th February Curtin cabled Churchill urging that immediate consideration be given to the question whether the Australian Corps should return to Australia, now the main Allied base. Curtin was acting on the advice of his Chief of the General Staff, Sturdee, who, also on the 15th, wrote that the object should now be to ensure the holding of 'some continental area from which we can eventually launch an offensive in the Pacific, when American aid can be fully developed'. He doubted whether Java could be held, and in any event it did not provide a suitable base for an offensive. The return of 100,000 men of the A.I.F. would more than double the security of Australia. He recommended the diversion to Australia of I Australian Corps and the recall of the 9th Division. On the 17th Curtin asked Churchill that the 6th and 7th Divisions and the 7th Armoured Brigade be diverted to Australia and the 9th Division also shipped home. Wavell on the other hand recommended to Churchill that one Australian division or both be sent to Burma.

Heavy pressure from Washington and London was now brought to bear on Curtin in an effort to persuade him to change his mind. Page and Bruce urged that the 7th Division should be allowed to go to Rangoon. Harry L. Hopkins, Roosevelt's adviser and envoy, told Casey at Washington that the President was worried; would Australia agree to send two divisions to India or Burma if America agreed to send considerable forces to Australia? On the 19th the non-Government (non-Labour) members of the Advisory War Council said that the 7th Division should go to Burma. Next day a telegram arrived from the Dominions Office announcing that an

American division would sail for Australia early in March; Churchill addressed a strong plea to Curtin to allow 'the only force that can reach Rangoon in time to prevent its loss' to continue its voyage; and Roosevelt sent a similar plea. Assuming a 'favourable response', Churchill on the 21st ordered the diversion of the leading Australian convoy to Rangoon. On the 22nd he informed Curtin that the ships were on their way and 'too far north for some . . . to reach Australia without refuelling'; this, he said, gave a few days for Curtin to review the position should he wish to do so. On the 23rd Curtin repeated the decision that the Australian Corps should return to Australia, and that day the leading ships turned back towards Colombo.

Although several of the multitude of telegrams exchanged between the political leaders implied that the convoy contained the 7th Division, in fact it contained one brigade group (the 21st) of that division. The ships containing the second brigade (the 18th) of the division arrived at Bombay, 2,500 miles from Rangoon, on 19th February, did not finish trans-shipping until the 23rd, and were still there on the 25th; the third brigade did not arrive at Colombo from Aden until the 23rd. The commander and part of the headquarters of the division were, on the 23rd, in the *Orcades* steaming west from Java towards Ceylon. Lavarack had stated early in February that the whole division would not be ready for operations in Sumatra until 21st March, and it must be assumed that it could not have been ready in Burma any sooner than that. Meanwhile what had been happening in Burma?

The Japanese *55th* and *33rd Divisions* had thrust the defenders from Martaban in the second week of February, and, a few days later, from the line of the Bilin River. The next stand was made on the Sittang River about sixty miles from Rangoon. The British-Indian force was pushed out of this line with heavy loss. On 24th February the 17th Indian Division possessed only 80 officers and 3,404 other ranks with 1,420 rifles and 118 automatics. Meanwhile the flight of labour from Rangoon since the first air raid on 23rd December had made it difficult to work the port. Thousands of Indians streamed from the city and began walking home. Most of the police and the fire brigade were evacuated and there was much looting. Round Rangoon Burman nationalists, some under Japanese officers, were causing disorder. By 27th February the air and naval staffs were opposing any attempt to bring a convoy into Rangoon—the 63rd Indian Brigade was expected. When Wavell landed at Magwe on 1st March, however, he ordered that Rangoon be held long enough to enable this brigade to land, and it did so a few days later. General Sir Harold Alexander arrived on 5th March to take command of all troops in Burma. The British-Indian force, comprising the survivors of the 17th Division, the remnants of the 1st Burma Division, the 7th Armoured Brigade and the 63rd Brigade (whose vehicles were still in the transports), was deployed east and north of Rangoon; and the troops at Pegu were heavily engaged. On the 6th the Japanese were only a few miles from the road and railway from Rangoon to Prome, the only line of withdrawal. Late on the 6th Alexander decided that Rangoon must be abandoned and that demolitions should begin next day. The first Japanese patrols entered Rangoon before dawn on the 8th.

It is now evident that a brigade of Australians if landed at Rangoon about 26th February, and perhaps another brigade about the 3rd or 4th

March, could not have turned defeat into victory in Burma, but would only have taken part in the 600-miles retreat northward to Assam. Two Japanese divisions drove out of Burma a force of five Indian brigades, two Burma brigades (these seven including between them four British battalions) and a British armoured brigade.

Burma did receive reinforcements, however, from another direction—China—and this deployment caused some alarm at Japanese General Headquarters, where there was a great respect for the Chinese Army which for years had frustrated them. Late in December one Chinese division began marching into northern Burma, and it had been agreed that two more should follow. Wavell had been unwilling that three more divisions offered by the Chinese leader, Chiang Kai-shek, should follow preferring, as he wrote later in a dispatch, 'that a country of the British Empire should be defended by Imperial troops rather than by foreign', and believing that the Chinese would move too slowly to be of any great value to the defence of Burma.

Meanwhile, although most of I Australian Corps was diverted to Australia, about one-third of its fighting troops were in fact landed in Ceylon at the suggestion of the Australian Government. On the 24th Page suggested to Curtin that the 7th Division should remain in Ceylon at least until the 70th British Division arrived there. (The garrison of Ceylon which might be one of Japan's next objectives included two Indian brigades and a local one.) The Australian Chiefs of Staff agreed that the 7th Division should stay in Ceylon if the British Government wished. On 2nd March however, when a decision was made, the first two convoys of I Corps were already on their way south from Colombo and it was agreed that a later convoy, containing the 16th and 17th Brigades, due at Colombo on 25th March, should disembark its troops in Ceylon.

In the three weeks between the fall of Singapore and the fall of Rangoon the Japanese conquest of the Netherlands Indies was completed.

A convoy carrying reinforcements Wavell had sought for Timor left Darwin on the 15th February. It contained an Australian battalion and two American artillery battalions (part of the American force diverted from the Philippines). The convoy was attacked by Japanese aircraft but not damaged. Wavell decided, however, that a Japanese attack on Timor was imminent and ordered the ships back to Darwin.

Since 12th December a force of 1,320 Australians, including the 2/40th Battalion, 2/2nd Independent Company and other detachments, had been in Dutch Timor, whose garrison had hitherto consisted of some 500 Indonesian troops with Dutch officers; Brigadier W. C. D. Veale was in command. Based on Penfui field near Koepang since December was No. 2 Squadron R.A.A.F. On 17th December, as mentioned above, the 2/2nd Independent Company with about 260 Netherlands Indies troops were shipped to Dili and, despite the protests of the Governor, were landed on a beach near the town. The Dutch troops occupied the town, whose inhabitants proved friendly, and the Australians the airfield a mile and a half away.

At Koepang Lieut-Colonel W. W. Leggatt, commanding the 2/40th and attached troops, deployed two companies along the beaches north-east from Koepang, one round the airfield and one in reserve. The Dutch troops defended the beaches west of Koepang. Like Colonel Roach on Ambon Colonel Leggatt was convinced that his small force could not effectively defend even the Koepang area against the kind of attack the Japanese were likely to launch. The Penfui airfield (six miles to the south-east) was, however, serving its main purpose—to be a staging ground for aircraft being flown into Java. Seven Japanese aircraft appeared on 26th January and strafed the airfield, and forty-two on the 30th (the day of the Japanese landing on Ambon). In the latter raid one Hudson was destroyed on the ground and a Qantas flying boat shot down over the sea. On 19th February the main R.A.A.F. force at Penfui was evacuated to Darwin.

At this time the Japanese *Second Fleet* and *Carrier Fleet* were steaming south. They included two battleships and four carriers. Vice-Admiral Kondo's plan was to attack Darwin from the air on the morning of the 19th February and land his troops—an infantry regiment and a force of marines including a battalion of paratroops—on Timor that night. At dawn the carriers launched 188 aircraft which attacked the crowded harbour and town of Darwin. They sank the American destroyer *Peary*, American transports *Meigs* (12,568 tons) and *Mauna Loa* (5,436 tons), the British tanker *British Motorist* (6,891 tons) and the following Australian vessels: the transport *Zealandia* (6,683 tons), merchant ship *Neptuna* (5,952 tons), lugger *Mavie* and coal hulk *Kelat*. Later in the day the *Florence D* (2,638 tons) was sunk and *Don Isidro* (3,200 tons) was beached after an air attack off Bathurst Island. In the morning raid, and a second raid by fifty-four land-based aircraft from Kendari and Ambon which reached Darwin about midday, 243 were killed, including 191 in the ships, 35 civilians ashore, 8 American troops and 9 Australian air force or army men. In addition

Timor

about 350 were wounded. Twenty-three Allied aircraft and probably seven Japanese aircraft were destroyed. There was much confusion ashore. Many civilians, expecting invasion, retreated southward and some air force units were temporarily dispersed.

About midnight on the 19th-20th February the Japanese fleet began shelling Dili and soon Japanese troops were ashore and advancing towards the airfield. The section of the Independent Company which was round the airfield was ready for them, and inflicted severe casualties, until at dawn the Australians cratered the airfield and withdrew inland. In the following days the whole company was withdrawn into the hills about twenty miles from Dili with patrols forward. On 2nd March the enemy advanced inland in strength, and after some sharp fights the Independent Company withdrew to Hatu-Lia, south-west of Dili.

Meanwhile on the 20th the Japanese had landed near Koepang. The first landing was made at an undefended place on the south coast of the peninsula on which Koepang stands. In the face of this threat the airfield was cratered and the reserve company deployed astride the road leading south. Soon many Japanese aircraft appeared. They destroyed the two coast guns and Japanese transports entered the bay. The companies defending the beaches were then withdrawn. Soon Japanese, including paratroops, were thrusting the Australians inland. After three days of confused and costly fighting the Japanese commander on 23rd February sent Leggatt a message that he was surrounded and demanded surrender. After consulting his officers Leggatt surrendered, though some officers and men made off and either joined Brigadier Veale, who had moved his headquarters some twenty-five miles to the east, or marched eastward independently. During this fighting Veale's headquarters was cut off from wireless communication with both the 2/40th and 2/2nd. With some 250 Australians Veale now moved to Atambua near the border of Portuguese Timor and at length joined the Independent Company.[3]

By taking Timor and neutralising Darwin the Japanese had ensured that no reinforcements could reach Java from the south. It remained to launch the final big offensive: the *XVI Army's* assault on Java. On 21st February the advanced parties of the Australian corps and divisional headquarters had been ordered to embark in the *Orcades*, and Lavarack signalled Curtin that he was flying to Australia to report. That day the Combined Chiefs of Staff informed Wavell that Java should be defended to the last by all combatant troops then on the island, but instructed him to withdraw his own headquarters from the island. Wavell replied that ABDA Command should not be withdrawn but dissolved, and command of all forces in the Indies taken over by Netherlands commanders. This was agreed to and ABDA Command ceased to exist on the 25th, Wavell flying to India where he again became Commander-in-Chief.

There remained round Java a naval force of eight cruisers (the Netherlands *Java* and *De Ruyter*, British *Exeter*, *Dragon* and *Danae*, Australian *Perth* and *Hobart*, and American *Houston*), with sixteen destroyers. Vice-Admiral Conrad Helfrich divided this force into an Eastern and Western

[3] The Australian casualties in Dutch Timor were eighty-four killed and about twice that number wounded.

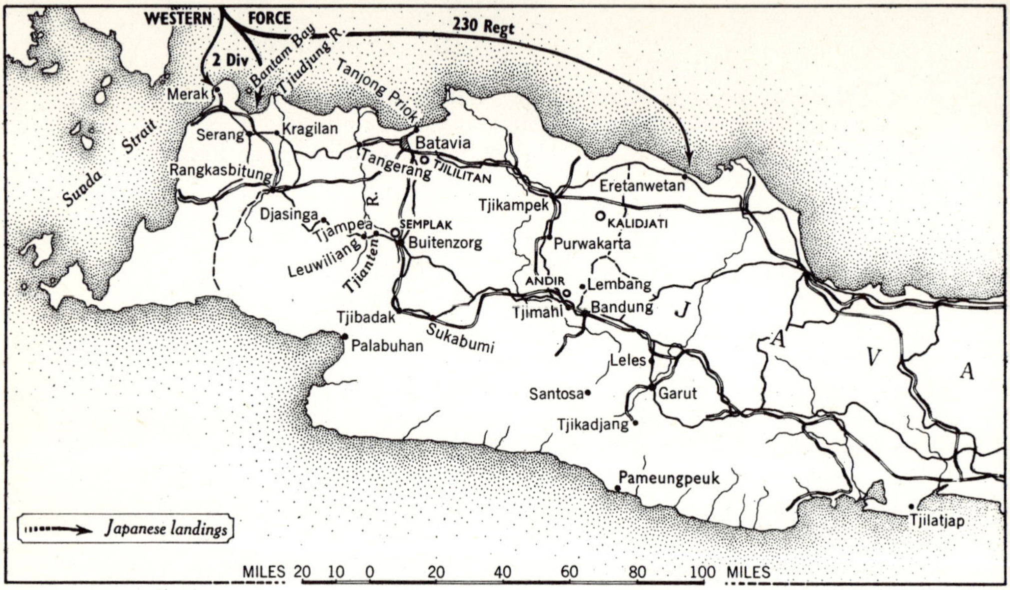

West Java

Force, based respectively on Surabaya and Tanjong Priok. There were also a Netherlands and an American submarine flotilla. The Allied Air Force included some ten Netherlands squadrons and the remnants of the air force from Malaya, reorganised by Air Vice-Marshal P. C. Maltby into three bomber and two fighter squadrons though it numbered over 12,000 men. There were also a few American long-range bombers in east and central Java. The Netherlands army in Java included five three-battalion regiments of native troops; the units contained about one European to forty Indonesians. The British force, which was placed under the command of Major-General H. D. W. Sitwell, who had been Wavell's senior anti-aircraft officer, included 3,500 United Kingdom troops, mostly belonging to five anti-aircraft regiments, two of which had no guns, and about 3,000 Australians. The II/131st American Artillery Battalion had also arrived in Java from Australia.

The Australians (landed from the *Orcades*) included the 2/3rd Machine Gun Battalion without its machine-guns or vehicles and less some 200 men, the 2/2nd Pioneer Battalion, 2/6th Field Company, 2/2nd Casualty Clearing Station, 105th General Transport Company, and a platoon of the Australian Guard Battalion. Also in Java were the 2/3rd Reserve Motor Transport Company, and some reinforcements who had been on their way to Malaya. Before he left Java General Lavarack appointed Lieut-Colonel Blackburn to command all A.I.F. men in Java and promoted him to the rank of brigadier. Blackburn organised his force as a brigade, forming a small third battalion from the engineers and others. It was decided that Blackburn's force should concentrate in west Java, about Buitenzorg, on the road between Batavia and Bandung, where the Netherlands headquarters were situated.

On 25th February Allied aircraft saw two convoys making towards Java, one evidently aiming at the eastern end and the other at the western. Admiral Doorman took out his 'Eastern Force'—cruisers *De Ruyter*, *Java*, *Houston*, *Exeter* and *Perth*—and nine destroyers against the easternmost convoy. They reached the convoy on the afternoon of the 27th, and in the ensuing action the Netherlands cruisers *De Ruyter* and *Java* and four destroyers were sunk. Meanwhile Commodore Collins (the former captain of *Sydney*, who had remained in Java after the dispersal of ABDA Command to command the British naval forces) had sent the cruisers *Hobart, Dragon* and *Danae* and two destroyers against the westernmost convoy. They found nothing. (A Japanese aircraft had reported them as three battleships and two cruisers and the convoy turned away.) In accordance with its orders, this force then steamed through the Sunda Strait. *Houston* and *Perth* were following them on the night of the 28th February-1st March when they unexpectedly came upon part of the western Japanese convoy anchored and landing its troops. There was a fierce mêlée in the course of which a Japanese transport and a minesweeper were sunk and other transports were damaged and landing craft destroyed, but *Perth* and *Houston* were sunk. *Perth's* captain, Waller, who had so ably led the Australian destroyer flotilla in the Mediterranean, was among the 350 who were lost. Later on 1st March the cruiser *Exeter* and two American destroyers were sunk while trying to reach Sunda Strait. During the fight for the Netherlands East Indies and the subsequent Allied withdrawal, of the Allied cruisers only *Hobart* and the small *Dragon* and *Danae* survived; five cruisers and nine destroyers had been lost.

Another Australian ship was lost on 4th March when the *Yarra* (Lieut-Commander R. W. Rankin) escorting a convoy south of Java fought with three heavy cruisers and two destroyers and was sunk, only thirteen of her crew surviving. The previous day nine Zeros had appeared over Broome in Western Australia and sunk sixteen flying boats that were being used to rescue people from Java; eight other aircraft were destroyed. About seventy people were killed including many Dutch women and children.

By 4th March the British air force in Java had been reduced to ten Hurricanes, three Hudsons and five torpedo bombers. The British and Netherlands bombers, including No. 1 Squadron R.A.A.F., had attacked the Japanese convoys. They reported many hits and over fifteen sinkings, but in fact the only Japanese ships sunk in the Java Sea between 26th February and 1st March were two transports and an aircraft ferry. By 5th March some 7,000 air force men had been shipped or flown out of Java. No. 1 Squadron flew its three remaining Hudsons to Australia carrying all the air crew they could hold.

The Japanese invasion force had landed at three places in Java on the night of the 28th February: the *48th Division* and *56th Regiment* landed west of Surabaya, the main naval base; the *230th Regiment* (part of the *38th Division* from Hong Kong) east of Batavia; and the *2nd Division* at the north end of the Sunda Strait. The central force advanced rapidly and in the morning tanks and infantry had overrun Kalidjati, the main British bomber airfield; few of the defenders survived.

In the west the Netherlands regiment deployed at the western end of Java fell back along the two roads leading east—one to Batavia and the other to Buitenzorg. Blackburn's force (to which the American artillery battalion and a squadron of light tanks of the 3rd Hussars had now been added) was ordered forward to deliver a counter-attack next day. The plan, proposed by Blackburn and agreed to by Major-General Schilling, the Netherlands commander of the forces in western Java, was that the counter-attacking force should advance along the southern road, attack the Japanese there, and then come in behind the force advancing west along the Batavia road.

In the course of the night (28th February-1st March) General ter Poorten ordered that the Netherlands forces which were to have taken part in the attack must be sent east to resist the Japanese advance on Bandung from the south and that all Netherlands forces in Buitenzorg must withdraw on Bandung; at length, however, two Netherlands companies were left about Buitenzorg. It was 4 a.m. before these points were decided. Thereupon 'Blackforce' hurried forward to a defensive position at Leuwiliang on the River Tjianten, some fifteen miles from Buitenzorg. As the leading Australians arrived the local Netherlands commander, not knowing the plan, blew up the bridge, thus making it impossible to execute the counter-attack.

Blackburn, having perused some notes on Japanese tactics provided by Australian corps headquarters before its departure, had decided that the way to counter them was to deploy part of his force (only two companies) in depth along the road and hold the rest of his force in reserve for rapid employment in a counter-encirclement role; and to hold his artillery fire until the maximum surprise could be gained. Thus Lieut-Colonel J. M. Williams and the 2/2nd Pioneers stealthily watched Japanese troops collecting on the opposite bank of the river from 11.15 a.m. until 2 p.m. on the 2nd, then opened fire and caused heavy loss. Blackburn then sent out his counter outflanking forces which that night and next day kept moving wider and wider and prevented the Japanese from crossing the river, except for one party which was destroyed. The enemy force increased in strength and, on the afternoon of the 3rd, after twenty-four hours of fighting, Blackburn ordered his artillery to open fire. This fire quietened the enemy in the centre. During the night (3rd-4th) the flanking units of Blackforce continued to outflank the attackers.

At 9 a.m. on the 4th Schilling told Blackburn that all forces were falling back on Bandung and asked him to hold the vital road and rail junction at Buitenzorg for another twenty-four hours. Blackburn undertook to do this. That afternoon a considerable body of Japanese crossed the river south of the Australian south flank, and a company of the Pioneers was sent to dislodge them. The withdrawal to a position covering Buitenzorg began at 2.15 a.m. on the 5th. This was carried out without mishap except that the detached company became heavily involved and was cut off. (At length, after hard fighting, it fell back into the hills and was not rounded up by the Japanese until some months later.) Blackforce guarded the roads through Buitenzorg until 3 p.m. on the 5th, having held off about one-third of the *2nd Japanese Division* for three days. Its own losses, killed and wounded, numbered about 100.

After being warned by Sitwell that the Netherlands forces would probably soon capitulate Blackburn spent the 6th March reconnoitring the mountain country south of Bandung with a view to continuing resistance and perhaps eventually being evacuated. At 10 a.m. on the 8th Blackburn's staff heard a broadcast that the Netherlands had capitulated. With Sitwell's approval Blackburn withdrew his force to the Tjikadjang area and it remained there from the 9th to the 11th. On the 8th, however, Maltby and Sitwell had decided that they must order a cease fire; three days earlier the Netherlands leaders had assured them that guerrilla warfare would be impossible because of the hostility of the Indonesians. On the 11th Blackburn, to whom Sitwell had given freedom to decide what course the Australians followed, decided, largely influenced by medical advice, to join in the surrender. In Bandung on the 12th an instrument of surrender was signed. The Japanese were convinced that a whole Australian division was in Java and in an effort to persuade Sitwell to reveal the whereabouts of this force and the movements of I Australian Corps kept him in handcuffs for ten days.

With the fall of Rangoon and the surrender in Java in the second week of March the Japanese objectives had virtually been obtained. Except that a doomed force survived in Luzon, a company of Australians was resisting in the mountains of Timor, and the army in Burma was making a fighting retreat to India, the Japanese held a line from the Kuriles through Wake, New Guinea, Timor, Sumatra to Burma and all that lay within it. They had counted on spending six months in achieving this task and had actually done it in three; their naval losses had been negligible: to the end of March eight destroyers, seven submarines (in the sinking of one of these, near Darwin on 20th January, the Australian corvette *Deloraine* had played a leading part) and a number of small vessels; only thirty-eight transports and merchant ships. Of the destroyers or submarines only one had been sunk by Allied aircraft.

Thus by the second week in March the Japanese had occupied the perimeter which was their objective. Within that line the forces in the Philippines and Burma attracted forces totalling seven divisions. (At the outset only ten had been allotted to the whole of the *Southern Army's* operations.) After the event it could be seen that the Japanese High Command would have been wiser to plan vigorous thrusts beyond the self-imposed confines of the perimeter more promptly, leaving minimum forces to mop up in Burma and Bataan; and that in March, April and May it missed opportunities of establishing forces across its enemy's lines of communication in the South Pacific and the Indian Oceans.

The reason why the Japanese had won their objectives so swiftly and relatively at such small cost in blood and equipment was simply that at every level and in almost every department they surpassed their enemies. Their strategy and their tactics had been far superior to those of their opponents. In the Far East their naval forces were not only overwhelming in size but more efficient than those of the Allies. Their fighter aircraft in particular and their pilots were far better than had been expected. Their troops were for the most part battle-hardened, well trained for the tasks they were given, and capable of rare feats of endurance. Their landings of whole armies on surf beaches were of a magnitude then only dreamt of in the West.

The Allied naval forces in the Far East were ill-balanced and uncoordinated, and so weak in numbers that if each had gone to the bottom taking a Japanese ship with it the loss would not have been crippling. Their air forces were weak in fighters; their bombers achieved some successes, but not many.

If the defending armies had mainly comprised trained European troops the invaders would have undoubtedly suffered some calamities, but in Malaya, the Philippines and Java the defending troops were mostly Asians, many of whom had not much stomach for a war against troops who were not only Asians too but soon proved they were deadly opponents. In every area some Asian troops as well as civilian leaders soon changed over to the

Japanese side. The strongest resistance came from Western troops or well-indoctrinated Asian regulars.

It was ironical that the Japanese forces whose destruction of Western power in east Asia had the effect finally of releasing the east Asian people from Western government were by temperament and training ill-equipped to win friends on the Asian continent and in the islands to the south. Throughout the Greater East Asia Co-Prosperity Sphere they soon proved far harsher overlords than the Europeans had been.

Australian War Memorial

The Japanese air raid on Darwin, 19th February 1942. The Australian ships *Neptuna* and *Barossa*, berthed at the wharf, are shown here during the attack. Both ships were hit and *Neptuna* later sank.

Chapter 7 South-West Pacific: the first six months

In January and February 1942 the Australian leaders and people had been making energetic preparations for a possible Japanese invasion. Their resources seemed slender and the time when the American fleet from the east or the British from the west would be willing to challenge Japanese command of the western Pacific seemed remote. The Australian Air Force had few modern bombers and no modern fighters, and the only reinforcements so far received had been a few American heavy bombers flown out of the Philippines and some inexperienced and poorly-equipped American squadrons from the convoys diverted to Australia. The land forces in Australia comprised an armoured division with virtually no tanks, a few other A.I.F. units, and the militia divisions. Until the second half of February the 6th and 7th Divisions of the A.I.F. were destined for either the Indies or Burma, and the 9th was still in Syria.

As the danger developed the Government introduced increasingly stringent regulations for the control of the citizens and of industry 'so that (as it announced on 10th February) the production of war materials will be speeded up, the manpower of the community mobilised in the interests of the nation'. These controls and others introduced during the critical year will be outlined later. Their effect on the mass of the people was that men and women might be ordered into any occupation, civil or military; wages and prices were pegged; goods were rationed and some were becoming scarce; preparations for air raids became more elaborate, and more and more people were drawn into spare-time tasks in air raid and first-aid organisations. Round the coast and particularly in the area stretching from Newcastle to Port Kembla defences were being dug and wired.

Because of a decision made before the Japanese war broke out, the Australian home army had lately received a contingent of senior officers with recent experience in action in the Middle East. Brigadier Rowell had returned in September to become Deputy Chief of the General Staff. In December five former brigade commanders of the A.I.F.—Savige, Robertson, Murray, Plant and Vasey—and C. A. Clowes who had commanded the artillery of the corps, returned to Australia. Vasey became General Mackay's Chief of Staff, Plant was appointed to the isolated Western Command, Murray to command the 'Newcastle Covering Force', Clowes the 1st Division, Savige the 3rd, and Robertson the 1st Cavalry. As a result of the plans and preparations made in earlier years the militia formations were now receiving a steady flow of new and modern weapons,[1] but the seven divisions had been fully mobilised only in December and needed some months of training before

[1] In February 1942 the army possessed, for example, 353 field guns of 1914-18 type, 101 modern 25-pounders, 129 3.7-inch anti-aircraft guns, 1,268 Bren carriers, 1,157

Australian War Memorial

Members of the Volunteer Defence Corps loading a 3.7-inch anti-aircraft gun during training on the Kensington golf course near Sydney. The Volunteer Defence Corps, or the 'Home Guard' as it was alternatively known, developed from the Returned Soldiers League Volunteer Defence Corps which was formed in June 1940 and became a part of the Australian Military Forces in May 1941 with an establishment of 50,000, later increased to 80,000.

they could be considered fit for operations against an enemy who had won such rapid victories over apparently well-trained forces farther north.

Behind the militia stood a keen Volunteer Defence Corps led and largely manned by veterans of 1914-18. Enthusiasts, some inspired by the Spanish Republican resistance and the Russian guerillas and others by the Boer commandos and the Australian bushrangers, advocated or actually began to organise irregular groups to such an extent that, early in February, the Minister for the Army declared that 'private armies' would not be permitted; if a citizen wished to serve he could find a place in the A.I.F., the militia, the V.D.C., or a factory.

It had long been accepted by Australian Army leaders that if Australia

Continued from p. 171.

Bren guns. There was, however, a shortage of some types of ammunition. Deliveries of some important weapons in, for example, January and April 1942 were:

	25-prs	*2-prs*	*Carriers*	*Brens*	*Rifles*	*Sub-machine-guns*
Jan	29	87	115	236	7,040	25
Apr	71	87	225	460	8,600	303

was threatened with invasion at a time when help from overseas was likely to be delayed she should concentrate on holding the arc embracing Newcastle, Sydney, Port Kembla and Lithgow, whence came most of her black coal, all her steel, and many of her manufactures, and in which lay her best-equipped naval base. On the 4th February General Mackay produced and General Sturdee 'generally concurred in' a memorandum stating this principle. Mackay wrote that he understood that the Chiefs of Staff had advised and the Government had agreed that the area most vital to the continuance of the war effort of Australia was the Port Kembla-Sydney-Newcastle-Lithgow area. The importance of Brisbane had been enhanced by the decision to develop an American base there, and the economic and military importance of Melbourne was recognised. The Melbourne-Brisbane region, 1,000 miles from north to south, had scarcely five divisions to defend it. 'I do not propose, therefore, whilst the main areas remain equally threatened, to attempt to defend either Tasmania or Townsville with more troops than are in those areas now.' The troops then in north Queensland (a few battalions) should remain there for reasons of 'morale and psychology'. 'It may be necessary to submit to the occupation of certain areas of Australia by the enemy should local resistance be overcome, and I remind the Government that it may be necessary to accept such a possibility.' He asked that the Government either confirm his proposal not to reinforce Townsville or Tasmania or give 'some further direction regarding the degree of such defence'.

Australian War Memorial

Martin Place, Sydney, 18th February 1942. Service detachments and portion of the crowd at a Liberty Loan rally.

The Minister for the Army, Mr Forde, whose electorate was in north Queensland, recommended that the Government decide to defend 'the whole of the populated area of Australia'. This discussion was still in progress in the second half of the month when knowledge that the 6th and 7th Divisions were returning and that an American division would come to Australia transformed the prospect.

Reviewing the altered situation on 27th February, the Australian Chiefs of Staff advised the Government that an attack on Darwin might be expected early in April. In such an attack the Japanese could employ two divisions, supported by carrier-borne and shore-based aircraft. Darwin was defended by two brigades, two Australian bomber squadrons, one Australian squadron armed with Wirraways and two American bomber squadrons. By April three American fighter squadrons were due to arrive. The Chiefs of Staff added that the Japanese might advance towards Port Moresby in a week. There they could employ a division supported by aircraft against one brigade group (the 30th) supported by twenty-five aircraft. They did not expect an attack against the east coast of Australia until Port Moresby and New Caledonia had been lost, and this might occur in May. The Chiefs of Staff recommended that Port Moresby, Darwin and Tasmania be not immediately reinforced, but that the garrisons of Townsville and Fremantle should be increased. By May, however, when the three A.I.F. divisions and one American division should have arrived, the garrison of Darwin could be increased to a division, that of Western Australia to a division, and a brigade group could be sent to Tasmania, leaving two of the new divisions to reinforce the vital area.

The War Cabinet, at a meeting attended by D. G. Sullivan and J. G. Coates of the New Zealand Cabinet, had decided that the Australian and New Zealand Chiefs of Staff should combine to make an appreciation. A substantial naval force was now in the Anzac Area—three Australian cruisers, two New Zealand, one American—and a British aircraft carrier, *Hermes*, was on the way. On 28th February these combined Chiefs of Staff emphasised the need to plan an offensive with Australia and New Zealand as the bases, mentioned the possibility of a Japanese advance down the west coast, and advised that a Supreme Commander, preferably an American, should be appointed. This commander should be appointed by a United States-United Kingdom-Anzac Council sitting in Washington, whose chairman would be the American President or his deputy. This proposal was sent to Churchill to be passed on to Roosevelt. Australia indicated that the appointment as Supreme Commander of Lieut-General George H. Brett, then commanding the American troops in Australia, would be welcomed.

The raids on Broome and Wyndham seemed to underline the warning of the Chiefs of Staff that there might be an advance down the west coast. In fact this was not the Japanese intention, but the prediction by the Australian Chiefs of Staff on 27th February that the Japanese might advance 'towards' Port Moresby within a week and in May might attack Port Moresby and New Caledonia proved remarkably sound.

On 29th January Admiral Yamamoto had been ordered to take Lae and Salamaua in the near future, and later, if possible, Port Moresby. A Liaison Conference in Tokyo on 7th March decided that Japan should enlarge her gains with the object of establishing 'a political and strategical structure capable of withstanding a protracted war'. But a three-sided struggle was soon being waged to decide in what directions new thrusts should be made: westward against British sea power in the Indian Ocean and perhaps to join hands with the Germans, southward to Australia, eastward against the Pacific Fleet. The army, always anxious to bring the long war in China to a successful end, and always conscious of the threat from the Russians, who might sweep out from Siberia, push back their *Kwantung Army* and drive into China, wanted to leave any new moves west, south or east to the navy. It planned to reduce the *Southern Army* and increase the garrisons in China and Manchuria and at home, by transferring the *Guards, 4th* and *5th Divisions* to Japan, the *33rd Division* to China, and the *16th Division* to Manchuria, thus leaving only six divisions round the southern perimeter.

The navy's attitude was more aggressive. Two days after the Liaison Conference Yamamoto had ordered Admiral Kondo of the *Second Fleet* to send the Carrier Force into the Indian Ocean in April to destroy the British naval forces round Ceylon in a surprise raid. And soon naval leaders were advocating two more ambitious ventures: invasion of Australia and a thrust towards Hawaii. Conquest of Australia would deprive America of a well-equipped base from which to mount a counter-offensive. The army staff maintained that the Australians would bitterly resist attack on their vast country, twice the size of China, and the invasion would demand ten more divisions and 1,500,000 tons of shipping. This would entail drastic reductions of the army preparing to resist attack by Russia, and of the forces in China. A compromise was reached: to sever communications between America and Australia by seizing New Caledonia, Fiji and Samoa.

Late in March the staff of the *Combined Fleet* drew up plans for the seizure of Midway Island and a landing in the Aleutians 2,000 miles to the north. Yamamoto's staff advocated deferring the New Caledonia-Samoa thrust until after Midway, which was planned for early in June. The naval general staff in Tokyo protested that the Midway project was unwise, arguing that the island would be under attack by land-based aircraft from Hawaii and it would be difficult to keep such a distant base supplied. Yamamoto stood firmly by the Midway plan. He maintained that the most effective way to sever the America-Australia route would be to destroy the American carriers, and the Midway operation would probably draw them into a battle. Yamamoto's plan was agreed to in principle by the naval general staff ashore on 5th April, but opposition to it continued.

Meanwhile on 8th March one Japanese battalion had landed at Lae and another at Salamaua, on the mainland of New Guinea, and a detachment went ashore on Buka Island in the Solomons. News of these Japanese moves reached the American carrier force at a time when it was making its second excursion into the South-West Pacific. The carriers *Lexington* and *Yorktown* and Rear-Admiral Crace's squadron were covering the transport to New Caledonia of the long-awaited American force of 16,000 men which was to garrison that island. This convoy had arrived at Melbourne on 26th February, and it sailed for Noumea on 6th March. Vice-Admiral Wilson Brown of the carrier force, who had planned a raid on Rabaul, now decided to fly his aircraft over the Owen Stanleys and attack the Japanese at Lae and Salamaua. The carrier aircraft, American Flying Fortresses and Australian Hudsons on the 10th found much Japanese shipping off the New Guinea coast and met no opposition. The pilots claimed to have sunk three cruisers, five merchantmen and a destroyer; in fact a transport and two small naval vessels were sunk—it was not a great result, but the raid gave experience and confidence to the carrier crews. The carrier force then steamed back to Pearl Harbour, leaving Crace's squadron to dispute command of the South-West Pacific. The Pacific Fleet now included seven battleships and five aircraft carriers—*Lexington, Yorktown, Enterprise, Saratoga, Hornet.*

By mid-March American or New Zealand garrisons had been stationed along a chain of islands on the shipping route from America to Australia and New Zealand: Palmyra, Christmas, Canton, Bora Bora, Samoa, Fiji, Tonga, New Caledonia and the New Hebrides were now all defended.

On 9th March, nine days after Australia had proposed the appointment of an American as Supreme Allied Commander in the South-West Pacific, President Roosevelt sent Churchill a telegram containing comprehensive plans for a world-wide rearrangement of command—an outcome of general discussions at their conference in December. He suggested that the whole responsibility for the Pacific Area should rest on the United States, the Supreme Commander being an American; that a middle area including India and the Mediterranean should be a British zone; and that the Atlantic-Western European area be shared between Britain and the United States.

Meanwhile, in response to instructions by President Roosevelt, General MacArthur, with a small staff and his family, had been flown out of the Philippines to Darwin. MacArthur and his party had been taken to Mindanao by motor torpedo-boats. There they were picked up by Flying Fortresses from Townsville and flown to Darwin. From Darwin the party travelled to Melbourne by air and rail, arriving on 21st March. On the 17th Curtin had told his Cabinet that Roosevelt had informed him that MacArthur had arrived in Australia and had assumed command of all American troops there; Roosevelt had added that, if Australia wished, 'it would be highly acceptable to him and pleasing to the American people for the Australian Government to nominate MacArthur as Supreme Commander of all Allied Forces in the South-West Pacific Area'. Curtin consulted the Advisory War Council, which agreed with enthusiasm, and the nomination was made.

The Combined Chiefs of Staff in Washington had been working on the proposals outlined in Roosevelt's telegram of the 9th, and on 25th March they made their recommendations, which were later adopted. The Pacific Theatre was subdivided into a South-West Pacific Area under General MacArthur and a South Pacific Area directly under Admiral King, who in April appointed Vice-Admiral Robert L. Ghormley to command it. Ghormley was directly under Admiral Nimitz, Commander-in-Chief of the whole 'Pacific Ocean Area'. The boundary was drawn so that the Solomon Islands were in the S.W.P.A., the New Hebrides and New Caledonia in the South Pacific Area. Thus the boundary between the two areas was a boundary also between control by the American Army and by the American Navy; the main fleet was to operate as a concentrated force under a single commander. It was an advisable arrangement because, between the American Army and Navy, there was, in the words of Henry L. Stimson, the Secretary for War, 'a traditional mutual mistrust'; towards MacArthur in particular the navy felt an 'astonishing bitterness'.[2] The New Zealand and Australian Governments protested against the placing of New Zealand and Australia in separate areas, but in vain, the Americans being determined to place the lines of communication to Australia under naval control.

Evatt, who had been sent to Washington to present Australia's point of view, on 3rd April sent Curtin copies of the directives issued to the new commanders. MacArthur's required him to hold 'the key military region of Australia as bases for future offensive action', to check the Japanese advance by destruction of their ships, aircraft and bases in eastern Malaysia, New Guinea and the Solomons; to maintain the American position in the Philippines, protect the communications within his area and finally to prepare to take the offensive. The Combined Chiefs were to control grand strategic policy while the American Joint Chiefs were to control operational strategy. When replying to Evatt, Curtin agreed to the terms of the directives (with the reservation that Australian forces should not be moved outside Australian territory without the consent of the Australian Government). Curtin accurately remarked that 'it does not appear that the Commonwealth Government has any place in the set up as laid down'.

Roosevelt was somewhat influenced in his decision to order MacArthur to Australia by a fear that Australian morale was gravely declining. The decision of the Australian Government—wise as it turned out—not to allow its troops to go to Burma had disturbed him greatly and, later, disagreement between Churchill and Curtin when Churchill against Curtin's wishes appointed Casey, then Australian Minister in Washington, as British Minister of State in the Middle East, led Roosevelt on 22nd March to address a reproving message to Churchill. In it he said: 'It would be desirable all round if any way can be found to avoid all further public discussion of this, which, it seems to me, plays right into the hands of our enemies. I realise that the Casey appointment is only an incident. The more important issue is the basic relationship of Australia to Great Britain. I sense in this country a growing feeling of impatience at what publicly appears to be a rather strained relationship at this critical time between the United Kingdom and Australia.' 'It was this "strained relationship", and the desperate predicament of Australia that caused it', wrote R. E. Sherwood in *The White House Papers of Harry L. Hopkins*, 'which influenced the orders to MacArthur.'[3] One aim was to 'bolster the morale' of the people of Australia and New Zealand. Moreover, Admiral King had advocated placing the Solomons in the S.W.P.A. 'as he felt it was essential to engage the attention of Australia to the defence of the approaches to their country and shake them out of their isolationist attitude'.

The scale on which Australia had sent military, naval and air contingents overseas in 1940 and 1941 should have indicated that Australia was not 'isolationist'; and, indeed, Curtin's argument for placing the boundary of the S.W.P.A. farther east was that 'it was essential that New Zealand, Fiji and New Caledonia should be in the same area as Australia' because they were interdependent and Australia's line of communication with America

[2] H. L. Stimson and McG. Bundy, *On Active Service in Peace and War* (1948), pp. 503-23.
[3] Vol II, pp. 513-14.

Ninigo Is.
Manus I.
Lorengau
ADMIRALTY
ISLAN
BISMARCK
Hollandia
Vanimo
Bewani Mts.
Aitape
Torricelli Mts.
But
Wewak
Maprik
Angoram
Sepik
River
May R.
Hansa Bay
Bogia
Karkar I.
Adelbert Range
Karawari R.
NEW
GUINEA
Central
Range
Telefomin
Hindenberg Range
Ramu
Alexishafen
Madang
Long I.
Bismarck
Range
Bogadjim
RAI
COAST
Saidor
Vitiaz
Strait
Umboi I.
Muller
Range
Mt. Hagen
Chimbu
Dumpu
River
Finisterre Mts.
Sio
HUON
PENINSULA
Bena Bena
Kaiapit
Aure R.
Markham
Nadzab
R.
Sattelberg
Lae
HUON
GULF
Salamaua
Hegigio
River
Purari
River
PAPUA
Strickland
River
Fly
River
Bulolo
Mubo
Wau
Nassau Bay
Morobe
Waria
R.
Bulldog
Lakekamu R.
Mambare R.
DUTCH NEW GUINEA
Merauke
GULF OF
PAPUA
Daru
Popo
Kokoda
Owen
Port Moresby
Donadabu
Torres
Strait
Thursday I.
Horn I.
CORAL
SEA
CAPE
YORK
PENINSULA

New Guinea

C I F I C O C E A N
Mussau I.
Emirau I.
New Hanover
Kavieng
SEA
NEW IRELAND
Namatanai
St George's Channel
Rabaul
Green Is.
Open Bay
Tol
Wide Bay
Kessa
Buka I.
Buka Passage
Gloucester
Talasea
C. Hoskins
NEW BRITAIN
C. Orford
Jacquinot Bay
Numa Numa
BOUGAINVILLE
Kieta
Torokina
Empress Augusta Bay
Arawe
Gasmata
Buin
SOLOMON ISLANDS
Shortland Is.
Faisi
Fauro I.
Treasury Is.
SOLOMON SEA
Hunt
Trobriand Is.
Kiriwina I.
D'ENTRECASTEAUX ISLANDS
Porlock Hbr.
C. Nelson
Woodlark I.
Goodenough I.
Musa R.
Collingwood B.
Wanigela
Fergusson I.
Goodenough Bay
Normanby I.
Milne Bay
Mullins Hbr.
Misima I.
China Str.
Samarai
Louisiade Archipelago
Rossel I.
Tagula I.
MILES 50 50 100 150 200 MILES
HUGH W. GROSER

went through New Zealand, Fiji and New Caledonia. The fact that the Government had found it advisable to forbid cross-enlistment from militia to A.I.F., and in February the Army had to appeal to 18-year-olds from the country not to come to town to enlist since they were too young to be accepted for the A.I.F., suggests that Australian morale was not in urgent need of 'bolstering'.

Evidence that American estimates of Australian morale and opinion were sometimes wide of the mark was provided also by an Intelligence Summary prepared by American headquarters in Melbourne on 14th March. It said:

> A certain lack of individual self-reliance, resourcefulness and initiative, due primarily to the fact that traditionally they have to look to England for detailed direction . . . a touchy inferiority complex . . . too willing to lay the burden of responsibility on someone else and, lacking prospects of effectual direction and support from England, they are turning to the U.S. to assume that responsibility.

Indeed, it was difficult for the American leaders and staffs to comprehend the relationships between Britain and the Dominions, and the free exchange of proposals and argument indulged in by the British countries was outside the experience of Roosevelt and his advisers. The American President regarded the installation of MacArthur in Australia as a successful manoeuvre on his part towards restoring Australian morale, whereas the Australian Government regarded it as a response to *its* efforts to establish a unified command and to attract American reinforcements into the Australian zone. The Australian people, knowing next to nothing of the melancholy facts of the operations in the Philippines, welcomed MacArthur as a strong leader whose forces had fought back while one disastrous defeat after another was occurring in other theatres. He was described as having given the Japanese 'the only thorough beating they have suffered in three and a half months of war'.[4] A leading American publicist was reported to have described him as 'the outstanding hero of the war, and so far the ablest general'.

For the Australian people as for the Government, February and March had been months of deep anxiety. The Japanese advance continued; the enemy was established in New Guinea and his bombs were falling on outpost towns on the Australian mainland. In the newspapers appeared constant appeals for the formation of an all-party government as had been done in Britain in the crisis of 1940, for the appointment of a unified command of all forces, for sterner air raid precautions, for younger and more vigorous generals. Round the coast, the citizens could see the troops digging and wiring defences and preparing demolitions. In March the navy was given power to immobilise all small craft which might be commandeered by an invading force.

As in 1941 propaganda was intensified. One development in this field—the broadcasting by Government stations of a series of short exhortations in which the Japanese were vilified in extravagant terms (they were dubbed 'hate broadcasts')—produced strong protests and these broadcasts were eventually stopped. Fearing direct attacks on the cities along the coast, some parents sent their children to the country, and some of those adults who were free to go retired to inland towns. Four main factors seem to have

[4] *Sydney Morning Herald*, 19th March 1942.

produced a rapid diminution of Australian anxieties between the last week of March and the first week of May. These were, in the order of their occurrence, the news of the arrival of General MacArthur and the reorganisation of command which followed, the return of men of the A.I.F. whose nonchalance calmed the people in tens of thousands of homes, the fact that the weeks passed and no large-scale attack occurred, and the Coral Sea battle, described later in this chapter. On 2nd May Blamey said in a newspaper interview that 'it would take a very serious expedition indeed to make any impression on this continent as a base for future operations', and that the chief aim was now 'to move forward carrying the fight into enemy territory as soon as possible'.

Numbers of resident aliens had been interned from the outbreak of war onwards, and in 1942 these internments reached a maximum; there were 3,651 Italians, 1,036 Japanese, and 1,024 Germans. Some Australians too were detained. The army also held at various times a total of 7,861 internees from other countries, including 2,542 from the United Kingdom, 1,949 from the Netherlands Indies, and 1,124 from New Caledonia. Among these were seventeen people belonging to or believed to belong to the Australia First Movement, a nationalistic organisation formed in Sydney in 1941. These men were detained in March 1942 because of a suspected relationship between some of them and four people in Western Australia charged with conspiracy to assist the Japanese. Fourteen of the seventeen were released later in 1942, two in 1944 and one in 1945. In 1945 a Commissioner appointed to inquire into the detentions reported that eight of them had been unjustified, that the original aims of the movement were legitimate, and that the people detained were unaware of the alleged conspiracy in Western Australia. Certain members, he reported, had acted in a way likely to cause disaffection and prejudice the war effort.

By accepting the appointment of MacArthur and the consequent directive the Australian Government had made a notable surrender of sovereignty. Australia had become the base of the South-West Pacific forces, and so far ahead as could then be seen would provide most of its sea, land and air forces. At least in the immediate future the land battles would be fought in her territory. But the commander-in-chief was an American and he was responsible to and directed by the American Chiefs of Staff. A strange aspect of this alliance of an Australian Government and an American commander was that their views on international and local politics were far apart.

> American generals have rarely been as nonpolitical as they have pretended, nor as political as they have sometimes hoped. MacArthur was accounted from the start a Republican general. He had been Herbert Hoover's Chief of Staff . . . and Franklin Roosevelt, while retaining him in office for two extra years, later passed over the MacArthur line of descent to make George Marshall, anything but a MacArthur man, the head of the Army. In the thirties MacArthur's ringing martial rhetoric struck a responsive chord in the Hearst and McCormick press . . . For his part, MacArthur welcomed their support and shared at least some of their ideals.[5]

[5] R. H. Rovere and A. M. Schlesinger, *The General and the President* (1951), pp. 228-9.

Before he arrived in Australia MacArthur had received a severe rebuke from Roosevelt over the proposed 'neutralisation' of the Philippines. He and his senior staff officers were extremely critical of Washington and its policies; and they shared the traditional American mistrust of British aims and policy. Later a visitor from Washington to MacArthur's headquarters would record that 'to hear some of the Staff Officers talk one would think that the War Department, the State Department, the Joint Chiefs of Staff—and, possibly, even the White House itself—are under the domination of "Communists and British Imperialists". This strange misapprehension produces an obviously unhealthy state of mind, and also the most unfortunate public relations policy that I have seen in any theatre of war'.[6]

Marshall suggested to MacArthur that he should appoint some Australian and Dutch officers to senior posts on his staff and informed him that this was the President's wish. MacArthur, however, appointed Americans to lead every branch of his staff, eight of the eleven heads being officers who had come from the Philippines with him. When pressed by Marshall he replied that the Australians did not have enough staff officers for their own needs. In fact the Australian Army possessed senior specialists in all fields of staff work who were at least as highly qualified academically as the Americans concerned and had the advantage of recent and varied active service against the German, Italian, French or Japanese Armies; but MacArthur did not ask for any of these. Some Australian liaison officers were attached to G.H.Q. and a number of the specialist organisations on the headquarters were chiefly Australian.[7]

The formation of a combined staff would have presented some difficulties; each group would have had to master a different vocabulary and learn to understand new administrative and tactical doctrines and methods. But at that stage a combined staff was particularly desirable because Australia was providing the greater part of the strength of the command, and also the Australians possessed local knowledge. Under MacArthur the Australian General Blamey was appointed to command the Allied Land Forces, the American General Brett the Allied Air Forces and the American Vice-Admiral Herbert F. Leary the naval forces.

The army was now, in April, vastly stronger than that which the Australian Chiefs of Staff had at their disposal in February. In the last half of March the I Australian Corps, except for two brigades left in Ceylon, had disembarked in Australia—about 46,000 veterans, fully equipped; the number of American troops in Australia had increased to 33,000, including air force men. By 25th April there were in addition 63,000 men of the A.I.F. who had not been out of Australia and 280,000 militiamen. The return of the A.I.F. formations led to a rapid re-allocation of commands and re-deployment. On the 24th March the War Cabinet, on the advice of

[6] Sherwood, Vol. II, p. 867.

[7] General Robert L. Eichelberger of the American Army afterwards wrote: 'I had been told before leaving Washington that General MacArthur had asked for key American officers to assist the Australians with their staff work. The Australians didn't think they needed much help from anyone. Many of the commanders I met had already been in combat with the British in North Africa, and, though they were usually too polite to say so, considered the Americans to be—at best—inexperienced theorists.' *Our Jungle Road to Tokyo* (1950), p. 7.

the Advisory War Council, had appointed General Herring of the 6th Division to command the Darwin area. A few days later General Blamey arrived, and on 31st March he attended a meeting of the War Cabinet in Melbourne and presented proposals, partly based on those drawn by General Lavarack, for a reorganisation of the now-expanding army. His object, he said, was to have a completely mobile corps in the east and a mobile division in Western Australia, and to secure a suitable distribution of protective troops. To this end he proposed the establishment of First Army (Lieut-General Lavarack) with headquarters in Queensland and including Lieut-General Rowell's I Corps (7th, 3rd and 5th Divisions) and Lieut-General J. Northcott's II Corps (1st, 2nd, 10th and 1st Motor Divisions). A Second Army (Lieut-General Mackay) with headquarters in New South Wales would include the 2nd Motor and 41st American Divisions. In the west the III Corps (Lieut-General Bennett, from Malaya) would include the 4th Division and local troops. There were two other main forces under Blamey's command: Northern Territory Force and New Guinea Force, the latter then including only one infantry brigade. Blamey's reserve was the 1st Armoured Division.[8]

On 10th April Blamey issued his first Operation Instruction as Commander-in-Chief to the commander of the First Army. It stated that the retention of the Newcastle-Melbourne area was vital but the probability of a major attack thereon was not then great because the enemy's main concentrations were in Burma and the Indies. The enemy's first effort southwards from the Mandates would probably be 'an attempt to capture Moresby followed by a landing on the north-east coast with a view to progressive advance southwards covered by land-based aircraft'. It added:

> In view of the limitations of resources, it is not possible at present to hold the coastline from excluding Townsville to excluding Brisbane. As our resources increase it is intended to hold progressively northwards from Brisbane.

Among the tasks given to First Army was: 'Defence of Townsville by a garrison which is to be built up to a division at an early date.'

On 17th April, the day before MacArthur assumed command, the War Cabinet formally assigned to him the five field formations of the Australian Army, those of its naval ships which were then under Admiral Leary's command, and all operational units of the air force. In the air force the Chief of the Air Staff (in May Air Vice-Marshal Jones replaced Air Chief Marshal Burnett in this appointment) remained responsible for a 'all matters associated with R.A.A.F. personnel, provision and maintenance of aircraft, supply and equipment, works and buildings and training'; these were not assigned to MacArthur.

General Brett organised an air staff on which, for a time, his chief of staff was an Australian (Air Vice-Marshal Bostock); the deputy chief and senior air staff officer were Americans; and of the five directors, three were Australians and two Americans. Since, however, an Australian commanded each of the five areas, American air units were generally under Australian command. But Brett could not yet seek to allot American officers to the field commands because he lacked officers of suitable rank and experience. The

[8] There were then 185 tanks in Australia, including forty-four heavy and medium.

shortage of experienced officers extended down through the American force and in May the plan was adopted of using Australian co-pilots in bomber aircraft. The newly-arriving Americans had a substantial number of first-rate aircraft, though they were handicapped by a shortage of spares, but mostly lacked training and experience. The Australian force contained tried veterans of the war in Europe and the Middle East and other well-trained air crew, but had relatively few first-line machines.

Admiral Leary's force at the end of April included 2 Australian heavy cruisers and one American, 2 American light cruisers, one Australian and one Dutch, 11 American destroyers and 4 Australian, 31 American submarines, and a large number of smaller Australian ships.

The Americans had now decided to send a second division to Australia. On 4th March Mr Churchill had asked President Roosevelt to send not one but two divisions to the South-West Pacific so that the 9th Australian and the New Zealand Division might remain in the Middle East, and on 28th March the 32nd Division was ordered to Australia. The main body of the 41st Division had sailed from San Francisco the day after MacArthur's arrival in Australia.

According to his biographers MacArthur was stunned to learn that there were only some 25,000 American troops in Australia and no immediate prospect of opening a counter-offensive to relieve the forces on Bataan. Nevertheless he addressed the Advisory War Council on 26th March in tones of restrained optimism. He said that the Japanese fighting machine was well co-ordinated but they had over extended themselves and could be beaten. He was one of those who considered the Pacific theatre the principal one. The Allies should take chances in other theatres and strike a main blow in the Pacific. Australia must stand firmly by its view that the Pacific was the predominant theatre. The Allies still lacked enough resources to open a second front in Europe. The American and British fleets should be concentrated in the Pacific for an offensive against Japan which might prove decisive. He proposed that in Australia the first step should be to make Australia secure. Then it should become a base for a counter-stroke to the Philippines and thence to Formosa. He asked the Prime Minister to help him to obtain from the United States whatever assistance that country could give. He doubted whether the Japanese would undertake an invasion of Australia as the spoils were not sufficient to warrant the risk. He proposed that he should 'function through the Prime Minister' in matters of general co-ordination, but that matters involving detail should be dealt with through the usual channels.

A few days later MacArthur sent Marshall a telegram saying that he had suggested that all Australian units be brought to full strength, intensive training initiated and all incompetent officers eliminated. There had been 'complete acquiescence and prompt action' by the Australians. With these positive signs of action, he said, 'the general public attitude of defeatism was replaced with a growing feeling of confidence and relief'. This did less than justice to the Australian Army and its leaders. In fact the units were at full strength and engaged in intensive training when MacArthur arrived, and the reorganisation of the army commands had been carried out. On 25th April MacArthur issued his first directive relating to a general plan. It proposed no alteration of Blamey's dispositions, and gave the Allied Land

Australian War Memorial

American servicemen, part of the 41st Division, arriving at Port Melbourne in April 1942 to strengthen Australia's defence forces and later to take up the fight with the Japanese in New Guinea.

Forces the task of preventing 'any landing on the north-east coast of Australia or on the south-western coast of New Guinea'. But no additional combat troops were sent northward to help carry out these tasks.

As mentioned, the Japanese time-table provided for a foray by the *Carrier Fleet* into the Indian Ocean early in April. After having supported the invasions of Rabaul, Ambon, Timor and Java the Japanese carriers had spent some time at Kendari refuelling and on 26th March they sailed from Kendari to raid Ceylon. Two days later Admiral Sir James Somerville, commanding the British Eastern Fleet, who had arrived in Ceylon on the 24th, learnt from intercepted signals that the carrier force would attack his bases in Ceylon about 1st April. The Eastern Fleet had been hurriedly reinforced until it included five old battleships (*Warspite*, *Resolution*, *Ramillies*, *Royal Sovereign* and *Revenge*) and three aircraft carriers (*Formidable*, *Indomitable*, and the small *Hermes*), five cruisers, fifteen destroyers and five submarines. These were all in the Indian Ocean but not yet all assembled round Ceylon.

Late in March the 16th and 17th Australian Brigades had landed in Ceylon, where the garrison had hitherto comprised three brigades. Earlier two squadrons of Hurricanes intended for Java had been diverted to Ceylon, making a total of three fighter squadrons on the island, with one squadron of bombers and two of flying boats.

Somerville decided that the enemy force would approach from the south-east and set about concentrating his force in that area. By 2nd April his battleships, designed for North Sea and Mediterranean service, were running short of water and there was no news of the main enemy force. Somerville took his main force to Addu Atoll south-west of Ceylon but detached the *Hermes*, with Australian destroyer *Vampire* and cruisers *Dorsetshire* and *Cornwall*, to

Australian War Memorial

Indian Ocean, March 1942. The Australian destroyer *Norman* off Trincomalee, Ceylon, photographed from H.M.A.S. *Nizam*.

Ceylon for repairs and escort duties. At Addu on the 4th Somerville learnt that the enemy force was 350 miles to the south-east, and took such of his ships as were ready steaming through the night in that direction. At 8 a.m. next morning about ninety Japanese navy bombers with thirty-six fighters attacked Colombo, where they damaged the port and sank a destroyer and an armed merchant cruiser. Of the defending aircraft twenty-seven were lost (including six naval Swordfish which arrived at the height of the fighting); although the defenders believed they had shot down at least nineteen enemy aircraft, the Japanese reported a loss of only seven. At 1.40 p.m. Japanese aircraft attacked *Dorsetshire* and *Cornwall*, now on their way from Colombo to rejoin Somerville. In a few minutes both ships had been sunk. Somerville, who had two carriers equipped with inferior aircraft against the five Japanese carriers with their Zeros, decided to withdraw his main fleet lest his battleships share the fate of the *Prince of Wales* and *Repulse*, but first sent out a cruiser and two destroyers to rescue survivors of *Cornwall* and *Dorsetshire*. They picked up 1,122 men and the fleet retired, part to East Africa and part to Bombay. On the 9th the Japanese struck at Trincomalee with about 110 aircraft. The few defending aircraft attacked gallantly and shot down some enemy machines but lost eleven of their own. The attackers damaged the naval base, but delivered a more severe blow out to sea, where they found *Hermes*, which had been hurried away from Trincomalee—escorted by the Australian destroyer *Vampire*—without her fighter aircraft. Both ships were sunk, *Vampire* losing her commander, Commander W. T. A. Moran, and eight others. Meanwhile a detached Japanese force including the carrier *Ryujo* and six cruisers had in one day sunk twenty merchant ships in the Bay of Bengal, and off the west coast submarines sank 32,000 tons of shipping. Well satisfied the Japanese *Carrier Fleet* set off for Kure, having in four months sunk five battleships, one carrier, two cruisers and seven destroyers.

That month the American carrier forces made another raid out from Pearl Harbour. The *Hornet*, bearing sixteen medium bombers (Mitchells) and escorted by *Enterprise*, cruisers and destroyers, steamed to a point 670 miles from Tokyo. There on 18th April the bombers took off, attacked Tokyo and other cities, and flew on towards China where most of them crash-landed. Fourteen of the crews survived, among these being the leader, Lieut-Colonel James H. Doolittle. 'This raid', wrote the American naval historian, 'gave a tremendous lift to American morale, which badly needed assistance at that moment.'[1] It had another important result, for it ended the Japanese naval staff's opposition to the offensive towards Hawaii, and strengthened Yamamoto's determination to destroy the American carriers and establish advanced bases at Midway and in the Aleutians. The Midway operation was now given priority over the advance into the south Pacific. On 5th May Imperial General Headquarters issued a formal order that the navy and army would co-operate in occupying Midway and key points in the western Aleutians. The army agreed to provide one brigade, but it was to be withdrawn after the island group had been taken, leaving the subsequent defence to a naval garrison. The operation was to take place some time before 20th June.

The last painful scenes in the defeat of British and American power in

[1] Morison, *The Rising Sun in the Pacific*, p. 398.

the Far East were now being enacted. In Burma the weary retreat of Indian, British and Chinese troops continued during the last half of March, during April and part of May. The Japanese in March had three divisions in Burma or on the way there. General Alexander had the shattered 17th Indian and 1st Burma Divisions and an armoured brigade, the 17th Indian Division and the armoured brigade now forming a corps under Lieut-General Slim. On 14th March Lieut-General Joseph W. Stilwell arrived to take command of the Chinese V and VI Armies (36 battalions) in northern Burma. The Japanese commanded the air and there was little possibility of halting their advance short of the Indian frontier. On 1st May the Japanese crossed the Chindwin which flows north to south through the mountains between northern Burma and India. By 17th May the survivors of the British-Indian force were out of Burma.

In the Philippines there had been virtually no fighting from early February, about a week before the fall of Singapore, until 3rd April, a month after the fall of Java. This was a result of the withdrawal of troops from the Japanese *XIV Army* to take part in the invasion of Java, and the weakness and weariness of the remaining formations. The Filipino and American defenders, holding along a line half way down the Bataan Peninsula were as badly off. Their food supply dwindled until the men were getting only a quarter of the peacetime ration. The cavalry ate their last horses in March. Fishing had ceased because of gunfire round the coast. The Filipinos hunted monkeys, iguanas and snakes and gathered jungle fruits and vegetables. Malaria and deficiency diseases flourished. In some units half the men were sick and none were truly fit. In February Tokyo became very concerned about the deadlock in Luzon. They replaced General Homma's chief of staff and other officers on his headquarters and began to reinforce the *XIV Army*. The *62nd Regiment* was sent in, and by 15th March the *4th Division* had arrived from China—the first fresh formation allotted to the *Southern Army*.

Homma issued orders for an offensive that would open on 3rd April. After ten days of air bombing and strafing the attack went in at 3 p.m. after five hours of intense artillery fire. The nerves of a division of Filipino troops were shattered by the bombardment and they were put to flight. By nightfall the attackers had penetrated 1,000 yards. Homma had ordered a slow, systematic advance, but when he learnt of the day's successes he decided to press on swiftly. By the end of the third day his men had broken a wide gap in the defenders' line. On the 6th the defenders made abortive counter-attacks. But the Japanese drove deeply between the two American corps, and the way to the south coast lay open. The Japanese then thrust along the eastern side of the peninsula against a disintegrating defence, and by the 8th were only a few miles from the American headquarters and their hospitals, crowded with 12,000 patients. Major-General Edward P. King, commanding on Bataan, surrendered next day. About 2,000 men escaped to Corregidor; 76,000 remained as prisoners.

In April, although there were 19,000 American air force men in Australia, the long-range bomber force capable of supporting the army in the Philippines totalled only six Flying Fortresses and fourteen Mitchells, of which six were under repair. Out of these resources Brigadier-General Ralph Royce on 11th April assembled a force of three Fortresses and ten Mitchells and led it to Mindanao, whence it raided Japanese shipping and other targets and returned to Australia on the 14th having lost only one aircraft.

From December until early April the Japanese maintained a base at Davao taken in December but otherwise made no attempt to gain the vast archipelago south of Luzon, where a force of three Filipino divisions was distributed. Homma simply lacked the troops needed to occupy the southern islands. But when Imperial General Headquarters ordered him to take Bataan and sent him new formations to make this possible, they also ordered him to move against the southern islands and allotted him two forces, each built round one regiment, to do this. On 16th April one of these landed unopposed on Panay. Homma did not trouble about the remaining islands of the Visayas—the central group—but sent both forces straightway against the big island of Mindanao, where since late December one lonely battalion had been round Davao Gulf, 900 miles from Manila. By 9th May organised resistance on Mindanao was over.

Homma's plan for reducing Corregidor was to assemble 116 guns, bombard the island for about three weeks with these and with all available aircraft, and then put the *4th Division* plus tanks ashore, one regiment at the eastern end on the night of 5th-6th May, and four battalions at the western end the following night. The final bombardment was concentrated against the north shore and lasted five days. As darkness fell on the 5th the assaulting troops embarked and the craft set off across the four-mile-wide channel. The tide swept the craft eastward and they went ashore in scattered formation 1,000 yards or so from the intended spot, and under heavy small arms and artillery fire. Perhaps half of the troops in the first wave of 2,000 men were killed or drowned; more than half the landing craft were wrecked. But the survivors pressed on with their usual gallantry, and by 1 a.m. some were on the south shore, the island here being only 500 yards wide, and some had advanced about the same distance west. There on a narrow front they beat off counter-attacks and clung on until reinforced. By mid-morning the defenders had lost perhaps 1,800 killed or wounded. Later in the day General Wainwright accepted defeat, and on 7th May was taken to Manila where he broadcast surrender instructions to his subordinates throughout the archipelago.

On Corregidor and the other islands in Manila Bay 12,000 prisoners were taken, including about 8,700 American troops; the island fortress had been won by two Japanese battalions, though more arrived after the decision to surrender. Throughout all the Philippines the Japanese held about 140,000 prisoners.[2]

[2] In 1942 the legend was established that, while British forces had been swiftly overcome in Malaya, on Singapore Island and Hong Kong, American forces had maintained a comparatively prolonged resistance in Luzon and on Corregidor. And so it appeared to Allied leaders at the time and later.

Since the war both British and American historians have compared the British resistance in Malaya adversely with the resistance on Luzon. For example (others could be added): 'Malaya was a steady retreat, unrelieved by the prolonged resistance that marked the fighting on Bataan—Singapore, unlike Corregidor, falling almost without a struggle in a single week.' Such comparisons leave out of account that the main body of the Japanese invading force did not land on Luzon until about a fortnight after war began and that, after the seven weeks of hard fighting that ended in the first week of February, there was little contact between the opposing forces for

Between 12th and 20th April the Japanese strengthened their grasp on western New Guinea by occupying nine points including Manokwari, Sarmi and Hollandia. Major-General Horii, commanding the *South Seas Force* at Rabaul, now issued orders for the attack on Port Moresby. A force including the *144th Regiment* and the *3rd Kure Special Naval Landing Force* would leave Rabaul on 4th May and land on both sides of Port Moresby on the 10th. The convoy would be protected by a force including two aircraft carriers. As a preliminary the Japanese would land at Tulagi in the Solomons to establish a seaplane base.

India and Australia were now the advanced bases in which forces might be concentrated for a counter-offensive. MacArthur told Curtin that he was 'bitterly disappointed' with the 'meagre assistance promised' which, he said, would not even ensure the adequate defence of Australia. At his request Curtin late in April asked the British Government for an aircraft carrier, and for the diversion to Australia, until the return of the 6th and 9th Divisions, of an infantry and an armoured division which were on their way to Egypt and which Churchill had recently offered to divert to Australia should she be invaded 'by, say eight or ten Japanese divisions'. Churchill sent Curtin's request to Roosevelt and asked whether MacArthur had 'any authority from the United States for taking such a line'. MacArthur was rebuked by Washington for having made a request through incorrect channels, and Churchill replied to Curtin, on 1st May, that there were no signs of a mass invasion of Australia, but India was in increasing danger; the diversion of the two divisions to Australia would waste and dislocate shipping; and none of the three aircraft carriers in the Eastern Fleet, *Illustrious, Formidable* and *Indomitable*, could be spared. He hoped, however, to relieve the Australian brigades in Ceylon about the end of May.

MacArthur continued to press for more reinforcements from America, and also suggested that Evatt, then in London, should ask for the dispatch to Australia of enough aircraft to re-equip thirteen squadrons of the R.A.A.F., bring the remaining squadrons to strength, and enable the formation of five more fighter squadrons. This would entail the supply of 616 aircraft. Evatt was unable to obtain all this, but on 28th May Churchill agreed to send to Australia three Spitfire squadrons—two Australian and one of the R.A.F.

While these appeals were being made the time arrived for the next Japanese thrust. Two large carriers, *Shokaku* and *Zuikaku*, were sent southward to assist the planned invasion of Port Moresby. These, with two cruisers and six destroyers, formed a striking force to protect the expedition; there was also a covering group including the small carrier *Shoho* and four cruisers; the troops were embarked in eleven transports. While the convoy steamed round the eastern end of Papua, the large carriers were to sweep through the Coral Sea and bomb the airfields at Townsville, Cooktown and Thursday Island.

Continued from p. 189.

about two months. When the Japanese resumed the offensive on 9th April they overcame the defenders of Bataan in four days. And when they attacked Corregidor in May, after long and devastating bombardment, two Japanese battalions overcame the fortress with its garrison of about 12,000 in a day. It cost the Japanese more days of actual fighting to take Malaya and Singapore Island than Luzon and Corregidor.

By 20th April Admiral Nimitz's staff at Pearl Harbour knew from intercepted signals that the Japanese would strike at Port Moresby about 3rd May. Nimitz decided to send *Lexington,* then near Pearl Harbour, and *Yorktown,* then near Noumea, with five attendant cruisers and eleven destroyers, against the Japanese. Admiral Crace's cruiser squadron (*Australia, Hobart* and the American *Chicago*) were ordered to join. The opposing forces were fairly evenly matched.

On the evening of 3rd May Vice-Admiral Frank J. Fletcher in *Yorktown* learnt of the landing at Tulagi and set off north to attack next morning. When his aircraft arrived over Tulagi early on the 4th they found only small vessels and landing craft there. They attacked, and sank some of them, but the Japanese carriers had withdrawn northward. Both carrier forces spent part of the 5th and 6th refuelling but on the 6th, after receiving news that the Port Moresby convoy was on the move, Fletcher steamed north-west. At dawn next day Fletcher was 100 miles south of Rossel Island, the two large Japanese carriers 200 miles to the east. Japanese aircraft searching to the south found an American oiler and destroyer, reported them as a carrier and a cruiser, and the carrier's air strength was sent out against these targets. The destroyer *Sims* was sunk and the oiler mortally damaged.

Meanwhile Fletcher had ordered Crace to attack the convoy as it turned the eastern corner of Papua while he himself sought out the enemy carriers. Crace's squadron, speeding north, was reported by Japanese aircraft at 10 a.m. In the next half hour the Japanese admiral learnt also the whereabouts of the American carriers. Thereupon the convoy was turned about and made off northward. Meanwhile Crace's force was attacked first by Japanese aircraft and then by American aircraft from Townsville, but without receiving a hit. Crace continued cruising south of Samarai all day and into the night, but the enemy was making off to Rabaul.

Meanwhile the carrier battle in the Coral Sea—the first of its kind in history—had begun. About 11 a.m. on the 7th the American carrier aircraft—ninety-three in all—having been launched in error against some small vessels came by chance upon the small carrier *Shoho* and four cruisers. They sank *Shoho.* At the end of the day, however, each main carrier force had failed to find the other. Next morning searching aircraft from each opponent found their enemy and the striking forces were sent in. The *Shokaku* received some damage, *Zuikaku* was not hit; but the Japanese hit *Lexington* both with bombs and torpedoes and sank her, and damaged *Yorktown,* but not seriously. Thereupon both carrier forces withdrew, the Japanese to Truk, the American to Pearl Harbour. The Japanese losses were greatly over-estimated at the time; it was believed that *Zuikaku,* two cruisers, two destroyers, and other light craft had been sunk, and *Shokaku* damaged.

It was indeed fortunate for the Allies that the American Intelligence organisation had broken the Japanese codes and, in consequence, that the American carriers were on the spot to oppose the Japanese in the Coral Sea. If the convoy had reached Port Moresby it would have found there the same garrison of one brigade which General Sturdee had established by early January, four months before, and would almost certainly have overcome it. In Washington there was now much anxiety. Admiral King pointed out at a meeting of the Joint Chiefs on 11th May that until the end of June there would be only two serviceable American carriers in the Pacific, whereas the

Japanese had from seven to ten, and Intelligence had intercepted information that a large naval force was due to leave Japan on 20th May and could be at some point on the line Alaska-Hawaii-Australia between 1st and 5th June. On 16th June the Japanese objectives were identified: Midway Island, and Dutch Harbour (Alaska).

The Coral Sea battle caused anxiety also in Australia. On 12th May MacArthur sent Curtin an appreciation in the course of which he said that he believed the enemy could strike 'a new blow of the most dangerous potentialities against the S.W.P.A. or against India', and that a Japanese offensive against the S.W.P.A. should precede a movement against India. He urged haste in developing the Australian 'defensive bastion'. 'The Territory to be defended is vast'; he added, 'the means of communication are poor; the defensive forces are few in number and only partially trained. The enemy . . . if supported by major elements of his fleet, can exercise control of the sea lanes and consequently can strike with a preponderance of force on any chosen objective. We have present, therefore, in this theatre at the present time, all of the elements that have produced disaster in the Western Pacific since the beginning of the war.' He informed Curtin that he had asked

Australian War Memorial

Japanese midget submarine raid on Sydney Harbour on the night of 31st May-1st June 1942. Part of one of the midget submarines is shown being brought to the surface the day after the raid.

Marshall for two aircraft carriers, a corps of three divisions and a first-line strength of 1,000 aircraft. In fact the Coral Sea battle had not caused the Japanese leaders to aim at more modest objectives than before. At Rabaul on 18th May Lieut-General Hyakutake of the newly-formed *XVII Japanese Army* was ordered to take New Caledonia, Fiji and Samoa, and, in July, to resume the advance against Port Moresby. Using these bases, naval and air forces were to sever communications between America and Australia and bomb Australian and New Guinea bases. The forces allotted to the conquest of the three island groups included the *Second Fleet* and the *Carrier Fleet.* Fiji was to be attacked by a force of 9,000 built round the *124th Regiment,* New Caledonia by Horii's force—5,500 men including the *144th Regiment*—and Samoa by a battalion group about 1,200 strong.

Meanwhile Evatt was finding that there was not much that he could achieve in Washington and London. It was not until 28th May that he learnt that in February the British and American leaders had decided to defeat Hitler first, and informed Curtin of this fact. He reported to Curtin that the policy was to deploy minimum forces against Japan; in London the defence of India was preferred to that of Australia partly because Washington was responsible for the defence of Australia; invasion of Australia was considered unlikely.

The Japanese now delivered two attacks by midget submarines, one against Sydney and the other against Diego Suarez in Madagascar, which had been seized by British forces on 5th May. Five Japanese submarines, between them carrying three midget submarines and possibly two aircraft, set out for Sydney. About 20th May and again on the 30th a Japanese aircraft flew over Sydney. On the night of the 31st the three midgets were launched seven miles east of Sydney Heads. One became entangled in the boom and her occupants blew her up. A second entered the harbour and fired torpedoes at the cruiser *Chicago.* They missed the *Chicago* but one hit the barracks ship *Kuttabul* (a converted ferry) killing nineteen men. This midget was destroyed by some means either inside or outside the harbour. A third midget also entered the harbour but was destroyed by depth-charges before it had fired any torpedoes.

The large submarines did more effective work, sinking merchant ships off the east coast between Newcastle and Gabo. On 3rd June the *Iron Chieftain* was sunk, on the 4th the *Iron Crown.* On the 7th-8th, soon after midnight, one of the large submarines fired ten shells, mostly 'duds', into the Sydney suburbs of Rose Bay and Bellevue Hill, and another fired shells into Newcastle, but without doing serious damage. On the 12th the Panamanian ship *Guatemala* was sunk off Sydney. At this stage the submarine flotilla departed.

Meanwhile, on 27th May, the Japanese Midway Occupation Force, about 5,000 strong in twelve transports, set out from Saipan, with close cover of two battleships, cruisers and destroyers. The main attack force—with Admiral Yamamoto commanding the operation—comprised the battle fleet of seven battleships with *Yamato* as flag, and Vice-Admiral Nagumo's carrier force (*Akagi, Kaga, Hiryu, Soryu*) and two battleships, each with cruisers and destroyers. Light carriers *Zuiho* and *Hosho* were with the Occupation Force and battle fleet respectively. Two additional light carriers—*Ryujo* and *Junyo*—were detached with Rear-Admiral Kakuta's *Second Mobile Force* of two heavy cruisers and destroyers, to strike at the Aleutians, and perhaps at the same time draw the American carriers away from Midway. Nimitz was able to concentrate three carriers (*Yorktown*, *Enterprise* and *Hornet*) and cruiser and destroyer forces somewhat weaker than the enemy's; although some battleships were available Nimitz did not send them out.

The Japanese troop convoy and its escort advanced on Midway from the west, the main carrier force keeping pace with it far to the north. Admiral Fletcher concentrated his carriers about 300 miles north-east of Midway. An American aircraft sighted the enemy convoy early on 3rd June. Fletcher had information that the Japanese carriers would attack Midway from the north-west at dawn on the 4th, and decided to hit the carriers while their aircraft were away. More than 100 Japanese carrier-borne aircraft duly attacked Midway on the 4th; ten torpedo aircraft from Midway made a vain attack on the carriers. The leader of the invasion force now called for a second strike on Midway, and Admiral Nagumo of the *Carrier Fleet*, whose reconnaissance aircraft had not found the American carriers, began to re-arm his remaining aircraft with bombs instead of torpedoes. Meanwhile the American carriers had located the Japanese, and from 7 a.m. on the 4th all *Hornet's* and *Enterprise's* aircraft had been dispatched against them. From 8 a.m. onwards the Japanese ships were under attack first by land-based and then by carrier-borne aircraft. By mid-morning most of the American carrier-borne torpedo bombers had been shot down without scoring a hit, but their dive bombers remained. *Hornet's* bombers failed to find the enemy, but when the other two groups arrived, flying at 19,000 feet, the Japanese fighters had drawn down to low level to meet the torpedo bombers. The dive bombers attacked practically unopposed and hit *Akagi*, *Kaga* and *Soryu* and set them afire. *Kaga* sank that day and the wounded *Soryu* was finished off by a submarine; *Akagi* sank next morning. The aircraft from *Hiryu*, the remaining Japanese carrier, hit and severely damaged *Yorktown* on the 4th, but that evening *Enterprise's* dive bombers hit *Hiryu* which sank next morning. On the 5th Yamamoto ordered a general withdrawal. An American aircraft sank the damaged heavy cruiser *Mikuma* on 6th June; the disabled *Yorktown* was attacked by a Japanese submarine and sank early on the 7th.

A decisive battle had been fought. The Japanese had suffered their first naval defeat, and had lost the better part of their carrier fleet. Hitherto, except for the *Shoho* in the Coral Sea, they had not lost a ship of the heavy cruiser category or above. In this one engagement the Japanese had been robbed of any likelihood of maintaining a supremacy over a United States Navy now expanding at a rate Japan could not hope to maintain. In the twelve months after Midway 3 battleships, 9 cruisers, 4 large carriers, 4 light cruisers and 16 escort carriers would be added to the United States Navy; in the two years after December 1941 America would have built enough ships in every category to equip a navy considerably stronger than the Japanese. An important and immediate result of the Midway battle was the postponement of the Japanese plan to advance southward from Rabaul and take New Caledonia, Fiji and Samoa, and a decision to advance overland against Port Moresby. Another outcome was a Japanese decision to abandon the building of battleships and concentrate on carriers.

From May until July, while these crucial aircraft carrier battles were being fought, Allied troops were in contact in only three areas on the vast

Australian War Memorial

Battle of the Coral Sea, 5th-8th May 1942, which turned back a Japanese attempt to capture Port Moresby from the sea. The United States Navy aircraft carrier *Lexington* is on fire with other ships standing by to pick up survivors.

Japanese perimeter stretching from the Aleutions to Burma: in the Philippines where guerillas were active, about Lae and Salamaua in New Guinea, and in Timor where the almost isolated 2/2nd Independent Company was still in action. In March and April the Independent Company had been out of touch with Australia but had been fighting on with remarkable success. In March the company was joined by Brigadier Veale and his headquarters and the survivors of the force which had been overcome at Koepang. During the month the platoons and sections of the company were deployed over the rugged interior of Portuguese Timor from the north, where they were close to the Japanese at Dili, to the south coast; the men were learning the native tongue, and, in co-operation with the natives and some friendly Portuguese officials, established control of a wide area. In April the Japanese sent strong forces southward into the mountains. The Australian tactics were to wear down these expeditions by withdrawing slowly from one carefully-prepared ambush position to another, inflicting sharp casualties on the enemy. On the night of 14th-15th April a party made a raid on Dili itself.

Signallers, including M. L. Loveless, an expert radio technician, contrived from parts of several wireless sets one which could reach Darwin, and on 20th April Darwin heard them and replied. Thenceforward the air force

Australian War Memorial

Hudsons of No. 13 Squadron withdrawing after bombing a Japanese post, on 17th December 1942, at Mindelo in central Portuguese Timor where Australian guerillas had been holding out since the Japanese invasion of February 1942.

squadrons of North-Western Area and small ships of the navy supported the company, the aircraft dropping supplies and bombing targets indicated by the troops, and the navy running in by night to land supplies and remove the sick. Brigadier Veale and the senior Dutch officer were taken out by a Catalina late in May, and for some months the force as a whole was commanded by Lieut-Colonel A. Spence, formerly commander of the company, with Captain B. J. Callinan commanding the company itself.

Early in June General Blamey suggested to General MacArthur that either Timor should be recaptured by an oversea expedition or most of the force should be withdrawn. MacArthur replied, on 11th June, that he lacked the forces necessary for an attack: perhaps a division with suitable landing craft supported by strong air and naval forces. On the other hand to retain the forces in Timor would greatly facilitate an offensive when the necessary means were at hand; thus the isolated force remained where it was.

Guerilla warfare continued, the Japanese losing heavily when they ventured south. By July they were concentrated in Dili with Australian outposts in a half-circle round them. Early in August, however, they began a big push south from Dili and east from Koepang with 2,000 troops supported by aircraft which strafed every village where Australians or their native supporters were believed to be. The Australians fell back in a well co-ordinated withdrawal, ambushing the enemy at intervals. Soon the company was in a perilous position, but after ten days the Japanese abandoned the operation and withdrew.

On 23rd September the 2/4th Independent Company was landed in Betano bay by the destroyer *Voyager*. Edging close to the shore to expedite unloading she ran aground and next day was found and disabled by Japanese aircraft. Her crew destroyed the stranded vessel and were taken off on the 25th by the corvettes *Warrnambool* and *Kalgoorlie*. Meanwhile on the 24th, in one of the most elaborate ambushes yet carried out, a platoon dispersed a column of 350 Japanese. In this and another smaller ambush on the previous day about ninety Japanese were thought to have been killed or wounded.

Above the men of the Independent Company in Timor and the garrison round Darwin, now equal to a division, a persistent air struggle had been in progress. Japanese bombers continued to bomb the harbour of Darwin and the airfields. On 2nd April, in the most damaging raid since the first one, an oil tank was hit and burnt out. The Australians of No. 2 and No. 13 Squadrons, in Hudsons, retaliated with raids against Japanese bases and shipping. In March and April at Darwin, as at Moresby, a force of Kittyhawk fighters arrived, but whereas Moresby received one squadron (R.A.A.F.), North-Western Area, now commanded by Air Commodore F. M. Bladin, received three (of No. 49 Group, U.S.A.A.F.). These fighters, with the help of newly-installed radar, made it possible to hit back, and losses were inflicted on the Japanese bomber forces and escorting fighters.

Since 8th March when the Japanese had landed at Lae and Salamaua they had been firmly established on the mainland of Australian New Guinea; the expedition against Port Moresby had shown that they wished to gain the whole island. It seemed likely that heavy fighting in the jungle-clad coastal plains and mountains of New Guinea lay ahead. In such warfare the local knowledge of the Australians who worked in New Guinea as administrators, planters and miners and in other jobs, and particularly their ability to hold the respect of the natives and exact obedience from them, was to prove an immense asset. In 1940 about 7,200 Australians and others of European origin were settled in Papua and New Guinea. Many of these were now serving in the Australian New Guinea Administrative Unit (Angau) which carried on the government of the territories and assisted the army by organising native carriers, gaining information and in other ways. Others were in Intelligence organisations such as the Coastwatchers, and others in the New Guinea Volunteer Rifles or the Papuan Infantry Battalion.

When Japanese forces landed at Lae and Salamaua on 8th March the only force in the neighbourhood was four platoons of the New Guinea Volunteer Rifles and an officer and twelve men who had extricated themselves from New Britain a few days before. After a skirmish the defenders at both Salamaua and Lae fell back. The N.G.V.R. were based on the goldfield town of Wau on a high plateau inland from Wau and Salamaua and their forward platoons were supplied by native carriers along difficult mountain tracks. When it became evident that the Japanese did not for the present intend to march far inland the N.G.V.R. established observation posts close to the enemy's bivouacs. The men of the N.G.V.R., with their faithful native followers, knew the country so well and some of them were such skilled scouts that they were able to move and live in the bush within earshot of the Japanese without being detected. By April the enemy was under close observation.

Blamey decided to reinforce the N.G.V.R. with more guerilla troops; he had several Independent Companies ready to hand. The 2/5th Independent Company was sent to Wau where a platoon of the 1st was already established. These with the N.G.V.R. were formed into 'Kanga Force' under Lieut-Colonel N. L. Fleay, an infantry officer of 24 who had served in two Middle East campaigns. Kanga Force's first task was to reconnoitre, but later it was to make surprise attacks on Lae and Salamaua.

In May the Japanese began patrolling inland from Lae and Salamaua and some sharp skirmishes followed. By the end of the month the 2/5th Independent Company was deployed at points along the Bulolo Valley leading from the goldfields to the Lae and Salamaua areas. Henceforward Japanese shipping and camps round Lae and Salamaua became important targets for the small bomber force in New Guinea.

Raids were now ordered on Japanese at Heath's Plantation inland from Lae, where there were some 2,000 Japanese and on Salamaua, where there were about 300. About seventy men of the N.G.V.R. and the 2/5th Independent Company descended on Salamaua before dawn on 29th June, each of seven parties being guided by expert scouts of the N.G.V.R. The raiders achieved a good deal of destruction and captured documents and specimens of Japanese equipment; they killed perhaps 100 Japanese; no Australians were killed and only three wounded.

On the night of the 30th June-1st July some sixty men raided Heath's. Again the Japanese were surprised. The raids caused the Japanese to reinforce Salamaua and patrol the tracks and foothills, with the result that the N.G.V.R. forward posts had to be abandoned and the riflemen's secret tracks were discovered. On 21st July about 100 Japanese advanced against the base at Mubo where sixty Australians were established. The Australians ambushed the enemy force and killed more than forty; the remainder withdrew. On the same day a similar Japanese force advanced up the Markham Valley and thrust the Australian outposts back towards Nadzab. Also on the 21st strong Japanese forces landed about Buna on the north coast of Papua. In the meantime both the Allies and Japan had been making plans which would swiftly terminate the four-months lull in the fighting on land.

In June MacArthur had continued to press for reinforcements, but the Allied leaders saw no great danger of a large-scale offensive by Japan. On the other hand in April Roosevelt and his Chiefs of Staff had presented a plan for invading Western Europe in the spring of 1943 with a force of forty-eight divisions, including eighteen British, supported by 5,800 aircraft; and possibly making a smaller invasion in 1942 as an emergency measure. The British leaders urged that while big forces were slowly being built up for the invasion of Western Europe, a less formidable undertaking—the occupation of French and Italian North Africa—should be carried out. After much discussion this plan was adopted. It had much to recommend it. It might divert German forces from Russia, it would give raw American commanders and troops active experience, it would enable landing craft and amphibious tactics to be tested on a larger scale than had been possible at Madagascar and in other smaller landings, it could be a prelude to invasion of southern Europe, and it should encourage the people.

But while these discussions were in progress the German-Italian army in

North Africa opened an offensive. On 20th-21st June it captured Tobruk and took about 35,000 South African, Indian and British prisoners. By the end of the month Field Marshal Rommel had advanced to within seventy miles of Alexandria. This reverse following so soon after the calamities in the East, had a crushing effect in America and Britain. In the House of Commons Conservative leaders moved a vote of no confidence in Churchill, but it was defeated by 475 votes to 25. Inevitably the crisis in Africa led to an even more decided effort to concentrate against the enemy in the West.

There could now be no question of the British divisions then at sea being diverted to Australia. The 9th Division in Syria was due to sail for Australia as soon as shipping was available, but instead it was hurried to the El Alamein front.[3] On the advice of MacArthur and Blamey the Australian Government decided not to press for its return, but they did urge the need to return the two Australian brigades from Ceylon. When Rommel attacked in Africa, forty-two aircraft to arm the three Spitfire squadrons which Churchill was sending to Australia were at sea off the West African coast. The Dominions Office asked Curtin to allow these to be unloaded at Freetown and flown to North Africa, another consignment of Spitfires being sent to Australia later. After consulting MacArthur, Curtin refused to agree, on the ground that Australia's needs were no less urgent. However, the British Government controlled the ship, and Churchill declined to accept Curtin's refusal.

In Australia on 14th and 15th May the 32nd American Division and the balance of the 41st landed. On the 15th Blamey sent the 14th Brigade and 700 anti-aircraft troops from Townsville to Port Moresby, now under frequent air attack. Thus, very belatedly, New Guinea received its first substantial infantry reinforcements since January; but, although there were veteran A.I.F. brigades available, New Guinea was given an inexperienced militia formation.

MacArthur's immediate plan was now to establish a defensive front through Merauke, Wau, Kokoda and Milne Bay, and on 8th June it had been decided to make an airfield at Milne Bay at the extreme eastern end of this front. For the present the defensive line was to be but thinly manned: two companies at Merauke, Kanga Force (two companies) at Wau, a battalion of Papuans round Kokoda, a force not yet decided at Milne Bay. In support at Port Moresby were the two militia brigades. The mass of the South-West Pacific army, now nominally of fifteen divisions, though not all these were ready for action, lay in south Queensland, New South Wales and Victoria. There had been some movement of troops northward and westward. Whereas in January there had been three brigades in Queensland and one in Western Australia, in June, after three new divisions had landed in Australia, there were eight brigades in Queensland and three in Western Australia.

On 29th June Blamey submitted a proposed reorganisation of the Australian Army, which then included ten infantry and two motorised divisions and one armoured division. He proposed, as a force adjusted to the flow of equipment and within the capacity of the population, a force of nine infantry

[3] The experiences of the 9th Division and other Australians in the Middle East are described in Chapter 9.

divisions and three armoured divisions each of one armoured and one motor brigade (the 1st Armoured then possessed two armoured brigades and one motor brigade). Probably another division would be abolished later. This organisation was adopted. In the next month Blamey obtained approval of some changes in the senior commands. Lieut-General Northcott became his Chief of the General Staff, Lieut-General Sturdee going to Washington as Australian Military Representative. Major-General Herring, commanding Northern Territory Force, became commander of II Corps.

Before Blamey had made the reductions mentioned above, a departmental committee had found that existing commitments involved providing 270,000 men and 48,000 women up to the end of December 1942. To the end of June 105,000 of these had been found, but in the meantime the requirements had been revised and it was estimated that the Services, the departments producing warlike supplies and civil industry would need, from July to December, 139,000 men and 80,000 women, not counting an army requirement of 40,000 in the event of large-scale fighting. The committee decided that to provide these 219,000 people would necessitate 'a series of measures which in scope and severity transcend any hitherto contemplated'. These measures will be described later.

In response to these proposals Blamey pointed out that under the reorganisation then in progress the army formations available by the end of the year would be eight infantry and two armoured divisions with a third armoured division being organised. (This did not include the two American divisions.) 'Should there be serious naval reverses . . . the forces available may easily

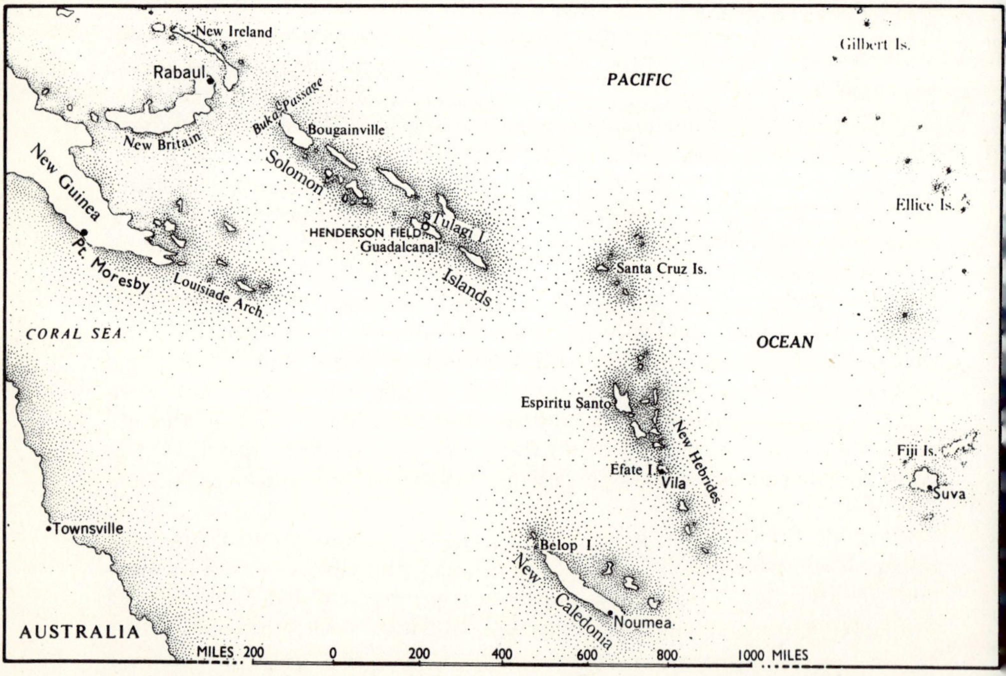

Noumea to Rabaul

prove inadequate to the task of defeating the enemy,' he added. In fact, in September, the army received only 6,523 men although its quota was 13,000.

The American success at Midway not only destroyed Japan's means of undertaking a new long-range offensive but encouraged the American leaders to plan an offensive. On 8th June MacArthur recommended to the Joint Chiefs of Staff that the time had come to attack the enemy in New Britain and New Ireland. He asked for an amphibious division (presumably of marines) and a naval task force. With these, and with the 32nd and 41st American Divisions and the 7th Australian Division he would seize the New Britain-New Ireland area. MacArthur was now in more buoyant mood. In June he described the militia as 'a sound and efficient force', ready in three months for any task. The defence of Australia was now assured. After the recapture of Rabaul, he proposed a further thrust either towards the Philippines or towards Malaya, but preferably the Philippines.

The Japanese, however, were now established well to the south of New Britain and New Ireland—at Tulagi which they had occupied at the time of the Coral Sea battle and Guadalcanal near by. The 'Americal Division' in New Caledonia had placed a detachment on Efate in the New Hebrides, 700 miles south of Guadalcanal, and later Espiritu Santo was occupied. Thus when, on 2nd July, the American Joint Chiefs ordered an offensive, its *ultimate* objective was to be the occupation of the New Britain-New Ireland-New Guinea area, including Rabaul, but the first step was to be the seizure on 1st August of 'the Santa Cruz Islands, Tulagi and adjacent positions', the second the occupation of the remaining Solomon Islands and, in New Guinea, of Lae, Salamaua, and the north-east coast. On 10th July, after it was learned that the Japanese were making an airfield on Guadalcanal, Admiral Ghormley, commanding in the South Pacific, was given more precise orders: to seize Tulagi and Guadalcanal, using the 1st Marine Division then arriving in the area. There were now three American divisions—1st Marine, 37th and Americal—in the South Pacific.

After the arrival of the Joint Chiefs' directive of 2nd July MacArthur ordered, as a preliminary to the achievement of the task allotted to him—the advance to Salamaua, Lae and north-eastern New Guinea—the assembly of a 'Buna Force' of some 3,200 men to prepare and defend an airfield in that area. It was to begin operations between the 3rd and 5th August in step with the projected landing on Guadalcanal. In mid-July the 41st U.S. Division began to move from Melbourne to Rockhampton and the 32nd from Adelaide to Brisbane. On 20th July MacArthur advanced his own headquarters from Melbourne to Brisbane, 800 miles nearer to New Guinea.

As early as February Major-General Rowell, then Deputy Chief of the General Staff, had warned Major-General B. M. Morris, commanding at Port Moresby, that the Japanese might land on the north coast and advance over the mountains against Port Moresby. The first sign of possible Japanese interest in the Buna-Gona area, the nearest likely landing place east of Salamaua, had appeared on 10th March, when a floatplane shot at two Anglican mission vessels off Buna and alighted on the water but took off when fired on.

On 6th June Morris had decided to send the Papuan Infantry Battalion (of 30 officers and 280 men) to the Kokoda-Awala area; and on the 24th,

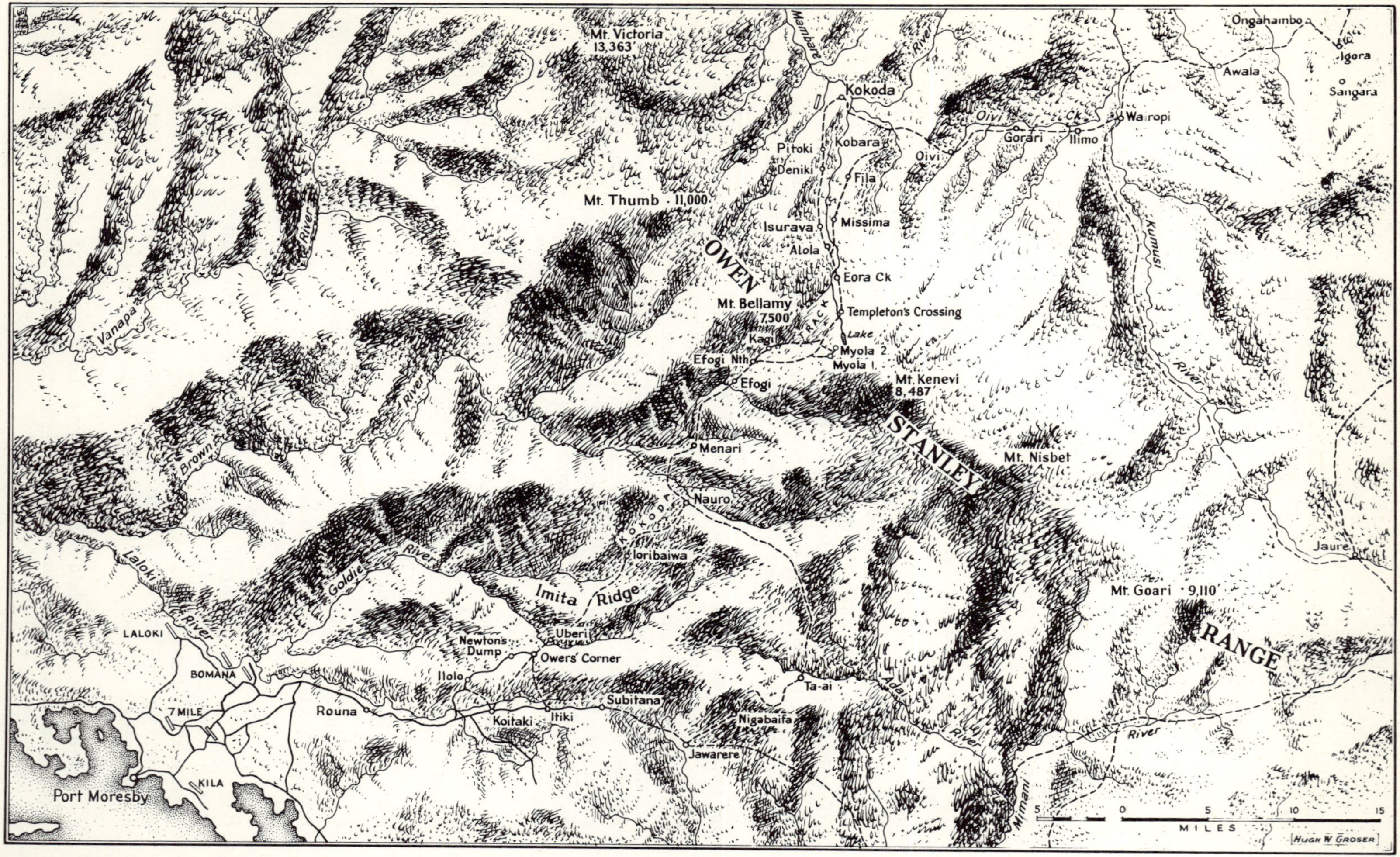

The Kokoda Track

after Blamey had given him the role of denying the enemy the possible airfield sites round Buna and holding the Kokoda pass, he gave to the Papuan Battalion and the 39th Battalion the task of preventing any movement across the mountains through the Kokoda gap. The leading company of the 39th set off towards Kokoda on 7th July. Meanwhile, on 29th June a company of American engineers joined a small force of Australian infantry that had arrived at Milne Bay a week before. Early in July the 7th Brigade was sent to Milne Bay and a squadron of Kittyhawks of the R.A.A.F. established itself on the new airfield.

Of the battalions in Papua the 39th, now moving forward to Kokoda, was probably the best, but a lamentable error had been made in sending to Port Moresby in 1941 and early 1942 not the best battalions in Australia but some of the least ready. In July 1941 the Chief of the General Staff had described the 49th Battalion, then the only one in Papua, as 'quite the worst battalion in Australia'. The 53rd when it arrived in January had had only about three months training. The task of training these units in New Guinea was made difficult because they were employed manning defences, building roads, unloading ships, transporting supplies, and building habitations. Soon about 10 per cent were off duty each day because of sickness of one kind or another.

From Buna the seldom-used track which climbed over the Owen Stanley mountains to Moresby travelled up fairly easy slopes through Gorari and Oivi to Kokoda, where a village stood on a small plateau 1,200 feet above sea level and flanked by mountains rising 7,000 feet. Thence the track climbed over steep ridges and through deep valleys to Deniki, Isurava, Kagi, Ioribaiwa, Ilolo, and at Owers' Corner linked with a motor road leading from plantation areas in the hills above Moresby down to the coastal plain. Between Ilolo and Kokoda the track often climbed up gradients so steep that it was a heart-breaking labour for burdened men to climb even a few hundred yards. Generally it travelled through dense rain forest which enclosed the narrow pad between walls of thick bush, but for a distance it rose above that level into an area of moss and stunted trees, usually clothed in mist. It was in this setting that a bitter four-months campaign was to be fought out.

For six months Japanese aircraft had been bombing the base at Port Moresby, the attacks generally being made by twenty to thirty bombers with fighter cover. The Hudson bombers of No. 32 Squadron and the Catalinas of Nos. 11 and 20, in twos and threes, had retaliated with raids against Rabaul and other Japanese bases. After a month of such raiding a few American Flying Fortresses had made their first attack on Rabaul on 23rd February. On 21st March, much to the delight of the troops round Port Moresby, who had been under air attack for two months, a squadron of fighters arrived—No. 75 R.A.A.F. with Kittyhawks. This fine squadron fought the Japanese raiders for six weeks, destroying, they believed, eighteen enemy aircraft in the air and seventeen on the ground (in a strafing at Lae), but losing twelve pilots, including the commander, Squadron Leader J. F. Jackson, and twenty-two aircraft. They were replaced on 3rd May by the 8th Pursuit Group—the first American aircraft to be based in New Guinea. By 21st July there had been more than seventy bombing attacks on Port Moresby.

Meanwhile, General Hyakutake of the *XVII Army* was planning the overland attack on Port Moresby, using Horii's *South Seas Force*. Its main com-

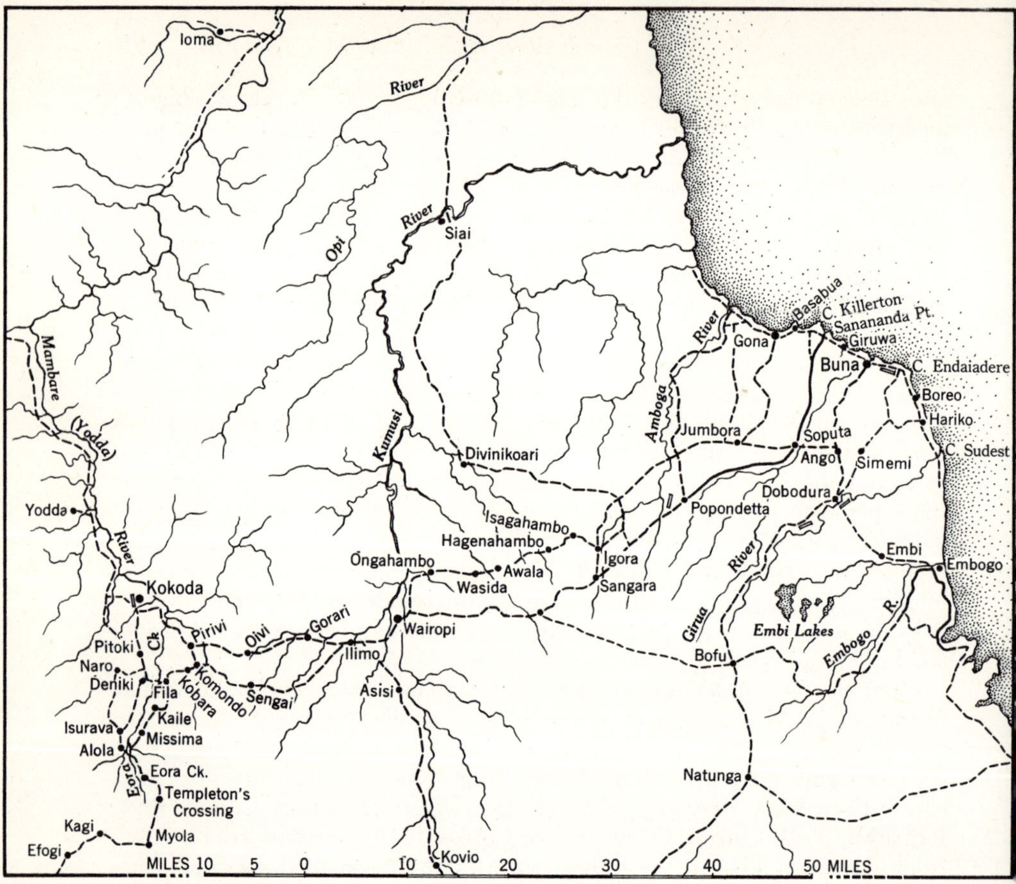

Kokoda-Buna

ponents were an engineer regiment to make roads and two infantry regiments which were to advance over the Owen Stanleys. The leading troops landed near Gona on the night of the 21st-22nd July. MacArthur's plan to establish a base on the north coast had been too leisurely. The Japanese got there first.

At this time the Papuan Infantry Battalion, only 300 strong, was spread out between Kokoda and the Buna coast, and a company of the 39th Battalion was arriving. On 23rd July there was a clash east of Awala. The foremost platoon of the 39th and the Papuans fell back. On the 25th they linked at Gorari with Lieut-Colonel W. T. Owen, commander of the 39th, and part of his leading company, Morris having ordered the remainder of the 39th forward into the mountains as soon as he learnt of the Japanese landing. The Japanese pressed on and thrust the small and weary defending force back through Oivi to Kokoda. There on the 28th-29th July in a confused night engagement in which Owen was killed, the Japanese again pushed the defenders back. The Australians consolidated about Deniki where Major A. G. Cameron arrived to take command. By 6th August the 39th Battalion was 460 strong round Deniki, the Papuan Battalion forty-three, and there was a group of Angau officers with fourteen native police. Cameron decided to retake Kokoda. Three companies advanced on the 8th. One company reached and occupied Kokoda without opposition, but the flanking companies encountered Japanese and inflicted and received severe casualties. On that day and the next they fell back to Deniki. On the 9th they repulsed an attack by perhaps 200 Japanese and on the 10th they beat off another attack; but they were now isolated and food and ammunition were running low. They defeated a third attack that evening. On the 13th and 14th August the whole force was strongly pressed, and gradually forced into a smaller and smaller perimeter. That night Cameron began a withdrawal to Isurava.

The Japanese landing in Papua had been accompanied by a renewal of Japanese submarine attacks on shipping off the east coast of the continent. Between 20th July and 3rd August three merchantmen were torpedoed and sunk and a trawler damaged by gunfire and abandoned. Three Japanese flying boats dropped bombs on Townsville on 25th-26th July and single flying boats attacked on the 28th and 29th, but no damage was done. Off Port Moresby on the 29th the transport *Malaita*, escorted by the destroyer *Arunta*, was damaged by a torpedo. Later *Arunta* sank the submarine *RO* 33 near by.

Meanwhile the storm had broken in the Solomons. A strong fleet had been collected to support the Guadalcanal undertaking: the carriers *Saratoga*, *Wasp* and *Enterprise*; battleship *North Carolina*; fourteen cruisers, including a squadron of five American and three Australian cruisers (*Canberra*, *Australia* and *Hobart*) under Rear-Admiral V. A. C. Crutchley now commanding the Australian Squadron.

At first all went fairly smoothly. By nightfall on 7th August 11,000 of Major-General Alexander A. Vandegrift's marines were ashore on Guadalcanal, where the defenders numbered about 2,000, mostly labour troops, and next day the marines occupied the airstrip. At Tulagi there was stronger opposition, but by midnight on the 8th the marines had occupied the little island. Coastwatchers looked on from their observation posts in the eastern Solomons at this encouraging indication that the tide was turning. The American leaders and people were delighted by the success of this their first full-scale offensive operation on land in a war now eight months old; but within twenty-four hours the attackers were to suffer 'one of the worst defeats ever inflicted on the United States Navy'.[4]

There were then five Japanese heavy cruisers and two light cruisers in the Bismarck Sea or at Rabaul, part of the new *Eighth Fleet*, formed in July to take over operations south of the Equator. On the night of the 7th they were steaming south to the attack. At 6 p.m. on the 8th Fletcher, commanding the carrier force, signalled Ghormley that he recommended immediate withdrawal of his carriers and without awaiting a reply set off south-eastward. Crutchley's eight cruisers and eight destroyers remained to protect the transports and the troops ashore. He divided his force into three divisions and stationed one on the northern side of the entrance to the 20-miles-wide channel between Guadalcanal and Florida Island, another (including *Canberra* and *Chicago*) on the southern side, and the third covering the eastern approaches. Two destroyers patrolled across the main entrance west of the cruiser forces. About midnight an enemy plane began circling over the

[4] S. E. Morison, *The Struggle for Guadalcanal* (1950), p. 17, a volume in the series *United States Naval Operations in World War II*.

Allied ships, but it was assumed to be a friendly one. About an hour later the Japanese cruisers entered the channel between Savo Island and Guadalcanal in line ahead at about 25 knots. About 1.40 Japanese aircraft dropped flares illuminating the transports and silhouetting *Canberra* and *Chicago*. In about two minutes *Canberra* was hit by twenty-four shells. Her captain, F. E. Getting, was mortally wounded, his gunnery officer was killed instantly, and in a few minutes the ship was listing and doomed. Then a torpedo hit *Chicago*. The Japanese cruisers now turned north in two columns towards the northern group of cruisers. Soon *Astoria* had been fatally hit, and *Quincy* and *Vincennes* were sinking. By 2.40, an hour after opening fire, the Japanese ships were speeding west, having sunk or mortally damaged four heavy cruisers.

After she had been hit *Canberra* was dead in the water, lacked light or power of any kind, and there were fires on board and ammunition was exploding. At 5 a.m. Rear-Admiral Richmond K. Turner, commanding the amphibious force, and Crutchley's senior, ordered Commander J. A. Walsh, who now commanded *Canberra*, that he must either join his force at 6.30 a.m., when it would leave the area, or abandon his ship so that it could be destroyed. Walsh had no choice and began to transfer the survivors of his crew to two American destroyers which were standing by; eighty-four had

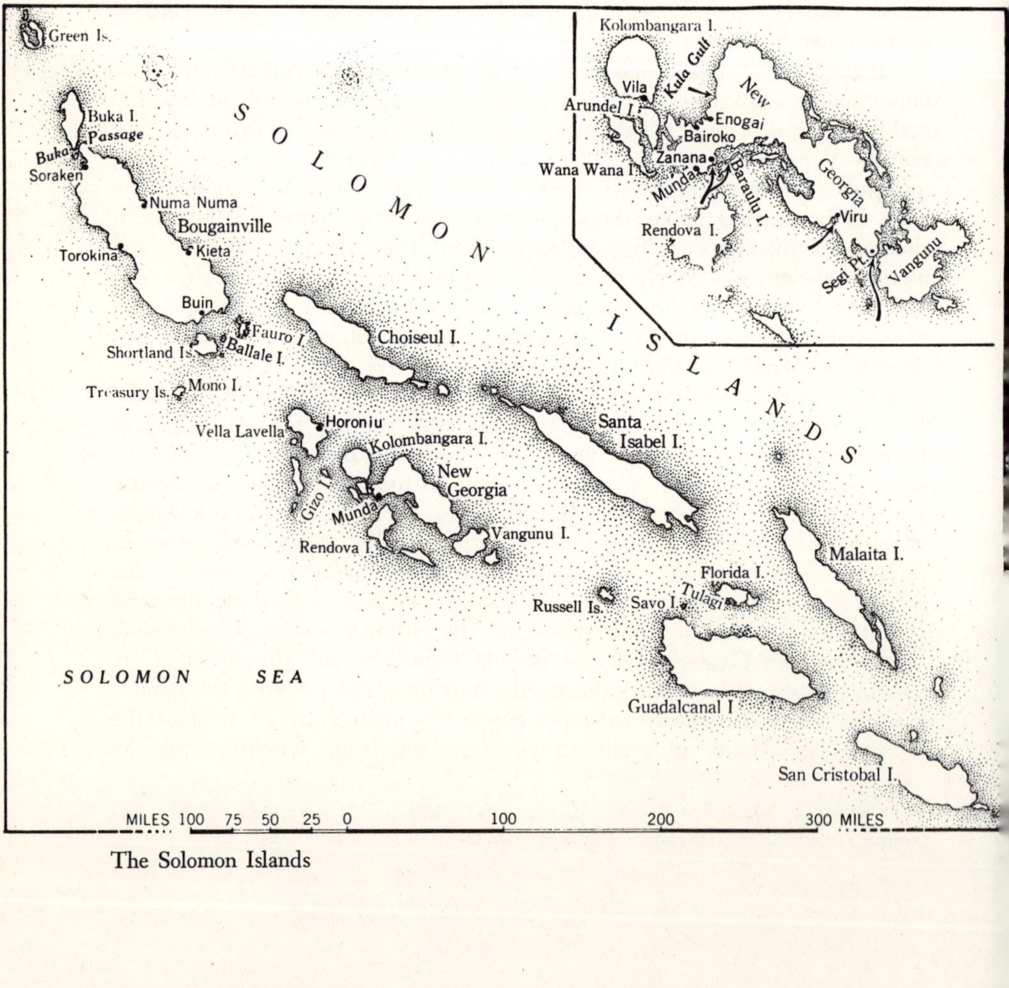

The Solomon Islands

been killed or died of wounds. About 8 a.m. an American destroyer sank the abandoned *Canberra* with a torpedo. A long effort was made to save the *Astoria* but on the afternoon of the 9th she heeled over and sank.

The Japanese ships suffered little damage in the encounter off Savo Island, but on the 10th an American submarine fired four torpedoes into the heavy cruiser *Kako* off Kavieng and sank her.

The American occupation of Guadalcanal produced a strong and continued reaction by the Japanese and led to a long campaign of attrition in the eastern Solomons, at sea, on land, and in the air. The marines were now being supplied by occasional convoys of destroyer-transports. General Hyakutake at Rabaul, underestimating the American strength, decided to land about 1,000 men on Guadalcanal and drive the Americans off. These were put ashore on 18th August but on the 21st they lost heavily in an attack on the perimeter which the Americans had flung round their airfields. Hyakutake continued to send in or try to send in reinforcements. The marines continued to await the new arrivals in their perimeter defences. In the last week of August 1,500 Japanese troops set out for Guadalcanal supported by a formidable fleet: 3 carriers, 3 battleships, 9 cruisers and 13 destroyers. Coastwatchers and aircraft reported this concentration and Admiral Ghormley sent his three carriers and their attendant vessels into the area. On 24th August ensued a carrier versus carrier action — the third of its kind — in which *Enterprise* was damaged, but the Japanese convoy was turned back. In the next three weeks the Japanese kept up their pressure and by 15th September *Saratoga* had been damaged by air attack, *Wasp* sunk, *North Carolina* damaged by submarines, and four American destroyers sunk. The Japanese had lost one carrier, *Ryujo*. But the Americans now had only one serviceable carrier, *Hornet*.

Another attack on the American perimeter had failed. The Japanese now commanded the sea round the island by night, the Americans by day. More reinforcements having been dribbled in by night some 3,400 Japanese attacked on 14th September, but again lost heavily in a wild attack on a well-dug-in, heavily-armed American unit.

In the meantime the Japanese offensive in New Guinea had attracted land forces considerably larger than those on Guadalcanal and somewhat heavier fighting had developed there. Early in August, when the Japanese had reached Kokoda, the 7th Division was on the move to New Guinea from south Queensland. The leading battalions of its 18th and 21st Brigades embarked at Brisbane on the 6th. The 18th was to reinforce the 7th Brigade at Milne Bay, the 21st to reinforce Port Moresby. On the 12th Lieut-General Rowell, commander of I Corps, took command at Port Moresby; Brigadier Porter of the 30th Brigade went forward to take command in the Owen Stanleys; Lieut-Colonel R. Honner, an outstanding infantry leader, was hurried to New Guinea to take over the 39th Battalion, which was now being joined by the 53rd.

From the 16th August until the 26th the Australian force round Isurava in the Owen Stanleys had not been hard pressed. The 21st Brigade was ordered forward into the mountains and on the 23rd August its commander, Brigadier A. W. Potts, reached Isurava, with two of his battalions strung out along the mountain track behind him.

In Moresby, before General Rowell's arrival, General Morris had been trying hard to obtain transport aircraft to supply his steadily-growing forces in the mountains. On 3rd August he signalled that their supply situation was 'most serious' and if aircraft and parachutes were not provided 'operations will be jeopardised and forward troops liable to starvation'. On the 5th the two transport aircraft which had been available at Port Moresby returned to the mainland; Allied Air Force headquarters promised, however, that another would be stationed there permanently.

On the previous day a new commander, Major-General George C. Kenney, had replaced Brett at that headquarters. Kenney was a vigorous and buoyant commander who quickly won the confidence of MacArthur and of the air forces. A few weeks later MacArthur obtained permission to give Kenney's command the title 'Fifth Air Force'. It then possessed, on paper, three groups of fighters and five of bombers, an American 'group' usually including two to four squadrons, and thus being equivalent to a British 'wing'. The available fighters numbered 250, but only 30 out of 70 Flying Fortresses were serviceable, and only 20 to 25 medium bombers. The bombers were still beset by shortages of spare parts, lack of maintenance tools, and production faults.

When Brigadier Potts was going forward into the Owen Stanleys he also soon discovered that the supply of the force then toiling painfully along the track behind him would be a main problem. Some 600 natives were carrying cargoes forward but they would not be enough. There was no airfield between Kokoda and Moresby but there was a dry lake east of Kagi which would serve as a dropping ground. It was named Myola. Hudsons of No. 32 Squadron did regular 'biscuit-bombing' flights, and by the 16th a useful quantity of supplies had been collected there. Between the 16th and 22nd August, however, after a Japanese raid on the Seven Mile airfield at Moresby had destroyed the transport planes there, no supplies were dropped.

Rowell was now pressing for supply aircraft, as Morris had done. Air supply was a commonplace conception in the minds both of old New Guinea hands, many of whom had lived on the Bulolo goldfields which were entirely air supplied, and of Australian officers who had served in the Middle East. MacArthur and his staff, however, knowing little of conditions in New Guinea took much persuading.[5] At length on 24th August, when about two brigades were in the mountains, MacArthur informed Blamey that two transport aircraft and six attack aircraft would be stationed at Port Moresby to supply both Kagi and Wau. He complained that there were only thirty transport aircraft in his command and as a rule only half of these were available at one time. 'Air supply', he added, 'must necessarily be considered an emergency rather than a normal means of supply.' The Australians considered that the right place for the thirty transport aircraft was New Guinea.

It became evident that the force in the forward area would have to be reduced for lack of supplies. Rowell ordered that the tired 39th Battalion

[5] The degree to which, at this stage, General MacArthur's staff was handicapped by lack of knowledge of New Guinea was baldly indicated on 13th August, when General Rowell received a message from Major-General Richard K. Sutherland, General MacArthur's Chief of Staff, urging that the Japanese advance be halted by demolishing the Kokoda Trail at selected points.

be withdrawn. At length Potts deployed the 2/14th and 53rd forward round Isurava and Alola with the 2/16th in reserve covering Myola.

The Japanese, who had also been delayed by supply difficulties, renewed their advance on 26th August. There were patrol clashes that day, and in the evening the Japanese were pressing hard. Next day, on Potts's orders, the 53rd advanced on Missima to counter-attack. The leading companies came under sharp fire and were dispersed, and Lieut-Colonel K. H. Ward, the commanding officer, was killed. Enemy attacks increased in intensity along the two-battalion front during the 28th and 29th. That evening the 2/14th was forced back from Isurava after suffering sharp losses, its withdrawal being covered by the 2/16th. The Japanese followed up next day and pressed hard round the flanks. In the afternoon Potts ordered a withdrawal to Eora Creek, under cover of a counter-attack. As this thrust went in it ran into a strong thrust by the enemy. There was a close and confused engagement in the course of which several large parties of the 2/14th were cut off; at the end of the day 172 of that battalion, including Lieut-Colonel A. S. Key, its commander, and eight other officers were missing. By the morning of the 31st what remained of the 2/14th was in position 1,000 yards south of Alola, part of the 2/16th was astride the track forward of them, the 39th were holding at Eora Creek, and the 53rd, which Potts now considered unreliable, was moving out of the battle. There were 130 wounded men and no means of removing them except by native stretcher bearers along the cruel track to the road-head.

The Japanese thrust against the 2/16th on 1st September but were stopped with heavy loss. The Australians, however, were now weary and undernourished. Potts informed his divisional commander, Major-General Allen, now in charge of the forward area, that he intended to withdraw to Templeton's Crossing at dawn on the 2nd. At this stage Potts's men

> had had nearly a week of constant fighting and during that time most of them had been unable even to brew themselves a mug of tea and certainly had not had a hot meal. Now, shelterless, their feet pulpy and shrivelled from the constant wet, they were soaked by continuous rain. They were worn out by fighting in a country where movement alone for even unencumbered men was hardship. They were burdened by their own wounded; desertions by carriers aggravated that difficulty and the supply problem.[6]

The Japanese attacked the flanks of the brigade as it withdrew and threatened to bypass Myola along a track through Kagi and Efogi. Myola had to be abandoned. On 5th September the retreating Australian column, now joined by the leading companies of the 2/27th, was at Efogi.

On the 7th the Japanese began to probe the positions held by the 2/27th which was now astride the track, and attacked in strength before dawn on the 8th. This frontal attack was beaten off, but they worked round the flanks and soon were threatening brigade headquarters and had encircled the rearguard force. Potts ordered the 2/16th, which was itself now under heavy fire, to thrust along the track towards him. Three companies attacked and, though they lost heavily, some platoons reached Potts. That night the survivors of the three battalions began to extricate themselves along a side

[6] D. McCarthy, *South-West Pacific Area—First Year* (1959), p. 217.

track to the east to Menari. The 2/14th and 2/16th—but not the 2/27th—arrived next morning; on the 10th the two units now only 307 strong were in position between Nauro and Ioribaiwa. There Porter took command again and thither some reinforcements—the 2/1st Pioneer Battalion, 3rd Battalion and 6th Independent Company—were moving forward. Porter withdrew to Ioribaiwa, where on 11th September the Japanese attacked the 2/14th and 2/16th. The Japanese advance was now losing its impetus. By the 14th they had made no progress and that day two fresh battalions—the 2/31st and 2/33rd of the 25th Brigade—arrived. The Japanese advance on Port Moresby had almost reached its limit. In the following days several large parties of the 2/14th cut off in the earlier fighting and all that remained of the 2/27th came in, weary and starving, after long marches round the flanks of the advancing Japanese.

On 12th September No. 30 (Beaufighter) Squadron, under the forceful Squadron Leader B. R. ('Blackjack') Walker, reached Port Moresby, armed with twenty-three of these twin-engined and heavily-armed fighters. During the 17th, twelve Beaufighters surprised and struck effectively at a group of barges engaged on supply at Buna-Sananda for the Owen Stanley force. Thereafter the long Japanese supply route was punished daily by these swift, low-flying aircraft. The arrival of the Beaufighters represented direct aid to Australian air defence by the United Kingdom, which had sent sufficient aircraft to form two squadrons.

Meanwhile at Milne Bay on the right flank of the defensive line in New Guinea there had been a decisive success. As mentioned, the 7th Brigade Group (Brigadier J. Field) from Townsville began to arrive on 11th July. That day a Japanese aircraft reconnoitred the area. Nos. 75 and 76 Squadrons R.A.A.F., armed with Kittyhawks, arrived on a completed airstrip on 25th July and a radar set was emplaced to assist the fighters. On 4th August four Zeros and a dive bomber strafed the strip; the bomber was shot down by a Kittyhawk. On the 11th twelve came over and were engaged by the Australian fighters. On 12th August (the withdrawal in the Owen Stanleys had then reached Deniki) Brigadier Wootten and advanced parties of the 18th Brigade arrived and its battalions and one battery of the 2/5th Field Regiment landed soon afterwards. That day Major-General Clowes, hitherto commanding the 1st Division, was appointed to command the augmented Milne Force.

Clowes deployed the 7th Brigade on the north-east coast of the bay, the 2/10th Battalion about Gili Gili, and the remainder of the 18th Brigade to the west. At 10.10 a.m. on the 25th Clowes learnt that a Japanese convoy including two transports had been seen by aircraft, evidently making for Milne Bay. Fog veiled the convoy for some hours but it was attacked by Hudsons, of which one flight was now at Milne Bay, and bomb-carrying Kittyhawks. A corvette received a direct hit. Earlier in the day Kittyhawks discovered and set fire to seven barges beached at Goodenough Island. The remainder of the main convoy entered Milne Bay that night and the ships put their troops ashore about Ahioma east of the area of the easternmost company of the 7th Brigade—a company of the 61st Battalion which was deployed round K.B. Mission. A small standing patrol fell back after skirmishes with Japanese advancing westward with a tank in support. About dawn the Japanese advance-guard reached the main positions of the company.

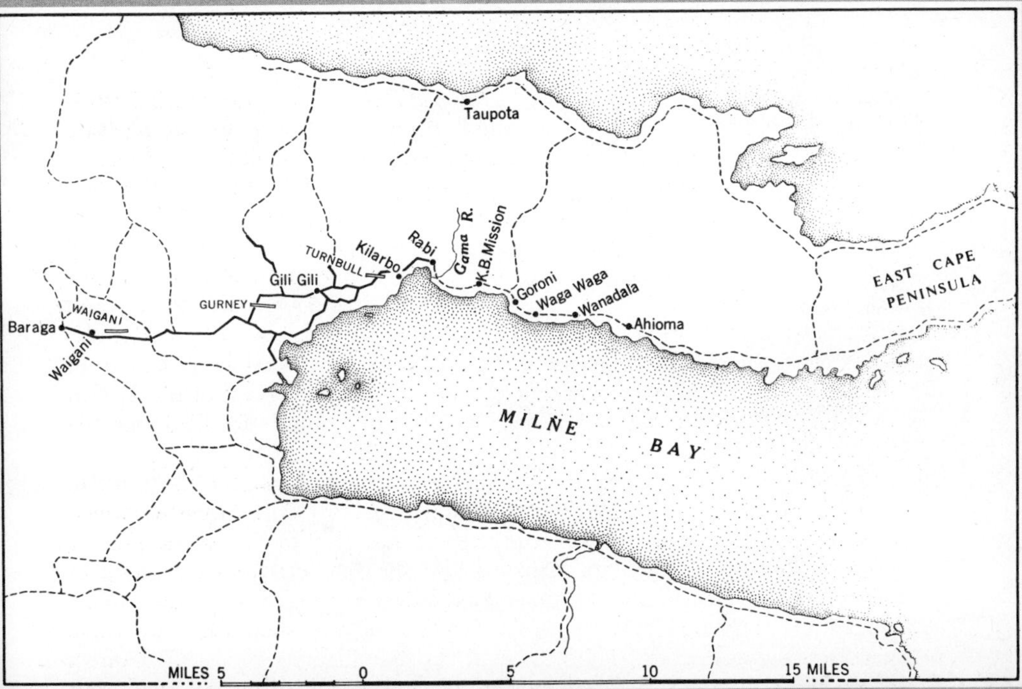

Milne Bay, where Japanese forces suffered their first defeat on land, at the hands of Australians, during the 1939-45 war.

Australian War Memorial

Australian War Memorial

Milne Bay, September 1942. Fellow pilots of No. 76 Squadron lend a hand to push Squadron Leader K. W. Truscott's Kittyhawk into the dispersal bay. Truscott (Commanding Officer of the squadron) can be seen stepping from the cockpit.

The Japanese tank was ditched and withdrew for a time. When it was light the Australian fighter and bomber aircraft found and strafed the Japanese landing craft and set fire to petrol dumps.

Two infantry companies and part of another were hurried forward to reinforce the forward company. At 4.45 p.m. on the 26th the Japanese had still not reappeared, and, supported by artillery and strafing aircraft, two companies of the 61st went forward and drove Japanese out of a position about 600 yards from the Mission. It was now becoming dark and the Australians had no anti-tank weapons; they withdrew to the Mission again. There at 10 p.m., in moonlight, the Japanese attacked, and a long fight ensued. The Japanese brought up a flame-thrower but the Australians silenced the crew with grenades. At 4.30 a.m. when the Japanese were moving round the flank and casualties were increasing, the weary Australians were withdrawn to the Gama River one mile farther west and a probable tank obstacle. At 1 p.m. on the 27th the Japanese had not followed up and the veteran 2/10th Battalion was advancing through the 61st towards K.B., thus relieving a battalion which had now been fighting for two nights and two days.

During the 27th Japanese dive bombers escorted by Zeros attempted to make No. 1 airstrip (Gurney) unserviceable, but were met by six Kittyhawks, whose pilots shot down perhaps two bombers; elsewhere two more bombers and two Zeros were destroyed. The air force also kept strict watch on the Taupota area to the north to block any attempt to outflank the defenders.

Clowes's problem was to discover whether additional Japanese ships entering the bay by night were landing more troops and where and how the enemy intended to use his main force. At length on the 27th he had given Field the 2/10th, now advancing on K.B. There the newcomers found no Japanese and settled into a defensive position for the night, with their right flank on the sea. Again the Japanese had been waiting for night before attacking. About 8 p.m. they advanced, with two tanks, which got among the forward positions and led their infantry into them, but did not break through the defensive zone. Sticky bombs, the Australians' only anti-tank weapons, failed to stick. Artillery fire was brought down on the enemy but they attacked repeatedly, inflicting sharp losses, and in the early hours the South Australians fell back in some confusion to the Gama River line. There at 2 a.m. on the 28th the Japanese delivered the strongest attack so far, and pushed along the road through the Australians on the river line. The 2/10th thus being thrust aside, the Japanese column next encountered the 25th Battalion deployed in defence of No. 3 Strip (Turnbull) its fire power augmented by machine-guns of the 43rd American Engineer Regiment which was working there. The forward platoons of the 25th halted the Japanese until daylight when, as usual, they pulled back to await darkness. By late afternoon on the 28th the 25th Battalion and now also the 61st were firmly in position covering the strip and awaiting a night attack.

After the Japanese reached the edge of this strip the Kittyhawks were ordered back to Moresby and spent the night of the 28th-29th there, returning at dawn, but the wing did not repeat this manoeuvre on subsequent nights lest it discourage the troops.

The Milne Bay landing had caused great anxiety at MacArthur's headquarters. MacArthur ordered that the 25th Brigade be shipped from Brisbane to Milne Bay. On the 28th he had instructed Blamey that Clowes must 'at once clear the north shore of Milne Bay without delay'. 'You possibly do not realise', wrote General Vasey (then at MacArthur's headquarters) to Rowell, 'that for G.H.Q. this is their first battle and they are, therefore, like many others, nervous . . . My view is that the decision to send 25 Brigade to Milne Bay is either precipitate or too late.'

Clowes continued to act with deliberation—a sound course in view of the fact that the Japanese had the freedom of the sea and could make other landings if they wished, and that they had not yet seriously threatened the airstrips, the defence of which was Clowes's main task. The Japanese too bided their time. They made no attack on the 29th, when Australian patrols found both the enemy tanks bogged and abandoned; nor on the 30th.

At length at 3 a.m. on the 31st the Japanese launched their attack on the strip. Flares showed them bunched near the seaward end of it shouting loudly. They charged three times across the open into intense fire which withered each attack and inflicted disastrous losses. Then they tried and failed again at the north-eastern end of the strip. Meanwhile, in accordance with Clowes's orders to attack towards K.B., the 2/12th was advancing. It passed through the forward positions about 9 a.m., and pushed through the Japanese survivors, killing some seventy. The battalion was counter-attacked by about 300 Japanese that evening but drove them off, and it continued its advance on the 1st, 2nd and 3rd September. On the 3rd, now reinforced by part of the 2/9th, it came upon a strong delaying position. A costly attack ensued and the Japanese were not manoeuvred out of the position until nightfall. That night Japanese ships were again in the bay.

On the 4th the Australians pressed on against a stubborn enemy, one bitter attack following another. Corporal J. A. French of the 2/9th advanced alone and silenced three enemy machine-gun posts, dying in front of the third gun. He was posthumously awarded the Victoria Cross. The fighters dive-bombed the Japanese through the 4th and 5th September. By the 6th the 2/9th were in the midst of what had evidently been the main Japanese base; in the six-day advance the two battalions together had lost about 200 killed and wounded.

Advanced elements of Nos. 100 (Beaufort torpedo bomber) and 30 (Beaufighter) Squadrons had now arrived at the base. Supported by Hudsons and Kittyhawks they attacked a cruiser and destroyer approaching Milne Bay but obtained no hits. The Japanese ships, which had entered the bay each night during the operation, went on to Milne Bay where they sank the steamer *Anshun* (3,188 tons), unloading at Gili Gili on 6th September, and shelled the troops ashore.

It was learnt later that the Japanese had estimated the garrison of Milne Bay at a few companies. Their expedition had been undertaken initially by about 2,000 marines. These were loaded into two transports escorted by two cruisers and three destroyers and had left Rabaul on 24th August. The convoy landed its men about four miles east of K.B. Mission on the night of the 25th-26th. A second convoy arrived on the 29th and landed some 800 marines. On 4th September the admiral commanding the expedition ordered an evacuation and that night and the next two nights about 1,200 out of 2,800 who had landed were taken off. Probably 750 Japanese were killed. The Australian battle casualties were 373. The only Japanese naval loss in this operation was the destroyer *Yayoi*, sunk by heavy bombers when trying to rescue troops stranded on Goodenough Island. Milne Bay was an epoch-making success strategically, tactically and psychologically. The Japanese plan to capture Port Moresby by a two-pronged thrust had gone amiss; for the first time in a war now nine months old a Japanese invading force had been thrown back into the sea; and the defenders had proved themselves man for man the equals of the Japanese infantry. The news of the Japanese defeat heartened Allied commanders and troops far and wide.

It was a matter of no small importance that at Milne Bay, as with the 39th Battalion on the Kokoda Track, a militia battalion which had had no more than eight months continuous training had proved itself able to put up a sturdy defence. If the militia divisions, now laced with a considerable number of officers who had served in the Middle East, could be considered adequately trained, that signified that in the South and South-West Pacific were twelve Australian and five American divisions, all of which should be ready for action.

The elements of two Australian divisions were now in New Guinea, but the senior commanders were planning to send more. On 29th August Rowell, learning that the 25th Brigade had been ordered to Milne Bay, urged that it be sent to Port Moresby instead. After the success at Milne Bay this wish was granted. On 5th September Blamey told Rowell that he might also have the 16th and 17th Brigades, just home from Ceylon.

The Australian air force squadrons in New Guinea had now been combined in a new formation, No. 9 Group, whose commander was Group Captain W. H. Garing, who had served with the Australian flying boat squadron in England in 1939 and 1940. By the end of September his force included two squadrons of fighters (75 and 76), and three of bombers (6, 30 and 100). In August and September the American long-range bombers based in Queensland had been striking at Rabaul and Japanese convoys in stronger force than hitherto, but, at least so far as the convoys were concerned, without much effect.

Early in September MacArthur decided to send an American regiment to Papua to be used to cross the island by an alternative track to the one through Kokoda and advance against the Japanese rear—a large undertaking.

Meanwhile, on the northern flank, Kanga Force had been under heavier pressure, and was having difficulty in keeping up supplies to the forward troops for lack of carriers. Sickness was increasing among the forward troops. On 29th August Colonel Fleay, at Wau, received information that 300 Japanese were at the village of Busama seeking natives to guide them to Wau, and more troops were landing at Salamaua. He asked for reinforcements but was told by New Guinea Force that none could be spared: the battle at Milne Bay was in progress and the 21st Brigade was being thrust back in the Owen Stanleys. On the 31st Mubo was attacked in force and the thirty Australians there fell back. The previous afternoon Fleay had ordered that the Bulolo Valley be 'scorched' preparatory to withdrawal to Winima and Kudjeru. Buildings, equipment, bridges and machinery in Wau were blown up or burnt and the main body of Kanga Force withdrew, the forward groups following in the next few days.

In this phase spirits were at a low ebb at MacArthur's headquarters. He informed the Joint Chiefs on 30th August that 'unless moves are made to meet the changing conditions a disastrous outcome is bound to result shortly; it is no longer a question here of preparing a projected offensive; without additional naval forces . . . and unless steps are taken to match the heavy air and ground forces the enemy is assembling, I predict the development shortly of a situation similar to those that have successively overwhelmed our forces in the Pacific since the beginning of the war'. Curtin sent a cable to Roosevelt on 11th September supporting a request by MacArthur for reinforcement by an American corps of three divisions.

In fact, after the Midway battle there was no danger of a large-scale Japanese offensive. In June the *10th Air Group* was withdrawn to Manchuria; the *4th Division* returned from Luzon to Japan. General Terauchi of the *Southern Army* was ordered to defend Burma, the Indies and Indo-China, to press towards Chungking from Burma, but to wage mainly a propaganda and Fifth Column campaign against India, Australia and China. However, the Japanese forces based on Rabaul were reinforced. As the fierce struggle developed in the Solomons the *XVII Army* and *III Air Army* were given the

2nd Division from Java, the *38th Division* from Sumatra and an air group from Manchuria.

In the first six months of the South-West Pacific Command its land forces had been greatly strengthened. The Australian Army plus the five American divisions in the South and South-West Pacific now numbered more divisions than Japan had employed in her whole offensive drive east, south and west. The Australians had 750 heavy and medium tanks to equip two armoured divisions and a tank brigade, and the factories had produced more than enough weapons of all main types to arm the fighting formations. There was, for example, a surplus of 25-pounders, mortars, sub-machine-guns, and carriers above the initial needs of the fighting units (not taking into account training units and reserves). From March to September, however, the struggle with Japan had been mainly a naval-air operation, fought out between the fleets, and particularly the carrier fleets, in the Coral Sea, the central Pacific and round the Solomons. Wisely the Joint Chiefs had refrained from detaching carrier forces to the South-West Pacific Command, but had left them under purely naval control, concentrated and mobile.

In the first half of 1942 the Australian political leaders faced heavier and more complex problems than any Australian wartime Government had met so far. They were no longer responsible only for overseas forces serving on remote battlegrounds: the commander-in-chief of the main Pacific theatre of war was established in their territory and the forces he controlled were chiefly Australian; they were no longer organising a circumscribed war effort but one into which maximum resources had to be flung.

Once American forces had landed the Government hastened to prove Australia a good ally by providing them with all they needed and as quickly as possible. To this end they established first an Administrative Planning Committee (it outgrew its usefulness by April), the Allied Works Council (which is discussed below) and—to co-ordinate the various American supply organisations and their Australian counterparts—the Allied Supply Council and the Allied Supply Standing Committee.

Early in 1942 measures which the economists had put forward earlier, but which were thought politically impracticable—for example, full-scale manpower regulation, restriction of non-essential industry, heavy taxation—were translated into action. The Japanese advance southwards produced a threat so evident that the country was prepared to accept almost any government action intended to combat it.

The blueprint which was being evolved by the Manpower Priorities Board in 1941 was implemented by the Manpower Directorate, created in January 1942. The Directorate adopted the principle of declaring protected undertakings, numbering 5,334 in June 1942, 8,585 in September 1942, 13,445 in December 1942. Movement in or out of these was controlled as was call-up to the forces from them. The Manpower Priorities Board had insisted that policy could not be successful unless based upon reliable and detailed statistics, and to acquire these the registration of all persons above the age of 16 was instituted, followed by the issue of identity cards which people had to carry with them. In February the Cabinet established the Allied Works Council with E. G. Theodore, a former Federal Treasurer, as Director-General. Its task was to carry out the big constructional jobs now necessary, and Theodore was given wide powers. A Civil Constructional Corps to supply some of the labour needed by the Allied Works Council was approved in April; into it were pressed men over military age (men of 45 to 60). In May aliens were recruited by the Council, forming a Civil Aliens Corps. By June 1943 the C.C.C. had 53,500 men, of whom 16,600 had been conscripted, and the Aliens Corps had 4,000.

In 1942 production of munitions and the fulfilment of the forces' needs in manpower and materials were seen as the first objective. Nevertheless there were signs that in pursuing this policy rural production was being denuded. The Manpower Priorities Board had recognised and studied the problem at the end of 1941.[7] In the balance sheet of total manpower the Directorate found that by February 1942 the forces (including their women members) accounted for 520,000, but civil employment was only 20,000 less than in July 1939. The resources which had produced the 500,000 were estimated at: 248,000 unemployed, 102,000 increase in the total working population, 150,000 persons not normally seeking employment. For 1942 it was estimated that 318,000 more persons would be needed (including 48,500 women and, for the Allied Works Council, 50,000 men). To provide these numbers the employment of women, the cessation of non-essential industries and the rationalisation of those remaining, were recommended, and it was affirmed that there could be no justification in producing for export anything not urgently required for war purposes.

By August 105,000 had been found, and in the light of revised figures the needs to the end of 1942 were set at 139,000 men and 80,000 women. The same methods of finding people were advanced, but with more vigour, and with the disconcerting assurance that the War Cabinet must expect the manpower program to be in arrears. Rural manpower was to be further searched, but the greatest emphasis was on the need for the Department of War Organisation of Industry's policy of economy in production, transport and consumption to be carried through with ruthlessness and speed. Despite its formal existence since June 1941 this department was not doing much effective work until February 1942.

On 10th February, five days before Singapore fell, the Prime Minister had announced 'a complete charter for a total war effort in Australia'. To carry this out regulations were issued which gave the Minister for the Army power to declare an emergency in any part of Australia; gave the Minister for Defence Co-ordination power to require any person in Australia to perform any specified services for the nation, and to require the use of any property (although he might not confiscate); and gave power to the Treasurer and the Minister for Labour and National Service to limit profits, control the transfer of land and shares, fix rates of interest, and peg wages. Armed with these unprecedented powers the Government set about its task.

[7] Movement away from primary production is shown in the following estimates:

	Owners Relatives, etc.	*Permanent Employees*	*Temporary Employees*	*Total*
1939	292,000	100,000	102,000	494,000
1940	294,000	101,000	102,000	497,000
1941	284,000	96,000	92,000	472,000
1942	256,000	83,000	62,000	401,000
1943	239,000	76,000	45,000	360,000

The efforts of the Department of War Organisation of Industry were soon successful in transport (the restriction of retail deliveries and of dry cleaning, the zoning of bread and milk deliveries), in the reduction of packaging, and in the simplification of clothing manufacture.[8] The department endeavoured to promote voluntary action by industries. It chose to direct its efforts first at distribution, commerce and finance, because these sections of the community were judged to give the 'greatest results in terms of manpower'.

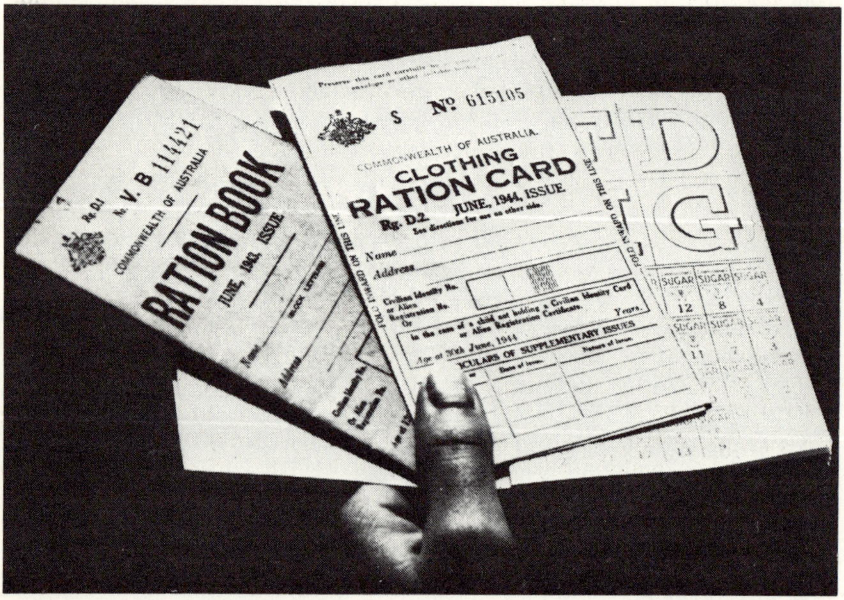

Australian War Memorial

Rationing of clothing began in June 1942 and food rationing followed. The scale varied from time to time, as did the format of the ration books. In 1944 the weekly ration scale for each adult was: tea, 2 ounces; sugar, 16 ounces; butter, 6 ounces; meat, $2\frac{1}{4}$ pounds. All rationing had ceased by July 1950.

A move to control the use of materials by order, as distinct from the informal arrangements which had sufficed in 1941, had begun in December and emerged in the Control of Essential Materials (Goods) Order of 23rd February 1942. Except under permit, the use of iron, steel, copper and industrial chemicals and 126 other items was 'prohibited', and of eighty-six others was 'restricted'.

As early as August 1941 discussion had occurred about the possibility of rationing, and clothing was mentioned as the most likely item. Early in 1942 an acute shortage was developing, and a buying rush was already occurring because rationing was expected and it was impossible to keep preparations

[8] For example, an order of 31st July provided: for men no double-breasted suits; buttonholes only for fastening; no welted or raised seams; and for women, no full or balloon type sleeves; one pocket; no embroidery. From April to December 1942 the making of civilian hats was prohibited.

secret. By an order of 9th May permissible sales were set at 75 per cent of the weekly figure for 1941, and on 15th June clothing coupons were introduced. These enabled adults to buy about two-thirds of the amount of clothing normally acquired each year, and for children about four-fifths. Rationing of tea at the rate of half a pound a person in each five weeks' period followed from 6th July, because Japan's advance had cut off the East Indian plantations and had left only Ceylon and India to supply the world. Sugar rationing (one pound a week) resulted from difficulties in transport from northern areas, reduced production due to inadequate supplies of fertiliser, lack of manpower, shortage of storage space, and the threat of enemy attack.[9]

In September 1942 the people generally began to feel the various shortages keenly. In that month 'austerity meals' in hotels and restaurants were ordered: a maximum of 4 shillings for lunch and 5 shillings for dinner.

Restricted deliveries, difficult shopping conditions, shortages, all rebounded on the housewife. But the Government was attempting also to reduce the labour and material involved in industries such as racing, liquor and tobacco —obviously more appropriate subjects for attack. On 17th September 1942 regulations were issued which permitted race meetings on Saturdays only, limited the number of events, and restricted the publication of racing information: on one Saturday in each month there would be no races, but holiday and carnival meetings were exempted. The production of beer and other liquors was cut by from 28 per cent to $33\frac{1}{3}$ per cent as early as March 1942; now the Prime Minister persuaded the State Governments to further reduce trading hours and to introduce other restrictions on drinking. The saving of manpower was offset by the fact that much time was wasted by men leaving work early to queue for drinks before the beer was 'on' at a particular hotel. From June 1942 the 'quota' of cigarettes and tobacco (it was calculated on the amount of supplies received during 1940) was reduced by a quarter and in September 1943 still further. Black marketing soon became a waster of time for the dishonest and an irritation to the honest. In September a Bill was introduced providing up to twelve months imprisonment for an individual convicted of black marketing and fines of up to £10,000 for a convicted firm, although enforcement proved to be very difficult because of legal complications and the lack of manpower to enforce the legislation effectively.

After Japan entered the war special tax resolutions were introduced which reduced the statutory exemption to £156 and introduced a special tax of sixpence in the £1 rising to a shilling in the £1 on incomes over £300. Company tax, already increased in the November proposals to 3 shillings, was brought to 4 shillings in the £1. A new source of tax—on entertainments—was invaded by the Commonwealth Government. But the most notable feature of taxation arrangements was the introduction in May 1942 of uniform tax proposals by which the Commonwealth would become the sole income taxing authority.

Despite price control it was inevitable, all other factors considered, that prices should increase, but control prevented steep and uncontrolled rises.

[9] The 1942-43 crop was 649,000 tons against a pre-war crop of 823,000; the 1943-44 crop would drop to 523,000 tons.

The effect of reduced supplies and of rising wages and increased purchasing power, however, was a degree of inflation. Total wages and salaries paid in factories almost doubled between 1939 and 1943. By June 1942 the 'C' series retail price index had risen 17.9 per cent, and the rate of increase was becoming alarming. The Prices Commissioner, aware of the trend, had introduced a far-reaching order on 15th April 1942 by which profit margins were pegged at those of 15th April 1942.

While the Government was instituting these various methods of controlling civilian and non-essential production, and providing money for the war effort, the production of war equipment, towards which these actions were largely directed, continued steadily, the organisation created in June 1940 remaining substantially unaltered. By the middle of 1942 some weapons had been produced in such quantities that immediate needs were satisfied and production was tapered off. The output of 2-pounder anti-tank guns was reduced from twenty-five a week in June 1942 to seven a week in December 1942, but the 6-pounder anti-tank gun, which began production with two a week in August 1942, rose to sixteen a week in December 1942. By December 1942 production of the following weapons stood at:

	Per week	*Total*
Austen sub-machine-gun	217	2,283
Owen sub-machine-gun	570	15,198
Bren machine-gun	135	6,693
Vickers machine-gun	72	6,497

Private industry had joined the government factory in the production of 25-pounders and by December 1942 the private factories' rate was seven a week and the government factory's twelve a week; the totals were 217 and 853 respectively. Steady production of the 40-mm Bofors gun began in July 1942 (eleven had been made by the end of the year), and of the new 17-pounder gun in December 1942.

Tanks continued to occupy money and manpower for only small return. The first experimental model of the AC.1 tank was produced in January 1942 and in August 1942 the first model produced to mass production methods was assembled at Chullora, New South Wales.[1] The Victorian and South Australian railways concentrated on making carriers.

Shipbuilding continued—eleven merchant ships were being built in December 1942—but only slow progress could be made because of the demand for repairs to ships and later because the needs of the Services for small craft cut across the merchant shipbuilding program.[2]

Shipping was one of the greatest problems of 1942 because of the extraordinary demands on coastal as well as overseas shipping, the increase in shipping casualties, the appearance of refugee ships and cargoes in Australian ports, the congestion and confusion in those ports, and the number of separate authorities in Australia who sought to control some part of shipping. America was as much interested in shipping in Australian waters as

[1] The NSW railways became the major assembly contractors for tanks. By the end of 1942 twenty-two AC.1 tanks, armed with 2-pounders, were completed; discussion and design of the AC.3 (25-pounder) and AC.4 (17-pounder) proceeded.

[2] By December 1942 orders received for self-propelled craft were: USA 450; RAAF 70; RAN 13.

Australia herself and the establishment in March of the Allied Consultative Shipping Council recognised the need for constant liaison.

Demands on coastal shipping resulted in appeals for vessels from overseas, but the Americans, to whom these pleas were addressed, were not convinced that Australia was making the most of the tonnage already available to her and urged that it must be handled more efficiently. The upshot was the establishment in October of a new department—Supply and Shipping—and within that department the appointment of a Director of Shipping. He planned a small central secretariat which co-ordinated the specialised activities of the various authorities controlling shipping.

The railways were heavily burdened as a result of the diversion of freight normally carried by sea, the military decisions which landed troops in southern ports and sent them by rail to threatened areas in the north, and the difficulties inherent in a change-of-gauge system. Wider powers than those which had been wrung from the States on the eve of Japan's entry were needed, and these were arranged in March 1942. They provided for a Director of Land Transport with a Director of Rail Transport and a Director of Road Transport. Restriction of civilian use of railways was the first need in order that carrying capacity should be reserved for essential use. Interstate travel was prohibited except by people holding a permit; in September transport of racehorses and racing dogs was prohibited, and to speed up the return of trucks demurrage rates were sharply increased. Cross traffic was closely studied and in consequence transport between States of items such as breakfast cereals, chilled and frozen meat, grain and potatoes was restricted.

Control of road transport had to be through the State authorities, there being no pre-war liaison such as existed between Commonwealth and State railway authorities. Restriction of road transport was achieved partly by control of fuel, tyres, spare parts, repairs and new vehicles.[3] From 1st February 1942 private users' and business cars' petrol ration was reduced by about 20 per cent and that for commercial vehicles 10 per cent.[4]

The disappearance of overseas markets for some primary products was now accepted; efforts turned from trying to get extra ships to questions of storage and restrictions of production. But before the end of the year it was clear that the future was not only reassuring, but actually promising, for primary production. The presence of American troops meant increased consumption of produce within Australia. Incidental influences were a drought in 1940-41

[3] Through close relation with the Department of Supply in whom rested control of the supply of these items. The fall in registrations was:

	Motor cars	*Motor cycles*	*Commercial vehicles*
1938-39	562,271	79,237	258,025
1939-40	559,533	74,496	260,994
1940-41	538,483	70,918	262,141
1941-42	450,851	49,467	250,515
1942-43	471,742	48,321	255,933

Control of tyres proved the most effective weapon.

[4] Eight horse-power cars came down to a two-monthly ration of 3 gallons, 30 h.p. cars to a two-monthly ration of 8 gallons. The estimated mileage allowed to private users was 16 miles a week.

and reduced supplies of fertilisers, which combined to bring down production. It was clear that for most primary products the worst effects of war were over.

An Australian Food Council came into existence in April 1942. It adopted the suggestion of the Department of War Organisation of Industry that production goals should be compiled so that the supplies from the various industries should have some relation to the estimated demands. These goals were submitted in September.

Early in 1942 butter production was in the process of partial conversion to cheese production at the request of Great Britain, but when the Japanese advance interrupted Britain's supplies of vegetable oils and thus her supplies of margarine Australia was asked to increase her butter production. The American's predilection for pork made an increase in pig-farming desirable. A contract was made with the United Kingdom for the supply of 110,000 tons of frozen meat but the drought now took a hand, and by August 1942 there was doubt whether the 110,000 tons could be supplied; canning was in arrears.

Wheat had been in need of stabilisation from the beginning of the war; the first wartime Government's plan (three shillings and tenpence a bushel f.o.b bagged on a crop of 140,000,000 bushels) was now replaced by what was known as the 'Scully' plan of August 1942 (4 shillings a bag at sidings on crops of licensed growers up to 3,000 bushels; any production above that was to be at market realisations).

After the loss of Nauru and Ocean Island the Combined Food Board in America had allocated 480,000 tons of fertiliser to Australia, but her normal consumption was 1,000,000 tons. Fertiliser allotted to sugar growers in 1942 amounted to only one-third of their needs.

Chapter 8 **The tide turns in the Pacific war**

In late September 1942 both the Allied and the Japanese leaders viewed the immediate future with great anxiety. The Japanese were able to man but thinly the arc of outposts flung around their recently-acquired Greater East Asia Co-Prosperity Sphere. From the Aleutians to the Burma-India frontier the line was about 12,000 miles long. Now two severe land battles had developed for the possession of airfields or potential airfields by means of which the Japanese had hoped to extend the range of their protecting aircraft. These were at Guadalcanal, where an American force had taken an airfield from the enemy and so far had succeeded in defending the tight perimeter flung round it; and in the Buna-Moresby area where, at the second attempt, Horii Force had not succeeded in reaching its objective.

A minor cause of Japanese anxiety was a conviction, established firmly in the mind of the High Command in Tokyo, possibly partly as a result of the enterprise of some 300 Australians fighting in Timor and the efforts of a few air squadrons operating from Darwin, that an attack from Australia into the Indies was imminent. It was to counter this expected offensive that the Japanese in August began moving the *48th Division* into Timor and, in November, sent the *5th Division* into the Ambon area.

The leaders in Washington, on the other hand, feared lest they might be compelled to abandon their foothold on Guadalcanal, and thus, within a few months of the surrender in the Philippines, accept another disheartening defeat.

In the South-West Pacific General MacArthur was alarmed at the turn of events in New Guinea, particularly as his own reputation was not likely to survive a second set-back. He now had a new American corps commander in Australia and his reaction to news of the continued Japanese advance towards Port Moresby was a decision to send him to the front. He was Lieut-General Robert L. Eichelberger, who had arrived in Australia late in August to command the I American Corps which would include the 32nd Division, now near Brisbane, and the 41st, at Rockhampton. Like many senior American soldiers he had not seen active service in Europe in 1918; in that year and until 1920 he had served on the staff of the American force in Siberia. He was a practical, kindly, modest soldier, who rapidly became on the best of terms with his Australian colleagues. On 14th September MacArthur summoned him to his rooms at Lennon's Hotel in Brisbane and told him that he was to go to New Guinea about 1st October in command of a force including the 32nd Division and was to capture the Buna-Gona area. Next day, however, MacArthur's Chief of Staff told Eichelberger that this plan had been abandoned, though two regiments of the 32nd would go to New Guinea.

General Blamey had visited New Guinea from the 12th to the 14th September, and on the 17th had told a meeting of the Advisory War Council that the 25th Brigade was in New Guinea and the 16th Brigade on its way there, that a regiment of American troops was being sent forward, and that he shared the confidence which both Generals Rowell and Allen felt that the Japanese would not take Port Moresby by land.

From MacArthur, however, the Australian Ministers received less hopeful counsel. Also on the 17th he spoke to Curtin by telephone and said that he had lost confidence in the efficiency of the Australian troops in New Guinea. The Australian command, he added, had the utmost faith in its ability to deal with the situation, but he, MacArthur, no longer had confidence, and he proposed therefore to send American troops to New Guinea. He considered that Blamey should go to New Guinea and take personal command 'not only to energise the situation but to save himself because in the event of the situation in New Guinea becoming really serious it would be difficult for General Blamey to meet his responsibility to the Australian public'. The problem was to fend the enemy off for some months, he said. Support was coming but the question was whether it would be too late.

Meanwhile Kenney, the new Allied Air Force commander, was rapidly making his presence felt. Recent arrivals were two brigadier-generals, Ennis C. Whitehead and Kenneth Walker. Walker replaced Royce in command of the bombers at Townsville, and Whitehead took over the American squadrons in New Guinea. Kenney insisted on improvement of the American maintenance system, which was failing to get supplies and spares forward to the right places at the right time. He organised heavier long-range bomber raids on the Japanese bases. To encourage the American fighter pilots of No. 35 Group in New Guinea he offered a decoration for every enemy fighter shot down.

Although it was implied in MacArthur's planning that he considered the 32nd and 41st Divisions fit to take the field, Eichelberger was less confident. Soon after his arrival he had told MacArthur that the divisions were not sufficiently trained to meet the Japanese on equal terms. This was despite the fact that the 32nd Division had been mobilised since October 1940 and the 41st since September 1940. They were handicapped, however, by inadequately-trained and inexperienced leaders, soft training methods in camps which had most of the amenities of urban life, and unsuitable equipment.

By the third week of September a force equivalent to three divisions was assembled in New Guinea. Whereas when the Japanese attack opened late in July there were three brigades in New Guinea there were now nine.

The 7th Division was now concentrated on the operations north of Port Moresby. The task of the 30th Brigade was to prevent penetration on the left flank and with the 14th Brigade (one battalion) to provide defence against seaborne landings. Allen also had sent out small forces wide to the east and west. On 19th September Vasey opened the 6th Division's headquarters at Port Moresby and took command of the troops protecting the base.

The 25th Brigade had been moved forward with a minimum of delay. It had arrived in Port Moresby on 9th September after eight days at sea, and it set out along the track next day dressed in the new jungle-green uniform. By the 14th the 25th Brigade was deployed with the 21st. Brigadier Eather's orders were to halt the enemy and then advance on Kokoda. He sent the 2/33rd Battalion round the right flank of the 21st, the 2/25th Battalion

Australian War Memorial

Sydney gave the 16th Brigade a tumultuous welcome on its march through the city on 5th September 1942. The brigade was newly returned to Australia after hard fighting in the Middle East and a period of sixteen weeks when it was retained in Ceylon (together with the 17th Brigade) for the defence of Colombo. Six weeks later the 16th Brigade was in action in New Guinea.

Australian War Memorial

Port Moresby, the Allies' main base in Papua in 1942-43. The corvette H.M.A.S. *Bendigo* is ferrying Australian wounded and sick to the hospital ship *Manunda*, in September 1942, at the height of the Japanese threat to Port Moresby.

straight along the track and the 2/31st round the left flank to come in on Nauro. The flanking moves met effective Japanese opposition and made little progress; in the centre the enemy pressed hard. Severe fighting continued on the 16th and that morning Eather asked Allen for leave to withdraw to Imita Ridge if he considered it necessary. Allen agreed, but told him he must fight it out at Imita. Rowell confirmed this, telling Allen that any further withdrawal was out of the question. The brigade, with the 3rd Battalion and the 2/1st Pioneers, was deployed on Imita Ridge by 11 a.m. on the 17th.

From the 18th onwards the brigade sent out strong fighting patrols from Imita Ridge, but the enemy had not closely followed up this last withdrawal. On the 21st guns of the 14th Field Regiment sited at Owers' Corner began harassing the Japanese. Eather began a general advance down the thousands of roughly-cut steps leading from Imita Ridge on the 26th and on the 28th made an encircling attack on Ioribaiwa. It had been abandoned by the enemy.

About 20th September MacArthur and Kenney had discussed a plan for sending three converging columns against Buna: the Australians through Kokoda, another (American) along the Jaure track which travelled over the Owen Stanleys east of the Kokoda Track, and a third (part of the 32nd Division), after being landed by aircraft at Wanigela, an undeveloped landing ground some 80 miles south-east of Buna, along the coast. Blamey agreed and said that he would send a battalion from Milne Bay to occupy Wanigela and prepare it for the arrival of the Americans.

Meanwhile, as an outcome of MacArthur's proposal that Blamey should take command in New Guinea, Blamey had returned to Port Moresby on 23rd September, and on the 25th went to Milne Bay and ordered Clowes to prepare to fly the 2/10th Battalion to Wanigela. Next day Rowell wrote Blamey a minute saying that his authority as commander of New Guinea Force needed definition, and instancing Blamey's order to Clowes. A strong disagreement developed. Rowell later suggested a *modus operandi* and Blamey accepted it, but, on the 28th, Blamey told him to return to Australia, and issued an order-of-the-day stating that he had assumed command of the forces in New Guinea on the 24th. He then telegraphed to Curtin stating that Rowell had been unco-operative and recommending that General Herring, then commanding II Corps, or General Mackay, of the Second Army, should replace Rowell in command of the corps in New Guinea. Herring was chosen.

As an outcome of the Government's anxiety about the set-backs in New Guinea, the Minister for Air, Drakeford, and the Minister for the Army, Forde, flew to Port Moresby on 1st October. On 2nd October MacArthur visited the island for the first time. Next day he was taken by jeep to the ridge overlooking Uberi, spent about an hour there, and was able to see from a distance the tangled mountainous country in which the troops were operating; on the 4th he flew back to Brisbane. Forde also returned on the 4th.

Two regiments of the 32nd Division—the 126th and 128th—had now reached Moresby, some men by air and some by sea. The detailed plan was that the 25th and 16th Australian Brigades should press on astride the Kokoda Track, secure the line of the Kumusi River and close in on the Japanese base at Buna. At the same time a battalion of the 126th American Regiment would advance through Jaure, and a battalion of the 128th American Regiment would advance on Buna from Wanigela, being joined

Australian War Memorial

General Douglas MacArthur with General Blamey in New Guinea early in October 1942. General MacArthur was paying his first visit to New Guinea after arriving in Australia in March 1942.

later by two battalions of the 126th which would be flown into the Pongani area, still nearer to Buna.

The 25th Brigade, with the 3rd Battalion leading, followed up the Japanese withdrawal from Ioribaiwa, and by 2nd October had reached Menari without opposition. Abandoned equipment lay along the track, and there were signs that about 2,000 Japanese had been in the forward area and that they had been reduced to eating grass, roots and wood. Efogi, where the cold, wet region began, was reached on 4th October. It was not until the 8th that contact was made with a Japanese rearguard, forward of Templeton's Crossing.

The dropping of supplies at Nauro in the Owen Stanleys had begun on 4th October, but a disturbing percentage was lost. On the 7th Allen had signalled to Herring that if the dropping of 50,000 pounds daily plus an additional quantity to build up a reserve was all that would be forthcoming a large proportion of the forward troops would have to be withdrawn to Imita Ridge. It became evident that the rate of the advance would depend on the establishment of adequate dumps of air-dropped supplies and the ability of the men to carry supplies forward from those dumps.

Having been assured of reasonably-adequate supplies, Allen ordered Eather to establish a battalion at Eora Creek, two at Templeton's Crossing and one at Kagi; Brigadier J. E. Lloyd's 16th Brigade, now arriving forward, was later to move through the 25th and take Kokoda.

Australian War Memorial

Papua, 1942. The 'Golden Stairs', one of the many steep rises in the Owen Stanleys, climbing towards Imita Ridge, each step battened at its edge by a rough log, sometimes broken and therefore treacherous, and cradling mud and water from the afternoon rains.

On 12th October the 2/33rd and 2/25th Battalions, pressing on, were converging on the Japanese round Templeton's Crossing. The enemy, however, was firmly dug in astride the tracks well forward of the Crossing. That day and on the 13th and 14th the attackers thrust forward but suffered sharp casualties and did not gain much ground. On the 15th the 3rd Battalion was sent round the left flank of the 2/33rd and found that the Japanese there had withdrawn from their rearguard position. Templeton's Crossing was secured on the 16th.

On 17th October Allen, now at Myola, received from Blamey a signal stating that General MacArthur considered that 'extremely light casualties indicate no serious effort yet made to displace enemy', and ordering him to attack with energy and speed at each point of resistance. Allen replied that round Templeton's fifty men had been killed and 133 wounded; in the 25th Brigade 730 officers and men had been evacuated because of sickness. He was sending the 16th Brigade forward to relieve the 25th. The Japanese were being attacked and were themselves counter-attacking.

During the advance through the mountain range the troops toiled along or astride a track sometimes deep in mud, at others climbing or dropping almost vertically in giant steps hewn from the side of a cliff face, the steps battened with rough logs and worn by countless feet so that they cradled mud and water. The service troops, drenched by the daily deluge, panted and sweated by day and froze at night, their light clothing, seldom dry, supplemented only by a half blanket with a ground-sheet to lie on and a gas cape to keep out the all-pervading damp. For the fighting soldier, burdened with weapons and ammunition, frequently hungry and always fatigued, it was far worse. Perhaps in no other phase of this slow painful advance across the mountains was the spirit of the riflemen more manifest than in the conduct of forward scouts—those men who led the advance along tracks where there was seldom room for the troops to move except in single file. Each day it was almost certain that one or more of the forward scouts, probing ahead for Japanese positions would fall killed or wounded by unseen snipers. Yet volunteers were always ready for the job.

The plan for building up a force north of the Owen Stanleys and east of Buna was now developing. The 32nd American Division was given the general role of attacking Buna from the south-east. On 14th October aircraft began to fly from Moresby into Wanigela (where the 2/10th Battalion had now been established for nine days) the 2/6th Australian Independent Company and later the 128th American Regiment.

As soon as it arrived at Wanigela the 2/6th Independent Company set out overland towards Pongani to establish the second landing ground to which the Americans were to be ferried forward. Soon after this advanced-guard had crossed the Musa, the river came down in flood and cut across the line of advance of the 128th Regiment, which had to be taken along the coast in luggers to Pongani. Meanwhile the II/126th Battalion had set out on its march through the Owen Stanleys along the Jaure track to Buna. The battalion reached Jaure about 22nd October, but the going proved very hard.

There was a small Japanese detachment of about 350 on Goodenough Island due east of Wanigela. It was important to occupy this island which would be a suitable site for a radar station and perhaps a fighter strip in the coming operations. On the night of 22nd-23rd October the 2/12th Battalion was landed by the destroyers *Arunta* and *Stuart*. The battalion attacked Japanese positions on the 23rd and 24th but on the 25th they found that Japanese craft had arrived and embarked the survivors.

Blamey at this stage was thinking ahead towards an offensive. On 18th October he wrote to MacArthur that plans must be developed to attack Lae and Salamaua. It might be possible to land troops from the air at Nadzab, in the wide Markham Valley, and advance thence on Lae. MacArthur replied on the 20th that the enemy commanded the sea and could bring overwhelming force to bear on the north coast of New Guinea. Great caution was needed. The garrison at Milne Bay (where Blamey proposed to leave only one brigade) should not be reduced below two brigades. (The airborne advance to Nadzab would take place but not until eleven months later.)

The Japanese too were pressing on with plans and preparations. On 5th October Hyakutake of the *XVII Army* issued orders that Guadalcanal was to be taken in that month, whereupon the army was to concentrate against eastern New Guinea, take Port Moresby by the end of December, and establish a strong defensive line embracing the Solomons, Milne Bay, Samarai and Port Moresby. Hyakutake decided that he would launch most of the reinforcements which had been sent to him in August and September—chiefly the *2nd* and *38th Divisions*—in a full-scale attack on the American perimeter on Guadalcanal. There in October 20,000 Americans were entrenched round a perimeter about four miles and a half wide protecting Henderson Field, while a Japanese force of about six battalions had the run of the rest of the island. Both sides were striving to land reinforcements in the face of the other's naval and air squadrons. Thus, on 18th September, a fifth regiment of American marines was landed; and the *XVII Japanese Army* trickled in reinforcements from Rabaul until in October most of the *2nd Division* had been landed there, bringing the total strength to about 20,000. In the course of this movement an American naval force covering the transport of a regiment of the Americal Division to Guadalcanal encountered a Japanese flotilla escorting Japanese reinforcements to the same place. In actions on 11th and 12th October the Japanese lost a cruiser and three destroyers, the Americans a destroyer. Later in October, in response to Admiral Nimitz's request for a more aggressive commander in the South Pacific, Vice-Admiral William F. Halsey was appointed to succeed Admiral Ghormley.

In the intermittent naval and air campaign of attrition over and round Guadalcanal the American defenders were helped by Intelligence of vital value. From Guadalcanal itself, after the Japanese landing, coastwatchers including Martin Clemens, District Officer on Guadalcanal, had sent out information about the Japanese occupation. It was not until January that the last of the coastwatchers on Guadalcanal came into the American perimeter. Along the 700-miles route from Rabaul to Guadalcanal in the northern Solomons other coastwatching parties were at their posts—W. J. Read's and P. E. Mason's far away on Bougainville, and others farther south. The Japanese air forces flying south to attack the Americans on Guadalcanal could be seen by Read and Mason, and—in plain language to avoid delay in coding—they broadcast information about the strength and the direction of these flights, giving the American ships and aircraft about two hours to prepare to receive them. Farther south was D. G. Kennedy on New Georgia, 160 miles from Guadalcanal, whose reports, following Read's and Mason's, enabled the speed and consequently the precise time of arrival of the enemy aircraft to be predicted. In October the line of coastwatchers was supplemented by landing men from submarines on Vella Lavella and Choiseul.

The main Japanese offensive began on 23rd October and lasted four days. At all points it withered under the fire of the American garrison. The defenders estimated that 2,200 Japanese were killed. On the 26th and 27th the supporting fleets clashed in a sea-air battle in which the Americans lost the carrier *Hornet* and a destroyer, and the Japanese lost no ships sunk but the carrier *Shokaku* was severely damaged.

The October battles on and round Guadalcanal increased MacArthur's anxieties. On the 17th of that month he had sent a telegram to Marshall stating that it would be necessary to prepare for possible disaster in the Solomons, and, if that occurred, 'the entire South-West Pacific area will be in danger'. He added that he had Intelligence that another Japanese attack on Milne Bay was contemplated for November, and he urged that the entire resources of the United States be used temporarily to meet the critical situation: that shipping be made available from any source and a corps be sent from America immediately, all available heavy bombers be sent to him, and the British Eastern Fleet be moved to the west coast of Australia. The American leaders at home shared MacArthur's anxiety. Also on the 17th Roosevelt confessed his fear of defeat in the Solomons to Queen Wilhelmina of Holland and on the 19th to Churchill; on the 21st he told the Pacific War Council that it seemed questionable whether Guadalcanal was not too far from a supply base to be permanently tenable.[1] But next month anxiety faded.

A new Japanese attempt to send large reinforcements to Guadalcanal led to a major fleet action between 12th and 15th November. Three American naval task forces included 2 battleships, the carrier *Enterprise*, 8 cruisers, and 24 destroyers; the Japanese deployed 4 battleships, 2 carriers and 20 to 30 destroyers, to protect 11 transports. In the long battle the American ships and aircraft sank 11 transports, the battleships *Hiyei* and *Kirishima*, a cruiser and 3 destroyers; and lost 2 cruisers and 7 destroyers. Only 3,000 of the 10,000 troops on the transports were landed. This was a notable victory. After the battle 'the United States Navy', writes its historian, 'felt it could never be defeated'. Roosevelt declared that 'it would seem that the turning point in the war has at last been reached'. It was not only in the South Pacific that the tide was turning. In Papua the Japanese invaders were being pursued towards the north coast. In North Africa about a fortnight earlier the Axis army had been put to flight at El Alamein and a few days later Allied armies had landed in French North Africa. In about a week the Russians would open a successful and epoch-making offensive at Stalingrad.

The contrast between the American operations on Guadalcanal and the Australian in New Guinea was indicative of a difference in the tactical outlook of each army that was to become more marked as time went on. On Guadalcanal the American marines had established a defensive perimeter round their airfield and there, except for some patrolling, awaited the enemy's attacks. At Milne Bay and in the Owen Stanleys the Australians set out to push the enemy back and finally destroy him.

In the Owen Stanleys on 20th October Brigadier Lloyd of the 16th Brigade had taken command in the forward area, and that morning the two leading companies of the 2/2nd Battalion attacked the enemy rearguard positions beyond Templeton's with success. Next day the leading battalions pressed

[1] The Pacific War Council in Washington was composed of representatives of the United States, United Kingdom, China, Australia, Canada, New Zealand, the Netherlands, and the Philippines. There was a similar council in London.

on and found the enemy strongly deployed about Eora Creek which flows through a wooded ravine. On the 22nd the Japanese were discovered to have abandoned this position but to have occupied another stronger one beyond the village.

Allen was still being urged on by his seniors. On 21st October Blamey had complained that in five days there had been practically no advance against a weaker enemy and that the attacks for the most part had been 'by single battalion or even companies on a narrow front'; and he passed on a signal from MacArthur declaring that the tactical handling of the troops was faulty. Allen replied pointing out, among other things, that the country did not lend itself to wide encircling movements and shortage of native carriers confined him to one line of advance.

On the 23rd the 2/1st Battalion attacked at Eora Creek, but by nightfall, having lost about fifty killed and wounded, were still held by Japanese on higher ground. They maintained their position until the 28th when under galling mortar and machine-gun fire the 2/3rd, having worked round the left, launched a ferocious charge through the bush from above the enemy stronghold and routed them. The captured position was found to be an immensely strong one concentrated about a central keep some 300 yards across. The Japanese left sixty-nine dead around the keep alone. Since its advance had begun the 25th Brigade, in 37 days, had lost 203 killed and wounded; the 16th, in 9 days, had lost 228.

On the 28th, the day on which this success was won, Blamey sent Vasey forward to Myola to relieve Allen in command of the 7th Division. Next day (as a result of the fight on the 28th) the pursuit of the broken Japanese rearguard began, and on the 30th the 2/1st entered Alola and Isurava. The plan was to send the 25th Brigade against Kokoda and reserve the 16th to take Oivi and establish a bridgehead over the Kumusi. By 2nd November the leading battalion of the 25th Brigade entered Kokoda, whence the enemy had departed two days before; the 16th, weary and hungry, was preparing a dropping ground at Kobara on the eastern track.

The supply problem would now soon be solved. It was expected that in two days aircraft would be able to land at Kokoda, and meanwhile supplies could be dropped there and at Kobara. Lloyd sent the 2/1st Battalion out from Kobara on 3rd November carrying three days' rations. About 1,000 yards along the track Lloyd himself, having moved ahead of the forward scouts, came under fire—the first contact since the 28th. When darkness fell this Japanese rearguard was still in position. On the 4th it had gone, but there were clashes farther on, and on the 5th the 2/2nd Battalion, advancing on Oivi from the west while the 2/1st followed a parallel track to the south, was heavily committed on the high ground a mile from Oivi. Here in relatively open country a large-scale engagement soon developed. By nightfall both the 2/2nd and 2/3rd Battalions were dug in facing a strongly-manned enemy position some three miles in extent, and the 3rd Battalion was moving up. Next day the Japanese counter-attacked in strength, but were driven back.

Meanwhile on the 5th the 2/1st, pressing on along the southern track, had reached the junction with a track leading north to Gorari. Lieut-Colonel P. A. Cullen left a company there and pushed on towards Ilimo, where he would come in across the Japanese line of communications. They missed their way, however, and returned to the junction where Cullen learnt of the impasse at Oivi, and soon afterwards met the head of the 25th Brigade approaching the junction.

Vasey now decided on a bold manoeuvre that might prove decisive: he would send the whole 25th Brigade round the southern flank to cut the Japanese communications at Ilimo and take the enemy in the rear while the 16th maintained pressure at Oivi. Consequently the 25th Brigade fought its way north along a well-guarded track and on the 9th were pressing hard against a determined Japanese defence round Gorari. That day the 2/1st moving on the left cut the Gorari-Ilimo track. The enemy was trapped. On the 10th they made frantic efforts to break out, but the Australian battalions closed tighter and tighter. On the 11th the 16th Brigade found the main Oivi positions abandoned. Soon only remnants of the defending force remained and they were fleeing north and east through the bush, repeatedly strafed by Beaufighters. Vasey left the 16th Brigade about Oivi to rest and refit and ordered the 25th to pursue.

The 2/31st with a detachment of engineers reached the wide, swift Kumusi River on the 13th at a point where a wire-rope bridge had spanned it until destroyed by Allied aircraft. Swimmers carried a line across the river and a ferry was contrived. By the 14th two flying foxes had been erected at

Australian War Memorial

Papua, November 1942. Australian troops crossing the Kumusi River at Wairopi during their advance towards the strong Japanese coastal defences in the Buna-Gona area.

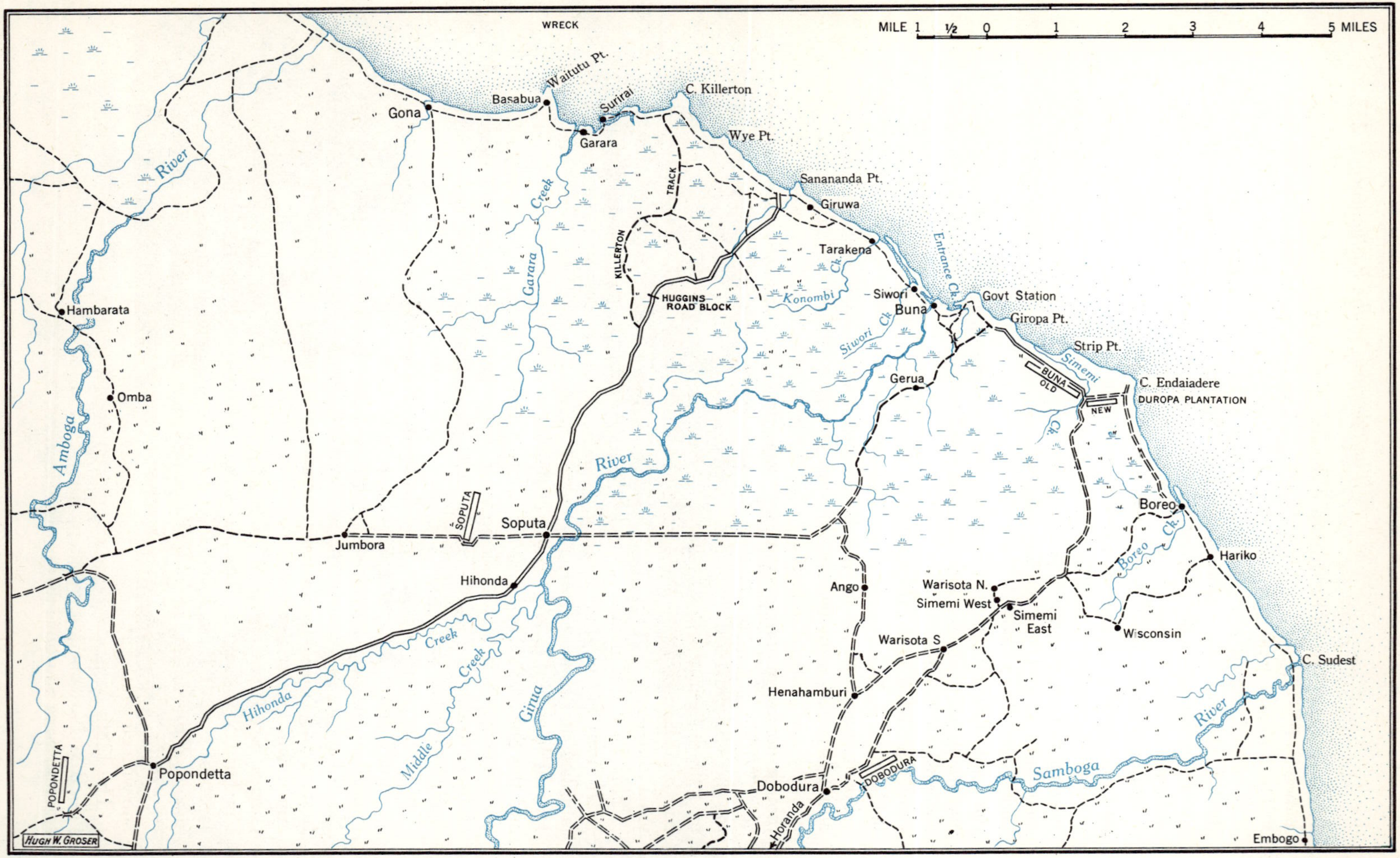

Buna, Sanananda and Gona

Wairopi and a foot-bridge farther downstream, and most of the 2/33rd was across. By the 17th all seven battalions were over.

The four-months fight for the Owen Stanleys and Moresby had finished. In it the four brigades employed had lost 625 killed and 1,055 had been wounded—a slightly heavier loss than that suffered by the Australians in the Syrian campaign, when seven of the twelve battalions involved had last been in battle.

From the foothills of the Owen Stanleys to the sea the country was flat and wet. Away from the sea it was clothed either with dense bush or patches of rank kunai grass, and near the coast there were sago and mangrove swamps and some coconut plantations. At Buna there had been a Government station, at Gona an Anglican mission. Into the Buna-Gona area the wide Girua River flowed from the south-west and lost itself in swamps near the coast. The tracks through this area were boggy, and the land so flat and overgrown that observation was difficult. In relatively well-drained areas covered with kunai grass, such as those at Dobodura, seven miles inland from Buna, and Popondetta, thirteen miles inland, there was land on which airfields might be built.

Along the coast from Gona to Cape Endaiadere the Japanese, now thrown on the defensive as their attack force was thrust back through the mountains, had dug and timbered a fortified line which stretched for about twelve miles, though not continuously because in some areas the country seemed impassable. Within this perimeter were the survivors of about one division, including the *41st* and *144th Regiments*, and part of the *38th Division*, equivalent to a third regiment. In October and November some 4,000 reinforcements had been landed. In all there were about 9,000 men in the quickly improvised fortress.

This force was now commanded from Rabaul not by Hyakutake of the *XVII Army* but by a more senior commander; in November, Tokyo had established at Rabaul *Eighth Area Army* headquarters, under Lieut-General Hitoshi Imamura, to take control of operations in both eastern New Guinea and the Solomons, Hyakutake's command thenceforward being confined to the Solomons. The local commander of forces in eastern New Guinea, west of Buna, was now Lieut-General Hatazo Adachi, whose *XVIII Army* eventually had its headquarters at Wewak.

In October and November the Allied Air Forces had made conditions increasingly uncomfortable for the Japanese forces both round Buna and round Lae and Salamaua. Group Captain Garing had seven squadrons in his No. 9 Group—No. 30 with Beaufighters, No. 6 with Hudsons, No. 22 with Bostons and No. 100 with torpedo-carrying Beauforts; and Nos. 75 and 76 armed with Kittyhawks, and No. 4 with Wirraways, were also in New Guinea. Brigadier-General Whitehead now had eleven American squadrons based in New Guinea. The American bombers were harassing the main Japanese base at Rabaul, but their long-range bomber force was not strong enough at this stage to be more than a nuisance: in late October, for example, only two squadrons of Flying Fortresses were available, one with nine and one with eight aircraft.

The 128th American Regiment was, in mid-November, concentrated about Oro Bay. No American artillery had yet been sent to New Guinea. Four columns were now advancing on the Japanese perimeter: Warren Force (four

American battalions and the 2/6th Australian Independent Company) towards Cape Endaiadere, Urbana Force (two American battalions) against Buna, the 16th Brigade along the track to Sananandа, and the 25th Brigade along the track to Gona.

On the 14th November Herring ordered that the Girua River, which flows north-east and enters the sea near Buna, should be the boundary between the Americans to the south and the Australians to the north; Buna would be the American objective, Gona and Sananandа the Australian.

On the southern flank the plan of Major-General Edwin F. Harding of the 32nd Division was that the 128th Regiment should follow to Cape Endaiadere, and the 126th should advance along an axis farther inland to Soputa. Beyond Porlock Harbour the Americans were to be supplied by seven luggers and a captured barge. On the 16th the barge and three luggers were attacked by Zeros, and the four vessels were sunk. This temporarily disrupted the American supply plan and delayed their concentration.

Meanwhile, marching from the Kumusi towards Gona across the forty miles of lowland stretching to the coast, the weary 25th Australian Brigade passed signs of hurried retreat—abandoned huts and stables and dumps of rice and barley. On 18th November the 2/33rd Battalion was at Jumbora, and next morning the leading company was fired on just south of Gona. That afternoon the foremost Australians—now a depleted battalion plus a company—pushing on to complete their success were in a semi-circle about Gona and under deadly fire from well-organised Japanese posts. Soon Lieut-Colonel J. Miller of the 2/31st had lost thirty-two men including four company commanders. Suddenly more and more men were going down with malaria. Food was running short and Eather ordered Miller to fall back while the brigade awaited supplies. Supply aircraft dropped food, ammunition, quinine and tobacco at Jumbora on the 21st, but they were so short of parachutes that these were used only for medical supplies, and other stores were dropped free with the result that only about 50 per cent were recovered. Eather decided to advance next day with the whole brigade except for a strong guard at the dropping ground. The 2/33rd advanced directly on Gona with the 2/31st moving round its right to come in from the east. In the evening the 2/31st delivered an assault, cheering as they charged the enemy posts. They reached the Japanese pits but lost sixty-five men in the advance—perhaps one-quarter of their rifle strength—and formed a defensive perimeter. It now seemed that the enemy was strongly entrenched in an area about 300 yards by 300 yards.

These depleted battalions of the 25th Brigade, the men who remained on duty worn out by the long fighting march through the Owen Stanleys and now contracting malaria in increasing numbers, continued to spend themselves against this Japanese stronghold. On the 23rd the 2/25th attacked from the east but gained little ground. In five days the brigade had lost 204 in battle for small gains, and was now only 736 strong.

On the 24th Gona was bombed from the air, and next day Eather's men plus the 3rd Battalion, only 180 strong, attacked from the south-west. They had the support of four field guns firing from Soputa, but though the attackers penetrated the defences at one point they later withdrew.

The 21st Brigade, flown into the forward area in the last week of November, reinforced the 25th. In this brigade, now commanded by Brigadier I. N.

Dougherty, the losses suffered in the retreat from Kokoda had not been fully replaced and the three battalions totalled only about 1,000 men. On the afternoon of the 28th, after an air bombardment, the 2/14th Battalion thrust at Gona from the east but was repulsed. Next day the 2/27th and 2/14th Battalions attacked, again from the east, while the 3rd and 2/33rd of Eather's brigade pressed forward from the south. In the main attack the 2/27th and 2/14th gained little ground. On the 30th all three battalions of the 21st Brigade were heavily engaged, their strength now rapidly dwindling as a result of battle losses, malaria and heat exhaustion, until the tired 2/14th, for example, had a fighting force of only seven officers and 152 others—less than one-fifth of a battalion's proper strength. The Australians now held a wide stretch of the beach east of Gona but the Gona position was still resisting firmly. On the 1st the 2/27th and part of the 2/16th attacked westward with fixed bayonets after a 15-minute bombardment and some men reached the centre of the Japanese position, but few survived. The losses being endured by the infantry were reaching disastrous proportions, particularly the loss of some of the finest among the young leaders whom two years of campaigning had brought to the fore.

A fourth brigade—the 30th—was now arriving to join Vasey's division. On 3rd December he sent the 39th Battalion of that brigade with the 2/14th eastward along the coast towards Sananda while the 25th and the remainder of the 21st Brigade contained Gona. The 2/14th found the swampy country impassable. Thereupon Vasey gave the 21st Brigade, plus the 39th Battalion, the task of relieving the 25th and pressing on Gona while the 30th Brigade (with only its 49th and 55th/53rd Battalions) advanced on Sananda along the main track.

The 21st Brigade, its four battalions now only 800 strong, attacked again on 8th December. About midday, after fifteen minutes of artillery and mortar fire the militiamen of the fine 39th Battalion thrust forward with great resolution and by evening half the Japanese defences were in their hands. The combined 2/16th and 2/27th advanced along the shore and gained some ground. The enemy was now confined to a small area from which that night they began frantically trying to break out, at least 100 being killed in these attempts. Next day patrols moved through what remained of the Japanese keep. Few living Japanese remained there, but the Australians buried the bodies of 638. The four battalions of the 21st Brigade had lost in this whole battle 530 killed and wounded, more than 40 per cent of their strength at the outset.

To the west the Japanese reinforcements moving towards Gona, not knowing it had been overcome, were still fighting hard. On the 10th the 39th Battalion reinforced the 2/14th there. The enemy was dug in round a village near the seashore. Captured papers suggested that the enemy comprised about 500 men of a battalion landed between the Kumusi and Amboga Rivers about 2nd December and perhaps 100 or 200 who had escaped from Oivi. The 39th pressed in steadily until by 15th December they were east, south and west of them. On the 18th the village was taken. In it lay 170 unburied dead, and documents showed that at least as many more had been killed and wounded earlier. In these final operations the 39th had lost 107 killed and wounded and the 2/14th had lost twenty-two.

The column next to the south was formed by the depleted 16th Brigade, which, following on the heels of the 25th Brigade, had reached Popondetta on 19th November. On the 20th Colonel Clarence M. Tomlinson's 126th American Regiment also began to arrive there, its II and III Battalions having been flown into the area while its I Battalion was toiling on foot along the Jaure track from southern Papua. That day the 2/1st Battalion advancing on Sanananda came under artillery fire while still some miles from the coast. Cullen promptly sent three companies out on wide outflanking moves. Two of these, together ninety one strong, under Captain B. W. T. Catterns, toiled through the bush and reached the track two miles behind the forward Japanese positions and then wheeled south against their rear. They moved stealthily and were fifty yards from the enemy rearward positions before they were seen. In the mêlée which followed perhaps eighty Japanese were killed but the Australians lost heavily, five of the 10 officers being killed. The Australians then dug in, and on the 21st withstood repeated attacks. The battalions pressed on from the south until they were near Catterns' position, and his men, of whom only twenty-four remained unwounded, rejoined the main body. The 16th Brigade had made a long stride towards Sanananda but its strength was failing. It now numbered only 1,040 men and those were weary and ill. Vasey ordered that the brigade should not advance until Tomlinson's fresh American regiment had secured the Soputa-Sanananda-Cape Killerton track junction which lay ahead.

On 22nd November Tomlinson's II Battalion had been transferred to Harding's command. The III Battalion moved confidently into the area held by the forward Australians and an encircling attack was set in motion but the companies lost their way in the swampy bushland and nothing was gained.

At length, on the 26th, the Americans attacked behind an artillery and mortar barrage, and on the right some 350 yards were gained but elsewhere little. Meanwhile a strong patrol of the 2/3rd Battalion, moving round on the left, cut in on the Killerton track well to the north but was then blocked by swamps. On the 30th the Americans attacked again, made no progress on the right and in the centre, but on the left swung round the Japanese flank and in a dashing attack established themselves about 250 strong in a Japanese bivouac area astride the track just south of the Killerton junction, a position that became known as 'Huggins Road-Block'. The Allied line now formed a deep arc with the road-block lying between its extremities.

Herring, whose corps headquarters was now at Dobodura, decided that Tomlinson should rejoin the 32nd Division and Lloyd should command both the Americans and the Australians on the Sanananda track. The Americans attacked again towards Huggins Road-Block on the 5th, this time with two young Australian officers attached as advisers. This attack made no progress, and at the end of the day two men had been reported killed, twenty-five missing and sixty-three wounded. Huggins Road-Block was still under frequent attack but holding out.

Vasey now decided to employ the 30th Brigade on the Sanananda track, and on the 6th its two battalions—the 49th and 55th/53rd—began the relief of the 16th Brigade, now worn to a skeleton by sickness and battle casualties. It had lost 209 killed and 400 wounded, 978 had been evacuated sick, and virtually all the survivors—about 800—were infected with malaria and many also with dysentery. The incoming battalions had not been in action as units before but both contained a cadre of veteran A.I.F. officers and the 55th/53rd had absorbed part of what remained of the 53rd after its action in the Owen Stanleys. Porter planned to capture the area between his main force and the road-block by attacking first with the 49th on the right of the track and then with the 55th/53rd on the left of it. The 49th advanced on the morning of 7th December following up a bombardment by guns and mortars. The infantrymen soon began to lose heavily but at some points advanced as much as 800 yards. In the afternoon the 55th/53rd attacked, also into the heavy fire from well-concealed posts. It consolidated only about 100 yards forward of its former position, having lost 130 men, including twenty-eight N.C.O's. The 49th whose losses had been shattering—229, which was about 60 per cent of the attacking force—withdrew from most of the ground it had gained. Herring and Vasey agreed that no more full-scale attacks should be made towards Sananada for the present.

Meanwhile on the right flank one battalion of the 128th American Regiment on 15th November had advanced on Buna along a strip of sandy ground on the coast, and another on the track from Dobodura. By the 17th the battalion on the right was forward of Hariko and the one on the left at Simemi. The only supporting artillery were two howitzers of the 1st Australian Mountain Battery.

Herring decided to concentrate maximum forces west of the Girua River and placed the 126th American Regiment (so far with only two battalions forward) under Vasey's command. Thus these battalions were switched to the Sanananda sector as mentioned above. The third battalion of the 128th took over the left flank of the American advance east of the Girua.

In drenching rain one battalion advanced along the coast on 19th November, was fired on as it neared the edge of the Japanese position on the fringe of a plantation flanking the Buna airstrips and thrown into confusion. As a result of inadequate fire control—a serious defect in American training at this stage—the troops soon spent practically all their ammunition. On the left a second battalion advanced along the Simemi track, which was bordered by swamps. As they neared the airstrips the Japanese defenders fired and they were halted. MacArthur, who had flown to Port Moresby on 6th November and established an advanced headquarters there, at this time told General Blamey that his forces must attack the Buna-Gona area on the 21st and that 'all columns will be driven through to objectives regardless of losses'.

The American attack on 21st November got off to a bad start. Bombers attacked the Japanese defences at 8 a.m. in preparation for the infantry assault ten minutes later, but the battalion commanders did not receive their orders until 8.40 and 8.50. Some bombs landed among the Americans. In the afternoon after a second air attack in which eighteen Americans were hit the infantry began to advance but made little progress. On the left the II/128th Battalion advanced from Ango to the forking of tracks to Buna village and Buna station and were halted there by enemy fire.

By the 21st the Dobodura strip had been improved sufficiently to allow transport aircraft to land and supplies were soon coming in rapidly.

It was now evident that the Japanese were resolute and well dug in and that heavier weight must be put behind the Allied attacks than could be provided by four guns and by aircraft which had difficulty in finding the enemy's well-concealed bunkers—dug-outs roofed with coconut logs and beaten earth. Two troops of guns of the 2/1st Field Regiment were now flown from Moresby, one to join Harding's divison and the other Vasey's. No craft were yet available to move tanks into the area from Milne Bay where a troop of medium tanks had arrived, and instead a platoon of thin-skinned Bren carriers was sent forward.

Thus on the 23rd when the Americans south of the airstrips (Warren Force) attacked again they had the support of somewhat heavier artillery fire, but not enough to have much effect on the Japanese bunkers. The attack gained only about 100 yards on the east and in the centre, and less on the left. On the Ango track, where the II/126th Battalion had joined the II/128th (Urbana Force), the attackers pushed forward through the swamps and on the 24th attacked after an inaccurate air strike by a few fighters. They were halted by fire after a short advance, the companies on the right falling back in disorder.

On 26th November Warren Force attacked with the III/128th Battalion forward on the right and the I/126th on the left. From 7.30 to 9 a.m. American and Australian aircraft bombed and machine-gunned the enemy and then eight guns and twelve mortars brought down fire. The attack of the III/128th, however, petered out after negligible gains, while on the left the I/126th advanced east instead of north-west and ended up where it had begun.

On the 27th Harding placed his chief of staff, Colonel John W. Mott, in command of Urbana Force, which had lain hungry and fatigued in the swampy area south of Buna during the four days since the last attack. He ordered a night attack on the 29th-30th which would precede an attack by Warren Force early on the 30th. The six Australian guns now had the advantage of Wirraway aircraft to observe their fire and report targets. The crews of these aircraft flew sometimes below tree-top level, often drawing fire, and themselves machine-gunning and even grenading likely targets. The leading companies of Urbana Force crossed the start-line four hours late and made little progress.

Warren Force's attack began at 6.30 a.m. on the 30th after a 15-minute bombardment, but was halted after 100 yards by fire from the Japanese bunkers along the New Strip and thence to the sea. Men of the 2/6th Independent Company patrolling on the left of the infantry attack got close enough to the Japanese bunkers to describe them and their camouflage in some detail. The 32nd Division had now lost 492 men killed or wounded but had gained virtually nothing.

On 30th November MacArthur summoned General Eichelberger to Port Moresby and ordered him to take command of the Americans in the Buna sector. MacArthur told Eichelberger that he had reports that Americans were throwing their weapons away and running. 'Bob', he said, 'I want you to take Buna or not come back alive.'[2]

When he arrived on the north coast Eichelberger found that already the troops were 'riddled with malaria, dengue fever, tropical dysentery, and were covered with jungle ulcers'. At the end of his first day at the front he wrote to Major-General Richard K. Sutherland (MacArthur's Chief of Staff) that 'the rear areas are strong and the front line is weak'. The men were

[2] Eichelberger, *Our Jungle Road to Tokyo,* p. 21.

dirty and in rags. One regimental command post was four miles and a half behind the front line; only 150 of its men were in the forward positions and the remainder of the 2,000 were scattered in the rear.

Harding was replaced by Brigadier-General Albert W. Waldron, his artillery commander. Eichelberger placed one officer of his staff, Colonel John E. Grose, in command of Urbana Force and another, Colonel Clarence A. Martin, in command of Warren Force. He then reorganised his five-battalion division for an attack on 5th December. The III/128th Battalion was on the seaward flank, the I/126th between the Strips, the I/128th in reserve; in Urbana Force the II/128th was forward on the right, the II/126th on the left. The plan was again to make a frontal assault after air, artillery and mortar bombardment, but five Australian Bren carriers (proof against small-arms fire if not too close) would take part. Six Bostons and eight guns bombarded the Japanese posts from 8.20 a.m. and at 8.42 Warren Force attacked with the carriers leading the III/128th. One carrier bellied on a log; another (Sergeant D. R. Taylor's) reached a post and circled it while the crew fired into it with their machine-guns and hurled grenades. At length the post was silenced, but a mortar bomb hit the vehicle and killed one of the crew of four. Taylor's carrier then silenced another post. At a third post Taylor's arm was shattered, the carrier's engine failed and the other two members of the crew were hit, one mortally. Two men in the third carrier were soon killed; one was killed in the fourth, and later it and the fifth bellied on concealed logs. Just behind the wrecked carriers the leading infantry lay halted. The left of the I/128th Battalion was similarly held up on the fringe of New Strip; on the left, between the Strips, the I/126th dislodged the enemy from several forward posts but at dusk was still 200 yards south of the bridge. Patrols of the 2/6th Independent Company crossed the New Strip but, being unsupported, withdrew again.

On the Urbana front that day the II/126th advanced towards Buna village with three companies forward. In the centre company Sergeant H. J. F. Bottcher, a man of German birth and upbringing who had served with the Republicans in the Spanish Civil War, led eighteen men right through to the beach east of Buna village where they remained, shooting down Japanese who tried to drive them out. Bottcher was promoted to the rank of captain on the spot. Farther left a company got to within fifty yards of Buna village, which was now effectively cut off from help by land. The success in this sector seems partly to have been due to the efforts of Eichelberger himself and officers on his staff who took charge of groups of forward troops.

The losses being suffered as a result of malaria, dysentery and battle casualties were now becoming calamitous. And about this time Curtin informed Blamey of Churchill's continued unwillingness to spare the 9th Australian Division from Egypt. Thereupon, on 4th December, Blamey wrote to Curtin from New Guinea to explain that losses, chiefly from malaria, were so heavy that he considered that he should break up one division. He added that 'in the tactical field' the operations in Papua were proving 'a very sorry story'. It had been revealed that

> the American troops cannot be classified as attack troops. They are definitely not equal to the Australian militia, and from the moment they met opposition sat down and have hardly gone forward a yard. The action, too, has revealed

> a very alarming state of weakness in their staff system and in their war psychology.

Thus, he continued, in replacement of the 9th Australian Division, Australia had been given two American divisions of low fighting quality. Unless the 9th Division returned the position would be 'definitely one involving considerable risk and danger'.

Blamey informed his Chief of the General Staff, Northcott, on 7th December that he had it in mind to withdraw the 16th, 21st and 25th Brigades and possibly also the 18th and send them to north Queensland to recuperate. He would replace them with militia brigades.

On the 8th he ordered Brigadier Wootten to bring forward to Buna two battalions and two troops of tanks recently landed in New Guinea, and clear the Japanese from the area stretching from Cape Endaiadere to Buna; it was agreed that Wootten would take under command the three American battalions in the Warren Force sector and control the whole attack.

To augment the transport aircraft available to fly men and supplies to the north coast a motley collection of machines had been flown to Moresby early in December. There were sixteen aircraft from training units, and eleven civil aircraft of six types. In seven days these flew in 3,000 men and 600 tons of freight including jeeps and field guns.

The American attack, whose early success had been reported just before Blamey began to consider relieving the Australians, had not continued to prosper. In the six days after 5th December Warren Force made no progress and the units were becoming weaker and the men more weary; on the 10th the division was only 3,186 strong. On 9th December, however, the fresh 127th Regiment was arriving at Dobodura from Port Moresby and its leading battalion was in the line two days later. At 7 a.m. on the 14th two companies of the III/127th advancing behind an artillery and mortar bombardment entered Buna village. It was empty of living men, the defenders having been ferried away by night. Fifty dead lay unburied.

Brigadier-General Clovis E. Byers, who had been appointed to command the 32nd Division when General Waldron was wounded in the attack of 5th December, now ordered an attack by the II/128th on Japanese entrenched in a coconut plantation east of the captured village. The depleted battalion pressed forward on the 16th and 17th and by noon on the second day held the plantation, Byers being wounded during the attack. The Japanese still held an area to the south.

Blamey's plan to bring forward the 18th Australian Brigade to add weight to the attack was now developing. The corvettes *Colac*, *Broome* and *Ballarat* carried the 2/9th Battalion (Lieut-Colonel C. J. Cummings) to Oro Bay. By the 17th the 2/9th Battalion and a squadron of the 2/6th Australian Armoured Regiment equipped with eight American M3 tanks (fast 14-ton vehicles but only lightly-armoured) were concentrated in the Buna area and the 2/10th (Lieut-Colonel J. G. Dobbs) was coming forward. There were now eight 25-pounders, three 3.7-inch howitzers and one American 105-mm gun in support. Wootten's plan was first to capture the area between the coast and the Strips; this task was to be carried out by the 2/9th with the tanks and supported by artillery and mortar bombardment.

Early on the morning of 18th December the 2/9th moved north through the Americans, on a front of about 600 yards and with their right on the sea. At 7 a.m. tanks and infantry advanced, their weapons blazing, against the line of close-set Japanese bunkers. They pressed on, though soon many were hit by the Japanese fire. On the right one post after another was shelled or bombed into silence and the leading men reached Cape Endaiadere. The left company, however, at first without tanks, lost more than half its eighty-seven men in an advance of only about 100 yards and was pinned down. In the afternoon three tanks were sent to this flank and the attack was resumed. The shells set the dry logs in some Japanese bunkers on fire and soon the enemy began to leap out and run. In half an hour sixteen bunkers had been taken. The battalion had lost 171 officers and men—about half the strength of the attacking companies. Two tanks had been burnt out.

On the 20th Wootten sent the 2/9th in again, plus one company of the 2/10th. This time three bombers gave support. The advance began at 7 a.m. with the four tanks which were still serviceable spaced among the infantry. They moved through the coconut plantation without great opposition, the shell of the enemy's defences having been broken on the 18th. At 10 a.m. they were advancing into the bush and kunai grass clothing the marshy country beyond the plantation. Here the tanks bogged and could travel only along the beach. Soon the attackers came under heavy mortar and machine-gun fire. The day's advance ended on the general line of Simemi Creek. On the 20th and 21st no crossing was found but early on the 22nd an officer managed to wade through marsh and creek near the Old Strip and led his company across. That day the 2/9th attacked again to take the tongue of land between the mouth of the creek and the sea, and, after a costly day's fighting in which fifty-eight were killed or wounded, succeeded in doing so. In six days the first phase of the attack had been completed.

On the 23rd the Japanese on the left, evidently bewildered by the fact that the Australians had managed to cross the creek in that area, abandoned their positions and by nightfall the 2/10th held about one-third of the Old Strip. Wootten ordered the battalion to continue the advance along the Old Strip next day and gave it the four tanks which were still 'runners'.

It was known that there were Japanese anti-aircraft guns just west of the Strip, but they had been silent for several days. The attack opened at 9.30 a.m. on the 24th, the tanks spaced at intervals of fifty yards, the Australians on and astride the Strip and a battalion of the 126th American Regiment extending the left flank. Tanks and infantry advanced steadily for half an hour. Then a concealed Japanese anti-aircraft gun opened fire at short range and knocked out the tanks in quick succession. The infantry were now under heavy fire. At the end of the day they had gained some 500 to 700 yards.

On the 25th and 26th little progress could be made. The 2/10th's companies were now no stronger than platoons, and the desperate Japanese were counter-attacking more frequently. At length on the evening of the 29th the 2/10th, strengthened by a company of the 2/9th and four newly-arrived tanks, attacked the area between Giropa Point and the mouth of Simemi Creek, but gained nothing. On 31st December the 2/12th Battalion (Lieut-Colonel A. S. W. Arnold) from Goodenough Island relieved the 2/9th and was ordered by Wootten to attack next day with the 2/10th and III/128th on the right and the I/128th on his left. Six tanks would be in support.

Australian War Memorial

Giropa Point, in the Buna area, 1st-2nd January 1943.
Australian Bren gunners fire on Japanese fleeing from a wrecked pill-box 100-150 yards ahead.

The advance began at 8 a.m. on New Year's Day. The tanks, working with precision, rolled close to the enemy's bunkers and lashed them with fire while the infantry rushed forward and hurled charges of ammonal through the loopholes. The strongposts thus overcome were found to contain from ten to seventy bodies. At the end of the long day few Japanese posts east of Buna still held out. In the next two days these posts too were reduced, only nine Japanese, of whom six were labourers, surrendering. The 2/12th lost 191 killed and wounded out of a total strength of 615 in this final drive. In sixteen days the 18th Brigade had lost 55 officers and 808 men, including 22 officers and 284 others killed.

For more than a week after the attack on 7th December no great pressure was exerted along the Sanananda track. On 15th December Porter estimated that he had 646 fighting men in his three Australian battalions and 545 in the 126th American Regiment. Two fresh units were now brought forward from Moresby. They were the 7th Cavalry Regiment, trained as infantry, and the 36th Battalion, the remaining battalion of the 14th Brigade. Vasey ordered that the 7th Cavalry should thrust from Huggins Road-Block to Sanananda Point while the 30th Brigade, now including the 36th Battalion, overcame the Japanese between its position and the road-block and then wiped out the Japanese between Giruwa and Garara. Porter had the 49th on his right, the 36th in the centre and the 55th/53rd on the left. He ordered the 49th to advance to a point about 500 yards north of the Killerton track junction, the 55th/53rd to advance due east to clear the road up to the Killerton track, and the 36th to be ready to exploit the success of either of the other battalions.

On the morning of the 19th after a bombardment by four field guns and by mortars the troops moved forward. The 49th made good progress and Porter promptly reinforced it with a company of the 36th. At the end of the day the 49th was a few hundred yards south-east of the road-block. The 55th/53rd on the left, however, met strong opposition and at the end of the day had made little progress and was in some confusion. Little progress was made on the 20th, and on the 21st the 36th Battalion attacked but lost fifty-five killed and wounded and gained little ground.

Meanwhile, the 7th Cavalry had reached Huggins and before light on 18th December advanced against the Japanese facing the road-block. The leading squadron had moved 450 yards when it came under heavy fire which caused disastrous losses. The Japanese then closed in on the following squadrons, and at the end of the day about 100 cavalrymen were in a perimeter about 400 yards forward of Huggins, some groups were between this perimeter and Huggins, and others at Huggins itself. Among the killed was the commanding officer, Lieut-Colonel E. P. Logan. On the 22nd two groups were still isolated forward of Huggins.

On the 21st Vasey had ordered Dougherty to bring his headquarters and the 39th Battalion from Gona to the Sanananda track and there take command also of the 49th Battalion and the cavalry. On the 23rd a way was found to the group of cavalrymen 400 yards forward of Huggins and the main body of the regiment was concentrated there.

Herring and Vasey had met on 20th December and agreed that it would be impossible to end the impasse round Sanananda with the troops available there, and impossible to bring in tanks and fresh infantry for at least nine days. Where could fresh infantry be found? All the A.I.F. brigades had been used except the 17th at Milne Bay and the 19th which formed the core of the garrison of the Northern Territory. At this stage MacArthur sent a fourth American Regiment, the 163rd (Colonel Jens A. Doe), to the Papuan front, and Blamey ordered it to Sanananda.

Herring made his plans on 29th December: when Buna had been overcome he would concentrate the 7th Division (14th, 18th and 30th Brigades and 163rd Regiment) and 'Buna Force' (the three regiments of the 32nd Division) against Sanananda. The 7th Division with tanks would capture the Sanananda Point-Cape Killerton position and contain the Japanese in the Amboga River-Mambare River area while Buna Force defended Buna and advanced up the coast against Sanananda by way of Tarakena. Herring ordered Buna Force to begin its advance at once. By 8th January the Americans had made some progress, but found that further advance was blocked by mangrove swamps.

Vasey's plan for reducing the Sanananda position was to place two fresh American battalions in the road-blocks and astride the Killerton track and then use the 18th Brigade to destroy the Japanese thus hemmed in. The Americans reached their objectives, and on 12th January the 18th Brigade began pressing the encircled enemy. On the right the 2/9th advancing through the swamp and undergrowth overcame the Japanese outer defences but on the left the three tanks with the 2/12th came under unexpected fire from a Japanese gun which destroyed one and holed another, while the third was set on fire, possibly by a mine. The infantry lost more than 100 men and hardly advanced at all.

It was a disheartening day. Vasey wrote that to send in infantry to attack perimeter localities studded with well-concealed pillboxes was to repeat the costly mistakes of 1915-17. Tanks could be used only along the main track and the Japanese had effective anti-tank guns. Berryman at New Guinea Force headquarters favoured a close blockade of the surviving Japanese, and Eichelberger was inclined to agree.

However, that night and on the 13th the Japanese began to withdraw from their forward positions. Vasey ordered Wootten to thrust swiftly to Cape Killerton and attack Sanananda and the track from the west. Meanwhile patrols of the 36th Battalion on the extreme left crossed the Amboga on the 12th and found abandoned camps. Later patrols found that the Japanese were withdrawing also from the Kumusi and that barges were taking them away.

The 2/10th advanced through bush and swamp to Cape Killerton, meeting only isolated parties; by 17th January the 2/12th was on the track behind the Japanese who were holding the Americans farther south; and on the 18th the 2/9th had taken Sanananda village and point and had a company at the mouth of the Girua. They captured forty-three men, mostly Chinese and Korean labourers.

On the track from the south on the 19th a company of the 2/10th in a skilful and resolute attack broke into a strong Japanese base killing about 150. Soon the remaining Japanese were almost encircled but still refused to yield and continued to kill or wound fifty or sixty Australians each day. On the 21st, however, patrols reported little opposition and a prisoner announced that only sick and wounded remained. The Australians closed in, killed the 100 survivors and found an equal number of dead. On the 21st the 127th American Regiment advanced to Giruwa, which was a scene of death and desolation. To the west a stubborn Japanese force remained at bay until, on the 22nd, after artillery bombardments the 2/9th and 2/10th broke organised resistance in this area.

However, there were still many resolute Japanese moving about. Some had swum round the Australians on the coast, some had made their way westward through the bush, despite the efforts of the 14th Brigade to block them. Probably about 3,400 escaped overland and about 1,200 sick and wounded were taken away by sea. Others had been taken away by sea from the Buna area before the fighting began.

It was learnt later that by 12th January the Japanese had no rice left and many were dying of starvation. On the 13th General Adachi told Major-General Yamagata to prepare to move his force from Sanananda to the Kumusi or Mambare River mouths and thence, overland or by sea, to Lae or Salamaua.

It seems likely that about 20,000 Japanese were employed in the operations in Papua. Of these probably 13,000 were killed or died of illness. In the operations in Papua 2,165 Australians and 671 Americans were killed and 3,533 Australians and 2,172 Americans wounded. It had been a period of grievously heavy loss for Australia, because in the same few months her 9th Division had suffered 5,800 casualties in the fighting at El Alamein described in the next chapter. Should the Japanese in their fortresses along the Buna-Gona coast have been attacked again and again until they were wiped out or should they have been besieged and blockaded while they dwindled away as a result of disease and starvation? The Australian historian of the Papuan campaign points out that it was vital to the Allied plan to secure airfields and develop a port on the north coast. For this reason and because MacArthur could not 'afford to allow any appearance of victory to remain with the Japanese' he had to take Buna. But by 2nd January, with the airfields secure, the Japanese at Sanananda might well have been sealed off and allowed to perish. For the Australians and Americans this course would have obviated three weeks of nightmarish and costly fighting in the swamps of Sanananda. However, because of the desire to raise Allied morale throughout the whole command the 'decision to press the coastal fighting to the bitter end was probably inevitable'.[3]

While the ground forces had been locked in the desperate struggle for the Gona-Buna stronghold the air forces had increased pressure on the enemy air force and shipping. In company with American aircraft, Beaufighters and Bostons of the R.A.A.F. continued the attacks on Huon Gulf airfields which, added to the attacks on Rabaul by American heavy bombers, the fierce fighting in the Solomons, and the growing American fighter strength over Papua, resulted in a noticeable lessening of Japanese air activity after December. The Australians also shared in onslaughts on the bunker positions along the embattled foreshore, and devoted much effort in maintaining a watch on seaborne traffic. On 14th December the Bostons joined the Beaufighters in harassing Japanese troops near the mouth of the Mambare River and forestalling another possible eleventh-hour attempt by the enemy to assist the besieged force to the east.

Throughout the Papuan campaign the Hudsons of No. 6 Squadron and the Beauforts of No. 100 were engaged in seaward reconnaissance and strikes against seaborne supply lines. Six torpedo Beauforts on 9th January succeeded in damaging a light cruiser near Gasmata. However this partial success did not compensate for numerous failures with the torpedo, caused not by lack of skill and daring, but by an unsatisfactory type of torpedo.

All through November and December neither side felt strong enough at sea to give full and close support to its land forces. Transports and corvettes brought in men and supplies and every night two American motor torpedo boats from a flotilla based on Milne Bay patrolled off the Buna shore. On 24th December one of these sank a Japanese submarine, the *I* 22, and another sank two barges. For their part the Japanese ran their reinforcements and supplies into the Buna area in barges if and when they could.

The struggle in the Solomons and New Guinea and the fear of an offensive against the Indies had continued to draw strong Japanese reinforcements into the area north and north-east of Australia. In addition to the *2nd* and *38th Divisions* sent to Rabaul in August and September 1942 and the *48th* and *5th* sent to Timor and Ambon, the *6th* and *51st Divisions* came to Rabaul from China in December, the *41st* to Wewak from China; and, in January

[3] McCarthy, pp. 531-3.

1943, the *20th* to the Wewak-Lae coast from Korea. Thus, by January, three divisions were deployed against the Americans in the Solomons; and, across the Australian front from Buna to Timor, six, including Horii Force, whose survivors were then still fighting round Buna. Farther west the *Guards Division* was in Sumatra. Four divisions (*55th, 33rd, 18th* and *56th*) were in Burma; and the *21st* was in Indo-China. It had required about eleven divisions to attain the initial Japanese objectives; in January 1943, fifteen were proving not enough to hold them.

To Guadalcanal in November three more American regiments, including two from the Americal and 2nd Marine Divisions, had been ferried in and Vandegrift now had some 40,000 men. He thrust out the eastern flank of his perimeter until by 20th November the defended area was about six miles in width. The 1st Marine Division was now feeling the effects of four months of active service on a tropical island. It had, to 10th December, lost 1,472 killed and wounded, and 9,000 men had fallen sick, 5,700 with malaria. At the end of November the Joint Chiefs decided to send the 25th Division from Hawaii to Guadalcanal where it and the remainder of the Americal and the 2nd Marine Divisions would form the garrison, enabling the 1st Marine to be withdrawn to Australia to rest and eventually be available to MacArthur as the amphibious division for which he had been asking. The 43rd American Division had also now arrived in the South Pacific, enabling the Americal to be relieved of garrison tasks south of Guadalcanal.

These reinforcements landed in December and early January and the 1st Marine departed for Brisbane but, finding conditions there unattractive, moved on to Melbourne.[4] Major-General Alexander M. Patch of the Americal Division took command of the Guadalcanal garrison, now named XIV Corps, and about 50,000 strong. Hyakutake had concentrated most of the *2nd* and *38th Divisions* on Guadalcanal, but was finding it impossible adequately to supply this force and troops were sick and hungry. In the three months from 16th November only eleven convoys of destroyers reached the island, and in these efforts ten destroyers were sunk and nineteen damaged. In the second half of December and in January the Americans again pushed westward and by the end of January were established eight miles west of the former boundary of their perimeter. On 4th January, four days after the decision to attempt withdrawal from the Buna area, the Japanese High Command decided to admit its inability to supply and reinforce its troops on Guadalcanal and ordered evacuation.

A gradual embarkation by ships which ran in by night began late in January, but Nimitz and Halsey thought the Japanese were reinforcing not evacuating, and Halsey sent into the disputed area a fleet including 3 battleships, 4 carriers, 12 cruisers and 25 destroyers, to attack the Japanese and cover the landing of fresh American troops. Japanese aircraft on 30th January sank the cruiser *Chicago*, but the transports landed their men without interference.

[4] A history of the Marine Corps in the war—J. A. Isely and P. A. Crowl, *The U.S. Marines and Amphibious War* (1951), p. 185—says: 'After a few hectic weeks in the hot malaria-infested environs of Brisbane, Southwest Pacific headquarters had moved the rehabilitation camp to the cooler and more salubrious region of Melbourne.'

Between 1st and 8th February the Japanese succeeded in secretly embarking about 12,000 troops from Guadalcanal. The American commander did not know that the evacuation was in progress until it was over.

In this campaign the Americans had employed 60,000 troops (of 1st and 2nd Marine, Americal and 25th Divisions),[5] the Japanese about 36,000 (mostly of the *2nd* and *38th Divisions*). The Americans had lost 1,592 killed, the Japanese perhaps 14,800, and 9,000 Japanese may have died of disease. On each side twenty-four naval craft had been sunk. 'By February 1943', wrote Admiral W. D. Leahy later, 'the Joint Chiefs could feel that the Pacific life-line to Australia was safe from dangerous attack.'[6]

Incidentally the operations had given immensely valuable experience and confidence to American leaders and men, at sea, on land and in the air. The navy and the air forces had learned useful tactical lessons. Two marine and two army divisions had been seasoned by active service. Two senior leaders—Patch of the Americal Division and later the XIV Corps and J. Lawton Collins of the 25th Division—would later reappear as an army commander and a corps commander respectively in the European theatre.

A first step forward from Guadalcanal along the Solomons was taken on 21st February when part of the 43rd Division and some marine units were landed on the Russell Islands, which the enemy had abandoned more than a week before.

By October 1942 Japanese air attacks on the Northern Territory fields had diminished in scale and frequency. All American squadrons had now departed and the force in Air Commodore Bladin's North-Western Area comprised the squadrons shown in the accompanying table.

Squadron	*Type*	*Aircraft*
No. 76	Fighter	Kittyhawk
No. 77	Fighter	Kittyhawk
No. 31	Fighter	Beaufighter
No. 2	Bomber	Hudson
No. 13	Bomber	Hudson
No. 12	General Purpose	Wirraway (converted to Vengeance dive bombers in December)

These had an establishment of about 120 aircraft and were distributed among eight fields. This small force, occasionally reinforced by some long-range American bombers, continued to attack Japanese shipping bases, particularly Dili in Timor. For example, during November targets in Timor were attacked almost daily by from six to sixteen aircraft. The Japanese now

[5] The 1st Marine lost 774 killed, the Americal 334, the 2nd Marine 268, the 25th 216. The battle casualties on Guadalcanal and in the Papuan campaign were:

	Killed	*Wounded*
Guadalcanal	1,592	4,245
Papua—Australian	2,165	3,533
Papua—American	671	2,172

It seems that the American figures include slightly wounded men and that the Australian figure omits these.

[6] W. D. Leahy, *I Was There* (English edn. 1950), p. 145.

had about forty aircraft in Celebes and about sixty in Timor but, except for one night raid by eighteen bombers on 23rd November and two dawn raids by twelve bombers each on the 26th and 27th, their attacks were on a small scale.

During December air fighting continued over Timor and the Banda and Timor Seas. On the 18th Beaufighters sank an enemy vessel. At regular intervals unescorted Hudsons of Nos. 2 and 13 Squadrons were attacked by Zeros, but in the month only one Hudson was lost.

On Timor itself the difficulties of the Independent Companies had increased in October and November. The discovery and destruction of the stranded *Voyager* in September combined with the reinforcement of the Japanese force in Timor, in August, September and October, made the prospect of maintaining an Australian force there seem dim. Not only had the Japanese garrison been augmented by a first-class division, but the wreck of the *Voyager* showed that Allied ships had been running in men and supplies and clearly marked one of their landing places. After ten months the 2/2nd Company was being affected by sickness and fatigue; the Timorese in the bush were going over to the Japanese side in increasing numbers.

On 24th November, after seeing a report from Callinan concerning the success of Japanese propaganda among the natives, General Blamey granted the request of General Stevens at Darwin that he should bring out the 2/2nd Company and authorised him to withdraw the remaining Australians.

As a first move the corvettes *Castlemaine* and *Armidale* and the naval tender *Kuru* sailed from Darwin to land some Indonesian troops and embark about 340 Dutch and Portuguese subjects; later they were to return and take off the 2/2nd Independent Company. *Kuru* embarked seventy-seven Portuguese but the corvettes, arriving later, received no signals from the shore and departed without putting their troops ashore. On the way back to Darwin the corvettes overtook *Kuru*, whose Portuguese passengers were transferred to *Castlemaine*. *Kuru* and *Armidale* then returned towards Timor, the last-named to land her troops and then, with *Kuru*, embark refugees for Australia. On their passage north Japanese aircraft attacked, and on the afternoon of 1st December *Armidale* was sunk 350 miles from the Australian coast. After strenuous efforts by aircraft and the corvette *Kalgoorlie*—which had been sent from Darwin to give support—to find and rescue the survivors, forty-nine were picked up but the rest were lost.

On 2nd December Stevens reported that the tempo of Japanese action had quickened, the Portuguese administration had been destroyed, Japanese troops were patrolling to the south coast and were training Timorese guerillas, two Japanese cruisers had been reported off the south coast and more aircraft than ever before had been counted at Koepang. He deduced (correctly) that the Japanese were preparing to meet an invasion. Meanwhile Captain C. J. Pope, Naval Officer in Charge, Darwin, had asked for a destroyer to carry out the planned evacuation of the 2/2nd Independent Company, and the Dutch *Tjerk Hiddes* was sent up from Fremantle. In three trips between 10th and 19th December she withdrew the 2/2nd Company and some hundreds of Dutch and Portuguese subjects, but Blamey was resolved still to leave the 2/4th Company on the island. On 4th January, however, Stevens reported that the force on Timor could no longer carry out its role and urged that it be removed as soon as possible. The company and some civilians were taken off a week later by the destroyer *Arunta.* Small parties were left behind as observers, but these were harried continually, and in February were taken off by submarine.

The main achievement of the Independent Companies on Timor and of the supporting aircraft and naval ships was to contribute greatly to Japanese fears of attack from north Australia and thus to tie up enemy land forces. The Japanese leaders had become so concerned at the prospect of a counter-attack developing from Australia that, early in January 1943 a new army—the *XIX*—including the *48th* and *5th Divisions* was formed to defend the islands round the Banda Sea. The responsibility of the *Eighth Area Army* was now limited to eastern New Guinea and the Solomons. The deployment of the new *XIX Army* was gravely hindered by American submarines and Australian and American aircraft.

Indeed, by April throughout the *Southern Army* area 'the shortage of shipping space and the raids of the enemy submarines and planes caused the break-down of (the Japanese) transportation and supply situation'.[7] American submarines, operating from Fremantle, were sinking many Japanese ships in the area north of Australia, and the American submarine flotillas generally were steadily intensifying those daring and destructive operations which at length were to prove a major factor in the downfall of Japan's overseas armies and the collapse of her war economy.

In the Indies the Japanese shipping problems were also partly a result of a general increase in Allied air strength in the North-Western Area. The American 319th Squadron (Liberators) arrived there in January and began to reconnoitre and attack as far afield as Kendari, Manokwari and Ternate. No. 18 Squadron R.A.A.F., a Dutch unit armed with Mitchells, began operations on 19th January. Soon afterwards arrived No. 1 Fighter Wing, comprising the three Spitfire squadrons sent out by Churchill. This reinforcement, combined with the increasingly efficient radar network, promised to provide effective defence for the Darwin area, which had so far received fifty raids. The new fighter wing was led by Wing Commander C. R. Caldwell, the most successful Australian fighter pilot the war had produced. It shot down its first enemy on 6th February. In a Japanese raid on 2nd March the Spitfire squadrons claimed three shot down, on the 7th one; on the 15th it claimed seven out of forty-four attackers, for a loss of four Spitfires.

Early in October Kanga Force in New Guinea was strengthened by the addition of the 2/7th Independent Company (Major T. F. B. MacAdie). Colonel Fleay spread his two companies from Kudjeru, through the Bulolo valley, and over the mountains towards Mubo, and throughout November and December patrolling continued.

The country lying between the goldfields, the coast and the Markham River is no less forbidding than that which lies between Port Moresby and Buna, and it presented the same obstacles to movement and supply: tangled steep-sided mountains clothed generally in dense bush but occasionally with long kunai grass. Usually the trees shut out the sun from the narrow tracks

[7] Southern Army Operations Record (a monograph compiled in 1946 by the Japanese General Staff, then entitled 'The Demobilisation Bureau').

so that these were like winding tunnels, their floors generally sodden. A divisional report described the country thus: 'Such conditions of rain, mud, rottenness, stench, gloom, and, above all, the feeling of being shut in by everlasting jungle and ever-ascending mountains, are sufficient to fray the strongest nerves. But add to them the tension of the constant expectancy of death from behind the impenetrable screen of green, and nerves must be of the strongest, and morale of the highest, to live down these conditions, accept them as a matter of course, and maintain a cheerful yet fighting spirit.'[8]

The main track leading from Wau to Mubo reached its highest point—6,400 feet—at the Summit Camp and thence wound along the ridges above the Buisaval River; the only other tracks leading east from the Wau area were the Black Cat and the 'Jap' tracks, both unsuitable as main supply routes. To the north another track led down from the goldfields to Salamaua. This route entered the Francisco Valley at Missim and thence wound on to Bobdubi and beyond. Northward from the goldfields area two main tracks led down to the wide Markham Valley at the mouth of which is Lae. A western track travelled through Wampit to the river south of Nadzab; an eastern one went through Wagau, where it branched, one track then descending through Gabensis and the other travelling to Markham Point.

In December Fleay planned an attack on Mubo by more than 300 troops, with 400 carriers, his intention being to kill as many Japanese as possible and, if it became feasible, to take and hold Mubo. The plan was to stealthily occupy five features round Mubo and suddenly pour fire into the enemy's positions from several directions. On the afternoon of 11th January the parties were in position and opened fire with machine-guns and mortars. Many Japanese were hit but they soon brought up reinforcements and drove the Australians back.

At the time that they decided to withdraw from Sananada the Japanese set out to reinforce Lae and Salamaua, and on 7th January, after a large-scale air battle, a convoy from Rabaul landed a strong force at Lae. It was fortunate that the last available A.I.F. infantry—the 17th Brigade—was still at Milne Bay ready to defend that base or to meet some new thrust. On the 8th Blamey informed Herring that, when the Japanese in the Buna area had been overcome, he intended to garrison that area with the 41st American Division, withdraw the worn-out formations, and bring two fresh Australian brigades from the mainland. One of these, the 29th, would replace the 17th Brigade which would be flown to Wau.

Brigadier M. J. Moten of the 17th Brigade was ordered to take over Kanga Force from 15th January. Shortage of aircraft and bad weather over the ranges slowed down the movement of troops and it was the 19th before the leading battalion—the 2/6th—was more or less complete round Wau. Soon its companies were deployed along either the track through Skindewai or the Black Cat Track.

Kanga Force had been reinforced none too early, for on the 21st a patrol saw troops moving in some strength along the Black Cat Track and it was soon evident that the Japanese were cutting their way along a disused track from the Black Cat to Wandumi. Moten decided to send the 2/6th Battalion

[8] Report on Operations of 3 Aust Div in Salamaua Area, 22 April 43 to 25 August 43.

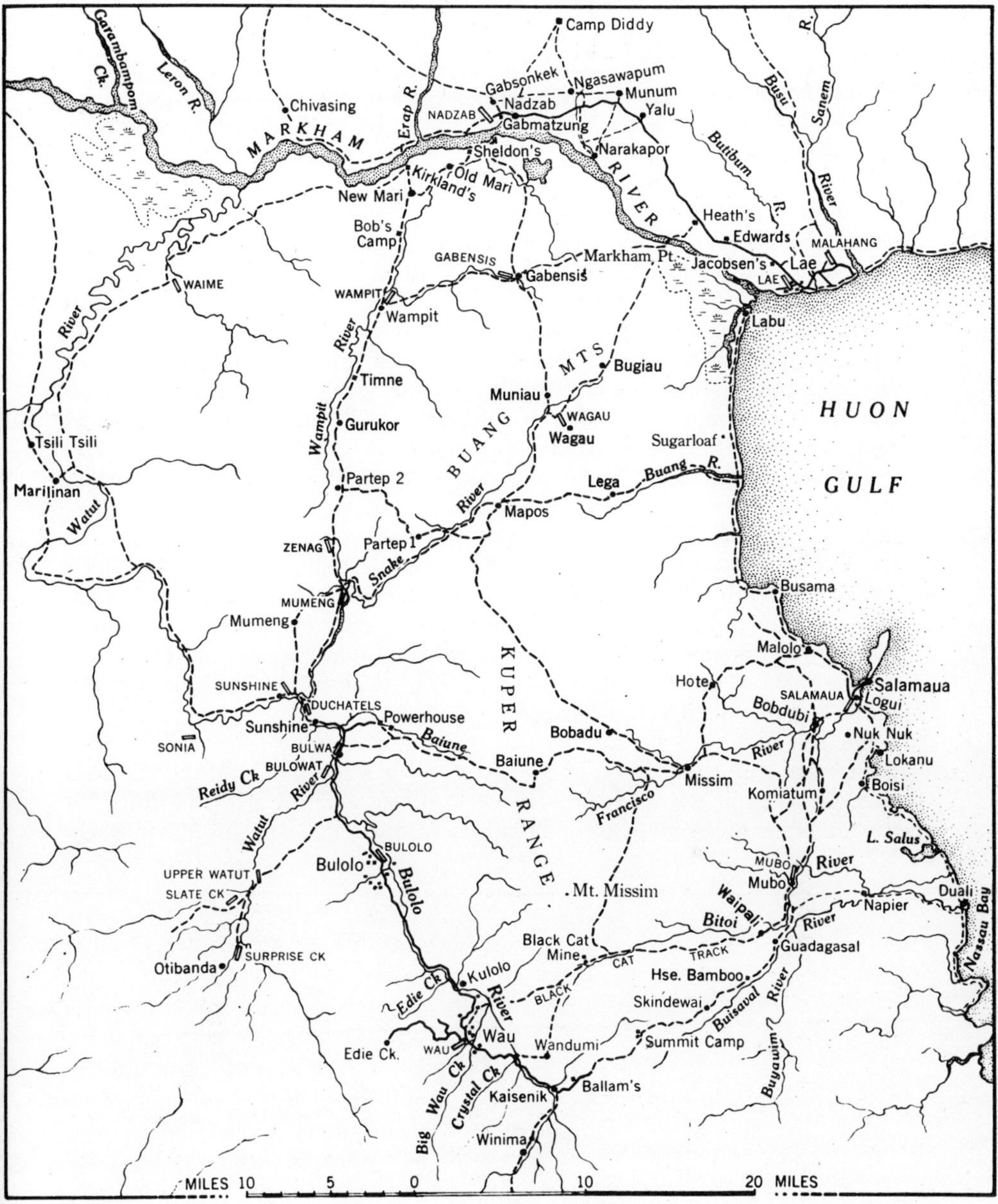

Wau-Lae area.

less three companies through the Black Cat area, and on the 26th Lieut-Colonel F. G. Wood of the 2/6th led this force out. The plan was that another company of the battalion would fall on the rear of the Japanese facing Wood while yet another would attack up the 'Jap' track from Wandumi. Next day the main body of the 2/5th arrived at Wau and its commander, Lieut-Colonel P. D. S. Starr, was given command of all troops on the Mubo track.

The Japanese moved fast, however, and early on the 28th attacked Captain W. H. Sherlock's reinforced company at Wandumi in strength. Sherlock's men held their ground under repeated attacks. By late afternoon their mortar bombs were exhausted, small-arms ammunition was running short, and Sherlock reported to Moten that hundreds of Japanese were moving swiftly past him towards Wau. A newly-arrived company of the 2/5th was sent out from Wau and reached Wandumi that evening. This force took up a new position between Wandumi and the Bulolo River intending to hold the track until morning at least and give time for the now-depleted force at Wau to be built up. That night the Wandumi force was under heavy fire and its communications were cut. Early next morning a relief force set out but it failed to reach Wandumi. Soon several forces of about company strength were more or less out of touch east of Wau, while the main Japanese column was approaching Wau itself, where few troops remained; and for twenty-four hours after 9 a.m. on the 28th the weather prevented troop-carrying aircraft from getting through.

At 7 p.m. on the 28th Japanese troops were only two miles from the Wau airfield and early next morning their fire was falling on its outer defences, then being hurriedly manned by two companies of the 2/5th. But at 9.15 the first of sixty aircraft-loads of troops began landing; that day 814 men arrived, including the 2/7th Battalion and the balance of the 2/5th. Before dawn on the 30th the Japanese attacked. There was hard fighting throughout the morning. Soon two field guns were landed, under fire, and by 11.30 a.m. were in action. In the afternoon the 2/7th attacked and the infantry and the field guns killed many Japanese.

On the 31st men began to come in from Wandumi whence little had been heard for several days. These told that when, on the 29th, the Japanese attacked in great strength both from the village and the river the force, in danger of being overwhelmed, broke its way through the bush and made

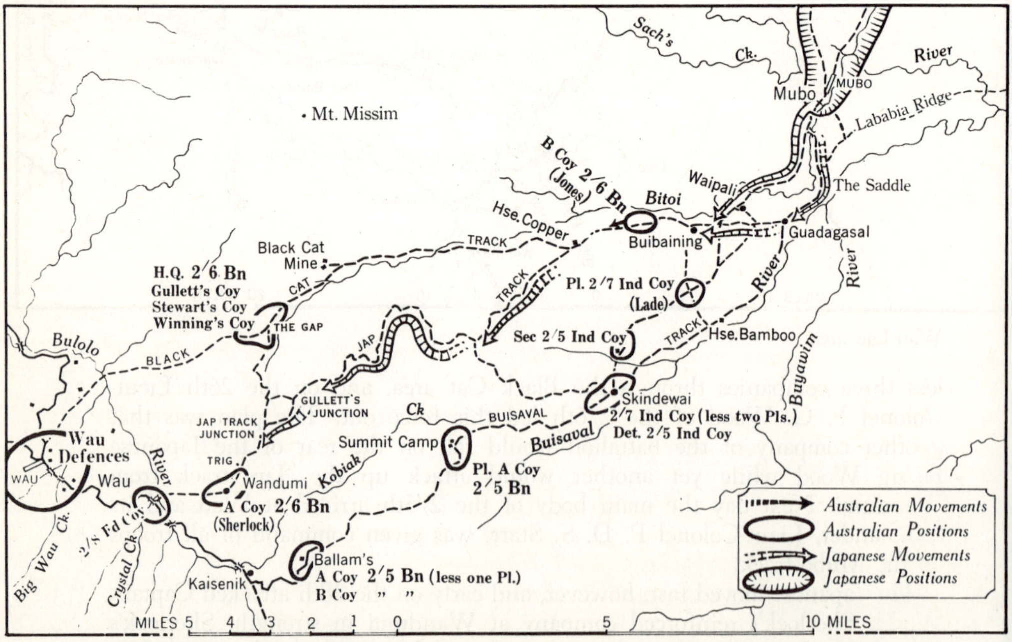

Wau-Mubo

for the Bulolo River near Crystal Creek. At the creek the pursuing Japanese poured machine-gun fire into them, killing seven including Sherlock, and causing them to break up into several groups.

From 1st February onwards the Australians made persistent attacks on the Japanese, who had now lost the initiative and were suffering sharp losses. On the 6th nine Japanese bombers with many fighters attacked Wau as four transport aircraft were unloading, five others were approaching and Allied fighters were overhead. Two Australian planes were lost but two Japanese bombers and twenty-five fighters were shot down. By this time the Japanese had begun gradually to withdraw towards Mubo but fought back hard wherever they were found. By the 9th all who remained in the Wau valley had been destroyed, and by the end of the month the Japanese force was back round Mubo.

The Japanese based on Lae and Salamaua included the *102nd Regiment* and *2nd Maizuru Special Naval Landing Force* and probably numbered about 6,500. The attack on Wau had been made by the *102nd Regiment,* 2,500-3,000 strong. When their withdrawal began the Japanese had probably lost about 1,200 killed and were very short of food. Their only chance of success had been to capture Wau quickly and live on the supplies it might yield.

General Mackay, who had temporarily relieved Herring in command of New Guinea Force on 31st January, considered that the enemy might again thrust at Wau and on 13th February signalled to Blamey that he thought the area should be reinforced. Blamey informed Mackay that the 4th and 15th Brigades were to move to New Guinea and suggested that the headquarters of the 3rd Division (Major-General Savige) should take over at Wau.

Meanwhile, in an effort to facilitate the supply of Wau, engineers and natives under Lieut-Colonel W. J. Reinhold were developing a road from Bulldog on the Lakekamu River to Wau along which it would be possible to feed men and supplies into Wau overland.

Blamey now proposed 'a severe blow' against the enemy round Salamaua, but warned that the force must not become involved in siege operations like those in the Buna-Gona area. Moten thereupon gave orders for an attack on Mubo. The Australians edged forward to Lababia Ridge and the Saddle. Salamaua lay about twelve miles ahead but the intervening country was extremely forbidding.

In February General Imamura at Rabaul, having lost his Buna base and having been thrust back from Wau, decided again to reinforce Lae, this time with some 7,000 troops—a great part of the *51st Division,* part of which was already round Lae and Salamaua. On 1st March these set sail in eight transports, mostly of 3,000 to 6,000 tons, and escorted by eight destroyers, which also carried some of the troops. A storm concealed the ships until the afternoon of the 1st when they were in the Bismarck Sea about halfway to Vitiaz Strait. An American aircraft saw them that afternoon, and next morning twenty-eight American heavy bombers attacked from 5,000 feet and sank one transport. Two destroyers rescued 850 men and raced them into Lae that night. Later eleven more Fortresses attacked. Australian Catalinas shadowed the convoy during the night, and on the 3rd the strongest force the Fifth Air Force could assemble attacked: heavy bombers from medium altitudes, medium bombers, torpedo bombers, and Beaufighters (of No. 30

Squadron) strafing at deck height. High overhead the opposing fighter escorts fought it out. Most of the surviving transports were sunk or set on fire that day. At night five motor-torpedo boats went in and sank an abandoned transport. On the 4th the only ship which could be found was a destroyer; bombers sank it. All the transports had now been sunk and four of the eight destroyers. For some days afterwards aircraft strafed the survivors in the sea. It seems probable that about 3,000 troops were killed. American aircraft made 335 sorties and Australian aircraft sixty-seven; only five American aircraft and one Australian were lost. The Japanese commanders decided that henceforward reinforcements must be sent to Lae and Salamaua only in submarines and barges. Kenney's air force was now well on the way towards establishing air supremacy.

While the long battles in Papua and the southern Solomons were reaching their final stages the future strategy in the Pacific—and in Europe—was being discussed by the senior Allied leaders. In December Churchill and Roosevelt agreed that they and their advisers should meet at Casablanca in North Africa to discuss the next moves. At this conference, in January 1943, it was decided that the invasion of Western Europe could not be undertaken until the spring of 1944. A problem that remained was where to apply the main effort in the meantime. Churchill wished to complete the mastery of North Africa and then, from African bases, to strike at 'the under-belly of the Axis'. King and Marshall urged that more weight should be put into the war against Japan, which, King estimated, was receiving a perilously low proportion of the total resources. These commanders wished to concentrate as much force as possible during 1943 against Japan while the build-up for the invasion of Europe continued. A compromise was reached whereby the operations in the Mediterranean would continue as opportunity offered, but operations against Japan should be pressed, and, particularly, an effort should be made to retake Burma and reopen a road to China; it was also decided to take Rabaul, and advance from the east on Truk and Guam.

So far as the South and South-West Pacific areas were concerned this decision did little more than confirm the Joint Chiefs' directive of 2nd July 1942, when they had ordered the seizure of New Britain, New Ireland and the occupied parts of New Guinea. Those projects had been interrupted by the Japanese offensive from Buna and the stubborn opposition in the Solomons. In February MacArthur and his staff completed new plans for the attainment of the old objectives. MacArthur proposed a mutually-supporting advance: by the South Pacific forces through the Solomon Islands to Kavieng and by the South-West Pacific forces along the New Guinea coast to Wewak and north-eastward to the Admiralties. This done there would be a combined assault on Rabaul. It was estimated that these operations would require twenty-one divisions and a force of 1,800 aircraft. In January MacArthur had prepared and handed to the Australian Government a statement of the conclusions he had reached as a result of the recent operations:

> The outstanding military lesson of this operation was the continuous calculated application of air power, inherent in the potentialities of every component of the Air Force, employed in the most intimate tactical and logistical union with ground troops. The effect of this modern instrumentality was sharply accentuated by the geographical limitations of this theatre. For months on end, air

> transport with constant fighter coverage moved complete infantry regiments and artillery battalions across the almost impenetrable mountains and jungles of Papua, and the reaches of the sea; transported field hospitals and other base installations to the front; supplied the troops and evacuated casualties. For hundreds of miles bombers provided all-around reconnaissance, protected the coast from hostile naval intervention and blasted the way for the infantry as it drove forward. A new form of campaign was tested which points the way to the ultimate defeat of the enemy in the Pacific. The offensive and defensive power of the air, and the adaptability, range and capacity of its transport in an effective combination with ground forces, represent tactical and strategical elements of a broadened conception of warfare that will permit the application of offensive power in swift, massive strokes, rather than the dilatory and costly island-to-island advance, that some have assumed to be necessary, in a theatre where the enemy's far-flung strongholds are dispersed throughout a vast expanse of archipelagos. Air forces and ground forces were welded together in Papua and with proper naval support their indissoluble union points the way to victory through new and broadened strategic and tactical conceptions.

These strategic and tactical conceptions were in fact not new. Against Crete the Germans had employed air transport on a considerably larger scale than had been done in New Guinea; and the last sentence but one of MacArthur's statement would have served equally well as a description of the principles followed by the Japanese in the first phase of their war 'in a theatre where the enemy's far-flung strongholds were dispersed throughout a vast expanse of archipelagos'. They had advanced where possible from one potential air base to another, in stages of about 500 miles—the range of their fighters—and where this was not possible they employed carrier-borne aircraft to cover their attacks. In Malaya, Java, Luzon, Rabaul, Ambon and Timor, and now at Guadalcanal and in Papua it had mainly been a fight for airfields.

On 3rd January 1943 Blamey wrote a statement of army policy in the immediate future. The requirements were three: the development of offensive action, the provision of defence against possible invasion, and the maintenance of the forces. In order to build up a force for offensive action the 6th and 7th Divisions would be concentrated on the Atherton Tablelands to be refitted and to undergo further training. The 6th Division would have only one brigade since the 17th Brigade would remain in New Guinea and the 19th was in the Northern Territory. (A new brigade would be formed for it including the 3rd and 39th Battalions and the 2/3rd Pioneers.) The 32nd American Division would probably also return to Australia. Two divisions—the 5th at Milne Bay and 11th at Moresby and Buna—would remain in New Guinea, as would the 41st American Division. Defence against possible invasion required maintenance of the present garrison at Darwin, but in Western Australia the arrival of the 1st Armoured Division made it possible to reduce the garrison by two infantry brigades.

In future two corps headquarters would be necessary in addition to the American Corps. One of the Australian corps headquarters would control operations in New Guinea and the other the force training on the Tablelands. The two Army headquarters in Australia would continue 'until such time as there is no possibility of a Japanese recovery that is likely to defeat the forces in New Guinea and other forward areas'.

As mentioned earlier, the policy of Churchill and Roosevelt was to concentrate first on defeating Hitler and then on defeating Japan. However, the necessity of stopping the Japanese thrust into the South Pacific and the influence of the American naval leaders, combined with the fact that invasion of Europe was not yet possible, had produced by the end of 1942 a stronger concentration of American forces against Japan than against Germany and Italy. In December the main strength of the American Navy was in the Pacific. And in Hawaii, the South Pacific and the South-West Pacific there were eleven American divisions, compared with six in North Africa and one in the United Kingdom. The European and Mediterranean zones had received forty-seven groups of the United States Army Air Force compared with twenty-three in the Pacific and Asian zones but, on the other hand, in the Pacific were the big carrier-borne air force and the U.S. Marine Air Corps.

By September 1942 a substantial American contingent had settled down in Australia and relationships had taken a shape which was not to be altered greatly in the coming three years. On the higher political, military and administrative levels there were relatively few points of contact—a consequence of the thorough way in which strategical control had been surrendered to the American Joint Chiefs of Staff and their local subordinate, General MacArthur. As has been seen MacArthur dealt directly only with the Prime Minister, Blamey and Blamey's chief of staff on matters of the first importance. The few Australians on MacArthur's staff were mostly liaison officers rather than executives. For the present there was closer integration of the two contingents in the Allied Air Force, but already there were signs that the Americans would prefer greater independence. The Australian Navy, experienced in fitting itself into British forces, was well qualified to link with an American force; and in any event the integration of naval forces presents fewer problems because of the relatively large size of the units and squadrons.

It is certain that no Australian Government would have so completely surrendered control of its forces in its own territory to a British commander and staff. This was not because there was greater affection for the Americans. On the contrary, except among a minority, there was a far warmer sentiment about the mother country. It was simply that the Americans appeared to possess the power which Britain now lacked, and the Australian leaders were willing to take extreme measures to attract that power across the Pacific. The completeness of the surrender of control had been an unforeseen and disappointing outcome: the Australian Government had hoped to have a share in strategical decisions but, in the event, had virtually none, although for the first year of the existence of the South-West Pacific Command it contributed the greater part of its forces.

In the Burma-India frontier during the second half of 1942 the opposing armies were virtually out of touch. Within Burma the Japanese had four divisions. In Assam and Bengal General Wavell had a force of about the same size, though less well trained: in the middle part of the year it included the 17th Indian Division and 1st Burma Division, both recuperating after the long retreat of March to May 1942, and the somewhat raw 14th and

26th Indian Divisions. In reserve in eastern India was the 70th British Division, less one brigade in Ceylon. The monsoon season lasts from June to October and this gave Wavell and his subordinates time to organise and train new formations and allowed time for reinforcements and equipment to arrive from Britain and for the building up of the Eastern Fleet and a more adequate air force. The defeats in Malaya and Burma had made a profound impression on leaders and men in India and a feeling of military inferiority to the Japanese was widespread.

When the monsoon ended in Burma in October neither side moved immediately. Wavell would soon have five Indian divisions (14th, 17th, 23rd, 26th, 39th) in Assam and Bengal and elsewhere in India and Ceylon five Indian infantry divisions (7th, 19th, 20th, 25th and 34th), two British (2nd and 70th), and two Indian armoured divisions forming. Most of the Indian divisions, however, were considered incompletely trained and some were short of adequately-trained officers. Wavell, not for the first time directing operations in which his resources seemed inadequate, decided that in the northern winter of 1942-1943 he would undertake two operations: on the right the recapture of Akyab; on the left a foray into northern Burma by a brigade trained on commando lines by Brigadier O. C. Wingate, an unorthodox leader who had led guerilla groups in Abyssinia and who possessed an evident singleness of purpose and an uncompromising eloquence which immediately impressed many of those about him. The advance on Akyab by the 14th Division, later replaced by the 26th, did not succeed. These operations lasted from December to April, and when the monsoon came in 1943 the attacking force was back where it had begun.[9] Wingate's column crossed the Chindwin on 18th February, advanced to the Mandalay-Myitkyina railway and carried out demolitions. On its return journey it was severely harassed by the enemy, and broke up into small groups. These returned into India in May and early June, the force as a whole having lost a third of its strength. Valuable experience was gained, and it was discovered after the war that these limited offensives deterred the Japanese from themselves undertaking a similarly limited offensive into Manipur and northern Assam.

On 8th April 1943 Churchill wrote to his Chief of Staff: 'This campaign [in Burma] goes from bad to worse, and we are being completely outfought and out-manoeuvred by the Japanese. Luckily, the small scale of the operations and the attractions of other events has prevented public opinion being directed upon this lamentable scene.'

General Slim, at this time a corps commander and soon to become an army commander in Burma, later recorded that Australian success against the Japanese in New Guinea had raised morale in India:

> If the Australians, in conditions very like ours, had done it, so could we. Some of us may forget that of all the Allies it was Australian soldiers who first broke the spell of the invincibility of the Japanese Army; those of us who were in Burma have cause to remember.[1]

In retrospect it can be seen that a major achievement of the Australian Army in 1942 was to establish a tactical superiority over the Japanese troops.

[9] The British and Indian force lost 331 killed, 625 missing and 1,678 wounded.
[1] Field Marshal Sir William Slim, *Defeat Into Victory* (1956), pp. 187-8.

Australian War Memorial

New Guinea, 1943. A carrier line setting out from the Mubo area with supplies for the forward troops. The Allied forces in New Guinea owed much to the native carriers, both in the maintenance of supplies to the forward troops and the evacuation of the severely wounded.

At Milne Bay Australian soldiers had defeated a Japanese amphibious operation; in Papua they had defeated the Japanese in a long campaign fought over big areas of mountain and bush; finally, with American aid, they had wiped out the enemy in fixed positions round Buna and Gona; and for a year they had maintained a small guerilla force in Japanese-held Timor. The Guadalcanal operation had chiefly demonstrated an ability to hold a perimeter against Japanese attack; the Australian operations demonstrated ability to attack and defeat the Japanese after they had been repulsed and thrown on the defensive.

In this period the Australians had certain great advantages. The Australian formations concerned had not taken part in the debacles of December 1941 to March 1942 but came fresh and confident to the Pacific from hard and mostly-successful campaigning in the Middle East. They were the first large bodies of troops the Japanese had encountered who were not only finely trained but had had recent experience of battle. In addition the Australians were able to adapt themselves more quickly to campaigning in the tropical bush than the American and British soldiers.

Most of the veteran Australian brigades now needed a long period of rest and recuperation particularly while malaria ran its course. From the Australian viewpoint the Japanese had abandoned the initiative none too soon. When the 17th Australian Brigade was flown into Wau to counter the last big offensive in this phase of the war in New Guinea only one A.I.F. infantry brigade—the 19th in the Northern Territory—remained unspent; but the 9th Australian Division was then at sea and would soon arrive home from the Middle East.

Chapter 9 The war in the West and Middle East, 1942

During 1942, while Australia's main strength was employed against the Japanese, she still maintained substantial contingents in the operations against Germany and Italy. By January 1942 no Australian naval vessels remained in the Mediterranean but the 9th Division was still in the Middle East, and, by the end of the year, there were ten R.A.A.F. squadrons in the United Kingdom and seven in the Middle East; in these squadrons, however, only a minority of the 14,500 men of the R.A.A.F. outside the South-West Pacific Area were serving, the remainder being in R.A.F. squadrons, at schools and so on. The Australian Government had not been entirely willing to have such big forces serving against the distant enemies. It will be recalled that for a time it had suspended the sending abroad of air crew; it also continued to seek the return of the 9th Division.

Throughout 1942, however, the 9th Division was retained in the Middle East where it was destined to play a notable part in the decisive battles in North Africa in the second half of the year. When last mentioned the division, except for one battalion, had been withdrawn from Tobruk to Palestine and it was there when Japan attacked. One immediate effect of the Japanese onslaught was that reinforcements and supplies intended for the Middle East theatre were diverted to the Far East, and formations already in the Middle East (including, as we have seen, the 6th and 7th Australian Divisions) were sent to the new theatre of war.

This weakening of already battered forces drove General Auchinleck to adopt a policy of harrying the retreating enemy's rear rather than make an all-out attempt to destroy his armour. A scarcity of petrol and motor transport also hampered his efforts to press home the pursuit.

On the insistence of the Italian Supreme Command, Rommel reluctantly agreed that the Axis forces should attempt a firm stand at Gazala, blocking the way to Derna and the Cyrenaican 'bulge', but an encircling move around the southern flank by the British XIII Corps forced him to order a further withdrawal. The Axis forces made their next stand at Agedabia, on the plain south of Benghazi. British mobile forces entered Benghazi on Christmas Eve to find the enemy had stayed long enough to destroy everything they could not remove. To the south a small column of the Guards Brigade had made contact with the German armour two days earlier, but had been driven off. In two later armoured clashes battle honours went to Rommel. The British 1st Armoured Division arrived in the forward area on 6th January and the Axis forces retired to El Agheila in the Tripolitanian frontier area. On the Egyptian frontier the isolated Axis garrisons at Bardia, Salum and Halfaya were successively battered into surrender by 17th January, and 14,000 prisoners taken.

Rommel received strong reinforcements of tanks, guns, armoured cars and supplies of all kinds when a convoy arrived at Tripoli on 5th January. These enabled him to launch a counter-attack which drove back the British some

300 miles to a defence line running south from Gazala. In the retreat the 1st Armoured Division lost about half of its armour—ninety tanks—and vast quantities of stores and equipment fell into Axis hands.

Lieut-General N. M. Ritchie, then commanding the Eighth Army, established a fairly strong line behind a minefield running from the sea to the fortified strongpoint of Bir Hacheim, forty-five miles away in the desert to the south. The port of Tobruk was the British forward base, and the ridges running back towards Tobruk were guarded against enemy encroachment. The opposing forces now began a race each to build up its strength to attack the other, with Rommel, having a shorter line of supply, gaining the advantage.

When the war of movement ceased the character of the air operations changed. Fighters were mainly employed on defensive tasks over the Gazala line and their own bases; the light bombers attacked the enemy airfields and the port of Benghazi. The area from Gazala to Benghazi was now covered by an adequate radar system and this enabled some successful interception of enemy air forces, in which Australian pilots, in Kittyhawks, at times played a notable part.

Continued transfer of aircraft to the Asian theatre in the early months of 1942 had now greatly weakened the air strength of Middle East Command. The reduced force was highly efficient, however, and organisation and liaison were being improved. The fighters were now together in No. 211 Group which had three wings each of four squadrons, the two R.A.A.F. Squadrons—Nos. 3 and 450—being in No. 239 Wing, which contained also Nos. 112 and 250 R.A.F. in which were strong quotas of Australians. By May No. 239 had been converted to a Kitty-bomber wing, which made its first sortie of six aircraft equipped for this new fighter-bomber role on 16th May.

On 26th May 1942 the lull in the desert fighting was broken when Rommel attacked with the immediate object of capturing Tobruk and then moving on to the Egyptian frontier, where he was to halt and wait until the German capture of Malta safeguarded his supply lines. He was then to attack Egypt.

General Ritchie's instructions from General Auchinleck, the British Commander-in-Chief, were that every effort was to be made to hold Tobruk. If forced to withdraw, however, Tobruk was not again to be left to hold out as a fortress, but should be evacuated after maximum destruction had been carried out. In the event of the Battle of Gazala going against him he too was to make a stand on the Egyptian frontier.

Moving the full weight of four armoured divisions with great speed, Rommel wheeled around Bir Hacheim, struck north, and in one day's fighting smashed several isolated British formations and established a dangerous salient in the British positions, but not without losing more than a third of his tanks. A counter-attack launched by Ritchie in the early hours of 5th June against the salient was repulsed with very heavy losses; more than 100 tanks were knocked out and four battalions of infantry and four regiments of artillery were wiped out in the area known as the Cauldron.

Rommel now decided to remove the troublesome Bir Hacheim stronghold on the southern flank. There the Free French Brigade put up an heroic defence for five days against continuous assaults from the ground and air and then made a fighting withdrawal on the night of 10th June.

For the first five days of the Battle of Gazala the R.A.F. threw all its strength into the battle. Fighters and light bombers attacked the enemy's columns and the medium bombers concentrated on enemy airfields. Twice the fighter-bombers left more than fifty enemy vehicles burning. The fighters and light bombers made a tremendous effort on 16th June. For example, No. 3 Squadron R.A.A.F. flew sixty-two sorties.

The British line, extending from Gazala to Tobruk in the coastal sector, was still guarded by lines of fortified areas, termed 'boxes', scattered along the general line of the Trigh Capuzzo some twenty-five miles to the south. On 12th June Rommel struck at the centre of this line and three British armoured brigades of the 7th Armoured Division were routed. Ritchie withdrew most of his forces to the Egyptian frontier though, on orders from Auchinleck, he tried to hold a line running from the west of Tobruk south-westwards through El Adem. He was directed not to allow Tobruk to become a besieged fortress. But Churchill then asked Auchinleck for an assurance that Tobruk would not be given up, and Auchinleck authorised Ritchie to allow the Tobruk garrison to be isolated for brief periods if this became necessary.

Rommel attacked Tobruk in the south-eastern sector on 20th June with infantry and about forty tanks after heavy dive-bombing and artillery bombardments. The tanks swiftly overran the defenders' gun lines and by evening had captured the port. Deciding that further bloodshed would not remedy the situation, the garrison commander (Major-General H. B. Klopper of the 2nd South African Division) surrendered the fortress at dawn next day. About 35,000 men, including four infantry brigades and a tank brigade, became prisoners.

The Eighth Army now fell back to defensive positions at Mersa Matruh, 130 miles across the Egyptian frontier. On 25th June Rommel's forces contacted the Matruh outposts and that day Auchinleck relieved Ritchie of his command of the Eighth Army and assumed command himself. Auchinleck's desert forces at that stage consisted of the X Corps (Matruh fortress troops, the 10th Indian Division and the 50th Division); the XIII Corps (remnants of the 1st and 7th Armoured Divisions and the motorised New Zealand Division, less one brigade) responsible for the left flank; and the XXX Corps at El Alamein, a further 120 miles into Egypt, organising a defensive position with the 1st South African Division and 2nd Free French Brigade Group.

Auchinleck decided at once not to attempt to fight a decisive action at Matruh. He reorganised his divisions into 'brigade battle groups' with the aim of keeping them mobile and ready to strike at the enemy from all sides. He intended that the principal arm would be artillery, with detachments of other arms, and only sufficient infantry to provide close escorts. This change, made on the eve of battle, tended to increase the growing confusion within the ranks of the Eighth Army.

When Rommel cleared a way through the minefield south of Matruh on 26th June and attacked the New Zealand Division from three sides, Lieut-General Gott, commanding the XIII Corps, ordered the withdrawal of the remainder of the corps, believing that the New Zealanders had been overrun. The New Zealanders, however, fighting one of their greatest battles, broke through the armoured ring at Minqar Qaim and withdrew in good order to El Alamein. Next night the 10th Indian Division and the 50th Division also fought their way out but suffered such casualties in the withdrawal that they had to be pulled back to reorganise.

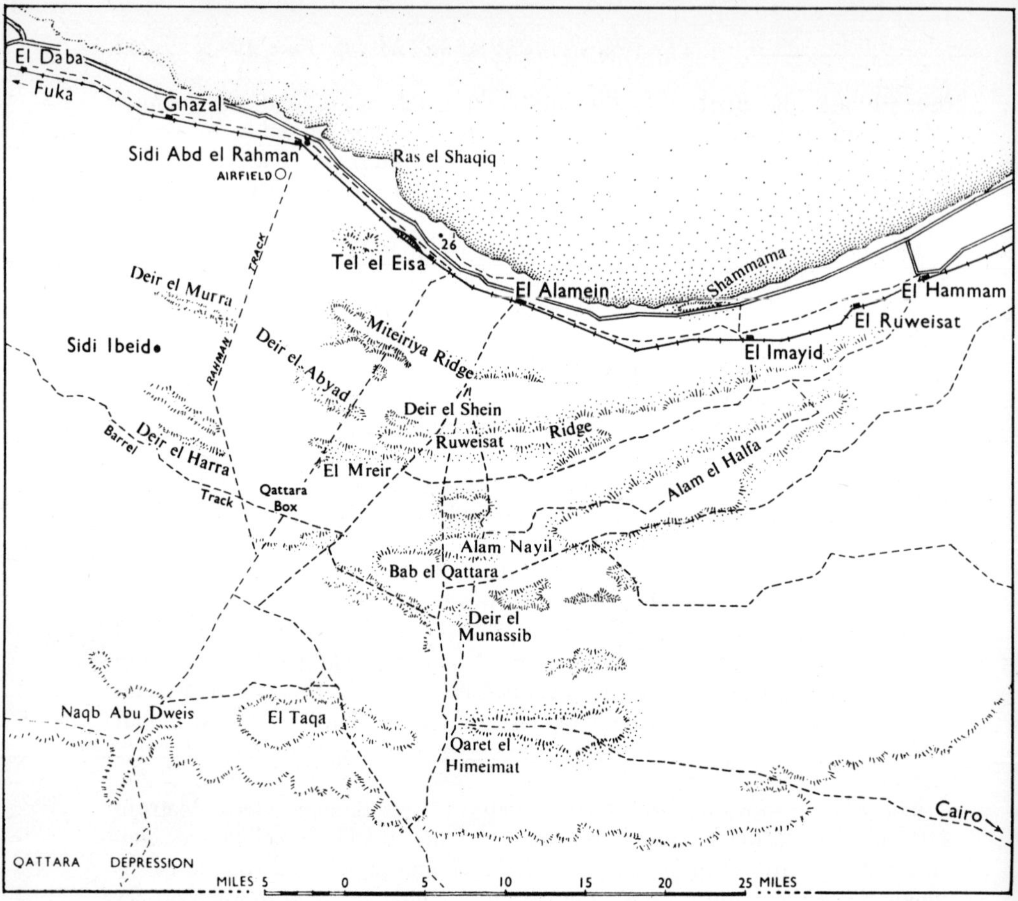

El Alamein area

Auchinleck now halted the long retreat in the defensive positions that had been established at Alamein, thwarting Rommel when he appeared poised for a triumphant entry into the Nile Valley. The area which was soon to become a vast battleground extended from the coast across forty miles of desert to the impassable salt marshes and sand-dunes of the Qattara Depression in the south. Alamein itself was a siding on the coast railway and road from Alexandria but there was no settlement there of any kind. The XXX Corps held the northern sector and the XIII Corps the southern. Insufficient troops were available to man a continuous line, and the British forces were therefore spaced at intervals in defended areas, or 'boxes', that were not mutually supporting.

On 1st July Rommel, still confident that he could smash his way through to Alexandria, launched a two-pronged attack on the British positions south of the El Alamein Box. The *90th Light Division*, after breaking through, was to swing north and encircle the forces in the Alamein Box while farther south the *Africa Corps* was to outflank the 18th Indian Brigade at Deir el Shein and attack it from the rear. In the north the 1st South African Division (Major-General D. H. Pienaar) repulsed the *90th Light Division*, but the *Africa Corps* overran the Indian brigade after five hours of bitter fighting.

Next day the *90th Light Division* resumed its attack at first light but made no significant progress. In spite of the loss of the Indian brigade Auchinleck had already decided to try and wrest the initiative from Rommel. He ordered the XIII Corps to thrust northwards and attack the rear of the enemy forces. The 1st Armoured Division, moving south-west to link up with the XIII Corps' attack, ran into the *Africa Corps* which was moving north-east to encircle the Alamein Box. The engagement was indecisive, but the German plan was thwarted.

Rommel tried again on 3rd July, throwing into the battle the greater part of his sorely-battered armoured and infantry divisions in a three-pronged attack, again with the purpose of overwhelming the Alamein Box. At the same time Auchinleck ordered the continuation of the drive northwards by the XIII Corps to take the enemy in the flank and rear. Nowhere did the German thrusts succeed. The New Zealand artillery, south of the Ruweisat Ridge, pounded the Italian *Ariete Division* so effectively that the 4th New Zealand Brigade commander decided to launch an all-out attack on the Italians. The leading battalion—the 19th—advanced with fixed bayonets and captured some 400 Italians, forty-four medium and field guns and many vehicles. Under British air attack the *Trieste Division,* which was to have assisted the *Ariete,* failed to get started at all. Astride the Ruweisat Ridge the German armour was halted by the 1st Armoured Division, and in the north the German-Italian infantry attacks were held.

The three days fighting convinced Rommel that he would need to reorganise his forces extensively before resuming the offensive. Auchinleck had won the preliminary phase of the battle for the El Alamein positions.

During July the German air force was gradually subdued by constant attacks, day and night, on its airfields and by losses in the air fighting. In this effort the two Australian Kittyhawk squadrons had a large share, flying 877 sorties in the four weeks. The number of fighter sorties made by the Axis aircraft dwindled in this month while those by the R.A.F. increased. An air offensive was now launched against the enemy's coastal shipping, largely tank landing craft. For example, between 1st and 17th August No. 459 Squadron R.A.A.F. in eighty-five sorties sank twelve out of a total of sixteen such craft on the Tobruk-Mersa Matruh run, whereupon the Germans ceased using them for this purpose.

Throughout 1942 the effort to keep Malta supplied was achieved only at heavy cost in naval and merchant ships sunk by Axis aircraft. Four of the Australian 'N'-class destroyers, which had been employed on the East Indies station earlier in the year, formed part of the escort of a convoy that set out for Malta in mid-June. They were *Nestor, Napier, Nizam* and *Norman. Nestor* was mortally damaged by bombs on 15th June and sank on the 16th after a fine struggle to keep her afloat. (In September the three surviving destroyers took part in the operation that ended in the occupation of the whole of Madagascar.)

On the night of 4th July Auchinleck issued an order that the Eighth Army 'would attack and destroy the enemy in his present position'. That evening he received very valuable reinforcements—the advance-guard of Lieut-General Morshead's 9th Australian Division. These first units were the 2/32nd and 2/43rd Battalions recently arrived from Syria. Next day they dug in on the eastern end of the Ruweisat Ridge, and came under command of XXX Corps. They were soon followed by the remainder of the division. In a highly successful raid along the ridge on the night of 7th-8th July a company of the 2/43rd Battalion, with twenty sappers, destroyed five German guns and inflicted forty casualties for the loss of one man killed and seven wounded. The raid created considerable alarm and caused Rommel to move half his available tank force to the area. On the night of the raid Auchinleck decided to close the gap between the two corps by withdrawing the New Zealand Division from Bab el Qattara in the south and close up on Ruweisat Ridge. When Rommel tried to move into the apparently deserted area his force was checked by light British and South African rearguards. Thereupon Rommel stormed the deserted 'box', employing two armoured divisions, dive bombers and artillery.

Deducing from the New Zealand move that Auchinleck was planning a general withdrawal, Rommel decided to resume the offensive in the south on 10th July—the very day Auchinleck launched an attack in the north. Heavy British artillery fire woke the German commander before dawn that day. It was the covering fire for the 9th Australian Division's attack on the high ground running along the coastal strip north of the main road and west of the Alamein Box. The 2/48th and 2/24th Battalions of the 26th Brigade (Brigadier R. W. Tovell), advancing behind a thunderous barrage, overran the positions held by the Italian *Sabratha* and *Trieste Divisions* and took 1,150 prisoners. It was the first British advance since the battle tide had turned against them on the frontier of Tripoli. Rommel hurried his armour north to the threatened sector and used it in two determined assaults on the Australian flank in the early afternoon and later again in a sustained attack at last light. Each attack was held. Eighteen German tanks were knocked out during the day.

Before dawn on 11th July the 2/24th Battalion, strongly supported by tanks and artillery, established itself on Tel el Eisa Ridge, south of the railway and captured 500 of the enemy without losing a man. But later heavy artillery and mortar fire inflicted severe casualties. The same morning a mixed column of tanks from the Australian 26th Brigade and British 6th Royal Tanks attacked enemy positions on Miteiriya Ridge, south of Tel el Eisa, and destroyed eight Italian field guns and captured 1,024 prisoners before withdrawing.

To Rommel the situation now appeared critical and on 13th July he mounted a heavy armoured attack on the salient the Australians had driven into his positions and against the Alamein Box itself. He used his *21st Armoured Division* and maximum artillery and air support. Both attacks were broken up by British artillery fire.

Next day the Australians became engaged in some of the heaviest fighting they were ever to experience when Rommel, again employing his *21st Armoured Division*, launched an all-out assault on the salient held by the 26th Brigade. German tanks overran some of the Australian weapon-pits in spite of a spirited defence and the two companies of the 2/24th Battalion on Tel el Eisa had to be withdrawn during the night. But when the German armour moved on to attack the 2/48th Battalion positions in the salient ten tanks were knocked out and the rest forced to withdraw. The attacks were resumed next morning on all positions in the salient, but the Australians beat off four separate tank and infantry attacks. Auchinleck now planned to break through the enemy's centre. On the night of the 14th the New Zealand Division and the 5th Indian Brigade attacked northwards, overran the German and Italian forward defences and secured their objectives on the commanding Ruweisat Ridge. This relieved for a time the pressure on the Australians, but next day the Germans counter-attacked with infantry and armour. The New Zealanders failed to gain adequate armoured support and lost 1,405 killed, wounded and captured. Their losses made the infantry sceptical thereafter of ever developing adequate co-operation with the British armour.

On the 16th the fight continued in the Australian salient. The 2/23rd Battalion recaptured the ground abandoned on Tel el Eisa, took 400 prisoners, but then had to retire before a storm of enemy artillery fire. This closed the first phase of the 9th Division's operations at El Alamein. With the aid of its own artillery and machine-guns the division had captured the high ground to the west of the El Alamein Box and had inflicted 2,000 casualties as well as taking 3,708 prisoners.

Next day Brigadier Godfrey's 24th Brigade took over the offensive in the north. The 2/32nd Battalion fought its way on to Makh Khad Ridge, south of Tel el Eisa, and the 2/43rd Battalion, passing through them seized the highest area of Miteiriya Ridge. Both units were driven off by enemy tanks later in the day, but next night the 2/28th Battalion recaptured Makh Khad Ridge, which was held thereafter.

In the last nine days of July Auchinleck mounted two further offensives aimed at compelling Rommel to withdraw his forces. In the first, again launched along the Ruweisat Ridge on the night of 21st-22nd July, the New Zealand Division and an Indian brigade secured their objectives, but once again the British armour failed to give support when German tanks counter-attacked at dawn. One New Zealand brigade and an Indian battalion were overrun.

The newly-arrived 23rd Armoured Brigade, in a gallant but ill-conceived attack soon afterwards on the enemy rear, lost eighty tanks, and a second thrust by the 2nd Armoured Brigade was also ineffective. Attacks by the South Africans and Australians in the north had limited success but a British brigade in the south reached its objective only to be pushed off when the enemy counter-attacked.

In the northern attacks the Australian 26th Brigade struck at the enemy's strongest points—along the coast road leading into his main headquarters and supply centre for the Alamein fighting, and south on to the hotly contested Tel el Eisa feature. In fierce fighting, distinguished by many individual acts of heroism—Private A. S. Gurney of the 2/48th won a Victoria Cross, awarded posthumously—the Australians suffered very heavy casualties, but held on to some of their gains, notably on Tel el Eisa.

A third—and final—attempt by Auchinleck to break through the Axis forces was made along the Miteiriya Ridge. It too started successfully and ended in disaster. On 26th-27th July the Australian 2/28th Battalion drove southwards and established itself on the ridge in an area known as Ruin Ridge, and the British 69th Brigade drove westwards along it. No British tanks arrived on the scene when German tanks overran the positions. The 2/28th Battalion lost two officers and sixty-three other ranks killed and twenty officers and 469 men missing, while the British brigade lost 600 men. Thus ended Auchinleck's attempts to drive off Rommel's forces from Alamein. Neither side was in a position to launch a major attack for more than a month, but Rommel's drive to the Nile had been effectively blocked.

Aircraft from Egypt and Malta and submarines continued to strike at Axis ships carrying vehicles and petrol to Africa, with the result that 38,000 of the 114,000 tons of shipping sent from Italy to Cyrenaica in August were sunk. Rommel reported to the High Command that his supplies were enough only to cover day-to-day needs, and asked for more fighters and anti-aircraft guns. On 18th August he reported that his stocks of fuel were sufficient only to meet normal requirements until the 26th, with none over for the offensive planned to open that day. The attack had to be postponed and when it began on the 30th it was largely because the German Air Force had handed over 1,500 tons of its fuel.

Churchill in London was becoming increasingly critical of the conduct of operations in the Western Desert. On 1st and 2nd July he had had to face a motion of censure in the House of Commons. It was defeated by 475 votes to 25, but next day Churchill announced to the Chief of the General Staff, General Sir Alan Brooke, his intention of flying to Egypt to see the situation for himself. Brooke persuaded him to wait until the position there had resolved itself. On 2nd and 3rd August, however, Churchill flew with a large entourage to Cairo. During the next three days he met the British leaders, visited the battle area and debated with Brooke, Field Marshal Jan Smuts and others what should be done to invigorate the command in the Western Desert. He urged Auchinleck to hasten an offensive, which in Brooke's view, as in Auchinleck's, the Eighth Army was then far from ready to undertake. Finally on 7th August he obtained the British War Cabinet's agreement to a proposal that General Alexander should replace Auchinleck as Commander-in-Chief, that General Gott should command the Eighth Army and that two of Auchinleck's senior staff officers and one of his corps commanders should be replaced. That day, however, Gott, flying to Cairo, was killed. Thereupon Churchill obtained the War Cabinet's approval of the appointment of General B. L. Montgomery to command the Eighth Army.

On the night of 30th August Rommel made his last attempt to break through to the Nile Delta. His main operation was to be a deep penetration of the British left flank with the German armour which was then to invade the British supply area. Alexander and Montgomery had anticipated such an attempt and had strongly fortified Alam el Halfa, south of Ruweisat Ridge, with infantry and tanks and supported by field and anti-tank guns. Rommel preceded his main thrust on 30th August with diversionary raids on the Australian positions in the north and against the 9th Indian Brigade on Ruweisat Ridge. The attacks were driven off with considerable losses to the enemy, though in the Ruweisat attack the German *Ramcke Brigade* did succeed in piercing the Indian defences.

As the main enemy force was assembling for the attack at dusk on 30th August it came under heavy attack from the air. The attackers were then delayed by bad going, unexpected minefields and renewed air attacks. Rommel ordered the attack to be switched to the western end of Alam el Halfa, not the more distant eastern end, as planned. It thus ran into the main concentration of British armour and made little progress. That night and throughout the next day the enemy were attacked by British bombers and artillery. Rommel broke off the offensive and went over to the defensive. Then on the night of 3rd September the New Zealand Division and the 132nd British Brigade attacked to close the gap Rommel had made in the British defences.

In this partially successful attack the New Zealanders suffered 275 casualties and the raw 132nd Brigade 697. But the air offensive decided the issue and Rommel withdrew to the protection of the British minefield where Montgomery, busy preparing for his own offensive, let him stay. The Germans had lost 1,859 men, the Italians 1,051 and forty-nine tanks had been destroyed. British losses were 1,750 and sixty-seven tanks. But the German General F. W. von Mellenthin, of Rommel's staff, later wrote that the German defeat at Alam el Halfa was 'the turning point of the desert war, and the first of the long series of defeats on every front which foreshadowed the collapse of Germany'.

While this battle was proceeding in the south the Australian 9th Division, employing the 20th Brigade, launched its diversionary attack, code-named BULIMBA, in the north.

Moving off before dawn on 1st September Lieut-Colonel R. W. G. Ogle's 2/15th Battalion crossed the German minefield through gaps made by the 2/13th Field Company of engineers and captured the objective from which a raiding force built around a squadron of the 40th Royal Tank Regiment was to cut the Axis supply route to the south. In heroic fighting (in which four men won Distinguished Conduct Medals), the 2/15th established a firm base, but before the tanks got under way the enemy counter-attacked in force, and the battalion withdrew under intense fire in text-book order.

Australian War Memorial

El Alamein area in September 1942. Australian positions near the sea.

Throughout September and the first weeks of October the Eighth Army was rapidly building up its strength for the planned El Alamein offensive. By 23rd October 7,029 tanks were ready for battle, with 200 replacements standing by and about 1,000 in the workshops. Enemy tanks numbered some 600. Infantry, artillery, transport of all kinds and bomber and fighter aircraft had been pouring into the battle zone in numbers never previously available to a British commander in this war.

The whole of the Eighth Army had been carefully trained for every role it was expected to play. Montgomery had evolved a plan differing widely from those prepared for all previous desert offensives. Instead of armour being employed to break through on an inland flank and drive into the enemy's supply centres, the main thrust this time was to be made by infantry driving forward in the coastal sector where each desert army had a firm flank on the sea and used the coast road as its principal supply line. After the infantry had crushed all opposition sent against it, and had opened lanes through the enemy defences, right up to the gun lines, the British armour would drive through, meet the surviving enemy armour 'on ground of its own choosing' and destroy it.

Elaborate steps were taken to deceive the enemy into believing that the main attack would take place in the south and much later than planned. In the north effective measures were taken to camouflage the build up of forces, and down south half-completed dummy pipe lines and other preparations were clearly visible from the air and desert vantage points.

For the great assault the main attack was to be made by Lieut-General W. H. C. Ramsden's XXX Corps, using four infantry divisions—the 9th Australian, 51st Highland, 2nd New Zealand and 1st South African, stationed in that order from north to south. On the first night they were to drive a corridor six miles wide and four miles deep through the Axis defences. Along two corridors, which the assault divisions would clear through the minefields, the 1st and 10th Armoured Divisions of the X Armoured Corps would later advance to deal with the enemy armour. The enemy guns, it was optimistically hoped, would be reached the first night. The Australians, in addition to their frontal advance to the west, were to establish a firm front facing north in the heavily defended enemy area near the coast road. Lieut-General Sir Brian Horrocks's XIII Corps, comprising the 7th Armoured and the 44th and 50th Infantry Divisions, was to undertake two thrusts in the south using the 44th Division and the 1st Free French Brigade. If a breach were forced the 7th Armoured Division was to exploit it but was not to become too heavily embroiled.

The British had superiority in tanks (about 1,100 to some 600) and in artillery (900 to 500 field and medium guns). The enemy line was held by seven divisions, including five Italian. In their rear the German and Italian armour was divided into battle groups spaced evenly across the whole front. General Stumme was in command when the battle opened, Rommel having gone to Europe for medical treatment.

In the period of preparation for the offensive the main tasks of the air force were to protect the British supply lines, attack the enemy's supply lines, gain an ascendancy over the German air force and continue to attack the enemy's land forces. The seven R.A.A.F. squadrons in the Middle East were Nos. 3, 450 and 451 armed with fighters or fighter-bombers and Nos. 454, 458, 459 and 462 with bombers or torpedo-bombers. (However, some R.A.F. squadrons in the area contained more Australians than two of the nominally R.A.A.F. squadrons.)

Enemy shipping maintaining the supply line between Italy and Africa were under frequent naval and air attack. In September 34,000 tons were sunk, and in October the score rose to 50,000 tons. Aircraft accounted for about half the total.

As the time for the opening of the offensive approached the German-Italian supply position became worse and worse and British air superiority improved. By 19th October the enemy had only enough fuel for eleven days.

On the night of 23rd October the whole of the Eighth Army was mustered between the sea and the Qattara Depression. All afternoon the steady throb of the army's transport filled the air as men, munitions and supplies were moved forward, but the sound had died away after nightfall. The night was clear, with a brilliant moon just one night from the full. When men talked there was excitement in their voices—elation mixed perhaps with fear of what was to come. In their front-line positions the men of the assault units were served a hot meal and then in the silence that fell over the battlefield they followed the marking tapes to the start-lines for the attack.

On the extreme right of the front the 24th Brigade of the 9th Australian Division had been allotted a semi-static role, holding the front line from the Tel el Eisa feature to the coast, but would stage a diversionary attack along the coast as its two sister brigades, the 26th and 20th, drove due west through the minefields on the right of the Eighth Army's advance.

As the moment for the opening of one of the great battles of history drew near flights of British bombers surged across the night sky, but the sounds soon faded. Then exactly at 9.40 p.m. the whole wide arc of the battlefield was rimmed with flickering yellow light as some 900 medium and field guns opened up against the enemy gun lines. Seconds elapsed before the first detonations reached the troops waiting on their start-lines. They could have believed they were watching a silent display of summer lightning, until the thunder burst upon their ear drums in a swiftly mounting crescendo. For fifteen minutes this counter-battery bombardment continued, then stopped as suddenly as it had started.

There followed five minutes of eerie silence while the men of the Eighth Army awaited the signal to advance. At 10 p.m. it came. Two parallel searchlight beams reaching high into the moonlit vault of the sky swung inwards and crossed. Instantly the guns belched fire again with a barrage of unbelievable intensity. The floor of the desert shook, vehicles shuddered without pause, men's bodies and their very voices quivered under the mighty shock waves. This time the barrage crept forward ahead of the infantry to assist them on to their objectives.

The first to cross the Australian start-lines were the 2/24th Battalion of Brigadier D. A. Whitehead's 26th Brigade on the right and the 2/17th and 2/15th Battalions of Brigadier W. J. V. Windeyer's 20th Brigade on the left. Almost immediately they ran into machine-gun and mortar-fire as they threaded their way through mines and booby traps. At the enemy wire the men were held up for a few minutes until the barrage lifted and moved on ahead of them through the enemy minefields. Where the barrage had failed to smash down the wire engineers blew gaps through it with bangalore

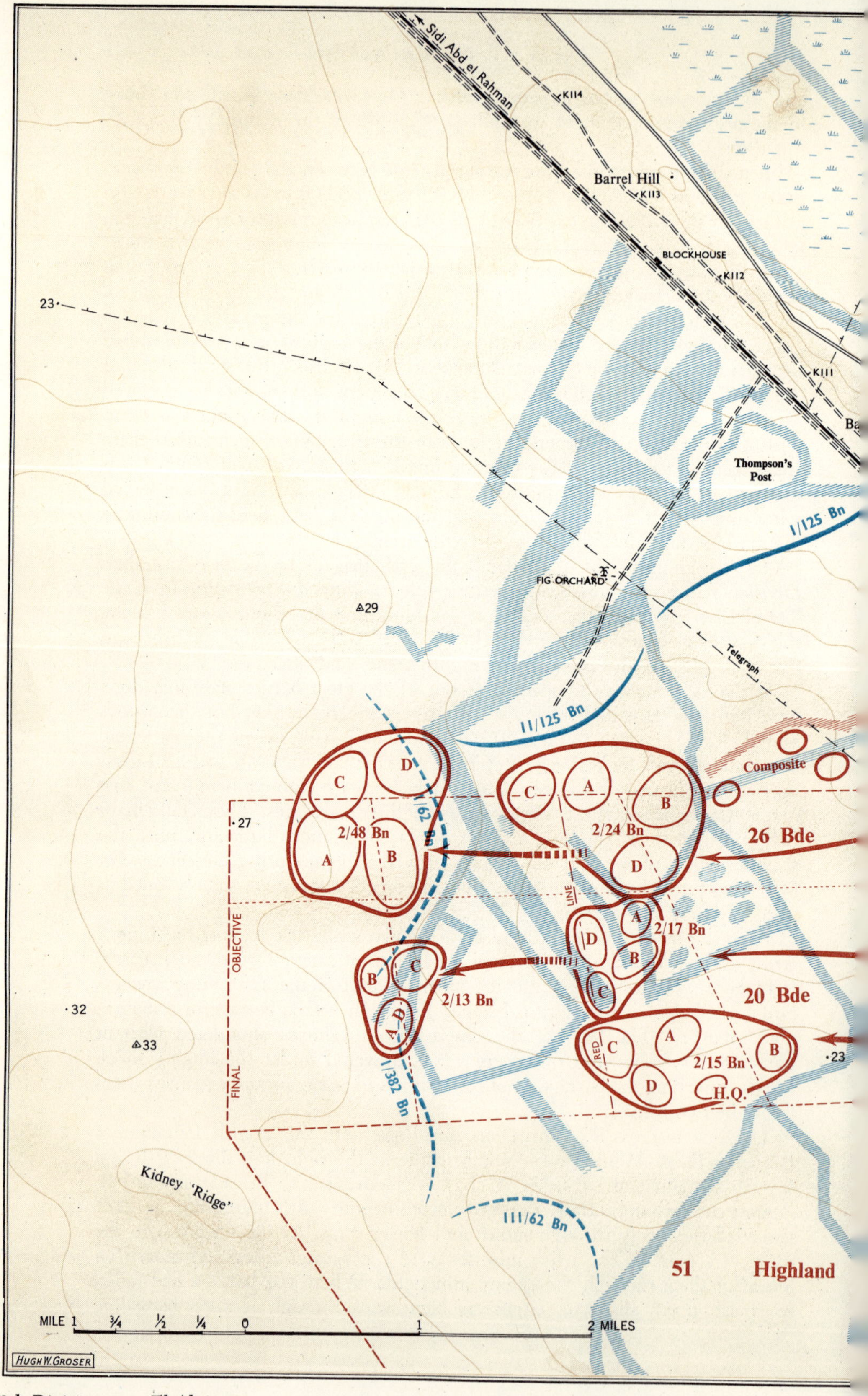

9th Division area, El Alamein

Cloverleaf
Egg
Mersa el Hamra
111/125 Bn
25
MINEFIELDS
White Knoll
C
33
A
2/28 Bn
K109
K108
B
D
K107
23
B
A
26
24 Bde H.Q.
CUTTING
B
24
Tel el Eisa
A
2/43 Bn
K106
2/32 Bn
D
Tel el Eisa
D
DIAMOND
ROUTE
K105
C
K104
LINE
Line
K103
C
2/23 Bn
ROUTE
SQUARE
Assembly Area
K102
Makh Khad Ridge
23
Cairn
K101
El Alamein
TRACK
MINEFIELDS
22
QATTARA
Div

Australian War Memorial

El Alamein, 9.40 p.m. on 23rd October 1942. The silence of the desert was broken by the British Eighth Army's artillery barrage at the opening of the great battle which was to defeat the Axis forces at El Alamein and finally to drive them from North Africa.

torpedoes, and the infantry passed through and started methodically mopping up the enemy posts. In the smoke and dust raised by the bombardment, visibility was limited to a few yards, but lines of tracer shells fired from the rear as guides helped to keep the attackers on their correct line of advance. Shortly after midnight the three battalions had reached their objectives and dug in. They had achieved a considerable success at a total cost of twenty-four dead and 140 wounded or unaccounted for. Indeed along the whole of the XXX Corps front the first objectives had been taken in about two hours without great opposition. The second phase of this opening night's attack was to prove more difficult. The assaulting divisions were soon to discover that the first line of defence, which on the British maps had been shown as bristling with obstacles and weapons of every kind, was in fact comparatively lightly held as an outer line to cover the main line of defence sited in rear at considerable depth.

As the battalions assigned the task of achieving the second—and final—phase of the night's attack were moving up to pass through the foremost battalions the artillery continued pounding the advanced enemy positions. An hour was allowed for the second wave of attackers to move into position. In the 9th Division's sector only one battalion in each brigade was employed in the final phase—the 2/48th Battalion on the right and the 2/13th on the left.

In the face of stiff opposition the 2/48th (Lieut-Colonel H. H. Hammer) fought its way to its objective, which it reached at 3.45 a.m. During this advance Sergeant W. H. Kibby attacked an enemy post which was holding up the advance, killing three with his Tommy-gun and accepting the surrender of twelve others.

Having penetrated 3,900 yards into enemy territory from the brigade start-line the 2/48th Battalion, like the 2/24th in its rear, had an open right flank which had to be protected as well as the front. Both battalions stationed companies facing north to protect this flank and linked up on the right with a composite force, commanded by Lieut-Colonel E. Macarthur-Onslow, which was in turn linked with the 24th Brigade to extend the northern flank to the coast.

On the left of the advance the 2/13th Battalion, having no open flank to protect, had to advance on a front thrice as wide as the 2/48th's—2,400 yards as against 800—and to the same depth. The strength of the enemy defences made the task beyond the capacity of the infantry, but the attack was to have been made with the 40th Royal Tank Regiment in support. The main enemy minefield in that area was expected to be about 250 yards deep, but it proved to be almost 1,600 yards. Despite Herculean efforts the engineers were unable to clear lanes through it in time for the tanks so the 2/13th attacked on time without their support. As the companies fought their way deeper into enemy territory opposition stiffened and soon they were taking very heavy casualties. Wounded officers and N.C.O's continued leading their men until they were killed or again wounded and put out of the battle. In one company the few survivors were forced back under their only remaining leader to the intermediate objective, where they were absorbed in another company. Dawn approached before the 2/13th could reach its final objective, and the companies were ordered to dig in where they were. At daylight the tanks finally got through and destroyed some posts threatening the 2/13th's positions.

While this fighting was going on the 24th Brigade carried out a series of successful diversionary attacks on both sides of the road and railway in the coastal sector.

The X Corps, which was to have effected the armoured break-through if the minefields were cleared before daylight, had assigned the northern corridor through the 9th Australian and 51st Highland Divisions' bridgehead to the 1st Armoured Division and the southern corridor through the 2nd New Zealand Division's bridgehead across the Miteiriya Ridge to the 10th Armoured Division. The sappers, toiling mightily, had cleared the southern corridor by 6.30 a.m. but the northern corridor could not be cleared in time, and the armoured sortie did not therefore take place. This was extremely unfortunate for the British, for at that stage the German forces were without direction, as the barrage had dislocated their communications and the German commander, General Stumme, was missing; he was later found to have died of a heart attack. Further, the German armour was dispersed across the desert, the German command still being unaware of the intended point for the British breakthrough. The thrust of the XIII Corps in the south had had only limited success.

Fighting and toiling throughout the day and night of the 24th and into the early hours of the 25th the British completed the consolidation of all the final objectives and cleared the corridors, but the enemy had by that time reacted and formed a new front. The British armour still failed to debouch, though armoured clashes developed at various points along the new front. Both sides sustained tank losses which the enemy, because of his inferiority in tank numbers, could afford less than the British. However, though the first night's attack had laid the foundation of the victory to come, it had not succeeded in its immediate objective. The armour had not been able to break out and its commanders were understandably reluctant to advance down the cleared corridors through the minefields into territory which still harboured guns and other anti-tank defences. Those tank brigades that debouched into the desert beyond the cleared lanes in the early hours of the 25th had to withdraw later in the day after suffering considerable losses, though they knocked out many German tanks.

On the Australian front soon after sunrise on the 24th the German *15th Armoured Division* moved in to stage the first counter-attack on the bridgehead. Three Australian field regiments, the 7th Medium Regiment and some British Sherman tanks engaged them. German lorried infantry entered the battle but the enemy finally fell back, leaving several tanks burning. Some Shermans were also knocked out. The 2/13th Battalion, still short of its final objective, was practically without officers. At 4 p.m. that day its commanding officer, Lieut-Colonel R. W. N. Turner, was mortally wounded and his adjutant seriously wounded. Major G. E. Colvin was sent forward to take command and he then obtained permission for the other left-out-of-battle officers of the battalion to join him. Starting at 2 a.m. on the 25th, the 2/13th and 2/17th Battalions, supported by the 40th Royal Tank Regiment, completed the 20th Brigade's task by fighting their way forward to the final objective and digging in.

Not all the tank battles on 25th October took place in the course of the abortive attempt of the British armour to break out to 'the ground of its own choosing'. Armoured clashes occurred when the enemy launched counter-attacks on the infantry holding the bridgehead. On the 20th Brigade's front artillery and British tanks smashed a morning attack by twelve German tanks followed by lorried infantry. In the afternoon tank attacks were launched almost simultaneously on the 2/17th and 2/13th Battalions. On the 2/17th's front fifteen enemy tanks were knocked out by artillery and tank fire, but the attackers then laid a smoke screen through which they advanced against the 2/13th. Colvin instructed the anti-tank gunners to hold the fire of their concealed 2-pounder guns until the tanks were within short range. Sergeant A. R. Bentley, commanding the anti-tank platoon, waited until the leading tanks were within forty yards of him and then fired, whereupon the other anti-tank guns opened up and the first wave, all hit, halted. Seventeen tanks were destroyed and the others drew back to assist the enemy infantry attack which followed. This attack, which was strongly pressed, caused severe casualties but was finally smashed. That evening Field Marshal Rommel arrived back from Europe to resume his command.

Montgomery now withdrew his armour behind the front, except on the north of the XXX Corps front, and in the far south ordered the XIII Corps to go over entirely to the defensive. He decided to put his 'crumbling' policy into effect, starting in the Australian sector. The aim was to employ the British artillery superiority both in conjunction with infantry attacks and in resisting counter-attacks to weaken the German and Italian defences and thus facilitate the planned break-out of the armour. There followed a week of bitter infantry fighting. The main brunt of it, which increased in intensity daily to a climax on 1st November, fell on the 9th Australian Division.

The task now given to the Australians was the tentative portion of the original El Alamein battle plan of cutting off and capturing the enemy between the XXX Corps' northern flank and the sea. To open the attack the 26th Brigade, already facing north as well as west, was to drive three-quarters of a mile northwards into the enemy salient to capture Trig 29, the highest ground in the area, and the slope that ran north-east from the Trig down to a feature called the Fig Orchard. Across part of the ground to be captured ran a switch defence line leading through the Fig Orchard to Thompson's Post, the scene of bitter fighting in the days to come. The attack on Trig 29 was to be carried out by the 2/48th, that on the Fig Orchard by the 2/24th. The successful conclusion of the 9th Division's task would extend the division's bridgehead to a three mile frontage on the west and to a two-and-a-quarter mile frontage on the north.

In an attack on the 2/48th Battalion's front at dusk on the 25th several Germans were killed and two German commanders were captured. One commander carried a map of the area to be attacked by the Australians that night, showing the enemy's minefields and the disposition of his troops—information that was highly valuable.

The attack opened at midnight with an artillery barrage. Pressing forward through heavy defensive fire two companies of the 2/48th stopped as planned 200 yards short of Trig 29 while carriers with another company aboard charged through to the dusty smoke-shrouded objectives where the infantry leaped among the enemy and overcame them with bayonets, grenades and small-arms fire. Advancing with the left-hand company Private P. E. Gratwick, a 40-year-old West Australian prospector, charged an enemy post with a rifle and bayonet in one hand and a grenade in the other. Throwing one grenade into the post, then another, he jumped in among the surviving defenders with his bayonet and killed them all, including a complete mortar crew. He then charged a second post but was killed by machine-gun fire as he reached it. He was posthumously awarded the Victoria Cross—one of the four V.C's to be won by members of the 2/48th Battalion in the war. All four men were killed in action. The 2/24th Battalion had the difficult task of advancing 3,000 yards along a line of enemy posts, one of the advanced companies moving down the left of the enemy wire and the other to the right of it. They captured the Fig Orchard post after heavy fighting, with severe losses on both sides; one company, overshooting its objective, reached the perimeter of Thompson's Post before the fourteen survivors of the sixty-three who had started were withdrawn to the Fig Orchard position. Lieut-Colonel C. G. Weir, commanding the 2/24th, found the forward companies surrounded by German dead, but at 4 a.m. decided the battalion was too depleted to hold such an extended front and withdrew the forward elements 1,000 yards back from the Fig Orchard, while the left company linked up with the 2/48th. Macarthur-Onslow's composite force on the right, which was also to have advanced its line to conform with the 2/24th's advance, had been held up by heavy fire from Thompson's Post, and now found a gap between its left flank and the 2/24th. The Australians were not left long in undisturbed possession of their newly-won positions. On the morning of the 26th they were heavily bombarded by a concentration of German artillery, but Lieutenant R. W. J. Menzies of the 2/7th Field Regiment, who maintained an observation post with little cover on top of Trig 29 for several days, had a view of 5,000 yards in every direction, and brought down fire that broke up several enemy counter-attacks. An attack on Trig 29 itself by 300 enemy infantry during the afternoon was dispersed by gunfire. The 2/48th had three field regiments and one medium regiment of artillery on call and was able to defend itself with devastating fire.

During the previous night of violent action the 20th Brigade, which had taken over the 26th Brigade's front, was attacked by tanks and infantry. Against the 2/13th Battalion the Germans followed up by dark the daylight attack that had failed earlier, but they were again routed, this time losing three tanks and two tracked troop carriers when they were within sixty yards of the Australians. Artillery and infantry-weapon fire broke up the attack. On the 2/17th Battalion front twelve enemy tanks appeared at dawn on a ridge to the north-west where they remained all day harassing the Australians.

That evening the South African and New Zealand divisions extended their penetration while at 11 p.m. the 7th Motor Brigade attacked Kidney Ridge, in front of the right flank of the 51st Highland Division, near the boundary with the 9th Division, and captured part of it. It was from this region that the armoured break-out later took place.

The 27th October was also marked by very fierce fighting. A pre-dawn attack on the 2/13th Battalion by infantry assisted by fifteen tanks was dispersed by a concentrated artillery bombardment with an infantry fire-curtain in front of it. A second attack was also dispersed. But it was on the Australians' new northern front that Rommel threw the main weight of his armour, artillery and infantry that day. While forming up for the attack near the Sidi Rahman mosque on the coast road in the afternoon the enemy concentration was pounded by British bombers, but an attack by an enemy infantry battalion supported by a heavy German artillery barrage was launched against the 2/48th Battalion on Trig 29. The artillery supporting the 2/48th put down a wall of fire and the battalion joined in with mortars, machine-guns and rifles. The enemy were driven back with very heavy losses. The German left wing came up against the 2/24th with tanks and infantry, but there too the attackers were dispersed with heavy losses. An attack on the 2/17th was also beaten off. Rommel later wrote of the attacks on the Trig 29 positions: 'Attacks were launched by elements of the *15th Armoured Division*, the armoured *Littorio Division* and a *Bersaglieri Battalion*, supported by all the local artillery and anti-aircraft. The British resisted desperately. Rivers of blood were poured out over miserable strips of land.' However, the enemy armour forced the British 2/Rifle Brigade off Kidney Ridge that night, but only after the anti-tank guns supporting the riflemen had knocked out seventy tanks and self-propelled guns.

On the 28th the British stood on the defensive during the day while regrouping, but at 10 p.m. the 9th Australian Division again struck northwards on the right flank towards the coast road. Brigadier Windeyer's 20th Brigade opened the attack with the 2/13th Battalion driving along the Switch Line through the Fig Orchard to the outskirts of Thompson's Post—the area from which the 2/24th had been withdrawn on the morning of the 26th—and the 2/15th Battalion taking over from the 2/48th and striking north from Trig 29.

The 2/13th was an exhausted and depleted unit, with its rifle companies down to thirty-five of all ranks. It had been attacking and beating off counter-attacks for five sleepless nights and had been on the march throughout the preceding night. Forced to advance on a narrow front because of its reduced numbers the battalion inevitably left unsubdued enemy posts on the left flank, which caused casualties among the Australians after they had advanced to their objective—across ground strewn with anti-personnel mines. A patrol of ten men led by Lieutenant S. C. F. North was hit by a mortar bomb which killed or seriously wounded all except North. North returned and organised another patrol which brought back the casualties while a patrol under Corporal R. V. McKellar moved through a minefield and attacked with grenades two machine-gun crews who were covering the troublesome mortar crew. This patrol then rushed the mortar crew, overcame them and returned with the weapons.

As the 2/15th was forming up for its attack on the left it was heavily shelled and its commanding officer, Lieut-Colonel C. K. M. Magno, and his adjutant were wounded, Magno mortally. Advancing through heavy machine-gun and mortar fire the battalion secured its objectives. In the attack the counted Italian dead numbered eighty-nine and 130 German and Italian prisoners were taken. Soon after dawn two enemy tractors towing anti-tank guns approached the 2/15th's new positions and the guns, with twenty-two Germans, were captured.

The 2/23rd Battalion (Lieut-Colonel B. Evans), which was to have driven through between the other two battalions to the coast road with the support of the 46th British Royal Tank Regiment, had mounted its assault company on the tanks, but the tanks missed the marked gaps in the Australian minefields and became immobilised at the start. The tanks came under heavy fire which caused severe losses among the infantry mounted on them and among the tank commanders. A warrant-officer rallied the survivors of the assault company and led them forward without the tanks to capture the foremost enemy positions and take forty prisoners. But elsewhere this attack with armour and infantry developed into a costly muddle. Evans collected about sixty or seventy of his men and after a hard fight captured the main German position with its six guns and 160 men. On his right a group of infantry, with fifteen tanks, unknown to Evans headed for the coast railway but nine of the tanks were knocked out and many of the infantry hit. Completely out of touch with the Royal Tank Regiment, and with few men left, Evans finally dug in 1,000 yards forward of the start-line. The battalion had lost twenty-nine killed, 172 wounded and six missing. The casualties included two majors, four captains and ten lieutenants.

At dawn on the 29th the 2/13th Battalion was heavily shelled in its isolated position. Three shells penetrated the dugouts of battalion headquarters, wounding Colonel Colvin, killing his adjutant and wounding his anti-tank officer. But it was on the 2/15th and 2/17th that the enemy's main efforts were directed that day. Fourteen enemy tanks stood hull down near Trig 29 and poured heavy fire into the Australian positions all day. But repeated attacks on the Australians by tanks and infantry were repelled by artillery and infantry fire which inflicted severe losses on the enemy. That night Brigadier Windeyer moved forward the 2/23rd Battalion, which had been placed under his command, to fill the gap between the 2/15th and the 2/13th.

These operations caused Rommel to concentrate even more forces in the north, and in the next four days the Australian sector became the focal area of the battle. The 9th Division was called on to maintain the relentless pressure on the enemy 'to eat the guts out of them', as Montgomery had expressed it, and open the way for the British armoured break-out farther to the south. In London, Churchill was becoming highly critical of Montgomery's apparent inactivity.

General Morshead attacked again on the night of 30th October, employing four battalions under the command of Brigadier Whitehead, with the intention of cutting the coastal road, sending two battalions eastwards along it to break through the enemy front-line from the rear, and then having another battalion turn north and drive to the coast, thus penning in the enemy between it and the 24th Brigade, which was still holding the coastal sector.

The 2/32nd Battalion (Lieut-Colonel J. W. Balfe) opened the attack, covered by a heavy barrage, at 10 p.m. and reached the railway (the intermediate objective) in good time, capturing 175 prisoners, mostly Germans, in the course of its advance. The battalion then moved on to the road in the face of stronger opposition but left two companies south of the railway to guard the left flank while engineers made a gap through the twelve foot high railway embankment to enable supply vehicles to pass through. The 2/3rd Pioneer Battalion (Lieut-Colonel A. V. Gallasch), the 2/48th and the 2/24th moved off at intervals and fought their way to positions near the 2/32nd, where they dug in shortly after midnight while preparing to move forward about their respective tasks. The area in which the battalions had gathered was a wide depression which the troops quickly named the Saucer. In the two days to follow the Saucer was to become the focal point in the bloody struggle between the two armies. The enemy had begun closing in by midnight and casualties were mounting among the Australians as the Pioneers toiled to complete the gap in the railway embankment.

At 1 a.m. the 2/48th and 2/24th Battalions left their start-lines. They were charged with the desperate task of fighting their way eastwards down the road and railway for 2,250 yards through the rear of the recently-reinforced enemy positions. They advanced into a receding British barrage laid down by guns massed farther east. After a week of almost continuous fighting the combined strength of these two battalions had been reduced from a total of some 1,300 officers and men to a meagre 450 between them. Now they became involved in some of the most bitter fighting of the battle. They stormed through machine-gun, mortar and 88-mm gun fire to subdue post after post, all of them stoutly defended. Companies were reduced to a few men without officers, but they were rallied by N.C.O's to join with other groups to continue the fight. On the left of the attack the 2/48th reached its final objective, where Sergeant Kibby, whose gallantry in this and earlier fighting could not have been surpassed, was killed attacking the last enemy post blocking the advance.[1] On the right the 2/24th found its final objective, Thompson's Post, strongly held, contrary to Intelligence reports. The depleted battalion, now deprived of artillery support, was unable to press on with the attack. Independently the two battalions had to retire to the Saucer as the last day of October dawned. Captain E. P. Harty led back the fifty-four

[1] He was posthumously awarded the Victoria Cross.

survivors of the 2/24th and Lieut-Colonel Hammer, himself wounded, brought back the forty-one men of the 2/48th still on their feet. Territorially their mission had failed but the division had captured 544 prisoners and a formidable array of weapons.

The 2/3rd Pioneer Battalion in its drive to the coast before dawn on the 31st was halted 1,200 yards from its objective. Later in the day its positions were overrun by enemy tanks and the survivors had to retire to the Saucer.

The Saucer position, by then the most hotly contested area of the whole battlefield, had been reinforced by a squadron of the 40th Royal Tank Regiment and a Rhodesian-manned battery of 6-pounder anti-tank guns which was attached to the Australian 2/3rd Anti-Tank Regiment. During the course of the day three enemy attacks with tanks and infantry were thrown back, with tank losses on both sides. In one German tank attack a company of the 2/32nd Battalion was overrun and most of the survivors of the company made prisoners. The Australian and Rhodesian anti-tank gunners suffered losses but they knocked out several of the attacking tanks.

During the early hours of 1st November Brigadier Godfrey of the 24th Brigade took over command of the units in the Saucer from Brigadier Whitehead. The 2/28th Battalion, rebuilt by Lieut-Colonel J. Loughrey after the Ruin Ridge disaster, relieved the 2/24th and the 2/43rd Battalion (Lieut-Colonel W. J. Wain) relieved the 2/48th.

At dawn the newcomers to the Saucer, who had taken up improvised positions in the darkness, found numerous enemy positions sited all round them at distances of between 800 and 1,000 yards. The enemy opened up with small-arms, mortars, 88-mm guns firing air-burst shells and a variety of field guns. At 10 a.m. British Intelligence intercepted a message from Rommel ordering his *21st Armoured* and *90th Light Divisions* to attack down the road and railway and capture the Australian position. At midday the attack began through clouds of dust and smoke raised by the shelling, aerial bombing and movement of tanks. Enemy assaults were maintained throughout the afternoon and well into the night, but every attack crumbled in the face of the spirited defence of the 9th Division. That evening, after about a half hour of continuous fire, an enemy shell scored a direct hit on the 24th Brigade's tactical headquarters, mortally wounding Brigadier Godfrey and killing three other officers.

Late that night all the divisional line communications were cut by British tanks moving through the area, but the battle continued to rage. It died down at 2.30 a.m. on 2nd November. An intense British barrage had started farther south signalling the beginning of Operation SUPERCHARGE. The long-awaited break-out was under way.

The 9th Division had completed its vital 'crumbling' mandate of drawing upon itself as much of the enemy's fighting strength as possible and destroying what it could. In the next few days patrols from the Saucer went out over a wide range of country to try to intercept enemy groups retiring from the east and north but with little success. They lacked the support to prevent the organised withdrawal that was then taking place in that sector.,

From 26th October, the night the Australians started their drive northwards and brought the whole weight of Rommel's *Africa Corps* against them, General Montgomery had been regrouping his forces to create a reserve for the break-out. Now, while the Axis reserves were concentrated against the

9th Division, Montgomery made his thrust through the bridgehead originally secured by the 9th Division on the opening night of the battle. General Freyberg had been given command of the infantry break-out operation, using his own New Zealand Division but employing two British brigades—the 151st and 152nd—and the Maori Battalion as infantry. The 9th Armoured Brigade, also under command, was to pass through the infantry after they had reached their objective. The attack started at 1.5 a.m. on 2nd November, with a supporting barrage fired by 192 guns, and an additional 168 guns shelling positions in front and on the flanks of the attack. By dawn the infantry had reached their objectives, lengthening the old bridgehead by 6,000 yards on a front of 4,000 yards. On the right the Maori Battalion had taken its objective west of Trig 29 and on the left battalions of the 51st Highland Division had captured an enemy strongpoint on Kidney Ridge.

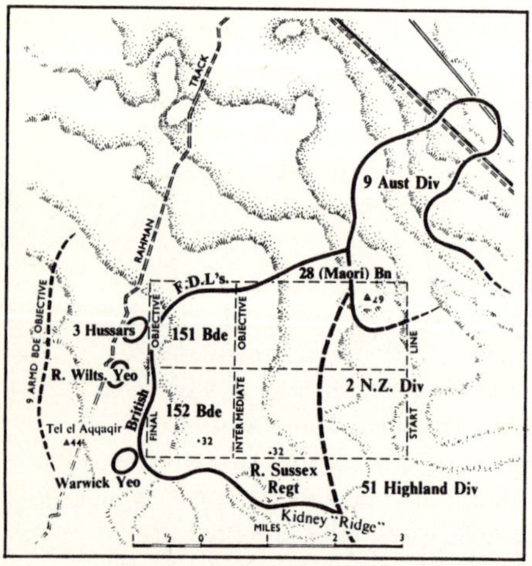

The next moves were for the 9th Armoured Brigade to drive on a further 2,000 yards beyond the infantry objectives to reach the enemy's strong Rahman track defences, where it was to hold the way open for the 1st Armoured Division to pass through, cross the Rahman track and defeat the enemy armour.

But all did not go according to plan. By the time the 9th Armoured Brigade had reached the infantry objectives it had lost thirty-eight of the 132 tanks with which it had started the battle, and in a series of heroic battles beyond the bridgehead (in the course of which its three regiments destroyed at least thirty-five guns) it ran into deadly fire from more deeply-sited enemy guns and from tanks of the German *21st Armoured Division*, around Tel el Aqqaqir, and lost a further seventy-five of its tanks. It had badly dented the enemy gun line, but had not broken through it. The 2nd Armoured Brigade, the spearhead of the 1st Armoured Division, arrived in the area too late to help the 9th Armoured and was itself badly mauled by the German armour. The enemy counter-attacked that afternoon—as Montgomery had hoped they would—and in a battle with the 1st Armoured Division that continued until nightfall seventy-seven German and forty Italian tanks were knocked out. The British tank losses were higher, but the Axis forces could afford their losses less than the British. The armoured cars of the Royal Dragoons succeeded in breaking through and went on a rampage, destroying dumps and vehicles and cutting telephone lines behind the enemy front.

However, the Axis command had succeeded in containing the British armour for the time being, and some British commanders were wondering if they were ever going to achieve the break-out. The truth, as known later, was that the battles fought by the armoured regiments debouching from the bridgehead that day had rendered it certain that the enemy must eventually break. In fact Rommel decided that night to start withdrawing to Fuka, some fifty miles to the west of the Rahman line, but the next afternoon, just after the withdrawal had been set in motion, Rommel received a personal message from Hitler ordering him to stand fast until 'victory or death'.

At dusk on 3rd November the 51st Highland Division launched an attack to breach the Rahman line south of Tel el Aqqaqir. It received a check in the centre, but in an attack starting at 1.30 a.m. on 4th November the 5th Indian Brigade, attached to the Highlanders, reached the Rahman track along a front of four miles, and burst through it on the south. At dawn the Argyll and Sutherland Highlanders captured Tel el Aqqaqir and the Axis defence ring had been sprung open. British armour and infantry poured through the gaps. Beyond the Rahman track the two German armoured divisions making their last stand checked the British 1st Armoured Division, but the 7th Armoured Division smashed the *XX Italian Corps*, including the *Ariete Division*. About midday the commander of the German *Africa Corps*, General von Thoma, was captured. By late afternoon the enemy was in full retreat. At 5.30 p.m. Rommel authorised a general withdrawal, despite Hitler's order. That was the end of the Battle of El Alamein and the beginning of the pursuit.

That morning the 9th Division found that only enemy stragglers remained in the coast salient, but the enemy was still holding a line west of the Australian positions. During the evening the Australians moved their front close to the new German line. While officers of the 2/43rd Battalion were holding a conference in connection with this move a shell landed in their midst, killing three and wounding four—the last Australian casualties in the battle.

At dawn on the 5th it was found that the enemy had gone from the 9th Division's front. A carrier patrol from the 2/15th Battalion followed up swiftly and captured 143 Germans waiting for transport at Sidi Abd el Rahman. A company of the 2/15th then occupied the high ground around the abandoned German headquarters. The division's cavalry moved on to El Daba, capturing 200 prisoners on the way. Divisional engineers cleared the two landing grounds at Daba, in addition to five others between Daba and Rahman, and that evening the cavalry handed Daba over to the Highlanders who had come up from the south-east. About the same time the 2/15th reported the capture of the last prisoners taken by the division—five Germans and three Italians.

The Australians had completed their last battle operation in North Africa. Of the German and Italian armies, the force that now remained and was in flight comprised little more than one composite division and fewer than 150 tanks (of which seventy were Italian and were soon abandoned along the road). The Eighth Army's losses in winning the battle were 13,560 killed, wounded or missing. About 27,000 prisoners were taken, 450 tanks destroyed or abandoned, and much equipment captured.

In the next two days of the pursuit, in which the 9th Division did not take part, 5,000 more prisoners were taken and thirty more tanks destroyed, but Montgomery's attempt to cut off the main body of the retreating force was frustrated partly by rain, which fell on the afternoon and night of 6th November and bogged down the British transport and armour in the desert, and partly by inability to supply petrol at the rate needed to sustain the advance.

The Australian division's losses in the Battle of El Alamein between 23rd October and 4th November totalled 2,694, including 620 dead, 1,944 wounded and 130 taken prisoner. For the whole period of the Alamein operations from 7th July the losses were 5,809, including 1,225 dead, 3,638 wounded and 946 taken prisoner.

During the battle Axis shipping had suffered further disastrous losses. Bombers sank a tanker and a transport on 26th October, and a submarine sank a second tanker that day. On the 28th torpedo aircraft sank a tanker. Of eleven ships sent to Tobruk in this period seven were sunk and three seriously damaged. The enemy now ceased trying to land supplies at Tobruk.

No. 239 Wing, which included Nos. 3 and 450 Squadrons R.A.A.F., took part in the pursuit, and displayed the remarkable mobility that the Desert Air Force had now achieved. Despite the rain and the traffic congestion the Australian squadrons, for example, were established at Daba on 6th November, Sidi Haneish on the 9th, Mischeifa on the 11th, Sidi Azeiz on the 13th, Gambut on the 14th, Gazala on the 15th and Martuba on the 19th. Each squadron was now divided into two mobile flights and these leap-frogged, thus enabling operations in the air to be maintained without a check. From 20th October to 22nd November the two squadrons made 1,442 individual sorties.

The victorious army entered Tobruk on 13th November. Meanwhile on 8th November American and British armies under General Eisenhower had landed in French North Africa. While the Eighth Army pressed on from the east the Allied forces pressed from the west. But it was not until 13th May 1943 that the main Axis forces surrendered; about 250,000 German and Italian troops were captured. Defeat in Africa finally broke the spirit of the Italians and the campaign gave invaluable experience to American commanders and troops, in action against the Western enemies at last after nearly a year of preparation. An immediate effect of the landing in north-west Africa had been that the Germans occupied the southern half of France; when they entered Toulon the French scuttled their fleet there.

After 5th November the 9th Australian Division had taken no further part in the African operations. From time to time during 1942 the Australian Government, on the advice of Generals MacArthur and Blamey, had pressed for the transfer of the division from the Middle East to the South-West Pacific. When MacArthur first arrived in Australia he advised Curtin that the division might be allowed to remain in the Middle East provided that the naval and air strength of the Australian base were augmented; to save shipping, he said troops should be moved from non-operational to operational areas rather than from one operational area to another.

Curtin thereupon informed Churchill that his government was prepared to agree to the postponement of the return of the 9th Division until it could be replaced and the necessary transports and escorts could be made available.

However, when the British Government would not agree to divert to Australia two divisions destined for the Middle East, MacArthur advised the Australian Government to ask for the early return of the 9th Division. However, after the Battle of Midway had transformed the situation in the Pacific and Rommel had defeated the British forces in Cyrenaica, the Government, as mentioned earlier, decided not to press for the return of the division.

The difficulty of finding reinforcements and the fact that it was becoming necessary to disband infantry units in Australia led to a renewed request in October for the return of the 9th. On 17th October Curtin informed Churchill that Australia had disbanded eight battalions and contemplated disbanding eleven more. It would not be possible to maintain the necessary flow of reinforcements to the 9th Division and if it remained in Egypt it would in a few months cease to be an effective fighting formation. (This was the time when the 7th Division was fighting its way back to Kokoda and MacArthur was warning that it was necessary to prepare for possible disaster in the Solomons, in which event 'the entire S.W.P.A. will be in the greatest danger'.) On 20th October Curtin was informed through Bruce in London that because of the operation that was then imminent, and the role allotted to the division, the date of the division's withdrawal from the front line depended on developments in the immediate future.

On 29th October, when the Battle of El Alamein was six days old, Curtin cabled Churchill that it was of vital importance to have the 9th Division back and in good shape. Roosevelt intervened on 1st November with a proposal that he should send to Australia a division from Hawaii, where there were then four divisions, thus obviating the need to recall the 9th; however, the American division, he said, might have to be diverted to another locality where it could be employed to greater advantage. (In fact, the division in question was diverted to Guadalcanal later in November.) MacArthur advised Curtin to continue to press for the return of the 9th Division. On 21st November (when the division had been out of contact with the enemy for more than a fortnight) Morshead cabled the Australian Government that General Alexander had told him that the division was to return to Australia. After more exchanges, in which Roosevelt again took part, Churchill informed Curtin that shipping would be arranged at the end of January for the return of the 9th Division with minimum equipment. It reached Australia in February.

It will be seen later that by the time the division had been re-trained for tropical warfare it was needed to take part in the offensive which opened in New Guinea in September. If it had not been available the difficult tasks allotted to the 9th would have had to be undertaken at least partly by militia troops.[2] And after El Alamein only a few of the divisions that had fought the battle could be employed in the pursuit. The advance to Tripoli was carried out by the 51st Division, 2nd New Zealand Division and 7th Armoured Division. Three of the El Alamein divisions—the 10th Armoured and 1st South African and the 44th British—were not in action again during the war.

The outbreak of war in the East led to a serious weakening of Coastal Command, in which No. 10 Squadron R.A.A.F. was still serving. Four flying boat squadrons were withdrawn from the Command and sent overseas early

[2] One course could have been to employ the 6th Division with two of its own brigades and one brigade of militia. As will be seen the third brigade of that division—the 17th —was withdrawn from action only just before the offensive opened and was in urgent need of rest and reinforcement. In the event the 6th Division was not re-employed until the end of 1944.

in 1942 and the return of No. 10 to Australia was considered. It remained, however, and instead the Air Ministry sent nine Catalina flying boats to Australia. Numbers of experienced pilots from squadrons of all types returned to Australia where, as we have seen, a large proportion of the squadron leaders and wing commanders were soon men with active service experience in the United Kingdom or the Middle East.

Air Chief Marshal Sir Philip Joubert de la Ferté of Coastal Command decided to concentrate his depleted forces over the Bay of Biscay and the Strait of Gibraltar and, as one result, No. 10 Squadron returned to its former base at Mount Batten. Bad weather hindered anti-submarine operations in January 1942 and early in February the main centre of attention became the powerful German battle cruisers *Scharnhorst* and *Gneisenau* and the cruiser *Prinz Eugen* which had been sheltering at Brest since April 1941 and now were showing signs of putting to sea. The three ships sailed at 10.45 p.m. on 11th February and, despite intense attacks from the air, got through to the Baltic but not before *Scharnhorst* and *Gneisenau* had been damaged by mines, presumably laid by the R.A.F.

Throughout 1942 the Coastal Command squadrons continued their monotonous but vital task often in the worst of weather. No. 10 Squadron now had its third generation of aircraft captains. In April two more Australian squadrons joined the Command: No. 455, now a torpedo-bombing squadron, and No. 461, a newly-formed Sunderland squadron which trained at Mount Batten under the wing of No. 10. In May and June Australians damaged two German and three Italian submarines. In September Flight Lieutenant E. P. Walshe became the first R.A.A.F. man to achieve, unaided, an indisputable sinking of a submarine: the Italian *Alabastro* sunk north-east of Algiers.

In the first nine months of 1942 from 250 to 450 Australian air crew were actively engaged in operations in Bomber Command, which in February included two Australian squadrons—Nos. 455 and 460—and by the end of the year three more—Nos. 464, 466 and 467. In Bomber Command, as elsewhere, despite the agreement to concentrate Australians in their own units, relatively few of the intended Australian squadrons had been formed and the R.A.A.F. was represented in practically every unit of the Command. This was partly an outcome of changes in the composition of bomber crews, with the result that the Empire Air Training Scheme was producing too many trainees in some categories and too few in others. Early in 1942 the policy of Bomber Command was radically altered and a new commander—Air Marshal A. T. Harris—appointed. Instead of concentrating against transport targets the bombers, aided by 'Gee', a new navigational device, would mainly attack large industrial areas and, in particular, Essen, Duisburg, Dusseldorf and Cologne. A major aim was now to depress the morale of industrial workers. At the end of May came the first 1,000-bomber raid on a single target—Cologne. Of the 868 bombers which reached the target seventeen were from No. 460 Squadron, the one R.A.A.F. Squadron taking part.

German bombing of Britain had fallen away in 1941; at the beginning of 1942 Fighter Command, then including seventy-five squadrons of single-engined fighters and twenty-three of night fighters, was better equipped to cope with the German bombers and with its task of exerting pressure on the German forces in western Europe in the hope of attracting German air units from the Russian front. When Nos. 452 and 457 Squadrons departed for Australia in June 1942, after a period of strenuous operations, the only R.A.A.F. Spitfire squadron in England was No. 453 which began to re-form in that month after having been disbanded after the Malayan campaign. In 1942 Australians played a relatively smaller part in Fighter Command than in the others.

During the second half of 1942 Australian destroyers and corvettes were serving in the Indian Ocean and the Mediterranean. The destroyers *Napier*, *Nizam*, *Norman* and *Nepal* were part of the naval force supporting the operations in Madagascar in September. The destroyers *Quiberon* and *Quickmatch* were at the North African landings in November, when *Quiberon* shared in the sinking of the Italian submarine *Dessie*. Twelve corvettes of the R.A.N. were employed on arduous Persian Gulf escort work.

Chapter 10 **Toward Salamaua**

In the South-West Pacific by March 1943 the Japanese thrust towards Wau had been defeated, and they had abandoned Guadalcanal. It was a year since they had completed their conquest of the Greater East Asia Sphere, and they seemed finally to have lost the initiative. How soon could the Allies undertake a large-scale offensive?

As a sequel to the decisions made at the conference of Allied leaders at Casablanca, General MacArthur, as mentioned earlier, had in February outlined a plan whereby in 1943 the South Pacific forces would advance northward through the Solomons to New Ireland, and the South-West Pacific forces along the New Guinea mainland to Wewak. Then the Admiralties were to be taken, followed by a combined assault on Rabaul.

In planning so large an achievement in 1943 the Combined Chiefs of Staff and MacArthur appear not to have seen the full significance of the long battles round Buna and Gona and on Guadalcanal. If in other areas the Japanese were to resist with equal valour, the reconquest of the Solomons, most of New Guinea and the Gilberts, Marshalls and Carolines was not likely to be achieved in 1943. Moreover these proposed Pacific offensives were given only fifth place in a list of priorities drawn up by the Combined Chiefs of Staff. First came 'security of sea communications'; second, assistance to Russia; third, the capture of Sicily; fourth, the building up of forces in Britain for an offensive in western Europe.

The Australian leaders considered that to give the Pacific so low a priority would entail (as Curtin said in a broadcast on 28th March 1943) 'a prolonged attrition . . . It may mean two, three or even more years.' In April in another broadcast he said that 'the holding war imposed on Australia by the decisions of the Casablanca Conference . . . means that our resources will be used up in many cases . . . and strained to a serious extent in others'. He declared that the Australian Government 'does not accept a flow of war material, notably aircraft, which does not measure up to the requirements of a holding war'.

MacArthur also had indicated that he would need far larger forces to reach his objectives. Just before the Casablanca Conference opened, when the Joint Chiefs had asked him to submit plans for the capture of Rabaul, MacArthur had replied that his forces could not undertake further operations without a long period of rest and preparation. The 7th Australian, 32nd American and 1st American Marine Divisions were all recuperating; the 9th Australian Division was preparing to embark for home from the Middle East. Soon after Casablanca Admiral Nimitz met Admiral Halsey at Noumea and they confirmed an earlier conclusion that an assault on Rabaul at that stage would be too costly. They considered that the next move in the South Pacific Area should be a northward advance to Munda in New Georgia where the Japanese had made an airfield.

At length, in March, a conference of representatives of the three principal

Pacific commanders—Nimitz, MacArthur and Halsey—was held at Washington. King's deputy urged that a unified naval command over the whole Pacific area should be established (in effect that MacArthur like Halsey be placed under Nimitz's command). Marshall proposed a compromise, which was accepted: that Halsey should control operations in the Solomons under general directives from MacArthur, while the naval task forces remained under Nimitz. It was learnt at the conference that the reinforcements sought by MacArthur were not available. Thereupon General Sutherland (representing MacArthur) suggested that the tasks for 1943 be limited to the capture of the Solomons as far as southern Bougainville, of the New Guinea coast as far only as Madang, and of western New Britain; and the establishment of airfields on Kiriwina and Woodlark Islands. This was accepted by the Joint Chiefs.

For the coming offensives MacArthur regrouped his military forces in the South-West Pacific into two main bodies: 'Alamo Force' (the code name of the Sixth American Army) under Lieut-General Walter Krueger (at first it contained two American divisions and part of a third); and New Guinea Force (nominally five Australian divisions). In reserve were three American divisions, an Australian armoured division, and an American parachute regiment. One effect of this rearrangement was that General Blamey in fact ceased to command the 'Allied Land Forces', though his title was not changed. The Sixth American Army, and later the Eighth, became 'task forces' directly under MacArthur's command. Neither Blamey (at this stage) nor the Australian Goverment (which was not consulted) protested. The regrouping had solid practical advantages: it virtually separated the Australian and American armies thus simplifying staff work; and to have left an Australian in command of the whole of MacArthur's army would doubtless have been politically unacceptable at Washington.

The Australian Air Force also had a command problem; but it was not solved so smoothly. As mentioned earlier, when the commander of the Allied Air Forces was appointed in April 1942 the Australian Chief of the Air Staff remained responsible for personnel, maintenance, supply, training, etc. This led to friction between Air Vice-Marshal Bostock, whose 'R.A.A.F. Command' controlled most of the Australian squadrons then in action against the Japanese, and Air Vice-Marshal Jones, who was Chief of the Air Staff. The Ministers tried to solve this problem by appointing Jones as an over-all commander of the R.A.A.F. with powers similar to Blamey's, but MacArthur would not agree; nor would he accept either of two senior R.A.F. officers whom the Ministers sought to bring from overseas to command the whole R.A.A.F. Divided control continued and there were frequent sharp disputes between Jones and Bostock on a variety of subjects, with consequent damage to the team spirit of the force as a whole.

MacArthur's outline plan provided for three mutually-supporting operations: Krueger would occupy Kiriwina and Woodlark Islands; the South Pacific force would infiltrate into New Georgia and/or Santa Ysabel Island, and then seize positions on Bougainville; New Guinea Force would take Lae, Salamaua, the Huon Peninsula-Markham Valley area and Madang. Later Alamo Force was to occupy western New Britain, and the South Pacific force was to seize Kieta on the east coast of Bougainville and neutralise Buka on the north.

The task of New Guinea Force was divided into three phases: capture of Lae; capture of Salamaua and Finschhafen; capture of Madang. Lae was to be taken by converging advances by the force then advancing overland, a sea-borne force landed near the objective, and an airborne force put down in the Markham Valley; thereafter Salamaua and Finschhafen were to be taken by forces landed from the sea. Madang was to be captured by an overland advance through the Ramu Valley and a shore-to-shore advance through Vitiaz Strait. On 7th May orders were issued that the landings on Woodlark and Kiriwina off New Guinea and on New Georgia would take place on 30th June; that is, 30th June 1943 would be the first day of the series of big offensives in the South-West Pacific.

Arrayed against the Allied forces of the South-West Pacific and South Pacific was Lieut-General Imamura's *Eighth Area Army* with headquarters in Rabaul, controlling Lieut-General Hyakutake's *XVII Army* (*6th* and *38th Divisions*) in the Solomons and New Britain and Lieut-General Adachi's *XVIII Army* (*20th, 41st, 51st Divisions*) in New Guinea; in September and October 1943 the *17th Division* would arrive at Rabaul. The strength of the *Eighth Area Army* was between 80,000 and 94,000 and it could be reinforced by about 60,000 within three weeks. About 320 combat aircraft were immediately available and about 270 others could be flown in within forty-eight hours.

After the defeats at Wau and on the Bismarck Sea General Adachi decided on a long term plan to establish a land line of communication from Madang south over the Finisterres to the Ramu and Markham Valleys and Lae. He would then attempt to capture Wau and move south to Port Moresby. Fresh troops were ferried into Lae during May 1943 by submarine, destroyer and motor landing craft until the main body of the *51st Division* and other smaller formations were there.

MacArthur was still anxious lest the Japanese open an assault against northern and western Australia in general and the Merauke-Torres Strait area in particular. In fact the Japanese reinforcement of their garrisons in the Timor-Aru Islands area and in north-western New Guinea, which caused MacArthur's fears, were defensive measures aimed at meeting a possible Allied offensive from northern Australia. On 22nd March MacArthur's headquarters issued a plan for meeting this possible Japanese offensive. The garrison at Merauke was to be increased to a brigade, and two brigade groups were to be concentrated in the Horn Island-Thursday Island area, with smaller forces round centres in Cape York Peninsula. The air force at Merauke and Horn Island was to include at least four fighter squadrons and there were to be at least four fighter and nine bomber squadrons at Darwin. In April, however, MacArthur decided that all these reinforcements need not be deployed immediately but must be ready at short notice.

Early in March a stroke of fortune had immensely improved Allied knowledge of the Japanese Army's organisation and deployment. After the virtual destruction of the Bismarck Sea convoy several boats and barges carrying Japanese survivors came ashore on Goodenough Island. These parties were rounded up by Australian patrols one of which captured some boxes of documents including a detailed account of the enemy's Order of Battle and other information which enabled the Allied Intelligence staffs to compile a comprehensive and fairly accurate account of the organisation and whereabouts of Japanese formations and units and their commanders.

The tasks given to MacArthur by the Joint Chiefs would have to be carried out by an army that was chiefly Australian, supported by chiefly-American naval and air forces. The Allied naval and air forces were now superior to the Japanese both numerically and technically. The American Fifth Air Force had about 770 first-line aircraft, the R.A.A.F. about 680. The opposing armies, if allowance was made for the rawness of most of the American formations, were more evenly matched.

Although Japanese naval losses were inconsiderable in their first successful half-year of war, in the next ten months they had lost naval ships much faster than they could replace them. Up to the time of the destruction of the Lae convoy 2 Japanese battleships, 6 aircraft carriers, 6 cruisers, 37 destroyers and 25 submarines had been sunk. Losses at such a rate could not be replaced by the Japanese naval shipyards; the American yards on the other hand were not only replacing losses but soon would double their navy's pre-war strength. And from October 1942 onwards American submarines had been sinking Japanese transports at a faster rate than Japan could sustain for long. In that month they had sunk twenty-seven ships and other agents had sunk nine. In the next seven months Japanese merchantmen sunk by submarines numbered:

November	9	March	23
December	15	April	18
January	24	May	30
February	10		

The Japanese submarines were less effectively employed, though in the first half of 1943 they achieved some successes, particularly off the east coast of Australia.

Throughout the war against Japan the R.A.A.F. was responsible for the air defence of the continent against submarines and possible raids by carrier-borne aircraft. In the first half of 1943 these tasks employed more squadrons than were serving in New Guinea and North-Western Area. In April, for example, there were four squadrons in North-Eastern Area (Air Commodore A. H. Cobby), seven under command in Eastern Area (Air Vice-Marshal W. H. Anderson) two in Southern Area (Group Captain C. W. Pearce), and four in Western Area (Air Commodore R. J. Brownell). Of these seventeen squadrons six were armed only with Wirraways or Boomerangs, and three with obsolescent Ansons which had a small range and bomb-load.

Many of these squadrons were called upon for strenuous patrolling during the first six months of 1943 when, after a lull of about five months, Japanese submarines began to operate off the east coast. From 18th January until 16th June between Cairns in the north and Gabo Island in the south, but mostly between Coffs Harbour and Wollongong, twenty-one ships were attacked by submarines, eleven being sunk, including (on 14th May) the hospital ship *Centaur* in which 268 persons were lost. In one six-day period from 24th to 29th April four ships with an aggregate tonnage of 20,000 tons were sunk. The total tonnage of the ships sunk in the six months was about 50,000. Such losses were microscopic compared with those being suffered in the Atlantic, but if they had continued they might have become serious, particularly to Australian coastwise traffic, conducted at the best of times by relatively few ships. As it was the Japanese withdrew the four submarines that had operated off the Australian coast in 1943, and thenceforward their submarines were tied more and more to ferrying supplies to isolated garrisons. On 8th December 1943 convoying was discontinued between Australian ports south of Brisbane. This caused discontent among merchant seamen and many ships were held up until naval spokesmen addressed the seamen in Melbourne and explained the situation to them.

In March 1943 Vice-Admiral Arthur S. Carpender's naval force in MacArthur's command was renamed the Seventh Fleet and Admiral Halsey's the Third Fleet; Carpender's force hardly deserved the new title. Its only cruisers were those of Admiral Crutchley's squadron—*Australia* and *Hobart* and the American *Phoenix*. Into the area had now come a second seagoing force—Rear-Admiral Daniel E. Barbey's VII Amphibious Force, whose arrival was significant of the growing strength of the Allied navies in landing ships and landing craft. Indeed there was now an ally who had the resources to manufacture landing craft in far greater numbers than the British countries could, and could make possible the large-scale landings by which alone victory could be won both in the West and the East.

Although the South-West Pacific naval force was small, formidable American naval forces were now ready to support the advance along the Solomons. There were two task forces built round the aircraft carriers *Saratoga* and *Enterprise;* there was a battle-squadron of four new capital ships and another of three old ones; there were two cruiser-and-destroyer forces. Indeed, the strongest single American naval force was now in this area.

On 6th March light naval forces, skirmishing forward, bombarded Munda and Vila, in the Solomon Islands, surprising and sinking two Japanese destroyers off Vila, but it was the Japanese who began a real trial of strength at this stage.

In April Admiral Yamamoto of the *Combined Fleet* launched an air offensive throughout the South and South-West Pacific, employing the aircraft of his *Carrier Fleet* as well as those of the *XI Air Fleet,* based on Rabaul. The total strength was about 400 aircraft. On 7th April the Japanese aircraft attacked over Guadalcanal. The defending fighters, warned by the coastwatchers on the islands farther north, were ready. In the ensuing fight the American destroyer *Aaron Ward,* an American tanker, and the New Zealand corvette *Moa* were sunk; the Japanese lost twelve bombers and nine fighters; the Americans seven fighters.

The Japanese then switched their air forces against New Guinea bases. On 11th April some ninety aircraft attacked small ships at Oro Bay. They hit one ship and damaged the corvette *Pirie.* Allied fighters claimed to have shot down seventeen Japanese aircraft without loss. On the 12th about 150 Japanese aircraft in two formations attacked the Port Moresby airfields, where they damaged about twenty aircraft on the ground. On the 14th more than 100 Japanese aircraft attacked Milne Bay. The Netherlands transport *Van Heemskerk* was sunk and two other ships were badly damaged. The Kittyhawks of Nos. 75 and 77 Squadrons and American Lightnings shot down thirteen Japanese planes.

Yamamoto decided to visit the northern Solomons to observe the results of the air offensive. American Intelligence staffs decoding Japanese signals learned of this intended tour and the time-table, and when on the 18th two bombers carrying Yamamoto and his staff, escorted by nine fighters, were about to land at Buin four American Lightnings from Guadalcanal shot them both down. American hopes were confirmed on 21st May when Tokyo announced Yamamoto's death. He was succeeded by Admiral Mineichi Koga.

Whence would the divisions be drawn to carry out the planned offensives in New Guinea? In March the formations which had fought round Buna and Gona having returned to Australia, and the 9th Australian Division having arrived from the Middle East, the main formations of Blamey's army on the mainland of Australia had been distributed thus:

FIRST ARMY (LAVARACK):
3rd Armoured Division, 4th Division

II CORPS (MORSHEAD):
6th (16th and 30th Brigades), 7th and 9th Divisions

SECOND ARMY:
1st Division, 3rd Army Tank Brigade

III CORPS (BENNETT):
1st Armoured Division, 2nd Division

NORTHERN TERRITORY FORCE (ALLEN):
12th Division

RESERVE:
3rd Brigade, 4th Armoured Brigade

In Australia were also the headquarters of the Sixth American Army and I American Corps and the 32nd and 1st Marine Divisions.

New Guinea Force (Mackay acting), some 54,000 strong, included the following formations:

WAU-BULOLO:
3rd Division (Savige)—17th Brigade

BUNA-ORO BAY:
41st American Division (H. H. Fuller)—162nd, 163rd and 186th Regiments

PORT MORESBY:
11th Division (Clowes)—7th and 15th Brigades

MILNE BAY:
5th Division (E. J. Milford)—4th and 29th Brigades

BENA-MOUNT HAGEN PLATEAU:
2/7th Independent Company, etc.

In April and May, in accordance with MacArthur's decision to reinforce the extreme left flank in New Guinea, the headquarters of the 11th Brigade (Brigadier J. R. Stevenson), the 31st/51st Battalion and part of the 26th arrived at Merauke, joining the 62nd Battalion.

The Australian armoured forces, which for a time had comprised two big divisions, had now been reduced to two divisions of the new smaller establishment (one armoured brigade and a support group instead of two armoured brigades and a support group); but the independent tank brigades were retained. The ranks of the armoured brigades had been filled with first-class men; many of the leaders were young veterans who had distinguished themselves in the mechanised cavalry in North Africa and Syria. The regiments were well trained and now were strongly equipped. The danger of invasion having almost disappeared and no role for complete armoured formations being likely in the Pacific area, it was perhaps unfortunate that the 1st Armoured Division was not shipped to Africa at this stage, perhaps in the transports which brought the 9th Division home.

The Australian Ministers, however, were becoming so anxious about the lack of manpower, and also were campaigning so vigorously for greater concentration of Allied forces against Japan that they would have been unlikely to look with favour on acceptance of new commitments in the West. The events of the last few months had made it evident to them and their advisers that unless malaria was subdued it would be impossible to maintain the army at its present strength. Early in March the War Cabinet was informed that in November, December and January the battle casualties in New Guinea had totalled 4,137, the casualties from tropical diseases 14,011, including 12,240 cases of malaria and 1,248 of dysentery. From 95 to 100 per cent of the troops of the 7th Division were infected with malaria. It was estimated that the monthly wastage rate in hyper-endemic malarious areas was 7 per cent of the troops actively engaged. Thus not only was Australia maintaining an army of twelve divisions—a far larger number in proportion to population than Britain, America or Japan were—but her forces were employed in a theatre where casualties were proving exceptionally high. On the face of it, it would be unlikely that Australia with a population of 7,000,000 and now in her fourth year of war, would be able to maintain so large an army. The United States, for example, with a population of 120,000,000 was then aiming at 100 divisions and later reduced this objective to eighty-nine.

The Government's growing anxiety about manpower caused it on 23rd March to address a strong direction to the Defence Committee. It reminded the committee that in January it had pointed out that maintenance of the existing forces and of the production program demanded an intake of 35,000 men and women a month of whom 22,000 were for the Services, but that it had been decided that only 10,000 a month could be found and those only by 'continual extension of restrictions on non-war uses of manpower'. Chiefly as a result of tropical disease the army was 79,000 short of its full establishment. In spite of this, munitions production was being continued at full capacity and the surplus was being sent to Britain. Australia was attempting to accomplish an impossible number of tasks. The Defence Committee was instructed to re-assess its needs.

In consequence on 13th April General Blamey submitted his views on a reduction of the size of the army. The successes in New Guinea and the Solomons since September, he said, had improved the position, though it had not removed the danger of invasion. He proposed to reduce the army to nine infantry divisions, two armoured divisions, one armoured brigade and one army tank brigade, with appropriate ancillary units. Of these, three infantry divisions would be needed in New Guinea; three infantry and two armoured divisions would be needed for the defence of Australia and three infantry divisions as a reserve to the New Guinea Force. (For every division in the field there would need to be another recuperating at home.) There would be an infantry division at Darwin, an infantry and an armoured division in Western Australia, an armoured division in Queensland (not including the offensive force of three divisions in training on the Atherton Tablelands and in reserve to New Guinea Force) and an infantry division in New South

Wales. In New Guinea, for the present, one division would be in the Milne Bay area, one about Buna, and three brigades divided between Wau and Port Moresby. An intake of 11,800 a month would be needed to maintain the reduced army and the actual intake was only 4,000. He recommended further releases of men from industry; if this could not be done the offensive force would have to be reduced by one division.

In July Blamey wrote to Curtin and Forde pointing out that a very great increase of the air force was under consideration, and urged that, as man-power could not meet existing requirements, the Government should determine the exact forces to be maintained by the army and the air force. He pointed out that he had broken up the following field formations between November 1942 and July 1943: the 2nd Motor Division, brigades of the 10th Division, the 14th Brigade, 30th Brigade, 1st Motor Brigade, 3rd Tank Brigade; also seven artillery regiments, two cavalry regiments and other units had been disbanded.[1]

At length, on 13th July, the War Cabinet decided if possible to maintain three infantry divisions for offensive operations and 'adequate forces for the defence of Australia and New Guinea and for relief of units in New Guinea'; one infantry division was to be disbanded within the next six months and perhaps another one later. The War Cabinet decided to maintain the Air Force 'at the strength authorised under the 72-squadron program to the extent to which aircraft can be provided'. The Navy was to remain at its present strength. It would receive 500 men a month, the Army 4,000 men and 1,000 women, and the Air Force 3,000 men and 1,000 women; an intake of 500 men and 2,000 women a month was allotted to Munitions and Aircraft Production and of 2,000 men to the Allied Works Council.

Earlier in the year the Government had achieved legislation which would increase the flexibility of its army. Until February the possible future deployment of that army was still limited by the provision of the *Defence Act* which required that Australian conscripts should not serve outside Australian territory. Curtin had now decided that this provision was a luxury which the nation could no longer afford. At that stage 820,000 men had been enlisted in the army and 530,000 of these were volunteers willing to serve anywhere. (An order had been given that any militia unit in which three-quarters of the men were volunteers would be described as a unit of the A.I.F.) Many leaders of the Labour Party were still bitterly opposed to conscription for overseas service, but Curtin, without consulting his Cabinet or some of his closest associates, took his political life in his hands and between November 1942 and January 1943 sought and won the approval of Federal Conferences of the party for a proposal that conscripts should become liable to serve outside Australian territory.[2] Thereupon the Government in February secured the passing of a Bill which provided that militiamen could thenceforth be

[1] The selection of the 14th and 30th Brigades for disbandment was perplexing. These were two of only three militia brigades that had fought in Papua and included one outstanding battalion—the 39th.

[2] But on 5th April MacArthur's senior Intelligence officer, C. A. Willoughby, sent a memorandum to MacArthur's Chief of Staff, Sutherland, in the course of which he said that Curtin favoured an amendment of the *Defence Act* to enable the militia to be employed outside Australian territory and, if the Labour Party 'made an issue of it', would cross the floor of the House and set up a National Government.

sent to any part of the South-West Pacific Area that lay south of the Equator.[3] It turned out that the new provision possessed no great practical importance: until the end, the fighting outside Australian territory was done by the entirely-volunteer A.I.F., except that militia units served at Merauke in Dutch New Guinea.

Relatively few people seem actively to have objected to conscription. For instance, by August 1944 2,791 applications for registration as conscientious objectors had been lodged. The fate of these was as follows:

Granted unconditional registration	41
Granted conditional registration	973
Employed on non-combatant duties	1,076
Rejected	636
Not finalised	65

Throughout most of these months of conferences and planning in Washington, Pearl Harbour, Brisbane and Canberra, Japanese troops were engaged on only two land fronts outside China: in Burma, and by the 3rd Australian Division facing Salamaua and Lae. On 23rd April Major-General Savige, as commander of the 3rd Division, had assumed command in the Wau-Bulolo area and Kanga Force had ceased to exist. For the present Savige's force included only the 17th Brigade (which he had led in the Middle East) and three Independent Companies. His immediate senior was Mackay under whom Savige had served in the 6th Division in Africa and Greece, and who had been temporarily in command of New Guinea Force since January. Mackay instructed him that his area was to be turned into 'an active operational zone for mobile defence' in such a way as to facilitate offensive operations. The staff estimated the Japanese around Lae and Salamaua at about 5,500 with between 6,000 and 8,000 at Madang and from 9,000 to 11,000 at Wewak. Mackay told Savige that he was not yet to attack Salamaua directly.

On the right, guarding the Mubo area, was the 17th Brigade (2/5th and 2/7th Battalions); in the centre round Missim was the 2/3rd Independent Company; on the left from Bulolo to the Markham Valley area was Lieut-Colonel Wood's 2/6th Battalion Group which included also the 24th Battalion. Savige decided that his general policy should be to establish 'firm bases' as far forward as possible and to harass the enemy with patrols. The incomplete 3rd Australian Division was facing the similarly-incomplete *51st Japanese Division*, which then included the three battalions of the *102nd Regiment*, some depleted units that had survived the destruction of the Lae convoy, and about 2,500 marines, but, as mentioned, reinforcements would soon arrive.

In the last week of April two units were in contact with the enemy—the 2/7th Battalion (Lieut-Colonel H. G. Guinn) about Mubo, with headquarters at Guadagasal and companies forward at Mat Mat and Lababia Ridge; and the 2/3rd Independent Company (Major G. R. Warfe) patrolling in the Missim area to the north. Part of the 24th Battalion was deployed on the extreme left round Gabensis and Kirkland's Dump on guard against a Japanese advance from the Markham. Astride the main track the Japanese were dug in on the Pimple, Green Hill and Observation Hill.

3 For the purposes of the Act the eastern boundary of the area was moved somewhat to the east so as to embrace the eastern Solomons.

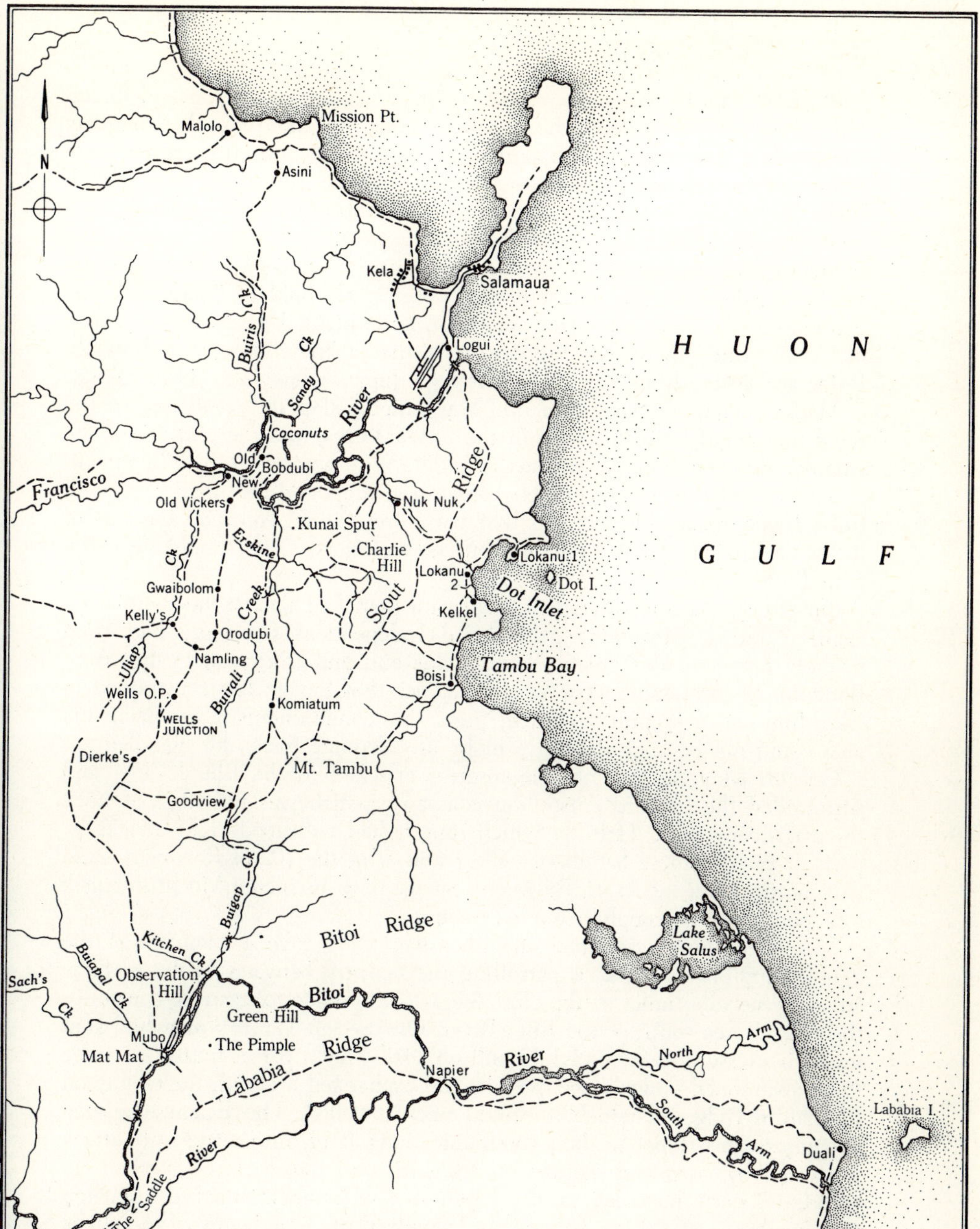

Salamaua area

On 24th April a company of the 2/7th attacked the Pimple and Green Hill. Four aircraft strafed the Japanese positions and then the company advanced in two columns supported by mortar fire, but the enemy were firmly entrenched on the precipitous feature and the Australians were halted. Next day another attack, supported by aircraft and the 1st Mountain Battery, limited to fifty rounds a gun, also failed.

Meanwhile the 2/3rd Independent Company had been probing deeply. Warfe decided that the Japanese were only lightly holding Bobdubi Ridge, dominating the main track from the west, and obtained permission to attack it. On 3rd and 4th May a platoon thrust the Japanese off part of Bobdubi Ridge and in the following days drove back Japanese moving up to retake it.

Mackay wrote to Savige on 6th May emphasising the small size of the force that could be maintained in the forward area, and the tenacity of the enemy, and concluding that no useful military purpose was served by attacks and raids which were not properly organised, supported by superior fire and fully driven home. He directed that patrolling should continue forward of the main Guadagasal-Waipali line but no strong positions should be maintained forward of it.

On 7th May a company attack was again launched against the Pimple but again it failed. Meanwhile, the 2/3rd Independent Company had been severely harassing the Japanese with raids and ambushes and by fire from Bobdubi. So successful were Warfe's tactics that Savige felt constrained to warn him not to attempt too much; 'premature commitments in the Salamaua area could not be backed at present by an adequate force', he signalled.

On 9th May the Japanese themselves attacked in the Pimple area and surrounded the forward Australian company, which was not relieved until the afternoon of the 11th, by which time it had withstood eight attacks by parts of two Japanese battalions—the *I* and *II* of the *102nd Regiment*—and two companies of the *115th Regiment.* Savige now instructed Moten to attack soft spots and not strongly defended positions.

Moten continued to probe on either flank. He gave a company of the 2/6th Battalion the task of patrolling the country between Mubo and the coast—some nine miles as the crow flies—as a prelude to securing control of the coastal area south of the Bitoi River. On the left Warfe's men had kept up their pressure round Bobdubi and on 11th May a patrol found the ridge to be abandoned, quickly occupied it, and exchanged fire with the enemy on Komiatum Ridge on which the main track travelled. The Japanese reacted strongly to this threat to their communications, launching a full-scale attack supported by guns and mortars on the 14th and forced the Australians to withdraw. Early next day twenty Japanese dive bombers attacked, then ten dive bombers and twenty fighters, and finally thirty-four bombers and thirty fighters—the heaviest Japanese air attacks for some time. No Australian was hit; and the third and heaviest attack struck Japanese positions.

The Japanese maintained their air attacks in the following days, but generally against targets farther to the Australian rear. On 17th and 18th May large formations of Japanese aircraft raided Wau airfield.

The 2/6th Battalion now, late in May, relieved the 2/7th; and the 15th Brigade headquarters and another battalion of that brigade began to arrive in Savige's area. In the same period the Japanese were reinforced by two battalions, the *I* and *II* of the *66th Regiment*, more men of the *115th Regiment*

Australian War Memorial

New Guinea, 1943. Looking north along Komiatum Ridge to the Francisco River. The Komiatum Ridge was a dominating feature during the arduous long-drawn-out Wau-Salamaua campaign.

and others—1,750 in all. Lieut-General Nakano's *51st Division* now possessed its three infantry regiments—the *66th*, *102nd* and *115th* and its divisional troops. Some of the reinforcements were transported by submarines forty at a time, others in barges to Lae, others in barges to Finschhafen and thence overland to Lae.

In the air, whether over New Guinea or over the Timor and Arafura Seas, neither side then possessed a decisive superiority. Kenney still lacked sufficient bomber power to knock out the bases used by the Japanese air forces. Indeed much of the bomber effort was absorbed by reconnaissance, anti-submarine patrols and convoy escort. An uncommon success was achieved on 1st and 2nd April when bombers attacked a Japanese Kavieng convoy and sank a 5,854-ton transport, put the heavy cruiser *Aoba* out of action and severely damaged a destroyer.

During May Australian Beaufighters and Bostons with American Mitchells attacked Madang and Lae, maintaining steady pressure on these bases. The R.A.A.F. now had three squadrons tied more or less to the Salamaua operations; and four squadrons based on Milne Bay and engaged chiefly in attacks on shipping and in reconnaissance. The seven Australian squadrons in New Guinea were part of No. 9 Group (Air Commodore J. E. Hewitt), now about 10,000 strong. Two Catalina flying boat squadrons based on Cairns also played a part in the operations in New Guinea by dropping mines in the enemy's harbours, making night raids and supporting coast-watchers in enemy-held territory.

These Catalina squadrons, with an American Catalina squadron based near Perth, were sometimes employed against Japanese bases north of Darwin. In April the air force in North-Western Area included six Australian squadrons, one British, one American (heavy bombers) and one Dutch. The Spitfire wing became heavily engaged when Japanese attacks recommenced on 2nd May. At 9.26 a.m. that day a radar station on Bathurst Island reported a large formation closing Darwin from the north-west. The thirty-three Spitfires, led by Wing Commander Caldwell, climbed up sun as fast as they could and were at 26,000 feet when they noticed eighteen bombers at 27,000 feet covered by twenty-seven fighters some 4,000 feet higher. Caldwell resolved not to attack immediately and the enemy let go 100 bombs over the Darwin air station, but caused only slight damage. The anti-aircraft guns fired 219 rounds, but without scoring a hit. The Japanese were now gradually losing height and the Spitfires were in a position to attack. The first squadron (No. 54 R.A.F.) dived almost vertically and less-experienced pilots found difficulty in aiming. The Japanese fighter escorts turned in and deflected the Spitfires from the bombers, and this happened again when No. 457 attacked. Now Caldwell led No. 452 Squadron down and one pilot got through and probably destroyed a bomber, but in turn was forced to parachute. At this stage six enemy aircraft were believed to have been destroyed and perhaps four more, but five Spitfires had gone, along with two pilots. The Spitfires were now short of fuel and many made forced landings. Most were salvaged, but in all eight Spitfires were destroyed.

This affair set off a series of raids and counter raids into which Catalinas from Nos. 11 and 20 Squadrons were also drawn. Enemy bases were repeatedly attacked. Beaufighters from Millingimbi made a series of successful strikes against float-plane anchorages in the Aru Islands, and the Japanese on

9th May were provoked to attack Millingimbi, with seven bombers, killing ten airmen, a soldier and an aboriginal. In anticipation of further attacks, Spitfires were stationed there, and next day nine Japanese fighters approached; six engaged five Spitfires which shot down two Zekes, while three Zekes strafed the airfield destroying a grounded Beaufighter and damaging three others, and destroying one Spitfire. On 28th May an attack by eight bombers and five fighters was met by six Spitfires, and ended in the destruction of three Japanese aircraft and two Spitfires. Air supremacy in the North-Western Area had not been gained by either side, but the early arrival of American Liberator heavy bombers now gave hope for the future.

After Blamey had received MacArthur's plans for the main offensive, he instructed Mackay that an advanced base on the coast should be seized within sixty miles of Lae, this being the farthest distance landing craft could carry troops in one night; Nassau Bay was chosen. Its occupation would enable the force round Mubo to be at least partly supplied by sea. Blamey on 17th May instructed Herring, soon to take over from Mackay, to seize not only the bay but the high ground round Goodview Junction and Mount Tambu and the ridge running thence to the sea. This operation might draw Japanese forces away from Lae to Salamaua. He did not want Salamaua to be assaulted until after the Lae operation; until the blow fell at Lae the Japanese were to be led to believe that Salamaua was the objective.

Savige was informed of the impending occupation of Kiriwina and Woodlark Islands and instructed to be ready by 15th June to threaten Salamaua; on 27th May he was told that his tasks were to drive the enemy north of the Francisco River and to establish a beach-head at Nassau Bay to which an American force—a battalion group was then envisaged—could come in. Savige decided that the coming operation would be carried out in three phases: first, the American battalion would land at Nassau Bay; next day the 15th Brigade on the left would assault Bobdubi Ridge and then that brigade would advance south to Komiatum and prevent the enemy's escape from Mubo; finally a battalion of the 17th Brigade and the American battalion would assault Mubo and advance thence on Komiatum and Lokanu. The day before D-day the 24th Battalion was to establish a position astride the coastal track. The task of reconnoitring Nassau Bay and ensuring an unopposed landing was given to the 17th Brigade.

In the Salamaua area preparations for the attack continued. In the last week of May a patrol of three men of the 2/6th Battalion and two natives had reconnoitred Nassau Bay. Early in June another patrol of the 2/6th Battalion re-examined the route. In the succeeding days other patrols explored the area over which the coming attack would take place.[4] At a final conference at Summit Camp on 15th June, attended by Generals Herring, Savige and Berryman, Brigadier Moten, Colonels Kenneth S. Sweany (Chief of Staff of the 41st Division) and Archibald R. MacKechnie (commanding the 162nd American Regiment, allotted to the Nassau Bay landing), Moten

[4] On 28th May, in long-range preparation for the advance on Madang along the upland valley of the Ramu, the 2/7th Independent Company (Major MacAdie) was flown into the Bena Bena area, where hitherto only a platoon of the 2/7th Battalion had been stationed.

outlined a detailed plan for the landing at Nassau Bay and the capture of Mubo: the Americans with an Australian company would advance from Nassau Bay to Napier; then the Australians would capture Observation Hill, and the Americans Bitoi Ridge; together they would take Green Hill and the Pimple; a fresh Australian battalion would then pass through to link with the 15th Brigade round Komiatum; finally Lokanu and Boisi would be taken. The operation was to begin on 30th June, the day of the proposed landing on Woodlark and Kiriwina Islands. In the final days before the attack the remaining battalion of the 15th Brigade and two companies of the Papuan Infantry Battalion arrived in the area.

On 19th and 20th June there were signs that the enemy was about to anticipate the Allied attack. They were patrolling aggressively; during the 20th enemy aircraft made more than eighty bombing sorties against the Australian positions, with the result that at this critical stage over 500 native carriers went bush and it took Angau officers three days to reassemble them. The right forward company of the 2/6th, holding its wide area towards Nassau Bay, was under sharp fire on the afternoon of the 20th. Next morning an attack in strength was dispersed; in the afternoon a stronger attack was made and soon the Australians were closely engaged. A fresh company reinforced the one under attack. At nightfall the Japanese withdrew having lost an estimated 100 men, but they renewed the attack on the 22nd and 23rd, when the beleaguered troops were heartened by the sight of Beaufighters strafing along the track. That afternoon the Japanese attacks ceased. Of the eighty Australians on Lababia Ridge at the outset, later reinforced by seventy more, eleven were killed and twelve wounded. It was later discovered that about 1,500 Japanese (two battalions of the *66th Regiment*) had made the attack and had lost forty-one killed and 131 wounded.

The landing craft available to carry the leading American battalion to Nassau Bay numbered thirty-two—fewer than MacKechnie had been led to expect. A company of Papuan infantry under Captain E. P. Hitchcock, a veteran infantryman of 1914-18 and an old New Guinea hand, was sent forward to a point on the coast between the Americans at Morobe and their destination, and its patrols probed as far as Nassau Bay itself. On 29th June the Papuans advanced to the bay immediately south of Nassau. By the 28th the right company of the 2/6th had moved east towards Bitoi Ridge, and from it a platoon set out on the 29th for Nassau Bay to guide the Americans in. After misadventure it reached the beach about midnight.

The American landing craft were already at sea, lashed by rain and in a heavy swell. The Australians ashore arrived in time to show the three prearranged landing lights for about half an hour before they heard the craft coming in. The night landing was a scene of confusion. Craft lost direction; the first and second waves became mixed; the craft broached in the heavy surf and twenty-one were left swamped on the beach. A group of craft, one of which carried the commanding officer, Lieut-Colonel Harold Taylor, went far north of Nassau Bay, turned back at 3 a.m. and finally went ashore far to the south, whence Taylor reached Nassau Bay about midday on 1st July. On the night of the 29th-30th only 770 were landed. MacKechnie was among them. He asked the Australian platoon commander, Lieutenant R. D. Urquhart, to site defensive positions for the Americans and Urquhart did so. Fortunately the Japanese were not ready to attack.

The swamping of the wireless sets during the landing made it impossible for any information to reach Savige or Moten on the night of the 29th-30th and next morning. On the 30th American companies set out north and south; the northern company came under fire and halted. The Americans were raw and ill-trained. On the evening of the 30th the outlying companies came back to the beach and, that night, which was pitch black, thinking they were being attacked, fired indiscriminately; eighteen Americans were killed and twenty-seven wounded. It seems probable that some Japanese were about, but certain that no concerted attack was made.

On 1st July the easternmost company of the 2/6th Battalion advanced to the coast along the south arm of the Bitoi driving off a company of Japanese, and Hitchcock's Papuans skirmished with some Japanese on the Cape Dinga peninsula. About midday, as mentioned, Colonel Taylor arrived by barge and soon afterwards a small party of Australians arrived from the Bitoi area. It was now evident that few Japanese remained south of the river.

On the morning of the third day ashore—2nd July—MacKechnie's force remained clustered round the beach, but that afternoon one company advanced to the Bitoi. Next day four 75-mm guns were landed at Nassau—a most important reinforcement—and by the 4th more than 1,400 troops were ashore. By the 6th three American companies were about Napier, but MacKechnie was unwilling to send more troops inland until he had more supporting weapons and supplies.

Also on 30th June three companies of the 58th/59th Battalion had advanced against Bobdubi Ridge on a wide front. They encountered fairly strong opposition and gained only parts of the objective, but drew substantial Japanese reinforcements into the area. On the 3rd, however, a company reached the track along the ridge and carried out a successful ambush. Brigadier Hammer, formerly a battalion commander in the 9th Division, and an uncommonly forceful leader, took over the 15th Brigade that night. By 6th July the brigade should have been pressing on to Komiatum to sever the track behind the Japanese round Mubo, but it was still far from that objective. The 2/3rd Independent Company had been given the task of going in on the south flank of the 58th/59th and preventing the escape of the enemy from Mubo. It secured Wells Junction on the Bobdubi track and pressed on.

Papuan soldiers advancing along the coast ahead of the 162nd American Regiment reached Lake Salus on 9th July and were instructed by MacKechnie to push on to Tambu Bay.

The occupation of Kiriwina and Woodlark Islands on the same day as the landing at Nassau Bay was in the nature of an exercise for American staffs and troops as the islands were not occupied by the Japanese. (Indeed an R.A.A.F. radar station had been operating on Kiriwina since May.) Advanced parties went ashore on 23rd and 24th June and the main forces—a regimental group in each instance—on 30th June. An American fighter squadron was operating from Woodlark by 23rd July and an Australian fighter squadron from Kiriwina by 19th August. In June No. 73 Wing with 79 Squadron (Spitfires) and Nos. 76 and 77 (Kittyhawks) was established on Goodenough Island.

Late in May Air Commodore Bladin, in North-Western Area, had been instructed that his force's role in the coming offensive would be 'to increase the show of force in North-Western Area'. It was for this purpose that the four additional American Liberator squadrons were sent to Darwin. These were able to penetrate far deeper into Japanese territory than the Australian Hudsons and Mitchells and bombed the big enemy bases at Kendari and Macassar. In response, on 20th June the Japanese dispatched a strong air force against Darwin. This time the Spitfires had greater success, destroying nine bombers and five fighters. On the 30th fifty enemy aircraft were sent against the Liberator base at Fenton. The Spitfire wing received good radar warning and in the ensuing fight eight enemy aircraft and six Spitfires were destroyed; three Liberators were destroyed on the ground and seven damaged. In a second raid on 6th July another Liberator was destroyed and three damaged, while in the air fighting eight Spitfires and nine Japanese aircraft were destroyed. This was the last heavy raid on the Darwin airfields.

Throughout this period the Catalina squadrons (Nos. 11 and 20) based at Cairns continued their mining campaign. Kavieng, Lorengau, Babo and Kaimana were enemy supply ports so attacked. These aircraft also continued supply missions which enabled coastwatchers to remain at their all-important tasks, and continued their night-bombing attacks.

In May 1943 the Allied staffs had been reminded of the possibility of further attacks on West Australian bases. The American Navy established a submarine base at Exmouth Gulf, 750 miles nearer the submarines' objectives in Indonesian waters than Fremantle. A fighter squadron, later replaced by a flight of Boomerangs, was established at Exmouth Gulf. On the nights of 20th and 21st May two Japanese aircraft dropped bombs which did no damage. Soon afterwards the Americans abandoned the Exmouth Gulf base, which offered no protection to submarines from the occasional cyclones.

In the Solomons the next objective in the American advance northward was New Georgia. There Major Kennedy, mentioned earlier, was in touch with agents among the natives throughout New Georgia and on the islands of Rendova and Kolombangara. He and his men round Segi, his main base, had waylaid three Japanese barges, killing all their occupants except two whom they took prisoner. They then ambushed a party which advanced against them overland. In all these engagements fifty-four Japanese were killed, and in a few months Kennedy and his men rescued twenty-two American airmen and captured twenty Japanese pilots. Kennedy himself was wounded but treated his own wound and carried on. There were in March 1943 coastwatchers also on Rendova, Kolombangara, Santa Ysabel, Vella Lavella, Choiseul and Bougainville. Their presence made it possible for one reconnaissance party after another to explore new Allied objectives in the Solomons before the attacks opened. For example, various parties of up to nine technicians secretly passed through Kennedy's base at Segi; on 20th-21st June two companies of American marines were landed to garrison this outpost, and next day two companies of infantry were landed.

On 30th June (the day of the landings at Nassau Bay, Woodlark and Kiriwina) the main landings on New Georgia and Rendova were made. There was little resistance by Japanese land forces. Admiral Halsey ordered that

Australian War Memorial

H.M.A.S. *Hobart* damaged in the quarter-deck and after turrets from a Japanese torpedo hit on 20th July 1943. Seven officers and six ratings were killed and seven other men were wounded.

troops be ferried across to Munda, the site of a Japanese airfield and apparently fairly well defended, on 5th July. The Japanese, however, had decided to reinforce and hold New Georgia and early in July began to send destroyers loaded with troops from Rabaul towards that island. An American naval force consisting of three cruisers, *Honolulu*, *Helena* and *St Louis*, and four destroyers set out against the Japanese destroyers and destroyer-transports—ten in all—and off Kolombangara on 6th July the cruiser *Helena* and two Japanese destroyers were sunk. On 12th and 13th July off Kolombangara another similar engagement took place between the same American force (in which the New Zealand cruiser *Leander* had replaced *Helena* and to which six more destroyers were added) and a group including the Japanese cruiser *Jintsu* and nine destroyers, four of them carrying troops. This time the *Jintsu* was sunk, the Allied force lost a destroyer, and all three of its cruisers were severely damaged by torpedoes. When these cruisers were put out of action Admiral Crutchley with *Australia* and *Hobart* was sent in to fill the gap. Approaching Espiritu Santo on 20th July *Hobart* was hit by a torpedo which put her out of action until December. (Only two Australian cruisers were now serviceable on the Australia Station, but the 8-inch cruiser *Shropshire*, presented by Britain to replace *Canberra* would arrive at Fremantle in September.)[5]

[5] At 30th June 1943 there were 83 ships in the Australian Navy, excluding auxiliary minesweepers and other small craft. They included 3 cruisers, 10 destroyers, 3 sloops, 48 corvettes, 16 Fairmile motor launches and 3 landing ships infantry. Six of the destroyers and 13 corvettes were under British command in the Indian Ocean.

Meanwhile the troops ashore near Munda were in difficulties. They were hungry, dispirited and weary, but more men were landed, until at length the 37th and 43rd Divisions, part of the 25th, and some marine units were ashore. The Japanese were cut off from supplies and their resistance gradually waned. On 5th August after a big bombardment the American tanks and infantry occupied Munda airfield unopposed. On the night of 6th-7th August six American destroyers intercepted four Japanese destroyers, of which three were ferrying troops to Kolombangara. These three were sunk, and perhaps 1,500 men drowned, without loss to the Americans. This advance of 300 miles from Guadalcanal—about a third of the way to Rabaul—had engaged for six weeks a corps of three divisions which lost 1,090 killed and 3,870 wounded.

The experience at Munda underlined the desirability, where possible, of choosing as stepping-stones along the line of advance those places where the enemy was weak—an age-old military concept. In the vast archipelagos between Australia and Tokyo the Japanese could not be strong everywhere. Thus Halsey decided to bypass Kolombangara which was strongly held and seize Vella Lavella where there were only about 1,000 Japanese and where two coastwatchers with native scouts were posted. On 21st July an American reconnaissance group was landed, and on 15th August a reinforced regiment of the 25th American Division was put ashore unopposed at the eastern end. On 18th September a new force entered the field—a brigade group of Major-General H. E. Barrowclough's 3rd New Zealand Division. These pressed northward and by 1st October had pinned the surviving 600 Japanese in a small area on the north-west shore. Thereupon Japanese barges and destroyers in a few days lifted nearly 10,000 men, mainly of the *6th Division,* from Kolombangara to Bougainville, and then set out to save the 600 on Vella Lavella. On the night of 6th-7th October six destroyers covering three destroyer-transports and other small troop-carrying craft sallied out, and were intercepted by three American destroyers. In a night engagement one American and one Japanese destroyer were sunk, but the Japanese transports succeeded in taking off their troops.

This account of the American advances in the Solomons has far outrun the narrative of events on the other main front round Salamaua. There on 2nd July Moten had issued orders for the capture of Observation Hill five days later by two companies of the 2/6th Battalion; that done the attacking companies would link with the Americans on Bitoi Ridge. On the 8th the I/162nd American Battalion would capture small hills forward of Bitoi Ridge.

The troops on the ground were now being far more effectively supported and supplied by the growing air force. Wirraways covered the fighting, dropping food and ammunition, dropping messages, spotting and so on. In June the Boomerang fighters made an appearance and soon most of the sorties were flown by this Australian-made machine. At the same time Kenney received, as part of his reinforcement for the 1943 campaign, considerable numbers of transport aircraft. Six new squadrons came in July, and by September he would possess fourteen such squadrons. By the end of July he had also received substantial reinforcements of Liberators and Mitchells. On paper his fighter strength rose to 565 aircraft, but half of these were well-used Kittyhawks and Airacobras, and usually half of these again were under repair. By July the inflow of ancillary units to No. 9 Group R.A.A.F. had been on a large scale. It now controlled four wings—two operational, one works and one radar—and included ten squadrons, a torpedo-bomber flight and three fighter control units.

The air force gave evidence of its growing strength on 7th July when Mitchells bombed and strafed the objectives—Observation Hill and Mubo areas—and Liberators and Flying Fortresses bombed and Bostons strafed the enemy far and wide. These attacks by more than 100 aircraft were accurate; a cloud of smoke filled the Mubo Valley. On the right the American battalion began to advance to Bitoi Ridge along tracks marked by Australian scouts, and were on top of it by the afternoon of the second day.

On the morning of the 7th the 2/6th had attacked Observation Hill and by nightfall held most of it. Next day the leading Australian company advanced a stage farther towards a creek where it was to link with the Americans from the Bitoi. On the 9th, now supported by the American field guns whereas formerly there had been only two mountain guns behind them, five Australian companies pressed on with aggressive patrols until, on the 10th, only seventy-five Japanese survived in the area, and their line of retreat was cut. On the 12th the Pimple was occupied. Next day there was a general advance and on the 14th Mubo airfield and Green Hill were taken.

To the north, however, the enemy was still stoutly defending Old Vickers where they were strongly dug in to defend the track to Salamaua, and there they defeated attacks by the relatively-inexperienced 58th/59th Battalion on 7th and 9th July.

In the meantime patrols of the 24th Battalion were probing deeply in the Markham area. One was out for three weeks in May seeking likely airfields, and picked sites at Marilinan and Tsili Tsili. Another established an ambush at the mouth of the Buang River, north of Salamaua, on 29th June. The Japanese, fearing an advance down the Markham, formed a main line of resistance from Heath's Plantation to Narakapor with patrols forward to Nadzab.

The 3rd Division had now driven the enemy out of the Mubo area and his hold on the heights defending the track to Salamaua as far north as Bobdubi was insecure. Savige next sought to invest Salamaua and block the track leading thence to Lae. To this end he ordered Hitchcock's Papuans to establish themselves about Lokanu, the 2/3rd Independent Company to occupy a position on Mount Tambu and cut the escape route from Mubo, and one of Moten's battalions, assisted by the 15th Brigade, to push on to the high ground south of the Francisco River. Later the 2/3rd was to move forward to Hote and a company of the 24th Battalion was to establish a base near Malolo and harass the coastal track. Finally Moten would move into the Lokanu area and bombard the Japanese base at Salamaua.

On 11th July Herring informed Savige that the 3rd Division's immediate task was still to drive the enemy north of the Francisco. He asked, however, for an outline plan for the capture of Salamaua when the time came. Savige said that he needed another Australian brigade, and three regiments of artillery—one of field guns, one of medium guns and one of light anti-aircraft guns—to undertake the capture of Salamaua. His plan would be to send in three Australian battalions to capture the high country overlooking the town north of the Francisco, and if possible to press on to the airfield and harbour, while the American regiment secured a position along the south bank of the Francisco. Thence, after a long bombardment, the combined force would seize the Salamaua peninsula.

A preliminary move, now undertaken, was to establish artillery at Tambu Bay. The III/162nd American Battalion (Major Archibald B. Roosevelt) was assembled at Nassau Bay by 12th July to occupy this area. At this time the Papuans had discovered that no Japanese remained south of Tambu Bay.

A touchy command problem now developed. On 12th July General Horace H. Fuller of the 41st American Division placed the units round Nassau Bay under Brigadier-General Ralph W. Coane, his artillery commander, leaving MacKechnie in command only of the forward units round Napier. On the same day Moten was informed that Roosevelt's battalion was responsible directly to Fuller, but Herring informed his subordinates that all units of MacKechnie's force were still under Savige's control, and Savige passed this on to Moten. On the 14th, however, when Moten sent a signal to Roosevelt, Roosevelt replied: 'I obey no orders except those from my immediate superior' and added, among other remarks, 'As a piece of friendly advice your plans show improper reconnaissance and lack of logistical understanding.' Savige promptly informed Roosevelt that Herring's instructions showed that he (Roosevelt) was under MacKechnie's command and thus under Moten's. Roosevelt replied that he took orders only from Fuller. At length Herring arranged that MacKechnie's force should remain under Moten's command, while Coane's (including Roosevelt's battalion) was under Savige's. Thereupon, on 15th July, Savige sent instructions to Coane, and welcomed him to the command, but on the 19th he received a copy of Fuller's instructions to Coane of 11th July which, in effect, made Coane's force an independent one operating on orders from New Guinea Force conveyed through 41st Divisional Headquarters at Oro Bay. Finally, on the 23rd, Herring gave an instruction that Savige would command all troops round Nassau Bay and north of it. The confused situation had taken twelve days to straighten out.

By the 17th Roosevelt's battalion was tramping north from Lake Salus towards Tambu Bay with the Papuans still far ahead. On the 19th its leading companies were half way from Salus to Boisi; at Boisi Hitchcock attacked a Japanese outpost, and next day occupied the village. On the 21st the American battalion reached Tambu Bay and supplies were being unloaded there. The Americans' task was to capture Scout Ridge, overlooking the bay. Attacks on the 22nd failed. Savige advised Coane to outflank the Japanese, and arranged that a second battalion (the II/162nd) be sent in.

Meanwhile, on the 16th, a company of the 2/5th Battalion had assaulted Mount Tambu with great dash and captured all but the main northern knoll. The Japanese counter-attacked again and again that night, supported by mortar bombs and shells from a mountain gun. A second company reached the area next morning. On the night of the 18th the Japanese attacked and almost encircled the two companies on Tambu, and next day a fierce struggle developed. By 2.30 p.m., after much slaughter of the Japanese, they accepted defeat and left the Australians in possession of the southern slopes. An estimate that 350 Japanese were hit was considered conservative. In the two Australian companies thirty-nine men were killed or wounded.

Farther north, on 15th July, after mortar and Vickers-gun fire, two

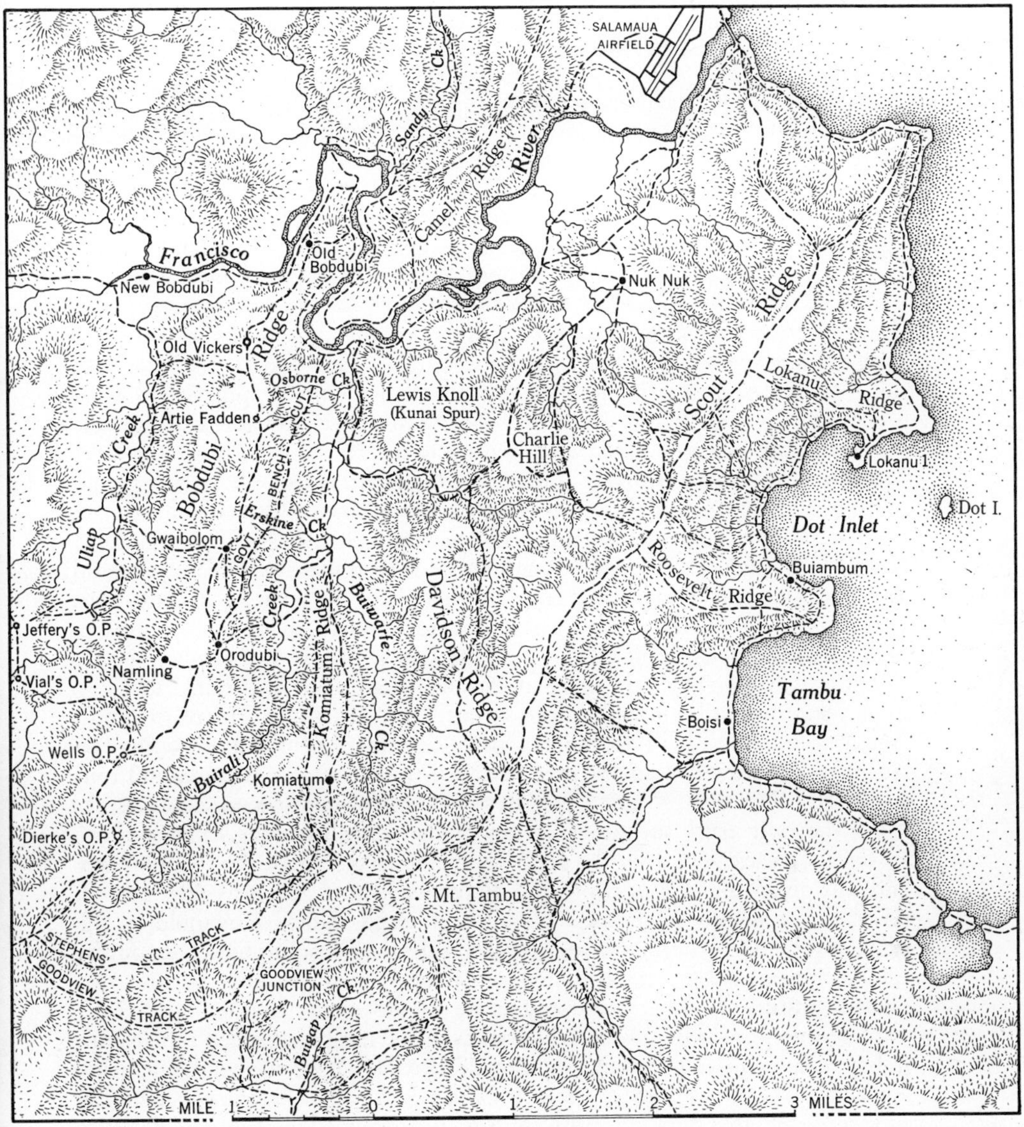

Komiatum and Salamaua

platoons of the 2/3rd Independent Company attacked Ambush Knoll south of Namling, while the 58th/59th Battalion attacked towards Bobdubi in another effort to cut the Japanese communications. One platoon of the Independent Company drove the Japanese from their forward positions, the other thrust them from Orodubi, and that night the Japanese abandoned Ambush Knoll. The attack by the 58th/59th was upset, however, by Japanese counter-moves. In a renewed attack on the 17th the Independent Company again carried out its task but the 58th/59th was held up.

The Japanese in this vital area had now been reinforced from Salamaua. They opened a counter-attack towards Ambush Knoll, but were repulsed. The enemy's main line, which had run through Old Vickers, Orodubi,

Buirali Creek, Goodview Junction and Mount Tambu, had now been deeply dented in the southern sector and they seemed resolved to re-establish it. On the 20th Savige agreed to free the 15th Brigade of responsibility for the area south of Namling, and the 2/6th Battalion was sent north to extend the flank of the 17th Brigade. Japanese counter-attacks continued, and the Independent Company had to withstand twelve assaults on Ambush Knoll on the 20th, but by the 23rd the Japanese not only abandoned these onslaughts but withdrew from strong positions farther north.

About this time there were increasing signs that the Japanese were patrolling aggressively along the coast between Salamaua and Lae; in this area the 24th Battalion was holding widely-separated positions, and patrolling on a wide arc from Hote and Malolo to the Buang River, thence to the Snake River and the Wampit River, and forward to the Markham. On the night of 18th July the troops near the Buang mouth heard much barge traffic, and twice in the next few nights one of their booby traps was exploded and there were signs that Japanese and their native guides had been hit. After some clashes with about 150 Japanese marines, the Australians were forced inland to Lega. Documents captured later showed that the Japanese commanders were concerned at signs of an advance down the Buang to facilitate a landing in that area and had sent a depleted battalion to secure the area.

The establishment of the Nassau Bay base had made it possible to bring in and supply a substantial quantity of artillery. By the 23rd there were two American field artillery battalions, two Australian field batteries, the 1st Australian Mountain Battery, the 2/6th Australian Survey Battery, and four anti-aircraft batteries.

On the right flank the American regiment was still making little progress. In the fourth week of July the II/162nd completed its arrival at Tambu Bay and was given the task of capturing 'Roosevelt Ridge' as it was now named. A well-led company of the new battalion attacked, gained a foothold on the ridge and held it. The Japanese were well dug in and not to be driven out by frontal attacks. Roosevelt's battalion, aided by Papuan patrols, was now employed cutting the enemy's supply route to the west.

The American leaders were still restless at having been placed under Australian command, and Coane on the 28th sent Savige a signal criticising Savige's instructions. Savige flew to Coane's headquarters, explained the situation, and told him he must capture Roosevelt Ridge without delay to protect the guns and the base at Tambu. Savige emphasised that it was not necessary to hold a continuous line, and that when ground had been gained it must be held; the troops should not withdraw at night to their perimeter camps or to the beach.

Nevertheless the Americans made no gains in the next few days, and on 4th August Coane signalled Savige and Fuller that his infantry strength had dwindled to 708, and some fifty sick and wounded were going out each day; in a few days he would not be able to hold the area. Savige in his reply pointed out that in proportion to his task Coane's force was stronger in men and weapons than those in the other sectors. Meanwhile Hitchcock and his Papuans were doing what they could to guide and encourage the Americans. On 24th July, after a 15-minute barrage, the 2/5th Battalion attacked on Mount Tambu with the object of gaining the heights still held by the Japanese and enabling the attached American battalion to patrol north-east to

Coane's force. The attack, over extremely rugged country, failed. This was a disappointing setback, and when the news reached Port Moresby it caused great concern at Herring's headquarters. On the 28th, however, a flanking attack by a company of the 2/6th took a feature forward of Ambush Knoll. During the July fighting 1,238 tons of bombs were dropped by American and Australian aircraft compared with 119 in June.

Herring now gave Savige an account of the plan for a large-scale offensive against Lae by the 7th and 9th Divisions before the end of August. The role of the 3rd Division, he explained, would be to hold the maximum number of Japanese in the Salamaua area, where they would be isolated when Lae fell. He was considering sending the headquarters and one battalion of the 29th Brigade (Brigadier R. F. Monaghan) into Tambu Bay; at length the whole brigade might relieve the 17th which had been in action for six months. Savige decided that the incoming battalion should relieve Coane's force of the task of operating against Tambu from the north-east. Meanwhile Brigadier Hammer had given the 58th/59th the task of driving the Japanese from Bobdubi Ridge by capturing Old Vickers. Four platoons attacked on 28th July, supported by some artillery, mortar and machine-gun fire, and at last took this stubborn position. The pressure was continued. It was estimated that in the six weeks to 6th August the 15th Brigade had killed 400 Japanese for a loss of forty-six killed and 152 wounded, an indication of the increasing tactical superiority of the attackers.

Australian War Memorial

At Timbered Knoll in the Bobdubi Ridge area, 29th July 1943.
An Independent Company corporal giving aid to a wounded mate.

Australian War Memorial

During the Salamaua and other operations in Papua-New Guinea troops in the forward areas were largely dependent on air droppings for food and ammunition. Here a 'biscuit bomber' is shown dropping supplies to the Australians at Goodview, 600 yards from the Japanese lines, on 1st August 1943.

The six Australian and three American battalions and one Australian Independent Company had now broken the enemy's outer defences and were pressing close to Salamaua. In July they succeeded also in attracting Japanese forces from Wewak to Salamaua, where four new battalions had now arrived. They were: the *I/80th* Battalion of the *20th Division* and the *238th Regiment* of the *41st Division.* Thus all three Japanese divisions in the *XVIII Army* were now represented round the enemy base.

Colonel MacKechnie resumed command of the 162nd Regiment which was now detached from the 41st Division and placed under Herring's control. The leading battalion of the 29th Australian Brigade—the 42nd—was moved forward into the Nassau Bay area and thence marched northward, and at length went into position between the Americans on the right and the 17th Brigade, of which it became part.

It was at this stage that, on 9th August, plans were issued for the second phase of the big offensive, to open on 4th September. But meanwhile the 3rd Division had its own preliminary tasks to complete: before 16th August the Americans were to take Roosevelt Ridge; then Moten was to take the Mount Tambu-Goodview Junction area, and Hammer was to advance east to the Komiatum track to prevent the enemy from moving north or south along it.

As a preliminary to the capture of Mount Tambu the 42nd Battalion occupied Davidson Ridge between Tambu and Roosevelt Ridge. Then on 13th-14th August the II/162nd Battalion took Roosevelt Ridge after a heavy artillery barrage which bared it of vegetation. The 15th Brigade's attack opened on 14th August. Twenty-nine heavy bombers accurately bombed Coconut Ridge with devastating effect, and guns, mortars and machine-guns brought down a barrage. A company of the 2/7th Battalion then attacked up a cliff so steep that the men had to crawl on hands and knees, but by early in the afternoon they had gained the North Coconuts position. On the night of the 16th-17th the Japanese abandoned South Coconuts.

The 2/6th Battalion opened its attack on Komiatum Ridge on the 16th. After about 500 shells had been fired into the Japanese positions two companies attacked and in twenty-five minutes had occupied the objective, the Japanese fleeing. The enemy in the Mount Tambu area were now surrounded, their routes to the north being cut on Komiatum and Davidson Ridges. Moten expected that lack of rations (patrols had discovered they were delivered every three days) would cause the Japanese to attempt the break out on the third night. On the 19th patrols of the 2/5th found Goodview Junction deserted. Moten, convinced that Tambu also had been deserted, ordered the I/162nd to occupy it, and it did so that morning without opposition.

At this stage a Japanese force, later learnt to be 180 strong, made a daring foray into the Allied territory on the coast. It was seen moving through the bush on the 12th and the conclusion was reached that its objective was the artillery. A strong American patrol set out in pursuit and other precautions were taken. On the 13th the Japanese force was nearing Lake Salus; next day it ambushed and dispersed an Australian platoon at the north-west end of the lake. Before dawn on the 16th a troop of the 2/6th Field Regiment, guarded by a platoon of infantry, was attacked. The guns were successfully defended, but before the raiders had been driven off they had destroyed some equipment and captured some packs and documents. That night the raiders clashed with an American patrol. The Japanese were now starving, and they dispersed. Several parties were intercepted on the return journey and probably few of the raiders survived.

The 15th Brigade now pressed in towards the track leading to Salamaua. On 17th August after a bombardment two platoons of the 2/3rd Independent Company advanced; one occupied the junction of the Bobdubi-Salamaua track and another track from the south without opposition, but the other was held. Heavy fighting developed, the Japanese launching strong counter-attacks.

On 19th August Savige ordered that every effort must be made to close the enemy's avenues of escape between Komiatum and Bobdubi Ridges. Next day the brigade attacked on a wide front, and the 58th/59th succeeded in cutting the Komiatum track in several places.

Herring had told Savige on the 13th that he would soon be relieved of responsibility for the outlying northern areas in which his 24th and 57th/60th Battalions had been patrolling with great success. Two new independent forces were to be established: Wampit Force, chiefly Lieut-Colonel G. F. Smith's 24th Battalion; and Tsili Tsili Force, chiefly Lieut-Colonel R. R. Marston's 57th/60th. Then, on the 19th, Savige was told that his headquarters would soon be relieved by that of the 5th Division, under Major-General Milford. At the same time Herring instructed Savige that his force should be so organised that by 28th August it could be maintained from the sea and without air supply. From 21st August the 29th Brigade began to relieve the 17th Brigade (not including the 2/7th Battalion now in the 15th Brigade) which had been fighting its way through the jungle-clad tangle of mountains from Wau towards Salamaua since January.

Hammer now set out to gain the inner defences of Salamaua before the Japanese could establish themselves firmly there, but, because the larger plan was to delay the fall of Salamaua until the big offensive opened, Savige ordered Hammer to limit his objective to Camel Ridge, north of the Francisco River, with patrols farther forward. North and south of the river the pursuit continued on the 21st; so rapid was the advance that Savige warned Hammer not to do anything which might cause the enemy to evacuate Salamaua too soon.

The next phase of the operations round Salamaua, after General Savige and his headquarters went out, on 26th August, and General Milford and his headquarters came in, belongs to the next chapter.

The strategical gains achieved by this long campaign through the winter of 1943 had been worth the great effort demanded of the troops. The *XVIII Japanese Army* had been kept employed and in the process had diverted a great part of its strength away from the areas which were to be the objectives of the big offensive which could not be mounted until the spring, when veteran divisions would be rested and retrained, landing craft available, and air superiority increased. At the same time immensely valuable experience had been gained in jungle tactics and in methods of supply. For the first time Australian infantry and commando units had worked closely together in a lengthy campaign and each had learnt from the other. Artillery had been used on a scale hitherto unattained in mountain warfare in New Guinea, and in a manner that would be repeated elsewhere in later years. Two more raw brigades had been tried in battle and had gained in skill and confidence. Part of an American division had been given some experience and there were now three American divisions in the South-West Pacific Area—1st Marine, 32nd and 41st—which had seen active service; and four others—Americal, 25th, 37th and 43rd—in the Solomons. In the six months to August 1943 the strength of the Japanese *XVIII Army* had been depleted and dispersed while, behind the front on which the 3rd Australian Division fought, the Allied strength in the South-West Pacific had greatly increased.

The Australians had now developed doctrines which gave them decisive tactical and administrative superiority over the Japanese in bush warfare. The supply of the Australian forward troops was maintained by three means: by wheeled vehicles to the 'jeep-head' where the road ended and thence by native carriers; by dropping stores from the air on prepared grounds equipped, if possible, with storage sheds; and coastwise by small craft. Much labour was spent on draining the tracks, corduroying low-lying sections with logs laid side by side, and cutting steps on steep pinches. The carriers bore 40-pound loads; thus one 'boy' could carry 600 rounds of rifle ammunition, or three 3-inch mortar bombs, or twelve days of field rations for one man, or ten blankets. The carriers were controlled by an Angau officer, often an 'old New Guinea hand', attached to each brigade.

In attack and defence the track and any high features commanding it were the vital ground, and particularly any razor-backed hills over which the track travelled. On such hills the flanks were protected by the steep slopes and the front was narrow. Frontal attack on such positions was costly and wide outflanking movements were made. In such deployment, however, the Australians were more successful than the Japanese because of the Japanese tendency to concentrate their strength forward with insufficient depth.

Tall dense timber often prevented aircraft crews from seeing the tracks, and reconnaissance by infantry patrols, generally of two, three or four men, was therefore most important. These had to employ the same kind of navigational aids as those used by night patrols in open country. Artillery support was often very limited because of the difficulty of bringing ammunition forward, ten natives being needed to carry fifteen rounds of 25-pounder ammunition. Henceforward the guns were generally sited near the coast and supplied by sea, though their fire might be supporting infantry miles inland and high in the hills. Before an attack all men were briefed with the greatest care because of the difficulty of using visual signals in dense bush. The attackers advanced firing from the hip; careful mopping up was essential because of the ease with which individual enemy soldiers could conceal themselves while the attackers passed through. Prompt organisation of a captured position was particularly necessary.

In defence a battalion was generally deployed in a series of company or platoon perimeters sited on high ground if any. Within each company or platoon perimeter the men occupied two-man slit trenches, each stocked with perhaps three days' food and ammunition, sited so as to give mutual support if possible, and with fire lanes cleared through the encircling bush, and booby traps round the whole area.

Booby traps and ambushes were employed by fighting patrols, the ideal ambush site in hill country being on a track round a steep slope and with the ambush party on the high ground. Ambush was used particularly by the Independent Companies (now given the unwieldy title of 'Cavalry Commando Squadrons'). The possession of native troops able to move silently through the bush and almost invariably to detect the presence of the enemy before he revealed himself gave Australian patrols an immense advantage over the Japanese.

The need for strict attention to hygiene, preventive medicine, and measures to preserve high spirits and self-respect was being increasingly recognised. The responsibility was placed on each leader of seeing that men took their atebrin against malaria, used powder to fend off skin disease, regularly washed clothes and body, and shaved. Strenuous efforts were made to ensure one hot meal a day, and dry sleeping places, and to establish fairly comfortable rest areas well forward. The value of Y.M.C.A. and Salvation Army posts with hot drinks and other amenities was recognised, as was the need to keep the troops informed about and interested in affairs in the world at large by the distribution of news bulletins and *Guinea Gold*, the army newspaper. Soon an education officer would be attached to each brigade to circulate news and books, give lectures and teach classes even among units in a forward area. Remarkable ingenuity went into preserving cleanliness and improvising buildings, furniture and other amenities in the most unpromising places, in the fighting area and out of it.

At the beginning of 1943 about 485,000 Australians and 116,000 American servicemen were in Australia; 125,000 more Australians and Americans were serving elsewhere in the South-West Pacific Area. All these were looking to Australia for part or all of their supplies.

The Production Executive, pursuing its task of making the best use of manpower, had pointed out in September 1942 that while 'it is not possible . . . to plan and control primary production anything like as accurately as secondary production . . . it is necessary especially for purposes of manpower policy to decide which types of agricultural production must be stimulated and to what extent'. The co-operation of State departments of agriculture, and of the Commerce Department (renamed Commerce and Agriculture in December 1942) was sought, and an Interdepartmental Committee on Production Goals emerged, which also included representatives of the Manpower Directorate. At first goals had been set only for butter, cheese and wool. But the policy of setting production goals was begun in earnest for the 1943-44 harvests. Rice, fish, peanuts, wheat, potatoes, field peas, vegetables, tobacco, eggs and barley were included. It was soon realised that to budget for only two dairy products was not much use and the goal for 1943-44 covered all such products; in terms of milk the goal was 1,210,000,000 gallons. Butter had fallen short of the 1942-43 goal by 25,000 tons and the goal for 1943-44 was set at 175,000 tons as against a previous figure of 190,000 tons.

With wool the committee had no success; from the start it was obvious that plans to rationalise this powerfully entrenched industry would be vigorously resisted; and reorganisation, improved methods, restriction as well as expansion of production were implicit in any policy for production goals. Despite 'exploratory' meetings of the Departments of War Organisation of Industry and of Commerce, and of graziers' representatives, no mention of goals for wool appeared on Production Executive agenda after June 1943.

In almost every item production was below the desired figure. Food production was growing ever more important. In April 1943 a Food Executive Committee was set alongside the Australian Food Council (which had been an advisory body only) and was charged with 'production control and distribution of foodstuffs at the highest pitch of efficiency'. In June 1943 the Prime Minister announced that 'for all purposes of priority the production of essential foods is to be regarded as a war activity'.

This shift of emphasis to food production meant a new demand for manpower. Mention has already been made of the drift of workers from rural production; men from the country provided fine types for the forces, and country workers were attracted by more highly paid jobs and shorter working hours in the city. In July 1942 a Women's Land Army had been formed under the encouragement and guidance of the Manpower Directorate from among the auxiliary and voluntary land-army organisations in existence from the beginning of the war. It was given improved status in January 1943 with a planned membership of 6,000 permanent and casual workers (in fact at the end of 1943 there were about 2,500 permanents and 1,000 casuals). This did something to fill the gap. After May 1942 men in rural industries were no longer called up for the army, and finally in October 1943 the War Cabinet directed that of 40,000 men to be released from the Services and from munitions, 15,000 were to go to rural industries.

That the limits of Australian manpower were being reached had been recognised in 1942, and it will be recalled that by August 1942 a committee was already investigating the problem of finding enough people to man industry and the Services. This proved the forerunner of a permanent War Commitments Committee which first met in January 1943. Through it the

War Cabinet was to be informed each month of the numbers of people to be allocated to direct war activities, and the progress made in obtaining these requirements. Moreover no new commitments needing manpower were to be undertaken until it was clear where the people were to come from.

The fact was that for the first six months of 1943 the Services and munitions and aircraft production wanted 24,000 men and 11,000 women each month, but the likely supply of people to fulfil these needs was 5,000 men and 5,000 women. Even these would be available only if inessential production was further restricted, industries were further rationalised, and sources like the retail trades and 'white collar' occupations carefully gleaned.

To assist the Manpower Directorate the Government finally agreed, on 29th January 1943, to give it the power of 'direction'. By the end of December 1943 nearly 3,500 of these 'directions' had been issued and by publicity, and some calling-up, the directorate prompted men, and more particularly women, not employed or in inessential jobs, to find work in war industry, in the forces, and especially in food processing, in order to avoid being called up by the directorate and 'directed' to whatever job the officials thought fit.

The problem was no longer to make an adjustment between essential industry and the Services on the one hand and inessential activities on the other; this time the adjustment would need to be between the claims of equally essential sections of the war effort. We have already seen how the army was compelled to reduce its Order of Battle and ultimately, by a decision of War Cabinet in October 1943, to release a net total of 20,000 men to industry, but industry also was compelled to release men and adjust its organisation.

At the end of 1942 the Services had been directed to review their demands for supplies. Some orders had been fulfilled and the completion of other objectives of the munitions program was approaching. The Cabinet was especially concerned at the excess production which, despite complaints from the Services and Munitions about lack of manpower, was still available for assignment overseas. When the consolidated program of the Services came before it in April 1943, the War Cabinet stipulated that 2-pounder ammunition production was to cease as soon as possible, and other items were to be 'depressed': 25-pounder guns and 17-pounders to a combined total of forty a month; 40-mm anti-aircraft guns to thirty a month; 3.7-inch anti-aircraft guns to four, or perhaps eight, a month; 6-pounder anti-tank guns to twenty a month; and there were similar reductions in various types of ammunition. The tank program disappeared in July 1943 having delivered, at that date, sixty-six tanks and having cost over £4,000,000. It released some 2,000 men. In June 1943 the army's stock of carriers was sufficient for the next twelve months.

These reductions were not made without opposition. The Minister for Munitions, Makin, underlined the needs of India, Burma and Malaya, and pointed to the advantages of maintaining production on a reduced scale. In his view people could not be suitably redistributed, he questioned the wisdom of breaking up manufacturing plants, and asked whether the closing of factories, specially in the country, would have a good effect on morale. Actually twelve ammunition factories, two explosive factories, five small-arms factories and two ordnance factories began production in 1943 as part of the plan to disperse munitions production into satellite factories throughout the country, thus tapping new sources of labour. Eight of these had closed before September 1944.

The munitions organisation was called on to produce new items as the result of the changing war situation in 1943. With the aid of imported machinery it set about producing ball bearings, and was doing so by June 1944; production of mobile refrigerating equipment, water-supply and excavating equipment was followed in July 1943 by the introduction of an Agricultural Machinery Division to supply special machinery not provided by proprietary firms.

Construction of small craft continued under the supervision of the Shipbuilding Board until 23rd October 1943 when the program was handed over to the Small Craft Construction Directorate in the Department of Munitions. At that date 3,619 craft had been launched. Three of the River-class cargo vessels which the Shipbuilding Board was supervising were launched in 1943 and the building of 300-ton wooden ships in Tasmania and Western Australia was begun.

In considering the reductions in the production of warlike equipment it is necessary to note that the flow of Lend-Lease goods into Australia had increased considerably. By June 1943 the total was 552,000,000 dollars (American) and 61 per cent comprised munitions. After prolonged negotiation an exchange of notes with the United States on 3rd September 1942 had established Australia's acceptance of the principles of the Mutual Aid Agreement entered into between England and America in February 1942. Australia's contributions to the maintenance and equipment of United States forces was accepted as reciprocal Lend-Lease, and by the end of 1943 Australia's contribution had reached £112,000,000.

In February 1943 the Treasurer, Chifley, had introduced additional taxation aimed at finding £40,000,000 for a national welfare scheme covering maternity allowances, pensions, etc. To do this he reduced the figure for exempt incomes from £156 to £104; rates began at 6d in the £1 and rose to 18s 6d in the £1 on incomes of £5,000 and over, and property rates were increased. From 1st April 1943 income tax could be paid in instalments.

Included in the expenditure for 1943-44 was an estimated £12,000,000 for subsidies. This indicated an important step and its origin lay in the continuing efforts to prevent prices rising. Implicit in the scheme was the declaration of 'ceiling' prices—that is prices above which goods might not be sold—and the order providing for these was made on 13th April 1943. By September 1943 subsidies were being paid on tea, potatoes, coal, firewood, whole milk and linseed; in addition a wide range of imported goods—with special attention being given to clothing—were being subsidised so as to isolate cost increases originating abroad.

The Government's design was to prevent rises in the costs of everyday needs (those affecting the 'C' series index on which basic wage adjustments would normally be made). Their concern was for the average citizen. But the Government had asked also for a special effort on the part of the people themselves. Speaking in Brisbane on 19th August 1942 the Prime Minister had asked the citizens to 'reconcile yourselves to a season of austerity, to make your habits of life conform to those of the fighting forces. The civil population can learn to discipline itself; it can learn to go without.' The

Prime Minister had taken on himself as a personal burden the whole weight of care of a nation at war, and he sought by vehement and sincere appeals to persuade the people to forego indulgence.

Earlier efforts at restriction have been noted. Manufacture was now controlled of electrical appliances, furniture, glass, domestic hardware, radios, sporting goods, toilet preparations, carpets, fancy foodstuffs and ice cream. Certain automobile servicing, beauty treatments and interior decorating services were also prohibited. These efforts were aimed at providing the manpower which was so urgently needed, but they were received with considerable criticism and some resentment, at least by the newspapers. They did, however, release men—300 to 400, for example, by the rationalisation of the pastrycooks' trade alone. An effort to reduce 1942 Christmas advertising and so remove some of the incitement to spend was presented by newspapers with their financial interest in advertising as an attempt to 'abolish Father Christmas'.

The action to reduce the number of domestic servants revealed more serious opposition—this time within the Cabinet itself from those Ministers who valued the goodwill of the 'middle class' vote—and the original order of 3rd December was replaced by one on the 29th which allowed not more than one domestic servant without the approval of the Manpower Directorate.

Two basic items—butter and meat—had to be rationed in 1943. Production of butter had fallen because of shortage of labour and reduction of herds. There seemed no prospect of supplying Britain with the quantity asked for in 1943-44—70,000 tons—and at the same time maintaining unrestricted Australian consumption. Accordingly from 7th June 1943 a weekly ration of 8 ounces a person was instituted. The increased demands from the Services and from the United Kingdom—particularly for beef—were important factors in the introduction of meat rationing also. To begin with a Controller of Meat was appointed in March 1943 and he was given power to acquire meat and to restrict slaughterings. Further restrictions became necessary, and to ensure equitable distribution it was decided at the end of October 1943 to introduce consumer rationing from 17th January 1944. The 1944 production was estimated at 1,080,000 tons; unrestricted civilian consumption would be 700,000 tons; Britain wanted 200,000 tons and the Services 320,000 tons. Some saving was obviously necessary. A coupon scale covering various types of meat was adopted. Following British experience it was considered advisable to leave some items uncouponed to 'cushion' the rationing; these were sausages, edible offals and cooked smallgoods, canned meats, bacon and ham, poultry, fish and rabbits.

In 1942 production of black coal, 14,903,000 tons, was an Australian record but this rate was not maintained and in industrial relations, with the miners particularly, the Government was forced to take drastic action. The ban on the Communist Party had been lifted on 18th December 1942; left-wing groups were vigorous in their support of any effort which would help Russia. Both the Labour Party and the Communist Party joined in castigating those who stayed away from work. The miners' president, himself a member of the Communist Party, was quoted by *Common Cause*, the miners' journal, as saying: 'Already (in early 1943) there have been numerous stoppages, and, comrades, I must advise you that someone is going to get hurt if this same irresponsibility continues.'

In April 1942 the Coal Control Regulations had provided that if, when a mine was open, men refused or failed to work they could be directed either into the forces or into a labour corps. In July 1943 regulations were introduced which provided that men could be fined for taking part in stoppages. Ultimately the power to garnishee was provided. In November the Government announced that a Royal Commission would conduct an investigation into the coalmining industry.

The following table indicates the progress of disputes in the coal industry:

	Number of Disputes		*Working Days Lost*	
	Australia	*N.S.W.*	*Australia*	*N.S.W.*
1942				
March quarter	123	114	55,394	51,019
June quarter	181	168	137,763	113,928
September quarter	129	119	85,731	78,556
December quarter	169	151	99,307	77,632
1943				
March quarter	218	192	275,593	237,762
June quarter	212	192	285,645	226,367
Total	1,032	936	939,433	785,264
Corresponding six quarters 1940-41	592	531	1,763,075	1,429,066

The total number of days lost in 1942-43 might be less, but the numbers of disputes were considerably more, and the centre of trouble continued to be New South Wales. Absenteeism, which troubled the munitions factories as early as April 1942, was responsible for the loss of as much coal as were strikes. Various efforts were made to provide better machinery for settling disputes, and for consultation between the Government, employers and employed. The Government enjoyed the special advantage of being a Labour one, and the unions frankly admitted that restrictions and regulations now in force would not have been tolerated from a government of another political colour. Nevertheless a Trade Union Advisory Panel failed to emerge now, as on an earlier occasion when the Menzies Government tried to form one. Trade union representatives, however, were appointed in great numbers—to the various industrial committees in the Manpower Directorate, to production boards, to the Prices Commission and the Department of War Organisation of Industry.

By insisting that union labour be used on all government contracts the Cabinet advanced the cause of unionism. Increased employment of women had renewed the old problem of the relation of their pay to men's; especially when, as now, they were undertaking jobs not attempted by women before. In the unions was an ever-present fear of cheap female labour, and the consequent displacement of men. The Women's Employment Board was established in March 1942, and it was decided that women's rates were to be not less than 60 per cent of men's. The board had a chequered career; the regulations establishing it were successfully challenged (the board, it was alleged, 'subtracted from the functions of the Arbitration Court') and the Government was forced to introduce legislation to reinstate it.

By June 1943 there were 190,000 women in direct war work (including the Services), and the total women in employment (again including the Services) had risen to 840,000. There had been a considerable drift from women's work to men's work which left gaps in those essential services which were traditionally filled by women; and the rates for skilled women's work compared unfavourably with those new rates being paid unskilled women in factories.

It seems possible to trace at least some of the slackening of effort by civilian men and women to the removal of the threat of invasion. Darwin continued to suffer air raids during 1943, and it was not until June 1943 that the Prime Minister announced publicly that he considered that the threat of invasion had passed. Nevertheless there were obvious signs that things were better; in December 1942 the civilians had learned that there could be a reduction in black-out provisions, and that the immobilisation of small craft no longer applied; in February 1943 some planters were allowed to return to their properties in Papua; in August 1943 the restriction on holidays was removed. In June the United Nations Relief and Rehabilitation Administration was announced. For the civilian, as for the soldier, the summer of 1942-43 was the turning point, and it then became fashionable to think in terms of 'post-war reconstruction'.

Significantly a government department of Post-War Reconstruction appeared in the last week of 1942, though its Director-General was not appointed until January, and its functions approved only in April 1943. The divisions of this department (some of which would later become separate authorities) illustrated the likely post-war problems as they were viewed in 1943: Central Reconstruction Training Committee (February); Demobilisation Committee, Rural Reconstruction Commission, Housing Commission (April); Secondary Industries Commission (October); National Works Council (October).

Post-war reconstruction was linked with the United Nations Charter, especially where the document referred to improved labour standards, economic advancement and social security. Quite early the Government's advisers foresaw constitutional difficulties; these matters were not within the province of the Commonwealth, and accordingly on 24th November 1942, after a draft bill had been prepared, a Constitutional Convention was held so that representatives of the various States might discuss the proposed transfer of the necessary powers. At this convention the States agreed to introduce and do their utmost to carry into law a Bill giving the Commonwealth powers for five years after the end of the war covering reinstatement of ex-servicemen, employment and unemployment, marketing, uniform company legislation, trusts, profiteering and prices, primary production, oversea exchange, air transport, railways, national works and health.

The State legislatures demurred, and the matter dragged on through 1943. Ultimately there was a constitutional referendum on 19th August 1944 and the Australian people, as usual, voted 'no'. The manner in which the Commonwealth dealt with the new situation belongs to the last year of war and the transition to peace.

In 1943 the Labour Government was confirmed in power: on 21st August 1943 Curtin's Government was returned with forty-nine seats in the House of Representatives—more than ever before in the history of the party—and a majority in the Senate. The U.A.P.-U.C.P. coalition won twenty-three seats, and there were two Independents. In September the coalition of the U.A.P. and U.C.P. was dissolved.

Chapter 11 **From Lae to the Philippines**

In spite of the formal adoption by the Allied leaders of the principle that they should concentrate against Hitler first, the Pacific continued in 1943 to attract a large share of the American forces. When Churchill, Roosevelt and their staffs met at Quebec in August there were, for example, ten American divisions in Britain and the Mediterranean, but there were six army divisions (1st Cavalry, 25th, 32nd, 41st, 43rd and Americal) and three marine divisions in the South and South-West Pacific commands, one army division (7th) in the Aleutians, and others in reserve in Hawaii. As for air power, behind the relatively modest Allied air forces in the Pacific were ranged the powerful American carrier-borne forces.

The Australian component in the combined South-West and South Pacific armies was still larger than the American, including as it did one armoured division and nine infantry divisions (6th, 7th, 9th, 2nd, 3rd, 4th, 5th, 11th, 12th). In the South-West Pacific Area (in October 1943) the strengths of the contingents were: Australian—land forces 492,000, air forces 136,000; U.S.—land forces 198,000, air forces 55,000.

The combat strength of the American air force was, however, greater than the Australian, whose numbers included those in the training organisations: there were now fifty-nine American squadrons and forty-three Australian. For some months the Allied air forces in the Pacific had been considerably stronger than the Japanese, and this superiority was increasing fast. In 1943 Japan was producing aircraft at the rate of about 1,300 a month and would increase this to about 2,300 a month in 1944, but at the end of 1943 the United States was producing 8,800 a month. More important, the Japanese economy and the Japanese forces, so greatly dependent on seaborne supplies, were suffering from lack of shipping while the Allied shipping pool was increasing. In 1943 Japan ran so short of steel that the building of battleships and aircraft carriers was discontinued.

The principal purpose of the Quebec Conference was to consider plans for the invasion of Europe. The invasion day was fixed tentatively as 1st May 1944. Future policy in the Burma theatre was discussed. Churchill recommended the appointment of acting Vice-Admiral Lord Louis Mountbatten as Supreme Allied Commander in South-East Asia—an abrupt promotion for a naval officer aged forty-three who, in 1941, had been commanding a destroyer flotilla in the Mediterranean; but he possessed great drive and confidence and had lately been close to Churchill as Chief of Combined Operations. This appointment was agreed to.[1]

[1] At the Quebec conference Churchill, aware how far out of touch London was with the South-West Pacific command (and after consulting Evatt and then Curtin) obtained American agreement to the attachment of a British general as his liaison officer on General MacArthur's staff. Lieut-General H. Lumsden, formerly a corps commander in North Africa, was chosen. At the same time Lieut-General Sir Adrian Carton de Wiart was appointed to a similar post on the staff of Chiang Kai-shek.

Two important decisions concerning the Pacific theatre were made about this time. The Combined Chiefs decided that the strongly-held fortress of Rabaul should be bypassed, a proposal that had been under discussion at Washington since June. They wished instead to encircle it by seizing Kavieng, Manus and Wewak. MacArthur was opposed to attacking Wewak before Rabaul but the Joint Chiefs of Staff overruled him, and decided also that in the summer of 1943-44 western New Britain and the Gilbert and Marshall Islands should be attacked, that Ponape and the Admiralties should be taken in the southern winter of 1944, and Truk and the Marianas in the following spring and summer.

At this time, in response to the Allied pressure westward in New Guinea, the Japanese *Fourth Air Army*, 10,000 strong, was moved from Rabaul and Ambon to Wewak, But, and other airfields in that area, where by August some 200 aircraft were concentrated. On 17th August the Fifth Air Force attacked in strength. The Japanese were caught on the ground on four airfields and about 100 aircraft were destroyed. This was described by the Japanese commander after the war as 'a decisive Allied victory'.

As part of the preparations for the coming offensive Kenney arranged that his Lightning squadrons would escort bombers operating against the *XVIII Japanese Army* and its supporting air forces at bases on the New Guinea mainland while the Australian fighter squadrons remained at Milne Bay, Kiriwina and Goodenough. By September three of the Kittyhawk squadrons were at Kiriwina, a fourth remaining at Goodenough.

The role of the squadrons of North-Western Area, now commanded by Air Vice-Marshal A. T. Cole, recently returned from posts in the Middle East and Great Britain, was to protect Allied shipping, attack Japanese airfields and ships, and generally to try to draw enemy strength away from New Guinea. Cole, in September, had four Australian and four American squadrons (all equipped with Liberators), one British squadron and one Dutch. The opposing air force was the *23rd Air Flotilla*, based on Kendari with forward airfields at Penfui (Timor), Ambon and the Kai Islands. On 6th August Japanese float-planes sank the steamer *Macumba* (2,526 tons). This led to spirited attacks on Taberfane, a float-plane base in the Aru Islands. Although the Japanese sent reconnaissance aircraft over Darwin by day their bomber raids were now made only by night. There was a clash with twenty-one enemy fighters over Darwin on 7th September, but thereafter the three Spitfire squadrons were seldom in action. During the early days of the Lae-Nadzab offensive the bomber squadrons increased their attacks to the maximum and the enemy responded with two night raids on Darwin—the 62nd and 63rd since the war began.

While this air fighting was going on over Darwin and the Japanese bases an inconspicuous little craft was sailing northward from Exmouth Gulf towards Singapore. She was the *Krait* and on board were a crew of eight and a raiding party of six under Major I. Lyon of the Gordon Highlanders. The raiders were equipped with three canoes and with limpet mines which they planned to attach to Japanese ships in Singapore harbour. They succeeded in fixing mines to seven ships on the night of 26th-27th September, returned safely to the rendezvous with the *Krait* and reached Exmouth Gulf on 19th October.

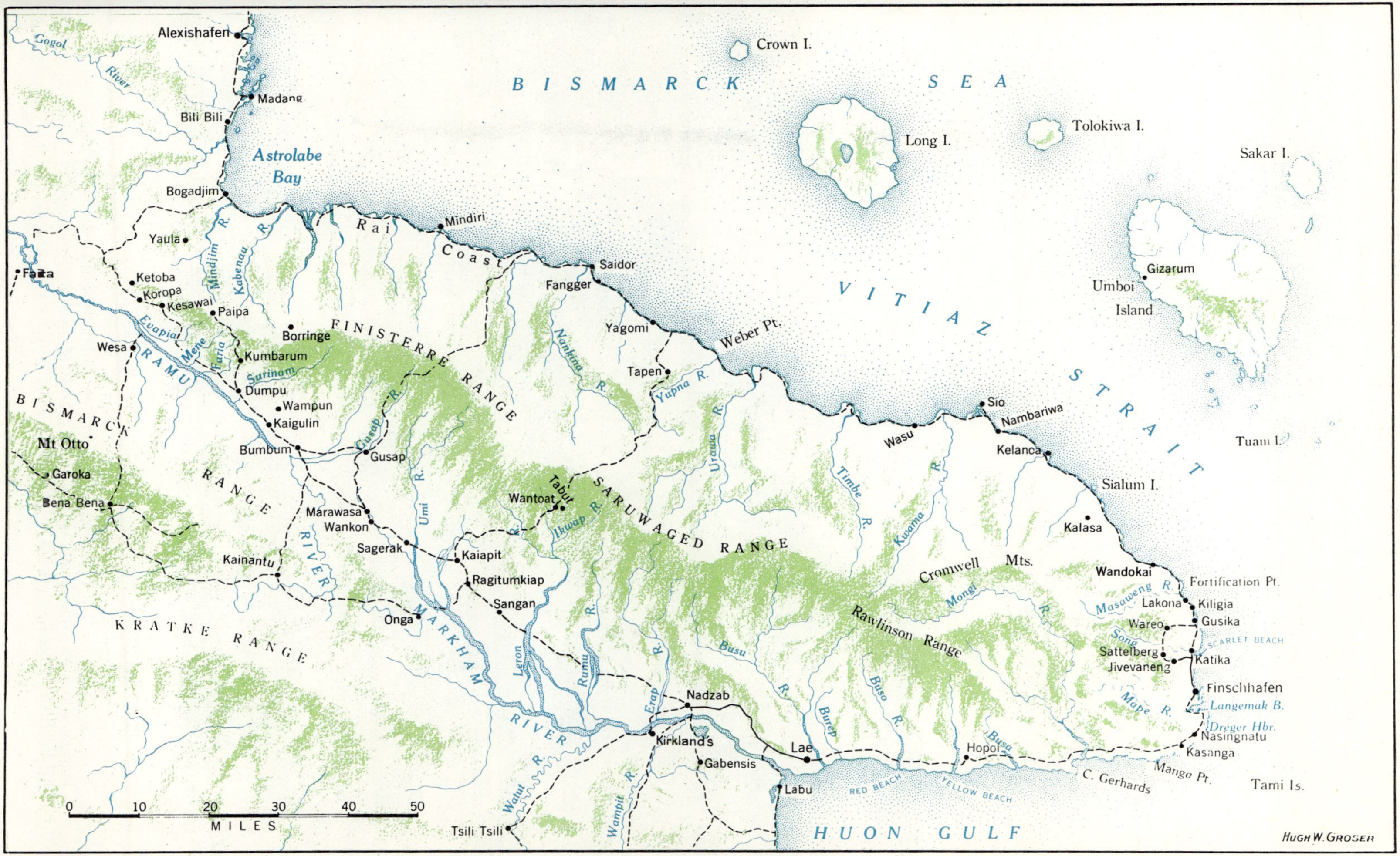

Huon Peninsula

The plans for the main New Guinea offensive had now been drawn up. The 9th Division, after strenuous training for jungle and amphibious warfare, was to be landed from the craft of Admiral Barbey's Amphibious Force and of the U.S. 2nd Engineer Special Brigade at beaches east of Lae and advance thence on Lae itself. At the same time a regiment of American paratroops with some Australian artillerymen and their guns were to descend on Nadzab in the Markham Valley, where, as soon as an airfield had been prepared, part of the 7th Division would be landed in aircraft. Both divisions would then converge on Lae.

Blamey reorganised the command for the coming operation. He himself remained in New Guinea, but Mackay took command temporarily of New Guinea Force, which comprised the I Corps (Herring), the 3rd Division, Bena Force, and Tsili Tsili Force. The I Corps included the 7th, 9th, 5th and 11th Divisions, and the 4th Brigade, but the command of the 11th

Australian War Memorial

On 4th September 1943 the 9th Australian Division landed east of Lae, New Guinea, to advance along the coast to the town. This picture shows Red Beach on the Huon Peninsula where the landing was made. The beach was carpeted with wire mesh to help vehicles cross the soft sand.

Division would pass to New Guinea Force when the I Corps moved away from the Lae-Salamaua area.

There were about 11,000 Japanese troops in the Lae-Salamaua areas. Against them would be sent a larger force than had hitherto been launched at the opening of an offensive in the Pacific theatre.

The 7th Division (Major-General Vasey), rested, retrained and reinforced after its Papuan campaign, landed at Port Moresby and the 9th (Major-General Wootten) arrived at Milne Bay, now a big base, in July and August. Later the 24th Brigade of the 9th was moved forward to Buna.

The leading brigades of the 9th Division—the 20th and 26th—were embarked in L.S.T's and L.C.I's on 1st and 2nd September. At 6.30 a.m. on the 3rd the convoy of nearly 100 vessels reached Buna where all except the troops in the larger and less uncomfortable A.P.D's and L.S.T's disembarked for exercise and hot meals. When they re-embarked at 3 p.m. the men were told their exact destination and objectives. After dark about fifty vessels carrying a shore battalion of the Engineer Special Brigade joined the convoy, which, with its escort, now numbered 152 vessels.

At 6.18 a.m. on 4th September two destroyer-transports were in position off each of the two beaches east of Lae on which the landing was to be made, and five destroyers began shelling the jungle-fringed shore at a range of two miles and a half. The assaulting battalions—the 2/13th, 2/15th and 2/17th of the 20th Brigade (Brigadier Windeyer)—clambered down nets from the four destroyers into sixteen landing craft. The bombardment ceased when the barges were 1,200 yards from the shore and the craft sped forward, their machine-guns blazing at the beaches. When they struck the shore and lowered their ramps the men filed on to the beach, spread into line and hurried across the sand to the jungle fringe. Neither the 2/13th at Yellow Beach nor the remainder of the brigade at Red Beach encountered any opposition at that stage. But thirty minutes after the first landing, as L.C.I's were putting the 26th Brigade ashore at Red Beach, nine Japanese aircraft attacked. Seven L.C.I's were then about 100 yards from the shore. A bomb hit one of these killing the commander of the 2/23rd Battalion, Lieut-Colonel R. E. Wall, and six others and wounding twenty-eight; another L.C.I. was holed by a near-miss. At 7.30 American bombers attacked Japanese positions in the battle area while R.A.A.F. Beauforts and Bostons struck at Gasmata on New Britain where enemy aircraft from Rabaul might stage on their way to the battle area.

Soon after this the American shore battalion was landed, with tractors and graders. At 8.14 a.m. six big L.S.T's hit the beach, opened their bows, dropped their ramps and disgorged vehicles, guns and men. By 10.30 7,800 troops were ashore and by 2.30 p.m. 1,500 tons of stores had been landed. Japanese aircraft from Rabaul attacked in force during the day, inflicting about 120 casualties, and severely damaging two L.S.T's. Three squadrons of American Lightnings intercepted and shot down many enemy aircraft.

The infantry advanced without interruption all that day. From Red Beach the 2/17th Battalion, moving in two columns, crossed the Buso, as did the 2/23rd and 2/24th later in the day. The westward advance continued on the 5th without opposition. That night the 24th Brigade (Brigadier Evans) was landed at Red Beach. General Wootten's orders to Brigadier Whitehead of the 26th Brigade were to secure crossings over the Busu on the 6th and reconnoitre as far north as a kunda bridge. The 24th Brigade was to move west and take over from the 26th which would swing northward. That night a patrol from the 2/23rd Battalion when 4,000 yards ahead of the main body observed about 100 Japanese advancing.

The 7th Division's plan provided that the 2/2nd Pioneers and a company of engineers should advance overland from Tsili Tsili to Kirkland's and across the Markham, a three-day march beginning on 2nd September. Two days earlier an advanced party including forty-five natives set out to improve the track for the main body, which reached the Markham on the 4th. They crossed the wide river on a bridge of folding boats that had been navigated down the Watut and Markham Rivers from Tsili Tsili. Since 1st September a detachment of No. 4 (Army Co-operation) Squadron had been established at Tsili Tsili with ten Boomerangs or Wirraways, for reconnaissance, supply dropping, ferrying senior officers and strafing. Meanwhile the 24th Battalion, which had been patrolling the Markham area for months, prepared for an attack on Markham Point, a dominating position overlooking the river eight miles west of Lae. On the 4th a company made the attack, but found the position occupied by about 200 Japanese and withdrew, after a hard fight.

At Moresby next morning at 7.30 a.m. the parachute troops were loaded into eighty-seven transport aircraft. Above Moresby they joined their escort of fighters and then flew across the Owen Stanleys at 9,000 feet in intense cold. About 10.15 a.m. the pioneers near Kirkland's saw them overhead. The three battalions of paratroops descended on their dropping grounds at Nadzab where they met no opposition and whence they moved to their assembly areas. Two hours later the pioneers and engineers crossed the bridge that had been flung across the Markham. At this stage the Australian paratroop-gunners of the 2/4th Field Regiment floated down with their guns. Meanwhile a company of Papuan troops which had long been patrolling in this area was advancing on Nadzab.

Thus by the night of the 5th the 5th Division was closing in on Salamaua, the 9th Division was ashore and its leading troops were watching the first Japanese the division had met, and at Nadzab the paratroops, pioneers, engineers and Papuan soldiers were preparing for the arrival of the airborne 7th Division.

There was now no need to delay the assault on Salamaua. General Milford had directed the fresh 29th Brigade to break through south of the Francisco while the 15th Brigade, by intensive patrolling, harassed the enemy north of the river. In the coastal sector on 29th August the western end of Roosevelt Ridge was found abandoned. The 15th Battalion was then sent through the Americans to try to seize the crest of Scout Ridge, exploit to Nuk Nuk, and cut off Japanese forces to the south. On 31st August the battalion captured a position near the crest of the ridge and held it against several counter-attacks. Stubborn resistance prevented any further movement, but the Australians could see the Japanese artillery positions and these were shelled. On 1st September the 47th Battalion captured Kunai Spur.

For the next week the Australians harassed the enemy with patrols, ambushes, and bombardments. On the 9th, five days after the opening of the assault on Lae, the 42nd Battalion captured Charlie Hill and the end

Australian War Memorial

Nadzab, New Guinea. The landing of the 503rd American Parachute Infantry Regiment on 5th September 1943. One battalion is landing in the foreground and in the left background another battalion ringed by smoke can be seen dropping. After the capture of Nadzab the 7th Division was flown in to support the advance on Lae.

was in sight at Salamaua. By the evening of the 10th Japanese resistance had collapsed south of the Francisco River. Heavy rain and flooded streams delayed the advance and enabled the Japanese to escape. On the 11th the 42nd Battalion occupied Salamaua and the 47th brushed with an enemy rearguard near the airstrip. The 15th Brigade moved forward on the same day and by the 12th had reached the coast north of Salamaua. On the 15th patrols from the 2/7th Battalion and 24th Battalion met at Malolo. The advance was then taken over by the 15th Battalion and the Papuans, who mopped up along the coast, joining forces at Labu on 18th September with the 24th Battalion patrolling from Markham Point. The Salamaua operations, now completed, had admirably succeeded in drawing the enemy's strength away from Lae. After the assault on Lae opened from 5,000 to 6,000 Japanese troops had been hurried from Salamaua to Lae in barges.

The advance on Lae from the east continued on the 6th. A company of the 2/23rd that morning attacked the 100 or so Japanese opposing them; a second company was sent north and then west to cut off these Japanese, but most of them withdrew before this could be done. About sixty, however, were intercepted by a platoon which had got astride the track behind them. Heavy rain hindered the advance on the 7th and 8th. At 4 p.m. on the

8th the 2/28th Battalion reached the Busu, an imposing obstacle, swollen by the heavy rains and five feet deep in the main channel. Orders demanded that a base be established on the west bank by dawn on the 9th but patrols failed to find a place where the river could be forded.

Wootten, anxious lest the Japanese should take advantage of this delay and dig in on the far bank, ordered Whitehead to seize bridgeheads not later than dawn on the 10th. This order did not reach Lieut-Colonel C. H. B. Norman, commanding the 2/28th, until 12.50 p.m. He ordered his company commanders to form their men up on an island in the stream, and thence wade the river in four columns, beginning at 5.30 p.m. This bold stroke succeeded. The men never faltered, although the Japanese opened fire when the leading men were half way over; thirteen were drowned during the crossing, and about a quarter of the automatic weapons were lost.

By 6.30 p.m. the battalion held a bridgehead 650 yards by 150, and it clung on there during a night of heavy rain which caused the river to rise still higher and by next morning had made it quite impossible for the next battalion, the 2/24th, to wade across. At midday, however, engineers arrived with rubber boats. Under fire sappers swam the river with ropes and secured them on the far bank.

Beyond the Busu the 2/28th pressed on that day. Anxious not to waste the 20th Brigade in a static role, Wootten asked for and obtained the 4th Brigade (Brigadier C. R. V. Edgar) to protect the beach-head. It arrived from Milne Bay on the night of the 10th.

Meanwhile, west of Nadzab, strenuous efforts had been made to prepare the airfield. Early on the 6th a small aircraft landed; at 11 a.m. the first three transport aircraft; and during the afternoon about forty more. Next morning General Vasey's headquarters and an infantry company were flown in. At Moresby, as part of the 2/33rd Battalion was assembling on Jackson's airfield in the darkness ready to emplane at dawn, a Liberator bomber crashed into trees after taking off and hit five trucks containing men of the 2/33rd; its four 500-lb bombs exploded and burning petrol was sprayed far and wide. Fifty-nine infantrymen and drivers were killed or mortally injured and ninety-two were injured. The depleted battalion was flown to Tsili Tsili, but the third battalion of the brigade could not be moved that day because clouds descended over the mountains.

On the morning of the 8th the remainder of the 2/25th and the 2/33rd Battalions were flown to Nadzab and Vasey sent the 25th Brigade, with the 2/25th Battalion leading, down the Markham Valley towards Lae. Next day the 2/25th passed through the paratroops and reached Munum; at 1 p.m. on the 10th it made first contact with the enemy about a mile and a half short of Heath's Plantation.

The 2/28th Battalion was across the Busu, but farther north the 26th Brigade could not cross the river despite many attempts to bridge it. There was some sharp fighting on the southern front as the 24th Brigade made slow progress against a stubborn defence. The 26th Brigade finally crossed the Busu on 14th September by which time the 7th Division had captured a document indicating that the Japanese intended to give up and march overland to the north coast. The 2/4th Independent Company, already guarding one supposed escape route, was reinforced by the 2/24th Battalion, but it was later discovered that the Japanese had escaped farther to the west. The advance now proceeded more rapidly and with little opposition, so that by the 15th both brigades were near the Bumbu River, which was crossed next day by the 24th Brigade.

In the Markham Valley on 10th September the 2/25th Battalion forced an enemy outpost to withdraw. Next day about 200 Japanese held up the advance, but after an artillery bombardment followed by severe infantry fighting the position was cleared. By the 14th Heath's was captured and the 2/33rd Battalion took over the advance.

As the 7th Division neared Lae opposition increased and enemy artillery shelled the advancing troops. A combined attack by the 2/31st and 2/33rd Battalions cleared Edwards' Plantation on the 15th after fierce fighting in which the two battalions lost fifteen killed and forty-two wounded, but killed over 100 Japanese. There was no more opposition; during the morning the 2/25th Battalion entered the ruins of Lae only to be forced out by artillery fire from the guns of the unwitting 9th Division and by an Allied aerial bombardment. Patrols from the 24th and 25th Brigades met that afternoon and the Australian flag was hoisted over the town. Among the defenders of Lae had been the *66th, 102nd* and *115th Japanese Regiments*, already battered during the Salamaua campaign, and elements of the *80th* and *238th Regiments*. All units were below strength. At least 1,500 Japanese were killed round Lae. In return they inflicted 547 casualties, including seventy-seven killed and seventy-three missing in the 9th Division and 142 casualties including thirty-eight killed in the 7th Division (not including the larger losses suffered by the 2/33rd Battalion in the aircraft accident at Moresby).

Parts of the 21st Brigade which arrived at Nadzab on 15th September tried hard to trap the Japanese but were too late. Only in the valley of the Sanem in October was any substantial Japanese force found, and there some 150 stragglers were killed. It was learnt later that General Adachi on 8th September had ordered General Nakano of the *51st Division* to abandon Salamaua and concentrate round Lae, and, when the threat to Lae became dangerous, he ordered him to abandon Lae but hold in the Finisterres and the Ramu Valley and at Finschhafen. About 7,800 Japanese from Lae survived the long march over the mountains to the north coast about Sio, where they were rested and reorganised.

Lae had fallen sooner than expected, and MacArthur and Blamey decided to press more rapidly along the coast of the Huon Peninsula to secure the Vitiaz Strait and thus facilitate the forthcoming attack by the Sixth American Army against New Britain by capturing an air and naval base at Finschhafen. Intelligence estimates of the number of Japanese round Finschhafen varied from 350 to about 4,000. The 20th Brigade was again selected to carry out the landing, this time at 'Scarlet Beach' about six miles north of Finschhafen. The 22nd Battalion from the 4th Brigade was ordered to march on Finschhafen overland.

The Americans who were to provide the craft from which the brigade would be landed were anxious to unload and to leave the beach before dawn because of the danger of attack from the air but Wootten and Windeyer doubted whether the navy could land them on the right beach in moonlight. Finally it was agreed to begin landing at 4.45 and to reduce the loads carried by the L.S.T's so that they would be able to get away the sooner. As a result the brigade would have at the outset fifteen days' rations instead of twenty.

Planning of the new operation was swift and efficient. Windeyer was informed of the general plan on 18th September, and the landing had to be made early on the 22nd. The plan demanded a night landing on a hostile shore and a night advance through jungle against an enemy about whom information could hardly have been more nebulous. The first task was to capture the Finschhafen-Langemak Bay area; a secondary and later objective was Sattelberg, a mountain mission station about five miles inland from Scarlet Beach and about 3,000 feet above sea level.

Windeyer's plan was to make the initial assault with two battalions; when the beach-head had been secured his third battalion would advance south towards Finschhafen. Scarlet Beach, only about 600 yards long, was bounded to the north by the Song River and to the south by a little headland beyond which was a small cove into which Siki Creek flowed.

For eleven minutes before the landing five destroyers shelled the shoreline. Before this was over sixteen barges carrying the first wave—four companies—sped towards the shore, their machine-guns exchanging fire with Japanese machine-guns ashore. As had been feared the craft did not reach the shore at the intended places. The whole wave was well to the left and the companies were mixed with one another. The men came ashore partly on Scarlet Beach, partly on the headland to the south, partly in Siki Cove and partly on coral cliffs farther south. They were trained, however, in such an event to wipe out any enemy posts they encountered and then to reorganise and make for their correct objectives. This they did.

Fortunately there was no heavy opposition immediately after the landing. By 6.30 a.m. the beach and the adjacent jungle had been cleared, and Windeyer was ashore and in touch by telephone with his battalion commanders. There was sharp opposition at Katika. The fact that a company from each of the three battalions was engaged in the Katika area indicates the degree to which the units had become intermingled. In the afternoon the Japanese were found to have abandoned the Katika position, and by dusk the leading troops were three miles south and south-west of Scarlet Beach and on North Hill.

During the day the Japanese staged their heaviest air attack for some months when they sent sixty to seventy bombers and fighters against the beach-head. They were beaten off by ninety American fighters, which destroyed perhaps half the enemy force.

The 20th Brigade advanced down the coast towards Finschhafen on 23rd September without opposition until it encountered Japanese deployed in strength along the southern bank of the Bumi River. Leaving two companies at the mouth of the Bumi, the 2/15th Battalion moved inland over rugged country and, on 26th September, gallantly forced a crossing farther upstream. This enabled the 2/13th Battalion to move through in an attempt to approach Finschhafen from the west. With every move towards Finschhafen Windeyer's lines of communication were extended and his flanks more exposed. From Scarlet Beach the 2/17th Battalion, with attached troops, had to watch the approaches to the beach-head and also hold the main track towards Sattelberg through Jivevaneng. A company of the 2/17th occupied Jivevaneng about the same time that an operation order was captured stating that a Japanese battalion would attack from Sattelberg towards the coast.

Beyond Jivevaneng the Australian company encountered a strong Japanese position astride the road. It was soon evident that Sattelberg could not be effectively attacked until the primary objective—Finschhafen—had been taken, and so the company advancing on Sattelberg was pulled back to Jivevaneng under orders to hold the road there. The 26th was a day of bitter fighting all round the front. The 2/15th made a brilliantly successful attack on the Japanese marines facing them and put them to flight. But meanwhile the enemy was pressing in towards Scarlet Beach, threatening a base area protected by one battalion whose companies were distributed from Kamloa in the south to the Sattelberg Road to the north. The actual beach-head was guarded from the Song to Siki Creek by a machine-gun company, a platoon of infantry and a few other detachments.

By this time Windeyer was convinced that parts of at least three enemy battalions were moving down from Sattelberg. An order captured on the 26th indicated that the Japanese would attack down the Katika and Sattelberg tracks from daybreak that day. On the 27th Windeyer signalled Wootten asking for an additional battalion to guard the beach-head and enable him to concentrate the 20th Brigade for the capture of Finschhafen; he asked also for a squadron of tanks.

Already on 22nd September Blamey had directed Herring to reinforce Finschhafen with the headquarters of the 9th Division and an additional brigade, but MacArthur's staff were convinced that the Japanese facing the 20th Brigade were weak and G.H.Q's instructions were that 'obligations for over-water supply and air force support will be kept to a minimum'. After several days, during which the Australian leaders appealed for the reinforcement of Finschhafen and the Americans who alone could provide the necessary craft demurred, three A.P.D's were allotted to carry the 2/43rd Battalion forward; the battalion arrived on the 30th, eight days after the original landing, and relieved the 2/17th in the Jivevaneng area.

Meanwhile the 2/15th and 2/13th Battalions had been pressing on beyond the Bumi towards Kakakog, possession of which seemed likely to give control of Finschhafen. On 1st October the 2/13th fought its way to the edge of Kakakog supported by air and artillery bombardment. The Japanese marines resisted doggedly and from 80 to 100 were killed that day. Already on the 1st the 22nd Battalion advancing from the south had seen indications that the Japanese were evacuating Finschhafen. On the 2nd the 2/13th and 2/15th met no opposition, and in the afternoon men of the 2/17th and 22nd Battalions spoke to one another across the Mape River.

The main task now was to secure the gains by getting possession of Sattelberg as soon as possible. From captured documents it appeared that there were more than 5,000 enemy troops in the general Finschhafen-Sattelberg area when Finschhafen fell. Opposing the landing at Scarlet Beach had been parts of the *80th Regiment* of the *20th Japanese Division* and the *238th Regiment* of the *41st Division* and, across the Bumi, had been the *7th Naval Base Force*. While Windeyer had been pressing southward to Finschhafen and had been guarding his western and northern approaches

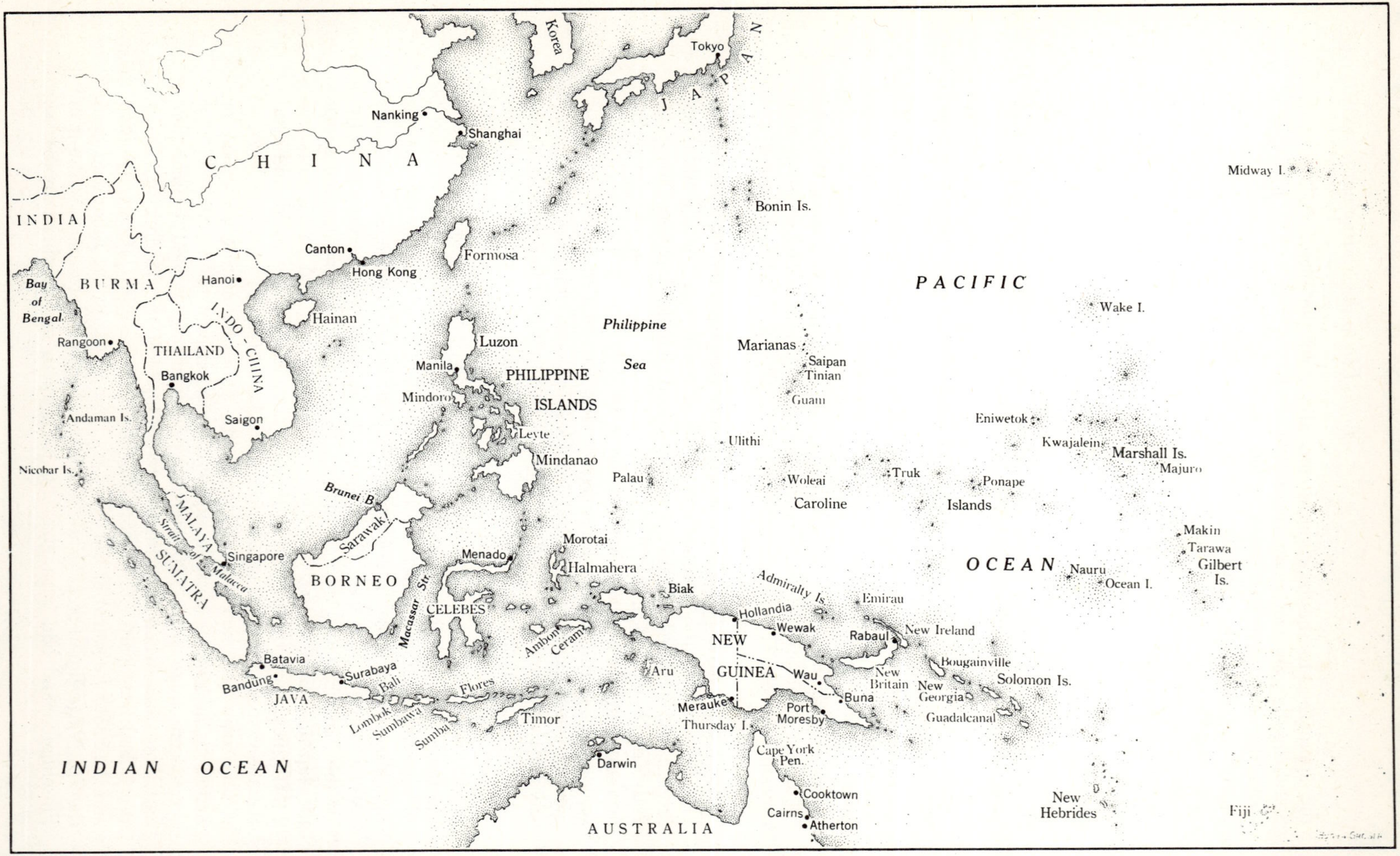
Korea
Tokyo
J A P A N
Nanking
Shanghai
C H I N A
Midway I.
Bonin Is.
INDIA
Canton
Hong Kong
Formosa
Bay of Bengal
BURMA
Hanoi
PACIFIC
Wake I.
Hainan
INDO-CHINA
Rangoon
THAILAND
Luzon
Philippine Sea
Marianas
Saipan
Tinian
Guam
Manila
PHILIPPINE ISLANDS
Bangkok
Mindoro
Andaman Is.
Saigon
Leyte
Eniwetok
Kwajalein
Marshall Is.
Majuro
Ulithi
Mindanao
Nicobar Is.
Palau
Woleai
Truk
Ponape
Caroline
Islands
Brunei B.
Sarawak
MALAYA
Strait of Malacca
Makin
Tarawa
Gilbert Is.
Morotai
Singapore
Menado
Halmahera
OCEAN
Nauru
Ocean I.
SUMATRA
BORNEO
Macassar Str.
Biak
Admiralty Is.
Emirau
CELEBES
Hollandia
Wewak
Rabaul
New Ireland
NEW GUINEA
Ambon
Ceram
Batavia
Surabaya
Aru
Wau
Bougainville
New Britain
Solomon Is.
Bandung
JAVA
Bali
Flores
Merauke
Buna
New Georgia
Lombok
Sumbawa
Sumba
Timor
Port Moresby
Thursday I.
Guadalcanal
Cape York Pen.
Darwin
INDIAN OCEAN
Cooktown
New Hebrides
Cairns
Fiji
Atherton
AUSTRALIA

with mere skeleton forces, the main body of the *20th Japanese Division* had been hurrying along the coast from Bogadjim to assemble at Sattelberg and attack the Australians.

Soon after the opening of the offensive the Japanese commanders made a series of crucial decisions. The Prime Minister, Tojo, favoured withdrawal of the south-east forces to a line through the Marianas, Truk, and Wewak. Admiral Koga contended, however, that the Bismarck Archipelago must be held to gain time while an inner line was strengthened and a decisive fleet action was fought. Koga's plan was adopted and thenceforward the intention was to defend all existing positions and fortify a line through the Marianas, Truk, the Solomons, New Guinea, Timor, the Indies and Burma; wear out the Allied offensives; engage the American Pacific Fleet at an opportune moment; and prepare a counter-offensive in the central and south Pacific in the northern spring of 1944.

The 7th Division was now moving up the Markham River Valley into the Ramu Valley. In the preceding five months steps had been taken to make airfields on the highlands whence fighters could protect the long-range bombers and close air support be given to the coming offensive. Thus an airfield was built at Tsili Tsili in the Watut Valley and an emergency landing ground at Garoka on the Bena Bena Plateau. The 57th/60th Battalion was flown into Tsili Tsili in June to protect the American engineers working there. On the plateau Bena Force (Lieut-Colonel MacAdie aged 23) was formed round the 2/7th and 2/2nd Independent Companies. It guarded the passes across the Bismarck Range into the Ramu Valley, and had several clashes with the enemy from May onwards.

When it had seemed that Lae would fall more easily and quickly than expected, Blamey had been instructed by MacArthur to seize areas in the vicinity of Kaiapit and Dumpu and establish airfields there. Because of supply difficulties the force employed on the highlands would be limited to two brigade groups. Since the landing at Nadzab, Papuan Infantry patrols had been probing the area to the west, and patrols from Bena Force had been across the Ramu River to reconnoitre enemy positions on the north bank.

On 17th September the 2/6th Independent Company was landed on an improvised air strip about thirty-five miles north-west of Nadzab. Patrols had found that perhaps 100 Japanese were established at Kaiapit, and on the 18th Vasey ordered Captain G. G. King of the 2/6th Independent Company to take that place as soon as he could. The company made a rapid march through high kunai grass in stifling heat and attacked late in the afternoon of the 19th. In a series of determined charges the 190 Australians, sometimes using grenades and bayonets, put the Japanese to flight. Two Australians were killed and seven, including King, wounded; the Japanese left thirty dead, and during the night six unsuspecting Japanese were killed as they walked into the captured area. On the 20th the Japanese attacked and were driven off. The Australians attacked again and after hard fighting in the course of which some 170 more Japanese were killed—the counted dead now included forty officers and N.C.O's—they were in control of the Kaiapit area. The Australians had lost fourteen killed and twenty-three wounded. That afternoon an enterprising American pilot landed a light aircraft on the strip and announced to King that transports would seek to land next morning. King's wireless sets had been out of action since the 19th, but fortunately his signallers succeeded in making contact later that afternoon and he informed General Vasey how things stood: Japanese patrols were moving about the newly-captured area, and the Australians were now only 139 strong and had little ammunition left. Vasey told King that he would fly in part of the 21st Brigade on the 21st if the strip was ready. Next morning some of the weary Australians, with natives, worked to prepare the strip while others fended off enemy patrols. At 3.30 p.m. a transport aircraft of the Fifth Air Force made a successful test landing, took off, and returned later with Brigadier Dougherty and part of his staff. Vasey had already landed in a Piper Cub. By 6 p.m. six aircraft had brought in a company of the 2/16th Battalion.

In the Ramu Valley patrols from Bena Force had been thrusting far and wide and occasionally clashing with enemy parties. A patrol from the 2/2nd Independent Company ambushed a large enemy party near Kesawai on 29th September and killed forty-five of them. The Independent Companies had thus cleared the way for a long advance by the 7th Division. Against only sporadic opposition the 21st Brigade crossed the imperceptible divide between the Markham and Ramu Rivers on 30th September and occupied Dumpu on 4th October. The Markham and southern Ramu Valleys were now in Australian hands and already the Fifth Air Force was building a big air base at Gusap.

So, by early October, the Allied offensive in New Guinea had achieved notable success. Lae was being converted into a major Allied base. The 9th Division had Finschhafen and the 7th Division Dumpu. The tasks of the two divisions, as ordered by corps headquarters, were now to hold what they had and to exploit. The 9th Division was to advance round the coast of the Huon Peninsula to Sio while the 7th was to hold the Markham and upper Ramu Valleys and guard the airfields and radar stations.

When Finschhafen fell the 20th Brigade was responsible for an area from Bonga on the north to Dreger Harbour on the south. The *20th Japanese Division (79th* and *80th Regiments)* was then arriving in the Sattelberg-Wareo area while the remaining regiment of the division—the *78th*—was moving into the Finisterres to block the advance of the 7th Australian Division. The broken *51st Division* was struggling across the inhospitable mountains between Lae and the north coast. As mentioned, part of one regiment of the *41st Division*—the *238th*, which had shared in the Salamaua fighting—was already in the Finschhafen area. As far as was then known the other two regiments of the *41st Division* were at Madang and Wewak.

On the Sattelberg Road the newly-arrived 2/43rd Battalion was soon under severe attack. Its forward company near Jivevaneng was isolated. Windeyer ordered the 2/17th Battalion to move through Kumawa and Sisi and cut the enemy's communications. On 3rd October the Japanese began to threaten the beach-head from the north also and a company of Pioneers was hurried to the area north of the Song to reinforce a company of machine-gunners there. To these were added two companies of the 2/17th.

When the main body of the 2/17th seized Kumawa (on the 5th) the enemy counter-attacked hard. The 2/15th began to arrive in Kumawa on the 8th, the intention now being to concentrate the 2/17th on the Sattelberg Road, the 2/43rd being brought into reserve. On the 9th the leading company of the re-deployed 2/17th drove the Japanese from a commanding knoll beyond Jivevaneng.

As information about the arrival of the *20th Japanese Division* became more definite, Allied misunderstandings about the reinforcement of the 20th Brigade rapidly disappeared, and American craft transported the remainder of the 24th Brigade to Finschhafen to meet the threat from the flanks. By 11th October, when General Wootten had established the headquarters of the 9th Division on the shores of Langemak Bay, he had two brigades, with attached troops, under his command. General Morshead's II Corps headquarters had relieved General Herring's I Corps headquarters on 8th October. This marked the end of Herring's active service. In February 1944 he became Chief Justice of the Supreme Court of Victoria. Indeed the Australian Army, now reduced in size, possessed a surplus of able and widely-experienced senior leaders.

Wootten decided that the vital ground was the Sattelberg feature and the narrow Wareo-Gusika ridge along which the main Japanese supply line ran. If he could capture these he could complete his task of driving the Japanese from the east coast of the Huon Peninsula and capturing Sio. His plan was first to take Sattelberg and cut the enemy's tracks in the Bonga area, and then to attack Wareo from the east. The 24th Brigade was given the task of protecting Scarlet Beach from attack from the west or north-west and gaining control of the Bonga track junctions. The 20th Brigade was to press towards Sattelberg.

Wootten was preparing to open this offensive when he learned from various sources that the enemy was making rapid preparations for a full-scale counter-attack. As Wootten would not be ready to launch his offensive in time, he temporarily assumed the defensive, in which task he was aided by the capture of a Japanese operation order signed by the commander of the *20th Division*, Lieut-General Katagiri. The counter-attack would consist of an assault by the two regiments in the Sattelberg-Wareo area towards the Australian positions in the Arndt Point-Scarlet Beach area. The *79th Regiment*, supported by a landing from the sea, would attack on the north and the *80th Regiment* would attack down the track through Jivevaneng towards the coast. Wootten allotted the northern defensive sector to the 24th Brigade and the southern to the 20th. Brigadier Evans of the 24th Brigade had the 2/43rd Battalion on the high ground south from Bonga, the 2/3rd Pioneer Battalion on the high ground to the west of Scarlet Beach, and the 2/28th Battalion defending the beach dumps and installations. The field guns were in the Heldsbach-Katika area. The third battalion of the 24th Brigade—the 2/32nd—was in divisional reserve. On Windeyer's front the 2/15th and 2/17th were in the Kumawa and Jivevaneng areas respectively, while the 2/13th and 22nd Battalions were about Langemak Bay.

The first enemy attack was on Jivevaneng early on the morning of 16th October but Jivevaneng was held and the *80th Japanese Regiment* could make no headway. About 3 a.m. on 17th October Japanese aircraft heavily bombed the Finschhafen area. The raid heralded the expected seaborne attack. In rain and darkness three Japanese barges with muffled motors approached

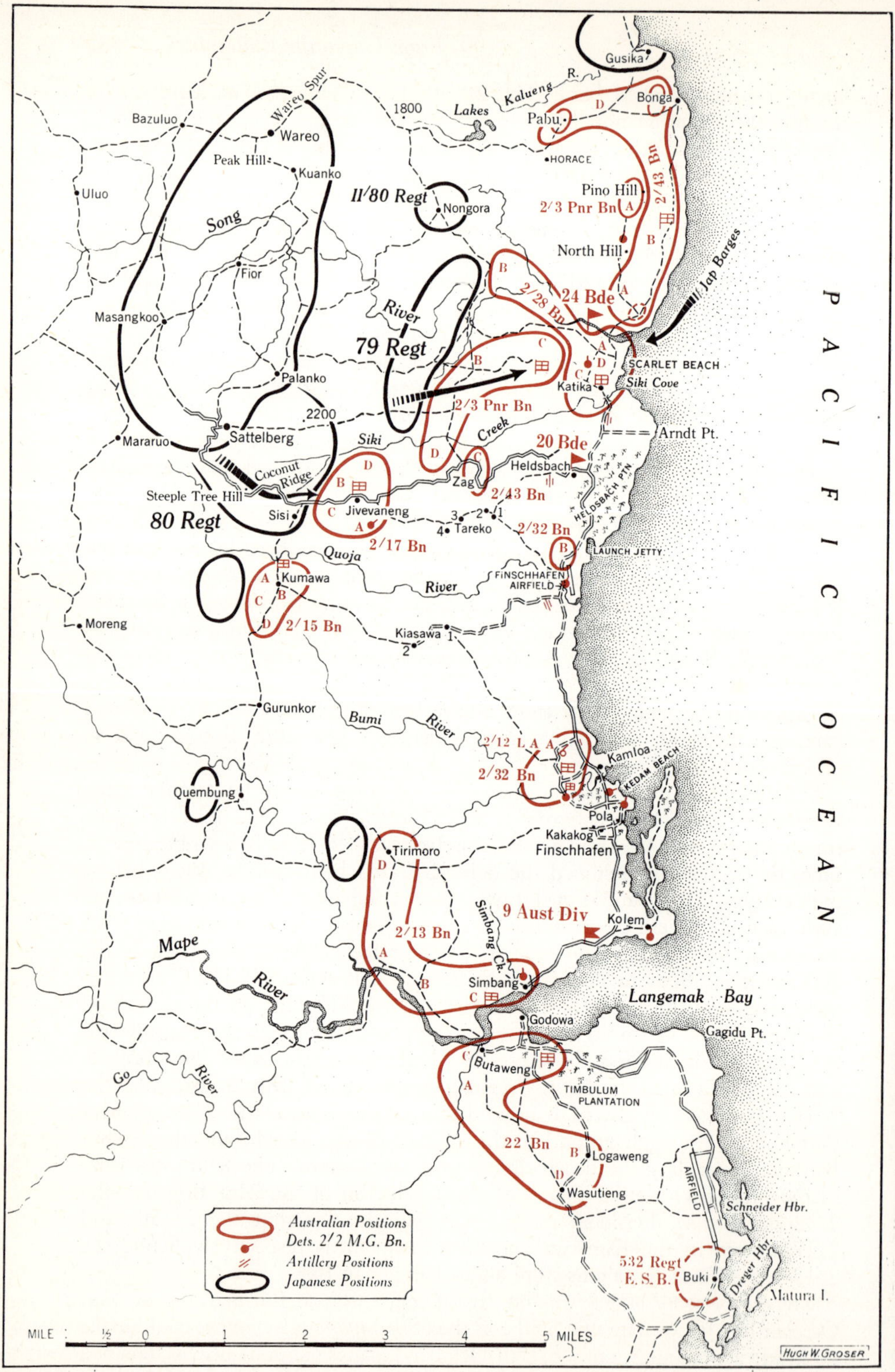

Finschhafen area

the northern end of Scarlet Beach. They were met by a combined force of Australian infantry and anti-aircraft gunners and American gunners from the Engineer Special Brigade, and the enemy force of about seventy was almost completely wiped out.

The main enemy attack came later in the morning, when the *79th Regiment,* having crept silently through the scattered forward positions of the 2/3rd Pioneer Battalion on the previous day, attacked round Katika and captured dominating ground less than 3,000 yards west of Scarlet Beach. Here they came up against a rugged defence by the 2/28th Battalion. The Australian situation was now disturbing because Wootten had little except part of one battalion in reserve. Morshead therefore asked that the 26th Brigade should be sent forward from Lae immediately and G.H.Q. provided the craft to make this move possible.

So far the Japanese had managed to keep up their momentum but, probably because of supply difficulties, they did not now press forward. Wootten therefore decided to regain the initiative and, early on the 18th, the 2/28th Battalion formed up for an attack at Katika; however, while they were preparing, the Japanese themselves attacked. Heavy and determined fighting continued throughout most of the day with the 2/28th holding its ground and exacting severe losses from an enemy who made repeated frontal assaults.

In face of such determined opposition the enemy sought other means of reaching the beach-head. Guarding the northern approaches was the 2/43rd Battalion which had carried out a rapid, though difficult, night withdrawal from the Pino Hill area. The battalion had hardly dug in when the enemy attacked. Here again dogged defence held the advance of this northern prong of the *79th Regiment.* South of Katika was Siki Creek and the Australian gun positions. Finding Katika strongly held, the Japanese moved to the south and attacked the guns but suffered heavy casualties when the guns fired into them over open sights. By the end of the 18th bands of Japanese had infiltrated through the Australian positions—a relatively easy task in thick jungle and kunai—and had reached Siki Cove, cutting the Australian positions in two. Late on the 18th the Japanese also occupied Katika and the 2/28th Battalion was withdrawn to join a narrow perimeter extending from North Hill southwards to the promontory just north of Siki Cove.

The 24th Brigade was now cut off from the 20th Brigade to the south, and if the Japanese attacked towards the main gun-area at Heldsbach they would be able to isolate also the two battalions of the 20th Brigade along the Sattelberg and Kumawa tracks. Half of the 2/13th Battalion was therefore rushed north from the Langemak Bay area in an attempt to reach the area immediately south of Siki Creek before the Japanese pushed south.

In the event the tactical moves and fighting qualities of the 9th Division proved decisive, and the Allies' possession of adequate sea transport enabled the Australians to build up their strength, whereas the *20th Japanese Division* had reached its limit. While the units of the 24th Brigade were meeting the thrusts of the *79th Regiment,* the 2/17th Battalion, aided by aggressive patrolling from the 2/15th to the south, held the Jivevaneng position astride the Sattelberg Road. During the night of 18th-19th October, by which time the main body of the 2/13th Battalion had reached its position south of Siki Creek, the *80th Japanese Regiment* established a road block east of Jivevaneng and the 2/17th was thus almost isolated. The use of an alternative supply route, however, enabled this resourceful garrison to retain the vital Jivevaneng position throughout the period of the Japanese counter-attack and to prevent the *80th Regiment* from reaching the coast.

After these few days of anxious defence the 9th Division was able, on 19th October, to go over to the offensive. That day the 2/28th recaptured Katika. The Japanese clung to their positions at Siki Cove, however, and were still there when a patrol from the 2/28th Battalion, north of Siki Creek, made contact with the 2/13th south of the creek and re-established telephone communication. It was not until the night of the 21st that the Japanese garrison at Siki Cove withdrew after having been harassed continuously by artillery and small-arms fire.

The Japanese counter-attack had finally been defeated by 20th October, the day on which the 26th Brigade Group with one squadron of the 1st Tank Battalion disembarked at Langemak Bay. By 23rd October American engineers had landed at Langemak Bay, and thereafter stores and heavy engineering equipment continued to arrive for use on airfields.

Despite a brave effort the *20th Japanese Division* had failed to achieve its object and had suffered heavily. The Australians counted 679 Japanese dead; many more must have been killed by artillery or mortar fire or dragged away at night and buried, and others must have perished and remained undiscovered in the jungle and the kunai. Wootten's staff thought that at least 1,500 casualties had been inflicted on the enemy. To the 9th Division the cost of this vital battle was 228 men including forty-nine killed.

Wootten now decided to carry out the offensive he had planned before the Japanese attack opened. He would clear the enemy from Sattelberg and then seize the track junctions on the eastern end of the Wareo Spur and threaten Wareo from the east. The 26th Brigade, supported by nine infantry tanks, would capture Sattelberg from the Jivevaneng-Kumawa area. The 20th Brigade in the centre and the 24th Brigade on the northern front would continue aggressive patrolling in an attempt to drive back the enemy's outposts and to deceive him as to the direction of the main thrust. The 24th Brigade would also be ready to cut the Wareo track and threaten Wareo from the east. For about five days before the projected offensive, aircraft and patrol torpedo-boats would batter the enemy lines of communication to prevent reinforcements and supplies reaching the forward area. As the whole division would be employed on this operation the remainder of the 4th Brigade (Brigadier Edgar) was lifted from Lae to Finschhafen to take over the defence of the growing base; and 1,000 native labourers were brought in.

Before the offensive could begin the enemy road block east of Jivevaneng had to be dislodged, and this was done by 5th November after bitter fighting by the 20th Brigade. Next day there was a change in the higher command when Morshead became commander of New Guinea Force in place of Mackay, now aged 61, who was appointed Australian High Commissioner in India, and Berryman hitherto Chief of Staff of N.G.F., became commander of the II Corps.

On 16th November the 2/48th Battalion captured a ridge ahead of the Jivevaneng positions and a suitable point from which to jump off for the attack on Sattelberg. Next day, with heavy supporting fire and accompanied by the tanks, the 2/48th Battalion began the advance along the main track, the 2/23rd Battalion prepared to move up from Kumawa in the south, and the 2/24th Battalion to capture a feature east of Sattelberg. With the 2/48th and the tanks pressing strongly along the Sattelberg Road, and the 2/23rd advancing over rugged forest country from Kumawa north to the main track, the first objective, Steeple Tree Hill, was taken on 20th November from tenacious enemy troops in positions of great natural strength along the steep-sided track. Thanks largely to the tanks the 2/48th's casualties were comparatively light.

Meanwhile the 24th Brigade, now led by Brigadier Porter, was carrying out its part of the offensive. On 20th November the 2/32nd Battalion (Major K. F. Mollard) occupied, against little resistance, a wooded knoll astride the Gusika-Wareo track at a position named Pabu. Pabu was to have a vital influence on the outcome of the fighting—an influence much greater than was foreseen when it was seized. The approaches on all sides lay through open kunai with the result that the Australians could the more easily defeat the many counter-attacks which the Japanese aimed at Pabu from both sides. Pabu was, indeed, a small fortress which dominated the enemy's territory to the north.

By 22nd November Wootten had the great advantage of a fairly detailed and comprehensive knowledge of the enemy's strength, dispositions and plans. The *80th Regiment*, about 2,000 strong, was round Sattelberg; the *79th Regiment*, about 2,400 strong, with the headquarters of the *20th Division* in the Nongora area, where there were also some 800 artillerymen. The fresh *II/238th Battalion* was moving south 'to annihilate the enemy north of the Song River', while the *79th* would attack from the north-west with a detachment thrusting at Scarlet Beach from the west. Thus the 26th Brigade was to be attacked by a force considerably stronger in infantry than it was itself.

In conformity with Wootten's plan to capture the feature ('Horace the Horse') overlooking Pabu from the west, Mollard sent a company on an expedition thither early on 22nd November and penetrated into the Horace feature where there were several encounters with groups of Japanese. That evening Japanese artillery and mortars began shelling Pabu. The Japanese advance had now swept right round the 2/32nd; patrols found an enemy battalion staging in the area whence they had advanced on the 17th. The 2/32nd was 'an Australian island in a Japanese sea'. Indeed, that morning the *II/238th* probed the right of the 2/43rd round North Hill, and as patrols discovered later, suffered heavy losses. Farther to the left Japanese artillery was firing and about ten enemy aircraft bombed and strafed the area. There was sharp skirmishing all along the front and the remaining company of the 2/32nd, moving forward to Pabu, ran into the attacking Japanese and appears to have disorganised their advance. At the end of the day it seemed that instead of launching a co-ordinated attack the Japanese had employed the now-antiquated tactics of 'infiltration', and had dispersed their effort, with the result that their counter-attack died out before it gained any real impetus.

On the 23rd attempts to infiltrate continued and were soundly defeated, largely as a result of the presence on Pabu of the 2/32nd which was still killing unwary Japanese moving along the tracks it controlled—evidence again of the slow circulation of Intelligence among Japanese units. By the 23rd eighty-two Japanese dead had been counted round Pabu. The 2/32nd, however, were steadily losing men, mainly as a result of artillery fire from guns on Pino Hill.

This counter-attack had none of the ferocity of the October onslaught. Like General Nakano at Salamaua and Lae, General Katagiri of the *20th Division* had contributed to his own defeat by sending in his units piecemeal and not developing a single major thrust. Thus he allowed the defenders to seize the initiative. The *80th Regiment*, now bitterly defending the Sattelberg Road, was exhausted and would inevitably be pushed back unless the pressure could be relieved. It was for this reason that Katagiri had decided to launch the *79th Regiment*, licking its wounds after October, and the newly arrived *II/238th Battalion* against the 24th Brigade. The *79th Regiment* had attacked with little determination and had easily been driven back but, along the coast, the battalion of the *238th Regiment* had attacked with great resolution and had only just been held by the 2/43rd.

The 26th Brigade in the meantime was inching slowly towards Sattelberg supported by daily air strikes, by the tanks, and by artillery, mortar, and small-arms fire. The 2/24th Battalion was unable to make much progress against the feature immediately east of Sattelberg but, along the main track, the 2/48th, followed by the 2/23rd, on 22nd November reached the southern slopes of Sattelberg about 600 yards from the summit. Fierce resistance was met both here and on the left flank where the 2/23rd Battalion, advancing across very rugged country, began to encircle the enemy position. On the road a landslide prevented further use of tanks and the final assault was left to the infantry. On 24th November Sergeant Derrick's platoon of the 2/48th Battalion after severe fighting gained a precarious toehold on the Sattelberg heights and, next day, Sattelberg was found to have been abandoned.[2]

The next step was to be the capture of the Wareo-Gusika spur, but before this could be done it was necessary to make contact with that part of the 2/32nd Battalion still isolated at Pabu. On 26th November two companies of the 2/32nd, with four tanks, captured Pino Hill and the supply route to Pabu was thus at length opened.

Wootten now ordered the 26th Brigade to exploit from Sattelberg to Wareo, and the 24th Brigade to secure the area from Gusika to the Lakes.

Between 27th and 29th November the 2/28th Battalion, supported by three tanks, advanced north along the flat coastal track and captured Gusika without loss, after which patrols moved inland and joined with the Pabu garrison. From Pabu the 2/43rd Battalion advanced west along the Wareo track and by 2nd December had reached the Lakes. From Sattelberg the 2/23rd advanced north down to the valley of the Song, forced a crossing over the river and began climbing the rugged slopes on the other side towards Wareo; it captured the Kuanko area against strong opposition on 7th December.

The 22nd Battalion secured a bridge-head across the Kalueng River at Gusika on the 3rd in preparation for the advance of the 4th Brigade. Next day the advance began but was bitterly opposed by the *II/238th Battalion*

[2] Derrick was awarded the Victoria Cross.

which had orders to hold the coastal track and so enable the escape of its comrades of the *79th* and *80th Regiments* from Wareo along the trail to the north coast.

Inland the Japanese rearguard heavily counter-attacked the 2/23rd Battalion at Kuanko and maintained pressure there for several days. By 8th December, however, the 2/23rd Battalion had occupied the abandoned ruins of Wareo. Two days later the 2/24th from Wareo joined hands with the 2/32nd from the Lakes, and thereafter patrols, including wide flanking patrols by the 2/4th Commando Squadron and the Papuan Infantry Battalion, scoured the general area and the Japanese escape route to Lakona. The enemy was now in full retreat, but with a rearguard was fighting stubbornly on the coast. This had little except its determination to help it, for stocks of food and ammunition were very scanty. The Japanese barge route for the supply of provisions and removal of casualties was under constant hammering by Allied aircraft and patrol torpedo-boats, and the inland routes were also regularly bombed and strafed. Against the Japanese rearguard the full might of the Australian artillery could now be concentrated, for there was no task for it elsewhere in the Huon Peninsula. Aided by tanks, the three battalions of the 4th Brigade (29th/46th, 37th/52nd and 22nd) advanced steadily, and by 20th December had occupied the high ground across the Masaweng River at Fortification Point.

On 21st December the 20th Brigade passed through the 4th to continue the pursuit. Large quantities of enemy equipment, ammunition and supplies were found, and abandoned barges littered the beaches. More and more Japanese who had died of sickness, starvation or wounds were found along the tracks.

Meanwhile forces of the South and South-West Pacific Areas had made their landings on Bougainville and western New Britain. Each lay within easy range of the Japanese bombers at Rabaul, and, as a preliminary to the landings, officers of the two commands had agreed to a program of heavy air attacks on Rabaul beginning in mid-October. On 1st November South Pacific forces were to land on Bougainville, where they would establish an air base whence fighter-escorted bombers would attack Rabaul by day, and between 25th December and January South-West Pacific forces would seize Saidor on the New Guinea mainland and Cape Gloucester in New Britain.

In early October the Japanese almost doubled their air strength at Rabaul and now had over 300 aircraft. No. 9 Group R.A.A.F. at Kiriwina was the Allied air formation nearest to Rabaul and it played a strenuous part in the operations against that fortress. For the opening attack, on 12th October, 308 aircraft, including twelve Australian Beaufighters, were mustered. Thereafter for eleven days the Fifth Air Force switched its main effort to New Guinea while the squadrons of No. 9 Group and later the three R.A.A.F. Catalina squadrons continued to attack bases on New Britain. They struck frequently at Gasmata, Cape Hoskins and Kavieng, and at Japanese ships and barges. Then from 23rd October onwards big forces of American bombers attacked Rabaul; there was fierce air fighting, and during October and November (it was learnt after the war) the Japanese lost 203 aircraft at Rabaul or in the Solomons. Naval aircraft were sent south from Truk to Rabaul and by 1st November there were 580 machines there. Next day 125 Japanese fighters were sent up to meet seventy-five Mitchells protected by Lightnings; eighteen American and twenty Japanese aircraft were shot down. Indeed, at that stage, the Allied effort to neutralise Rabaul by air attack had produced an opposite effect, and by early November the air force defending Rabaul was at its maximum strength.

The operation against Bougainville was commanded by General Vandegrift, who decided to land the 3rd Marine Division at Torokina in Empress Augusta Bay on the uninviting west coast so far away from the Japanese bases that the American staffs estimated that it would take three months for the enemy to organise a full-scale counter-attack. To establish an advanced base and radar stations close to the objective a New Zealand brigade was sent into the Treasury Islands on 27th October. There were only about 300 Japanese with mortars and one field gun in the Torokina area, but they succeeded in creating confusion among the American marines when they landed on 1st November. 'Boats were disabled, command of the assault wave broke down, several dozen casualties were suffered, and the men went ashore in a mixture of units. Tactical control by higher echelons was impossible, but the marines knew what to do. Rifle groups were quickly formed and the Japanese were dug from their crude pill-boxes.'[3]

After the landing on Bougainville Admiral Koga sent a strong naval force including six heavy cruisers to Rabaul. Admiral Halsey on 5th November dispatched aircraft from the carriers *Saratoga* and *Princeton* against this force and did it much damage. The Japanese air force at Rabaul was still unsubdued, and, in response to a request from Halsey, Nimitz sent him three more aircraft carriers, making a total of five, and their aircraft struck Rabaul on 11th November. Soon the Japanese naval force was sent back from Rabaul to the relative safety of Truk, and the first stage in the neutralisation of Rabaul had been achieved. By mid-December airfields had been completed at Torokina and on 17th December fifty-six American and twenty-four New Zealand fighters made a sweep over Rabaul. Similar sweeps and attacks by fighter-escorted bombers followed.

The 37th Division had now reinforced the 3rd Marine Division at Torokina and when Major-General Oscar W. Griswold of the XIV U.S. Corps took over on 15th December the perimeter was about fifteen miles long and extended about five miles inland at its widest point. The Americal Division relieved the 3rd Marine Division in January 1944. During all this period the Japanese had made only ineffective counter-attacks against the beach-head; their air and naval forces had been kept busy by land and carrier-based Allied aircraft.

In the Central Pacific Nimitz's offensive against the Gilberts proved more costly than the South Pacific offensive in the Solomons. Landings on Makin and Tarawa were to be the first of a series of large-scale and often costly amphibious operations that were to win Allied air bases closer and closer to Japan. Makin was captured between the 20th and 23rd November, with the loss of sixty-four Americans killed and an escort carrier sunk with 644 of its crew. In the same period the Americans invaded Tarawa and, in four days of fighting, suffered 3,110 casualties before they wiped out the Japanese garrison of 3,500.

[3] J. A. Isely and P. A. Crowl, *The U.S. Marines and Amphibious War* (1951), p. 181.

In preparation for the landings in western New Britain Kenney's air force carried out the heaviest and most sustained series of attacks yet made in the Pacific. These began on 20th November when fifty-one Liberators bombed Gasmata. In November and December No. 9 Group's activities were more intense than ever before. There were attacks on the western bases and on Rabaul, sometimes by three squadrons at a time.

Australian coastwatchers had been at large in New Britain throughout most of 1942 and 1943. Towards the end of 1942 three of them who had been established at posts along the north coast were withdrawn. But early in 1943, at the request of the American Navy, three officers, led by Lieutenant M. H. Wright, a former patrol officer in the administration, were landed by submarine near Cape Orford and remained in the area, sending back Intelligence. In September, in preparation for the offensive against New Britain, sixteen Europeans and twenty-seven natives were landed in Wright's area, the object being to establish posts across eastern New Britain and elsewhere so that they could send in warnings of coming air attack against the American forces which were to land farther west. Of five parties all reached their posts except one; it was intercepted by a Japanese patrol and all the Europeans in it were killed except one who was captured.

Late in November the plans for the landings on New Britain were defined. On 15th December there would be a landing at Arawe on the south coast and on the 26th one at Cape Gloucester on the north coast. The Fifth Air Force dropped 433 tons of bombs on Arawe on 14th December. An American dismounted cavalry regiment was embarked at Goodenough Island in four transports, including H.M.A.S. *Westralia*, now converted into an L.S.I., and about to take part in her first assault landing. The regiment was put ashore in L.V.T's (amphibious tractors) and other types of landing craft on the 15th. There was little resistance from the small Japanese force defending Arawe and 1,900 American troops were ashore the first day. The Japanese aircraft from Rabaul harassed the American landing craft severely for a few days.

The landing near Cape Gloucester was made by the veteran U.S. 1st Marine Division, which had been resting near Melbourne since its service on Guadalcanal. The operation was well managed and was supported by an effective naval bombardment in which the *Australia*, *Shropshire*, *Warramunga* and *Arunta* took part. On the first day, 26th December, 12,500 troops and 7,600 tons of equipment were put ashore. Japanese aircraft attacked the convoy and sank one American destroyer, but Rabaul was now under such severe bombing by American aircraft that its air force was not able to make sustained attacks on the forces moving in from the west. The marines fought their way through boggy country to their main objective, the Cape Gloucester airfield, which they secured on 30th December. They had much hard fighting, however, in almost continuous rain before they had driven the enemy out of positions dangerously close to their perimeter. By the middle of January the Japanese force had been broken and the survivors were retreating eastward. The 1st Marine Division lost 248 killed and 772 wounded.

In January No. 9 Group R.A.A.F. continued to send out relatively strong forces against targets on New Britain. For example on 17th January Air Commodore F. W. F. Lukis, now in command, dispatched thirty-two Beauforts with an escort of thirty-three Kittyhawks and eight Spitfires in daylight

Australian War Memorial

New Britain, 17th January 1944. A daylight raid by 32 Beauforts of Nos. 6, 8 and 100 Squadrons on an enemy camp and dump area on the Amgen River near Lindenhafen. The escort included 16 Kittyhawks from No. 77 Squadron, 17 from No. 76 Squadron and 8 Spitfires from No. 79 Squadron.

against enemy positions at Lindenhafen, near Gasmata. This was the strongest single force the R.A.A.F. had sent out up to that time. There was no opposition. On 21st January a still larger force of seventy-six aircraft struck Lindenhafen.

In mid-February the Japanese main fleet withdrew from Truk, just before it was heavily raided by American carrier-borne aircraft on 17th and 18th February. In this situation the Japanese accepted defeat in the air over New Britain and the Solomons and withdrew their serviceable aircraft from Rabaul. Only fifty-six damaged aircraft remained; but the garrison rebuilt eleven aircraft and they were used on minor tasks within the area. Thenceforward the great base with its large garrison was of small value to the Japanese, though General Imamura had the satisfaction of knowing that on New Britain and Bougainville his divisions were tying down Allied troops who might otherwise be taking part in the advance towards Japan. From Truk part of the Japanese fleet went to Palau and part to Singapore. It was purely a defensive move, but news that heavy naval units including five battleships and a carrier were in Singapore induced fear of an attack on the Fremantle naval base. On 8th March, after it was learned that the Japanese ships had left Singapore on 4th March and were sailing towards Surabaya, merchant ships at Fremantle were dispersed, submarines were deployed, the defences round Fremantle were manned, two fighter squadrons were moved from Darwin to Perth and three squadrons were sent to Exmouth Gulf. This operation, carried out at high pressure, proved unnecessary because the

Japanese ships went no farther south, and on 20th March Kenney ordered the return of all squadrons concerned to their former stations.

After the American landings on New Britain Lieutenant Wright, leader of the coastwatching parties farther east, recommended that he be allowed to wage a guerilla campaign against the Japanese retreating towards Rabaul. This was agreed to, and weapons for 100 natives were dropped to him. The natives in the area responded with enthusiasm, and soon parties of native guerillas had been trained and leaders appointed. In February 1944 when Wright's force was about 200 strong the ambushing of retreating Japanese parties began. In April a group of 180 was attacked and thirty-five were killed. In two months more than 300 Japanese were killed for a loss of two native guerillas.

Meanwhile on 17th December Krueger, commander of the U.S. Sixth Army, had been directed by MacArthur to seize Saidor, seventy miles west of Sio, about 2nd January 1944. Krueger gave this task to the 126th Regimental Team (which had fought at Buna). It landed unopposed on the 2nd and by the end of the day more than 8,000 troops were ashore and the infantry had formed a perimeter round the airstrip. Only skirmishes occurred in the next few days and thereafter the American force settled down to a defensive role. A second regiment, the 128th, arrived on the 16th and 19th. Unfortunately the orders to Brigadier-General Martin, commanding the Saidor force, did not include any instruction to cut off the retreat of the Japanese from Finschhafen and, while the Americans carried out their appointed task of protecting the Saidor airfield, the retreating Japanese bypassed them along inland tracks a few miles away.

As a result of the landing at Saidor and the pressure from the east Adachi decided that his two battered divisions—the *20th* and *51st*—should continue their retreat along the coast to Madang and Wewak. To guard the escape routes the *78th Regiment* was ordered to hold on in the Finisterre Mountains against the 7th Australian Division advancing along the Ramu Valley, and to send five companies to help the *239th Regiment* in the area west of the Americans at Saidor.

By 13th January the 20th Brigade had reached the main Japanese barge and supply point of Nambariwa on the north coast and, two days later, it took Sio. The 9th Division had now finished its task, and Major-General A. H. Ramsay of the 5th Division (who had commanded the 9th Division's artillery in North Africa) was ordered to take over the advance.

In the four months campaign from the landing at Scarlet Beach on the 22nd September 1943 until the handover to the 5th Division at Sio on the 21st January 1944 the 9th Australian Division had severely defeated the Japanese *20th Division*. At the time of the October counter-offensive there were about 12,600 Japanese troops forward of Sio. Of these 3,099 had been counted dead and thirty-eight were captured; if three were wounded to each two killed the total casualties of the *20th Division* would have been about 7,800. Many of the 4,300 who retreated from Sio, in company with the 6,000 or more men of the battered *51st Division*, died along the route to Saidor or on the inland trails beyond. The 9th Division had suffered 1,028 casualties including 283 killed.

The march of the incoming 8th Brigade (Brigadier C. E. Cameron) towards Saidor was led first by the 4th Battalion and then by the 30th.

Supply and maintenance difficulties, largely a result of monsoonal weather along the north coast, caused delay, and little opposition was met although many Japanese corpses were counted and a few prisoners were taken. The advance, preceded by Papuan patrols, began on 25th January and ended on 10th February when the Australians and Americans joined east of Saidor.

During February the 35th Battalion (of the 4th Brigade) and patrols from the Papuan Infantry Battalion pursued the enemy into the hills south-east from Saidor. Along the inland trails the Australians and Papuans hunted down and killed many of the Japanese rearguard, now so short of food that some resorted to cannibalism. The estimated Japanese casualties since Sio were 734 killed in action and forty-eight prisoners; 1,793 corpses had been counted along the tracks.

Meanwhile the 7th Australian Division, since its capture of Dumpu on the 4th October 1943, had been steadily improving its situation in the Finisterres where the *78th Japanese Regiment* was entrenched in strong defensive positions such as abounded in that rugged country.

Vasey's task was merely to guard the Markham and Ramu Valleys from enemy penetration towards the big Allied air bases built there and to guard various radar stations. Because the division had to be maintained by air, only two brigades could be employed. The Japanese had long been making a road to Bogadjim as the only practicable overland route from their base at Madang towards Lae, Salamaua and Wau, and by October the road had reached Yokopi. Thence the Japanese intended that it should follow the valley of the Mindjim River, cross the Kankiryo Saddle, a 4,800-foot watershed, and follow the valleys of the Faria and Uria Rivers to Dumpu. Kankiryo Saddle, eight miles north of Dumpu, was the key to the enemy's defensive position and completely blocked any Australian advance along the main track. The Japanese were strongly established there and also to the south, including defences along Shaggy Ridge, a steep-sided razor-back spur about four miles long running parallel to the upper Faria Valley and controlling the approaches from Dumpu.

After its arrival in Dumpu early in October, Dougherty's 21st Brigade was ordered immediately into the foothills of the Finisterres to guard approaches to the Ramu Valley. While establishing itself the brigade fought a series of fierce actions against those units of the *78th Regiment* already in position and others retreating after their defeat at Kaiapit. On the right flank the 25th Brigade skirmished with enemy outposts and on the left flank the 2/2nd and 2/7th Commando Squadrons harried the Japanese.

The 2/27th Battalion led the 21st Brigade's advance into the mountains. On 5th October, advancing along the valley of the Uria River, it occupied Kumbarum whence, after supplies had been carried forward, the battalion pushed on up the Faria River to get astride the main Japanese route towards Kankiryo Saddle. Attacking with great resolution the battalion drove deep into the enemy's area reaching the eastern edge of Shaggy Ridge. Hard fighting continued during the early days of October as the 2/27th and the flanking units strove to secure dominating positions in the foothills. On 11th October the 2/14th drove the Japanese from positions from which they were blocking the supply route to the 2/27th which was short of ammunition and rations. Next day the Japanese made heavy attacks on the 2/27th on Trevor's

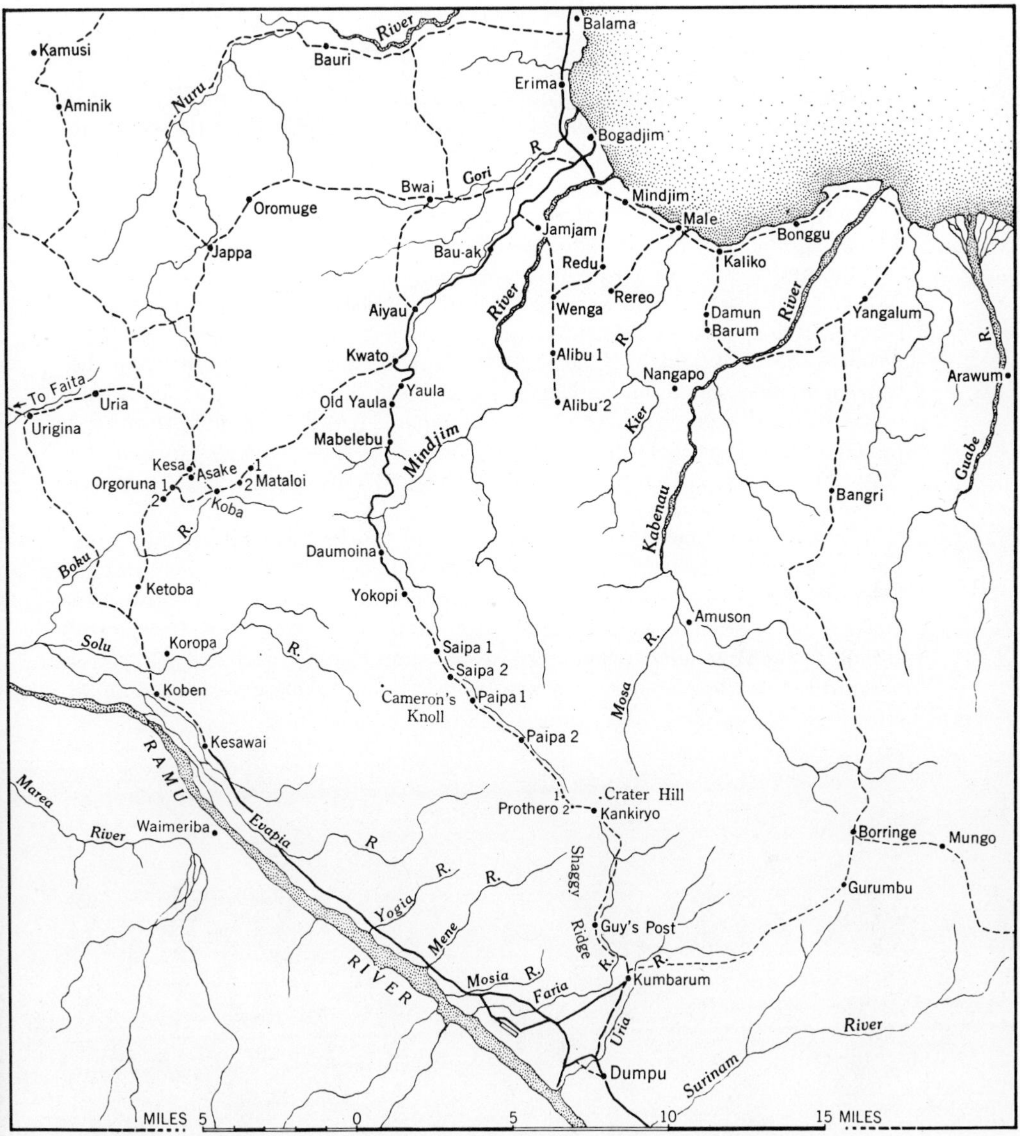

Dumpu-Bogadjim area

Ridge and Johns' Knoll but were beaten off in a fight that went on all day. Before dawn next morning a native supply train delivered rations and ammunition to the 2/27th and carried out the wounded; when this arrived the battalion had enough ammunition for only about a quarter-of-an-hour's fighting.

On the 14th the 2/16th Battalion relieved the 2/27th. Meanwhile the 2/33rd Battalion to the east had taken a commanding 4,100-foot feature (about 3 miles north-east of Kumbarum) and was probing forward in very rugged country.

From mid-October onwards there were weeks of arduous and hazardous patrolling. The 'front' was now more or less stabilised: the Japanese were clinging to Shaggy Ridge, Kankiryo Saddle and the upper Faria River, with outposts among the foothills protecting approaches from the west to Madang and Bogadjim.

Vasey's general plan was for one brigade to maintain contact with the Japanese on the Bogadjim track and block the head of the Ramu Valley, while the other brigade was held in reserve in the Ramu to improve the lines of communication and patrol into the foothills of the Finisterres. During November Eather's 25th Brigade (2/25th, 2/31st and 2/33rd Battalions) relieved the 21st, which guarded the valley. The 2/2nd Pioneer Battalion watched the right flank and, on the left, Papuan patrols and patrols from the two commando squadrons at Kesawai and Faita (about twenty miles to the north-west) clashed frequently with Japanese patrols. At this stage the Japanese moved part of the *239th Regiment* into the Finisterres to join the *78th*. The Australian army in New Guinea had now met in battle eight of the nine Japanese infantry regiments there.

By the end of November the engineers had finished two all-weather landing strips at Dumpu and roads had been pushed forward as far west as Kesawai. There were frequent exchanges of artillery fire, the Australian gunners being greatly aided by the pilots of the Wirraway and Boomerang aircraft. The Australian patrolling was constant, skilful and deep, a patrol often being out for a week or more. As usual the Japanese were content to

Australian War Memorial

New Guinea, 1944. Australian troops, on the way towards Japanese-held Bogadjim, rest after a hard climb in the Finisterre Mountains.

sit in their defences while the Australians reconnoitred and dominated no-man's land—a situation that would finally prove disastrous to their opponents.

So constant was Australian patrol pressure that the Japanese commander in the Finisterres, Major-General Nakai, decided to make a counter-attack with parts of the *78th* and *239th Regiments*. A drive launched on 8th December towards Kesawai disorganised the 2/6th Commando Squadron and the Papuans and, by reaching the Ramu Valley, isolated the 2/2nd Commando Squadron at Faita. The enemy continued to probe forward and on 13th December attacked the two forward companies of the 2/25th Battalion west of the Evapia River and forced the battalion back across the river. As had happened so often in the past the Japanese counter-attack now fizzled out, most probably because of poor staff planning and lack of supplies. Even had it been pressed there is little possibility that it could have succeeded, for the whole of the 25th Brigade was massed between Kesawai and Dumpu.

On 23rd December 1943 Blamey had issued a policy directive to his senior commanders informing them that the operational role of the Australian Military Forces in New Guinea was to be gradually taken over by American forces; the 6th, 7th and 9th Divisions would be allocated to I Australian Corps and would return to the mainland for training and rehabilitation. Three militia divisions—3rd, 5th and 11th—would be allocated to II Corps for garrison duties, training and rehabilitation in New Guinea and on the Australian mainland. The Atherton Tableland in North Queensland had been chosen as the principal rehabilitation and training area. It was well served by the port of Cairns, had a healthy climate, ample water and much rain forest suitable for jungle training.

Vasey now set out to improve his position in the Finisterres and, on 27th December, under cover of dive bomber and artillery bombardment, the 2/16th Battalion assaulted the southern slopes of Shaggy Ridge, captured the Pimple and held it against many enemy counter-attacks.

A new R.A.A.F. formation was now in action. In November 1943 No. 10 Group was created as a subordinate formation within No. 9 Group. This was done in response to a request by Kenney that a mobile Australian force be created. The new formation, commanded by Group Captain F. R. W. Scherger, included a dive bomber wing (No. 77) and a fighter wing (No. 78) and was to operate from Nadzab. It took a long time to assemble the units and on 13th January, when Kittyhawks carried out the group's first combat mission, only two squadrons were forward. These squadrons, and later the others, supported the 7th and 9th Divisions and attacked Japanese camps and communications farther north and west.

Early in the New Year Vasey's third brigade—Chilton's 18th, which had been at Port Moresby for more than six months—relieved the 21st; and Hammer's 15th Brigade, which had already fought hard in the Salamaua campaign, relieved the 25th. Although it was not in his orders that he should open an offensive, Vasey decided that the 18th Brigade should capture the key position of Kankiryo Saddle. Chilton planned an advance by his three battalions: the 2/10th would thrust forward on the right along Cam's Saddle and Faria Ridge, and the 2/9th along Shaggy Ridge; these moves

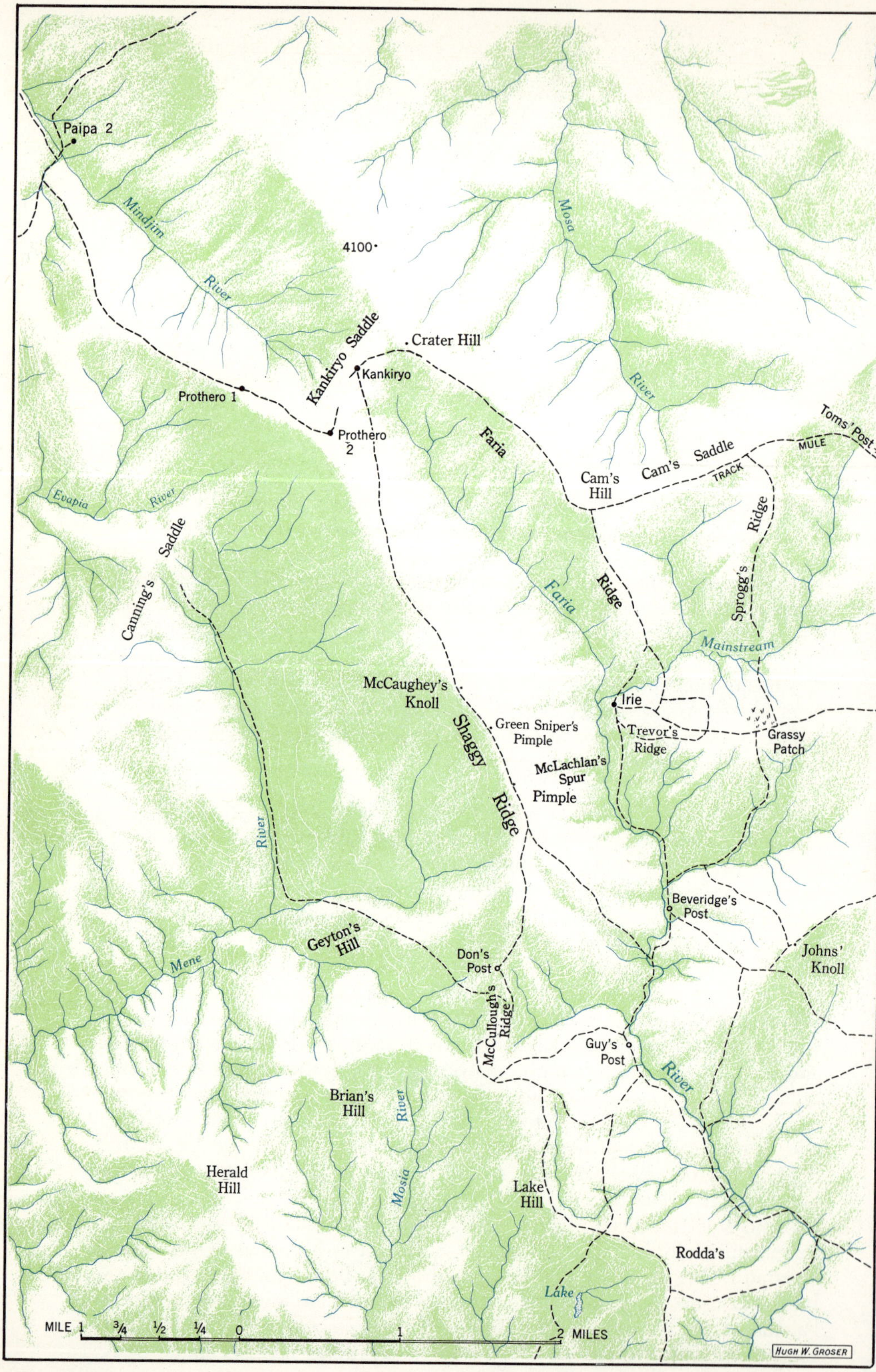

Shaggy Ridge

Australian War Memorial

Shaggy Ridge, looking south-west to the Ramu Valley. This was the scene of much heavy fighting for the Australians in December 1943-January 1944 during the Australians' offensive campaigning in New Guinea.

would support the main effort on the left flank by the 2/12th, which would advance secretly to Canning's Saddle and make a direct attack from there on the Protheros and Kankiryo Saddle.

From 17th January onwards squadrons of No. 10 Group bombed and strafed the Japanese positions. While the 2/12th began to assemble at Canning's Saddle on the 19th, the 2/10th that day openly advanced to Cam's Saddle, meeting no resistance. Next day the 2/10th met strong opposition along the Saddle but the battalion had been successful in diverting Japanese attention from the 2/12th, all of which had reached Canning's Saddle unobserved. On the 21st the 2/12th crept up the steep sides of Shaggy Ridge and launched an assault on Prothero 1 where there was stiff fighting. At the same time the 2/9th from the southern slopes of Shaggy Ridge began an advance north along the razor-back which again drew off strength from the enemy opposing the 2/12th. The 2/9th captured Green Sniper's Pimple and held it against counter-attacks. The enemy fought stubbornly but, in the face of continued pressure and artillery and air bombardment, they finally broke and by 26th January Kankiryo Saddle was in Australian hands with the enemy concentrated on Crater Hill overlooking the Saddle from the north-east.

Here the enemy was surrounded but he continued to resist in an effort to ensure the withdrawal of the *20th* and *51st Japanese Divisions* along the coast. Had the Japanese then completely broken it is possible that the 7th Australian Division might have got astride the escape route. After the bombardment from the air and from the ground and constant patrol pressure, enemy resistance collapsed on 31st January and they withdrew towards Paipa. In these actions the Australians counted 244 Japanese dead, and lost forty-six of their own men killed.

The 15th Brigade relieved the 18th in mid-February and, when the Saipa area was found abandoned on 13th March, the brigade moved forward to regain contact with the retreating Japanese. By the 14th March the 57th/60th Battalion concentrated in Yokopi where the Japanese road began, and a company of the 58th/59th was patrolling down the Kabenau River towards the coast. After clashes in the Yaula area the 57th/60th Battalion occupied Bogadjim on 13th April. Americans from Saidor had previously landed at Yalau Plantation east of Bogadjim on 5th March, and by the 21st the 58th/59th from its forward base at Nangapo in the valley of the Kabenau joined forces with their allies.

Meanwhile some changes in higher command had taken place. On 8th April Major-General A. J. Boase and his 11th Divisional Headquarters relieved the 7th Divisional Headquarters at Dumpu, and on 12th April Lieut-General Savige and his I Corps Headquarters from the Atherton Tablelands relieved Lieut-General Berryman's II Corps Headquarters in New Guinea. The title of the headquarters was changed and the three A.I.F. divisions (6th, 7th and 9th), now assembling on the tableland, were henceforth grouped in I Corps; and the militia divisions in II Corps.

On 24th April a mixed patrol from the 57th/60th Battalion (15th Brigade) and the 30th Battalion (8th Brigade) entered a deserted Madang. With the occupation of Madang the Huon Peninsula was finally secured and thereafter patrols moved north without opposition through Alexishafen to the former Japanese base at Hansa Bay. In July and early August Papuan patrols crossed the mouths of the Ramu and Sepik Rivers and once again clashed with the Japanese rearguard.

In the offensive that opened in September 1943 the Australian Army backed by strong air and naval forces and with the help of some American regiments had defeated the *XVIII Japanese Army* and driven it in disorder out of most of the mainland of Australian New Guinea. In these operations and the earlier fighting round Wau and towards Salamaua the Australians lost 1,231 killed and 2,867 wounded. Japanese losses in the same period seem to have numbered about 35,000. By March 1944, according to Japanese sources, the strength of the *XVIII Army* had dwindled from 105,000 to about 54,000; about 16,500 had died in Papua or at sea on the way to New Guinea. These losses were evidence partly of the tactical superiority that the Australians had now developed, partly of their superior staff work and equipment and the effective naval and air support, and partly of the rudimentary nature of Japanese staff work and medical care.

Meanwhile in the Solomons the northward advance had continued. On 15th February the 3rd New Zealand Division landed a brigade in the Green

Islands north of Bougainville and occupied the group with little fighting. This was the division's last major task. The New Zealand Government found that it could not maintain from a population of 1,700,000 two divisions in action in addition to an air force which in December 1943 numbered 38,000; and in 1944 the 3rd Division was disbanded, many of its men going to Italy to reinforce the 2nd New Zealand Division.

MacArthur now decided to accelerate the next move—the seizure of the Admiralty Islands. This had been planned for 1st April, but on 29th February part of the U.S. 1st Cavalry Division were landed at Los Negros. The Japanese resisted strongly but soon exhausted their strength in ineffective attacks; on 9th March Wing Commander G. H. Steege of No. 73 Wing R.A.A.F. landed on the Momote airstrip with twelve Kittyhawks of No. 76 Squadron, and twelve more Kittyhawks landed next day. As part of the U.S. Seventh Fleet, Task Force 74, commanded by Rear-Admiral Crutchley in H.M.A.S. *Shropshire,* maintained a covering patrol between the Admiralties and the Equator during part of these operations, and bombarded positions ashore; and a naval force commanded by Captain E. F. V. Dechaineux in H.M.A.S. *Warramunga* took part in the invasion. By 18th May the Americans were in control of the whole group of islands and all No. 73 Wing was established ashore. More than 3,300 Japanese had been killed; the American forces lost 330 killed and 1,189 wounded.

The plan had provided for the capture of Kavieng, a strongly-garrisoned Japanese base, on 1st April but Nimitz persuaded the Joint Chiefs to cancel that operation and let him take instead Emirau Island between Manus and Kavieng. At the same time the Joint Chiefs fixed earlier dates for the next group of operations. Emirau was occupied on 20th March. Rabaul, with its big garrison, was now thoroughly encircled. The leap forward to the Admiralties marked the opening of a new phase and one in which, in MacArthur's area, his American divisions, some now seasoned and all superbly equipped, would form the spearhead. Hitherto the steps towards Tokyo from the south had been relatively short, judged by the standards of those that were to follow. Henceforward MacArthur, and Nimitz, were to make giant and rapid strides, where possible bypassing and isolating strong Japanese forces and seizing bases—stepping stones for further advances—where the enemy was weak.

Already Nimitz's forces had seized Roi-Namur and Kwajalein in the Marshall Islands early in February at relatively small cost. Eniwetok, farther east, was taken on the 21st.

Looking far ahead the Joint Chiefs of Staff had decided early in 1944 that the first major objective of the two-pronged thrust towards Tokyo would be to gain a grip on Luzon, Formosa and the South China coast. As a preliminary MacArthur was, on 12th March, directed to continue to advance along the New Guinea coast in preparation for the occupation of Palau and Mindanao and Nimitz to occupy the southern Marianas whence long-range bombers could attack the Japanese mainland.

By the end of March nearly all the six Japanese divisions which in mid-1943 had stood along the South-West Pacific front had lost heavily and at least three were cut off from any supplies except what submarines might bring. Between December 1943 and April 1944 the Japanese brought forward two new armies to their new defensive line: to the Marianas the *XXXI*

Australian War Memorial

The Australian destroyer *Warramunga* approaching H.M.A.S. *Australia* during operations in New Guinea waters, March 1944.

Army (including *14th, 29th, 43rd* and *52nd Divisions*) and into western New Guinea the *II Army* (*32nd, 35th* and *36th Divisions*). The *Second Area Army* headquarters was sent south from Manchuria to Celebes, whence it controlled the *II Army, XVIII Army* and *XIX Army* (Ambon). East of Java and Borneo there were now seventeen divisions where, in November 1943, there had been only nine.

The bypassed Japanese forces to the south were resolved, however, to go on fighting hard. Thus on 9th March the *XVII Army* on Bougainville attacked the XIV U.S. Corps and did not desist until over 7,000 men had been killed round the defenders' perimeter.

The next move by MacArthur's army was to be a landing by formations of the Sixth Army west of the *XVIII Army* round Wewak, thus isolating that base and its garrison. On 22nd April American forces landed simultaneously at Tanahmerah Bay, Humboldt Bay and Aitape. There was at first little opposition to the 163rd Regiment at Aitape; within forty-eight hours No. 62 Works Wing, R.A.A.F., had the airfield there ready for Kittyhawks of No. 78 Wing.

At Hollandia and Humboldt Bay Eichelberger's I American Corps was landed. By 26th April the airfields in this area had been taken, and by 6th June 3,300 Japanese had been killed and 611 taken prisoner; the Americans lost 159 killed. Hollandia was rapidly developed into a big army and air force base.

Admiral Crutchley's Task Force 74, comprising *Australia, Shropshire, Arunta, Warramunga* and two American destroyers helped to give close support to the landings and the three Australian L.S.I's, *Manoora, Kanimbla* and *Westralia,* converted passenger ships, were among the nineteen trans-

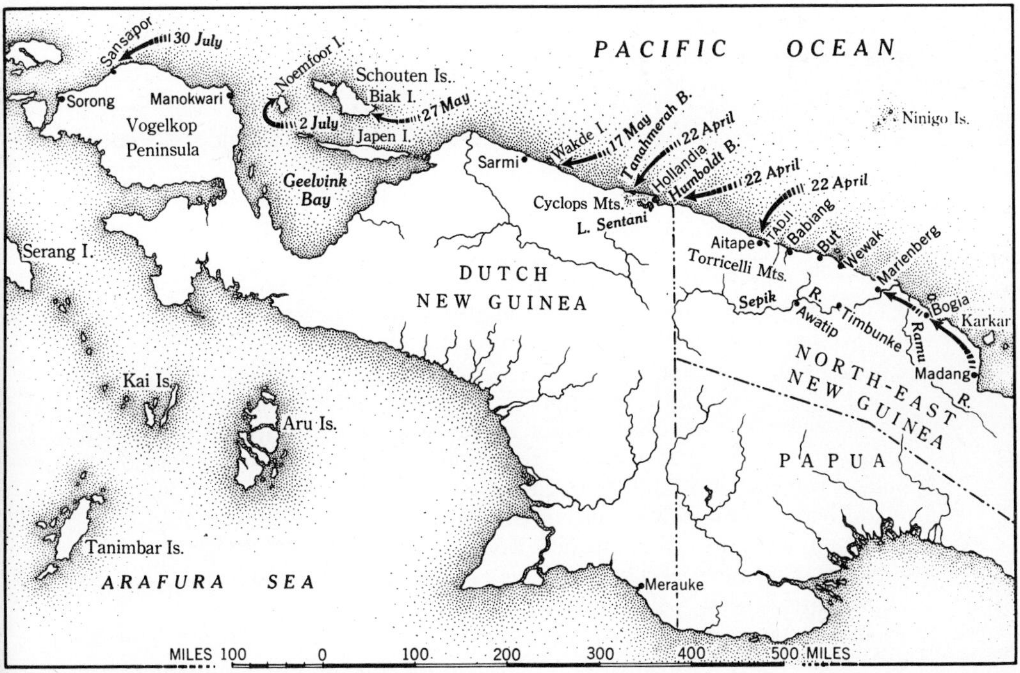

West New Guinea

ports employed. (About the same time, some 3,000 miles to the west, the Australian destroyers, *Napier, Nepal, Nizam* and *Quiberon* as part of the Eastern Fleet made a diversionary attack on Sabang off the northern end of Sumatra.)

The American force advancing into western New Guinea now faced the *II Japanese Army,* which had been depleted by submarine attacks on the convoys which had brought it to New Guinea. On 17th May the 41st U.S. Division was landed at Wakde Island; by 25th June it and the 6th American Division had secured both Wakde and the Sarmi area on the mainland. Biak Island was taken by the 41st Division, later reinforced, after heavy fighting lasting from late May to late July. Three R.A.A.F. Kittyhawk squadrons from Hollandia took part in the Wakde-Biak operations, providing air cover for the troops, bombing and strafing; and at Biak the naval Task Force 74 built round the principal ships of the Australian squadron was in support.

The next move was to seize Noemfoor Island. An American regimental team landed there unopposed on 2nd July. Air Commodore Scherger was to establish No. 78 Wing on the island as soon as possible and later bring Nos. 77 and 81 Wings forward. Four American groups (the equivalent of Australian wings) were also to be based on Noemfoor. No. 78 Squadron flew its aircraft to Noemfoor on 20th July and the remainder of the wing followed. Air Commodore Cobby took command of No. 10 Group at Noemfoor after Scherger had been injured in a jeep accident.

At Noemfoor naval support was again given by Task Force 74. It was now commanded for the first time by a graduate of the Royal Australian Naval College, Commodore Collins. The Australian Navy had now almost come of age. The first class to enter the college, in 1913, had been boys born in 1899. For the next thirty years the Chief of the Naval Staff and the admirals commanding the squadron had been officers lent by or transferred from the Royal Navy, though now and then these had been Australians by birth. In February the War Cabinet had decided to extend the term of Admiral Sir Guy Royle, R.N., as Chief of the Naval Staff for a further year, but, at the end of Admiral Crutchley's term in command of the squadron, to appoint Collins to succeed him. It instructed the Minister for the Navy that when Royle's term ended all senior appointments were to be held by Australians: Collins would become Chief of the Naval Staff and be followed in command of the squadron by Captain Farncomb, who meanwhile would be given experience of commanding a big ship in the Royal Navy—in the event this was only an escort carrier. And, as a result of the misfortunes of war, it was not until after the fighting ended that an Australian was in command both at Navy Office and of the squadron.

Round Noemfoor the Japanese counter-attacked, but lost heavily. Mopping up continued throughout July and August. On 30th July the 6th American Division took Sansapor.

To Aitape, garrisoned by the 32nd U.S. Division, supported by three squadrons of the R.A.A.F. and one American squadron, came information in June that the Japanese would soon counter-attack. The 43rd American Division plus two regiments were ordered to Aitape. The attack opened on 10th July and after heavy fighting was defeated, perhaps 8,000 Japanese being killed. During the counter-offensive the R.A.A.F. squadrons and an American Airacobra squadron were called upon to make a maximum effort over the immediate battle area. For a time Beaufort crews were flying four sorties a day, and in July four squadrons flew a total of 1,510 sorties and dropped 670 tons of bombs. On 14th July Collins' Task Force 74—the cruisers *Australia* and *Shropshire* and two Australian and two American destroyers—bombarded Japanese position east of Aitape.

Two more strides of about 400 miles would bring MacArthur's forces to the Philippines. But meanwhile Nimitz's forces were continuing their more deadly converging thrust through the central Pacific. MacArthur relied for air support usually on squadrons operating from the air base last captured, while Nimitz used mainly carrier-borne aircraft; and whereas MacArthur's troops belonged to the army Nimitz's were mainly marines. Nimitz's land forces had the harder task in that his stepping-stones were small islands where the Japanese were strongly entrenched and prepared to fight to the death, whereas on the long New Guinea coastline MacArthur had often been able to put his forces ashore at weakly-defended places.

In June and July 1944 the pincers began to close both in the East and the West. The final phase of the war opened. On 6th June, two days after the fall of Rome, General Eisenhower's Allied armies began to land in Normandy. There were 2,470 landing ships and craft to carry the assault troops, 1,656 for ferry services and 1,213 warships in support; by 5th July the millionth Allied soldier had been landed. On 23rd June the Russians opened the summer offensive that would carry them into Prussia and Poland by the end of the year.

In the Eastern theatre, in preparation for the big amphibious operations that lay ahead, the Pacific Fleet had been reorganised. In future command would be held alternately by Admiral Halsey, as commander Third Fleet, and Vice-Admiral R. A. Spruance as commander Fifth Fleet. While one was directing an operation the other, with his staff, would be at Pearl Harbour planning the next one. When the title of the fleet changed its components remained more or less the same. Whoever was in senior command, Vice-Admiral Marc Mitscher continued to lead the Carrier Task Force.

Realising that the loss of the Marianas would be fatal the Japanese High Command decided to send their *Mobile Fleet* in full force against the Americans. Vice-Admiral Ozawa, hitherto in command of the *Carrier Fleet,* had 9 aircraft carriers, 5 battleships, 13 cruisers, 28 destroyers; Admiral Spruance had 15 carriers, 7 battleships, 21 cruisers, 69 destroyers. On 19th and 20th June these forces met in what developed into the biggest carrier battle of the war—the Battle of the Philippine Sea. Three Japanese carriers were sunk, two by submarines, and the Japanese suffered irreplaceable losses in trained carrier pilots.

Meanwhile on 15th June a huge convoy of 535 ships carrying three marine divisions and one army division had arrived off Saipan, where the marines spearheaded the landing after a bombardment of hitherto unequalled intensity and weight. The Japanese resisted valiantly and for a time the invaders were in a perilous position, but counter-attacks were broken up and on 9th July resistance ended. The Americans lost 3,426 killed on Saipan and over 23,000 Japanese were buried and 971 taken prisoner. The landing of two divisions on Tinian took place on 24th July and the whole island was in American hands by 1st August. Next, after a fierce fight which opened on 21st July and cost 1,435 Americans killed, Guam was taken, and the Americans were in control of the Marianas. These defeats caused despondency in Japan. The Tojo Cabinet resigned and was replaced by one led by General Koiso; the Japanese leaders now realised that utter defeat was inevitable, but pride demanded that they must fight on.

The final operations in this phase were the taking of Morotai by MacArthur's forces, and of the Palau Islands by Nimitz—each a leap of about 700 miles. Morotai was but lightly defended. In the Palaus a reinforced division was landed on Peleliu Island on 15th September and another on Angaur on the 17th. Before the islands were secured about 1,800 Americans and 12,000 Japanese had died in battle.

Between January and September 1944 thirteen Japanese divisions had been destroyed or isolated. Also in these nine months the American fleets had developed overwhelming strength and the land forces had gained greatly in confidence and efficiency. When the drive began only eleven United States divisions had fought against the Japanese, now twenty had been in action, some several times.

In mid-1944 the problem had risen of deploying the very large air forces of the South-West Pacific Area. General Kenney now commanded the Fifth and Thirteenth Air Forces, R.A.A.F. Command, No. 10 Operational Group, R.A.A.F., some units of the American naval air arm, a marine air group, and units of the R.N.Z.A.F. These had a combined strength of more than 4,000 aircraft. In June 1944 a new headquarters, 'Far East Air Forces', was formed with Kenney as its commander. Through it he controlled the Fifth Air Force (Major-General Ennis C. Whitehead) and the Thirteenth Air Force (Major-General St Clair Streett); in his capacity as commander of 'Allied Air

Forces S.W.P.A.' he controlled R.A.A.F. Command and other units assigned to those forces.

Kenney decided that the Fifth Air Force would henceforth lead the air assault, while the Thirteenth filled supporting roles, and No. 10 Group, R.A.A.F., supported the Australian garrisons in New Guinea. Air Vice-Marshal Bostock discussed the future tasks of his forces with Curtin, who informed him that the first requirement was adequate air support of Australian land forces; a tactical air force should be maintained to co-operate with Australian land forces in the forthcoming offensive operations. It was agreed that No. 10 Group be re-named First Tactical Air Force.

The main components of R.A.A.F. Command were thus at this stage First T.A.F., Air Commodore A. M. Charlesworth's North-Western Area (twelve squadrons), and Air Commodore Lukis's Northern Area (six squadrons). The task of Northern Area was to take part in the operations in Australian New Guinea, to be described in the next chapter.

First T.A.F., under Air Commodore Cobby, included in October No. 77 Attack Wing, No. 81 Fighter Wing, No. 78 Fighter Wing, and two airfield construction wings each of two squadrons. In addition one Beaufighter squadron and two Spitfire squadrons were under orders to join First T.A.F. from North-Western Area, where dwindling Japanese opposition made it possible to greatly reduce the fighter force.

The American forces were now poised for invasion of the Philippines. It had been intended that the next moves would be an attack by MacArthur's forces on Mindanao and by Nimitz's on Yap. In September, however, Halsey proposed to Nimitz and Nimitz to the Joint Chiefs that these two attacks be cancelled, and instead that MacArthur should invade Leyte not on 20th December as planned but as soon as possible. MacArthur agreed that he could land on Leyte on 20th October. On that day the Sixth American Army put one corps ashore on the north-east coast and another farther south. On Leyte the Japanese had one division; on Luzon, where Field Marshal Terauchi, commanding the whole *Southern Army,* had his headquarters were four; elsewhere in the Philippines three.

The three Australian L.S.I's were among the transports that carried the invasion forces to Leyte, and Collins' Task Force 74, including *Australia, Shropshire, Arunta* and *Warramunga,* were part of the supporting Seventh Fleet. On the 21st October, the day after the landing, a dive bomber crashed into the foremast of *Australia*—the first Allied ship hit by one of the suicide pilots who were to inflict increasing damage in the coming months. In *Australia* thirty were killed or mortally wounded and sixty-four others wounded; the captain, Dechaineux was mortally wounded and Collins wounded seriously.

As soon as the Japanese High Command knew for certain where the American force would land they set in motion a plan aimed at decoying the main American fleet away from Leyte while two forces converged on the transports and destroyed them. The weak remnant of the Japanese *Carrier Fleet* under Admiral Ozawa was to move south from Japan and draw off Halsey's Third Fleet, while Vice-Admiral T. Kurita with a force including five battleships advanced from the west through the central Philippines and

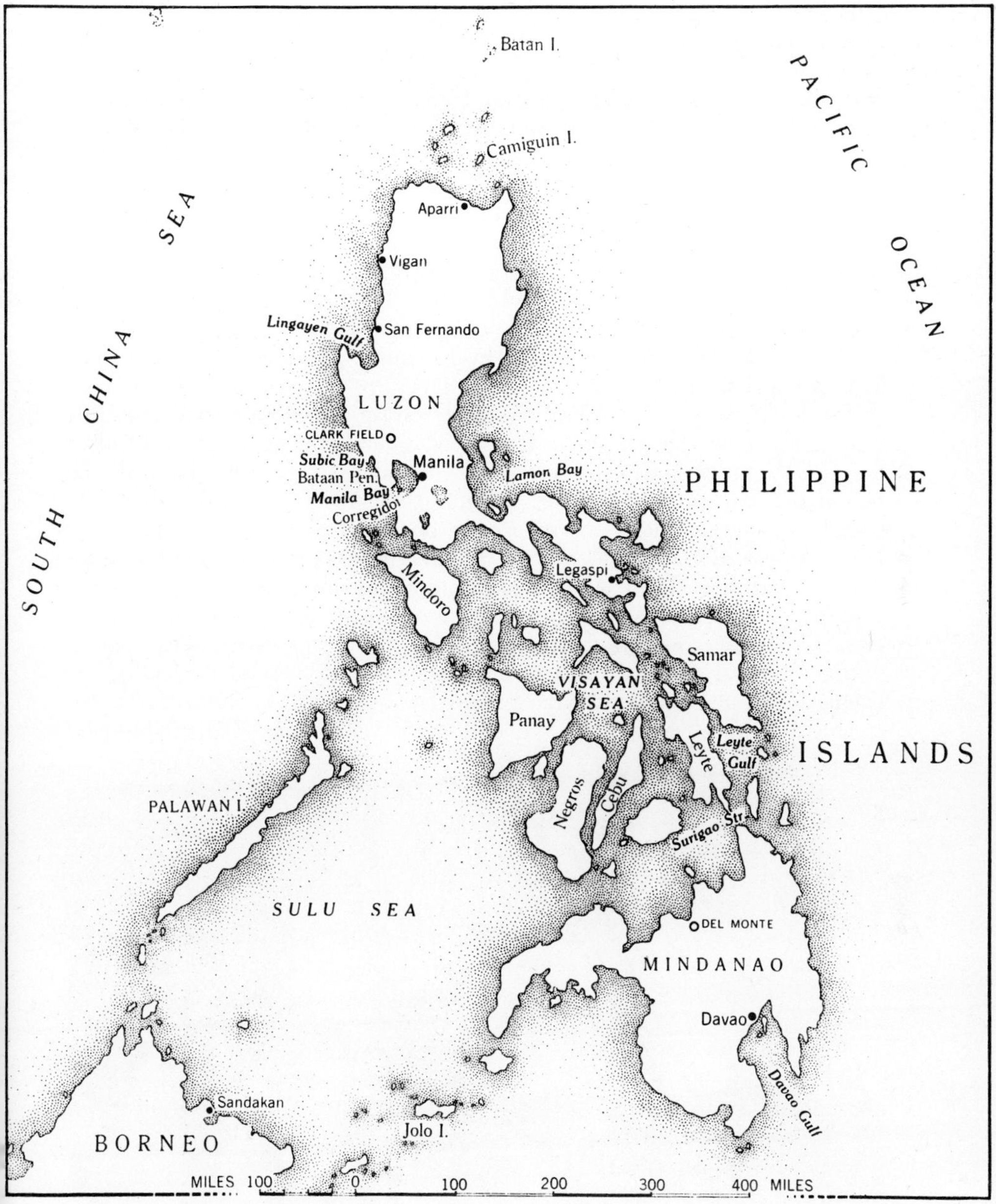

The Philippines

descended on Leyte from the north and Vice-Admiral Shoji Nishimura, with two battleships and a cruiser and destroyers, moved through the Surigao Strait and advanced on Leyte from the south. The battle opened on 23rd October when a submarine sank Kurita's flagship. Thereafter there was a series of engagements, ending three days later, and resulting in the final and decisive defeat of the Japanese fleet. The *Shropshire* and *Arunta* were part of a force that turned back Nishimura in Surigao Strait—the last 'battle line' engagement in history.

Henceforward the Pacific Fleet's command of the ocean after which it was named would be disputed only by *Kamikaze* pilots, and by a few ships making hopeless forays.

For weeks before the landing on Leyte the squadrons of First T.A.F. had made daily attacks on targets in the Vogelkop and Ambon areas. In October No. 77 Wing sank twenty-four vessels including barges. As planned, the role of the Thirteenth Air Force (including No. 10 Group) and of R.A.A.F. Command in this phase was to operate on the flanks while the Fifth Air Force supported the actual assault. Fighter opposition was rare, but some aircraft were shot down or damaged by anti-aircraft fire. On 25th October Cobby established a headquarters on Morotai and in the following weeks First T.A.F. was concentrated there. Thence the squadrons ranged far to the north, west and south. And there on the night of 22nd-23rd November the enemy struck a sharp blow. Nine aircraft bombed the two Morotai fields destroying fifteen Allied aircraft and damaging twenty-nine. Two nights later

Australian War Memorial

Australian Landing Ships Infantry at the invasion of Leyte, 20th October 1944. On board *Westralia* with *Kanimbla* and *Manoora* ahead.

Japanese bombers destroyed five more Allied aircraft and damaged others. These raids led to heavy and sustained attacks on all Japanese airfields within reach and particularly at those on Halmahera.

By mid-December the Americans had seven divisions ashore on Leyte, and the Japanese had landed two reinforcing divisions. By the end of December, after bitter fighting, the defending force had lost perhaps 56,000 men and was disintegrating; the Eighth U.S. Army, formed in September with General Eichelberger in command, took over in the southern Philippines and the Sixth Army began to prepare for the invasion of Luzon.

In September Lieut-Colonel Lyon had again led a raiding party from Australia to Singapore to sink ships there. This time the raiders were equipped with electrically powered submersible boats and were taken to their base in the Rhio Archipelago by a British submarine, *Porpoise*. When in November a second submarine, *Tantalus,* arrived at a rendezvous to pick up the raiders they found only signs of a hasty departure about a fortnight before. After the war it was learnt that on 6th October the raiders were outside Singapore ready to strike when a police launch approached and they fired on her. Lyon ordered his men in their four rubber boats to withdraw to Merapus Island. In a subsequent fight on one of the islands Lyon and one other were killed but the rest of the party reached Merapas. Here the Japanese found them on 4th November and a running fight followed from island to island until twelve had been killed and eleven taken prisoner. One man died soon after capture. The survivors were taken to Singapore and after being sentenced to death by a Japanese military court were beheaded on 7th July 1945.

In 1944 the tide had turned in Burma, where since November 1943 Admiral Lord Louis Mountbatten had been Supreme Allied Commander. Early in 1944 some 950 Australians of the R.A.A.F. were serving in this theatre, the aircrew dispersed among fifty-eight squadrons. In February and March the Japanese opened two big offensives. First in Arakan they succeeded in cutting the communications of two Indian divisions. But General Slim, commanding the Fourteenth Army, was ready; he supplied his beleaguered forces by air and sent in reinforcements. The tables were turned on the Japanese, who were eventually routed. This was the first British victory in Burma. Also in March General Wingate had led three mobile brigades into northern Burma; one marched in, the other two were flown in to strongholds behind the Japanese lines. The 'Chindits' got astride the Japanese communications but did not achieve their main aim, which was to cause the Japanese to withdraw from northern Burma. Wingate was killed early in the operation and at length the brigades withdrew after losing heavily. In April the second Japanese offensive had been launched in Assam. Here again they surrounded the Indian-British force round Kohima and again air supply was provided and by June the Japanese had been soundly defeated. The scene was now set for a decisive Allied victory in Burma after the monsoon.

German submarines had been operating in the Indian Ocean from August 1943 onwards, using Penang as a base. In the first quarter of 1944 the heaviest losses suffered by Allied merchantmen were in the Indian Ocean, where up to thirteen Australian corvettes were employed on escort duty. In February the Australian corvettes *Launceston* and *Ipswich* with the Indian *Jumna,* escorting a convoy from Colombo to Calcutta, sank the Japanese submarine *RO 110*. Off the Australian coast there had been no sinkings by enemy submarines for about eighteen months when on 9th December 1944 a Greek ship was attacked by a surfaced submarine off the South Australian coast. Air patrols wre intensified. On Christmas Day a submarine torpedoed the American ship *Robert J. Walker* off Moruya, New South Wales. The raider did not strike again until 6th February when it sank the motor vessel *Peter Sylvester* off the coast of Western Australia. The submarine was the German *U 862*, and the *Peter Sylvester* was thc last ship attacked by a submarine off the Australian coast and in the Indian Ocean.

We have seen how towards the end of 1942 plans for equipping the Australian forces from Australian factories were reaching fruition and the shortage of weapons had largely disappeared. In the next two years production of some munitions had been slowed down or discontinued, and new projects, some of them most ambitious, had been undertaken.

Thus at the end of 1943 the manufacture of 25-pounders ceased, 1,527 standard guns and 213 short guns having been delivered. Half this number would have sufficed for the reduced Australian Army of 1944. The army also now had far more anti-tank and anti-aircraft guns than it needed. During 1944 the rate of production of small-arms was slowed down. Production of all these weapons could safely have been either discontinued or reduced far sooner and the manufacturing resources put to better uses.

On the other hand the demand for operational aircraft was always far greater than the capacity of the Australian factories. By January 1945, 688 Wirraways and 248 Boomerangs had been delivered, production of Boomerangs was discontinued and of Wirraways reduced to a few replacements a month. Production of Beauforts had ceased when the 700th was delivered in August 1944, but Beaufighters were being turned out at an increasing rate which, in November 1944, reached twenty-seven a month. At the end of 1944 the thirtieth Mosquito aircraft had been produced. The Commonwealth Aircraft Corporation was now preparing to produce Mustang fighters and it had been decided to follow the Beaufighter with the Lincoln bomber, a far larger aircraft than the Australian factories had hitherto produced. The war ended, however, nine months before the first Lincoln had been delivered. In the war or soon afterwards the aricraft factories produced 3,500 aircraft of nine types, and nearly 3,000 engines.

Eight shipyards had produced corvettes of which a total of sixty were built. Six of the yards were now making 1,420-ton frigates, of which fourteen were built or building. Merchant shipbuilding was in full swing at four yards and a program of small-craft building, eventually to produce more than 33,000 craft of 162 different sorts, was in progress.

The production of naval mines had reached its peak in 1943 and was now tapered off. Much effort and skill had been put into the making of torpedoes, and the first of them passed its tests in February 1944. But once again, by the time Australia had succeeded in making a complex product it was not greatly needed, and Australian torpedoes were never used in action. However, the torpedo factory continued in peace to employ the skills and the tools it had acquired in war.

Chapter 12 **The end of the German war**

After the 31,000 Australian troops comprising the 9th Division and other elements of the A.I.F. departed from Egypt in the first quarter of 1943 the Australian contingents engaged in the German war included some 16,000 air force men, a substantial number of naval officers, and eight corvettes in the Mediterranean. There were then seven R.A.A.F. squadrons in the Middle East (though two of them contained few Australians). These were Nos. 3, 450 and 451, which were fighter squadrons; and Nos. 454, 458, 459 and 462, armed with bombers. There were 3,400 men of the R.A.A.F. in the area, about half of them being aircrew. In the United Kingdom were nine Australian squadrons: Nos. 10 and 461 were equipped with flying boats, Nos. 460, 466 and 467 with heavy bombers, No. 453 with Spitfires, No. 455 with Hampdens, No. 456 with Mosquitoes, and No. 464 with Venturas. No. 463, a heavy-bomber squadron, would be formed in November 1943. There would then be two regular and fifteen *Article XV*[1] squadrons in the European and Mediterranean theatres and two *Article XV* squadrons operating with the main body of the R.A.A.F. in the South-West Pacific.

To meet the new situation in the Mediterranean theatre Mediterranean Air Command was formed in February 1943 with Air Chief Marshal Tedder as its commander-in-chief. Under it were three formations: North-West African Air Forces (Major-General Carl A. Spaatz), R.A.F. Malta Command (Air Chief Marshal Sir Keith Park) and Middle East Command (Air Chief Marshal Sir Sholto Douglas). After the Eighth Army entered Tunisia Nos. 3 and 450 Squadrons R.A.A.F. became part of North-West African Tactical Air Force; Nos. 451, 454, 459 and 462 remained in Middle East Command; and No. 458 was in Malta Command.

No. 451 Squadron now found itself an unwanted army co-operation unit, so much so that its commanding officer applied for its transfer to Australia, but without success. Nos. 454 and 459 had more active employment on anti-submarine patrol along the African coast. No. 458 armed with torpedo-carrying Wellingtons was engaged in costly operations from Malta, losing eleven aircraft in the first three months of 1943.

Meanwhile the two Australian Kittyhawk squadrons in the Desert Air Force had been helping to support the Eighth Army's advance to Tripoli and onwards through Tunisia. Attacks both from the west and the east on Axis airfields gradually subdued the enemy air force and by mid-March it was unable to offer effective opposition. The Kittyhawks, sometimes now armed with six 40-lb bombs instead of one 250-lb bomb, attacked forward

[1] Of the four-party agreement in which Britain undertook that Canadian, Australian and New Zealand aircrews passing through the EATS would serve in Canadian, Australian or New Zealand squadrons respectively, within the RAF.

Libya-Tunisia

airfields and road traffic. There were bursts of intense activity. Thus, in late February, flying from Tripoli, the Australians made 159 sorties in a four-day offensive against enemy airfields. No. 239 Wing to which these squadrons belonged pressed on close behind the advancing army and at Medenine and El Hamma in the Mareth area was based within range of the enemy's heavier guns.

By mid-April the Axis forces were penned in behind a line hinged on Enfidaville and embracing Tunis and Bizerta; on 18th April No. 239 Wing moved to an airfield near Kairouan. The Desert Air Force began a campaign against seaborne supplies now mostly coming from Sicily in small ships. Wellingtons of No. 458 sank the *Fabiano* (2,493 tons) on 11th April and made night attacks on harbours on the south coast of Sicily. The Kittyhawks of No. 239 Wing flew hundreds of sorties over the Gulf of Tunis and soon were intercepting and bombing small vessels almost daily. Tunis fell on 7th May and between the 9th and the 13th the Axis forces, 250,000 strong, surrendered, their escape having been prevented by the air forces and light naval forces.

The conquest of French and Italian North Africa was accompanied by a new crisis in the Atlantic. The needs of the operations in the Mediterranean had been met partly at the expense of anti-submarine operations. The German submarines resumed mass attacks on the Atlantic convoys in August 1942 and in the last quarter of that year more than 1,600,000 tons of shipping were sunk in all areas. November was the most successful month of the war for German submarines, whose new tactics and equipment were making them very difficult to find. For example, in November and December the two Australian Sunderland squadrons made no sightings.

Admiral Karl Doenitz, the commander of the German submarine fleet, replaced Admiral Raeder as Commander-in-Chief of the German Navy at the end of January 1943. The Germans at this time were able to keep more than 100 submarines constantly at sea. At the Casablanca Conference in January the Combined Chiefs of Staff decided that in 1943 the defeat of the German submarines must be the first charge on the resources of the Allies. By April improved tactics and more aircraft were keeping the submarine wolf-packs away from the main convoys and by May Doenitz reported to Hitler that they were 'facing the greatest crisis in submarine warfare, since the enemy by means of new location devices . . . is causing us heavy losses'.

In this period Australians sank or shared the sinking of the submarines *U 632, U 167, U 332, U 109, U 227, U 447, U 266*. In May a total of forty-one German submarines were destroyed. It was a month of victory over the U-boats and successes continued. The submarines were now on the defensive. In the next phase from June to August Australians again sank or shared in the sinking of numbers of U-boats—*U 194, U 564, U 461* (sunk by a Sunderland numbered U/461), *U 454, U 106*. In six days in late July and early August nine German submarines were sunk in the Bay of Biscay and five more elsewhere, and two Italian submarines were sunk in the Mediterranean. Such losses could not be sustained indefinitely and Doenitz now ordered more cautious tactics.

In August 1942 the Pathfinder Force had been formed within Bomber Command. Its leader was a remarkable Australian, D. C. T. Bennett, who had been trained at Point Cook, joined the R.A.F. in 1931 and left it to become a commercial pilot. After war broke out Bennett, who was a navigator of great skill and knowledge, pioneered the Atlantic ferry route and then commanded bomber squadrons. Sir Arthur Harris has described him as 'the most efficient airman I have ever met'. Bennett's experience and drive made him the ideal commander for the new *corps d'élite*. By January 1943 the general practice when bombing German towns was for the leading Pathfinders to drop flares over the computed position of the target. As soon as the aiming point was seen visually a special flare was dropped and a second group would drop bundles of flares on this objective. Target indicators which would burn for about six minutes were then dropped, and these were renewed by later Pathfinders. When cloud hid the ground, sky-marker flares were used. Thus the individual bomb aimer in the main bomber force was required to find and bomb a visible light, and the bombers could pass through the dangerous areas without delay.

Of the four nominally Australian squadrons in Bomber Command in January 1943 only No. 460 was manned predominantly by Australians, and each of the four was in a different group. Australia had sent overseas only 40 per cent of the ground staff needed for her *Article XV* squadrons. Air Marshal Williams, Air Officer Commanding R.A.A.F. Overseas Headquarters, proposed to the Air Board that it should send more ground staff for R.A.A.F. bomber squadrons as a step towards achieving a truly Australian force in England. However, the Government decided that, because of the manpower shortage, no more ground staff should be sent abroad. Williams then made proposals aimed at the concentration of a number of R.A.A.F. heavy-bomber squadrons in one group analogous to No. 6 (Canadian) Group in Bomber Command, and some senior regular officers of the R.A.A.F., including two group captains, were sent to England to command new squadrons or staff the group should it be formed. Such efforts to concentrate Australians in the oversea theatres failed to inspire much enthusiasm among the wartime flying men as distinct from the senior regular officers for whom such concentration might provide more opportunities of service in the air war against Germany. Most preferred to mix with men of other nations of the Commonwealth, or men of other Allied nations. Incidentally, since casualties in Coastal and Fighter Commands were now light, most Australians arriving in Britain were henceforth absorbed by Bomber Command.

The Combined Chiefs of Staff in January 1943 restated the aims of the Anglo-American bomber offensive. The main objective was to destroy and dislocate the German military, industrial and economic system and undermine the people's morale; the targets were to be submarine building yards, the aircraft industry, transport, oil plants and other targets in war industry. In March a sustained offensive against the Ruhr began. In April, May and June 11,000 sorties were made over the Ruhr and Rhineland, which was equal to the total number of heavy-bomber night sorties throughout the whole of 1942.

The offensive opened with a raid on Essen on 5th-6th March in which 369 aircraft, out of 412 sent out, actually bombed the target. Of these thirty-three were from Nos. 460, 466 and 467 Squadrons. For the next four months forces ranging from about 300 to about 800 struck Essen, Duisburg and other industrial networks, the R.A.A.F. squadrons providing up to sixty aircraft on individual raids. Between March and July No. 460 (Lancasters) operated on forty-six nights, making 597 bombing and twenty minelaying sorties; No. 466 (Wellingtons) sent out 345 aircraft on twenty-seven nights against towns and made 121 minelaying missions on twenty-six nights. No. 467 sent 555 Lancasters on forty-two area raids and fourteen to lay mines. No. 460 lost twenty-nine crews—more than its total strength at the outset—No. 466 lost twenty crews, and No. 467 lost thirteen.

Throughout 1943 one day-fighter (Spitfire) squadron of the R.A.A.F. and one night-fighter (Mosquito) squadron served in Fighter Command, and other Australians were scattered among R.A.F. squadrons. No. 453 made sweeps over France, escorted convoys and bombers striking targets in France and attacked ships. The German fighters were now greatly outnumbered and not eager to give battle. In May No. 453 flew 308 sorties without meeting German fighters; in June the squadron lost its first pilot in combat in more than six months.

In a new Empire Air Training Scheme agreement signed on 31st March 1943 Australia had arranged not to increase her *Article XV* squadrons beyond the original quota of eighteen—actually only seventeen were formed—though she would continue to send most of her trainees overseas for service in the R.A.F. The main reason for this was the difficulty of providing ground staff for her squadrons, and a result was that an ever-increasing number of Australian aircrew would be sent to non-Australian squadrons. It was agreed that so far as practicable Australians would be sent to one or other of certain selected R.A.F. squadrons. Australia's desire to concentrate her men in her own squadrons plus certain others was by no means fully attained, however; in May 1943 some 8,400 Australian aircrew were scattered among 135 squadrons in Britain alone; in India 330 Australians were serving in forty-one different squadrons only nine of which had more than ten Australians. Efforts were made at the highest levels to achieve greater concentration but in practice little was achieved. The weak efforts to integrate senior R.A.A.F. officers into Bomber Command had achieved little; as late as October 1943 no R.A.A.F. officer filled a staff post at either Bomber Command or a group headquarters.

There was a similar but far smaller sprinkling of Australians in the Royal Navy. By June 1944 about 500 Australians, including more than 400 officers of the R.A.N.V.R., were serving on loan with the Royal Navy. Of the R.A.N.V.R. officers six were commanding ships and four were commanding flotillas of landing craft.

It was decided at Casablanca in January 1943 that Sicily should be invaded soon after final victory in North Africa. The capture of Sicily would provide a stepping-stone between Tunisia and Italy and open the shipping routes through the Mediterranean. The operation would also divert some enemy strength from Russia.

The invasion was carried out from some 2,000 vessels on 10th July 1943 after the Allied air forces had driven Axis bombers from Sicilian airfields and virtually subdued the enemy fighters which remained. In two days

North-West Europe

DENMARK
BALTIC SEA
Sylt I.
Hornum
Pomeranian Bay
Kiel
Peenemunde
Heligoland
Heligoland Bight
Norderney I.
Is.
Trave
Lubeck
Wilhelmshaven
Bremerhaven
Hamburg
Politz
Stettin
Emden
Elbe
Bremen
Weser
Spree
Ems
Oder
Berlin
Elbe
Canal
Ruhr
Hanover
(Mitteland)
Gravenhorst
Brunswick
Rheine
Osnabruck
Ladbergen
Magdeburg
Munster
Dortmund Ems
GERMANY
Rheda
Hamm
Soest
Dortmund
Mohne Dam
Essen
Ruhr
Niedersachswerfen
Elbe
Leipzig
Kassel
Dusseldorf
Sorpe Dam
Diemel Dam
Eder Dam
Leuna
Dresden
Cologne
Bonn
Remagen
Giessen
Boundary
1937
Frankfurt
Hanau
Schweinfurt
CZECHOSLOVAKIA
Rhine
Mainz
Oppenheim
Aschaffenburg
Darmstadt
Main
Wurzburg
Pilsen
Mannheim
Ludwigshaven
Kaiserlautern
Nuremberg
Saarbrucken
Heilbronn
Karlsruhe
Danube
Pforzheim
Stuttgart
Strasbourg
Ulm
Augsburg
Rhine
Freiburg
Munich
AUSTRIA
Kembs Dam
L. Constance
Wurm See
Friedrichshafen
HUGH W. GROSER

about 80,000 men and 300 tanks of the Eighth British and Seventh American Armies were ashore. The fighter-bombers of No. 239 Wing operated in support of the invading forces from Malta where they arrived between 9th and 13th July. On 17th July the Kittyhawks moved from Malta to Pachino in the south-east of Sicily and immediately began to operate in close support of the army pressing on towards Catania. From Pachino the wing advanced on 1st August to Agnone, fifteen miles south of Catania, whence in the next four days the two Australian squadrons alone mounted 190 sorties against traffic on roads behind the Axis positions. Catania fell on 5th August, and soon among the Kittyhawks' main targets were craft ferrying German troops and equipment to the mainland. By 17th August, after a campaign that had lasted thirty-eight days, the conquest of Sicily was complete.

No. 458 Squadron was also heavily engaged in July flying 134 sorties on anti-shipping patrols and strikes round Sardinia and the Tyrrhenian Sea; it damaged an Italian cruiser and a destroyer and sank a merchantman.

By July 1943 it appeared both to the Allies and to the Germans that aerial bombardment of factories, which had not caused significant damage in the first three years of the war, might now play a decisive part. The German Air Force was unable to retaliate by effectively bombing English towns and could only strengthen her defences in the hope of making the Allied raids too costly to maintain. Germany increased her fighter force by withdrawing units from Russia, the Mediterranean and France and improved her night-fighter and anti-aircraft tactics. These reactions were meeting with some success, as is illustrated by the fact that, in the second quarter of 1943, British aircraft losses averaged 4.6 per cent of all sorties, a rate which prevented the rapid growth of Bomber Command.

From July 1943 Bomber Command began employing a device named 'Window' to confuse enemy radar. This consisted simply of dropping from bombers metallised strips which produced the same results on radar screens as did an aircraft and thus crowded the enemy's screen with a multitude of indications, some true some false.

The first big blow in a campaign against targets farther afield than the Ruhr was against Hamburg, which was hit by from 425 to 740 bombers four times between 24th-25th July and 2nd-3rd August, the three Australian squadrons providing from forty-nine to fifty-eight aircraft on each raid, and losing six in all. A total of 7,829 tons of bombs was dropped on the four nights. It gradually became evident that these repeated raids, supplemented as they were by daytime attacks by American Fortresses and nuisance raids by Mosquitoes, were achieving immense destruction. On the second main raid smoke rose from the burning city to 22,000 feet and firestorms raced through the streets. On 1st August photographs revealed that 74 per cent of Hamburg had been heavily damaged. Aircraft had never before caused such destruction in a city of that size.

In August No. 466 Squadron re-armed with Halifax aircraft, and in November No. 467 shed a nucleus which was expanded into No. 463 (Lancasters) making a total of four R.A.A.F. heavy-bomber squadrons in Bomber Command. As the nights grew longer the main bomber force began ranging farther afield. Munich and Berlin were struck, also Hanover and Kassel, and Ruhr towns were bombed again.

In the first half of 1943 No. 455 Squadron with its Hampdens played a vigorous part in attacks on enemy merchant and naval ships. It shared in the sinking of a 3,500-ton merchantman in January and sank a 468-ton trawler in June. Damage was done to many other vessels. In December the squadron was withdrawn to be rearmed with Beaufighters and form the anti-flak component of a new strike wing in which No. 489 Squadron R.N.Z.A.F. would be the torpedo force.

In September U-boats again began operating in packs. In this phase the boats were ordered to remain on the surface when set upon by aircraft and fight back, and to attack destroyers with acoustic torpedoes. These tactics did not achieve much success. In the first ten days of October, for example, the Germans lost six submarines and sank only one merchantman and a destroyer. After having lost twenty U-boats in the North Atlantic in October, Doenitz decided that they should cease engaging in surface warfare, and he withdrew the boats from the North Atlantic. In January 1944 a Sunderland of No. 10 Squadron sank *U 426* and one from No. 461 sank *U 571*.

In November 1943 Bomber Command opened a sustained offensive against Berlin. Raids were now restricted to moonless nights because of the danger from fighters, and in fact, for this reason or because of bad weather, raids were made on only six nights in November and six in December. On those twelve nights, however, the bomber force was about 900 strong, 86 per cent being four-engined aircraft. The use of Window had reduced the proportion of aircraft hit by ground fire from 10 to 4 per cent.

In eight raids on Berlin in November and December from 332 to 670 aircraft hit the target, the four Australian squadrons providing from thirty-two to sixty. About 14,000 tons of bombs were dropped on Berlin in this period. Over Germany 183 bombers were lost. In the first quarter of 1944 Berlin was hit nine times; the heaviest raid was on 15th-16th February when 806 aircraft (out of 891 dispatched) dropped a total of 2,643 tons of bombs. In this series of raids the R.A.A.F. squadrons lost twenty-seven aircraft. The main bomber force was now switched to other targets as part of the preparation for the invasion of Europe and the task of harassing the German capital and pinning down big defending forces was handed over to squadrons of Mosquitos. These, eventually carrying a 4,000-lb bomb, were fast enough to evade most enemy fighters.

From December 1943 to March 1944 a series of heavy raids by up to 800 bombers were made on Frankfurt, Leipzig and Stuttgart. In the last raid in March against Nuremburg Bomber Command suffered its worst single reverse of the whole war. Of 795 aircraft sent out 95 failed to return and 11 more were damaged beyond repair; the 4 Australian squadrons dispatched 75 aircraft of which 67 attacked and 5 failed to return.

By March 30 per cent of the built-up areas of German towns attacked by Bomber Command had been damaged. But the attacking force's losses had been grievous: in the first three months of 1944 alone 763 four-engined bombers had been shot down in major night raids against German cities—equivalent to 80 per cent of the aircraft in active squadrons of Bomber Command when the year began. The German High Command was convinced that such losses would compel the abandonment of large-scale night attacks, and in fact aircraft losses were outstripping production, but there was no shortage of aircrews.

Italy, Sicily, Corsica, Sardinia

Meanwhile Italy had been invaded. Tentative plans for the invasion received great impetus when a moderate Government assumed power in Italy on 25th July 1943 and Mussolini was deposed. On 3rd September the Eighth Army landed on the Italian mainland opposite Messina. On 8th September Italy's surrender was announced.

The Germans had about 1,000 aircraft which might oppose the landings but the Allies could bring 4,000 aircraft to bear. There were some 3,000 Australian air force men in the Mediterranean area (compared with about 10,000 in England) and seven R.A.A.F. squadrons. These were Nos. 3 and 450 (Kittyhawks), 451 (Hurricanes), 454 (Baltimores), 458 (Wellingtons), 459 (Hudsons), 462 (Halifaxes). The squadrons were widely scattered when the invasion of Italy opened: Nos. 3 and 450 were in Sicily, No. 458 in Tunisia, No. 459 at Gambut, No. 454 at Amiriya, No. 451 at Idku (Egypt), No. 462 near Benghazi. Only the three single-engined fighter units were truly Australian; each had arrived in the Middle East with almost complete ground crews and there was never a shortage of Australian fighter pilots in the area.

The Australian Kittyhawk squadrons gave close support to the troops advancing cautiously northward from the toe of Italy. In southern Italy the Germans had six divisions, two of them armoured. On 9th September two Allied corps landed in Salerno Bay, wither the Allied air forces flew about 1,300 sorties a day in support of the land forces. The Germans counter-attacked and for a period the bridgehead was in peril. Meanwhile the 1st British Airborne Division had landed from the sea at Taranto and soon occupied Brindisi. This made possible the basing of aircraft on the Italian mainland, and from the 14th September onwards the Kittyhawks of No. 3 Squadron were established at Grottaglie airfield, whence they helped to halt the German drive against Salerno. Soon other elements of No. 239 Wing had been flown in. On 22nd September the wing moved forward in the wake of the Eighth Army to Bari and by 3rd October was established on the main Foggia airfield, the seizure of which had been one of the main strategic aims of the Italian campaign. Throughout this and later operations No. 239 Wing gave effective close support. For example, on 5th October Australian Kittyhawks flew fifty-five sorties in the course of which they struck at a convoy of petrol lorries and considered that twenty-five were set alight and others damaged. Aided by powerful air support, now based well forward, the Allied armies took Naples on 1st October and Caserta on the 5th, and by the 6th the line ran along the Volturno and Calore Rivers. The aim was to pin down maximum German forces that might otherwise be used in France, and seize Rome, not only because it would be a political prize but because of its airfields from which targets in Germany could be kept under constant attack. It is arguable that it might have been wiser at this stage for the Allies to have stood on the line of the Volturno, concentrated on the coming invasions of France, and let Rome be. On the other hand the Allies had the power to press on in Italy without starving the forces needed for OVERLORD Operation (the invasion of north-west Europe) just as in the East they had the means of maintaining three separate offensives: Admiral Nimitz's, General MacArthur's and Admiral Mountbatten's.

From October onwards winter weather reduced the activity of No. 239 Wing but the fighters continued to harass enemy vehicles and attack strong-points and occupied villages. A new kind of task was undertaken on 24th October when the Kittyhawks operated off the Yugoslav coast in support of Yugoslav irregulars. Soon after this the wing moved forward to Mileni, where the weather was no better. In late November and in December the Kittyhawks were employed largely in close support of the New Zealand division on the line of the Sangro River. During this period No. 205 Group (Wellingtons), in which about 20 per cent of the aircrew were Australians, operating from Tunisia, were striking targets in northern Italy and in France. The group took part in a costly and ineffective attack on a ball-bearing works near Turin late in November, seventeen aircraft including four captained by Australians being lost. In December the wing moved to Italy.

In October 1943 the Australian squadrons based in Egypt and Palestine had become involved in the campaign in the Aegean that followed the Italian capitulation. After that capitulation the Germans swiftly reinforced their air force in the eastern Mediterranean to some 350 aircraft. Aided by effective air support their troops seized Cos, and then Leros and Samos. In this phase four Australian squadrons—Nos. 451 (Hurricanes), 459 (Hudsons), 454 (Baltimores) and 462 (Halifaxes) were engaged on convoy protection, attacks on targets in the Aegean islands and in Greece and Crete, and attacks on ships. The Allied Air Forces, however, were able only to somewhat delay the German assault on Leros, and when Leros had gone Samos was abandoned.

After unsuccessful efforts to make No. 462 Squadron truly Australian it changed its name to No. 614 Squadron R.A.F., an event that caused regret in the unit, as such changes generally do. A more unhappy squadron was No. 451 which, after a long period of strenuous activity in 1941 and 1942, had now been out of the front line for more than two years. In April, however, No. 451 was sent to Corsica. There were now only two R.A.A.F. squadrons in the Middle East—Nos. 454 and 459, which was converted from Hudsons to Venturas early in 1944, and continued mainly on convoy patrols, varied by occasional hunts for submarines and night bombing of targets in the Aegean area.

In July No. 459 was again re-equipped, this time with Baltimores. No. 458 Squadron in the western basin of the Mediterranean, re-equipped early in 1944 with Wellingtons carrying Leigh lights, was strenuously engaged in anti-submarine patrols and convoy escort; detachments from the squadron worked from bases in Corsica and from Malta. In May and June the whole squadron was transferred to Sardinia.

In Italy the Allies' aim was now to take Rome by a combination of direct assault and outflanking seaborne landings. As a prelude to landings at Anzio the Allied bombers made systematic attacks on the railway system and other supply routes. At the same time, and in keeping with the often irrational tactics adopted in these years, bombers were employed in bombing Sofia, Piraeus and Salonika. The Australian Kittyhawks struck at ships in the Adriatic, railway centres and road traffic. The landings near Anzio were made on 22nd January 1944 after preliminary attacks by the Fifth Army. The corps landed at Anzio displayed excessive caution and soon was strongly hemmed in by hurriedly assembled German forces.

The Germans had barely 450 aircraft available to operate over Anzio whereas the Allies had about 3,000. However, after the first day, the weather almost entirely prevented the Allied aircraft from intervening effectively. On the ground the Germans soon gained the initiative and the timidly-led Allied force was on the defensive. When the Germans launched a major attack on 16th February the weather had improved: on the 17th the Allied Air Forces mounted 1,700 sorties and dropped 1,000 tons of high explosive on the enemy's forward troops. This bombardment combined with artillery fire halted the enemy's offensive. The Australian fighter-bombers took part in a devastating bombing of the monastery at Monte Cassino forward of the Eighth Army's line, a bombardment which only impeded the attack because it created heaps of rubble each of which could be made a strongpoint.

On 1st May the Allied Air Forces began intensive preparations for a new offensive to open on the 11th. In the next eleven days the Australian Kittyhawks flew 307 sorties against communications, dumps and headquarters. From 23rd April No. 451 with its Spitfires entered the battle, flying from Corsica over areas of Italy north and west of those covered by Nos. 3 and 450.

In the new offensive the Desert Air Force gave close support to the Eighth Army, from the 13th adopting the time-honoured cab-rank system. There was no opposition to the cab ranks, the German Air Force being too preoccupied with home defence and preparations to meet the invasion of Europe. Backed by an almost ceaseless air offensive—for instance Nos. 3 and 450 flew 401 sorties in 8 days—the Allies broke the German line and American forces entered Rome on 4th June.

After much argument about the time, place and manner of the invasion of France, the Allied leaders had finally decided in December 1943 that Overlord and Anvil (the invasion of southern France) should have absolute priority over all other operations during 1944 and that both should be mounted in May of that year. The American General Eisenhower was chosen as Supreme Commander with the British Air Chief Marshal Tedder as his deputy, the British General Montgomery as commander of the Twenty-first Army Group and the American Major-General Walter Bedell Smith as Chief of Staff. The plan finally provided for an initial assault by five infantry and three airborne divisions; these were to be rapidly increased to twenty-three infantry, ten armoured and four airborne divisions.

The plan was to land on beaches in Normandy with the initial objective of capturing a group of airfields, the port of Cherbourg and other ports in Brittany. Australian participation in the campaign in north-west Europe was almost entirely in the air and therefore it is with the air operations that this account will be mainly concerned. More than 10,000 aircraft were available in England to support the offensive, yet even these were insufficient to meet all demands in full. The principal air commander was Air Chief Marshal Sir Trafford Leigh-Mallory who co-ordinated his requirements for forces not under his control—Bomber Command, American Eighth Air Force, Coastal Command, and Air Defence of Great Britain—through Tedder. In general terms the role of the air forces was to subdue the German Air Force, provide continuous reconnaissance, disrupt enemy communications, strike enemy land and sea forces and transport airborne troops.

Of the 292 squadrons in the home commands in April 1944 ten were Australian. The percentage of Australians in these squadrons ranged from 26 to 100; on the other hand there were about 1,500 Australian aircrew in R.A.F. squadrons. There were two Australian fighter squadrons, three squadrons in Coastal Command, four in Bomber Command, and one in Second Tactical Air Force. By January 1945 another Australian fighter squadron and another bomber squadron would be added, and by that time most R.A.A.F. squadrons were considerably more Australian, the percentages ranging from 47 to 100; and the number of Australian aircrew in R.A.F. squadrons had risen to 2,600, scattered among 214 squadrons.

Attacks on German aircraft factories in April and May not only had the effect of reducing production but forced the enemy to keep in Germany fighter squadrons that otherwise might have been deployed in France. In

Australian War Memorial

Above: A Lancaster of No. 463 Squadron awaits yet another load of bombs for a daylight raid on German military targets in France.
Below: A 4,000-pound 'cookie' and a load of incendiaries dropping from a Lancaster of Bomber Command.

May and early June 6,700 tons of bombs were dropped on German airfields. In western Europe the Germans had only some 800 aircraft of which 325 were long-range bombers and 315 were fighters. Nevertheless this force was considered large enough to make damaging raids aimed at upsetting Allied preparations. In the last week of April and in May, Australians were to the fore in countering raids aimed at Portsmouth and at shipping along the south coast of England; for example, in the six weeks to 5th June No. 456 Squadron R.A.A.F. shot down eight of the twenty-two German bombers destroyed by night fighters.

From 6th-7th March onwards systematic attacks on railways began, the aim being to put the railways out of action initially within a radius of 150 miles from the intended beach-head. In April and May attacks on railway targets were intensified, up to 350 bombers taking part in a single operation. R.A.A.F. squadrons contributed up to thirty-eight aircraft to individual raids. For example, in the most effective raid of this series, on Juvisy near Paris on 18th-19th April, Nos. 463 and 467 Squadrons provided thirty-seven of the 204 bombers that reached the target and dropped nearly one-quarter of the total weight of bombs. These attacks were backed by fighter strikes against locomotives, an average of more than 200 sorties a day being made from 19th May onwards.

Other main targets were radar stations, against which 1,668 sorties were made before 6th June; wireless stations; batteries of guns. At the same time bombers attacked military camps far from the beach-head area, buildings housing headquarters, munition dumps and factories. For example, Nos. 463 and 467 Squadrons sent twenty Lancasters against an explosives factory near Bordeaux; these bombed from 4,000 feet, caused terrific explosions, and damaged every important building.

The Australian squadrons in Coastal Command took part in a vigorous campaign against German submarines concentrating in readiness to oppose the expected invasion. In eleven days in May six U-boats were sunk, Australians sharing in the sinking of three. The strategic air offensive against Germany and her occupied territories continued in the months leading up to the invasion—a telling demonstration of Allied superiority in the air. Forces of up to almost 600 bombers attacked industrial towns in late April and in May, the R.A.A.F. squadrons contributing up to forty-nine aircraft to individual raids.

The time had now come for the landing in Normandy. Australians took part in the air operations designed to mislead the enemy as to the point of attack, but it was the assault by Bomber Command that concerned the greater number of Australians. In night attacks on coastal batteries on 5th-6th June 168 of the 1,136 aircraft that were committed belonged to the four R.A.A.F. heavy-bomber squadrons or had R.A.A.F. pilots. This onslaught was followed after dawn on the 6th by attacks by 1,661 day bombers.

After the leading troops had landed they had the close support of 171 squadrons of day fighters and fighter-bombers, about half being American and half British, and ten of night fighters. There were also sixty-four squadrons engaged on static defence, reconnaissance and other duties. The Australian contribution amounted to one day-fighter squadron (No. 453), one night-fighter squadron (No. 456) and about 200 individual pilots serving in British units—enough to man an additional seven or eight squadrons. Thirty-six squadrons, of which No. 453 was one, maintained thirty-six aircraft constantly in the air during daylight over the beaches. Only once that day did an Australian fighter pilot see an enemy aircraft.

Comforting as Allied air superiority was to the Allied land and sea forces, the opening day of the invasion once again demonstrated the limited offensive power of aircraft employed against a resolute and well-prepared army. The grand total of sorties flown on the opening day was about 11,000 not counting those by Coastal Command and transport aircraft. The Germans achieved only 319 sorties in the first twenty-four hours. Yet nowhere, on 6th June, did the Allied army attain all its objectives.

In the next six days, while the troops pressed forward and achieved a bridgehead up to twenty miles deep, the air forces made heavy and continuous attacks against enemy communications, one aim being to ensure that no reinforcements reached the defenders by rail. By 12th-13th June this result had virtually been achieved. Bomber Command aircraft made nearly 3,000 sorties against communications centres in this period, Air Chief Marshal Harris unwillingly accepting the diversion of effort from the attacks on industrial targets in Germany which he regarded as the proper role of the bomber force.

It was only at night that German bombers attacked and therefore it was the British night-fighter squadrons that had the greater opportunity for successful combat. Thus No. 456, one of the six Mosquito squadrons flying over the beach-heads, in the first week destroyed twelve German bombers. Indeed, during the first week the Allied air forces confined the German Air Force to defence of its own bases and ineffectual patrols over the Allied lines of communication; daylight attacks on the Allied supply routes were prevented and night attacks were rendered almost ineffective.

Admiral Doenitz had high hopes that his submarines and light surface craft would be able to severely damage the Allied invasion fleets. However, largely as a result of night and day patrols flown by endless chains of aircraft round a series of contiguous boxes, there was no interference by enemy naval craft during the first ten days of the invasion.

The hope that Caen and Cherbourg would be taken by the ninth day of the invasion was not fulfilled, but nevertheless the Allied armies had secured a firm foothold. Montgomery now concentrated for some weeks on regrouping and improvement of supply, while retaining the initiative by continued offensive probes.

The German light naval forces were still causing anxiety and No. 460 Squadron took part in an attack on Le Havre when 1,816 tons of bombs were dropped, 25 per cent more than in the first 1,000-bomber raid on Cologne two years before. The main result was the destruction of ten E-boats, three torpedo boats and numerous minor craft.

Meanwhile, for more than six months before the opening of the invasion, the Allied air forces had been heavily engaged in efforts to subdue a new German offensive, waged with long-range missiles. Since the 1930s the Germans had been experimenting with military rockets; production of long-range missiles and preparation of launching sites began in earnest early in 1943. From May of that year onwards a great part of R.A.F. photo reconnaissance was devoted to gaining information about German secret weapons.

By December 1943 75 launching sites for long-range missiles had been identified and in that month heavy bombing attacks on these sites began. In the next six months the Allied air forces dropped 36,200 tons of bombs on them. As a result German preparations were so delayed that the rocket offensive, instead of being a means of preventing an Allied invasion of France, became only a means of retaliating after the invasion should begin.

The first flying bombs were loosed on the night of the 12th-13th June six days after the beginning of the invasion. Only ten were fired, only four crossed the English coast and only one reached London, where it killed six people. By the end of June, however, 724 bombs had fallen in London. The Air Defence of Great Britain Command was placed in command of all fighter aircraft, anti-aircraft guns, searchlights and balloons in southern England so as to co-ordinate the defences against the new weapon.

At first the guns destroyed more bombs than the aircraft, but by the end of June the scores had been reversed: aircraft had disposed of 410, guns 169 and the balloon barrage thirteen. No. 456 Squadron, for example, armed with Mosquito night-fighters had no successes during June but sixteen out of twenty-eight Australian pilots in Spitfire, Tempest or Typhoon squadrons claimed victories in the first fortnight. On 23rd June an Australian employed a new method of attack. Flying Officer K. R. Collier used a wing of his Spitfire to tip up the wing of a flying bomb so violently that it upset the automatic controls and the bomb spiralled down into a field.

Anti-aircraft defences round the bomb sites were very strong. For example, on 22nd June when No. 466 sent fifteen Halifaxes in daylight against bomb sites six of the aircraft were hit, one being brought down. Two nights later Nos. 463 and 467 contributed thirty-four Lancasters to a force of 112 aircraft sent against a missile base. Enemy opposition led to delay and this gave the German fighters their chance. Five Australian crews were lost and all bombs were found to have fallen wide of the mark. In June German missiles struck London with 700 tons of explosive.

The missile offensive from sites in the Pas de Calais continued until 1st September when those sites had been captured or were closely threatened by the Allied army. In July and August the Allies spent over 10,000 sorties and 43,666 tons of bombs on missile targets in France, an immense subtraction from the weight of the attack on industrial targets and on the opposing army. Of 643 aircraft dispatched by R.A.A.F. heavy-bomber squadrons 585 found their targets and dropped 2,961 tons of bombs, losing nine aircraft.

While the missile sites were being bombed missile supply depots were also attacked with some success. Early in July Nos. 463 and 467 took part in two attacks by 455 Lancasters on supply depots, which reduced the daily average of flying-bomb attacks from about 100 to less than seventy. The relative lack of success of attacks on launching sites and depots led to a diversion of some of the bomber force to attacks on missile factories and research stations in Germany. Thus raids were made on Peenemunde, a main experimental station, the Opel factories and others. At this stage Bomber Command was spending 30 per cent and the American Eighth Air Force 20 per cent of their bomb-load against the flying-bomb offensive.

Soon after the defeat of the flying bomb, the first German rockets fell in England; within a week ten had exploded in Greater London. The rockets presented a new problem: they descended at five times the speed of sound and no fighter or gun could hope to destroy them: and launching points, if destroyed, could quickly be replaced. The heavy bombers were withdrawn from the anti-missile campaign and used against more profitable targets, and fighters and fighter-bombers were used to attack a wide range of missile targets—sites, communications, storage areas, and so on.

Thus No. 453 Squadron, which had been operating from continental bases since June, was brought back to England and, like many similar squadrons, employed principally against guided missiles. It made successful attacks on rocket-storage dumps in November and December, the Spitfires each carrying two 250-lb bombs. Late in December it was one of three squadrons which severely damaged a block of flats near The Hague reported to be the headquarters of rocket officers and technicians.

The guided missiles failed to achieve any notable military sucess. The 8,246 flying bombs that were launched killed 6,139 people in England and seriously injured 17,239; 1,115 rockets killed 2,855 and seriously injured 6,268. These represented 14 per cent of civilian deaths and 28 per cent of civilians severely wounded in the United Kingdom by enemy action throughout the war.

On 12th May 1944 the Eighth Air Force opened a new offensive against the synthetic oil industry in Germany, sending 900 heavy bombers against six plants. Such an offensive was much more to the liking of General Spaatz and Air Chief Marshal Harris, with their wholehearted belief in area bombing as a way to victory, than were the tasks in support of the army. Between 1940 and 1943 German synthetic oil production had risen from 7,500,000 tons to 11,250,000. Before May 1944 fewer than 4,000 tons of bombs had been aimed at the German oil industry. In the next twelve months 180,000 tons would be used against it.

Bomber Command began to take part in the campaign against oil on the night of 12th-13th June when 294 Lancasters attacked a plant at Gelsenkirchen in the Ruhr. No. 460 contributed fourteen crews and there were fifteen Australian pilots in R.A.F. squadrons that took part. The plant was severely damaged; seventeen bombers were lost, including one from No. 460. Such raids continued, against increasing opposition; on 21st-22nd June Nos. 463 and 467 provided thirty-four out of 130 aircraft for an attack on a plant near Gelsenkirchen, but the bombing was inaccurate because of heavy undercast and three R.A.A.F. aircraft were lost and others damaged.

By the end of June damage to oil plants was causing great anxiety in Germany and a labour force of 350,000 men was formed to work day and night on repairs. This force achieved remarkable results. At the same time it was now agreed on the Allied side that oil should be the main target of strategic bombing. In three months the weight of bombs dropped on oil targets nearly equalled the total tonnage dropped on all targets from the beginning of the war to the end of 1941. On occasions, however, the British losses were disturbingly high: in two consecutive raids in July, twenty-eight heavy bombers were shot down, but one of the two plants attacked was put completely out of action.

In eight raids in August Nos. 460, 463 and 467 sent out a total of 150 Lancasters and not one was lost. By this time the Germans had lost the Rumanian oilfields and the Polish fields were soon to fall to the Russian armies. Raids on plants in Germany were intensified: on 27th August 243 R.A.F. aircraft were sent against Homberg-Meerbeck in the Ruhr—the largest force yet committed by Bomber Command against a single oil objective. The raid was made in daylight and saw the first appearance over Germany of the newly re-formed No. 462 Squadron.

By December German aviation fuel production had been reduced to only 11 per cent of planned output, but motor-transport fuel was still about 45 per cent of what was planned. The campaign against oil hampered German operations but could not halt them, as the launching of a counter-offensive soon demonstrated. The raids continued through the winter. Thus on 21st-22nd December Nos. 463 and 467 contributed thirty-four to a force of 207 bombers that struck Politz; thirty-three reached the target. Nos. 460, 462 and 466 all took part in the final raids of the year, on Gelsenkirchen and Sterkrade in the Ruhr.

Meanwhile in Normandy in July the Allied armies had been halted in the difficult bocage country about Caen and air power had been called on to help resolve the problem. Leigh-Mallory was convinced that heavy bombers could break the deadlock. The plan was to saturate an area two miles and half by one mile, and 6,000 yards forward of the British troops, as a prelude to an attack on the ground. Nos. 460 and 466 provided thirty-four out of 467 bombers all but ten of which attacked, delivering 2,500 tons of bombs. This bombardment dazed the defenders and the infantry soon pressed forward to the outskirts of Caen only to find that the craters and debris caused by the bombers halted the tanks and gave the Germans time to reorganise.

Eisenhower again used heavy-bomber onslaughts in the next two attacks later in July. To the first of these, on 18th July, more than 2,000 bombers of all sizes were assigned. The Australians of Nos. 463 and 467 who provided twenty-seven Lancasters in the first phase were enthusiastic about the accuracy of the bombing. Nos. 460 and 466 contributed twenty-four heavy bombers in later phases. The final air attack was made by 920 American bombers. The troops made good progress at first but the Germans soon rallied, rain fell, the intended break-out was not achieved, and again the airfields necessary to an orderly deployment of the Allied Expeditionary Air Force in France were not taken. The next attack planned for 24th July was postponed because cloud and mist impeded the bomber force that day. On the 25th 4,790 tons of bombs were dropped west of St Lo; American troops advanced and by the end of the month had a foothold in Brittany.

Massive intervention by the heavy bombers continued at intervals. Thus on 7th-8th August No. 460 provided thirty-two Lancasters out of a total of 212 supporting the First Canadian Army. By mid-August the battlefront was mobile and there was no longer need for heavy bombers in close support. In this period Australian squadrons took part also in continued attacks on railway centres. Some of these proved costly, as when, on 18th-19th July, during an attack on Revigny twenty-four out of 110 bombers were shot down including nine piloted by Australians.

Complementary to massive onslaughts on railway centres were opportunist fighter-bomber attacks, particularly on bridges. The Mosquitos of No. 464, often employed on such operations, made 350 sorties in July and 400 in August from a temporary base on Thorney Island. Meanwhile No. 453 Squadron with its Spitfires had moved into the beach-head area on 25th June as part of Second T.A.F. and had been employed mainly in attacks on enemy vehicles just behind the battle area. For example, on 18th July the squadron flew sixty sorties—a record.

Throughout July the R.A.A.F. squadrons in Coastal Command continued to take part in the effort to suppress intervention by submarines. No. 10 Squadron scored its first big success for six months when one of its Sunderlands sank *U 243* 130 miles south-west of Brest. In the first half of August No. 461 had an extraordinary run of success: its crews sighted five submarines, attacked three and sank two—*U 385* and *U 270*. No. 455, armed with Beaufighters, operated in July and August against coastal shipping and small German naval craft, work that became increasingly hazardous as the enemy packed more and more anti-aircraft guns on to merchant ships and escort vessels. A typical strike was made on 21st July when No. 455 and a torpedo squadron attacked a convoy of at least nine merchant ships with thirty-one escorts. Despite 'the heaviest barrage . . . ever encountered' on such an occasion no R.A.A.F. Beaufighters were lost, but four merchantmen were hit with torpedoes and six escorts heavily damaged. Thus July and August brought ample employment to all R.A.A.F. squadrons operating from the United Kingdom or France, and all achieved or approached new records in terms of sorties flown. Morale was high, crews were expert, and the knowledge of the overwhelming strength of the combined air forces and the dwindling effectiveness of the *Luftwaffe* augmented the immense confidence of veterans and newcomers alike.

Two R.A.A.F. squadrons—Nos. 451 (Spitfires) and 458 (Wellingtons)—had some share in the invasion of southern France which opened on 15th August. No. 451 had been operating from Corsica escorting bombers, making armed reconnaissance and strafing sorties, and occasionally engaging in battle with enemy fighters, as on 25th May when six Spitfires shot down three out of four FW-190's encountered near Rome. On the other hand on 12th May 25 German bombers had attacked the airfield on which No. 451 was based and destroyed or damaged all but two of the squadron's Spitfires.

No. 451 met no opposition during the invasion and for some days afterwards and on 25th August the squadron began to establish itself on an airfield in southern France, but by that time the front line was out of effective range from this field and again No. 451 felt that the war was leaving it behind. In October the squadron was transferred to Foggia, where, however, it soon learnt that it was to be sent to England. It reached R.A.F. Station Hawkinge, near Dover, on 2nd December.

In the summer of 1944 No. 458 had largely been employed in preparations for and support of the invasion. It helped to counter submarines and small naval craft based on Marseilles, Toulon and Genoa, and bombed factories and oil targets. At the end of August, however, the squadron was ordered to move to Ancona to take part in night attacks on ships and ports in the northern Adriatic.

In mid-August there were strong hopes that the collapse of Germany was imminent, but these had faded by mid-September when the Germans had consolidated in good defensive positions forming a continuous front from the English Channel to Switzerland. In this period No. 460 took part in raids on submarine pens at La Pallice and on Le Havre in preparation for an

R.A.A.F.

Beaufighters of No. 455 Squadron took part in this two-wing strike on an enemy convoy off Mandal on the Norwegian coast on 15th July 1944.

assault by the First Canadian Army. In September No. 460 contributed nineteen out of 348 aircraft that attacked Le Havre on the 5th and next day contributed twenty-four; on the 10th Nos. 460, 463 and 467 sent sixty-seven Lancasters in a total gigantic force of 930 heavy bombers which struck Le Havre. Next day 218 bombers (including forty R.A.A.F.) attacked the port again, and a few hours later the garrison capitulated, having been blasted by 9,800 tons of bombs within a week. Similar treatment was given to Boulogne which was surrendered on 22nd September, and to Cap Gris Nez and Calais which were occupied on the 29th and 30th.

There was some criticism of such massive attacks on isolated garrisons on the grounds of diversion of effort from strategic tasks, the losses suffered by French civilians, and damage to port equipment (additional to that done by enemy demolitions). On the other hand some 30,000 Germans surrendered in the Channel ports at a cost of fewer than 1,500 British and Canadian casualties, and, except on one day over Calais when eight Lancasters were lost, the air force did not suffer heavily.

The Germans stood firm on the Siegfried Line and Rhine defences and in an effort to break the deadlock it was decided to use the First Allied Airborne Army (three divisions) against Arnhem, Nijmegen and Eindhoven, where it was to hold on until the advancing infantry linked with it and turned the enemy's flank. There were some 150 Australian aircrew in the two groups (fifteen squadrons) responsible for the British share of glider delivery and re-supply missions. The glider-borne troops and paratroops were landed successfully on 17th and 18th September. However, dogged opposition and

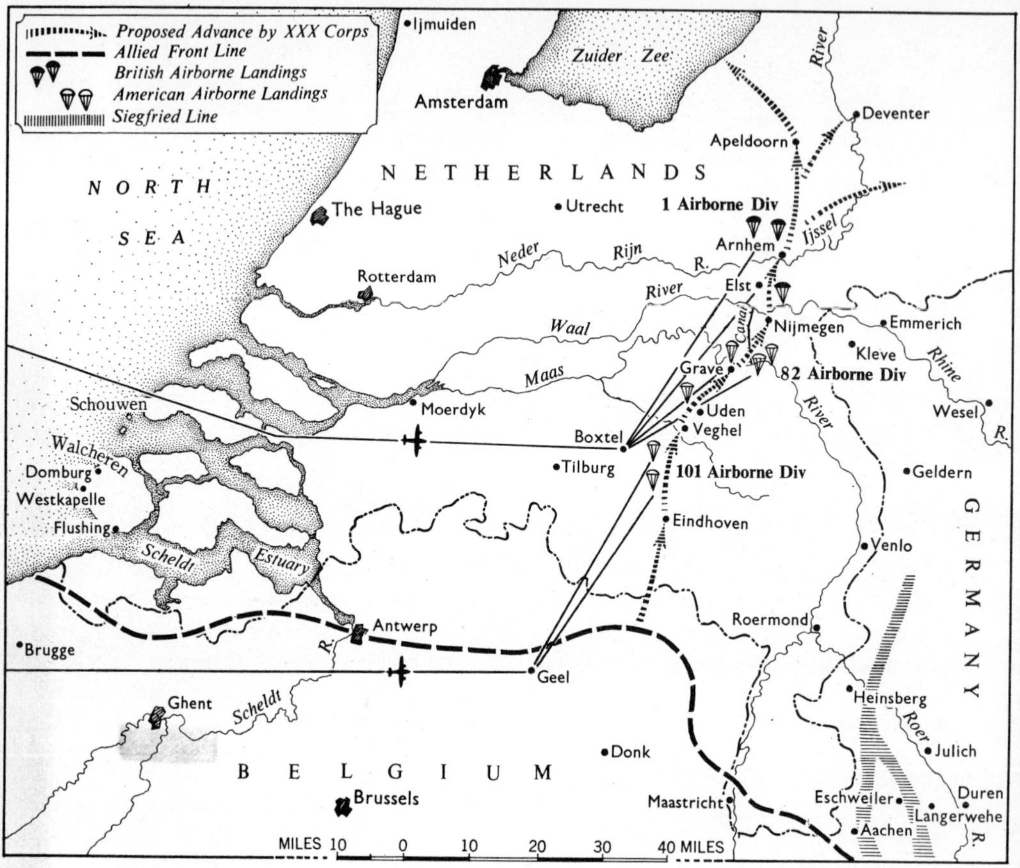

The Netherlands

bad weather were encountered. Contact was established with the airborne troops at Eindhoven by 19th September but the 1st British Airborne Division at Arnhem was isolated. Some 2,000 men from Arnhem managed to rejoin the main force but the airborne division lost about 7,000 killed, wounded or missing. No. 453 Squadron flew 210 sorties between Nijmegen and Arnhem from 17th to 26th September, and on the 28th, as mentioned, was transferred to Air Defence of Great Britain.

The Arnhem operation coincided with a change of role for No. 456, hitherto engaged on patrols against flying bombs. The policy whereby night fighters equipped with highly secret types of radar were forbidden to fly over enemy territory was abandoned on the ground that there would now be not enough time for the Germans to develop counter-measures against radar found in crashed aircraft, and the night fighters were made available for patrols over the battlefront. The R.A.A.F. Mosquitos of No. 456 flew in support of the airborne operations.

As from the end of June 1944 the dispatch of trained pilots from Australia to England was discontinued at the request of the Air Ministry; and after December 1944 no more men in other aircrew categories were sent. Before December 1943 the output of the R.A.A.F. schools had been 923 a month; from then onwards it was 701 a month, until, as a result of the above decision, the schools were reorganised to provide only for the needs of the

South-West Pacific Area plus those of Nos. 3 and 10 Squadrons, the two regular squadrons serving overseas, and the planned output was reduced to 439 aircrew a month.

On 1st July 1944 there were 14,000 men of the R.A.A.F. in the United Kingdom, 12,400 being aircrew, a majority of whom were in or destined for Bomber Command. Until the end of the war in Europe the numbers gradually declined as reinforcements did not keep pace with casualties and repatriation, but the numbers serving with combat units or commands rose as the reserve of aircrew at the Personnel Dispatch and Reception Centre, numbering 3,000 on 1st July, was slowly fed into the advanced and operational training units. One more *Article XV* squadron—No. 462, re-formed in August—joined Bomber Command in the course of the last ten months of the war and, as mentioned, No. 451 was transferred to England, bringing the number of R.A.A.F. squadrons there to twelve, but fewer than half the active Australian aircrew were with these squadrons. Only two squadrons were commanded by regular officers and efforts to place senior officers of the R.A.A.F. in appointments in the R.A.F. had not got very far. In the last eighteen months of the war two Australian air commodores, Bladin and McCauley, had arrived from Australia and been placed in staff appointments, but Bladin was recalled before the war was over. By the middle of 1944 the idea of a R.A.A.F. bomber group in Bomber Command had been dropped.

By August 1944 there were many Australians who, having completed two operational tours, were eligible for repatriation. Aircrew who had completed one tour were now also eligible for repatriation for further operational duty in the Pacific war; and in the last half of 1944 the repatriation of ground staff from England and the Middle East began at the rate of 150 a month.

In the first two months of the invasion period no heavy attacks were made on major German cities, but in July air planners became concerned at the respite afforded to German factories, and on the 23rd-24th heavy strategic bombing was resumed with an attack on Kiel by 629 bombers (of which twenty-eight were from Nos. 460, 463 and 467). Before the end of September the main bomber force had made twenty-nine more attacks. There were sixteen raids on inland cities, twelve on North Sea and Baltic ports and two (mentioned earlier) on the Opel factory near Mainz.

One or more of the R.A.A.F. squadrons took part in twenty-three of these raids. In the first raid on Kiel successful measures were taken to outwit the German defences and widespread damage was done for a loss of only four aircraft. Kiel was subjected to three more raids in August and September. In the four raids 1,780 aircraft attacked with nearly 4,800 tons of high-explosive and 2,200 tons of incendiary bombs.

Fifteen aircraft of No. 463 and nineteen of No. 467 took part in a very damaging raid on Bremerhaven on 18th-19th September when submarine and shipbuilding yards, warehouses and business areas and homes were hit. In August Bomber Command struck the Baltic ports of Stettin and Konigsberg. Of the 461 aircraft sent against Stettin fifty-seven were from Nos. 460, 463 and 467. The port was damaged and mines laid in the canal carrying most of the traffic supplying the northern part of the eastern front.

In this period Stuttgart was bombed four times and damage done to ball-bearing, machine-tool and engine factories, and to transport facilities. The

Australian squadrons took part in three of the raids, contributing from twenty-nine to fifty-one aircraft. Darmstadt was struck twice in this period, once without great success in August, and again in September when incendiaries were rained down and the whole centre of the city set on fire. Crews from Nos. 460, 462 and 466 took part in the heaviest raid in September when 549 aircraft dropped 2,660 tons of bombs on the railway and port area of Neuss.

The strategic air forces had reverted to the control of the Combined Chiefs of Staff on 15th September and plans were made to continue area raids despite the onset of winter. This was made easier by new navigation aids, a superfluity of crews, electronic radio counter-measures and shorter flights over enemy-held territory. Thus, whereas No. 460, for example, in October 1943 had operated only on nine nights and in November 1943 only on six, in the same two months of 1944 the squadron undertook twenty-eight operations. At this stage about half Bomber Command's effort was against German industrial cities, about one-quarter against oil and about one-quarter in more direct support of the armies. In the two months and a half before the German counter-offensive in the Ardennes, Bomber Command rained nearly 86,000 tons of bombs on industrial cities. This involved over 20,000 sorties, the rate of loss being only 1 per cent. The Australian squadrons sent out 1,233 aircraft which dropped 5,450 tons of bombs. Thus the contribution of the Australian squadrons was about 6 per cent, though, if the Australians in R.A.F. units were included, the Australian aircrew contribution would rise to about 10 per cent.

In October, November and December seven Rhineland and Ruhr cities were attacked, some of them four times, the heaviest raid being against Duisburg on 14th October when 1,007 aircraft attacked, including fifty-four from R.A.A.F. squadrons. Duisburg suffered a second 1,000-bomber raid within twenty-four hours. Losses were now less heavy. In an attack on Dusseldorf on 2nd-3rd November all five Australian heavy-bomber squadrons took part, contributing eighty-two aircraft, out of a total of 946 which reached the target; four were lost.

In the same period Bomber Command struck at nine towns in south and south-western Germany. The heaviest onslaughts were made on Stuttgart (2,446 tons), Karlsruhe (2,309 tons) and Saarbrucken (2,073 tons). This series of raids was performed by Lancasters because of their superior range, ceiling and bomb capacity; Nos. 463 and 467 flew in four of the series and No. 460 in six. No. 467 lost three aircraft and Nos. 460 and 463 each lost two.

In this period R.A.A.F. squadrons took part in raids on two North Sea ports, Bremen and Wilhelmshaven; and in a raid, mainly incendiary, on Brunswick, where the old part of the town was left in ruins; a raid on Giessen and one on Osnabruck. The Australian heavy bombers were also employed in operations against rail targets, and the internal waterways of Germany, notably the Dortmund-Ems canal, which had been breached in September and repaired, and was now, in November breached again, repaired, and breached once more.

The R.A.A.F. heavy bombers also took part in operations in direct support of the army in the Netherlands, including the breaking of the sea wall of the island of Walcheren to cause flooding, and the bombing of coastal batteries in the Scheldt estuary which barred the way to Antwerp now in Allied hands. By 6th November all Walcheren was captured, but the approaches to Antwerp were still blocked by minefields, and it was 28th November before the first Allied supply ships reached Antwerp.

Immediately after the fall of Walcheren Bomber Command and the Eighth Air Force were warned to be ready to attack enemy defences along the River Roer as a prelude to a large-scale attack. Thus on the morning of 16th November in one hour and a half 1,191 American and 1,188 British heavy bombers struck towns along the Roer and to the west of it. It was the heaviest tactical bombardment up to that time.

By the middle of 1944 the only R.A.A.F. squadron remaining in the Mediterranean area east of Malta was No. 459 (Baltimores). This veteran unit moved from Palestine to Cyrenaica in July and August. Thence it engaged in a variety of tasks including attacks on ships, anti-submarine escorts, road traffic in Crete and reconnaissance. So few enemy ships remained in the area that worthwhile targets were hard to find. Allied forces were landed in Greece early in October and thereafter No. 459 was largely employed in attacks on enemy airfields, specially Maleme in Crete, and on targets in Rhodes. The Germans had now withdrawn from Greece but had left resolute garrisons holding Crete, Rhodes, Milos and the Dodecanese. In February 1945 No. 459 was transferred to England where to its great chagrin it was disbanded in April—the only R.A.A.F. squadron to disband in Europe before the end of the war.

From September 1944 No. 458 operated one flight from Foggia and one from the Ancona area and later one from Rosignano, near Leghorn, mainly against enemy shipping. In January 1945 the squadron was moved to Gibraltar—a welcome change from the mud and cold of Italy—for anti-submarine duties, and was there when the war ended.

In Italy in the last year of the war Australian interest was concentrated mainly on two veteran fighter-bomber squadrons—Nos. 3 and 450—and No. 454 (Baltimores). After the fall of Rome on 4th June the United States Fifth Army advanced towards Siena and Leghorn and the British Eighth towards Florence. Enemy vehicles became the main target of the fighter-bombers; and the advancing army found many wrecked and abandoned vehicles. Support was close and devastating.

By 4th August 1944 leading units of the Eighth Army were on the edge of Florence. It was now decided to transfer most of the Eighth Army's strength to the Adriatic sector which offered an easier approach to the Po Valley and the plains of Lombardy. The overwhelming air superiority enabled this transfer to be made without the enemy's knowledge. The Allies hoped to force the enemy back to the Po but by October, when rain produced seas of mud, the Allies were still south of Bologna. The scale of the close support is indicated by the fact that the two Australian Kittyhawk squadrons were able to operate on twenty-one days in October and flew 823 sorties. But now that the fighting had become static aircraft influenced the battle less than they had during the fluid fighting that had followed the fall of Rome.

In November No. 3 Squadron was rearmed with Mustangs. At this stage both No. 3 and No. 450 were largely engaged in sorties over Yugoslavia, supporting the partisans and harassing communications.

An Allied offensive which opened on 9th April 1945 with massive air support, drove the Germans across the Po. Soon the enemy were in full retreat. In three days No. 239 Wing accounted for 500 motor vehicles on roads crowded with disorganised troops.

On 2nd May the German commander in Italy surrendered to General Alexander. The task of No. 205 Group in which numbers of Australians were serving changed from bombing to transport duties, including the ferrying of some 1,200 released prisoners to England and some 800 South African former prisoners to Cairo.

In mid-August 1944 German submarines were forced from their bases in ports in the Bay of Biscay to Norwegian bases. Thereafter the chances of a flying boat crew finding and sinking a submarine were greatly diminished but their patrols had to continue as before to ensure that any U-boat suspected of being in the area they were able to cover was harried so effectively that it could not get into a position to fire. Thus No. 10 Squadron, for example, flew fifty-eight anti-submarine patrols in August, but without finding a submarine.

By the end of August all German fighters had been withdrawn from western France and the Sunderlands, now able to operate without cloud cover and close inshore even in daylight, engaged in reconnaissance of ports and searches for ships moving along the French coast. In September part of No. 461 Squadron was transferred to the Shetland Isles and patrolled over Norwegian waters.

In the latter part of 1944 Australian interest in the campaign against enemy shipping centred mainly on No. 455 Squadron. In August this squadron first used a new 25-pound rocket projectile with a solid head. On 29th August four Beaufighter squadrons including No. 455 attacked five ships near Heligoland and, using rockets, cannon and torpedoes, sank two merchantmen. Throughout September Beaufighter formations sometimes fifty or sixty strong harassed shipping along the North Sea coast, attacking at such low altitudes that on one occasion a Beaufighter of No. 455 returned with three feet of a trawler's mast embedded in its nose. So effective was this offensive that during October Coastal Command failed to discover a single enemy cargo vessel moving by day off the Dutch, German and Danish coasts. This interruption of enemy coastal traffic occurred at a time when the Swedish Government had virtually stopped its ships from trading with German ports. Coastal Command now turned to the problem of night attacks on shipping.

After the German surrender Coastal Command aircraft continued armed patrols during May in case individual submarines should disregard their orders, but in fact no hostile acts occurred. No. 461 Squadron was disbanded on 4th June but No. 10, being a regular unit, continued training pending its return to Australia. No. 455 made many attacks on enemy shipping in Norwegian waters in the early months of 1945. On 7th May attacks on enemy ships were discontinued and on the 25th the squadron was disbanded.

Early in December 1944 the Allied commanders were convinced that the Germans could not stage a major counter-offensive. In fact Field Marshal von Rundstedt had withdrawn armoured divisions for rest and re-equipment and had received infantry reinforcements. Mostly by night he concentrated ten armoured and fourteen infantry divisions in the Ardennes sector, lightly held by five divisions of the First American Army. In thick fog on 16th December three German armies attacked. The offensive made swift progress and the attackers were nearing the Meuse before stubborn resistance at key road junctions slowed down their armour.

Fog and low cloud in the first few days greatly reduced close support by the Allied air forces. The best the heavy bombers could do was to attack the German communications system. Thus the Australian heavy-bomber squadrons were among those employed against such targets as Duisburg, Ulm, Trier, Bonn and Cologne. From 23rd December the weather was fine for five days and Allied bombers pounded German airfields, and the German formations were heavily attacked.

Nos. 460 and 466 took part in an attack on the enemy's communications centre at St Vith which was devastated by 1,139 tons of bombs of which the two Australian squadrons dropped 95 tons. At length von Rundstedt withdrew to a defensive line covering St Vith. The heavy bombers continued to deal damaging blows against rail targets. For example, on the last night of the year No. 466 took part in an attack on marshalling yards at Cologne when 1,750 tons of bombs were dropped. In the second half of December Bomber Command dropped 12,848 tons of bombs on rail targets.

January was a particularly bad month for night flying. There was much fog and snow fell on eighteen days. The main bomber force could operate on only eleven nights and the monthly total of 33,000 tons of bombs was the lowest since March 1944. However, on 14th-15th January 580 Lancasters, including forty-four from R.A.A.F. squadrons, took part in the heaviest raid made by Bomber Command on an oil target—a plant at Leuna, which was rendered quite inactive for a month.

The heavy-bomber force contributed directly to the opening of the Allied offensive in February 1945 by bombing key centres behind the front. Thus on 7th-8th February No. 460 contributed twenty-one Lancasters to a massive raid on Kleve and No. 466 sent eighteen Halifaxes against Goch, near Wesel. The bombing was too heavy, for craters and blocked roads delayed the advancing troops. In this phase communications were receiving the greater part of the Allied bombing effort. This bombing created traffic jams and thus helped to provide targets for the fighter-bombers and fighters.

In February Australian heavy-bomber squadrons took part in raids on Ludwigshaven, Dortmund, Duisburg and Pforzheim. Twenty-four Lancasters of Nos. 463 and 467 were included in a force of 188 which dropped bombs on the Dortmund-Ems canal on 7th-8th February, and on 3rd-4th March contributed forty-five to a force of 222 Lancasters that bombed the same target; four of the R.A.A.F. aircraft failed to return. In little more than a month No. 467 had lost two commanding officers, one flight commander and two gunnery leaders; and No. 463 lost its commander.

Allied fighters and light bombers were now swarming over the enemy's trunk roads. No. 464 was so employed, and on fourteen nights in February made 151 attacks. On 22nd February the Mosquito wing took part in a large-scale operation against communications throughout Germany but this proved a costly operation; twenty-one Mosquitos out of 143 failed to return. On 21st March the wing, protected by Mustang fighters, made a successful daylight precision attack on Gestapo headquarters at Copenhagen. The

Mosquitos continued to bomb Berlin night after night, to ensure that the Berliners had no respite from the wailing of sirens, anti-aircraft fire and the intermittent explosion of 4,000-lb bombs. In March, for example the fast, unarmed Mosquitos dropped 1,800 tons of bombs on Berlin.

Fifty-six R.A.A.F. Lancasters took part in a raid by 773 aircraft on Dresden on 13th-14th February to aid the Russian armies. A great part of the city was laid waste and civilian casualties were very high. Next day 310 Fortresses attacked showering 750 tons of bombs through a blanket of smoke rising to 15,000 feet. Public opinion deplored these raids on a city teeming with refugees from farther east and without adequate air raid organisation.

As the armies advanced Bomber Command was able at the one time to strike targets that were both important communication centres and industrial centres. Thus on 16th-17th March sixteen R.A.A.F. Lancasters took part in a raid on Nuremberg and thirty-three in a raid on Wurzburg.

On 6th March Cologne fell and on 7th March American troops crossed the Rhine at Remagen where the railway bridge was still intact. Bomber Command staged a gigantic attack on Essen in daylight on 11th March when over 1,000 bombers, including sixty-one from four R.A.A.F. squadrons, dropped 4,680 tons of high explosive against negligible opposition. Next day Dortmund was hit by over 1,000 bombers.

Oil targets were still being attacked during this final bombing onslaught and by the beginning of April practically the whole German oil industry was at a standstill.

By mid-March the early collapse of German resistance seemed inevitable. On 15th March General George S. Patton began a drive across the lower Moselle and on the 22nd forced a second crossing of the Rhine at Oppenheim. By that time the Remagen bridgehead was thirty-five miles wide and ten miles deep. On 24th March Field Marshal Montgomery opened his drive across the lower Rhine at Wesel. Bomber Command forces including thirty-two Lancasters from Australian squadrons gave massive support at Wesel. At the same time two divisions were landed from the air within the battle area. This operation was an outstanding success and soon a swift advance eastward was in progress.

It was indicative of the magnitude of the Allied air potential that R.A.A.F. squadrons were not particularly active on the day this offensive opened, nor during the next week when the armies swept forward and encircled the Ruhr. Another sign of the times was the announcement on 31st March that the Empire Air Training Scheme had ended; no longer was there need for air crew reinforcements either for the European or Pacific theatres.

On 25th April No. 460 Squadron, for example, made its last raid—on Hitler's 'Eagle's Nest' at Berchtesgaden, considered to be the headquarters of the National Redoubt where, according to Nazi propaganda, German armies would make a final stand. Other targets attacked by R.A.A.F. heavy-bomber squadrons in April were oil refineries, road and rail communications, oil tanks at Hamburg, ships in harbour. The only R.A.A.F. squadron of Bomber Command to operate in May was No. 462 which sent some aircraft out on a simulated raid while others were on a radar-jamming mission.

When Germany surrendered on 7th May there were 13,500 men of the R.A.A.F. in the United Kingdom, western Europe, Gibraltar, Iceland and the Azores; and 2,500 in the Middle East and Mediterranean Allied Air

Forces. An early step towards demobilisation was to transfer some 800 Australians from R.A.F. to R.A.A.F. squadrons. In June about 1,300 men were repatriated from England. By August the unscrambling of Australian aircrew had reached a stage where only 128 R.A.A.F. aircrew remained in forty-two R.A.F. squadrons whereas in May there had been 2,563 in 220 squadrons. As a general rule former prisoners were repatriated first, then Australians disgorged by R.A.F. units, then men from *Article XV* squadrons as they disbanded. About 2,500 men of the R.A.A.F. undertook educational courses in England and about 4,000 engaged in other civilian employment while awaiting repatriation.

Whereas when the German war ended about 16,000 men of the R.A.A.F., of whom 12,300 were aircrew, were engaged against Germany, in the Pacific area there were 138,000 members of the R.A.A.F:, of whom only 14,500 were aircrew. These figures illustrate the degree to which the Dominion contribution to the Empire air forces was a contribution of aircrew to a force for which the United Kingdom provided most of the ground staff, equipment, technical services and senior leaders. A Dominion's share in the total effort in the air is impossible to estimate precisely. Thus Australian squadrons in Bomber Command dropped 6 per cent of the total weight of bombs, but numbers of men in these squadrons were not Australians and on the other hand some 6,000 Australians served in R.A.F. bomber squadrons. Fatal casualties suffered by the R.A.A.F. were: in Europe 5,397, in the Middle East 1,135, in the S.W.P.A. 3,342, elsewhere 688. Of the total fatal casualties in the European theatre 3,486 were suffered in Bomber Command, 191 in Fighter Command, 408 in Coastal Command, 478 in other units, and 834 in training units. Those killed in action in other national forces in Bomber Command were: R.A.F., 38,792; R.C.A.F., 9,913; R.N.Z.A.F., 1,676; S.A.A.F., 27; other British countries, 34; Poles, 928; other Allies, 481.[1]

[1] These figures were derived from Sir Charles Webster and Noble Frankland, *The Strategic Air Offensive Against Germany, 1939-1945*, Vol. III: *Victory*, Part 5 (1961), p. 287, a volume in the military series of the British official *History of the Second World War*.

Chapter 13 **Plans and problems: looking forward**

From the last quarter of 1943 onwards post-war problems began to take up more and more of the time of the Australian Government. Already plans had been made for a Reconstruction Training Scheme for ex-servicemen, for their employment and settlement on the land, and for more generous 'social service' benefits, as they were now called. Plans were made to accelerate and assist the building of houses; the virtual cessation of house-building would lead to a grave shortage for years after the war. In October 1943 a Secondary Industries Commission was set up to which firms needing permits to make 'peacetime' goods could refer and which could assist the transition to post-war manufacture. The disposal of unwanted government-owned factories became one of the Commission's main activities.

In 1944 it was decided to set up an organisation to co-ordinate the disposal of the vast stocks of manufactured and raw materials that would be available when the fighting ceased—and some of it before then. It was feared that the dumping of such goods both in Australia and by oversea countries would flood the markets and imperil peacetime employment. Consequently in June a Disposals Commission was established. By May 1945 the Services were being urged to release their surplus holdings while a demand existed rather than later when they might cause a glut.

Indeed throughout the later years of the war there was a fear that demobilisation would lead to an over-supply of labour, raw materials, goods of some kinds and factory space. The time it would take to overcome the shortages created in a rapidly-growing population by years of hard living does not seem to have been foreseen even in regard to housing. The foremost aim for the period after the war was to be full employment. A paper put out by the Government on 30th May 1945 opened with the statement that 'full employment is a fundamental aim of the Commonwealth Government' and warned that in the period of transition control of prices, scarce materials, capital issues and imports would continue. After the war an effective employment service would be developed.

By 1944, though Parliament continued to pass laws, the nation was largely governed by regulation. In 1942, for example, 557 Statutory Rules were issued, apart from many other orders, delegations, proclamations, etc., mainly by the Prices Commissioner and Customs Department.

Moreover, whereas there had been twelve Commonwealth Government departments in 1938, there were now twenty-five, plus many primary-produce boards and committees and six commissions. Whereas in June 1939 there had been 32,429 permanent Commonwealth public servants and 14,614 temporary or 'exempt' employees, there were now 38,944 who were permanent and 60,540 who were temporary. New permanent appointments had been restricted with the object of protecting the interests of people in the armed Services who in normal circumstances might have sought appointment to the Public Service and most newcomers to the permanent service had been women and boys.

Numbers of senior administrators in the expanded service had been brought in from the universities, from State services, and elsewhere, and in the middle and junior ranks were many young economists and other graduates destined for rapid promotion after the war. These newcomers were grouped particularly in the Departments of Post-War Reconstruction, and War Organisation of Industry. The old-established departments were managed, and well managed, by permanent public servants.

Another change which the war brought to the Public Service was that the names of numbers of senior administrators became well known to newspaper readers, and the anonymity that had formerly cloaked the public servant largely disappeared. Some wartime departments set about explaining their tasks and their achievements to the public by means of books, periodicals and pamphlets to a degree hitherto unknown.

By 1943 and 1944 lawyers were beginning to express misgivings about rule by regulation and the increasing delegation of power by Ministers. For example Geoffrey Sawer, a teacher of law, wrote in 1943 that government was becoming 'more and more a matter of making and unmaking administrative regulations and administrative discretions. If the bureaucrat wants a power he gets it under the guise of a National Security Regulation. If he gets into trouble while exercising that power he can get out of trouble by making another regulation.'[1]

So strong were such anxieties that in June 1944 Evatt appointed a committee comprising three lawyers with a Member of Parliament as chairman to which he could refer questions whether to review, repeal or modify regulations under the *National Security Act*. This committee recommended the repeal or amendment of certain regulations and made other recommendations aimed at protecting the rights of individuals.

On the other hand the Government was convinced that it would continue to need extended powers in the unsettled times after the war. In December 1943 it announced that a referendum would be held to decide whether additional powers should be given to the Commonwealth for five post-war years to enable it to carry out the task of reconstruction. These powers numbered fourteen and covered: reinstatement and rehabilitation of returned servicemen; employment and unemployment; organised marketing; uniform company legislation; trusts, combines and monopolies; profiteering and prices; production and distribution of goods; control of oversea exchange and investment; air transport; uniformity of railway gauges; national works; national health; family allowances; and care of Aborigines.

The referendum was held on 19th August 1944 and the proposals were rejected by a margin of more than 340,000 votes. Only in South Australia and Western Australia was there a majority for 'Yes'. Australians have seldom been willing to vote for an extension of the powers of the central government. And in 1944 the people were probably weary of the strict controls to which they were being subjected and looked forward to the time when peace would bring them to an end.

The censorship of news and opinion also was coming under criticism.

[1] *Public Administration,* December 1943.

Australian War Memorial

A long queue of people waiting for bottled beer at The George Hotel, St Kilda, Melbourne on 31st December 1943. Such queues for beer, tobacco and cigarettes and other goods in short supply were a familiar sight in cities and towns throughout Australia during the war years and for some time afterwards.

Throughout the war and particularly since the Japanese onslaught the newspapers had complained about the manner in which, from time to time, the censors had performed their task. In April 1942 the Government had established a Press Censorship Advisory Committee consisting of two newspaper proprietors, and two (later three) journalists, with J. H. Scullin, a former Labour Prime Minister, as Chairman. At the meetings of this body the members were able to express their views on what they considered to be the shortcomings of news censorship. Typical complaints were made by the committee in March 1943 when it protested against censorship of criticism of the High Command and the inaccuracy of over-optimism in G.H.Q. communiqués, and described the dissatisfaction of certain war correspondents. Curtin, who was chairman on this occasion, declared that loose criticism would have a disastrous effect on morale, that the military leaders knew best what should go into the communiqués, and there was no justification for allowing criticism of the management of campaigns if the criticism was based on mis-statements.

The Australian censors would have avoided many complaints if they had refrained from censoring news on the grounds that it might adversely affect morale and from the outset had confined themselves to 'security' censorship. A radical difference between their outlook and that of the British censors was demonstrated when, at the request of the Australian publicity censorship, Curtin protested to the British Government because a London newspaper had published an article from Australia about the local censorship. The British Government replied that its censorship was based on security considerations only and no action would be taken concerning an article which merely embodied the private opinion of a journalist. 'Critical articles not dissimilar in character not infrequently appear in the press here,' said the British reply to the Australian complaint, 'and must be accepted as part of the price paid for the undoubted advantages of a free press.' Unfortunately this did not persuade the Australian authorities to follow the British example.[2]

In October 1943 both the Department of Information and Publicity Censorship were placed under one control, the Chief Publicity Censor, E. G. Bonney, becoming Director-General. The newspapers continued to complain and on 30th November the censor ordered the *Daily Telegraph* (Sydney) to submit all matter intended for publication. The order was withdrawn on 1st February but the dispute continued, the newspapers contending that security should be the sole object of censorship, while the censor demonstrated that he was concerned also with morale and the reputation of Australia overseas.

In April 1944 the *Daily Telegraph* appeared with three columns blank, thus implying that what was to have been printed therein had been censored; this defied the rule that no indication should be given of any excisions or modifications demanded by the censor. Next day the *Sunday Telegraph's* front page contained two blank columns. Commonwealth police entered the newspaper's office and impounded all copies still undistributed. The *Sydney Morning Herald* reported the suppression and announced that it and the *Telegraph* that day contained material that the censor had banned. All Sydney newspapers were suppressed that day—17th April—but on the 18th a High Court injunction was obtained restraining the Commonwealth from endeavouring to prevent publication of the articles on censorship that were objected to and the papers appeared as usual, with the suppressed issues as supplements.

At length on 19th May a code of censorship principles was announced by the Acting Prime Minister, the first clause being 'Censorship shall be imposed exclusively for reasons of defence security'.

During 1944, while the American forces were striding to the Philippines and the Australian Army was driving the Japanese in New Guinea to the Sepik, three large military questions were to exercise the Australian Government: how to distribute the waning supply of manpower, what role their

[2] In 1940 Cyril (later Baron) Radcliffe, a distinguished barrister employed in the British Press and Censorship Bureau, had drafted the following principles for the guidance of censors, and they were adopted and followed:

1. The powers of the Press Censorship were derived from Defence Regulation No. 3. Press censors had therefore authority only to ban from publication information which would *aid the enemy in his military effort,* the word *'military'* being interpreted in its broadest sense and not confined merely to the armed forces.

2. Information covered facts, but not opinions, comments, speculation or the use which the enemy might make of such information to further his propaganda against us.

3. The censors were not concerned with an editor's liability under other Defence Regulations; for example, the publication of subversive or other material which sought to undermine the people's morale or will to continue the war. The censor's 'Passed for Publication' stamp on such material was, however, to be accompanied by a note to the editor intimating that the article or passages passed contained no information of value to the enemy but the censorship took no responsibility for their publication in other respects.

4. The censor was authorised to pass on to an editor the views of the Foreign Office or other Government department concerned when they considered it undesirable in the national interest to publish an article or passage which was not censorable on security grounds. (Quoted in G. P. Thomson, *Blue Pencil Admiral* (1947).)

army would play in future operations, and what role United Kingdom forces would play in the Pacific. All these problems were interlocked; the size of the forces to be maintained would depend on the tasks they had to do, and would be influenced by the extent of the demands that United Kingdom forces in the Pacific might make on Australian civilian manpower. At the same time, as we have seen, the Government (in common with other Allied Governments, and, soon, sometimes in co-operation with them) was giving increasing attention to preparing for the peace which seemed likely to be achieved by 1945 or 1946.

On 1st October 1943, at the height of the New Guinea operations already described, the War Cabinet had decided that the army must by June 1944 release 20,000 men in addition to routine releases on medical, age and disciplinary grounds, and other releases arranged at the request of the Director-General of Manpower; that the munitions and aircraft industries must free 20,000 men in the same period; and that in both these quotas priority should be given to 15,000 men for rural industry, since there was growing anxiety about the ability of Australia to continue feeding her own people and those Allied forces that were largely dependent on her for rations. The monthly intake into the Services was to be limited to 3,000 men and 2,000 women allotted thus:

	Men	*Women*
Army	550	950
Air Force	2,450	1,050

The War Cabinet decided that Australia would continue to take in aircrew under the Empire Training Scheme but at a reduced rate, and that the air force in Australia should be stabilised at its present strength of forty-eight squadrons (including five reserve squadrons) plus such Australian squadrons as could be brought from the European theatre. (In November, however, the War Cabinet decided that the R.A.A.F. in the S.W.P.A. would be increased to fifty-three squadrons by the end of 1944.)

When making these decisions about allocation of men and women to the Services the War Cabinet had affirmed that

> it is of vital importance to the future of Australia and her status at the peace table in regard to the settlement in the Pacific that her *military effort* should be concentrated as far as possible in the Pacific and that it should be on a scale to guarantee her an effective role in the peace settlement.

The War Cabinet added that if necessary the effort in the Pacific should be maintained at the expense of commitments in other theatres. Thus the Australian Ministers had the notion that the nation's military effort and the nation's place in the post-war world were inter-related, and henceforth, in discussions of strategical policy, manpower, and other such problems, the Government looked to the future as well as the present.

'The Government', wrote Curtin to Churchill, after the meeting of the War Cabinet mentioned above, 'has considered whether it should sanction a further regimentation of the civilian economy in order to make available additional manpower. This would necessitate the imposition of such drastic restrictive measures as to involve in Australia a higher degree of regimentation than exists in any democratic country. In view of this, and having regard to the effect on morale and on the war effort itself, the Government has rejected this course.'

The reason why Curtin sent this communication to Churchill was that he wished to have the observations of the British Prime Minister on the question of returning to Australia 3,400 Australian naval men serving overseas, chiefly in destroyers and minesweepers of the Eastern Fleet, and also of some of the seventeen R.A.A.F. squadrons serving overseas, where about 20,000 Australian airmen were still posted. These were fifteen *Article XV* squadrons and two regular squadrons; two other *Article XV* squadrons were already serving in Australia.

On 21st January 1944 the War Cabinet approved a revised statement of the forces assigned to MacArthur's command, and decided that any future assignments should be 'specifically made upon the authority of the Government. The assigned forces were listed: 4 cruisers, 4 L.S.I's, 2 destroyers, 2 sloops, 35 corvettes, and numbers of smaller vessels; all mobile combat formations of the army, the divisions included being the 6th, 7th, 9th, 2nd, 3rd, 4th, 5th, 11th and 12th, and two armoured brigades; all combat units of the R.A.A.F.

It was proving impossible, however, to maintain so large an army from the available men and women and Curtin and MacArthur agreed between themselves that by the end of 1944 the military force that Australia should maintain for service in combat would comprise six infantry divisions and two armoured brigades.

Meanwhile Curtin and Evatt, looking ahead, had outlined ideas that they had been pondering concerning, in Curtin's case, the future co-ordination of British Commonwealth affairs and, in Evatt's, Australia's role in world affairs. On 14th August 1943 Curtin had announced that he believed that 'some Imperial authority must be evolved so that the British Commonwealth of Nations will have, if not an executive body, at least a standing consultative body'. Later he said that he had in mind a council with a structure similar to that of the Pacific War Council—a permanent body with regular meetings and a permanent secretariat.

In October 1943 Evatt had propounded ideas which he was to pursue vigorously in the following years. He claimed a place for Australia in world affairs. Leadership in the international sphere would naturally be assumed by the three great Powers, but the smaller nations should be brought within the framework of an 'organised family of nations determined to give effect to the declared objectives of the United Nations'. He quoted with approval a proposal of Churchill's for the establishment of a system of subordinate regional councils within the framework of a world organisation. Australia could and should make a very special contribution towards the establishment and maintenance of the peace settlement in South-East Asia and the Pacific. 'I regard', he said, 'permanent collaboration between Australia and New Zealand as pivotal to a sound post-war Pacific policy.' Thereupon he suggested to the New Zealand Government an early exchange of views between Ministers, and a conference was held in January 1944. Co-operation in four fields was sought: armistice preparations and arrangements; post-war questions such as security, aviation and migration; dependencies; relations with other Pacific Powers.

It was agreed that a defence zone based on Australia and New Zealand

Australian War Memorial

The new Labour Ministry photographed on the lawns of Government House, Canberra on 24th September 1943: *(front row)* N. J. O. Makin, J. A. Beasley, J. B. Chifley, John Curtin (Prime Minister), Lord Gowrie, F. M. Forde, H. V. Evatt, J. S. Collings, R. V. Keane; *(back row)* H. P. Lazzarini, E. J. Holloway, W. P. Ashley, E. J. Ward, A. S. Drakeford, D. Cameron, J. J. Dedman, W. J. Scully, C. W. Frost, J. M. Fraser, A. A. Calwell.

stretching through the arc of islands north and north-east of Australia to Western Samoa and the Cook Islands should be established, but within the framework of a general system of world security. Australia put forward a suggestion that Australia should take over from the United Kingdom the administration of the British Solomons and should share or undertake alone responsibility for the New Hebrides. New Zealand said she would not oppose such transfers to Australian administration but made it clear that she wished Britain to remain in the South Pacific and 'would not dream of seeking a change of British rule in Fiji'.

The Governments declared that the doctrine of trusteeship was 'applicable in broad principle to all colonial territories in the Pacific and elsewhere', and the Governments would encourage the establishment of a South Seas Regional Commission with advisory powers. It was agreed that Australia should take steps to call a conference of Powers with territorial interests in the South and South-West Pacific.

The proposal to call this conference provoked a protest by the United States Government, whose Minister to Australia wrote to Curtin to say that the President had considerable doubts that the time had arrived for such discussion. The war had still to be won; and it was necessary to agree on arrangements for a general international security system before attempting to deal with problems of regional security. The President feared that such a conference might bring into focus conflicting opinions on matters not yet requiring decision. The President hoped Curtin would take no steps towards calling such a conference until they had discussed the matters personally.

Evatt, who replied (not Curtin), welcomed this last proposal, but defended the conference plan with vigour and pointed out that the United States had often taken the initiative in matters of regional co-operation.

This, of course, was not the first occasion on which the President of the United States had been disquieted by Australian attitudes. Since early in 1942 Roosevelt had at times been perturbed by the sharp, though rare, disagreements between Britain and Australia; and on 3rd January 1944 he wrote to Curtin to suggest that Curtin and he should meet, and added: 'Incidentally and confidentially, while Churchill and I did not discuss the matter in any way, I do not think it would do anything but good if you could go to London for a short visit.' He said to Curtin that among the problems he wished to discuss were the future protection of Australia, the disposition of the Japanese islands in the central Pacific, and 'the future policing of the whole Pacific and Asiatic Area'.

A conference of Prime Ministers of the British Commonwealth in London in May offered an opportunity not only for the meeting Roosevelt sought but, more importantly, for Curtin and his advisers (he was accompanied by Sir Frederick Shedden and General Blamey) to discuss Britain's plans for participation in the operations in the Pacific or the Indies. Largely because of differences of opinion in London about those plans the Australians had only a foggy picture of what the British intentions were and were anxious to know more.

Late in 1943 the British Chiefs of Staff had intended that as soon as possible after the defeat of Germany, then assumed for planning purposes to take place by October 1944, the main British fleet should be sent to the Pacific and four British divisions should be based on Australia for service in the Pacific. As discussions of the plans for British participation developed in 1944 it became evident that there were various areas of agreement and disagreement between five groups or individuals: the British Prime Minister, the British Chiefs of Staff, the Australian Government, General MacArthur, and the American Joint Chiefs of Staff. (The Australian Government, however, was only dimly aware of the differences between the British Prime Minister and his Chiefs of Staff.)

These differences arose from the fact that Mr Churchill wished the main British effort to be made from the Indian Ocean against Malaya and the Indies—a 'Bay of Bengal' policy—and he was strongly supported by the Foreign Office, which wanted the British forces to appear in a strong independent role in the Far East. The British Chiefs of Staff, on the other hand, saw the Pacific as the decisive theatre of war against Japan and wished to contribute British weight there rather than in places remote from Japan. Curtin was most anxious that the United Kingdom forces should be prominent in the Pacific in the final stages of the war and constantly pressed for the dispatch of a British fleet to the Pacific. MacArthur and his staff would probably have preferred to go forward without British forces—they shared the traditional American suspicion of British policy and intentions—but they would welcome the support of a fleet tied to their command.

Lastly the American Chiefs of Staff, and particularly Admirals Leahy and

King, made no secret of the fact that they did not want the British fleet to have a share in the main operations in the Pacific. The American Chiefs of Staff wished the main British effort to be made not towards Sumatra and Singapore, which they regarded as a step in the wrong direction, but northwards through Burma to China, because they had high hopes of a bombing offensive against Japan by long-range aircraft based in China.

Curtin had talks with Roosevelt in Washington in April on his way to the London meeting which opened on 1st May. The London conference concentrated on post-war questions, and discussed the scope and nature of an international security organisation, colonial problems, regional commissions, commercial policies, international civil aviation, post-war migration, foreign policy, post-war employment.

Curtin took the opportunity to put forward his suggestions for improving the machinery for Empire co-operation. He suggested that the British Prime Minister should meet the High Commissioners and the Secretary of State for Dominion Affairs once a month to review current problems and to enable the Dominion representatives to raise any questions on which they thought they should be consulted. He went on to outline the proposal for improved machinery for Empire consultation and co-operation that he had made in Australia in December 1943, but he reported to his Ministers at home that he did not think that he would get far with this proposal after an address by the Canadian Prime Minister a few days earlier in which Mackenzie King mentioned suggestions for new methods of co-operation and praised the existing ones asking: 'What more effective means of co-operation could have been found than those which, in spite of all handicaps of war, have worked with such complete success.' However, the conference expressed general agreement with the proposal for monthly meetings.

The London talks gave Curtin an opportunity of describing Australia's manpower problems. He mentioned that in October 1943 United States demands were involving the employment of 75,000 Australians and this number was expected to reach 100,000 by June 1944. He pressed again for an indication of the size of the British forces that were likely to be based on Australia.

Curtin did not favour plans to send a British army into the South-West Pacific Area. More troops were not needed and their arrival would make demands on Australian military and civilian manpower and might upset the delicate balance of the command organisation in the S.W.P.A. For example, in March, before the London conference, a proposal that a British military mission should go to Australia to examine its capacity as a base was firmly opposed by Blamey, who maintained that this ran counter to a long-accepted principle of Imperial defence and that any such group should be integrated into the Australian staffs. And a much later proposal from Churchill for a 'British Empire task force under a British commander' brought a sharp protest from Curtin, who then and earlier had emphasised Australia's interest in preserving the existing command arrangements in MacArthur's area.

In Washington on his way home Curtin on 2nd June obtained the approval of the Combined Chiefs of Staff to the Australian proposal to reduce the combat formations of the Australian Army to six divisions and two armoured brigades.

As soon as Curtin returned he conferred with MacArthur, and later informed the Advisory War Council of the coming reduction of the army. It was decided to maintain the navy at its present strength plus men to man new ships, and the air force finally at the 53 squadrons agreed upon earlier.[3]

On 4th July Curtin told Churchill that, having heard MacArthur's strategical plan, and as British land and air forces would not become available for some time, the best manner of ensuring the earliest and most effective association of British forces in the war against Japan would be to assign to MacArthur the naval forces becoming available in 1944. The British fleet, he said, would be the naval spearhead in a large portion of MacArthur's coming campaign. 'It is the only effective means of placing the Union Jack in the Pacific alongside the Australian and American flags. It would evoke great public enthusiasm in Australia and would contribute greatly to the restoration of Empire prestige in the Far East.'

Before Curtin had returned Rear-Admiral C. S. Daniel of the Royal Navy and a staff arrived in Australia to examine the problems involved in basing British naval forces on Australia. On 2nd May Daniel informed the Advisory War Council of the various roles for the British naval forces that were under discussion. He said that, until Germany was defeated, Britain could send only a task force to the Pacific but, after the defeat of Germany a force of four to six battleships, four fleet carriers, twenty-five smaller carriers and appropriate numbers of other vessels would be available.

After considering further reviews of the manpower problem the War Cabinet on 23rd August directed that 30,000 men be discharged from the army and 15,000 from the air force by 30th June 1945, in addition to discharges from the Services as a result of normal wastage, which were expected to number 58,300 in that period.

As the year went on the conflicting claims on manpower became harder to satisfy. In September the monthly intake of the three Services was fixed at 4,020 including 1,020 women, the army's share being only 420 men and 500 women. General Blamey promptly stated that the army was already short of 26,000 men, and the new reduction would make it impossible to maintain the six divisions and two armoured brigades agreed to with Washington. He estimated that by June 1945 the army would be short of 63,000 men and women.

The arrival of preliminary information about the facilities needed in Australia by the British Pacific Fleet led to a further comprehensive review of manpower, and this came before the Advisory War Council in September and October 1944. It presented a disturbing picture: in 1944-45 155,350 men and 37,700 women would be needed for essential war tasks but only 117,650 men and 26,000 women would become available. Thus the supply of labour was inadequate by a wide margin without providing for the needs of the British forces. The War Commitments Committee recommended several cuts in works programs that had been adopted.

[3] There were now also three RAF squadrons in the SWPA—No. 54, which had arrived in 1942 with two RAAF *Article XV* squadrons (Nos. 452 and 457), and Nos. 548 and 549 which arrived in December 1943. Two Netherlands East Indies squadrons, Nos. 18 and 120 were incorporated in the RAAF.

In November Australia was informed that the British Pacific Fleet, to arrive in Australia towards the end of December, would include, to begin with, two battleships, four fleet aircraft carriers, and appropriate numbers of other vessels; and by July would include four battleships, ten fleet carriers, and, for example, forty destroyers. Such a force would require formidable land-based installations. By November Australia was being required to provide 4,875 men in respect of supply required for the Royal Navy, 8,700 for maintenance and repair work and 3,860 servicemen for shore-based Royal Navy aircraft. Works required included a depot at Warwick Farm, Sydney; new berthing facilities at Brisbane and stations for the Fleet Air Arm at Nowra, Bankstown, Schofields (all in New South Wales) and Jervis Bay. By June 1945 there would be a manpower shortage of 50,000 for high-priority needs, again not including those of the British forces. By the end of 1944 the Services had released about 20,000 of the 45,000 people that the War Cabinet had directed them to yield; the remainder were to be released by June 1945. Not only were the Services and the direct war industries competing for what each regarded as its necessary share of the inadequate number of people available, but by mid-1945 the program of house building to ease a shortage that must rapidly become critical needed some 20,000 men.

A contribution to the solution of the manpower problem was now being made by employment of Italian prisoners on farms and elsewhere. By August 1944 more than 10,000 of the 14,700 Italian prisoners then held were at work on farms or in hostels. The number of German prisoners at this time was 1,600, of Japanese 2,200.[4] All prisoners were a responsibility of the army, and were treated strictly in accordance with the Geneva Convention, at a time when it was known that many of the prisoners held by the Japanese, Germans and Italians were being badly treated. The prisoner camps in Australia functioned smoothly enough, except for one unhappy incident: a mass attempt by Japanese to break out from a compound at Cowra, New South Wales. There, in the early hours of the morning of 5th August 1944, about 1,100 Japanese armed with clubs and other improvised weapons broke loose. Four Australians were killed; 378 Japanese reached the surrounding country; 234 Japanese were killed or died by their own hands, and 108 were wounded. None succeeded in remaining at large for more than a few days.

Meanwhile one of the future tasks of the Australian Army had been fixed. The American component of MacArthur's land forces was greatly increased during 1944. Between March and September four additional corps were added, and he then commanded eighteen American divisions compared with seven (counting those in the South Pacific) a year earlier. Six of these, however, were tied to the defence of the bases on Bougainville, on New Britain, and at Aitape on the mainland of New Guinea. MacArthur would need either these, or a similar number of Australian divisions, for the coming assault on Luzon, and it soon became evident that he and his staff would prefer to regain the big American colony of the Philippines with American troops only. Also, in November 1943, Curtin had pointed out to MacArthur

[4] By August 1945 the number of Japanese prisoners had increased to 121 officers and 5,127 other ranks. These included 546 merchant seamen and 3,779 captured by American forces.

that Australia had a special interest in the employment of her own troops to drive the Japanese from her New Guinea territories.[5]

Blamey had expected at least since March 1944 that he would be required to garrison the New Guinea bases with Australian troops and in that month outlined a plan for employing militia brigades on this task. When, on 12th July, MacArthur asked him to take over responsibility for the northern Solomons (including Bougainville) from 1st October and New Britain and all of the mainland of Australian New Guinea from 1st November, Blamey proposed that he should perform these tasks with six brigades, not including the brigade already committed to patrolling the area from Madang to the Sepik. The American forces then deployed in those areas were three times as strong. MacArthur would not agree to so great a reduction and, after conferences, it was decided to use twelve Australian brigades—four divisions, or their equivalent. This meant that the three A.I.F. divisions would not all be available for operations farther north, since one would now have to be employed in New Guinea.

In each of the areas in which Australians would take over the American garrisons had been holding fairly small perimeters round their bases while the Japanese held the surrounding or the adjacent country. The Japanese forces were in October 1944 estimated at: 13,400 in Bougainville, 38,000 on New Britain, and 24,000 round Wewak. Although these estimates were revised upwards in the next nine months the true figures were not known until after the end of the war: in October 1944 the Japanese forces in fact numbered about 30,000 on Bougainville, 93,000 on New Britain with 13,000 more on New Ireland, and 31,000 round Wewak.

On 11th August Blamey issued instructions for the new phase: the headquarters of the First Army (Lieut-General Sturdee) would move to Lae and take command of all forces in the New Guinea territories; II Corps (Lieut-General Savige) would take over in the Solomons where it would command the 3rd Division and two independent brigades; the 5th Division was allotted to New Britain, and the 6th to Aitape. The 8th Brigade would continue to operate between Madang and the Sepik.

It remained to fix the task of I Corps, now reduced to the 7th and 9th Divisions and corps troops. Before the landing on Leyte MacArthur had proposed to Blamey that an Australian division be included in each of two American corps but Blamey had insisted that the divisions should be used as an Australian corps under their own experienced corps commander, and the proposal was dropped. In August and September 1944 MacArthur promulgated a plan in which a somewhat nebulous role was provided for the A.I.F. Corps. The American Joint Chiefs of Staff had decided that MacArthur's forces should land at Lingayen Gulf in Luzon in December 1944 and Nimitz's should seize Iwo Jima on 20th January and one or more positions in the Ryukyu Islands on 1st March 1945. The next step would be to Okinawa, only 300 miles from Kyushu, southernmost of the islands of Japan proper. From Okinawa the bombing of Japan could be intensified and long-

[5] In November 1944 there were about 600,000 American troops and 132,000 American Air Force personnel in the SWPA, the Australian Army was 423,000 strong (307,000 being members of the AIF) and the Air Force 163,000, including 24,000 serving in other theatres.

range fighters could fly over the southern cities. As a prelude to the landing at Lingayen Gulf I Australian Corps was to land at Aparri in northern Luzon on 5th December and establish a base whence aircraft could support the later operations against Manila. The Australian landing, however, was to be made only if Admiral Nimitz could not provide enough carrier-borne aircraft to ensure the protection of MacArthur's transports. Soon the necessary naval protection was guaranteed and the Australian operation at Aparri cancelled. After other proposals had been discussed another probable role for the Australian corps was announced: to swing westward from the axis of the American advance and thrust into the Netherlands Indies.

Already detailed planning was in progress for the rehabilitation of nations that had suffered in the war and for international co-operation in peace. Thus, in June 1943 the United States Government had sent to other Allied Governments a draft agreement for a United Nations Relief and Rehabilitation Administration (U.N.R.R.A.). It was to be controlled by a council on which each nation subscribing would have one representative, with a central committee comprising representatives of the 'Big Four'—United States, United Kingdom, Soviet Union and China—and a director-general. Australia signed the U.N.R.R.A. agreement and was represented at the first meeting of the council, in the United States in November 1943. Among the purposes of the organisation was relief 'through the provision of food, fuel, clothing, shelter and other basic necessities, medical and other essential services'.

More looking forward was done at a conference of the International Labour Office at Philadelphia in April 1944. The conference adopted a series of resolutions concerning the welfare of labour; in particular it recognised the obligation of the organisation to further programs which would achieve 'full employment and the raising of standards of living'.

At Bretton Woods in July 1944 an international conference on post-war monetary organisation was held. It was a meeting of official experts and its proceedings did not commit the governments represented.[6] The conference proposed an International Monetary Fund into which member countries would pay quotas, partly gold and partly currency, and from which they might draw—for example, when imports exceeded exports. The conference made recommendations also concerning reduction of trade barriers and orderly marketing.

In November there were discussions at Wellington between Australian and New Zealand Ministers in pursuance of the Australia-New Zealand Agreement. The two Governments agreed to play their full part in the establishment of a general international organisation to preserve peace and promote human welfare; immediate steps should be taken to establish the South Seas Regional Commission; colonial powers should undertake to make regular reports to an international body analogous to the Permanent Mandates Commission, which should be empowered to publish reports and inspect dependent territories.

[6] The Australian delegates included L. G. Melville, J. B. Brigden, F. H. Wheeler and A. H. Tange.

This last proposal was received in London with strong disfavour. Bruce informed Curtin that the United Kingdom Government was bewildered at a public declaration in favour of the mandates system because it had seemed at the Prime Ministers' meeting that Australia agreed with the United Kingdom about the defects of that system. The Australian-New Zealand policy had been announced without proper prior consultation. Nevertheless, the Australian and New Zealand Governments approved the conclusions of the Wellington Conference.

From 21st August onwards a series of meetings was held at Dumbarton Oaks, Washington, of representatives of the 'Big Four' nations and on 7th October a joint statement was issued setting out proposals for a general international organisation to consist of a general assembly of which all nations would be members, and a security council of which eleven nations would be members, the United States, Britain, the Soviet Union, China and eventually France having permanent membership. The Soviet Union had insisted on the right of the Great Powers to veto any proposals by the Council. There would be a secretary-general and a secretariat.

The next step was to hold a conference of the United Nations, at San Francisco from 26th April 1945. Forde and Evatt represented Australia. They said that they thought it wrong to over-emphasise the security or peace-preserving aspects of the proposed world organisation and wished to see more vigorous grappling with the economic and social causes of conflict. They considered that the distinctive position of the 'middle powers'—Australia regarded herself as one of these—should be recognised. The Economic and Social Council should be associated with 'the maintenance of high levels of employment and progressively increased standards of living'.

Churchill and Roosevelt and their staffs had met at Quebec in September 1944 to consider future operations against Japan. Here it was agreed that Britain's main role would be to take Rangoon and then advance eastward through the Bay of Bengal, but the United States accepted Britain's request that she should send a self-contained British fleet into the Pacific to take part in the main operations there, and that the R.A.F. be given a share in the long-range bombing of Japan.

The precise tasks to be given to I Australian Corps in the East Indies were subject to many changes of plan before it was agreed that a brigade of the 9th Division would attack Tarakan, the remainder of the division would later seize the Brunei Bay area, and finally the 7th Division would take Balikpapan. These operations were to be a prelude to an advance into Java.

Thus some time in 1945 six Australian divisions would be in action and, consequently, in this final phase of the war Australia would be more heavily committed than hitherto; yet in August the War Cabinet, as mentioned, had decided to reduce the monthly intake of recruits by the army to 420 men and 500 women. The army was able to survive only by breaking up some units to reinforce the others. Between September 1944 and January 1945 the number of battalions, for example, was reduced from seventy-three to sixty-eight. These losses were partly offset by raising more battalions of New Guinea natives. There were two of these in September 1944 but it was proposed to add four more in the next twelve months.

The question now arose what directions were to be given to the Australian forces which were to take over in the bypassed areas. The American policy had been to fling a perimeter round their bases wide enough to prevent the Japanese from shelling the airfields and depots and then to go on the defensive. If Blamey's proposal to employ six *brigades* to relieve the six and a half American *divisions* in the islands had been agreed to it seems inevitable that these would have had to adopt a similar policy, being too weak to undertake offensives. But the Australian commander had been required to allot four *divisions* to the task, and was presented with a choice of leaving these tied down on defensive duties or of attacking with the object of so reducing the strength of the enemy that he could make a corresponding decrease in the size of his garrisons. At a conference at his advanced headquarters on 11th August Blamey told his subordinate commanders that the primary role of the Australian formations would be the protection of the existing bases, but that he desired such offensive operations to be undertaken as would not commit major forces. He added that it might be possible for II Corps to undertake the elimination of the Japanese forces remaining on Bougainville.

Of the five army corps and divisional commanders to control the forthcoming operations three had not commanded forces in New Guinea before. Sturdee, leading the First Army, had been Chief of the General Staff and later head of the Australian Military Mission at Washington. Stevens had led a brigade in Syria in 1941 and held divisional commands in Australia since 1942. W. Bridgeford, commanding the 3rd Division in Savige's II Corps, had served in the operations in Greece, Syria and New Guinea in staff appointments. Savige, on the other hand, had had a long period of active command in New Guinea, first with the 3rd Division and later commanding the whole Australian force there; and Ramsay had commanded his 5th Division in the operations on the Rai coast in 1944. The forces to be employed would include the 6th Division, the senior formation of the A.I.F., militia brigades with long and arduous New Guinea service behind them, and a few brigades that had not yet been in action.

On the Allied side twenty-three American and six Australian divisions[7] and one New Zealand division had now (December 1944) been in action in the Pacific, and there were eight Indian, three African, two British and some small Chinese divisions opposing the Japanese in Burma. The Allied superiority on land was not great—indeed in the Burma-Indies area it was near equality. On the other hand, after the great naval battles of October the Japanese fleet had been reduced almost to impotence; and the forces of MacArthur and Nimitz possessed fleets of transports and landing craft which gave them great mobility.

In 1945 as in 1944 the main Australian contributions to the operations in Burma were made by aircrew dispersed among many R.A.F. squadrons and, in the early stages, by the Australian destroyers with the British Eastern Fleet. In January 1945 there were 923 men of the R.A.A.F. in the Burma-

[7] Not including the 8th Australian Division lost in Malaya and the Indies in early 1942.

India theatre, scattered among sixty squadrons. The air force supporting the army in Burma was ranging far afield in support of the Fourteenth Army now steadily driving the Japanese out of Burma. By December 1944 General Slim's army was across the Chindwin and firmly established on the central Burma plain, while the XV Corps was advancing southward in Arakan, where it occupied Akyab early in January. The supporting naval force at Akyab included the Australian destroyers *Nepal*, *Napier* and *Nizam*, of the 7th Destroyer Flotilla, commanded by Captain H. J. Buchanan, R.A.N. Buchanan's flotilla supported the seizure of Ramree Island later in the month, and then joined the British Pacific Fleet. The Fourteenth Army was now sweeping southward. Mandalay fell on 20th March, Toungoo on 22nd April, Rangoon on 2nd May. Air support was on a grand scale.

The Japanese divisions deployed in the areas in which MacArthur's troops would be fighting early in 1945, and in the adjacent Banda Sea and Palau areas were:

Luzon: *8th, 10th, 19th, 23rd, 30th, 103rd, 105th, 2nd Armoured*
Leyte: *1st, 16th, 26th*
Elsewhere in Philippines: *100th, 102nd*
Banda Sea Area: *5th, 32nd, 48th*
North-west New Guinea: *35th, 36th*
Aitape-Wewak: *20th, 41st, 51st*
New Britain: *17th, 38th*
Bougainville: *6th*
Palau: *14th*

The Sixth American Army landed in Lingayen Gulf on the west coast of Luzon on 9th January and that day 6,800 troops were ashore and were soon in control of a beach-head fifteen miles wide and up to three miles deep. In the bombardment and fire support group off Luzon were the Australian cruisers *Australia* and *Shropshire* and destroyers *Arunta* and *Warramunga*. The *Australia* (Captain J. M. Armstrong), now repaired after the damage done by a Japanese suicide aircraft off Leyte, was flying the broad pendant of Commodore Farncomb, like Collins a graduate of the Royal Australian Naval College. The minesweeping and hydrographic group off Luzon included the Australian frigates *Gascoyne* and *Warrego* and the three Australian L.S.I's were among the transports. Between 5th and 9th January *Australia* was struck five times in *Kamikaze* (suicide aircraft) attacks and forty-four of her crew were killed. This was *Australia*'s last action. She was withdrawn for repairs and Farncomb transferred his flag to *Shropshire*. The Sixth Army was pushing towards Manila when on 29th January a third corps was landed near Subic Bay, also on the west coast. Manila was entered on 3rd February but organised resistance did not cease until 3rd March. On 16th February troops were landed from the sea and parachute troops were dropped from the air on Corregidor, where the Japanese garrison fought on from the tunnels for two weeks and then blew up the tunnel system and themselves.

On 19th February, as planned, the Americans landed on Iwo Jima, defended by some 20,000 Japanese. Nimitz put ashore a corps of three divisions of marines, and, after very grim fighting, in which about 6,000 Americans were killed, secured the island, which provided a heavy-bomber base only 775 miles from the Japanese mainland. Okinawa, the next stepping stone, was garrisoned by 77,000 (though the Intelligence estimate before the landing was only 55,000). Against it was sent the Tenth American Army of seven divisions. The landing on Okinawa proper took place on 1st April. The Japanese fought as resolutely as ever, and organised resistance did not cease until late in June. The American forces lost 12,500 killed and missing, including nearly 5,000 in the supporting naval forces. About 61,000 Japanese were killed and 16,000 taken prisoner.

As mentioned earlier, the First Tactical Air Force was given a role in the Philippines but, in the second phase—the invasion of Luzon—it was a relatively minor one. The Fifth Air Force took part in the assault on Luzon with the Thirteenth Air Force in support; the task of the First T.A.F. based in Noemfoor and Morotai, was to attack the enemy forces bypassed in Celebes, Halmahera and the Vogelkop Peninsula. On 15th December 1944 No. 3 Airfield Construction Squadron R.A.A.F. took part in the landing on Mindoro which prefaced the assault on Luzon, and, with the help of an American engineer battalion, completed the first airfield there by the 19th.

The squadrons of First T.A.F. were busy against targets at Jolo, Celebes, Halmahera and elsewhere in December. Opposition by Japanese aircraft was inconsiderable though now and then one or two of them appeared. Even on Luzon only two Japanese aircraft contested the landing in Lingayen Gulf. It was at this stage that some of the Australians in First T.A.F. began to question the value of their efforts. They were working hard; they were losing aircraft—fifteen in October and November; they were expending much ammunition; but they doubted whether attacks against targets so far south of the spearhead of the Allied forces were of real value. Lack of targets plus a shortage of ammunition led to a decline of activity in February, when 1,324 sorties were flown by twelve squadrons compared with 2,037 by nine squadrons in January. The First T.A.F. felt that it was being left behind; as indeed it was.

At the same time the divided control of the R.A.A.F. continued to produce problems and disputes. The War Cabinet in August 1944 had tried once more to appoint an R.A.F. officer who would be senior to Air Vice-Marshals Bostock and Jones, but when the name of the chosen officer was submitted to MacArthur he said that it was too late to make such a change. Disagreements between Bostock and the Air Board continued, and the problem remained unsolved.

The discontent in First T.A.F., now nearly 17,000 strong, reached a critical stage in April, when seven officers including Group Captains W. S. Arthur and Caldwell and several young wing commanders and squadron leaders applied for permission to resign their commissions. One result was that Air Commodore Cobby and two of his staff were transferred to other appointments, and Air Commodore Scherger was given command of the force.

While the principal formation of the R.A.A.F. was simmering with discontent because it considered it was being left far behind the main battles, the largest formation of the Australian Army, deployed from 1,800 to 3,000 miles farther to the rear, had been engaged in bitter fighting against the Japanese armies bypassed in New Guinea.

Chapter 14 **Bougainville, Wewak, New Britain**

From October 1944 onwards, Australian troops had replaced American troops in the Solomons and New Britain and at Aitape. Of the six American divisions that were set free the Americal and the 32nd went to Leyte, the 37th, 40th and 43rd to Luzon, and the 93rd, a Negro division, to Morotai where it relieved another division that went to the Philippines. On 2nd October 1944 Lieut-General Sturdee, commanding the First Australian Army, with headquarters at Lae, assumed control of all operations in Australian New Guinea. In his command 900 miles separated the headquarters of II Corps to the east from the headquarters of the 6th Division to the west.

Whether examined from the Australian or the Japanese point of view each of the three main operations conducted by the First Army had very little influence on the others. The Japanese could not transport men or supplies from Rabaul to either Bougainville or Wewak. The *Eighth Area Army* on New Britain, the *XVII Army* on Bougainville and the *XVIII Army* on the mainland of New Guinea had to fight it out where they were with what they had. At the same time practically all Sturdee's forces were committed from the outset and any reinforcement of his three main formations—II Corps, 5th and 6th Divisions—could be only on a small scale; in two areas the opposing ground forces were about evenly matched at the beginning, and in the third—New Britain—the Australians were outnumbered six to one. The Australian command of the sea and air was not disputed, but the mainly-Australian sea and air forces that exercised that command were meagre, and shortages of shipping, barges and transport aircraft created persistent problems, and imposed severe limitations on the army commanders in all areas. In many respects they had to employ the tactics of 1942 rather than those of 1945.

Bougainville is about 120 miles in length and about forty miles wide at the widest part. The volcanic mountain chain which forms its spine rises to a height of 8,500 feet at Mount Balbi, and the coastal shelf is often very narrow and never more than ten miles wide. Rain forest with dense undergrowth covers the island except in the comparatively few cultivated areas. The rainfall averages 100 inches a year and was drained away by many short rivers up to eighty yards wide and subject to rapid flooding.

The Australian force on Bougainville was to include the II Corps headquarters, the 3rd Division (7th, 15th and 29th Brigades), and the 11th and 23rd Brigades. The 7th Brigade (Brigadier Field) had fought at Milne Bay in 1942, the 11th (Brigadier Stevenson) had garrisoned Merauke and had engaged in patrol actions there; the 15th (Brigadier Hammer) had seen long and arduous service in the Salamaua campaign of 1943; the 23rd (Brigadier Potts), as mentioned, had not been in action before; the 29th (Brigadier Monaghan) had seen considerable fighting in New Guinea. All the brigade commanders had led battalions in Middle East campaigns and brigades in action in New Guinea.

The air force task of neutralising Rabaul and providing support in the Solomons was to be done by No. 1 Group R.N.Z.A.F. (Group Captain G. N. Roberts), which in January included four New Zealand fighter-bomber squadrons with Corsairs, two bomber squadrons with Venturas; and by No. 84 Wing R.A.A.F. (Group Captain W. L. Hely) which included No. 5 Tactical Reconnaissance Squadron (Boomerangs and Wirraways), part of No. 36 Squadron for supply dropping, and No. 10 Local Air Supply Unit. Effective Japanese air action was unlikely, however, since the last bombs to be dropped on Torokina had been delivered in March 1944; no merchant ship had been seen off the island since January 1944.

The first American garrisons in the Solomons to be relieved by Australians were those on three outlying islands or island groups—Treasury, south of Bougainville; Green, north of it; and Emirau, far away between New Ireland and the Admiralties. American army and navy and New Zealand air force men were established on the Green Islands and Emirau. On the Green Islands, for example, there were in December, some 750 New Zealanders and 6,800 Americans. One battalion of the 23rd Brigade was placed on each of the island groups. Sturdee in October proposed that the islands be guarded by small detachments and that most of the 23rd Brigade be brought to Bougainville, and Savige favoured this. Three months were to pass however, before MacArthur's staff would agree that the garrison of the outer islands where they had been deploying a whole division should so soon be reduced to a few detachments.

Major-General Bridgeford opened the headquarters of the 3rd Division at Torokina on 6th October and General Savige opened his headquarters there on 22nd November. The relief of the Americans was completed by 12th December, its pace being determined by the availability of shipping, most of which was then busy supporting the operations in Leyte.

The Australian commanders found the XIV American Corps manning posts round a perimeter about fifteen miles by seven and some outpost positions beyond it. When deployment was complete, Savige had the 3rd Division in the south-eastern sector, through which the tracks led towards the main Japanese base round Buin, and astride the Numa Numa trail leading over the mountains into the perimeter; he allotted the northern sector to the 11th Brigade. Soon after it was known that the 3rd Division would be sent to Bougainville Savige had told Bridgeford that the ultimate role of his division would be an offensive aimed at reducing the enemy forces on that island; and before Savige took command Bridgeford had prepared a tentative outline plan for an advance along the coast towards Buin.

However the first task of the incoming force was to gain information. Until March 1944 parties of Australians and trusted natives had been operating behind the enemy's lines on Bougainville but the American commanders, no longer vitally interested in what the enemy was doing on the island, had withdrawn them. This was part of a policy of live-and-let live then pursued by both the Americans and the Japanese. The Australians, however, sent scouting parties in again: one under Lieutenant K. W. T. Bridge into the northern mountains, one under Lieutenant Mason above Kieta, and one under Flying Officer N. C. Sandford round Numa Numa.

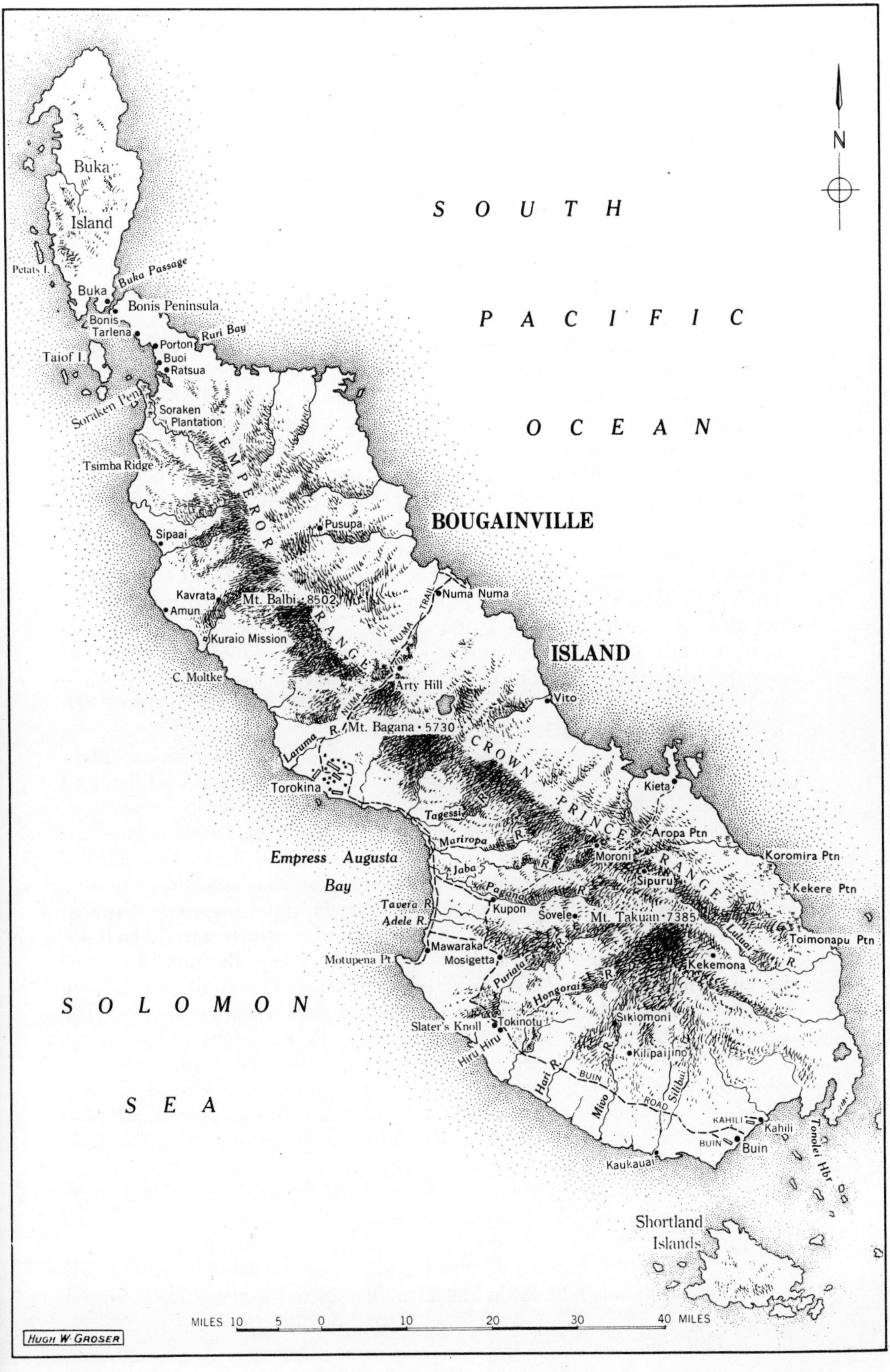

SOUTH PACIFIC OCEAN
BOUGAINVILLE ISLAND
SOLOMON SEA
Buka Island
Petats I.
Buka Passage
Buka
Bonis Peninsula
Bonis
Tarlena
Ruri Bay
Porton
Buoi
Ratsua
Taiof I.
Soraken Pen.
Soraken Plantation
EMPEROR RANGE
Tsimba Ridge
Pusupa
Sipaai
Kavrata
Mt. Balbi 8502
Numa Numa
NUMA NUMA TRAIL
Amun
Kuraio Mission
C. Moltke
Arty Hill
Vito
Laruma R.
Mt. Bagana • 5730
CROWN PRINCE RANGE
Torokina
Kieta
Tagessi
Aropa Ptn
Empress Augusta Bay
Maririopa R.
Moroni
Koromira Ptn
Jaba
Sipuru
Kekere Ptn
Pagana R.
Tavera R.
Adele R.
Kupon
Sovele
Mt. Takuan 7385
Luluai R.
Toimonapu Ptn
Mawaraka
Mosigetta
Motupena Pt.
Kekemona
Puriata R.
Hongorai R.
Slater's Knoll
Tokinotu
Sikiomoni
Hiru Hiru
Kilipaijino
Hari R.
BUIN ROAD
Mivo R.
Silibai
KAHILI
Kahili
Tonolei Hbr
BUIN
Buin
Kaukauai
Shortland Islands
N
MILES 10 5 0 10 20 30 40 MILES
HUGH W. GROSER

There was some uncertainty about the strength of the Japanese force. It was known that it was the *XVII Army* and included mainly the *6th Division* and *38th Independent Mixed Brigade;* it was not known that there were also about 7,000 naval men including some first-rate units of marines. MacArthur's staff estimated the total strength at 12,000, but the Australian staff believed it was about 25,000; they agreed to compromise with an estimate of 17,500 'effectives'. In fact there were then between 37,000 and 40,000 Japanese on Bougainville.

Lack of shipping handicapped the Australian force. By Christmas it had only three days' reserve rations apart from those held by units; and, mainly for lack of ships to carry them from Australia, it had barely enough landing craft to ferry supplies to forces along the coast or on outlying islands, much less carry out any large-scale opposed landing.

The first actions were fought in the central sector. Here the track across the island from Torokina to the east coast—the Numa Numa trail—travelled from the Torokina plain along a gorge, up an escarpment, and thence over a saddle in the main range. Above the escarpment the American and Japanese outposts had faced one another with only 100 yards between, but a tacit truce had long existed. The 9th Battalion (Lieut-Colonel G. R. Matthews) took over from the Americans here on 22nd November and, on the 29th, supported by a battery firing from below the escarpment, attacked and took the nearest Japanese outpost. On 18th December a company, supported by New Zealand fighter-bombers and the artillery, attacked and took the next enemy position, Arty Hill, where the Japanese left twenty-five dead. The 25th Battalion, having relieved the 9th, planned to attack the next feature, Pearl Ridge, on the 30th.

Meanwhile, in the southern sector too, the truce had been broken. Here the track along the narrow coastal plain crossed a series of rivers all liable to sudden flooding. At the mouth of one of these, the Jaba, the Americans had been maintaining an outpost on the northern bank facing a Japanese post. The 29th Brigade, with the 15th Battalion and a company of the 1st New Guinea Battalion forward, probed south of the Jaba and soon most of the 15th was across the river and driving Japanese patrols southward.

On 23rd December General Savige issued an instruction in which he described the ultimate role of the 3rd Division as the destruction of the Japanese forces in southern Bougainville, although for the present its objective would be to gain control only as far as the Puriata River. The 11th Brigade in the central sector was to capture Pearl Ridge, and establish a patrol base. It was to probe both here and along the north coast to a minimum depth of 4,000 yards. 'The ultimate aim in the north was to force the enemy garrison into the narrow Bonis Peninsula and there destroy it. In the central sector the offensive was to clear the enemy from the high ground near Pearl Ridge and then by aggressive patrolling to threaten the important enemy line of communication along the east coast. The main enemy concentration was in the garden area in south Bougainville and here the decisive battle of the campaign must eventually be fought.'[1]

In the event the capture of Pearl Ridge was carried out by the 7th Brigade before it was relieved by the 11th. The earlier thrusts had convinced

[1] Report of II Corps.

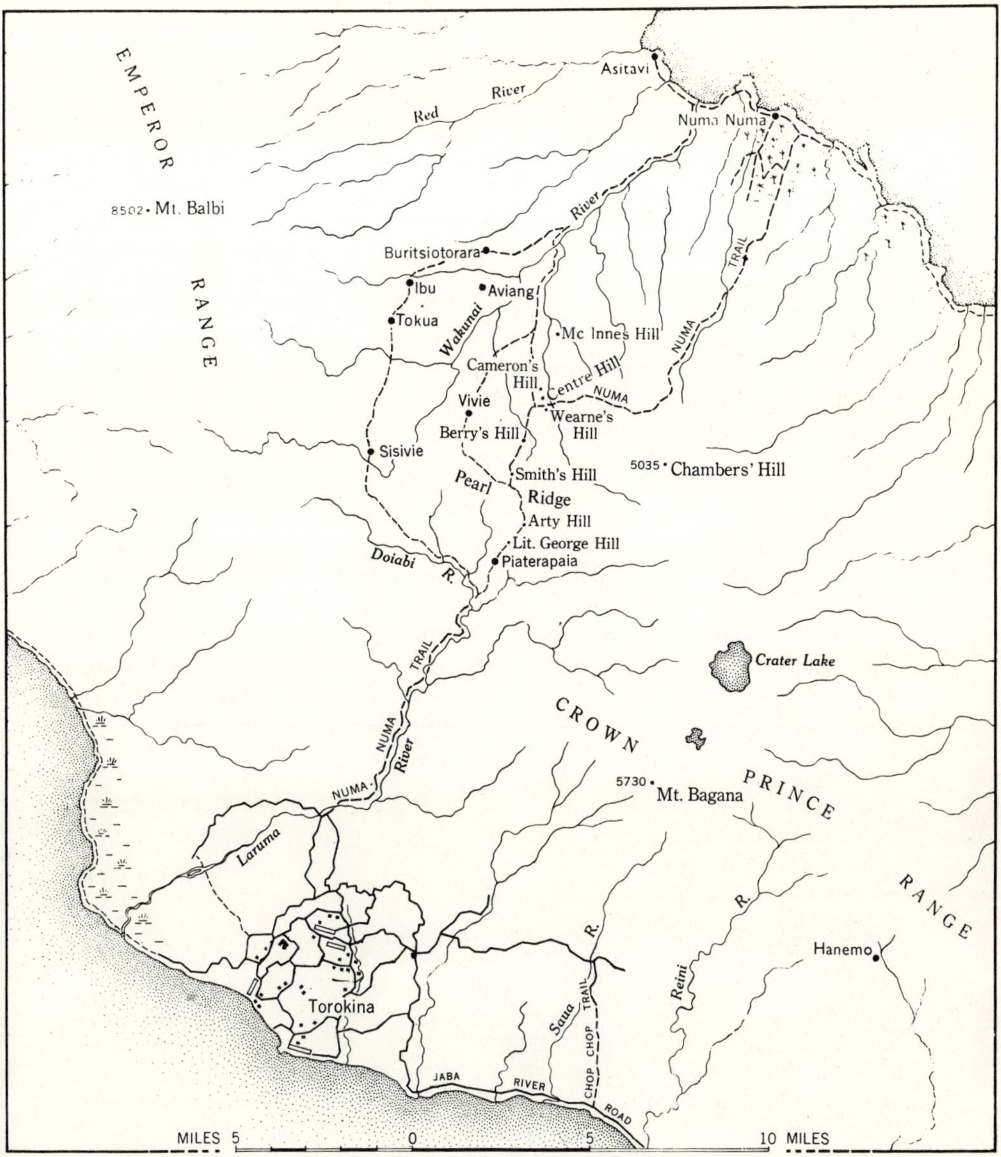

Numa Numa Trail

the Japanese that a determined attempt was to be made to push to the east coast and cut the island in half and they sent in reinforcements until there were more than 600 troops astride the Numa Numa trail. The 25th Battalion attacked with all four rifle companies, supported by air and artillery bombardment. That day the attackers failed to reach the objective but next day a flanking attack succeeded. From their newly-won positions the Australians could now see the sea on both sides of the island. It was not until later that they knew that the attack had been launched against a Japanese battalion, not a company as was believed.

A few days later the 11th Brigade took over this sector, where each of its battalions did a tour of duty of four to six weeks, first the 26th until 2nd

February, then the 55th/53rd until 15th March and finally the 31st/51st until 18th April. In this period the second battalion of the brigade was in the northern sector, and the third resting.

In the next three months patrols, often guided by native police, and sometimes with an artillery observer ready to signal for gunfire at short notice, stealthily probed deep into the enemy's territory. Some patrols were out for five days or more. In this period 236 Japanese were killed for certain, and four prisoners taken, but the finely-trained Australians lost only four killed and nineteen wounded. No better patrolling was done by Australians in the war than by these relatively untried troops, often led, however, by subalterns who had served in the ranks of the veteran divisions.

In the northern sector a new phase opened when Savige ordered Stevenson to gain control of the north-west coast up to Soraken Harbour. As a result the 31st/51st Battalion was concentrated about Sipaai with the intention of advancing against a Japanese force believed to be in position forward of the Genga River some five miles south of Soraken. On the 17th, 18th and 19th January the Australians had sharp fights against Japanese groups supported by artillery, and it was soon evident that the Japanese intended to stand on high ground just south of the Genga and particularly in a well-dug position on Tsimba Ridge. One company of the 31st/51st crossed the Genga

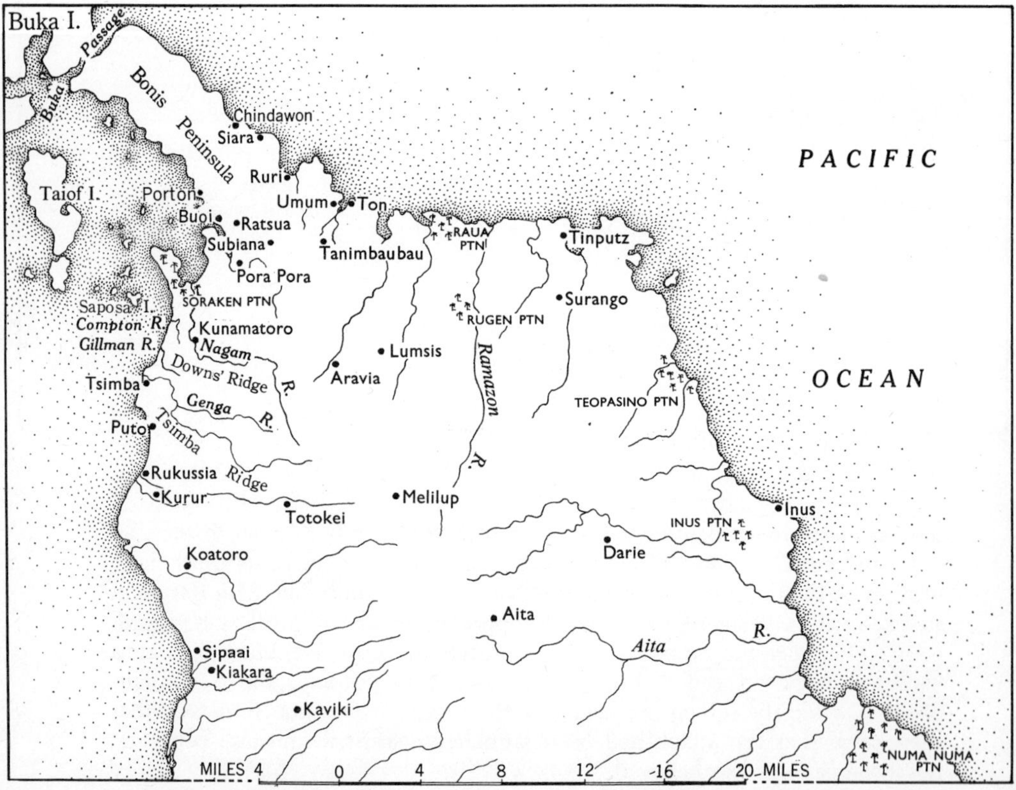

Northern Bougainville

inland from Tsimba and held on there against fierce attack but it was apparent that Tsimba Ridge itself could be taken only by a strong set-piece attack with supporting fire from all available heavy weapons: one mountain battery and some heavy mortars.

A company attacked on 6th February after more than 500 shells and mortar bombs had been rained on the small ridge. The Japanese were driven out except from a pocket on the western tip, and next day this pocket was captured. It was estimated that sixty-six Japanese had been killed; seven field or light guns and nine machine-guns were taken.

Lieut-Colonel J. L. A. Kelly of the 31st/51st, a veteran of Tobruk and El Alamein, now sent a company inland on a flanking move. It made good progress and dug in on a ridge overlooking Soraken and prepared an attack on Japanese positions there. This was delivered (against Downs' Ridge) on 19th February, with the support of aircraft, and of 25-pounder guns which had now been ferried forward. The Japanese were driven out and by the 21st were north of the Gillman River. Next day the 26th Battalion, which had been withdrawn from the Numa Numa sector on the 3rd, took over. The outgoing battalion had lost thirty-four killed and ninety-one wounded in this fighting, the heaviest so far experienced on Bougainville. Afterwards it was learnt that the 31st/51st had been opposed by about 900 Japanese, far more than was thought at the time.

While this firm thrust was carrying the Australians to within sight of Buka Passage, the 29th Brigade had been pushing southward. From the Pagana River to the Hupai the coastal plain was wide and there were two tracks: one along the coast and the other six to eight miles inland. On 28th December Monaghan ordered the 15th Battalion to seize the south bank of the Tavera, the next big river beyond the Pagana. It did so, and the 47th on its left advanced to the junction of the Jaba and the Pagana. The enemy reacted violently and forced the withdrawal of the forward Australian outposts. On 4th January Bridgeford ordered Monaghan to take Mawaraka and the peninsula to the south of it, and sent the 61st Battalion forward to guard his rear so that the whole 29th Brigade would be free for the advance. By the 6th a company had established a base at the mouth of the Adele and on the 9th, after a platoon of New Guinea troops had crossed, a company was landed by a barge south of the river. The Japanese attacked and the company was withdrawn. On 11th January, with the close support of field and anti-tank guns, part of the 47th crossed the Adele and pressed on to the mouth of the Hupai. Intelligence now suggested that a strong counter-attack was coming; Bridgeford ordered Monaghan to consolidate, and sent the 2/8th Commando Squadron to reconnoitre the inland track south from Kupon, on the Pagana eight miles from the mouth. The expected attack did not then develop. On 17th January patrols of the 42nd Battalion, now forward, entered Mawaraka without opposition and soon a patrol of the New Guinea Battalion reached Motupena Point and other patrols probed the Sisiruai area. In the last week of January the 7th Brigade relieved the 29th in positions already about half way between the Allied base at Torokina and the Japanese base at Buin.

On 25th January the 2/8th Commando on the inland flank had begun to form a new base at Sovele Mission. Here the squadron was in occasional touch with Angau patrols collecting information and succouring the natives

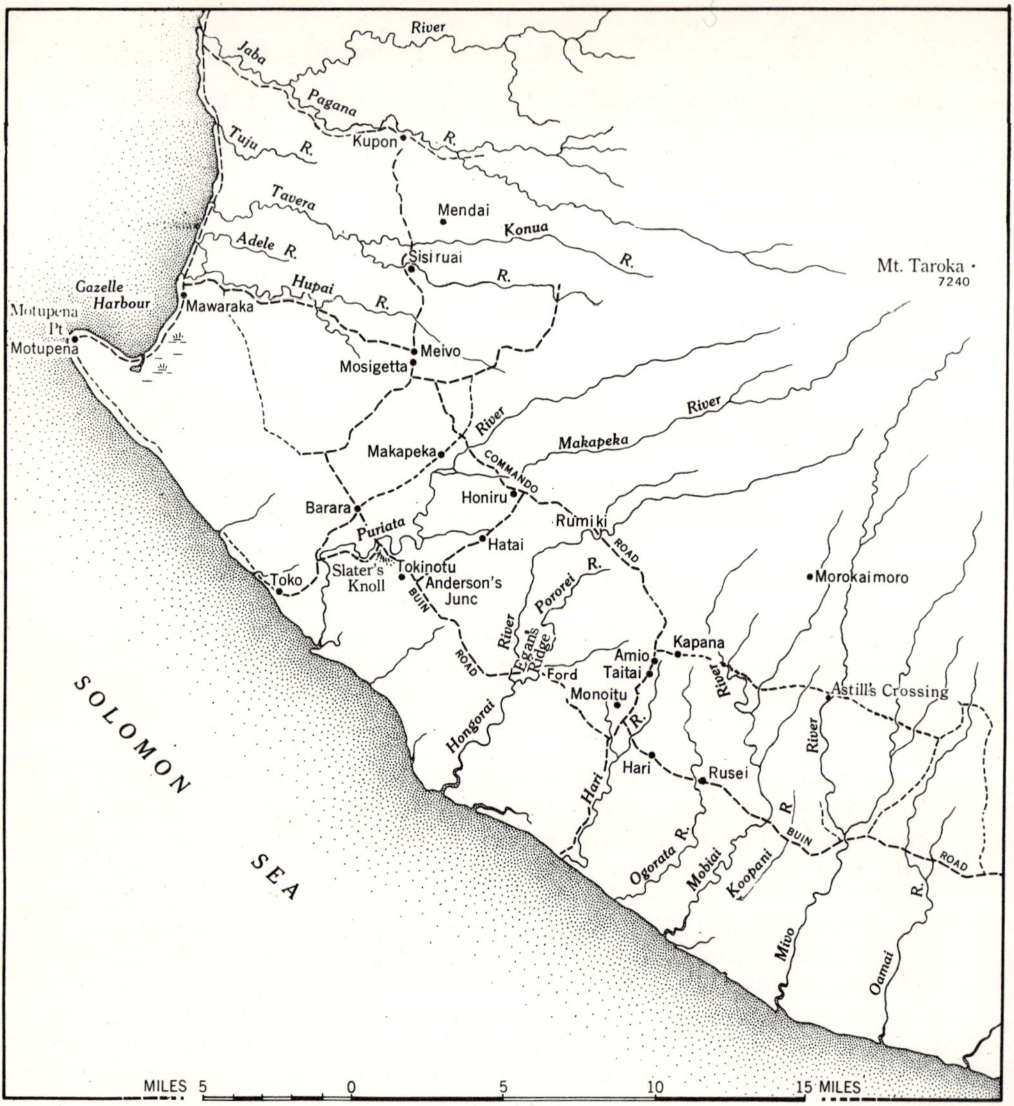

Southern Bougainville

and with Lieutenant Mason's guerilla force operating in the mountains above Kieta and harassing the Japanese with ambushes and by calling down air attacks on their bivouacs.

Savige considered that the hard crust of the enemy's defence would be encountered on the Puriata River. Bridgeford gave the 7th Brigade the task of advancing to the Puriata while the 2/8th Commando, maintained by air-dropping, protected its flank and reconnoitred crossings over the Puriata well upstream. Brigadier Field sent the 61st Battalion along the Pagana towards Kupon, the 25th along the Tavera towards Sisiruai, while the 9th protected the base at Mawaraka. Later the brigade was to be regrouped for an advance to the Puriata. The tracks along which this advance was to be made ran through thick bush and the country was low and swampy; in January and February rain fell almost every afternoon.

From 15th January onwards the 61st advanced systematically from one company base to another, each base ready to meet attack from any direction. A platoon entered Kupon on 2nd February and a patrol was at Mendai on the 13th. On the inland flank the 2/8th Commando patrolled the Sisiruai area and the upper Tavera. The 25th Battalion on the lower Tavera pushed through very swampy ground and on 14th February linked with the 61st. The 9th Battalion on the Hupai was in even wetter country than that through which the Tavera flowed and patrols were often waist deep in water. In all areas the advancing infantry encountered only Japanese rearguards, and the conviction that no solid opposition would be offered between the Pagana and the Puriata seemed to be confirmed. On 16th February the 9th Battalion entered Mosigetta.

Meanwhile, on 25th January, a company of the 25th had been landed by barges on the coast south of Motupena Point and by 4th February it was at Toko near the mouth of the Puriata. Soon the whole battalion had been ferried to Toko, and by 22nd February had marched inland to Barara making a jeep road behind it. Indeed it began to appear that the Japanese would not fight even for the Puriata, and Savige now decided that they would make their stand on the Hari to protect the gardens farther east. On 4th March the 25th Battalion crossed the Puriata and next day thrust the enemy off Slater's Knoll close to the meeting of that river and the Buin road.

It was not known to the Australians that in this phase there had been a crisis in the Japanese command. The *13th Regiment's* delaying tactics had not succeeded and the young reserve officers had uttered criticism of the policy of their professional seniors. In February the army commander, General Hyakutake, suffered partial paralysis and Lieut-General Kanda of the *6th Division* took command of the *XVII Army*.

In the second week of March it became evident that the Japanese intended to dispute the advance more vigorously than in recent weeks. They brought down much fire on Slater's Knoll and dug themselves in firmly astride the Buin road a few hundred yards away. The advance of the 25th Battalion from Slater's was strongly opposed. One company was surrounded and attacked persistently for three days. Soon a strong Japanese force was moving about between the forward and rear companies of the 25th. On 19th March Lieut-Colonel J. G. McKinna of the 25th began a thrust astride the Buin road on a two-company front with the object of clearing the road as far as Tokinotu where his forward company was deployed.

The 25th encountered an extensive system of pill-boxes at the junction of the road with the track to Hatai. Two platoons made a bayonet charge which drove the enemy from part of this stronghold. Positions to which the Japanese fell back were bombarded by aircraft and artillery and a company attacked. Corporal R. R. Rattey using a Bren and grenades knocked out four Japanese posts. (He was awarded the Victoria Cross.) In an hour the positions were taken.

On 14th March Field urged that tanks be sent forward to support his infantry's advance to the Hongorai River and three days later Savige agreed to move some tanks and medium guns to Toko. Next day a patrol of the 2/8th Commando Squadron captured an order dated 16th March indicating that a large-scale Japanese offensive would open early in April.

The Japanese now made a number of raids on the Australian lines of communication and rear areas. On the 27th the 25th Battalion was in depth along the Buin road from Tokinotu back to Slater's Knoll, with its rear echelon 400 yards behind protected by a company of the 61st. Then, about 8 p.m., the line from the battalion headquarters on Slater's Knoll to the rear echelon went dead; and at 8.15 about 100 Japanese charged Slater's Knoll from the rear, screaming and with bayonets fixed. This and later attacks were beaten off. The following night the rear echelon of the 9th Battalion at Barara was attacked by about 100 Japanese with fixed bayonets, and big raiding parties attacked other Australian positions. On the morning of the 30th the forward company of the 25th was severely attacked and forced back on to the next company to the rear; both were soon isolated, under frequent attack, and short of food and water. At 7 p.m. that night three tanks from Toko reached the rear echelon of the 25th Battalion, but were too late to thrust forward to the isolated companies that day.

Next morning the tanks advanced along the road to Slater's Knoll and thence set off forward with a bulldozer to haul them through creeks and improve the track. That afternoon the tanks and their escorting infantry reached the isolated and hungry forward companies and the Japanese fled. Round their perimeter and the abandoned one at the Hatai junction lay 110 dead Japanese not counting nineteen killed that evening by the tanks. At 6.50 p.m. eleven Japanese were killed after having ambushed a jeep train sent out to bring back wounded men; eight Australians had been killed and fifty-eight wounded in the three days from 30th March to 1st April.

Clashes were frequent in the next few days over a wide area, and soon captured papers revealed that the fresh *23rd Regiment* was round Barara and preparing a new attack. On the night of 4th-5th March about 200 shells fell round the Australian artillery positions near the river. Telephone lines were cut throughout the area and at 5 a.m. the perimeter at Slater's Knoll, manned by 129 men, was attacked from two directions by strong forces of Japanese who sacrificed themselves to devastating fire for more than an hour, some falling within four yards of the defenders' weapon pits. At dawn the Australians found that the enemy dead were 'literally, in heaps in front of the wire'; 292 bodies lay over an area about 200 yards square, with 219 rifles, forty-four machine-guns and twenty-two swords. Among the dead was Colonel Kawano, the commander of the *23rd Regiment*.

It now appeared that, when the offensive opened, the *13th* and *23rd Regiments* combined were about 2,400 strong in the forward area; after it, some 620 had been killed and at least 1,000 wounded. The Japanese patrols had been enterprising, and their riflemen had shown their usual courage and devotion. Once again, however, the staff work was unworthy of the men it served, the artillery ill-employed, the cutting of signal wires just before each attack warned the defenders of what was coming, and the practice of making repeated charges against strong enemy positions led to disastrous losses. In the ten days to 6th April the Japanese dead outnumbered the Australians by nearly twenty-five to one.

After Slater's Knoll, Bridgeford ordered the relief of the 7th Brigade by the 15th which had not yet been in action on Bougainville. The 29th Brigade would come forward to protect the lengthening lines of communication.

In this period Mason's guerillas in the mountains were killing more and more Japanese both in patrol fighting and in carefully-organised ambushes and surprise raids in which grenades proved the most effective missiles used. In the mountains farther south Flying Officer R. Stuart and others were based on Sikiomoni where they were collecting valuable information, indicating targets to the air force, and gaining the support of the local people.

In the northern sector in late February the 26th Battalion (Lieut-Colonel Callinan) relieved the 31st/51st and began an advance towards Soraken. The tactics were to sweep round the inland flanks of the enemy's forces, drive them on to the coast and make a series of landings behind their western flank. In hard fighting during March the Australians thrust the Japanese from the Compton River and Nagam River areas, twice employing the device of landing a company from barges behind the enemy's forward positions. By 26th March there were no organised Japanese in the Soraken Peninsula. Taiof and Saposa Islands were taken without much difficulty and good observation of Soraken harbour and Buka Passage obtained.

A comparative lull followed the defeat of the Japanese counter-attack in the south. The Australians built up their supplies in the forward area and strengthened the sodden roads; at the same time the Japanese reorganised after their defeat and made ready to defend the Hongorai. On 19th April Savige gave Bridgeford the task of advancing to the Hari River, with the Hongorai as an intermediate objective. Between the Puriata and the Hari the coastal plain was about ten miles wide and clad with dense bush above which rose high trees. About 5,000 yards from the coast ran the Buin road; the Commando Road ran parallel to it about 5,000 yards farther north. Hammer of the 15th Brigade sent the 24th Battalion along the Buin road, with the 58th/59th protecting the rear and flanks, and the 57th/60th along the inland route.

The fresh brigade opened its advance on 17th April when the 24th Battalion, moving behind a creeping barrage, and supported by tanks, after sharp fighting established itself beyond Dawe's Creek, south-east of Tokinotu, where it withstood a series of counter-attacks. It then sent out jeep patrols, which probed as far forward as the Hongorai. The advance was resumed on 26th April. Aircraft bombed and machine-gunned the enemy's positions and a creeping barrage preceded the infantry, who met little opposition. On the Commando Road the 57th/60th had been patrolling forward while a lateral track was made from the Buin road to Rumiki along which tanks could move into its area.

By 2nd May the 24th Battalion had advanced more than a mile without opposition and was nearing the Hongorai. From the 4th onwards, however, the Japanese opposed the tanks with mines—sometimes made from 150-mm shells—and concealed guns. The forward infantry were now under frequent artillery fire, and it was this which was causing most of the casualties. At this stage Savige learnt that a valuable reinforcement was on the way—the headquarters and one additional squadron of the 2/4th Armoured Regiment. This would enable the relief of the squadron then in action, whose men were feeling the effects of spending long hours in closed tanks in a steamy climate.

The Japanese continued to resist strongly. After an advance by the 24th Battalion on 5th May the enemy bombarded the battalion and staged the heaviest counter-attack since Slater's Knoll. After some hours they were

Australian War Memorial

Bougainville, 26th April 1945. Australian troops advancing with a tank along the Buin Road towards Hiru Hiru.

driven off leaving fifty-eight dead. This was their last effort to defend the line of the Hongorai, which the Australians reached on 7th May. It had taken the brigade three weeks to gain the 7,000 yards to the Hongorai and cost 120 killed and wounded; 169 Japanese dead had been counted.

Behind the forward infantry the engineers and the supporting infantry laboured to improve the road. By the end of the first week of May the 9,300 yards of road from Slater's to the Hongorai and 5,000 yards of the Hatai track had been corduroyed with logs. On 6th May a company of the 57th/60th on the Commando Road crossed the Hongorai. It now appeared that some 1,500 to 1,800 Japanese with about nine guns were forward on the Hari, and that 900 to 1,100 were just east of it. They were likely to fight hard for the line of the Hari to protect the fruitful gardens beyond. Savige now ordered an advance to the line Hari River-Monoitu-Kapana and, in a second phase, to the Mivo River.

In the middle weeks of May the 15th Brigade patrolled deeply. Hammer's plan was that the 57th/60th should begin a diversionary advance on 17th May and that the main thrust across the Hongorai should open on the 20th. Thus, on the 17th, the 57th/60th Battalion supported by thirty-two Corsairs and the fire of two batteries crossed the Hongorai on a wide front, dispersed the enemy, and next day reached the Pororei. The main attack, astride the Buin road, was supported by aircraft which dropped 132 tons of bombs and by a bombardment in which nearly 1,200 shells or mortar bombs were used. At 8.30 a.m. on 20th May the 24th Battalion advanced with two troops of tanks. The Japanese fought hard for their well-dug position on Egan's Ridge but were overcome and by the 22nd had been driven beyond the Pororei.

The advance was resumed on 2nd June, again behind a devastating air and artillery bombardment, and by the 5th some patrols were on the Hari. But when the main body of the 58th/59th began the final thrust to the Hari it met heavy fire, and the tanks were delayed by boggy country. The 57th/60th resumed the advance on the 11th and the 58th/59th on the 12th. The 58th/59th sent two companies and two troops of tanks on a wide flanking movement to a position astride the road 2,000 yards beyond the Hari. This force reached its objective with little opposition and in the next few days the Japanese between it and the Hari were squeezed out.

On the left Lieut-Colonel P. G. C. Webster of the 57th/60th organised three columns each about eighty strong and, beginning on 11th June, these cut their way through the bush towards Rusei beyond the Ogorata River. On 16th June a patrol from the 58th/59th reached the 57th/60th which had been out in the bush for six days. Next day traffic, including three troops of tanks, moved along the Buin road to the 57th/60th. The plan had succeeded brilliantly. It was soon evident, however, that the Japanese were still well organised and in strength west of the Mobiai River: on the 16th a concealed Japanese field gun destroyed the forward tank and halted the Australian advance. Meanwhile a strong patrol had penetrated to Astill's Crossing on the upper Mivo. On this inland flank patrols of the 2/8th Commando had been carrying out successful ambushes and establishing a new base near the headwaters of the Mivo; on the 24th this new base, at Morokaimoro, was established and a strip for light aircraft begun.

The guerilla forces inland from Kieta, led by Captain C. W. Seton since Mason had been brought out to rest, continued to inflict heavy losses on the Japanese groups in the mountain country; the leaders estimated that their native followers killed about 2,200 Japanese in eight months.

Since December Savige had been trying to have all or nearly all the 23rd Brigade withdrawn from the outer islands and concentrated on Bougainville. Winning agreement to this proposal, and obtaining shipping once agreement had been achieved took many weeks, but in April, May and June the 23rd Brigade arrived at Torokina. In April Potts had taken command in the central sector where his 27th Battalion was now forward, patrolling deeply but under orders not to attack in strength. When, after six weeks forward, the 27th was relieved by the 7th it had made forty-eight patrols and killed at least 122 Japanese, losing only four killed and nine wounded. Farther north Sandford's parties were harassing the enemy; he estimated that by the end of May they had killed over 200.

On the north coast the 55th/53rd had been forward since early in April. The next objective was Pora Pora. Brigadier Stevenson decided that the best course would be to make a quick advance through the swampy country with the object of splitting up the enemy's force. One company was sent along an inland track while the main body of the battalion moved along the coastal route. After some sharp clashes the enemy was forced out of his positions on the coast and at Pora Pora, where forty-one out of about 120 defenders were killed. Thence the Japanese gradually withdrew to a line through Ruri Bay-Ratsua inlet across the narrow neck of the peninsula.

Late in May the 26th Battalion relieved the 55th/53rd and continued the northward drive but met opposition so stern that Savige soon decided to put a second battalion (the 31st/51st) into this sector. Each battalion had a field battery and some heavy mortars in support. However the fresh Japanese naval troops from the Buka base were strong in numbers, skilful and aggressive. They doggedly resisted every advance, and made daring raids into the Australian area. The Australian battalions were now weary and far below strength. It was decided to solve the problem by landing a force at Porton Plantation behind the enemy's western flank. The attacking force was to be a reinforced company of the 31st/51st about 190 strong with six landing craft, and commanded by Captain H. C. Downs.

The first wave of three craft landed before dawn on the 8th June somewhat north of the intended point and soon held a perimeter extending up to 150 yards inland but not embracing the three jetties serving the plantation. Soon after the second wave of troops were ashore the Japanese opened fire. It proved impossible to land the heavy weapons from craft that had stranded seventy-five yards from the beach, but at 6 a.m. the group ashore had established communication with the artillery, whose fire was soon being brought down on the enemy. But it became evident that the Australians were hemmed within an arc of Japanese trenches and pill-boxes, and that the enemy was being rapidly reinforced. By dusk the Australians had made little progress, and it was estimated that about 300 Japanese were now manning the cordon round the beach-head. That night unsuccessful efforts were made to land stores and reinforcements, and in the morning it was decided to withdraw the force after dark. The Japanese had attacked persistently throughout the night and in the morning launched a full-scale attack but were beaten off. Throughout the day the Australians fought on, supported by accurate artillery fire and, in the afternoon, by aircraft. Late in the afternoon three bullet-proof landing craft beached under intense fire and in five minutes picked up the survivors. One craft backed out successfully but the others were so heavily weighted that they stranded. At 10.40 p.m. one of the stranded craft drifted off on the tide but sixty men, of whom twelve were wounded, remained in the third, now holed by coral and half full of water. Efforts to rescue these men continued that night and all next day. Early on the morning of the 11th three assault boats were sent in, while heavy artillery fire was poured into the Japanese positions. Before dawn these brought out every living man. The Australians lost twenty-three killed and 106 wounded. It was learnt later that there were about 100 Japanese at Porton at the outset and 150 were sent forward to reinforce them; twenty-six Japanese were killed.

At one time or another II Corps had been given eager but inevitably modest naval support by the frigate *Diamantina* and the corvettes *Kiama, Lithgow, Dubbo* and *Colac*. *Colac* in May was given the task of searching for and preventing barge traffic believed to be moving between Bougainville and Choiseul and of bombarding targets of opportunity. Off Choiseul on 26th May *Colac* became involved in a duel with a Japanese gun which hit her twice causing the engine room to be flooded. She survived and was eventually towed to the Treasury Islands and thence to Sydney.

In southern Bougainville the Japanese were now confined within an area about thirty miles by fifteen, and in the north they were hemmed within the Bonis Peninsula and Buka Island. It was estimated, however, that

19,000 to 20,000 Japanese remained on the island (actually there were about 24,000); the Australian strength was 32,000 including 7,600 in the base subarea at Torokina. With the object of providing an adequate force for the continued thrust towards Buin Savige decided that the 23rd Brigade must take over both the northern and central sectors, and on 28th June he instructed Bridgeford that after securing the line of the Mivo he should advance to the Silibai River, still moving astride the two main tracks—the Buin and Commando roads—as rapidly as the jeep tracks could be built. On the Mivo the 15th Brigade was to be relieved by the 29th.

From 17th June onwards the 57th/60th Battalion had thrust steadily forward and by the 23rd was close to the Mobiai where a strong enemy group with a 37-mm gun was entrenched. In two days these Japanese were forced out. Hammer now gave the 57th/60th the task of moving round the enemy's northern flank and the 24th the task of advancing to the Buin road beyond the Koopani River. This was achieved on the 28th, 29th and 30th June after some sharp fighting. The 24th now occupied a section of the Buin road about half way between the Mobiai and the Mivo, and the 57th/60th was astride the road at the Mivo. Japanese were west of each battalion, the 24th was pushing forward to join the 57th/60th and the 58th/59th was trying to link with the 24th. The 57th/60th was now under the fire of six Japanese field guns—an indication of the growing resistance to be expected on the Mivo.

The 29th Brigade, now commanded by Brigadier N. W. Simpson, taking over from the 15th Brigade had to fight its way into the area. The 42nd Battalion relieved the 24th, the 15th Battalion relieved the 57th/60th. The 47th placed a company on the Mivo. It was soon under fierce attack, as was the forward company of the 57th/60th. The plan was that the brigade should cross the Mivo on 3rd July but heavy rain caused a postponement to the 10th. Meanwhile all battalions sent out patrols. These met strong opposition but obtained a clear picture of the enemy's dispositions. Before 10th July arrived the persistent rain caused a second postponement, this time to the 24th. By the 10th even patrols could not cross the Mivo, and the Buin road was 'a series of islands between the various rivers'. On 17th July eight inches of rain fell in thirty-six hours, and soon the forward troops could be supplied only by air. The opening of the offensive was postponed until late in August. In this period a series of fine patrols were carried out, some moving well beyond the Mivo and engaging in sharp fights, with an almost-impassable river behind them.

On the inland flank the 2/8th Commando in June had found the Commando Road abandoned by the enemy from the Mivo to Kapana and patrols probed forward to the Silibai. In July they established a new base at Kilipaijino whence they hoped to gain control of the Buin natives, many of whom were working for the Japanese.

General Kanda had decided in June that the Australians would cross the Mivo early in August. He planned to launch an offensive early in September: one regiment was to make a thrust north of the Buin road and harass the Australian supply lines, a second was to operate from the Mivo ford towards the Mobiai, a third was to operate along the northern road, while a fourth force of 3,500, was finally to attack southward from the headwaters of the Muliko River. About 9,000 troops would take part in the offensive, and

Australian War Memorial

A sodden camp of an Australian battalion in southern Bougainville on 20th July 1945. Weeks of torrential rain brought operations almost to a standstill.

about 8,000 more were close behind in the Buin area. Having thrust the Australians back to the Mivo, Kanda intended to withdraw to his inner defences, where he had eighty-six guns, and there fight out the final battle.

In the central sector in June and July a fresh battalion not hitherto in action, the 7th (Lieut-Colonel H. L. E. Dunkley), had been given a more active role than its predecessors had been allowed in recent months. It was to take Wearne's Hill, Sisivie and other dominating positions and establish a company well forward in the Wakunai Valley from which the Japanese on the east coast could be harried. The battalion attacked and took Wearne's Hill in June after a series of sharp fights, Centre Hill early in July, and McInnes Hill in August. Sisivie was occupied in June and Tokua early in July and thence strong patrols probed deeply into Japanese territory.

When the 23rd Brigade took over in the northern sector Savige had ordered Brigadier Potts to contain the Japanese in the Bonis Peninsula and patrol towards Buka Passage, employing only one battalion group whereas the outgoing brigade had employed two. Potts, however, obtained permission to employ also his 8th Battalion, then arriving from the outer islands. By the end of June the 27th Battalion was in position on the right and the 8th on the left. One battery of field artillery was in support. The front was about four miles wide and it was impossible to protect all tracks leading south. Japanese patrols made deadly raids behind the Australian positions, ambushing ration trains and cutting signal lines. At length Potts obtained leave to withdraw his right and concentrate on a 3,000-yard front round Buoi Plantation. On

23rd July the 8th attacked a ridge where the Japanese seemed to be digging in strongly. One company was employed supported by aircraft and two tanks. The ridge was soon taken. On 24th July a further attack was launched. It encountered heavy fire and was halted until Private F. J. Partridge, a youth of 20, dashed forward, although wounded, knocked out one bunker and led the attack towards another. (He was awarded the Victoria Cross.) The whole position was not taken that day, but was abandoned by the Japanese soon afterwards. On 11th August active patrolling ceased in all sectors on Bougainville.

In the Bougainville campaign 516 Australians were killed and 1,572 wounded; about 8,500 Japanese were killed by II Australian Corps and the native guerillas and from October 1944 about 9,800 Japanese died of illness; 23,571 surrendered.

In New Britain, as in Bougainville, in August 1944 the American garrisons guarded their airfields, and the main Japanese forces had withdrawn far to the east; in the intervening country, patrols of Australian-led natives waged guerilla warfare against Japanese outposts. The Japanese force on New Britain, then believed to be between 32,000 and 38,000 strong but actually far larger, was concentrated in the Gazelle Peninsula, and mainly round Rabaul, still the principal Japanese base in the south Pacific and the site of the headquarters of the *Eighth Area Army*, which included the *17th* and *38th Divisions, 65th Brigade* and other smaller formations. The Japanese air strength was believed to have been reduced to fewer than thirty aircraft, and no vessels remained in this much-bombed area except about 150 barges, some large enough to carry fifteen tons or ninety men.

The Japanese were known to have prepared a fortified line across the north-eastern corner of the peninsula enclosing an area about twenty-eight miles by sixteen. Forward of this were several delaying forces of varying strength, the largest being at Waitavalo on Henry Reid Bay covering the track to Rabaul from the south; there were patrols and outposts west of the peninsula. As mentioned, Allied Intelligence Bureau parties had been at large on New Britain since before the American landings. In mid-1944 the parties on the south coast were placed under the command of Captain B. Fairfax-Ross, who was ordered to clear the enemy from that coast as far east as Henry Reid Bay, to gather Intelligence, and to help the natives and regain their confidence—a formidable task for a force of five officers, ten Australian N.C.O's and, at the outset, 140 armed natives. Fairfax-Ross, however, was a sage leader, who had worked in New Guinea before the war, had served in the infantry in the Middle East, and had been behind the Japanese lines on the mainland of New Guinea in 1943.

In July, after several parties of Japanese had been wiped out, the main Japanese outpost west of the peninsula was Milim. This was repeatedly bombed and was bombarded by the sloop *Swan*. Fairfax-Ross advanced against Milim on 12th August and, although his attack did not develop, the enemy (now about 150 strong) after firing off much ammunition withdrew to Waitavalo. Thence in September they sent against Milim a force which eventually was 700 strong and reoccupied their former positions, while the guerillas concentrated about Lakiri. By November there were no Japanese south and west of Henry Reid Bay, and, partly with the help of agents in

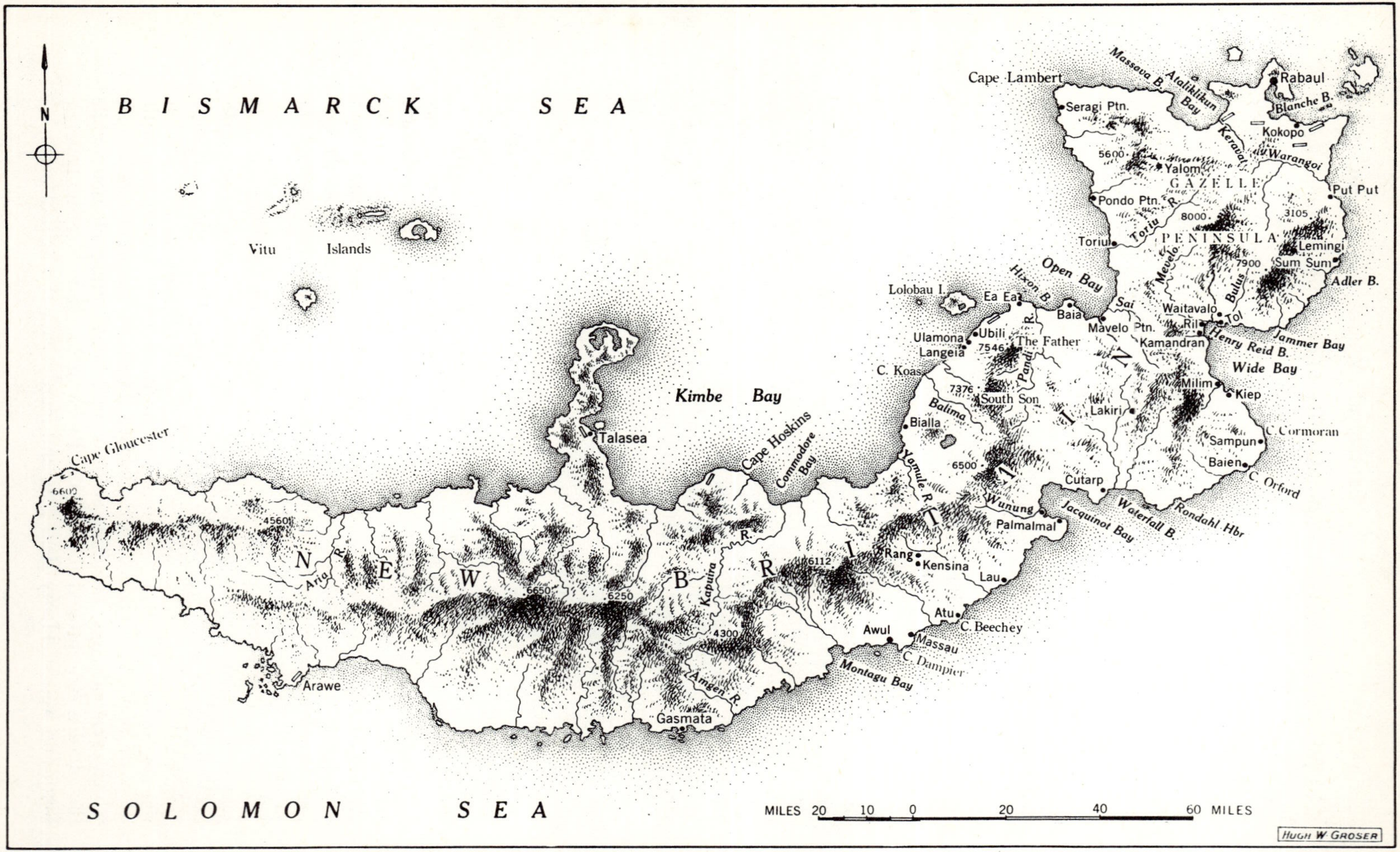
BISMARCK SEA
SOLOMON SEA
NEW BRITAIN
GAZELLE PENINSULA
N
Vitu Islands
Cape Lambert
Massava B.
Ataliklikun Bay
Rabaul
Blanche B.
Kokopo
Keravat
Warangoi
Seragi Ptn.
5600
Yalom
Put Put
Pondo Ptn.
Toriu R.
8000
3105
Toriu
Mevelo
Lemingi
7900
Sum Sum
Adler B.
Open Bay
Hixon B.
Bulus
Lolobau I.
Ea Ea
Baia
Sai
Waitavalo
Tol
Ril
Mavelo Ptn.
Henry Reid B.
Jammer Bay
Ulamona
Ubili
Langeia
7546
The Father
Kamandran
Wide Bay
Pandi R.
C. Koas
7376
South Son
Milim
Kiep
Balima
Bialla
Lakiri
C. Cormoran
Sampun
Baien
C. Orford
6500
Cutarp
Yamule R.
Wunung
Jacquinot Bay
Waterfall B.
Rondahl Hbr
Palmalmal
Rang
Kensina
Lau
6112
Atu
C. Beechey
Awul
Massau
C. Dampier
Montagu Bay
Kimbe Bay
Talasea
Cape Hoskins
Commodore Bay
Kapuira
R.
4300
Amgen R.
Gasmata
6250
6650
Aria R.
4560
Cape Gloucester
6602
Arawe
MILES 20 10 0 20 40 60 MILES
HUGH W GROSER

New Britain

the Gazelle Peninsula, the Australians had a fairly detailed knowledge of the enemy's strength and dispositions in the forward areas: there were about 700 round Kamandran and Waitavalo.

The incoming 5th Division (Major-General Ramsay) planned to establish its base far to the east of the existing ones. From 4th November the 6th Brigade (Brigadier R. L. Sandover)—the first to arrive—was landed at Jacquinot Bay, less one battalion, the 36th, which went to Cape Hoskins on the north coast. After having covered the initial landing at Jacquinot Bay the naval escort—H.M.A.S's *Swan, Vendetta* and *Barcoo*—bombarded Japanese positions in Wide Bay. It was decided that eventually the whole division less the battalion group on the north coast would be concentrated at Jacquinot Bay and east of it. Because of lack of shipping the 13th Brigade did not arrive, from Darwin, until late in November and December, and the 4th Brigade was not complete on New Britain until 24th February. All this time the equivalent of five Japanese divisions, well fed and equipped, idled around Rabaul.

Ramsay's tasks were to limit Japanese movement south-west from the Gazelle Peninsula, to harass them, and to collect information: rather similar tasks to those already largely carried out by Fairfax-Ross's little force.

On the north coast the 36th Battalion (Lieut-Colonel O. C. Isaachsen) promptly patrolled eastward by barge to Ea Ea, and in January was given permission to concentrate there, plus a company of the 1st New Guinea Battalion. In January and February there were patrol clashes about Mavelo Plantation and the Sai River. Early in March Ramsay instructed Isaachsen not to establish bases east of the Mavelo River but to patrol forward to the Sai. After seven months of arduous patrolling this battalion was relieved in May by the 37th/52nd.

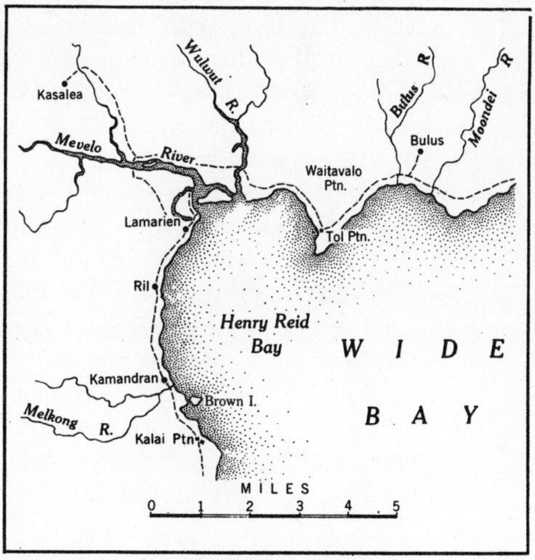

In January the leading battalion on the south coast—the 14th/32nd—was concentrated first at Sampun, and then at Milim. It patrolled forward to Kalai Plantation. In February after bombardment the Japanese abandoned Kamandran and by the end of the month the 19th Battalion, now forward, had crossed the Mevelo River and was patrolling towards the ridge overlooking Waitavalo and Tol Plantations at the eastern end of Henry Reid Bay. Here the Japanese were strongly dug in and artillery was soon harassing them.

On 27th February Sturdee instructed Ramsay to secure the Waitavalo-Tol area and hold a line not forward of the Moondei River. The fight for Waitavalo opened on 5th March when the 19th Battalion (Major J. A. Maitland) crossed the Wulwut River under heavy fire. For the next nine days it fought its way forward from hill to hill through rain forest against an enemy well dug in and supported by many mortars. By the 14th the Japanese were all concentrated on one hill in an area about 500 yards by 500 and had lost heavily, largely as a result of the

Australian War Memorial

New Britain, 7th February 1945. A sergeant of a New Guinea Infantry Battalion giving instructions to a patrol.

artillery fire provided by the 2/14th Field Regiment then in strenuous action for the first time since its formation in 1940. Sandover now replaced the 19th Battalion with the 14th/32nd which, in three days of hard fighting, destroyed or dispersed the surviving Japanese about Waitavalo. Many of those who escaped from Waitavalo were killed by patrols of a company of the 1st New Guinea Battalion astride the tracks leading eastward.

Air support was on a modest scale. Beauforts of the R.A.A.F. from Goodenough Island had bombed Rabaul in October and November. No. 6 (Beaufort) Squadron gave support during the operations on New Britain from November onwards. From February onwards a detachment of No. 5 (Boomerang) Squadron was based at Cape Hoskins and in May squadrons of the Royal New Zealand Air Force began operating from Jacquinot Bay. By that time infantry fighting on New Britain had almost ceased.

The 13th Brigade (Brigadier E. G. H. McKenzie) had relieved the 6th early in April. The 5th Division had achieved its main task and henceforward held the line it had gained and patrolled forward of it.

The strength of the Japanese force on New Britain, as mentioned, had been estimated at between 32,000 and 38,000. After the war it was found that the army imprisoned by a weak Australian division included 53,200 soldiers, 16,200 naval men, and 20,000 civilian workers; nearby on New Ireland were 11,100 army and navy men and 1,200 civilian workers. The combined force included nineteen generals, eleven admirals, 3,300 other army officers and 1,400 other naval officers.

Meanwhile the 6th Australian Division had been engaged in a long offensive on the mainland of New Guinea. There in October 1944 the *XVIII Japanese Army,* based on Wewak, was deployed westward along the coast to the Driniumor River and in the Prince Alexander Ranges and the Torricellis, whose gardens helped to feed a force now cut off from all outside supplies except those an occasional submarine might bring. East of Aitape the coastal plain is very narrow and, as in Bougainville, is cut by a series of rivers all subject to sudden flooding. South of the mountain ranges the rivers drain into the great Sepik River, a stream navigable for about 300 miles by vessels drawing up to ten feet. The spurs leading from the coast into the mountains were narrow-edged and offered excellent defensive positions.

The Australian Intelligence staff believed in October that the *XVIII Japanese Army* (*20th, 41st* and *51st Divisions*) had dwindled to about 30,000 (the true figure was about 35,000), and that some 3,000 base troops had been dispersed in small groups to live off the country in the mountains east of a defensive chain of posts held by the *41st Division.* Thus the 6th Division faced three Japanese divisions, each so reduced by losses in earlier fighting from Wau to Aitape that it had about the strength of a strong brigade group. The opposing formations were both veterans of several campaigns. The Australians had the advantages of fairly strong air support (though little air transport), some naval support, far more heavy weapons than the Japanese, and excellent medical services.

Not enough shipping was provided by MacArthur's headquarters to move the 6th Division to Aitape in one convoy. The 3rd Base Sub-Area, the division's housekeeper, began to arrive on 15th September, and the headquarters of the division opened on 8th November. By that time the 32nd and 31st U.S. Divisions had departed and the 43rd plus the 112th Cavalry Regiment were about to move. The 19th Australian Brigade had arrived by 19th November, the 17th was complete by 7th December and the 16th by 31st December. In November the north-west monsoon began and brought a heavy surf which made unloading difficult in the open roadstead at Aitape. There were not enough L.C.T's to cope with the unloading of the transports, and late in December 30,000 tons of cargo and 2,000 men were offshore in five transports awaiting disembarkation. Not until March could unloading be promptly carried out.

Air support was provided by No. 71 Wing R.A.A.F. (Nos. 7, 8 and 100 Squadrons) armed with Beauforts; it had been operating from Aitape since June 1944. There was also a flight of Boomerangs and Wirraways for tactical reconnaissance, and, at first, only one transport aircraft. Wing Commander E. W. Cooper commanded the wing from October until the end of March; Group Captain V. E. Hancock took over on 1st April.

At the outset Sturdee gave the 6th Division the role of defending the Aitape area, preventing the westward movement of Japanese forces, seizing every opportunity of destroying those forces, and helping the Allied Intelligence Bureau and Angau units to gain information, establish patrol bases and protect the natives. These A.I.B. and Angau parties had long been patrolling from Aitape deep into enemy territory.

When the Australians began to arrive, the 43rd American Division had two companies forward on the Driniumor River and some standing patrols outside the perimeter; otherwise it was either training or manning the 'main

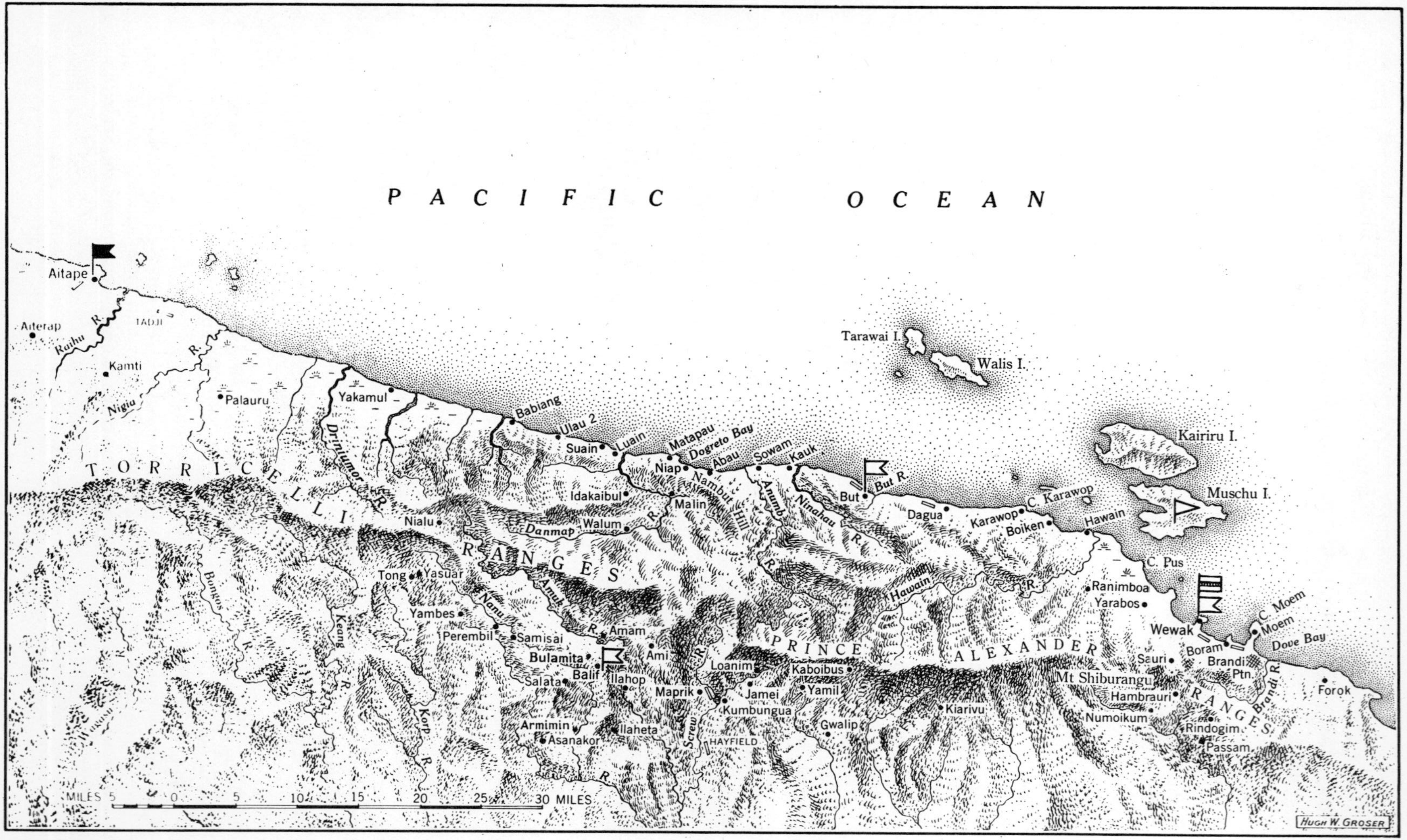

Aitape-Wewak

line of resistance'. General Stevens decided that the 2/6th Cavalry (Commando) Regiment should carry out vigorous patrolling mainly with the object of increasing the somewhat scanty knowledge of the enemy's dispositions. The cavalrymen early in November probed forward to Suain on the coast, and Yasuar Mission in the Torricellis. On the coast they found many small groups of hungry Japanese and took prisoners who gave useful information. By the end of the month they had killed seventy-three, taken seven prisoners and cleared a big area; their own losses were one killed and one wounded.

Already Stevens had obtained permission to embark on operations aimed at cutting the enemy's forward line of communication which ran from Malin to Amam and destroying the enemy east of the Danmap. Early in December the 19th Brigade (Brigadier J. E. G. Martin) relieved the cavalry, whose 2/7th Commando Squadron was sent inland to establish a patrol base about Tong. From Tong the squadron gained control of a wide area and soon patrol clashes were frequent. With the object of firmly securing the Tong area, whence he proposed to advance into the valuable gardens in the Torricellis early in 1945, Stevens now ordered the 17th Brigade to send a small force to that place. Initially it comprised two companies of the 2/5th Battalion. The first contact was made by this force on 27th December when a patrol ambushed twenty-two Japanese and killed fifteen. By the end of the month most of the remainder of the battalion had arrived forward and Lieut-Colonel A. W. Buttrose was in command. The Japanese had now been cleared from the country west of a line through Yambes, and the battalion was close to the enemy's main defences.

On the coast in the first half of December the 2/4th Battalion destroyed such small groups of Japanese as were west of the Danmap River; and on 14th December Stevens gave the 19th Brigade the larger task of capturing a line from Abau to Malin. It was believed that there were 700 Japanese in the Danmap-Malin-Abau triangle, and 2,000 to 3,000 in the inland area from Malin to Amam. The 19th Brigade was now in battle for the first time since Crete in May 1941. Martin's plan was that the 2/4th Battalion should cross the Danmap and then the 2/11th should march along the coast to Abau and the 2/8th advance on an inland route from Idakaibul to Malin. They now knew that they faced the *237th Regiment* of the *41st Division*.

The 2/4th crossed the Danmap on the 17th December and in five days drove the enemy back about four miles. One group of about forty Japanese, thrusting southward from the coast, ran into a standing ambush and twenty-eight were killed. The 2/11th now took over the advance. Round Matapau it met determined opposition but repulsed counter-attacks and pressed on, supported by artillery fire directed by observers who sent back their orders from positions very close to the enemy, and by accurate air strikes. On 6th January three tanks of the 2/4th Armoured Regiment went into action and with their support the infantry took Niap, on the 10th occupied Dogreto Point, and on the 20th Abau.

In the foothills the 2/8th Battalion had had to delay its advance because of shortage of native carriers. At first it could maintain only one company at Idakaibul, but by 5th January it was able to move forward. The 2/9th Commando Squadron patrolled the hills south of the Danmap and the 2/8th Battalion on 8th January entered Malin. There were several patrol clashes

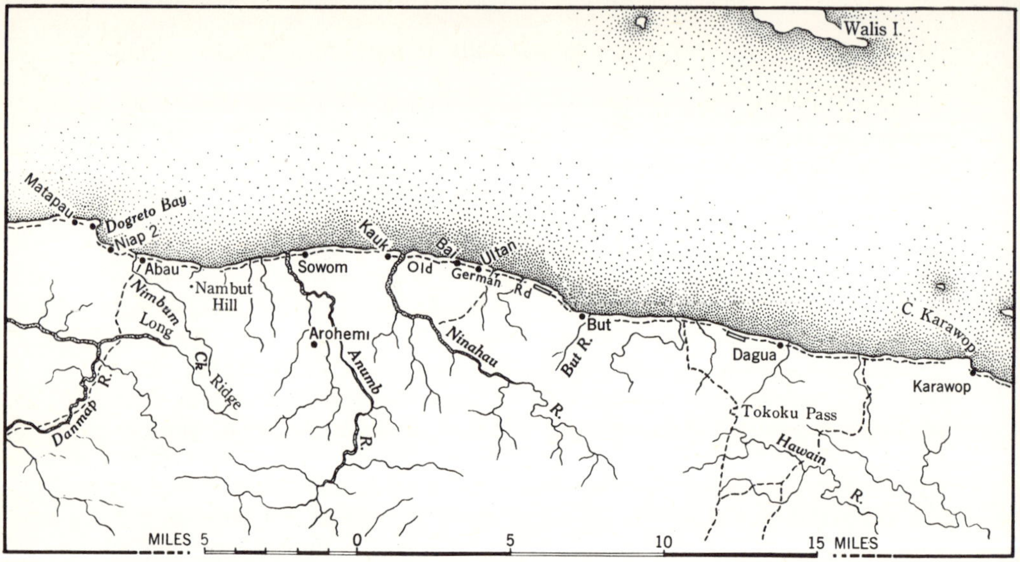

Matapau-Karawop

Aitape-Wewak campaign. Men of an Australian battalion moving through the jungle during an attack on Japanese positions on a hill feature beyond Matapau, on 2nd January 1945.

Australian War Memorial

in the rugged country round the upper Danmap, where communications were so difficult that written signals were sent back to brigade headquarters by carrier pigeon. On Long Ridge above Nimbum Creek there was a series of sharp fights with what turned out to be a large Japanese raiding detachment sent out to re-take Malin and advance thence to Luain.

Stevens sent the 16th Brigade forward to relieve the 19th, which had now killed 434 Japanese and lost only thirty-six of its own men killed in action. On 21st January the Danmap River was in flood and broke a bridge that the engineers were building; on the 26th rain fell almost continuously, the Danmap rose rapidly, and soon trees sixty feet high were being swept downstream. A platoon of the 2/3rd Battalion was cut off and swept downstream, and seven men were drowned. A cavalry troop upstream at Walum suffered a similar experience and four were drowned. Seven bridges were washed away between Aitape and the Danmap.

High in the Torricellis the 2/5th Battalion now faced the enemy's main outer defences. It was believed that there were 400 Japanese about Balif where the *41st Division* had its headquarters, 800 of the *238th Regiment* about Perembil, and 500 to 700 of the *239th* about Womsak (south of Amam) and Salata. Buttrose planned to press east and south-east. On 3rd January Perembil was taken after a sharp fight; Samisai was entered on the 11th; on the 20th a force of sixty Japanese was driven from Bulamita which became the battalion's advanced base. Almost every day, bombers from Aitape, guided by mortar smoke and radio telephone, made accurate air strikes ahead of the advancing infantry. By the end of January the 2/5th had driven the enemy, except for parties of stragglers, from a belt of country about twelve miles from west to east and eight from north to south.

As the advance continued on the coast and in the Torricellis it became increasingly difficult to supply the Australian forward units. The maintenance of the road along the coast was hampered by shortage of heavy equipment, and there was only one transport aircraft available to supply the force in the highlands. Early in January Stevens had told Sturdee that by the end of the month he would hold the line Abau-Walum, but would then have to halt because he could not maintain forces farther forward. But, in case more 'maintenance facilities and air support' were provided, he submitted plans for thrusts along the coast to Wewak and through the mountains to Maprik, and listed the transport and attack aircraft and landing craft that would be needed. Sturdee ordered that the advance be continued within the limits of the division's resources and without becoming involved in 'a major engagement'.

On the coast maintenance was now a little easier because of the capture of Dogreto Bay, the first point east of Aitape where landing craft could be run ashore; from 30th January onwards landing craft put supplies ashore every second or third day.

Ahead of the 2/1st Battalion, now forward in the coastal sector, lay a narrow shore cut every few hundred yards by creeks draining Nambut Hill, round whose southern side ran Nimbum Creek. Here for three weeks from 29th January onwards the battalion was engaged in a long fight with a strong Japanese force—one, it was soon learnt, which had been sent from Wewak to drive the Australians back across the Danmap. The hill was finally secured on 18th February. Meanwhile the 2/3rd Battalion on the inland coastal sector had on 31st January sent out a force against Japanese on Long Ridge where on 1st February it surprised and defeated a strong Japanese group.

Stevens, having now received Sturdee's decision that he might press on towards Wewak to the extent that his resources allowed, informed his brigade commanders that he intended to advance along the coast to Wewak, and, in the inland sector, to take Maprik and thence advance eastward. Brigadier R. King of the 16th Brigade was instructed to advance to the Anumb River; Brigadier Moten of the 17th was told that his advance to Maprik would have to be accomplished by one battalion plus one company and two commando squadrons—all that could be maintained in the mountains.

In the Torricellis in the first week of February the 2/5th Battalion took Salata and Balif. Next week it pressed on to Numango, and by the 17th had Malahun. A party of artillerymen, picked for their physical strength, had now carried two 4.2-inch mortars over the mountains to Balif and these went into action against the Japanese stronghold of Ilahop on 19th February. A strip for light aircraft had now been completed at Balif and henceforward wounded men were flown out instead of being carried over the mountains—a six-day journey. In this period the 2/10th Commando Squadron, protecting the left flank, was engaged in a series of sharp fights. Here, and in the 2/5th's area, the Japanese were now launching determined counterattacks. At Malahun on 23rd February a Japanese force totalling 130 attacked a company of the 2/5th but was driven off. In its two months in the

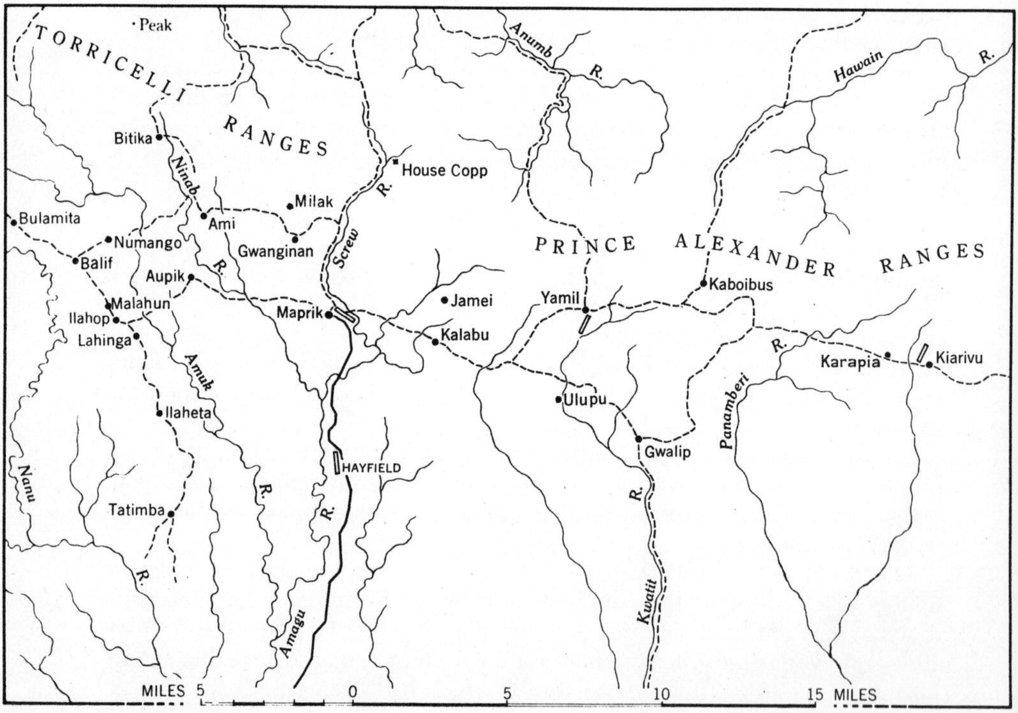

Balif to Kiarivu

mountains the 2/5th, now being relieved by the 2/7th, counted 376 Japanese dead, took twelve prisoners and itself lost only seven killed.

During the advance of the 2/5th a great part of the force opposing it had withdrawn southward into populous garden areas. These enemy troops could not safely be left on the flank. Moten therefore, on 17th February, ordered a wide sweeping movement to the south by a force moving slightly in advance of the main one. This task was given to a company of the 2/6th under Major D. O. Hay, which was to drive the Japanese in the south—perhaps 2,000, who were living off the country—eastward and away from their gardens.

The enemy had now been reinforced and was becoming more aggressive, patrolling widely, setting ambushes, and reoccupying villages from which he had been driven. An isolated cavalry troop, fifty strong, at Milak was attacked on 13th March by a strong force and besieged for five days, and two other troops were also attacked, though less severely.

In mid-March the 2/6th Battalion (Lieut-Colonel Wood) relieved the 2/10th Commando Squadron on the northern flank and there were then two battalions forward. To the south of the 2/7th Battalion (Lieut-Colonel P. K. Parbury) was steadily advancing, with Hay's company on its southern flank. On 9th March there was a general advance to Ilahop and Armimin (about five miles to the south-west). By 20th March Hayforce had advanced to Tatimba, and the enemy were withdrawing east and north-east. At Ilaheta the Japanese held out for three days under mortar bombardment and air attack. In the fourth week of March there was fighting round the Aupik villages, and by 3rd April the 2/7th Battalion was across the Ninab and ready for the final advance to Maprik.

In the coastal sector heavy rain had damaged the road from Dogreto Bay and the advance was discontinued for some days. Brigadier King now placed the 2/3rd Machine Gun Battalion, working as infantry, in the mountain sector, with the 2/9th Commando Squadron under command. On 4th March the squadron plus a company of the battalion marched on Arohemi where the enemy was well dug in and resisted for three days. The 2/2nd Battalion patrolled forward to beyond the Ninahau River.

It now became evident that the Japanese were not strong forward of But, once an important airfield, and King decided, despite the precarious condition of his roads, to make a dash for But, to establish a barge point there and then move the whole brigade forward and ferry vehicles and heavy equipment thither in landing craft. On 14th March the 2/2nd sent a company out towards But and by nightfall it was beyond Bai. West of Ultan it encountered a strong Japanese position which was bombarded and then taken after a dashing charge. A fresh company then moved through and, after being shelled by three guns, it dug in at the eastern end of the But airfield. Next day it established a beach-head round But jetty and by evening the whole battalion was forward round But. The swift advance had confused the enemy whose artillery were now lobbing shells a mile or two behind the forward troops. In the next three days the 2/2nd patrolled deeply, both inland and along the Old German Road, and destroyed four field guns.

The 2/1st Battalion now took over the defence of But and the 2/2nd pressed on to Dagua. The enemy's main strength was now not astride the coast road but in the hills to the south. The 2/3rd Machine Gun Battalion fought its way along the Ninahau River. The 2/2nd had the task of clearing the foothills south of Dagua and destroying the enemy in the Tokoku Pass through which a track led inland to Wonginara Mission, about five miles away. The Japanese made a resolute effort to hold this pass, which was not taken until a series of strong attacks had been made on Japanese forces dug in on razor-back ridges. In an attack on 25th March Lieutenant A. Chowne, an outstanding leader in this battalion, was killed leading his men in a bayonet charge.[2] It was not until 5th April that the forward company of the 2/2nd linked with the 2/3rd which had marched round to the south of the pass and attacked from that direction. Round Wonginara Mission the 2/3rd found few Japanese.

The first barges had arrived at But on 19th March and round this beach a large field maintenance centre swiftly developed.

Blamey visited But on 19th March and approved a plan for an advance overland to Wewak, now twenty miles ahead of the forward troops. At that stage there seemed little likelihood of obtaining landing craft for an amphibious attack, but on 24th March Stevens learnt that G.H.Q. had been persuaded to allot him ten additional L.C.T's, and later that he would be given the support of the sloop *Swan*, three corvettes, *Colac*, *Dubbo* and *Deloraine*, six motor boats, and a few additional aircraft. With this reinforcement, minute compared with the naval and air forces employed in the smallest operations farther north, Stevens planned to land a force beyond Wewak.

In the mountain sector on 3rd April Moten issued orders for the final thrust to Maprik. The 2/7th Battalion was to capture Maprik and the line of the Screw River on a three-mile front; Hayforce on the right was to capture the site of a proposed airstrip able to accommodate Douglas transports. On the left the 2/6th was to advance to the Screw and prevent the enemy escaping northward. The site of Hayfield, as it was named, was secured, and a Pioneer platoon with the help of about 200 natives using, of necessity, only hand tools and improvised graders and rollers, began forming the airfield.

The 2/7th opened its attack on Maprik on 15th April and there were ten days of hard fighting before the Japanese, dug in on dominating features round the area, had been driven out or had died where they stood. In this period the 2/6th continued its arduous probing forward on the northern flank.

The first Douglas aircraft landed on Hayfield on 14th May, and thereafter the 17th Brigade became a more formidable force. Tractors, graders, jeeps and field guns were flown in; practically all troops were henceforth moved in or out by air. Behind the troops advancing east from Maprik a road was rapidly formed.

The enemy was now holding strongly round Kaboibus, Yamil and Jamei. Jamei was taken on 25th May after heavy bombardment from the ground and the air. In this phase Captain C. M. Johnson's battery of the 2/1st Anti-Tank Regiment, armed as infantry, garrisoned Hayfield and patrolled deeply to the south where it fought some highly-destructive actions.

[2] He was posthumously awarded the Victoria Cross.

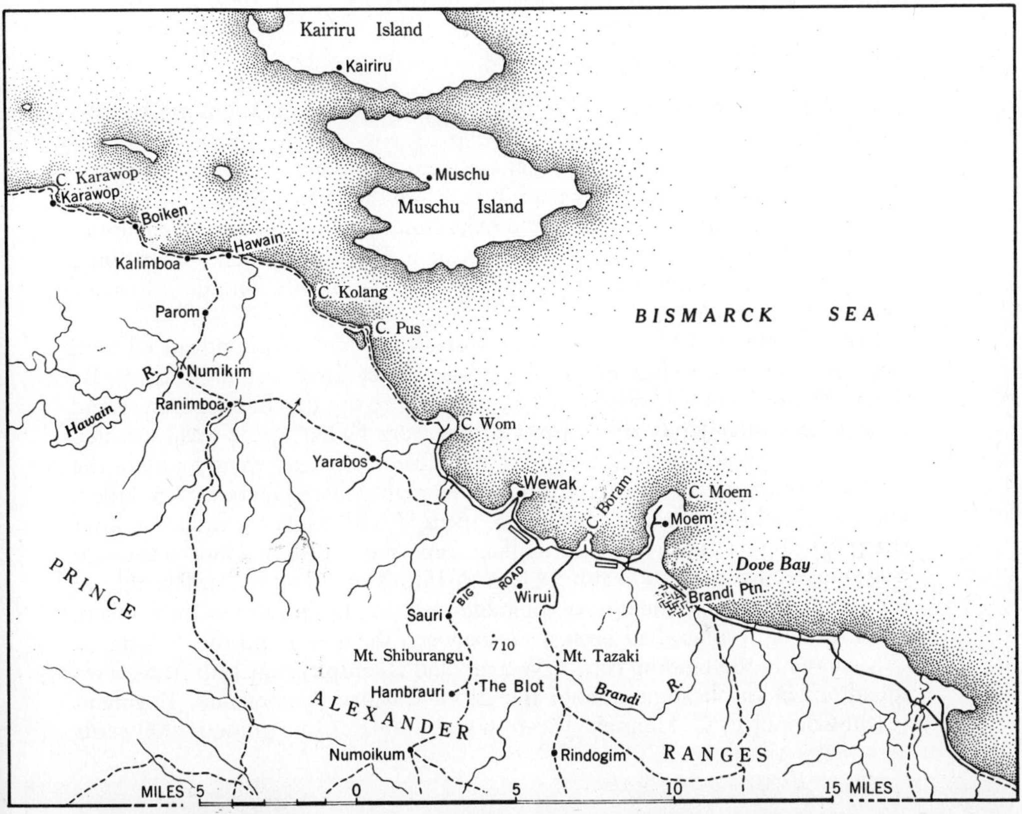

Karawop to Dove Bay

Meanwhile on the coast the operation against Wewak had been carried out. The 16th Brigade fought its way to Karawop and on through Boiken to the Hawain River, which a company of the 2/2nd Battalion and a squadron of tanks crossed in assault boats on 27th April. Wewak was then only twelve miles ahead in a direct line. The 19th Brigade now took over the advance from the weary and depleted battalions of the 16th, which had lost eighty-five killed and 192 wounded in the 35-mile advance from Abau to the Hawain; they had killed 909 Japanese and taken twenty-seven prisoners. The plan was that the 19th Brigade would advance to Cape Wom and thence attack Wewak from the west while the 2/6th Cavalry (Commando) Regiment plus other detachments landed ten miles east of that base.

The 19th Brigade's tasks were to advance from Boiken Plantation and destroy the enemy between Cape Wom and Yarabos and round Ranimboa, cut the tracks south of Wirui Mission, and finally destroy the Japanese round Wewak Point and Cape Moem. Brigadier Martin had the squadron of tanks and a commando squadron under command and, in support, nearly all the artillery of the division. The advance opened on 3rd May when the 2/4th Battalion marched six miles without meeting much opposition. By 7th May it had reached Yarabos, ten miles beyond the Hawain, and thus reached the outskirts of Wewak without having encountered any Japanese except a few stragglers. On the right the 2/8th Battalion had taken Ranimboa and Numikim after a few minor clashes. The tanks and artillery and Martin's headquarters were concentrated round Cape Wom on the 7th when a squadron of American Lightnings, sent out to strafe Wewak, by mistake attacked Cape

Wom (the next headland to the west) killing eleven and wounding twenty-one Australians.

It was now evident that the Japanese were abandoning their great base at Wewak and withdrawing their main forces into the Prince Alexander Ranges, leaving strong rearguards to hold the exits from the Wewak area. To counter this the 2/11th Battalion and the 2/7th Commando Squadron were sent on a wide encircling movement to the south while the 2/4th Battalion attacked Wewak Point.

Before dawn on 10th May the attack opened. The infantry advanced with two troops of tanks while five batteries of artillery fired over their heads. By 8 a.m. Wewak Point had been taken, and during the day bunkers, caves and tunnels in which Japanese were sheltering were blown up. It was estimated that about fifty perished in the caves; sixty-five other dead were counted; the attackers lost only two killed. Next day about eighty more Japanese were killed, and the airfield was taken. Meanwhile the 2/7th Commando Squadron after sharp fighting had taken the Sauri villages, and the 2/11th had moved through a swamp against the 710 Feature. Here on 15th May it had its hardest fight of the campaign against some forty Japanese well dug in, but the hill was taken. On 13th May contact had been made between the 2/4th and the 2/11th.

Meanwhile the landing east of Wewak had taken place on 11th May. Two squadrons of the headquarters of the 2/6th Cavalry (Commando) Regiment (Lieut-Colonel E. C. Hennessy) were taken from But to a point 10,000 yards

Australian War Memorial

Part of 'Farida Force' landing east of Wewak on 11th May 1945.

off Wewak in H.M.A.S's *Swan*, *Dubbo* and *Colac* and there loaded into landing craft. At 7.15 a.m. a naval force including the cruisers H.M.A.S. *Hobart* and H.M.S. *Newfoundland* (detached from the British Pacific Fleet) and the destroyers *Arunta* and *Warramunga*, all commanded by Commodore Farncomb, began to bombard targets ashore. Bombers from Aitape and mortars mounted on barges thickened the fire. The first wave of landing craft grounded about ten yards from the beach at 8.34 a.m. and the men waded ashore. There was little opposition, a perimeter was swiftly formed round the beach-head, and a strong Japanese group on the eastern flank was driven off. At 5.50 the troops cut the Wewak road. A patrol reached Forok on the 12th and thereafter steadily extended the area covered by its patrols. On the 20th 'Farida Force', as it was named, was placed under Brigadier Martin's command and ordered to be ready to link with the leading troops of the 2/8th Battalion at Brandi Plantation about 22nd May.

The 19th Brigade had been heavily engaged about Wirui Mission, situated on a steep kunai-covered hill above the airfield. On 14th May the 2/4th Battalion with tanks attacked it from the east and after a sharp fight took all but the north-western spur. Three posts remained. Next day a company of the 2/4th attacked again. Two of the posts were knocked out by Private E. Kenna, who stood in the open and fired with a Bren gun, then a rifle, and then with a Bren again.[3] Only about twenty out of some sixty Japanese escaped from Wirui, possession of which gave the brigade complete control of the Wewak coast. Captured documents and patrolling showed that three forces each about 300 to 400 strong were defending the exits from Wewak, but that no strong groups existed within about 1,000 yards of the coast. Martin now sent the 2/8th Battalion against Boram. It took Boram village on the 16th after heavy bombardment from sea and air but found the airfield strongly defended. After a very heavy bombardment in which every bunker and weapon-pit was hit, the 2/8th made a three-company attack on 20th May and took the airfield. On 22nd May the 2/8th occupied Cape Moem and linked with Farida Force. In this period the 2/11th was continuing its arduous advance into the mountain area where it drove the enemy from a series of strong positions.

By the end of May the 6th Division had driven the Japanese away from the coast into a fairly confined mountain area where they were now hemmed in between the 17th Brigade on the west and the main body of the division round Wewak. It soon became evident that the enemy, well fed and well armed, and concentrated in country offering many naturally strong defensive positions, would fight harder than ever to hold the ground that remained to him.

Up to the end of May a total of 1,458 sorties had been flown by the air force in support of the Australian troops and 1,236 tons of bombs had been dropped. There was a chronic shortage of bombs and by the end of May not only was this shortage curtailing the air support but many bombs were proving defective. No. 71 Wing used captured bombs, but about 40 per cent of these were duds. In July Group Captain Hancock reported that he had only enough bombs for three days of operations.

In the mountain sector the 17th Brigade had been strengthened by the equipment landed from aircraft on Hayfield. This support was the more

[3] Kenna was awarded the Victoria Cross.

welcome because the brigade was now encountering more elaborate defences than hitherto. The 2/5th and 2/6th Battalions, probing forward vigorously, broke into a strong defensive line in the Yamil area in the second week of June but the enemy held out round Ulupu and on Kunai Spur, about a mile to the north and a main stronghold in this area; Kunai Spur was abandoned on 3rd July after withstanding bombardment for nearly three weeks. On 28th June the 2nd New Guinea Battalion (Lieut-Colonel A. C. Murchison) had joined the 17th Brigade, and Moten gave it the task of thrusting deeply to the south and destroying the survivors of the *41st Division* there. Within a few days the New Guinea soldiers had killed twenty-five Japanese for a loss of three of their own men wounded.

On 8th July a strongly-held knoll in the Ulupu area was taken by the 2/5th Battalion after a hard fight. The enemy's defence system had now been broken and the 2/5th thrust rapidly forward about 2,000 yards with only minor clashes. During July the 2nd New Guinea Battalion and native scouts led by Angau officers continued to harass the scattered Japanese groups to the south, killing as many as thirty in a day.

Captured papers showed that the next main line of resistance was through Kaboibus and Gwalip. Moten decided that the brigade should accelerate the advance by making a wide flanking movement to Kiarivu. The plan provided that the New Guinea Battalion would converge on the Gwalip villages by 30th July, that the 2/7th Battalion should be flown to Hayfield and move to Gwalip whence it would advance south-east and then north to Kiarivu airfield and Karapia some ten miles behind the Japanese forward positions. Stores and heavy weapons would be dropped at Kiarivu to assist a further drive westward. Meanwhile the 2/5th and 2/6th would clear the enemy from the area west of Kaboibus. Finally the New Guinea battalion would prevent the enemy from escaping southward towards the Sepik.

In July the New Guinea Battalion attacked and took a series of villages in the south and then concentrated about Gwalip where it secured a base for the 2/7th. The 2/5th took the Kaboibus villages on 2nd August. In response to these thrusts the Japanese concentrated all the *20th Division* and the *41st Division* against the 17th Brigade. On the Australian side the 2/6th was moved out for a rest at the end of July, after having been in contact with the enemy for five months.

The 2/7th began its wide outflanking movement on 6th August preceded by a New Guinea company. After three days of hard marching it secured Kiarivu on 8th August and in the next few days guns were dropped there and light aircraft landed.

When fighting ceased it was found that the 17th Brigade faced a far stronger force than it had believed: 1,700 of the *20th Division*, and 1,150 of the *41st*; while 2,230 of other units were nearby to the south-east.

Meanwhile the main body of the 6th Division had been heavily engaged in the mountains south of Wewak. On 28th May Stevens had issued orders to the 19th Brigade for the capture of Mount Tazaki and Mount Shiburangu where the enemy held a series of positions dominating the routes through the mountains.

Along each line of advance the Japanese had deployed the equivalent of a battalion. An Australian battalion was sent against each: the 2/4th against Tazaki and 2/8th against Shiburangu. The 16th Brigade needed further rest, but the 8th Brigade less one battalion had been ordered to Wewak from the Alexishafen area where it had long been patrolling the country east of the Sepik. It was to help defend the base while the 19th advanced southwards.

The country round Tazaki and Shiburangu was far too rugged for tanks. The enemy held a series of strong positions on razor-back ridges, but the attackers had the immense advantage of air and artillery support. The 2/8th Battalion fought its way forward and by 16th June was close to Shiburangu itself. A series of subsidiary positions were taken and the assault on the main position opened on 27th June. Beauforts dropped bombs which almost cleared the forward slopes of trees, and the artillery fired 3,000 shells. The 2/8th attacked with great dash and took the position with small loss. There were twenty bunkers on the hill manned by sixty or seventy men of whom forty-four were killed.

Meanwhile the 2/4th had pressed on towards Tazaki in a series of platoon and company actions and by mid-June were close to the objective. The final assault was launched on 22nd June. Part of Tazaki was secured that day, and the southern crest on the 24th. The 2/8th now found that the highest ground round Shiburangu was not the position they had taken but was an eminence 1,000 yards farther south—'The Blot', 1,650 feet above sea level.

On 5th July the two battalions linked. On the 7th the 30th Battalion (8th

Australian War Memorial

Beauforts bombing beach positions in the Wewak area, early in 1945. During the period September 1944 to May 1945 Beauforts and Boomerangs of No. 71 Wing flew hundreds of sorties each month in the Aitape-Wewak area, many of which were in direct support of the ground operations of the 6th Division.

Brigade) took over and the weary 2/4th returned to the beach. On 13th July Brigadier Martin ordered the 2/8th Battalion to take The Blot. A company attacked on the 14th supported by a bombardment in which 3,500 rounds were fired. The men advanced swiftly through broken defences and fallen trees to the summit whence they saw the surviving Japanese making off to the south. By the 21st the 2/8th had exploited to the Hambrauri villages; between Shiburangu and Hambrauri it killed 146 and took eight prisoners.

The battalions of the 16th, 17th and 19th Brigades were now weary and depleted. Most of them had only about half their quota of riflemen; in some fewer than half the rifle platoons were commanded by officers. Even in the coastal areas the infantry had to do much patrolling and to keep on the alert, because the dogged Japanese persistently made raids down to the coastal plain, often in search of food.

Late in July Stevens decided that the 16th Brigade would relieve the 19th, which, after a spell, would relieve the 17th. The 16th began to replace the 19th on 25th July. The 2/2nd Battalion was given the task of taking positions south of Hambrauri in which the Japanese were defending Numoikum and their escape route through Rindogim. After a series of sharp fights they took Rindogim and were approaching Numoikum when news came that a cease fire was imminent.

About 13,500 survivors of the *XVIII Army* were alive at the end. There had been from 35,000 to 40,000 in October 1944; in the following ten months about 9,000 had been killed and 12,000 to 14,000 had died of illness.

Here ends the long and painful story of the Japanese armies in Australian New Guinea where, in three years and a half, about 100,000 Japanese soldiers died. After the war it was estimated that about 300,000 Japanese, including some 20,000 civilian workers, were landed in New Guinea and the Solomons from January 1942 onwards. Only 127,000 were alive in August 1945. Of the remainder perhaps 60,000 were killed in battle and 110,000 died of illness, many of these victims of the Japanese Army's neglect of medical care and the rudimentary nature of its staff work. These defects seem to have been an outcome of the Japanese military ethos with its scant respect for human life and its small regard for the multitude of lowly activities that are demanded of an effective military staff.

While the New Guinea offensives of 1945 were in progress the necessity for them was persistently questioned in Parliament and in the newspapers. Should not the American policy of allowing the bypassed Japanese to 'wither on the vine' have been continued? Many of the officers and men were convinced that the arduous and perilous operations they were employed upon in jungle and swamp and in forest-clad ranges against an enemy willing to die in the last ditch were not necessary. The criticism of the aggressive policy for which Blamey was responsible was accompanied by censure, often harshly expressed, of Blamey's character, his treatment of some of his senior subordinates, his public statements and so on. Seldom had a nation's senior military commander been subjected to such angry fault-finding. It is true that Blamey side-tracked some generals in whom he lacked full confidence, and that he answered some critics in terms as cutting as their own. But the main charge against him was that he had initiated needless and wasteful offensives against a strategically impotent enemy.

In the course of an explanation sought by the War Cabinet in May 1945 Blamey said that his policy had been to destroy the enemy where this could be done with relatively light casualties, and thus free Australian territory, liberate the native people, and reduce the army's commitments; but where the enemy could not be destroyed at low cost his policy was to contain him in a restricted area by the use of a much smaller force than his own. He considered that the American policy of leaving bypassed Japanese armies to wither on the vine had proved unsuccessful, since those forces were still strong and well-organised, and were living off the country; and though MacArthur had described the bypassed Japanese forces as 'strategically impotent' they had in fact tied up two American corps including six divisions and an infantry regiment, even though most of the patrolling beyond the perimeters was done by Australians and Fijians. He pointed out also that when the American armies reached the Philippines they sought the complete destruction of the Japanese forces—a change of policy evidently based on political rather than military grounds.

Blamey said that on Bougainville, lacking the naval forces necessary for a major offensive, he decided to systematically drive the enemy from their garden areas and eventually bring about their destruction. In New Britain, on the other hand, where the enemy was far stronger, he decided to drive them back into the Gazelle Peninsula and contain them there. In the Aitape area where the enemy had some 24,000 to 27,000 troops, fewer than half as many as on New Britain [actually only about a quarter as many] he decided to follow a somewhat similar policy to that on Bougainville. He hoped, he said, by the end of 1945 to be able to reduce the force in the Aitape-Wewak area and the force on Bougainville each to one brigade group; on New Britain, however, a division of two brigades would be needed. At length he planned to achieve the final destruction of the Japanese forces on Bougainville and in New Guinea chiefly with battalions of New Guinea natives and small guerilla groups.

When Blamey's explanations were placed before the Advisory War Council his policy was criticised by some members, but eventually both the War Cabinet and the Council approved his general policy: 'to destroy the enemy where it could be done with light casualties, but, where conditions were not favourable to the destruction of the enemy, to contain him in a restricted area by the use of a much smaller force'.

The wisdom of undertaking offensives on Bougainville and the New Guinea mainland in 1945 will probably always remain a subject of debate. On Blamey's side it can justly be claimed that in the Wewak area, after August 1945, the Australian garrison could have been reduced to perhaps one brigade, and native battalions with native partisans could have set about the grisly task of gradually destroying the remaining Japanese troops. On Bougainville, however, where the strength of the Japanese had been so greatly underestimated, it seems unlikely that the Japanese bases, north and south, could have been reduced without perhaps a year of hard fighting by II Corps, and then only if that corps had the support of far more aircraft, armour, landing craft and naval bombardment forces than hitherto.

Blamey argued also that to have committed the troops to a passive role would have destroyed their morale, and pointed out that so long as they remained in the islands they were subject to tropical diseases. So far as morale went, however, in New Britain and the central sector on Bougainville, where the forward troops spent a long period on the defensive but carried out systematic and constant patrolling, there seems to have been no decline in morale, although, inevitably, there was some sickness. Blamey contended also that it was desirable to liberate the natives. The number of natives who were rescued was greatly increased as a result of the recapture of wide areas. On the other hand many of these were recovered by expeditions behind the enemy's lines, and there were places where the advance brought death and destruction to natives as well as succour.

The operations in Bougainville and from Aitape cost 958 Australians killed in battle—grievous losses, including many fine soldiers then in their sixth year of service in the infantry. The losses suffered if a 'New Britain policy' had been adopted in the other areas would however not have been negligible.

In the bypassed southern Philippines the Americans, as Blamey pointed out, made it their aim to destroy the Japanese forces completely. These operations cost 454 killed in the Eighth Army which took over after the assault phase had been carried out by the Sixth Army, but appear never to have been subjected to criticism on the ground that they were unnecessary. Here as in the Australian territories the casualties were very few compared with those the American navy and armies farther north suffered in this period: in the Okinawa campaign alone 12,520 Americans were killed.

Whatever view is taken of the wisdom of the Commander-in-Chief's decisions and the Government's and the Opposition's approval of them, there can be no difference of opinion about the devotion of both the Australian and the Japanese soldiers who fought it out in these bitter campaigns.

Chapter 15 **Borneo regained**

On 8th May, eight days after the opening of the first of the series of Australian offensives in Borneo, the fighting ended in Europe. For the three major Allies (and for Canada and New Zealand) this meant a vast reduction of effort, but for Australia the fact that her 16,000 air force men in Europe and Africa now ceased fighting was offset by the knowledge that her commitments in the Pacific, already weighty, were due to increase in June and July, when her land forces would be more heavily engaged than at any time in the previous six years of war.[1]

Thus, after the cease fire in the west, Blamey wrote from New Guinea to the Minister for the Army, Forde, pointing out that the forces required by the Allies would now be on a much lower scale, and recommending that the 7th Division be not committed to the coming operation against Balikpapan. The Acting Prime Minister, Chifley, passed this proposal on to MacArthur, who stated that the withdrawal of the 7th Division would 'disorganise completely not only the immediate campaign but also the strategic plan of the Joint Chiefs of Staff'. The Australian Government accepted MacArthur's views; though it is difficult to see what important disarrangement of plans could have resulted from the abandonment of an attack on an isolated Japanese position on the east coast of Borneo. Meanwhile the landing on Tarakan had taken place.

The reasons for attacking Tarakan were to enable the establishment there of air and naval units to support the future operations of the I Australian Corps, to re-establish the Netherlands Indies government, and to conserve the oil installations. It was hoped that one wing of fighter aircraft would be established six days after the landing, a wing of attack aircraft nine days later, and staging facilities for four more squadrons by the twenty-first day after the landing. Air Commodore Cobby chose No. 78 (Fighter) Wing and No. 77 (Attack) Wing to garrison Tarakan. The systematic bombing of airfields in Borneo, Celebes and Java began twenty days before the day fixed for the landing—1st May—and air attacks on Tarakan and near-by targets in Borneo on 12th April.

The Allied Air Forces encountered only negligible opposition from Japanese aircraft as they pounded Tarakan itself and airfields as far away as Surabaya. All oil tanks on Tarakan were destroyed so that their contents could not be set on fire and used to hamper the landing.

Brigadier Whitehead's 26th Brigade Group, as reinforced for the Tarakan operations, was nearer to the strength of a division than a brigade. It included, in addition to the usual units, two pioneer battalions, a commando squadron, a squadron of tanks, and an anti-aircraft regiment and had a total strength of

[1] Of the 16,000 air force men some 12,300 were aircrew. In the Pacific-India area were 14,500 aircrew and 123,500 ground staff and others.

Australian War Memorial

Left: Tarakan Island. *Right:* Morotai, 1945. The fighter strip at Morotai, showing four Kittyhawks returning from an offensive sweep and many others parked closely together in the dispersal areas.

nearly 12,000. On the eve of the attack Allied Intelligence learned that one Japanese battalion had been transferred from Tarakan to Balikpapan, and it was then estimated that from 1,500 to 2,000 troops remained on the island. (The actual total proved to be about 2,100.) This was a small force against which to deploy five battalions, but experience had shown how difficult it was to overcome resolute Japanese troops in the kind of tangled hills that dominated Tarakan.

The initial task was to capture a covering position within which a beach maintenance area could be established, and to seize enough ground to enable the repair of the airfield to be carried out. The work on the airfield was to be done by Nos. 1 and 8 Airfield Construction Squadrons. Naval support was given by a force including H.M.A.S's *Hobart, Warramunga, Burdekin, Barcoo, Hawkesbury* and *Lachlan,* and the force was transported in fifty-six vessels and craft including the Australian L.S.I's *Manoora* and *Westralia.*

The day before the main landing the 2/4th Commando Squadron and a battery of the 2/7th Field Regiment were landed on Sadau Island so that their guns could protect the engineers, who from 11 a.m. onwards were to make gaps in the parallel rows of posts, iron pipes and rails extending 125 yards into the sea along the whole length of Lingkas beach. After a heavy naval and air bombardment, eight detachments each of six engineers went forward in amphibious tractors and, under fire, blew gaps in the obstacle, using 780 explosive charges in all.

Next morning, after another naval and air bombardment, the leading infantry—the 2/23rd Battalion on the right and the 2/48th on the left—landed on the beach, which until a few minutes before had been 'aflame from the crimson flashes of bursting bombs and shells', as one observer put it. There was no opposition on the beach.

The 2/23rd (Lieut-Colonel F. A. G. Tucker) did not come under heavy fire until it was approaching Lingkas Hill. The battalion pressed on and by nightfall was on the Glenelg Highway. The 2/48th on the left took Finch and then Collins Highway ridge and was astride Anzac Highway, having lost eleven killed and wounded in the day. By nightfall the Australians held an area 2,800 yards wide at the base and up to 2,000 yards in depth. (In the Australian maps every one of the many hills in the area had been given a name so as to simplify and speed up signals.) Whitehead's orders for the 2nd were that the 2/48th should take Lyons and the 2/24th, coming in on the left, Sturt and Wills. All three features overlooked the built-up area from the north.

Meanwhile strenuous efforts to establish a base on the beach had been hampered: the falling tide exposed a stretch of soft black mud 500 yards wide, and there were deep drains and soft clay pitted with water-filled craters farther inland. The water table was found to be only twelve to eighteen inches below the surface of the narrow coastal strip. Unloading proved so difficult

Tarakan, 1st-5th May

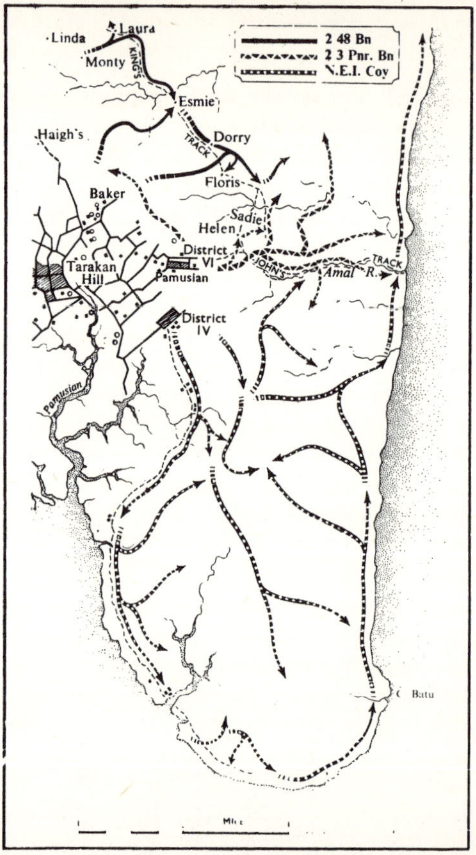

Tarakan, 6th-16th May 1945

Below: 'H.M.A.S. Margy' bombarding the Joyce feature during operations on Tarakan Island, off the east coast of Borneo, on 10th June 1945.

Australian War Memorial

that no field guns were in action until 2.50 p.m., hours later than was intended. In the first twenty-four hours, however, 1,562 tons of stores were put ashore, and by 8 a.m. on the 3rd the total was 2,640 tons.

On 2nd May the 2/23rd took Milko and thrust inland beyond Lingkas Hill, and the 2/48th secured Lyons. On the left the 2/24th (Lieut-Colonel Warfe) had the initial task of taking Sturt and Wills. After an artillery bombardment these were taken by the two leading companies but not before some resolutely-held bunkers had been destroyed with flame-throwers. Warfe now sent his remaining companies toward the airfield and by dusk they were on Essex. One company with a troop of tanks advanced on the airstrip next morning; by 6.45 a.m. they had passed through the forward troops on the left but were soon halted by heavy fire. Warfe now sent in two more companies but the opposition was very strong. It was considered imperative that the airfield be secured that day, and at 4.38 p.m. a company made a dashing attack under heavy cross-fire and through the explosion of two big Japanese mines. At the end of the day the forward troops were in the shelter of the aircraft bays. Next morning the 2/4th Commando Squadron made an attack on Tarakan Hill. This led to a fierce fight in which the commandos suffered severe losses but by nightfall they held most of the hill. On the 5th the Australian flag was hoisted on the airfield. The brigade had completed its main task but the Japanese still held a line of strongposts overlooking the town and airfield.

Information from prisoners and captured documents indicated that about 1,700 Japanese were manning a series of positions through Cape Juata, the Amal River area, Otway, Fukukaku—a central stronghold—and Mount Api. It seemed that the enemy's aim would now be to delay the attackers with mines, booby traps and suicide raids and by fighting to the death from deeply-dug positions.

Meanwhile the infantry had bypassed Japanese pockets, from one of which they could bring down small-arms fire on part of the Anzac Highway. There was a need for more space for the Indonesian refugees, 7,000 of whom were now under the care of the Dutch officials who landed with the attacking force. Whitehead decided to capture the high ground along Snags Track from Mount Api to Janet (1,200 yards north-west of Susie), the high ground overlooking the town, and Districts IV and VI. The 2/23rd, with tanks, seized part of Snags Track and on the 9th was relieved by the 2/24th Battalion. In the centre the 2/48th occupied Otway. The 2/3rd Pioneers, less two companies, were given the task of advancing along the Amal River. Just east of Pamusian on 7th May they came under heavy fire and were held up, but on the 8th and 9th forced the enemy back to Helen, which was found to be an important enemy stronghold.

The forward companies of the Pioneers, who had been in action on three successive days, were now relieved by the two other companies and the attack on Helen was continued. Here on the 12th Corporal J. B. Mackey commanding the leading section overcame the Japanese in one machine-gun post in a hand-to-hand struggle, charged another post and killed the crew by throwing a grenade through the firing slit, and then, armed with an Owen, charged a third post, which he silenced. At the edge of this post he fell, mortally wounded.[2] The fight went on until half the attacking company had been

2 Mackey was awarded the Victoria Cross posthumously.

killed or wounded, but the Japanese stood firm. Next day the Pioneers withdrew and aircraft, naval and field guns bombarded the feature, but the Japanese halted the infantry when they attacked. On the 14th aircraft bombed and then dropped napalm on both the Helen and Sadie features. This drove the Japanese from Helen and the track along the Amal River and thereafter was the kind of air support that was always asked for. On the 16th the 2/3rd Pioneers reached the coast.

In all the thickly timbered country increasing use was made of air support. The 2/24th was meeting strong resistance from Hill 105. Flame-throwers were used extensively here and the Japanese were systematically forced out of one position after another. In general, however, the task of the brigade was proving difficult and costly. By the 16th it had lost 523 killed and wounded and 252 were sick. The Japanese dead who had been counted numbered 479 but the survivors, estimated at 1,600 including probably 400 sick and wounded, were showing no tendency to surrender. It seemed likely that the Japanese were determined to make a last stand in their headquarters area round Fukukaku. On 18th May the remaining Japanese positions on Hill 105 were occupied by the 2/24th, after the hill had been blasted by bombardment.

The infantry, supported by aircraft and artillery, continued to press in upon the enemy's stronghold in the tangled country round Fukukaku, but the Japanese fought doggedly from every hill. Even after very heavy bombardment they would quickly emerge from their shelters and make the capture of their defence systems impossible except at too great cost. Japanese holding the Freda feature (1,000 yards north of Susie), for example, were rained with 500 mortar bombs on 21st May but remained unsubdued. On 22nd May, after a bombardment, two companies attacked behind a moving barrage. Fierce fighting followed in the course of which Lieutenant Derrick, V.C., D.C.M., a famous young infantry leader, was mortally wounded.

Whitehead now decided that his force was in a position to assault the stronghold, but emphasised to his commanding officers that no attack was to be made without maximum bombardment beforehand. His general policy would be to attack each position with eighteen Liberators carrying 500-lb or 1,000-lb bombs and then with Lightnings carrying napalm.

On 25th May the knolls still held by the Japanese on the Freda feature were given a devastating bombardment by twenty-four aircraft, and guns and mortars; then a company of the 2/48th followed the barrage in and took the knolls, round which sixty-seven Japanese were buried including twenty-one killed that day.

In the last ten days of May the enemy continued to fight back resolutely but were blasted on one feature after another by aircraft and artillery until the infantry were able to capture the positions with few casualties. For instance, Margy (1,500 yards north-west of Susie) where the Japanese had resisted two attacks, was finally hit by forty-eight aircraft and then taken by two platoons. Hill 102, another strongly held position which could be approached only along a razor-back three feet wide, was taken after air bombardment and after three flame-throwers had scorched the place. Guns, including a 3.7-inch anti-aircraft gun, were now being used only a few hundred yards from their targets.

A letter dropped to the Japanese naval and army commanders on 4th June suggesting a parley with the object of enabling the Australians to care for the

Japanese wounded was ignored. A half-hearted counter-attack was made by the Japanese on 10th June. For the next three days they continued to resist strongly. But on the morning of the 14th patrols found that the enemy had made a big withdrawal, though they were still holding firmly on the Essie track (about three miles east of the Juata oilfields) which was evidently their escape route. That day 112 Chinese and Indonesian labourers arrived from the enemy-held area bearing a note from the Japanese commander asking that they be treated well.

The pursuit of the retreating Japanese now began. It was estimated that about 1,000 were still at large (actually there were probably 1,300) and it was soon learnt that on 13th June their commander had given orders that the force should split into a number of independent groups each allotted its own area within which each leader was to choose the ground on which he and his men would fight to the death.

Whitehead decided that the Japanese should be pursued swiftly before they had time to dig new positions, and in particular that the rearguard at the Essie feature should be attacked from all directions. On 14th and 15th June companies of the 2/24th took Essie ridge and then pressed swiftly on for more than 2,000 yards through very difficult country.

It was now evident that the Japanese groups were mainly heading north and east. By 19th June pursuing patrols were radiating east, north and west. By 24th June a total of 1,131 Japanese had been killed and fifty-eight taken prisoner. It was estimated that only about 250 armed men remained, but actually more than 700 were killed or captured up to 14th August. Some of these were intercepted by patrols in L.C.M's and prahus while trying to sail from Tarakan to the mainland.

In the whole operation the Australian force lost 225 killed and 669 wounded. The Japanese dead who were counted numbered 1,540; 252 surrendered before the cease-fire and more than 300 after it. The main object of the seizure of Tarakan had been to establish an air base from which to support the later operations in Borneo. The two airfield construction squadrons had gone ashore on the first day and they began work on the cratered and water-logged airfield on the 6th. Constant rain, the high water-table and lack of suitable paving materials made the construction of the airfield very difficult. Throughout the early phase of the Tarakan operation most of the First T.A.F's combat strength remained at Morotai, where it could do nothing to contribute to the operation's success. At an early stage Air Vice-Marshal Bostock ordered Beaufighters of No. 77 Wing and Kittyhawks of No. 76 Squadron to Sanga Sanga whence they gave cover over Tarakan. It was soon evident that the Tarakan strip would not be serviceable in time for the opening of the air operations against Brunei Bay and Balikpapan. The results achieved did not justify the cost of the Tarakan operation.

For many months an important role in the Indies had been played by Catalina squadrons of the R.A.A.F. These aircraft had a variety of tasks: anti-submarine patrols, delivering supplies to coastwatchers, night bombing and so on. From mid-1943 onwards much of their effort was spent on laying mines in Japanese ports and shipping lanes in the Indies—Macassar, Surabaya, Kendari, Kau Bay (Halmahera), Balikpapan and Palau were among the ports often visited in 1943 and 1944. Up to September 1944 25 ships were considered to have been sunk or damaged by aerial mines in the waters of the Indies, and in that month Bostock assigned Nos. 20, 42 and 43 Squadrons solely to mine-laying, and sent No. 76 Wing Headquarters to Darwin to control the three squadrons. In three weeks in September and October the Catalinas flew ninety-eight sorties and laid 196 mines round Java and elsewhere. Damage from anti-aircraft fire was fairly frequent but relatively few Catalinas were lost: to May 1944 five crews had been lost in 1,000 sorties. After the capture of Morotai the Catalinas flew there from Darwin, refuelled, and then attacked targets hitherto beyond their range.

The main enemy of Japanese shipping, however, was the efficient American submarine force. Japanese merchant shipping losses in 1944 totalled nearly 4,000,000 tons most of which was sunk by American submarines, and by March 1945 only 1,800,000 tons of Japanese shipping remained, all but 150,000 tons being in the 'Inner Zone'. At this stage Catalinas were called upon to lay mines round Formosa, the Pescadores, Hainan, Hong Kong and Amoy, using a base on Luzon. They continued to attack these and other targets in that area until July 1945.

The next tasks of the Australians were to establish bases on the mainland of Borneo. By late in May 1945 the Japanese forces in north Borneo were believed to number about 650 on Labuan Island, 1,550 round Seria and Miri, and 6,600 round Jesselton, where the headquarters of the *XXXVII Army* were established. The total strength of the army forces in all Borneo was believed to be about 31,000.

The planning of the Brunei Bay operation was greatly hampered by shortage of shipping and consequent late arrival of units and equipment, and by changes in the dates for opening both the coming operations. Finally the Brunei Bay date was fixed at 10th June. The attacking force under Major-General Wootten included the 9th Division less one brigade, and corps, base and R.A.A.F. troops, the whole numbering nearly 30,000 men. The naval force that was to transport and support the expedition was commanded by Vice-Admiral Barbey: a naval force of three cruisers including H.M.A.S. *Hobart*, and twenty-three destroyers including H.M.A.S. *Arunta*, plus the frigates *Hawkesbury*, *Barcoo* and *Lachlan*, twelve motor torpedo boats, the L.S.I's *Westralia*, *Manoora* and *Kanimbla*, thirty-four L.S.T's and many other troop-carrying craft.

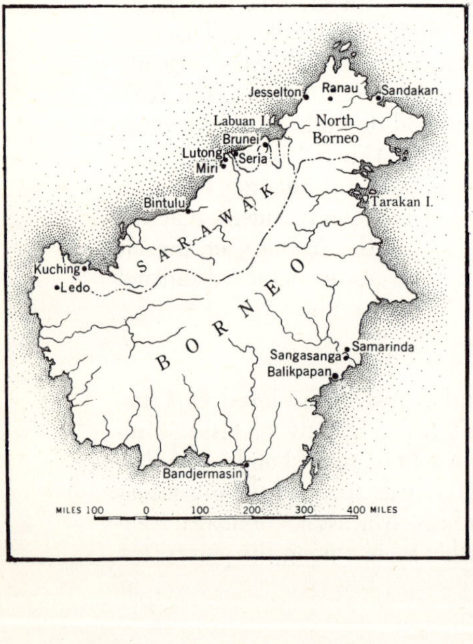

Air support was controlled by Bostock and was provided by First T.A.F. and the Thirteenth Air Force, with the Fifth Air Force lending two groups of bombers for the pre-assault bombardment. In addition the heavy-bomber squadrons of North-Western Area and Western Area had the task of neutralising enemy bases that were beyond the range of bombers based in the

Australian War Memorial

A group of Australian Spitfire pilots at Morotai in 1945 after operations in the Halmaheras. Group Captain C. R. Caldwell, Officer Commanding No. 80 Wing R.A.A.F., is fourth from left.

Philippines and at Morotai. The First T.A.F. was to establish on Labuan as soon as possible No. 81 (Fighter) Wing, a Spitfire squadron, No. 83 (Army Co-operation) Wing, No. 86 (Attack) Wing. The pre-assault air bombardment began early in May. It was not easy to find enough profitable targets for the big air force now available and it was later found that not a little of the bombing had caused far more distress to the people of Borneo than to the Japanese. In the five days before the landing 3,088 sorties were flown.

The assault troops carried out elaborate rehearsals at Morotai and then embarked for the uncomfortable 1,100-mile voyage in crowded L.S.T's and L.C.I's to Brunei Bay.

A novel feature of the naval fire program for the landing was that the ships instead of bombarding only the jungle fringing the beaches, from which the enemy had usually withdrawn, provided a moving barrage. *Hobart*, for example, fired more than 1,000 rounds of 6-inch and 4-inch. On the southern flank the 20th Brigade (Brigadier Windeyer) planned to put the 2/17th Battalion ashore on Green Beach to secure a beach-head on Brunei Bluff and the 2/15th on White Beach on Muara Island. In the second phase the brigade was to take Brooketon and the southern and western side of Muara Island, thus opening Yellow Beach and the approach to Muara harbour, and was to exploit towards Brunei. In the third phase the infantry would take Brunei town.

There was no opposition to the landings on these southern beaches on 10th June. By dusk the 2/15th had found that Muara Island was unoccupied; on the mainland the 2/17th encountered only a few Japanese, and by the end of the day were a few miles along the road to Brunei. By this time the 2/13th Battalion had landed and moved into reserve behind the 2/17th.

Next day the 2/17th again saw few Japanese, and on the 12th it marched on to the airstrip after a short fight. On the 13th, after an air strike, it entered Brunei town with little opposition. Meanwhile Windeyer had ordered the 2/15th to send a company in landing craft up the Brunei River. He now ordered that the main body of the 2/15th should pass through the 2/17th and advance to Tutong (thirty-five miles down the coast from Brooketon), and that its detached company should cross the river and block the Limbang road.

The plan of Brigadier Porter of the 24th Brigade was to land initially on Brown Beach at the southern end of Labuan Island and secure the port and airstrip as soon as possible. As expected, there was no opposition on the beaches when the 2/43rd and 2/28th Battalions landed, but in the afternoon strong fire was met. The 2/43rd on the right moved fast, giving the enemy no time to recover from the bombardment, and by the end of the day held the airfield, having lost only four men wounded during the day.

The 2/28th on the left quickly secured the town and met no opposition for

Australian War Memorial

North Borneo. Fires caused by rocket-firing Beaufighters at Brunei in June 1945. This photograph was taken by a member of the crew of an R.A.A.F. Liberator; another Liberator can be seen in the centre foreground.

Brunei Bay area

an hour and a half; then it came under fire near Flagstaff Hill. Thereafter resistance became stronger and a long fight took place at a canal at the junction of Callaghan and MacArthur Roads. It ended when two tanks were sent forward to support the infantry, who then drove the Japanese from the slopes overlooking the canal.

On the 11th and 12th the infantry pressed on and it became evident that the surviving Japanese had all been withdrawn into a stronghold about 1,200 yards by 600 where they were well dug in among a tangle of ridges covered with trees and dense undergrowth all round and fringed by swamps on the west and south. It seemed certain that the Japanese were resolved to make a last stand in 'The Pocket' as the position was now named.

Meanwhile Wootten had ordered the 2/32nd Battalion, part of his reserve, to seize Weston on the mainland east of Labuan and reconnoitre across country and by river towards Beaufort, which was eventually to be captured

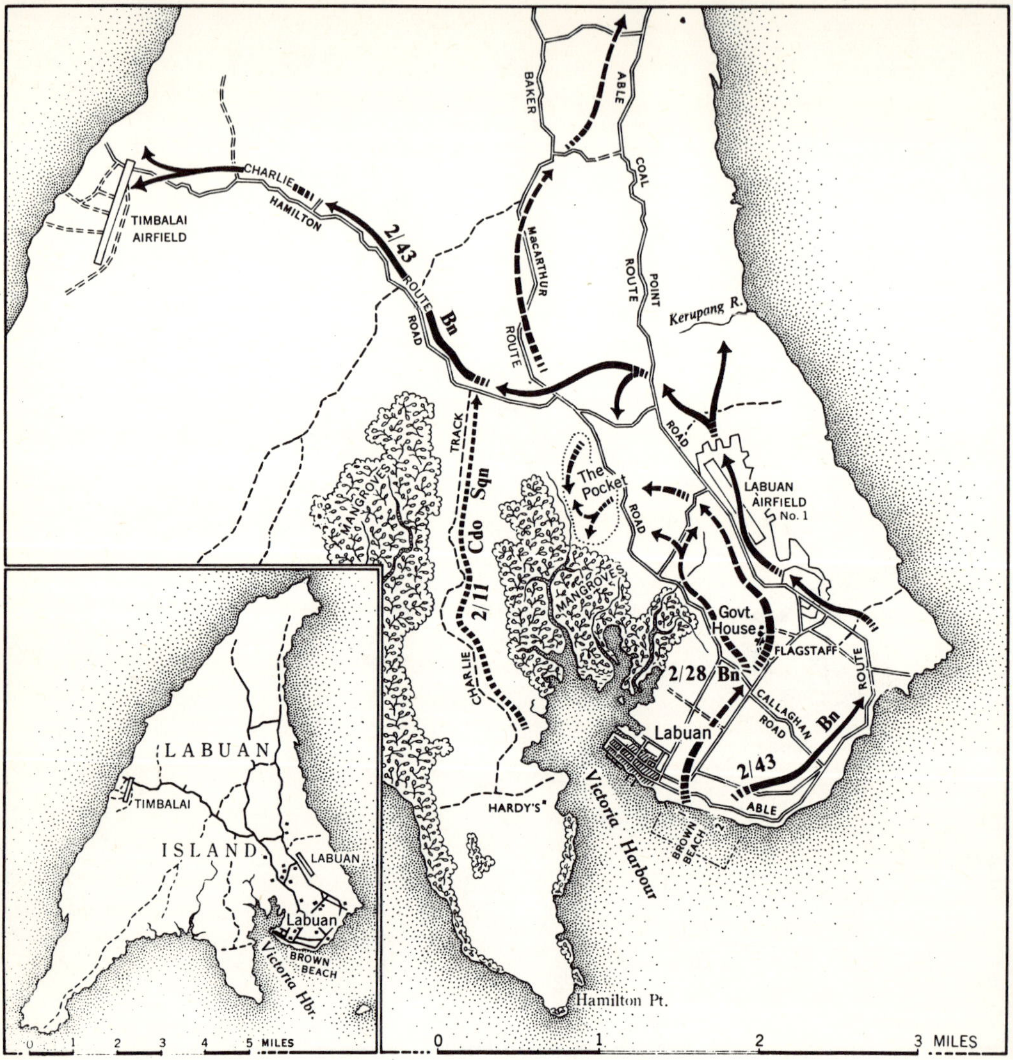

Labuan Island

by the 24th Brigade, thus confirming the division's grip on Brunei Bay. Weston was occupied without opposition on the 16th and a company began to advance along the one-metre-gauge railway leading to Beaufort.

The reduction of The Pocket necessitated a full-scale attack by infantry and tanks with heavy artillery support. In the five days and nights from 15th June onwards the 2/12th Field Regiment fired 140 tons of shells into it. On the 15th after hard fighting in which two tanks were hit and damaged, some positions were taken but the Japanese were resisting resolutely and it was decided to bombard The Pocket more thoroughly before continuing the assault. On the 18th the cruiser *Shropshire* joined in with her 8-inch guns, and on the 20th bombers blasted the Japanese positions.

Before dawn on the 21st, the day fixed for a renewal of the attack, about fifty Japanese from The Pocket raided Australian positions in and round the town of Labuan. The guards were alert, however, and almost all the raiders were killed whereas the Allies (an American boat detachment was also involved) lost only about five men.

The planned attack on The Pocket, by two companies supported by tanks including some armed with flame-throwers, was deadly, and soon bulldozers were burying about 180 Japanese. At this stage 400 Japanese had been killed or captured on Labuan and the 24th Brigade had lost thirty-four killed.

Wootten had now decided to gain control of the high country from Mempakul to Cape Nosong to prevent the enemy using the tracks north of the Klias River and to secure beaches for use as supply points during an advance northwards.

Meanwhile, after a few clashes, the 2/32nd had reached Lingkungan. However, Porter decided that it would be wiser to approach Beaufort by way of the Padas and Klias Rivers rather than along the railway, which presented a series of defiles with hills on one side and swamps on the other. Thus the 2/43rd and the 2/11th Commando Squadron secured most of the Klias Peninsula and patrolled along the Klias River, and part of the 2/32nd patrolled up the Padas in L.C.M's each carrying a platoon. On 21st June, about ten miles from Beaufort two platoons of the 2/43rd landed from L.C.M's firing from the hip and drove a party of Japanese from a house they were occupying. It appeared that there were from 800 to 1,000 Japanese round Beaufort; but they were without artillery, whereas Porter not only had a strong air force on call but had brought 14 guns of the 2/12th Field Regiment up the Padas in barges.

On the 26th two companies of the 2/32nd advanced along the railway and two along the Padas, while the 2/43rd moved on Beaufort north of the river. Next day the 2/43rd opened the decisive attack on the Japanese defending Beaufort. That night one company secured the town, and another, after a gruelling march over the hills, dug in at the junction of tracks along which the Japanese were likely to withdraw from the town. The Japanese counter-attacked the Australians in Beaufort and soon isolated them. Next morning (28th June) the company at the track junction left one platoon there and thrust towards Beaufort along a track strongly held by Japanese. A series of enemy posts along this track were overcome by a redoubtable soldier, Private L. T. Starcevich.[3] These troops did not manage to reach Beaufort that day. At night, after being bombarded, the Japanese began to withdraw along the track where the Australians were awaiting them. By the morning of the 29th the fight was virtually over and more than 100 Japanese had been killed along the track.

Porter now decided to pinpoint the Japanese in the hills east of Beaufort by constant patrolling, to bring down heavy fire on any position and follow up fast. As a result of these tactics the Japanese were pushed farther into the hills. The problem of supplying the brigade was eased when first a train drawn by a jeep and later one drawn by a steam engine began to use the Weston-Beaufort railway. On 12th July the 2/32nd Battalion occupied Papar, some troops having advanced along the railway line and some along the coast in barges.

Meanwhile the 20th Brigade too had attained its objectives. On 13th June Wootten ordered that the 2/13th Battalion should land in the Miri-Lutong

[3] He was awarded the Victoria Cross.

Australian War Memorial

North Borneo, June 1945. Australian signallers make contact with forward infantry on the Weston-Beaufort railway.

area, seventy miles to the south-west of Brunei, while the 2/17th advanced overland towards the same objective. Without meeting opposition a company of the 2/17th entered Tutong on 16th June and on the 21st the battalion, less two companies, was at Seria, its vehicles having moved from Tutong along the hard sand of the beach. As the troops neared Seria they could see a great blanket of smoke over the big oilfield there, and when they arrived they found that the Japanese had smashed the head of the thirty-seven wells and set them ablaze. A platoon of engineers promptly set to work extinguishing these fires.

On 20th June the 2/13th Battalion with attached troops had been landed near Lutong in amphibious tractors. There was practically no opposition, and natives reported that from 400 to 500 troops had abandoned Miri and Lutong some days before and were now deployed astride the road leading south. At this stage groups of emaciated Indian prisoners of war began to reach the lines of the 2/13th and 2/17th and the Australians found evidence that the Japanese had slaughtered other Indian prisoners.

The enemy's positions south of Miri were now being shelled from sea and land and strafed by fighters, and on 27th June a patrol made contact with the forward Japanese position. Patrol clashes at points along the road continued for the next few weeks. Elsewhere the enemy forces withdrew inland. The 2/17th and 2/15th Battalions, aided by Dyaks, who despised the Japanese and were treated with great respect by them, sent out deep patrols along the tracks and up the rivers and there were several sharp fights. It was not part of the plan, however, to pursue the retreating Japanese into the interior. Having secured the coast and the immediate hinterland from Miri in the south to Papar in the north Wootten had attained his objectives. Such patrolling as was undertaken was exploratory and aimed at ensuring that the surviving Japanese forces remained ineffective.

It was now known that there were six Japanese battalions in the Brunei Bay area when the offensive opened, one round Beaufort, one on Labuan, two round Brunei and two round Miri. These units had been greatly depleted, during an exhaustive march from the Sandakan area, but even so the Japanese infantry in the 20th Brigade area probably outnumbered the Australian infantry throughout the operations.

From the outset the 9th Division was busy with the task of caring for the civilians and re-establishing British government. To assist it in this task it had the British Borneo Civil Affairs Unit, staffed partly by Australians and partly by British officers, some of the British having served in Borneo before the war. In no other campaign had an Australian force faced such a heavy task of this kind. On Labuan, for example, the bombardment had destroyed practically every building and soon some 3,000 civilians had to be fed and otherwise cared for. Before long a large part of the resources of the division was being employed on relief and reconstruction. In a period of seventeen days 7,500 civilian patients were treated at Brooketon and Brunei. One field ambulance established six hospitals for natives, with average daily totals of 125 in-patients and 970 out-patients. By the beginning of September in the 24th Brigade's area civilians were consuming more army rations than the troops. The engineers, with the help of thousands of natives, repaired roads, bridges, buildings and drains.

In the operations in North Borneo 114 Australian soldiers were killed or died of wounds; 1,234 Japanese dead were seen and counted and 130 were taken prisoner.

The Australian Army's next task was to secure Balikpapan with its port and oilfields, a task which at this stage seemed even less necessary than it had in May when Blamey had proposed its abandonment. Balikpapan's only strategic value would be as a base from which to launch an expedition against Java, which was a purely political objective since it would not matter militarily whether that outlying part of Japan's crumbling empire was lost or held. It would take some months at least for Australia to prepare an invasion force, which would have to be drawn from I Corps. Meanwhile the cities of Japan were being systematically destroyed by air bombardment, the agreed time of the Soviet Union's entry into the war against Japan was approaching, and it seemed certain that Japan would soon surrender.

Balikpapan, built round the eastern headland of Balikpapan Bay, had a port with seven piers, a big oil refinery, and many warehouses. The hills rose steeply from the narrow coastal plain on which lay the two airfields, one at Sepinggang five miles east of the town, and the other at Manggar five miles farther on. The country was open for several miles round Balikpapan, but farther inland forest and jungle clothed the hills.

In June it was estimated that there were about 3,900 troops plus 1,100 Japanese and Formosan workers at Balikpapan, about 1,500 troops round

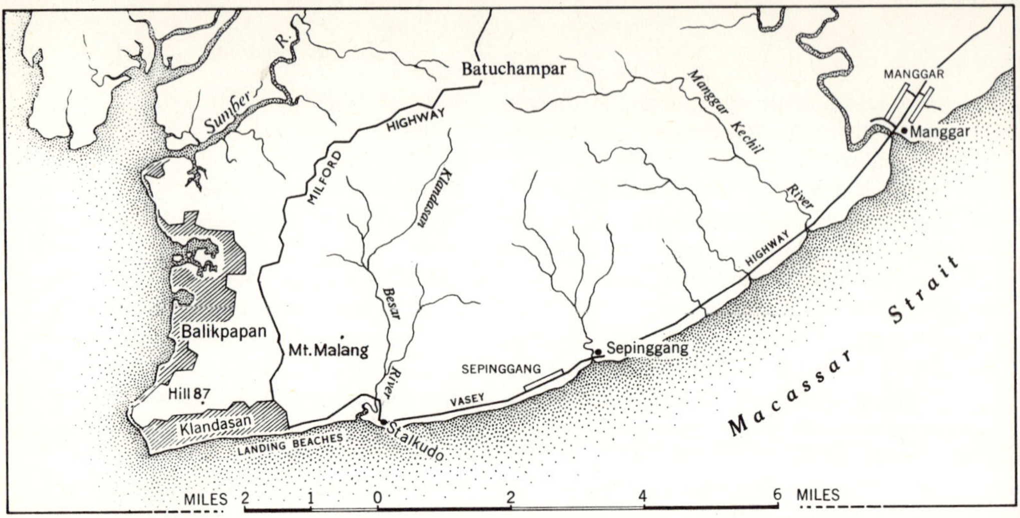

Balikpapan area

Samarinda, and at least 112 heavy, medium and light guns round Balikpapan. Offshore from Klandasan to Manggar were heavy timber obstacles, and ashore there were many concrete strongposts and bunkers.

General Milford of the 7th Australian Division decided to make the landing at Klandasan in the very heart of the enemy's defences rather than in a less strongly-held area whence he would have to fight his way to the objective. One reason was that the maximum fire support would be available on the first day. Milford thought that it would prove more economical in the long run to assault the key positions directly. The plan provided for the employment in the opening phase of 33,000 troops of whom 21,000 were of the 7th Division and the balance were base troops, R.A.A.F. and others.

So many mines had been laid off Balikpapan by both Allied and Japanese ships and aircraft that minesweeping was begun more than two weeks before the landing, and before the sweeping could be done it was necessary to subdue the powerful batteries of guns overlooking the sea.

The air attack on Balikpapan was commanded by Air Vice-Marshal Bostock, one of whose tasks was to establish at Balikpapan within six days of the landing a fighter wing and a flight of Catalinas, and, as soon as possible thereafter, a medium-bomber wing and a heavy-bomber wing.

Because the Tarakan airfield was not ready the air bombardment plan had to be recast at short notice. American Lightnings based on Sanga Sanga provided fighter cover, and the commander of the naval force was given three escort carriers armed with fighters. The Liberator bombers used against Balikpapan were based as far afield as Morotai, Samar and Palawan. In the second half of June Balikpapan was struck by up to 196 bombers a day. On the 28th the first aircraft were able to land at Tarakan and thereafter No. 78 Wing, with Kittyhawks and Spitfires, began flying from Tarakan in support of the Balikpapan operation.

In June Admiral Sir Louis Hamilton became Chief of the Naval Staff and on 22nd July Collins, recovered from his wounds, replaced Farncomb in command of the squadron, which was joined that month by the third Australian-built Tribal-class destroyer—*Bataan*.

The naval covering force, which had arrived off Balikpapan on 15th June when the sweeping of the outer minefields began, included four American cruisers and two Australian—*Shropshire* and *Hobart*—with thirteen destroyers including H.M.A.S. *Arunta.* In the next fifteen days the ships fired over 23,000 shells at targets ashore. From 26th June onwards underwater demolition teams made gaps in the shore obstacles; that day the convoy of more than 100 ships left Morotai and on the morning of the 1st July, under cover of naval and air bombardment, the assaulting troops were landed on a 2,000-yard stretch of beach, the 21st Brigade on the right and the 18th on the left. Pillars of smoke were rising 1,000 feet from the town and the refinery and now and then big bursts of flame would show where an oil tank had been directly hit.

The task of the 18th Brigade was to secure a beach-head about half a mile in depth and then advance north and north-west. Its main objective was 'Parramatta' ridge which dominated the entire landing beach area. A company of American L.V.T's disembarked the leading troops of the 18th Brigade, and thereafter carried forward heavy weapons and ammunition. The task of the 21st Brigade was first to secure a covering position 800 yards deep and then advance north and east to Sepinggang.

In the 21st Brigade's sector the leading battalion, the 2/27th, was soon on its first objectives, having met little resistance. The 2/16th met strong opposition but by the end of the day had secured Mount Malang and other features allotted to it, having lost only six men killed. The 2/14th, thrusting east, was dug in beyond Stalkudo ridge at nightfall; north-east of Stalkudo the 2/5th Commando Squadron came under heavy fire and also dug in.

In the 18th Brigade's sector the 2/12th Battalion on the right took its objective with the loss of three killed. The 2/10th had the vital task of taking the Parramatta feature. Lieut-Colonel T. J. Daly, who led this battalion, planned to secure high ground above the left of the landing beaches with his two leading companies, and then, with the other two companies, and tanks, to move through and take Hill 87 and Parramatta. Daly had been allotted the support of a cruiser's guns, a battery of field artillery and other heavy weapons, but by the time the first objectives had been taken and the thrust to Parramatta was ready to begin he had learnt that the naval fire and field guns were not yet available and the tanks were bogged near the beach. Nevertheless he decided to press on with what he had without giving the Japanese time to reorganise. One company, advancing boldly took Hill 87 despite heavy mortar and machine-gun fire. Nearly half the men in the leading platoon were killed or wounded. At this stage, about 11.40 a.m., tanks reached the forward area. Soon preparations for the assault on Parramatta itself were being made, six tanks were forward and the guns of the supporting field battery were in action. By 2.12 p.m. the infantry and tanks had secured the vital hill.

On the second day the 2/14th Battalion advanced swiftly to Sepinggang without opposition and the other forward units pressed on while, behind the front line, numbers of tunnels in which Japanese were sheltering were blown up. The enemy tried to infiltrate by night but by the end of the second day it seemed likely that the main objectives would soon be secured.

On 3rd July light aircraft began operating from Sepinggang airstrip and the port of Balikpapan was occupied. By that morning nearly 1,000 vehicles,

1,932 tons of equipment, and 17,000 men were ashore, and an L.S.T. was unloading from a pontoon jetty. The 25th Brigade had arrived on the 2nd and next day it was given the task of advancing inland astride the Milford Highway. It set off with the 2/33rd Battalion on the right and 2/31st on the left and soon met heavy opposition in the rugged hills.

On 4th July the 2/14th also met strong resistance. Two companies crossed the Manggar River and occupied the airfield without being fired on, but, when the command group of the battalion and a party of the 2/5th Field Regiment crossed, guns and mortars began a sustained bombardment and killed or wounded a number of officers and men. The battalion faced what was soon seen to be a heavily-armed stronghold commanding the airfield. Captured documents showed that when the landing took place one battalion was defending the Klandasan area, one was round Manggar and one astride the Milford Highway.

On the 5th the Japanese entrenched above the airfield were bombarded, but when three tanks were landed on the bank of the river the Japanese guns destroyed two and damaged the third. That night a 25-pounder was brought forward, and at dawn on the 6th it opened fire and soon silenced the Japanese guns. A small fighting patrol was now sent out to dispose of two powerful naval guns in the enemy stronghold. In the darkness they drove off some fifty Japanese and took both guns, using grenades, explosive charges and phosphorous smoke grenades. A company occupied the positions and defeated four strong counter-attacks during the remainder of the night. By the 9th Japanese resistance had been overcome. In this fortress 107 dead were counted and it was estimated that 150 were buried in underground shelters. The guns numbered fifteen ranging in calibre from 20-mm to 120-mm.

Numerically the Japanese defenders round Balikpapan had been far weaker than the 7th Division, but they had many heavy weapons, were strongly entrenched, and were as resolute as ever. The Australian commanders had reduced casualties in their own forces by lavish use of naval and field guns, and bombers. From the day of the landing onwards air bombardment had been intense; 31,000 shells and rockets were fired from the sea; and in the first ten days the 25-pounders fired 42,000 rounds.

Although the two Japanese battalions that had been in the coastal zone had now been virtually destroyed, the third battalion, dug in in the Batuchampar area on the Milford Highway, was stoutly resisting the 25th Brigade. On 4th July Brigadier Eather had instructed his battalion commanders 'to move forward slowly making utmost use of supporting arms'. The end of the war seemed not far off and all commanders, while pressing on with their allotted tasks, were specially anxious to avoid casualties. The brigade advanced steadily through heavily-forested country which offered good cover to the defenders. Despite the policy of making the maximum use of supporting arms the Australians were suffering sharp losses. On 5th July, for example, twenty-two killed and wounded, on the 6th thirty-four. At night small parties of Japanese emerged from the bush and raided the Australian positions but always at high cost to themselves. On the 9th, however, the 2/33rd Battalion and the 2/6th Commando Squadron found several features abandoned and it was soon evident that the enemy had withdrawn about three miles along the highway to Batuchampar.

The advance to Batuchampar was allotted to the 2/31st. After an unopposed advance the battalion, late in the evening of 9th July, struck strong opposition. As one leading platoon was moving along the highway five 500-kilo bombs were exploded by remote control killing three and leaving seventeen dazed by the blast; and the Japanese then opened fire with machine-guns. Next morning the forward Japanese positions were secured but there were strongposts among fallen logs farther on. These were attacked in the afternoon with the help of tanks and heavy supporting fire. A long fight followed in which a strong defence system armed with a field gun, eleven light anti-aircraft and anti-tank guns and other weapons was taken. Then Lieut-Colonel E. M. Robson of the 2/31st sent a company with a troop of tanks against the next feature. A sudden burst of intense fire from a group of posts among big fallen logs and standing timber killed or wounded many Australians. Some infantrymen pressed on swiftly and there was close fighting. At length the forward sections were withdrawn and the battalion took up a defensive position astride the road for the night. That day eighteen were killed and twenty-three wounded, all but twelve of the total being in the forward company.

The 25th Brigade probed forward in the next few days and there were several sharp clashes. On the evening of the 21st the Japanese abandoned their forward positions astride the highway, leaving twenty-six dead, and made a long withdrawal. Thereupon Milford, having attained his objectives in this direction, ordered Eather to stay put and send only patrols forward.

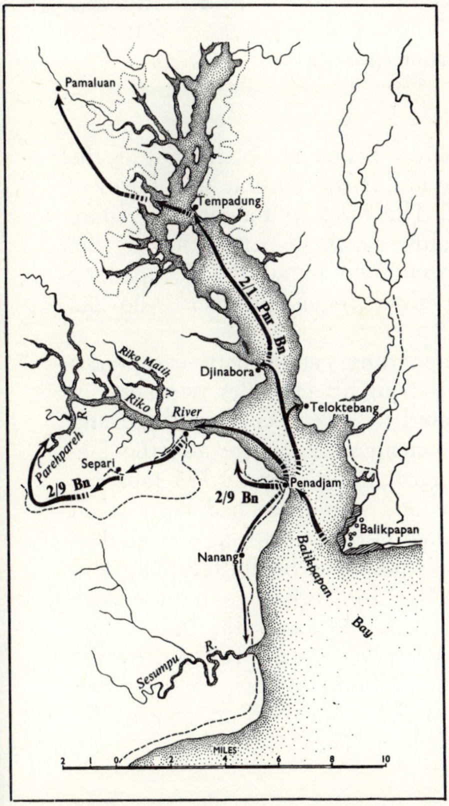

Balikpapan Bay area, 5 Jul-6 Aug

Meanwhile the 18th Brigade had been given the task of ensuring that the Japanese on the western shores of Balikpapan Bay could not interfere with the working of the port. The force allotted to this undertaking was the 2/9th Battalion (Lieut-Colonel A. J. Lee) with a commando troop, a troop each of tanks, field guns and mortars, and other detachments. After a bombardment two companies were landed by L.V.T's on the afternoon of 5th July and were soon followed by the remainder of the force. Little opposition was encountered until the 7th when patrols of the 2/3rd Commando found two well-manned positions.

On the 9th a company was landed at Teloktebang whence patrols probed northward. On the Riko River one of these captured a motor vessel of 300 tons and sank a Japanese motor-boat. A force built round two companies of the 2/1st Pioneer Battalion was allotted the task of protecting Balikpapan Harbour

Australian War Memorial

Balikpapan, 1st July 1945, the last large-scale landing operation of the war.

against possible attacks from the north. There was now much shipping in the port, the naval covering force had departed and it was possible that Japanese in small craft might attempt a night raid. The Pioneers fought some sharp platoon and company actions against resolute Japanese parties and by the 6th August the whole battalion was concentrated round the Tempadung area. Next day the Pioneers rescued sixty-three Indian prisoners who had been captured early in 1942.

Meanwhile the 21st Brigade had been sending patrols north-east, north and north-west. On 14th July Sambodja (about fifteen miles north-east of Manggar on the Vasey Highway) was found to have been abandoned and four days later it was occupied by two companies. Elsewhere also the Japanese withdrew farther into the hills. When fighting ceased 1,783 Japanese dead had been counted round Balikpapan and sixty-three had been taken prisoner. The Australians had lost 229 killed and 634 had been wounded.

When the natural strength of the enemy's positions, his fortifications, and the number of his heavy weapons are taken into consideration the Australian losses seem low, a result largely of the power of the Allied supporting arms. It is indicative that the heaviest losses were suffered by the 25th Brigade in the close country along the Milford Highway where their heavy weapons were less effective than in the more open country nearer Balikpapan.

From June 1944 onward the XX American Bomber Command from bases in China had struck at targets in Japan proper. A new phase opened on 24th November when 111 Superfortresses took off from Saipan to bomb Tokyo thus beginning a heavy-bomber offensive from Pacific Ocean bases. Eighty-eight of these aircraft succeeded in dropping their bombs on Tokyo. Thereafter for three months the heavy bombers mainly concentrated on daylight, high-altitude attacks on Japanese aircraft factories. Then General Curtis E. Le May, commanding XXI Bomber Command, changed his force's tactics with catastrophic results for the people of Japan. From early in March the Superfortresses were employed increasingly in burning Japanese cities and suburbs with napalm. The first raid of this series was made on Tokyo on 9th-10th March by more than 300 Superfortresses; it was discovered later that about a quarter of the buildings of Tokyo had been burnt out, 83,000 people had been killed, and more than 1,000,000 were homeless. No other raid of the war in Europe or Asia caused such loss of life and destruction of property. Similar attacks were made on other Japanese cities: Nagoya, Osaka, Kobe, Kawasaki, Yawata, Yokohama and others. Some cities, including Tokyo were struck again and again. Then attacks began on large numbers of smaller cities and towns. In nine months the Superfortresses caused 806,000 civilian casualties, somewhat more than the Japanese estimate of 780,000 combat casualties in her armed forces during the war. Later Prince Konoye said that 'fundamentally the thing that brought about the determination to make peace was the prolonged bombing by the B-29's'.

In July the United States Third Fleet, whose carrier aircraft had been striking targets on the Japanese mainland since April, bombarded targets round Tokyo and elsewhere. On the 16th the Third Fleet was joined off the Japanese coast by part of the British Pacific Fleet, including H.M.A.S's *Quiberon* and *Quickmatch* (and four N-class Australian destroyers in the big Fleet Train it had built up to enable it to dispense with reliance on shore bases for long periods). On the 17th there was a combined American-British bombardment of coastal areas north-east of Tokyo, and next day aircraft struck at the Yokosuka naval base, damaging *Nagato*, one of Japan's two remaining battleships. In late July what was left of the Japanese Navy was destroyed in Kure by carrier aircraft.

On 6th April MacArthur had assumed command of all American army forces in the Pacific. Soon his staff and Nimitz's were preparing plans for the invasion of Japan, where an army about 2,000,000 strong was deployed for a last desperate stand. The American plan provided for the seizure of southern Kyushu by the Sixth Army in the autumn of 1945—operation OLYMPIC. In the second phase, to be carried out in the spring of 1946, the Eighth and Tenth Armies (fourteen divisions), with the First Army (eleven divisions) in reserve, were to land on the Tokyo plain—operation CORONET.

While the Allied leaders were conferring at Potsdam in July Stalin informed Churchill and Churchill informed President Harry S. Truman, who had replaced Roosevelt on Roosevelt's death on 12th April, that the Japanese were seeking through the good offices of the Soviet Government to bring the war to an end. Terms of surrender drafted by the Americans and approved by the British and Chinese leaders were published on 26th July. On the 28th the Japanese Prime Minister announced that his Government would ignore the declaration. In Australia Evatt protested that Australia should have been consulted before the terms of any peace settlement were announced and New Zealand also protested. The Potsdam conference ended on 2nd August. Next day Truman ordered the dropping of atomic bombs.

On 6th August a B-29 dropped an atomic bomb on Hiroshima, killing some 60,000 people. Russia declared war on Japan on 8th August and invaded Manchuria next day. On the 9th a second atomic bomb was dropped, on Nagasaki.

On the 10th the Japanese announced that the Allied terms were acceptable provided that they did not prejudice the prerogatives of the Emperor. The American Government demanded that the authority of the Japanese Emperor and Government should be subject to the Supreme Commander of the Allied Powers. On the 14th the Emperor accepted these terms.

General MacArthur was appointed Supreme Commander in Japan and Admiral Sir Bruce Fraser was to represent the British Prime Minister at the formal surrender there; the British Government hoped that Australia, New Zealand, Canada and South Africa would arrange for a senior officer to be attached to Admiral Fraser. Evatt's prompt suggestion was that Australia's representative should go in his own right and not as an appendage to Admiral Fraser. After some exchanges it was agreed that representatives of Australia, Canada, Holland and France should sign the instrument of surrender in addition to representatives of the Big Four nations—United States, Soviet Union, Britain and China.

On the morning of 2nd September 1945 on the battleship *Missouri* in Tokyo Bay the surrender was signed, General Blamey signing for Australia.

Curtin had been very ill during the last quarter of 1944. From November 1944 to January 1945 Forde acted as Prime Minister but in the next three months Curtin was able to attend all Cabinet meetings. He then became ill again and in June it was made evident that full recovery from a heart condition was unlikely. He had proved a great leader of his nation during perhaps the most critical period of its existence. His high ideals were matched by the political skill which enabled him to retain the respect and support of his party in difficult times. Austere, sensitive, and devoted, it seems likely that worry and inner conflicts shortened his life. He died in Canberra on 5th July 1945, and, when the problems of demobilisation and reconstruction became immediate ones, there was a new Prime Minister—Chifley who took office on 13th July, Forde having been Prime Minister during the intervening week. Chifley retained the Treasury portfolio and Beasley became Minister for Defence; this post, now diminishing in importance, had been held since its establishment in 1939 by the Prime Minister, except during the short life of the Fadden Government.

It was indicative of the switch from the concentration on waging war to concentration on the problems of peace and reconstruction that, in July, the Department of War Organisation of Industry was formally abolished; in February its Minister, J. J. Dedman, had been placed in charge of the Department of Post-War Reconstruction. Also in July a Department of Immigration was established and the Department of Works became Works and Housing. The pressing tasks were now to bring fighting men home, house them, return them to civil employment, and at the same time decide what

Australian War Memorial

Canberra, 6th July 1945. The Memorial Service in King's Hall, Parliament House for the Prime Minister, John Curtin, who died on 5th July 1945, seven weeks before the war ended.

Australian War Memorial

Mr J. B. Chifley was appointed Prime Minister after the death of Mr Curtin. The new Ministry is shown here after being sworn in at Government House, Canberra, on 13th July 1945: *(sitting)* J. A. Beasley, J. B. Chifley, the Duke of Gloucester, F. M. Forde, N. J. O. Makin; *(standing)* H. V. Johnson, W. J. Scully, E. J. Holloway, A. S. Drakeford, C. W. Frost, R. V. Keane, J. J. Dedman, J. S. Collings, W. P. Ashley, A. A. Calwell, J. M. Fraser, E. J. Ward, H. P. Lazzarini. (Dr H. V. Evatt, who was overseas, and Senator D. Cameron are not in the picture.)

Australian War Memorial

H.M.A.S. *Junee* disembarking seriously ill Australian prisoners of war from Ambon at Morotai in September 1945. The recovery of the Australian prisoners of war from Japanese camps extending northwards from Java to Manchuria, most of them suffering from malnutrition and disease, was a major task performed with great skill and speed.

part Australian forces would play overseas in the period that must intervene between the cease fire and the transition to the sort of peaceful coexistence that had been achieved after the earlier war—if it was to be achieved again.

An urgent task was to bring home the 14,340 Australian prisoners who were in the hands of the Japanese, the survivors from about 22,400 who had been captured, mainly at Singapore in February 1942. For three years and a half these men, with some hundreds of thousands of other prisoners and internees, had endured semi-starvation and often brutal treatment in prison camps and in labour gangs throughout the Japanese Empire. When the war ended about 5,500 Australians were on Singapore Island, some 4,800 working in Burma and Thailand, 2,700 in Japan and Korea, and other smaller groups in other places. The swift and efficient recovery of the Allied prisoners had long been planned, and as soon as the fighting ceased the repatriation teams went into action. Hospital ships, transports, naval vessels and aircraft took part in the welcome job of bringing the prisoners home. By the end of September only a month after the parachuting of the first small rescue group into Changi, most of the prisoners recovered in Singapore, Java and Sumatra were on their way to Australia, and by mid-October all but a few Australian prisoners had been embarked or emplaned for home.

After the cease fire it was arranged that the Australian Army's area of

Australian War Memorial

On U.S.S. *Missouri* in Tokyo Bay on 2nd September 1945. General Sir Thomas Blamey signs the surrender document on behalf of Australia. Immediately behind him, from left to right, are General MacArthur, Lieut-General F. H. Berryman, Air Vice-Marshal W. D. Bostock, Rear-Admiral G. D. Moore and Lieut-Colonel D. H. Dwyer.

responsibility should include, in addition to the Australian territories, Borneo, all the Netherlands Indies east of and exclusive of Lombok, and Nauru and Ocean Islands. MacArthur had required that no surrender documents should be signed by the Japanese commanders in the field until he had taken the surrender of the Japanese Government in Tokyo Bay. After this ceremony was over Blamey on 8th September took the surrender of Lieut-General Teshima of the *II Japanese Army* at Morotai. Sturdee had taken the surrender of Imamura in the aircraft carrier *Glory* off Rabaul on the 6th and other Australian commanders, with the help of Australian naval vessels, mainly little corvettes, took the surrenders of their opposite numbers in other areas. There were 192,000 Japanese including auxiliaries in the Australian area of Borneo and the Indies and 152,000 in Sturdee's territory.

The Japanese in the New Guinea territories were concentrated in three main areas awaiting repatriation. Not until mid-1946 had they all been embarked, except for some 550 charged with various crimes.

The task of the Australians in the Netherlands Indies was more difficult. A smaller force than in New Guinea had a larger area to control and one containing not only more Japanese troops but a vastly greater civil population, much of it congregated in big towns in which the Indonesian independence movement was simmering.

In the 7th Division's area Milford sent forces to Samarinda and Bandjermasin, where they showed the flag and did their best to handle the Indonesian republicans with firmness and tact. In British Borneo five zones of responsibility were established in each of which an Australian force controlled the prisoners, helped the civilians and, in places, recovered Allied prisoners of war.

In the various parts of British Borneo military government ceased and the civil administration was re-established between April and July 1946. In acknowledgment of the debt owed to the 9th Australian Division in the period of reconstruction the division's sign was incorporated in the coat of arms of the Colony of British Borneo.

In the Australian zone of the Netherlands Indies, excluding Borneo, five occupation forces were formed. These were sent to Timor, Ambon, Menado, Macassar and Ternate. The Japanese army commander concerned was told that Allied forces would occupy only parts of his area and that elsewhere he would be responsible to the Allied commanders for maintenance of law and order.

In December 1945 the Indonesian nationalists became active on Sumbawa where there were then 21,000 Japanese troops and there were clashes between the Indonesians and the Japanese. In January the Japanese arrested some 250 Indonesians and the Australian commander instructed the Japanese to tell the local Sultan that he would be removed if he could not control his people. Later in January the Netherlands Indies Government was re-established on Sumbawa, and on 19th March 1946 the Australian responsibility for the rehabilitation of the islands north of the Timor Sea ended and Timor Force closed its headquarters.

Macassar Force, built round the 21st Brigade, and commanded first by Brigadier Dougherty and later by Brigadier Chilton, had the most difficult job of all the Australian occupation forces, as was to be expected since Macassar, with a population of about 90,000, was the largest Indonesian town under Australian control, and, indeed, the largest town and busiest port in the Indies outside Java and Sumatra. Here the Indonesian leaders refused to recognise the authority of the Netherlands officials, but said that they would obey Australian Army orders. Dougherty, however, refused to treat directly with the Indonesian leaders. In October there was a severe clash between Indonesian republicans and Ambonese, who supported the Dutch, but Australian patrols established and maintained order. Dougherty spoke to a general assembly of Indonesian representatives after the clash, and with tact and firmness he, and later Chilton, established the Netherlands authorities in control. In February 1946 Macassar Force handed over to an Indian brigade. The Australians were satisfied that their methods had not only prevented much bloodshed but had won the respect of Indonesian, Chinese and Dutch alike.

On 15th September Blamey reported to the Minister for the Army that he had been present at the surrender in Tokyo Bay and advised that there was no longer any need for him to exercise the powers of a Commander-in-Chief. He wished to lay down his office as soon as possible to make way for a transition to peace-time arrangements. On 15th November Forde informed Blamey that the Government had decided to reintroduce control of the army by the Military Board and that Sturdee would act as Commander-in-

Chief from 1st December until the Military Board was formed (which happened on 1st March 1946). In this abrupt manner the services of Australia's senior commander were terminated.

After much discussion it had been decided in September that the British Commonwealth's contribution to the occupation force in Japan should be a united force commanded by an Australian. Australia would provide a brigade group, three fighter squadrons, and two cruisers and two destroyers. The first substantial body of Australian troops did not reach Japan until February 1946. Lieut-General Northcott commanded B.C.O.F. until June 1946 when Lieut-General Robertson succeeded him.

When the war ended the army was 385,000 strong, the air force 171,000 and the navy 39,000. A big problem of demobilisation was to bring home about 167,000 soldiers who were serving in forward areas. Australia had ships enough to lift only 6,500 a month and transport aircraft enough to lift only 6,000 a month. However Britain made available ships that could move 12,000 a month, and three aircraft carriers of the British Pacific Fleet were used as troop carriers. By the end of the year only 20,000 were awaiting repatriation from New Guinea not counting 45,000 still employed in the garrisons. By the middle of 1946, as mentioned, virtually all the Japanese in New Guinea had been embarked, and on 24th June the New Guinea civil administration took charge of the last areas that had remained under military control.

Australian War Memorial

Crowds in Bourke Street, Melbourne celebrating the news of Japan's surrender which had been announced early that morning, 15th August 1945. Throughout the country jubilant crowds gathered in the streets of towns and cities.

Chapter 16 **Changed Australian attitudes**

The loss of young lives suffered by Australia in the six years war had been far smaller than in the four years war of 1914-18. Australia in common with most of the other belligerents was spared the appalling payment exacted in the second war from the Soviet Union, Germany, Japan—and the Jews. On the other hand the six years war wrought vastly greater changes in the Australian economy and in Australian attitudes than had the earlier and remoter one.

During the war of 1939-45 27,073 members of the Australian fighting services were killed or died of wounds or died while prisoners of war.[1] Of these 9,572 died in the war against Germany and 17,501 in the war against Japan. Nearly half of those lost in the war against Japan were killed or died of neglect while prisoners. The Australian Army suffered 18,713 fatal battle casualties, the Air Force 6,460 and the Navy 1,900. Of the Air Force's total 5,397 were suffered in the European war and of these about 3,500 were men serving in the R.A.F's Bomber Command. Indeed in this war it was more dangerous to serve in Bomber Command than in the infantry.

In money the cost to Australia of the First World War was assessed at £364,000,000, during the years 1914 to 1919. From 1939 to 1946 total 'war expenditure' was £2,494,380,000. At its peak, in 1942-43, war expenditure represented 40.1 per cent of the national income.

The total value of Lend-Lease received by Australia from the United States was about 1,500,000,000 dollars (about £A.466,000,000) and reciprocal Lend-Lease from Australia to the United States totalled about £A.285,000,000. An agreement reached in June 1946 provided that neither government would pay for goods and services supplied up to 2nd September 1945, that America would complete the transfer of goods selected by Australia from those in course of being procured on VJ-day and Australia would make no charge for goods transferred to American forces between 2nd September and 31st December 1945, that Australia would pay 27,000,000 dollars (American) for machine tools and other capital equipment and for surplus American property. Already Australia had paid 20,000,000 dollars; the remaining 7,000,000 was to be met by the delivery to the United States of real property and improvements thereto in Australia and by the establishment of a fund to be spent by the United States on educational and cultural programs of mutual benefit.

[1] The fatal casualties of the forces of other Commonwealth Nations and of India were:

United Kingdom	397,762
Canada	39,319
New Zealand	11,671
South Africa	8,681
India	36,092

In World War I Australia lost 59,342 killed. The United Kingdom lost 702,410, Canada 56,625, New Zealand 16,654.

Australian War Memorial

Patients and nurses line the rails of the hospital ship *Oranje* on her arrival at Darwin from Singapore with 760 former prisoners of war. The end of the war brought the release from Japanese hands of more than 14,500 Australians after three and a half years of captivity.

There had to be a similar financial settling up with Britain too. Early in September 1945 the Australian Government was informed that Britain intended to move the base organisations of the British Pacific Fleet from Australia to Singapore and Hong Kong. In the settling-up the British Government made a net payment of £3,000,000, for work on fleet bases estimated to have cost £5,642,000; and £4,250,000 for aerodromes, camps and so on constructed for the fleet 'leaving £1,150,000 as the residual value of the assets which will become the property of the Commonwealth'.

The Commonwealth Disposals Commission, established in 1944 to sell or give away surplus government property, sold some things through trade channels, some by auction, some by tender, some privately. In the five years to July 1949 the commission realised £135,000,000. It sold 124,000 motor vehicles, whole camps which were used to ease the shortage of houses, numbers of factories, more than £9,000,000 worth of machine tools, aircraft, ships, textiles and so on. Hundreds of thousands of garments and blankets were given to charitable causes.

When the war ended about 595,000 Australian men and women were serving in the forces. As a general rule they were given their discharges under a points system whereby length of service, age, and family responsibilities were taken into account. The Government directed that discharges should reach certain totals on certain dates and this was done. Thus, at the end of

Stage 1, on 31st January 1946, some 249,000 had been released; by 30th June the total was over 468,000; and by 15th February 1947 the forces had been reduced to the strength considered necessary in an interim period before a reduction to final peace-time establishments became feasible.

The details of demobilisation and rehabilitation had been carefully planned and the scheme worked smoothly. So far as possible men and women were sent to their own homes to await the completion of their discharge papers. They were given vocational guidance and detailed information about housing, land settlement, opportunities for training, repatriation benefits and so on. By 1951 some 94,000 candidates for university, technical or rural training had completed courses and 39,000 were still undergoing training, more than 15,000 being in universities (as full or part-time students); about 135,000 had withdrawn after beginning training, often having found that without more study they could find employment that suited them.

War service homes legislation provided that a loan of up to £2,750 might be made an ex-serviceman or his female dependants to acquire a home. A war gratuity was paid to members of the forces at the rate of £3.15.0 for each month of oversea service and of certain later periods in Australia, and at the rate of 15 shillings for each month of service in Australia after 6th December 1941. If a member had died on service at home or abroad and his family was totally dependent on him a minimum payment equivalent to three years of oversea service was made. There were other provisions. Most of the payments were made on 3rd March 1951, and in that financial year more than £61,000,000 was distributed under these arrangements.

In the sphere of government the passage from war to peace saw the disappearance of such departments as Aircraft Production, Munitions, Home Security, and others already listed and the appearance as separate departments of National Development and Supply.

As mentioned, the war drew into the Federal administration numbers of economists and other graduates. After the war there was an influx, larger in numbers, of men of mature age from the Services, who brought with them useful civil and service experience, and, in a Public Service which possessed relatively few who were in their age groups (as a result of the pre-war recruitment policy of preference to returned soldiers), some of these rose rapidly to the middle and senior ranks. At the same time post-graduate training along lines long followed in the fighting forces was developed in the Public Service.

During and after the war the scope of the Commonwealth Government's activities and the strength of its Public Service rapidly increased: from a total of about 47,000, including 'temporary' and 'exempt' employees in 1939 to about 162,000 in 1959. The wartime administration had been carried out with only a modest increase in the number of senior appointments held by permanent public servants. In the period immediately after the war the number of senior appointments steadily increased, and the Public Service provided rapid promotion for newcomers of enterprise and ability.[2]

[2] In 1943, for example, the Prime Minister's Department had a Secretary and two Assistant Secretaries; in 1965 a Secretary, Deputy Secretary, three First Assistant Secretaries and eight Assistant Secretaries. In 1943 the Treasury similarly had a Secretary and two Assistant Secretaries; in 1965 a Secretary, two Deputy Secretaries, five First Assistant Secretaries, and eleven Assistant Secretaries.

After the war the Commonwealth continued to be the sole collector of income tax, a situation which greatly helped it to retain the leadership it had attained in the war or soon afterwards in such fields as social services, economic planning and tertiary education.

The end of the war was soon followed by a radical change in the nature of the Australian Army. From the time of the organisation of Commonwealth military forces in the years immediately before the war of 1914-18 the regular soldiers had formed a cadre of staff officers, instructors and other specialists in the service of a predominantly citizen army. It was quite otherwise in the Navy, and later in the Air Force, where the citizen forces formed a reserve to assist the expansion of the regular forces in war, the regular forces providing the senior leaders. In Britain the Territorial Army provided a reserve force that was self-contained except that its senior commanders and staff were drawn from the regular army, the idea that a citizen soldier should command a formation larger than a brigade being not generally acceptable. The Australian Army tradition was very different. When war broke out in 1914 the brigades of the Australian Military Forces (there were no divisions) were all commanded by citizen soldiers. The regulars filled staff and training appointments, provided district commandants and officered the small permanent artillery and engineer units. Throughout the war of 1914-18 citizen soldiers held most of the commands in the A.I.F., and when the war ended six of the eight major-generals or lieut-generals in the A.I.F. were non-regulars.[3]

By 1939 there were eight citizen and seven regular generals, citizen soldiers commanding four divisions and regulars two. By 1945, however, the rank of general was held by twenty-three regulars and sixteen citizen soldiers, but (in the early part of the year) citizens commanded the two corps and three of the six combat divisons, and of the infantry brigades only one was led by a regular.

The gradual change to a system resembling the British or American one in which, though there was a numerically large citizen army, the senior appointments were all or mostly held by regulars occurred swiftly after the end of the war. It was accompanied by the formation by the Chifley Government of a small regular army along the lines of the one proposed but rejected in 1939. By 1950 eleven regulars held the substantive ranks of lieut-general or major-general and one was a temporary major-general; two citizen officers held the temporary rank of major-general.

The war produced a rapid increase in the quantity and variety of Australian manufactures. Between 1937-38 and 1944-45 the value of industrial production almost doubled and by ten years after the war the 1944-45 figure had been more than trebled, though allowance must be made for a big rise in prices in the meantime. This post-war development was largely built upon the skills and equipment acquired during a war in which Australians learnt to build aircraft and their engines, ships of greater complexity than hitherto, a wide variety of machine tools, optical equipment, a comprehensive range of electrical equipment and so on. As an outcome of a wartime decision an aluminium industry was established and later tin-plate was produced, thus

[3] One of these, Gellibrand, was a former regular. The Director of Medical Services, Howse, held the rank of surgeon-general and is not included above.

filling two big gaps in Australian self-sufficiency. Another gap was closed in 1949 when large-scale production of an Australian motor-car was begun by General Motors-Holden's. As part of the effort to provide more power for the growing industrial machine and water for irrigation the Snowy Mountains Hydro-Electric Authority came into being in 1949 to carry out an immense undertaking which when completed would produce more power than all generating stations then operating, and make available some 2,000,000 acre feet of water for irrigation in the Snowy and Murrumbidgee Rivers.

As mentioned earlier, the war revealed Australia's inadequate provision for scientific and technical training and research and produced strenuous measures to repair them. This process was accelerated after the war. Partly as a result of the contributions of the universities to the solution of war-time technical and scientific problems, governments were more easily persuaded to support scientific work than they had been before the war. Within a year or so after the end of the war were established the first Australian university devoted mainly to post-graduate studies—the Australian National University—and the first university devoted primarily to higher technological studies—the New South Wales University of Technology, later named simply the University of New South Wales.

In several fields scientific research establishments that had been developed during the war carried on increasingly intensive attacks on fundamental problems in the peace. The Radiophysics Laboratory, for example, was soon achieving important results in rain and cloud physics, radio-astronomy and radar. In 1957 an historian wrote: 'Australia's contribution to knowledge in the fields of physical sciences which had for so long been an insignificant trickle, now grew to proportions in keeping with the remarkable growth of her industries and the activity of her scientific institutions. For the first time students and scientists from other parts of the world began to come to Australia to work for higher degrees and to carry out researches in laboratories that had achieved a well-established international reputation.'[4]

The need for survey of the country's scientific and material resources had been felt and in some degree coped with in the war. Some years afterwards surveys of scientific resources along the lines of wartime counterparts were made. Investigations of mineral resources improvised in the war were followed in the peace (June 1946) by the formation of what was at length entitled the Bureau of Mineral Resources, Geology and Geophysics, within the Department of National Development. This department by 1952 had completed and published the first exhaustive survey of Australian secondary industry, dealing with some 43,000 factories.

As early as 1945 a British mission visited Australia in search of a desert area over which to test guided missiles. Soon a Long-Range Weapons Establishment was set up in former munitions factories at Salisbury, South Australia, and a base for a missile range was established at Woomera near the Transcontinental Railway, whence it was possible to test weapons over a land distance of more than 1,000 miles. The task of advising the Defence Department on the formulation of a scientific policy in the defence field was given to a Defence Research and Development Policy Committee whose chairman was Professor L. H. Martin, a leading physicist, and among whose

[4] D. P. Mellor, *The Role of Science and Industry* (1958), p. 687.

members were other senior scientists as well as senior officers of all the Services. But despite the demonstration by the Australian engineering industry during the war of their ability to produce the most sophisticated equipment of those days, the Government and its advisers gradually reverted to the dubious policies of the 1920s and 1930s when relatively simple jobs were given to Australian factories and the more costly and difficult ones to overseas firms, which (with their governments) might thus regulate Australia's armament by failure or inability to deliver re-orders for spare parts.

After the war Australia took a more active part in the affairs of the world at large than she had before 1939, but a less influential one than some of her leaders had hoped in the later years of the war. The efforts of Australia, side by side with Canada and New Zealand, at San Francisco in 1945 and on later occasions, to ensure that the middle Powers should be able to exercise influence on the great Powers did not achieve much success.

> The Commonwealth contribution at San Francisco was considerable but the conference was for most Commonwealth delegations a disillusioning experience. There they were brought face to face with the growing rift between the Soviet Union and the Western World . . . This rift was soon destined to widen into an open breach . . . the Soviet Union was inexorably resolved on a great-power peace, if indeed there was to be a peace at all, and not all the violent indignation of Dr Evatt nor the pained remonstrances of Mr Mackenzie King sufficed to qualify by one iota their resolve.[5]

However, Australia sought and accepted far greater international responsibilities than had been dreamt of before the war. Whereas, for example, in 1925 members of the Opposition in the House of Representatives had demanded the recall of an Australian cruiser serving on exchange on the China Station lest it be involved in an 'incident', in 1946 and later an Australian Labour Government was maintaining a contingent of an occupation force in Japan, and soon Australian naval, land or air forces would be engaged in action with other United Nations forces in Korea and in police operations in Malaya.

It was as a result of an Australian initiative that the Colombo Plan to assist economic development in countries of South and South-East Asia was instituted; and increasingly in the post-war years Australia gave technical assistance to Asian nations and received young Asians for training in schools, universities and elsewhere.

Measures of Australia's growing responsibilities in the field of external affairs were the increase in the number of oversea posts and the corresponding expansion of the diplomatic service needed to man them and the central office in Canberra. In 1943 Australia maintained four legations—in the United States, China, the Soviet Union and to the Netherlands Government in exile—and two High Commissions—in London and Canada. None of the Heads of these Missions was a career diplomat. By 1947 there were seven embassies or legations and six high commissions, plus other missions and consulates-general. By 1965 there were twenty-six embassies and twelve high commissions, and a majority of the senior appointments were held by career diplomats.

[5] N. Mansergh, *Survey of British Commonwealth Affairs—Problems of Wartime Co-operation and Post-War Change 1939-1952* (1958), pp. 320-1.

The change in Australia's attitudes towards her Asian neighbours was no less striking than the transformation of her migration policy. Up to 1939 the entry of non-British migrants had seldom been actively encouraged or else had been impeded, and the fact that about 97 per cent of the people were of British birth—though many of these were of foreign descent—was a source of pride. The four largest groups of foreign-born residents at the census of 1933 were: Italian, 26,700; German, 16,800; Chinese, 8,500; Greek, 8,300.

After the war all political parties supported a policy of assisting migrants from most European countries and from among the multitude of displaced persons. From the earliest years of assisted migration until 1939 about 1,100,000 people had been helped to migrate to Australia; between 1947 and 1959 785,000 were assisted. By 1961 the number of people born in foreign countries had increased to some 805,000 and there were 523,000 of foreign nationality in Australia, compared with 60,000 in 1933. In 1961 the largest groups of foreign-born people were: Italian, 228,000; German, 109,000; Netherlands, 102,000; Greek, 77,000; Polish, 60,000.

The main argument advanced in favour of large-scale immigration of European nationals (as distinct from refugees) was that Australia had to 'populate or perish', 'double or quit'. The voices which had maintained in the 1930s that, on balance, inconsiderable military strength was gained as a result of an influx of alien migrants were silent. Perhaps the main reasons for the new policy were the existence of fairly full employment, a desire for national aggrandisement, and a friendly sentiment that to limit immigration at least of Europeans, was ungenerous.

Indeed, as the years of war recede, their main early effects within Australia may be seen to be a drive towards more rapid and adventurous development and more assertiveness, a weakening of political and economic links with Britain and a strengthening of links with the United States, an increasing diversion of trade towards Asian countries, and a forgiving if not a forgetting of the ruthlessness of the enemies whose foolish ambitions produced the years of turmoil and destruction. The second war and its immediate sequels dispelled the dream of a community of friendly and tolerant nations seeking always to achieve 'the Parliament of man, the Federation of the world' and left in its place a nightmare in which mankind was faced with a choice between establishing an equilibrium among the nations or the large-scale destruction which was the price that henceforth would have to be paid for the unleashing of fanatical ambitions by a Power armed with modern explosives.

List of Abbreviations

AIF	Australian Imperial Force
Angau	Australian New Guinea Administrative Unit
Armd	Armoured
BCOF	British Commonwealth Occupation Force
Bde	Brigade
Bn	Battalion
Brig	Brigadier
Bty	Battery
Capt	Captain
Cdo	Commando
Cdr	Commander
Coy	Company
Cpl	Corporal
Div	Division
Fd	Field
F-Lt	Flight Lieutenant
F-O	Flying Officer
GHQ	General Headquarters SWPA
Indep	Independent
Inf	Infantry
Lt	Lieutenant
Lt-Cdr	Lieut-Commander
Lt-Col	Lieut-Colonel
Lt-Gen	Lieut-General
Maj	Major
Maj-Gen	Major-General
ME	Middle East
NG	New Guinea
NGF	New Guinea Force
NGIB	New Guinea Infantry Battalion
NGVR	New Guinea Volunteer Rifles
NZ	New Zealand
PIB	Papuan Infantry Battalion
Pte	Private
RAAF	Royal Australian Air Force
RAF	Royal Air Force
RAN	Royal Australian Navy
Regt	Regiment
RN	Royal Navy
Rt Hon	Right Honourable
Sgt	Sergeant
Sqn	Squadron
Sqn Ldr	Squadron Leader
SWPA	South-West Pacific Area
UN	United Nations
US	United States (of America)
W Cdr	Wing Commander
WO2	Warrant Officer, Class 2

Index

Text set in 10 on 11 pt Fairfield
on Shoalhaven Brochure Opaque 77 gsm

Designed by Richard Farmer, Design Section
Australian Government Publishing Service

R71/1868